Nannie

Her Ancestors, Life and Family Legacy

Carolyn Stier Ferrell

Edited by Janet Gooden Thompson

Previously published as *In Search of Nannie Tyler, A One Hundred Year History of a Family Who Helped Shape Clarksville.*

Photograph credits are listed when known. Permission has been requested and granted for every image that could be traced to the copyright holder. Other contributed photos are identified by the donor. Remaining photos are attributed to the author and may not be reproduced without permission.

PHOTO CREDITS
AP Austin Peay State University Archives
LOC Library of Congress
MB Mary Bodnar Collection
TSLA Tennessee State Library and Archives
MCA Montgomery County Archives
CMCPL Clarksville-Montgomery County Public Library
CHM Customs House Museum
GF Gill family
LC *Leaf Chronicle*
CV *Confederate Veteran*

Front cover graciously provided by Kitty Harvill.
Back cover photo provided by Valerie J. Linares, Montgomery County Government

Published by Kindle Books

Dedication

This book is lovingly dedicated to the memory of my grandmother, Irene Farrar Thomas and my grandfather, Carlyle Thomas, Sr., who instilled in me a deep love and respect for the history of Clarksville and Montgomery County. It was her request that I do what I could to save Clarksville's history that started me on this journey.

and to

Miss Marie Riggins who fought to save "Judge Tyler's" courthouse and to those today who dedicate themselves to preserving our history.

Acknowledgements

The interest in Nannie Tyler transcends generations, each succeeding one curious to know more about her. When the first book was written in 1906, this author compiled as much as was available about her short life. Since that time with new discoveries from journals and diaries, more details emerge about the Tyler family. With this information, a re-write of the book became desirable.

Sue Baggett Page was an absolute delight as she recalled her time living at the old city hall/jail on the Public Square. In fact, she was born there as was one of her sisters. Her father was the jailer. She provided insight to what it was like to live in a building with prisoners housed with them during the1950s. She is a treasure of memories of the old days of Clarksville.

I am grateful to Rosemary Klein who provided important documents on the Night Riders and as always, it was an honor to meet with Judge Tyler Gill and his daughter Emily whose family is the topic of this book. The three of us met at the public library genealogy room where Judge Gill showed me family documents that proved to be of great interest and so were included in this manuscript. In the process of delving into these historic papers and letters, the afternoon was not only informative but thoroughly enjoyable. The day was capped off by a visit to Judge Tyler's former home now owned by Kitty Harvill and her husband Christoph Hrdina. What a delight!

It has been the goal of this author to provide a "real time" exploratory account of the lives of the Tyler family, one in which it is hoped the reader captures a true sense of the era in which each generation lived.

While going up to the library's genealogy room to do my research, it was necessary to pass each time by the portrait of Judge Charles W. Tyler. The countenance of the judge's face reminded me of the serious manner in which he conducted his life and I could almost hear him admonishing me, in his judicial manner, to "get the facts straight" I endeavored every day to do just that!

I am always grateful to Jan Thompson, not just for being the most thoughtful and true friend one could ever have but also for suffering through the editing of my books like a Trojan warrior. Her comments, corrections and suggestions are to be credited for making my books readable and cohesive.

For me personally as stated in the first book, Nannie could never know that by her existence, once again in 2025, she helped me through a challenging time, but that's between Nannie and me!

Preface

Desecration of a child's grave is a crime so despicable, wicked and abominable that it is beyond a person's reasoning. This is brought to mind from several friends who have lost a child and who, after suffering the horrible loss, had to endure further unspeakable pain by having their loved one's gravesite vandalized.

When it was discovered that a rather well known grave in Clarksville, Tennessee was so disturbed, the outcry was immediate. The statue that stood watch over the grave of a four-year-old child who died over one hundred years ago had been stolen sometime in the early summer of 1996. The grave was that of Nannie Tyler, the beloved daughter of Clarksville Judge Charles Waller Tyler and his wife Mollie Settle Tyler. This endearing child's life began March 16, 1881, during the darkest days of her father's political career and ended a few years later on September 9, 1885, from a disease no one knew how to combat.

Nannie's story deserves to be told not only because of who she was but also because of an event that occurred 110 years after her death. Stories abound about her premature death and subsequent burial. What was the true cause of her death? Was her burial delayed due to the extreme grief of her parents? Was she buried in a metal casket with a glass top? Were her favorites toys placed in a glass case on top of her grave at her burial? These are the questions that will be addressed in this book. Her gravesite is probably the most visited one in Clarksville; people yearn to know more about her. This is an attempt to reveal the unknown facts behind the four-year-old child whose life like statue was stolen in 1996 and the history of her family's impact on the town in which she lived.

The idea for this manuscript formed in July of 1996 when a white station wagon with a tired but excited couple, pulled into Greenwood Cemetery. It was 11:30 in the morning and already showing signs of becoming a typically hot, humid summer Tennessee day. The purpose of their trip was to return something of importance to the Clarksville citizens awaiting its arrival. This is the story of a little girl, her family, her stolen statue and the people of a Southern town that loved her. For me, it began as an historical journey but became much more as I went in search of Nannie Tyler...and her family.

Vanished

She died; this was the way she died;
And when her breath was done,
Took up her simple wardrobe
And started for the sun.
Her little figure at the gate
The angels must have spied,
Since I could never find her
Upon the mortal side.

--Emily Dickinson, a contemporary of Nannie

Part One

Chapter One: Nannie's Ancestors: Immigrants, Pioneers and Settlers

> **All the past we leave behind,**
> **We debouch upon a newer mightier world, varied world,**
> **Fresh and strong the world we seize, world of labor and the march,**
> **Pioneers! O pioneers!**
>
> **--Walt Whitman**

Nannie's family story is a proud one. Her people were pioneers in the truest sense of the word. Some of her people crossed an ocean to settle in a new country, traversed hundreds of miles and a mountain range to integrate themselves in the farming communities of the Cumberland territory and became vital members of a new town's history.

Records indicate that families by the name of Tyler came to this country from London, England. The surname describes a person (tiler) whose job it was to bake clay into tiles in an oven, a common occupation in medieval times. These tiles were used to be placed on floors and roofs. The surname Duke has multiple origins, therefore difficult to know which is associated with this family.

According to Marshall Wingfield's book, *A History of Caroline County, Virginia,*

> **In 1202, there lived a Gilbert de Tiller, and in 1311, a Thomas le Tyler was a member of the English Parliament. The Tylers of Virginia trace their ancestry to Wat Tyler, who, in the reign of Richard, the Second about 1381, led the commoners of England in what is known to history as the 'Wat Tyler Rebellion.' So successful was this rebellion against oppressive taxation and other excesses of Richard's reign, that the king sued for terms and was forced to sign a charter abolishing serfage, (sic) reducing rent rates and taxes and giving freedom of commerce in market towns. While in an interview with the king, at the king's invitation and under promise of protection, Tyler was treacherously slain and the stout resistance against oppression, having lost the leader, weakened. The royalty-worshipping historians of the fourteenth century, regarding it outrageously insolent for a plebian to make any assertion of manhood, have caused Wat Tyler to fare poorly in history.**

On the left: The death of Wat/Walter Tyler at the hands of Walworth, Mayor of London, with the young 14-year-old King Richard II looking on.[1] On the right: Wat/Walter Tyler.

In the end, Wat was beheaded and his head placed in a pole on London Bridge. People honor his memory and his name is found on buildings and used as street names.[2]

For our purposes, we will start with the American Tyler ancestors. According to a manuscript by Quintus M. Tyler, the Duke side of the family had come to Hanover County some time before 1700. The Tylers, as well, had come over from England at an early date but settled in Caroline County which is located half

[1] This rebellion warrants further investigation by the readers of this manuscript.

[2] In the August 21, 1872 issue of the *Leaf* is an article on Wat Tyler. It is unfortunately, unreadable as the page is torn but it appears that Judge Tyler was quoted in the article about his "rebel" ancestor.

way between Richmond and Fredericksburg, Virginia, covering approximately 549 square miles.

Caroline County, Virginia

The Tylers were to become part of the rich heritage of Virginia and contribute to its history. Marshall Wingfield wrote "Caroline was the third most populous and affluent county in Virginia at the time of the Revolution. The descendants of its early families contributed, perhaps as much as any county in America, to the building of the United States." The Tyler line of Montgomery County, Tennessee is known to have started from Henry Tyler (1620-1697), and Margaret Joanes Tyler 1624-1959). Their son, Richard Tyler, Sr. born in 1659/60 in London came to Essex County, Virginia in 1678 after obtaining patents for land. Richard is referred to in genealogical records as "the immigrant." In 1684 he married Susannah Baxter (1660-1734), a daughter of Nathaniel Baxter.[3] They had the following children:

Richard Tyler, Jr. (1685-1761)
Mary Tyler (bef. 1700-1792) married James Boughan (1697-1749)
John Tyler (bef. 1707-1758) a lieutenant
William Tyler (1710-1794) married 3 times
Susannah Tyler (1718-1751) married John Phillips (1714-1751)

In 1704, Richard, Sr. owned 650 acres in Essex Quit Rent. In addition to farming, Richard was a justice of the peace and a major in the militia under Capt. Francis Tompkins with 59 men under his command. Richard himself could not read or write and signed his name with a mark, but he made sure his children were better educated. By checking several genealogical records, it can be verified that Richard Tyler's son Richard, Jr. first married Catherine Montague in 1724. They had a daughter, Frances "Franky" Tyler (1724-1785). His second wife was Katherine Williamson (1685-1781). In deeds from May 10, 1705, Richard, Sr. entered into a land transfer deal with Richard Jones of Essex, also a planter. He received fifty acres on the south side of Piscataway Creek in exchange for some land previously owned by Nathaniel Baxter, his former father-in-law.

Piscataway Creek, a tributary of the Rappahannock River. Photo from Wikipedia.

In tracing this family, the name Taylor is sometimes substituted for Tyler and such is the case here. The deed is signed Richard **X** (his mark) Taylor. Richard Tyler, Sr. died in 1734 and for some unexplained reason, his wife Susannah is recorded as relinquishing her dowager's rights. His will written in 1732 read:

-In the name of God amen. I, Richard Tyler of Essex County in Virginia, being weak in body but of perfect mind, sense and memory and knowing it is appointed for all men once to die do make this my last will and testament in manner and form following, that is to say, first I bequeath my soul into the hands of my Creator and for what worldly goods it hath pleased Almighty God to bestow upon me in this life after my decrease I give as follows:

-I give and bequeath unto my beloved son Richard Tyler after the decease of my beloved wife Susanna Tyler, the plantation whereon I now live with all the land belonging to me between Piscataway Creek and the Road together with a piece I purchased lately adjoining to it to him and his heirs forever. Also I give and bequeath unto my beloved son Richard Tyler at the time of my wife's decease the best feather bed & furniture belonging to me. Also I give to my said son Richard Tyler after my wife's decease a Negro man named Will to him and his heirs forever.

[3] The Tylers and Baxters will have interactions generations later.

-I give and bequeath unto my beloved son John Tyler the plantation whereon he now lives with all the land belonging to me on the south side of the swamp[4] that divides the land where he now lives and John Boughan's land to him & his heirs forever. Also I give and bequeath to my beloved son John Tyler a young Negro named Tony to his and his heirs forever.

-I give and bequeath unto my son William Tyler all the land that I am possessed with on the south side of the Road[5] by said swamp to him & his heirs forever.

-I give and bequeath unto my beloved daughter Mary Boughan a good suit of cloaths (sic) at the discretion of my beloved wife, Susanna Tyler.

-I give and bequeath unto my beloved daughter Susanna Tyler a feather bed and furniture belonging to it at the day of her marriage to her & her heirs forever. Also I give and bequeath unto my beloved daughter Susanna Tyler after my wife's decease my great looking glass to her & her heirs forever.

-I lend unto my beloved wife Susanna Tyler all the rest residue & remainder of my estate of what nature & kind whatsoever to her during her natural life and after her decease then to be equally divided between my beloved son William and my beloved daughter Susanna Tyler to them & their heirs forever.

-Last I constitute and appoint my beloved wife Susanna Tyler and my beloved sons Richard Tyler and William Tyler to be my full and wholly executrix and Executors of this my last will and testament revoking disannulling making void all former wills and bequeaths by me heretofore made and appointing this to be my last will and testament as witness my hand & seal this fourth day of December in the year of our Lord God one thousand seven hundred and thirty-two.

In presence of James Saint John
John Richard Tyler
Margaret Swiney
Thomas Barber

<u>Inventory of Richard Tyler, Sr.:</u> total value: 248 pounds, eleven shillings, one pence, ½. The inventory includes animals, household items, dishware, a looking glass, two old guns, kitchen utensils, 10 lb. pewter, 1 old Bible, 1 brick layer's trowel, various tools, a Negro boy named Tony, a Negro man named Will, a Negro man named Old Ned, 1 do[6] called young Frank, 1 Negro wench called Susan, 1 do girl called Moll, 1 old trunk, a parcel of wool.

In the end, Richard's son, William inherited his father's land because his two older brothers died without sons. In 1740, William served as a lieutenant in the militia. Records show that William sold one hundred acres of land in South Farnham, Essex County next to his brother John's farm. The records of Essex County, Virginia on February 3, 1749, states that "William Tyler, of Caroline County," has bargained and sold to Joseph Dunn one hundred acres of land lying in South Farnham Parish, Essex County. The land is described as adjoining that of John Tyler, and "as being the placed on which James Boughan now lives." William was probably a widower at this time since no wife is shown in the deed.

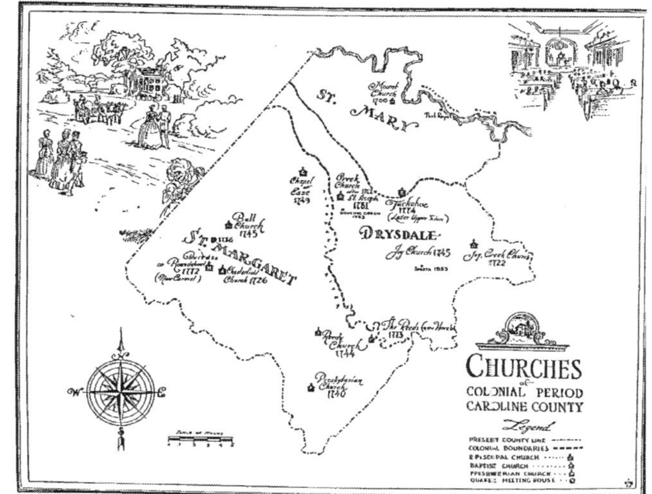

The three parishes of Caroline County as they were in the 1700s. From the book, *Colonial Caroline: A History of Caroline, County, Virginia.*

---

4 This is now named Drinking Water Swamp.
5 This is Highway 360 to Richmond.
6 The "do" written here is short for ditto.

In 1749, William was recorded as living in St. Margaret's Parish, one of the three parishes in which Caroline County was divided. This was the area between the Mattaponi and the north Anna-Pamunkey Rivers. The Mattaponi is a meandering tidal river, which means that twice daily, every day the salt water of the Chesapeake Bay reaches up the Mattaponi as far as Aylett in King William's County, Virginia and twice daily, every day, the fresh water of the Mattaponi flows past West Point. There it joins with the Pamunkey River, creating a pristine estuary, which is the York River. Its name is derived from the four streams in Spotsylvania County that creates the river: The Mat River and the Ta River join in Spotsylvania Co. to form the Matta River. The Po River and the Ni River join in Caroline Co. to form the Puni River. The Matta River and Po River join in Caroline Co. to form the Mattaponi River. It is still a lovely river today, monitored and fiercely protected by environmental groups.

William served as a magistrate, appointed by Gov. Robert Dinwiddie until 1757 when he resigned due to age. It is written that the greatest difficulty to law enforcement in Caroline County during Dinwiddie's last years was the apathetic attitude of the magistrates. William Tyler is listed among the four magistrates who "took their duties seriously." William did not serve in the American Revolutionary War however, he supplied food and pasturage for the Continental Army's livestock.

William, Sr. was married three times: the first wife's name is unknown yet her dates are recorded as (1714-1743) Their children were:

Catharine "Kitty" or "Caty" Tyler (1738-1779). Catharine was described as "very beautiful and a good weaver and entertainer." She used to "entertain her beaus after the war sitting at the loom weaving cloth like a sensible girl as she was." She married James Maulding/Mauldin (1734-1797), in 1754, the son of Richard Maulding (1694-1751) and Jane Maulding[7] (? -1744) and the couple had seven children. They moved to Logan County, Kentucky, settled on the Red River and established a station called Maulding's Station. James served as a judge and was a signer of the Cumberland Compact.

John Tyler (1740-?) died young and without issue.

Richard Tyler (1741-1802) no children.

William Tyler, Jr. (1742-1762)

Mary Tyler (1743-1814) married Henry Terrell, Jr. (1735-1811) in 1765. He was the son of Henry Terrell, Sr. (1695-1760), and his first wife, Ann Chiles.

After the death of his first wife, William married Susan Miller (1720-1750), abt. 1744 in St. Margaret's Parish. Their children were:

Ann "Nancy" or "Nannie" Tyler (1745-1805) married Charles Terrell (1748-1828), the son of Henry Terrell and his second wife Sarah Woodson (1716-1764), who owned a large plantation in Caroline County.

Richard Tyler (1746-1802) married Catherine Gatewood.

---

[7] This statement was read at the unveiling of the Ambrose Maulding monument in Hamilton County, Illinois on June 15, 1926: "Captain Richard Maulding was the father of James Maulding, who received a good education and wrote in a fine hand. He married Katy Tyler, a near relative of President John Tyler. James Maulding and his wife had four sons, Ambrose, Morton, Richard and Wesley and several daughters. James Maulding and his family moved to the backwoods country of North Carolina and his children were deprived of the advantage of good schools."

His third wife was Elizabeth Miller Keeling (1710-1790),[8] daughter of Richard Keeling (1682-1772), and Elizabeth Carraway Lovett Keeling (1678-1769). They married abt. 1748. The children from this marriage were:

Ann Tyler (1748-1805)

Frances "Franky" Tyler (1751-1813) Married William Redd (1750-1802), abt. 1769. He was the son of Capt. Samuel Redd and Lucy Rogers of "Cedar Vale."

"Cedar Vale" circa1729. Ancestral home of the Redds. Located today at 5623 Hewlett Road, Ruther Glen, Virginia.

John Tyler (1751-?) another son to be named John who also died young.

Elizabeth Tyler (1753-1837) married Lt. George Terrell.

George Thomas Tyler (1755-1833) a captain; married Judith Terrell (1750-?), a daughter of Henry Terrell and Sarah Woodson and brother of Henry Terrell who married his half-sister Ann Tyler.

Richard Keeling Tyler, Sr. (1760-1832) married Mary Cluverius Duke (1767-1846), the daughter of John Duke and Elizabeth Burnley. His land was called "Sampson."

In the year 1787, William was taxed for 1031 acres of land and so in Virginian records is described as a "prosperous planter." Tax records showed that he owned 23 slaves. His will was dated May 1, 1791, three years before his death. He named 8 children in his will. Each was left property and a certain part of the estate was "to be divided among my children to share and share alike. To them and their heirs forever." Note that his wife is deceased at that time.

It is my will and desire that my just debts and funeral charges be first paid and satisfied.

Item. I give and bequeath to my daughter, Caty the wife of James Maulden (sic), if she be living, the sum of seventy-five pounds, but should my said daughter be dead then and in that case, I give and bequeath the said seventy-five pounds to the children of my said daughter to be equally divided among them, share and share alike.

Item. Whereas I have from time to time given to my son, Richard Tyler, both money and tobacco in order to enable him to purchase land and for which money and tobacco my said son Richard stands charged on my books. It is my will and desire that my said son, Richard, have full credit and quittance for all charges for money and tobacco as I do hereby give and bequeath the same to my said son.

Item. Whereas I formerly lent to my daughter, Nanny, the wife of Charles Terrell, two Negroes, To Wit: Judy and Lucy, and whereas the said Judy hath had children since she has been in the possession of my said daughter, and the said Lucy hath had children since she has been in possession of my daughter, now it is my will that the said Negro Lucy together with all her children be returned to my estate to be divided as hereafter to be directed and I do give and bequeath to my said daughter, Nanny, and to her heirs and assigns forever the said Judy and all her children together with their future increase.

Item. I give and bequeath to my daughter, Franky, the wife of William Redd and to her heirs and assigns forever, one Negro woman named Delila and all her children and their future increase, which said Negro Delila and her children are now in possession of my said daughter.

Item. I give and bequeath to my daughter, Elizabeth, the wife of George Terrell, and to her heirs and assigns forever, one Negro woman named Letty and all her children together with their future increase, which said Negro Letty and her children are now in possession of my said daughter.

Item. I give and bequeath to my son, George Tyler, and to his heirs and assigns forever

[8] The repeat of names made research on the Tylers extremely difficult: There were two Capt. William Tylers who married two Elizabeth Keelings. They were cousins. The Elizabeth Keeling born in 1740 and who married Capt. William Tyler, Jr. was the only daughter of Richard Keeling (1684-1770), and Elizabeth Lovett (1678-1769), and granddaughter of Capt. George Keeling (1654-1720), and Ursula Flemming (1659-1697). The Elizabeth Keeling who married Capt. William Tyler, Sr. (1708-1794), was the daughter of Thomas Keeling II (1674-1714), and Elizabeth Lovett (1678-1710), and granddaughter of Capt. Adam Keeling (1639-1683), and Ann Martin (1640-1698).

all the Tract of Land I purchased of Charles Benness and on which my son now lives.

Item. I give and bequeath to my son, Richard K. Tyler, and to his heirs and assigns forever, all that Tract of Land lying in Caroline County called Sampson and for which my son has a deed.

Item. I give and bequeath to my son John Tyler, and to his heirs and assigns forever all that tract of Land on which I now live; also all that Tract of Land lying in Caroline County which I purchased of William Mason.

Item. I give to my son, George Tyler, one Negro woman named Nanny to be by him accounted for at her appraised value as a part of his portion of my estate hereafter disposed of.

Item. It is my will and desire that all the remainder of my estate, both real and personal, including the Negroes to be returned by my daughter Nanny and the value of the Negro Nanney bequeathed to my son George, be divided among my children, To Wit: Richard Tyler, George Tyler, John Tyler, Richard Keeling Tyler, Nanny, the wife of Charles Terrell, Franky the wife of William Redd and Elizabeth, the wife of George Terrell, to be divided equally, share and share alike to them and their heirs and assigns forever.

Lastly, I do hereby constitute and appoint any living son of Richard Tyler, George Tyler, and John Tyler Executors of this my last will and testament, hereby revoking and making null and void all other wills by me heretofore made, declaring this and no other to be my last will and testament.

In testimony whereof I have hereunto let my hand and affixed my seal this first day of May, one thousand, seven hundred and ninety-one.

W. Tyler

Signed, sealed, published and delivered by the testator to be his last will and testament.

Francis Tompkins, Richard Lowry, Jonathan Clark

Regrettably, there was a dispute over the will as seen in the document below. Chancery Court record in Caroline County-Richard K. Tyler v. Catharine Tyler Maulding. It reads

The Commonwealth of Virginia to the Sheriff of Caroline County greeting: You are hereby commanded to summon Catharine Maulding to appear before the Justices of our said County Court at the courthouse of the said County on the second Tuesday in next month to answer a bill in Chancery against them by Richard K. Tyler, George Tyler, Charles Terrell & Nanny his wife, George Terrell & Elizabeth his wife & Franky Redd complainants, and have them there this writ under the penalty of £100. William Nelson Clerk of the said court the 15th day of October 1804 and in the 28th year of the Commonwealth. -Wm. Nelson

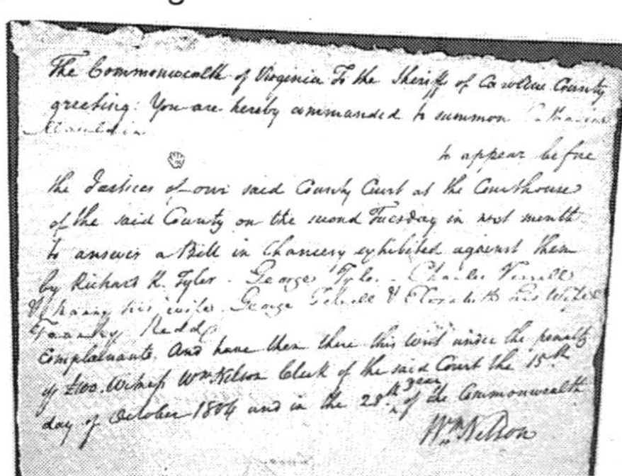

The Commonwealth of Virginia To the Sheriff of Caroline County greeting: You are hereby commanded to summon [illegible]

to appear before the Justices of our said County Court at the Courthouse of the said County on the second Tuesday in next month to answer a Bill in Chancery exhibited against them by Richard K. Tyler, George Tyler, Charles [illegible] & Nanny his wife, George [illegible] & Elizabeth his wife & Franky Redd Complainants. And have then there this writ under the penalty of £100. Witness Wm. Nelson Clerk of the said Court the 15th day of October 1804 and in the 28th year of the Commonwealth

Wm. Nelson

William Tyler was the last of Nannie's direct line to be buried in Virginia. Richard Keeling's name also appears later in his Aunt Catharine's will. According to the *Virginia Will Books,* he is shown as receiving two slaves and a silver watch from his Aunt Catharine Tyler in a will proved on August 12, 1816. Another relative, Phillip Redd[9] also received two slaves at her death. The Tylers and the Redds were two families whose histories would be intertwined for manifold years.

Nannie's great, great grandfather was Richard Keeling Tyler, (1760-1832), the son of William Tyler and Elizabeth Keeling Tyler. Richard was born at the old Tyler homestead near Chilesburg, Caroline County, Virginia. At age 16, he left to fight in the Revolutionary War and was later the captain of a company which surrendered at Yorktown. His two brothers George and John served as first and second lieutenants respectively.

When the war ended in 1781, Richard Keeling returned home to the family farm. By this time, he was twenty-one and realized that he was deficient in his education; others noted that he also lacked what some call "direction" in his life or "a bit wayward." This was due to the fact that he

---

[9] In a letter dated 1963 to a Tyler descendant, the writer states that the Tyler men liked the Waller girls and also the Redd girls as "we know of two Tyler men who married Miss Wallers and two Tyler men married Miss Redds."

had been raised with very few responsibilities. Before the war Richard never labored on his father's farm as slaves did all the work. Richard spent his days in leisurely activities occupying his youth with hunting or fishing which reduced his exposure to education.

Richard Keeling purchased land near Campbell's Mill sometime in 1780 or 1781 and reputedly settled down after his love match marriage on July 1, 1790 to Mary "Mollie" Cluverius Duke (August 3, 1767-1846). Mary was the twenty-three-year-old daughter of John Duke (1738-1782), and Elizabeth Burnley Duke (1739-1816), daughter of Hardin and Anne Winston Terrell Burnley from Hanover County, Virginia. It was said that Richard was "poor and hopeful" and she was "poor and trustful." People were pleased to see that he developed into a true gentleman,

> **A kindlier man or one with warmer heart you could not find and popular he was too with his neighbors. He was inclined to make the world easy and to make the very best of life while it was his, but he never knowingly wronged his neighbor or bore malice in his heart against any human being. As long as he lived-and he lived to a green old age- he never failed to take his morning and evening dram or to read his daily lessons in the prayer book.**

Richard did indeed mature into a responsible, caring husband and father. He and Mollie were inseparable and their long-term dedication to each other was evident to everyone who knew them. As an adult, Richard wore a full beard and had kind, hazel colored eyes. His hair was light brown, as was Mollie's. Her eyes were a lovely blue and her hair was worn in the simple style with a part down the middle and pulled back into a bun. Nannie Tyler, the subject of this manuscript, was to inherit her blue eyes from the Duke side of the family. These, her great-grandparents were to bring the Tyler family into Tennessee.

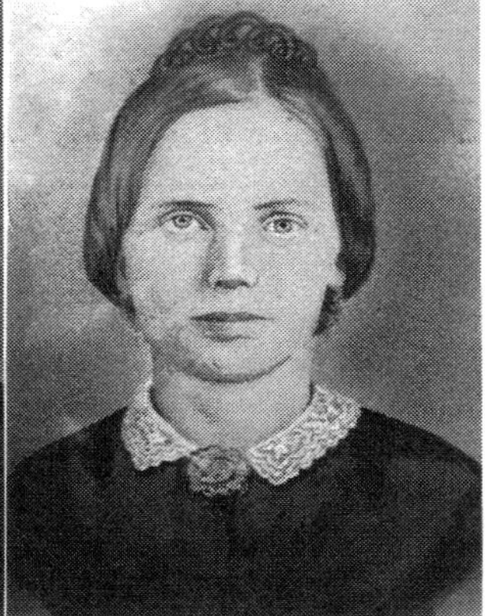

Richard Keeling Tyler and Mary "Mollie" Cluverius Duke Tyler. Courtesy John Duke Tyler IV.

Richard Keeling Tyler, Sr. and Mary C. Tyler had six children, two of whom died in infancy:

- **Elizabeth Tyler (died at 6 months old)**
- **Maria Tyler (died at two years old)**
- **Richard Keeling Tyler, Jr. (1782-1860)** His son Richard K. Tyler III (1801-1878), married Lucy Quintus Redc.
- **William Burnley Tyler (1791-1856)**
- **John Duke Tyler (1794-1860)**
- **Mary Cluverius Tyler (1798-1828)** married Henry C. Mockbee, a veteran of the Revolutionary War. She died the day after giving birth to their one child, Mary Cluverius Mockbee, who lived part of her life with her cousin John Duke Tyler's family at Hickory Wild.

The 1810 Census also showed two other free persons and 28 slaves listed with the family. For twenty-eight years, Richard and Mollie lived in Caroline County rearing their remaining children. During many of these years, Richard served, as his father had, in the capacity of a magistrate. Caroline County records also show that Richard was sworn in as a deputy sheriff in October 1796, a much-esteemed position in those days.

Their son, John Duke Tyler started school before he was 5-years-old, walking three miles each day to and from a little private school house, having to cross the small, but beautiful Mattaponi River by a log footbridge along the way. This was the year 1799. It must have been rugged country at the time with rich farmland fed by the numerous rivers in the area. Even before John Duke began school, his mother taught him lessons from a "horn book" which served as a primer for study.[10]

[10] The primer consisted of a sheet with the letters of the alphabet mounted on leather, bone, or wood. This was protected with a thin sheet of transparent mica. The primer usually had a handle to which it could be worn at the child's waist.

He was to become a scholar of both Latin and Greek, having been taught by a highly regarded Scottish schoolmaster named Peter Nelson[11] who considered it his duty to flog his students at regular intervals to "loosen their hides to stimulate growth and development of both mind and body." John Duke's practice of whipping undisciplined students was learned from this schoolmaster.

In 1786, the North Carolina General Assembly had passed an Act - Chapter LXIV - naming and authorizing trustees to build and manage a new school named the Warrenton Academy. The trustees were also authorized to establish a lottery to raise money to help fund the new academy. In January 1787, the state legislature chartered Warrenton Academy. In 1802 the Warren Academy building was a two-story, frame building with limited bedrooms upstairs for teachers and a few students. In 1802 the exterior of the Warrenton Male Academy was painted red and became known to the country people as "The Red Academy." John Duke taught at Warrenton Academy for one year, 100 miles from his home. Peter Nelson must have seen great promise in so young a pupil to give him the high recommendation needed to become a teacher with some students older than himself. Even then when boys his age were considered to be men, it must have been very lonesome for John Duke, being so far away from family and friends. At this time, he was described as six feet tall but extremely slender and delicate in his youth.

At age 18, he enlisted in a cavalry company at the start of the War of 1812 and was given the rank of captain. His company was never called into service but he retained the title of captain for the rest of his life.

One year later on December 15, 1813, he married his first wife, Harriett Redd (1791-1820), a first cousin of his father's. Harriett's parents were: William Redd (1750-1802), and Frances Tyler (1751-1813). Harriett's siblings were Ann Redd (1787-1868), George Redd (1770-bef.1813), Elizabeth Redd (1773-1812), Lucy Quintus Redd (1777-?), Frances Tyler Redd (1782-1868), Phillip Redd (1784-1819), William Redd, Jr. (1785-1856), Matilda Redd (1788-1841), and John Redd (1792-1830).

John Duke bought some land near his father and settled down to start raising their family. John Duke's apparent love of ancient languages is evidenced by the names of his early children. Five years later the Tylers would make their move to Tennessee out of necessity.

The increasing numbers of immigrants sailing into Chesapeake Bay and settling in the area negatively affected the area's economics. To make matters worse, the aftermath of the Revolutionary War adversely impacted the farmers of the Tidewater community as the demand for tobacco began to decline significantly. Depression spread as the credit system was overextended, until everyone owned everyone else to the point that debts were impossible to repay. The next generation of Tylers was not only faced with adapting to a new nation, but also still coming to grips with the effects of the war.

The repeated planting of tobacco in Virginia was taking its toll on the farmland by stripping many of the nutrients from the soil. Tobacco is one of the most labor-intensive crops grown in the South. It is a year-round crop, requiring constant attention from the moment it is planted until the day it is sold. Without artificial fertilizers and the failure to rotate crops, the acreage of useable tillable land began to diminish. By 1818, many farmers were forced by economics to pull up stakes and head west seeking better farming opportunities.

Another contributing factor to the westward movement was the practice of primogeniture laws in Virginia, which meant the oldest son inherited the estates while the other children received little or no inheritance at all. To remain in Virginia meant that a younger son would need to enter the clergy or the military. If not, the obvious solution for the younger sons was to seek their fortune elsewhere.

When Richard Keeling Tyler, Sr. passed away in 1794 the family farm was willed to his son, John. He divided up his 25 slaves and bequeathed them to his kinsman, Phillip Redd (b. ca.

---

[11] Rev. Peter Nelson (1757-1827), who graduated from William & Mary College; was ordained a minister of the Episcopal Church, taught a select Classical School at "Wingfield," in Hanover County and was ordained a minister of Congress (or Elder) in the Baptist Church. Burnley Duke Smith (mentioned later) was also a student of Peter Nelson's. He had to walk 8 miles to school.

1784): 4 slaves, George Tyler: two slaves and other relatives. One slave, his manservant, he emancipated, gave him $45, a mare and lent him fifty acres of his land for him to farm during his life. Richard Keeling Tyler, Jr. and his family found themselves in a most unenviable situation. After struggling for years, Richard Keeling and Mollie resolved to load up the wagons with their four surviving children and their families to move west. Harriett's sister Matilda Redd also decided to leave Virginia with the Tylers to settle in Tennessee.

At age 24, John Duke and his wife and their two young sons, Marcus Marcellus Tyler, born in 1814 and Quintus Marcellus Tyler, born 1816, would also make the journey. Harriett was pregnant at the time of the trip and upon their arrival in Tennessee, she would give birth to a daughter, Mary Frances Tyler.

At this time, the new state of Tennessee was considered to be the Far West. Land speculators were widely espousing it to be like the Biblical land of milk and honey. Already many relatives and friends had made the trip, so it must have been a solace for the Tylers to know that when they arrived in Tennessee they would see many familiar faces. This included the Minor, Fortson, Carney, Trigg and Hampton families. The journey was made by wagon with the exception of the senior Tylers riding in an old family carriage. They and their slaves began their long, arduous journey with as many furnishings and provisions as they could load into wagons and moved to the reputed cheap, fertile farmlands of Tennessee. This difficult journey must have tested every ounce of resolve.

What a sad parting this would have been! Saying farewell to friends and family members must have resembled the goodbyes at a funeral, for who was to believe that they would ever see their loved ones again over such a long distance, separated by a mountain range? Would it ever occur to these families that they were to become an integral part of the expansion of a new nation or that this new experiment of democracy was spreading into virgin regions because of their actions? Their stamina and hardiness would be tested, as would all others making the same decision to leave behind the familiar to endure whatever lay ahead.

The timing of the trip was important. It is estimated that their journey began in October or November, since it was recorded that it lasted two months and their arrival at their destination was in December. Waiting too late to travel meant risking unfavorable weather. It was imperative that grass be available for the livestock and that the rivers and creeks they were to cross were not hardened by ice. Setting out at this time also meant that they would have had time to harvest crops and dry fruits and meats for foodstuffs to take along with them. Much of what they owned had to be sold before they began the journey, certainly anything considered to be non-essential.

Heavy white fabric coated with oil to repel rain and snow was stretched over the tops of the wagons on wooden hoops, called bows. Everything the Tylers needed for the journey had to fit inside the wagons. Furniture, clothes, barrels of food such as flour, sugar, cornmeal, coffee, dried beans, rice, bacon and salt pork along with quilts, frying pans, iron skillets, knives and rifles with shot pouch and powder horns took up much of the wagon space, allowing room only for a child's doll, a pocketknife or book. On the outside of the wagons, tools such as axes, saws, hoes and augers were hung. A spare wheel was also a necessity. One item that Richard Keeling would not leave behind was the sword he carried with him in the Revolutionary War.[12]

Advice on which route was the best or safest to take would have been sought and the route planned out. The route they took required them to cross the Allegany Mountains, a substantial barrier to westward land travel.

To lessen the weight in the wagons, most of the group walked all day from sun up to sundown. Each day followed a routine of eating breakfast, packing and hitching up the wagons. Drinking coffee helped to warm the mornings and get them started; even the children drank coffee. Landscape and weather dictated the distance covered daily with some days more difficult than others, especially if the trail was washed out, muddy, or too steep or rocky. Whenever possible, the group would stop for "nooning," a short pit-stop to allow sore feet to rest, time to enjoy some type of lunch and give the animals a respite to enjoy some refreshment as well.

Everyone slept in make-shift tents except for the elder Tylers who, when they could, took

---

[12] His descendants were to recall the sword as one of his most cherished possessions.

shelter in any cabin or inn along the way. Sleeping in a tent also meant sleeping on the ground, but if it were dry, leaves would be collected and with a quilt thrown on top, the night would pass in relative comfort. If bedding was available, it too could be pulled from the wagons for use. The slaves probably slept under the wagons for shelter at night. What began for the children as a grand adventure must have turned weary in a short time. The travelers' lingering thoughts of their old beds back in Virginia and the warmer conditions of their former homes were replaced with speculation and expectations of the unknown future. Maybe it was during these moments that John Duke pulled out his fiddle and livened up everyone's spirits. He got his love of the instrument from his father, Richard Keeling.

As the campfires died out and they settled down to rest, sounds emerging from the surrounding forests might have sent a child scrambling into the arms of its mother or father! Children contributed to the journey by helping to find food such as berries, which they picked along the way. Older children might shoot rabbits or squirrels to add to the menu. The meals would consist of beans, bread, dried meat and any game that was shot. Deer and turkeys inhabited the forests and venison was always appreciated. Children also helped care for the work animals and gathered wood for the campfire. Responsibility was taught at an early age and everyone was expected to pitch in.

The roads they followed were generally nothing more than the former trails of Indians, traders, deer and bison. Pioneers going before them cleared the way for those to follow, their names forever ingrained in the history of the country. After a few weeks, the feat of crossing the mountains soon loomed before the Tylers.

Traversing the mountains was a methodical one. When the wagons were ready, one of the men would scout ahead to survey the best route. Preparations were made to move one wagon at a time up the steep incline. In all likelihood the Tylers used both horses and mules to pull the wagons. It would be difficult to imagine horses alone having the strength to make this ascent. It is said that one mule is worth two horses in strength. Mules were also more expensive than horses. They were purchased as a team since they worked in conjunction with each other. As a reward for their hard labor, mules often received special attention and pampering from their owners.

Quintus recorded the trip in a manuscript he wrote later in life. (Recorded here verbatim):

> **In the fall of 1818 our grandfather (Richard Keeling) and family consisting of wife, daughter Mary E. and son Richard K. and a good many Negro slaves; also our father's family consisting of his wife, her sister Matilda Redd, brother, (Marcus "Uncle Mark Tyler"), and myself and Negroes; also old Uncle Madison whose wife was sister of our grandmother (both Dukes) and his family, consisting of his wife, 3 sons, 1 daughter, and Negroes, ---all moved to the place occupied by the Redds near Hampton's Spring. Trip took seven or eight weeks in wagons and carriages.**

Like many of the settlers, the Tylers came down into Tennessee by way of the Cumberland Gap. This route was crucial to the westward movement since it was the only natural trail through the Appalachian mountain range. They would have met up with others moving west. Many friendships began on this journey and lasted for a lifetime. Added numbers also meant additional security and although attacks by Indians were not expected still, having the extra travelers with them made the trip less nerve wracking and boring.

To begin the ascent, the wagonloads were reduced and extra horses were added to help pull. Moving each wagon at a time involved a concerted effort by everyone. Someone would be positioned at each of the wagon wheels to help turn it. Two additional men were placed behind each wheel to "scotch" it. This meant that whenever the wagon had moved forward a short distance or the team hesitated, they threw a large stone (scotcher) under the wheels to prevent losing any of the valuable slope they had already gained. The team would be spurred on by the crack of whips and loud shouting. This routine was repeated over and over until all wagons reached the summit. Each instance must have felt like a major victory of man against mountain. Certainly descending down the slope was just as challenging as first going up and once a ridge was successfully conquered, yet another lay ahead of them.

The Cumberland Gap. Courtesy the National Park Service.

Another detail of this crossing comes from John Duke's son, Charles Waller Tyler, who in 1903 wrote a book describing the trek made over the mountains. As he was not born until many years later, his information had to have come from stories "passed down" from family members actually present on the journey. He wrote:

> **Notwithstanding locked wheels and constant tugging against the breeching on the part of the hindmost mules, the conveyance now went forward at headlong rate, bumping against huge boulders, and scattering the fearful housewife's plunder, with now and then a few of the children, promiscuously along the route. Often spokes and tires were smashed, axles broken, or tongues[13] shattered, and it took a few days to mend up and start afresh on the journey to a new home in the wilderness.**

Finally, from the last ridge, the vantage points of what lay before them must have excited every heart. Nearing the end of their journey, in what they later recalled to be a "bleak December," the Tylers arrived at about sundown in the diminutive town of Port Royal, Tennessee on the banks of the Red River. Ten miles away was the emerging town of Clarksville[14] if they wanted to sell their tobacco or buy goods.

Just a few miles down the road from Port Royal was the farm of John and Phillip Redd near Hampton's Springs.[15] These two brothers had left Virginia in 1817, one year ahead of the Tylers. The Redds welcomed their two sisters, Matilda and Harriett and the entire group of Tylers.[16] They settled ten miles from Clarksville, Tennessee which, within a year, would be incorporated as a town with elected officials. The Tyler family was to impact Clarksville in ways unimaginable for the next 100 years.

To begin their new life, Richard K. Tyler, Sr. rented "the Hampton farm" from the Redds. Quintus described the farm:

> **Grandfather rented this farm for one year. Single story log house with shed room, wooden chimney, rib pole roof and ladder to go up to the loft. Lived on the Hampton farm during 1819, 20, 21, 22. Hauled water from Hampton's Spring,[17] one mile off.**

The George W. Hampton house.[18]

The Tylers were able to purchase their own the farm in District One of Montgomery County in January 1823. Quintus obviously preferred this house to the cabin. He stated:

> **He (grandfather) and father bought the Hickory Wild place and moved there January 1823. Double room, hewed log house with a passage between. Story and a half, 2 brick chimneys, 3 entrance doors. Fine House! Aunt Mary (Mockbee) and Lucy Q. Tyler died**

---

[13] A "tongue" of a wagon refers to the long, wooden beam that extends from the front of the wagon body and connects to the draft animals, essentially acting as the point where the pulling force is applied to move the wagon forward; it's the part of the wagon that the horses or oxen would be harnessed to. -*Wikipedia*

[14] In 1785, the North Carolina Legislature designated Clarksville as a town.

[15] One of the first settlers in this area was William Trigg from southern Virginia who initially purchased 289 acres for $980 in 1811. His wife's name was Ann (Nancy) Hampton and it was for her family that this area was named after the Trigg farm was inherited by George W. Hampton, a relative of Ann's.

[16] A note of local interest here is that at the same time the Tylers were settling in Montgomery County, TN, in nearby Adams, the John Bell family was dealing with a haunting known as the infamous "Bell Witch."

[17] Formally known as Doe River Cove.

[18] George W. Hampton was also a cousin of Kate Wimberly Killebrew mentioned later in this manuscript.

in that house. Grandfather very popular, kind, sociable, not a good business man.

The land they now called home was a vast area of forests on gently rolling hills filled with turkey, deer and other game. Here they could raise all the crops they needed to feed their families as well as livestock to sustain them.

By 1819, the newly established town of Clarksville had 22 stores, including a bakery owned by Thomas Bray and a silversmith. The Montgomery County Census of 1820 lists the household of Richard Keeling Tyler, Sr.:

1 male age 16-18: Richard Keeling Tyler, Jr.
1 male age 18-26: John Duke Tyler
1 male age 45 and up: Richard Keeling Tyler, Sr.
1 female age 16-26: Harriett Redd Tyler
1 female age 45 and up: Mary "Mollie" Tyler

Additionally, the 1820 county slave records show that a Negro boy could be purchased for $13.50 and a Negro woman for as low as $50.00. However, this was not the norm. At the other end of the spectrum were these prices:

$1,450 for a 39-year-old Negro man
$580 for an 8-year-old Negro boy
$650 for a 10-year-old Negro boy
$755 for a 12-year-old Negro boy
$1,250 for a Negro woman and her children

While growing up, both John Duke and his father enjoyed playing a fiddle and giving large-scale house parties that went on for several days. Peter Nelson never appreciated music or saw its practical application, but in spite of this, John Duke became an accomplished musician. He played a fiddle his entire life and was often asked to provide the music at social events, which he did with zeal. A relative of John Duke's, born in 1790 in Virginia, also grew up loving to play the fiddle. His name was John Tyler, later to become the tenth President of the United States.

However, John Duke was known to differ greatly with his father on political views. His father was a staunch Federalist believing that the government was "of gentlemen, for gentlemen and by gentlemen." Of course, as any parent knows, children will take the opposite viewpoints just for the sake of arguing. Sometimes, their arguments became quite boisterous and loud and when John Duke was of age to cast his vote he would on occasion, ride for miles to the precinct in which his father voted in downpours of rain, just to negate his father's vote.

John Duke also had some strong views on the roles that soldiers played after their military service and it did not include politics. Therefore, he most certainly did not support Andrew Jackson's bid for President in the 1828 election. When the Robertson County votes were counted, Jackson won a resounding victory. The polls showed Henry Clay earning 1 vote... was it John Duke's? It is also interesting to mention here that Clay was from Hanover Co., Virginia where John Duke was born. Over time, it is said, the political differences of father and son mellowed out and became more agreeable.

In early 1820, John Duke rented some land from Maj. James Johnson upon which he started his school. He chose this property because there already existed a two-room log cabin, which could be used immediately for classes. Being the progressive individual he was: he had already taken out an advertisement in the December 1819 issues of the *Clarksville Gazette*. The ad read:

EDUCATION

THE SUBSCRIBER, residing on Spring Creek, Montgomery County, Tennessee, tenders his services to the public, the ensuing year, as an instructor of youth in the following branches of Literature, viz: The Latin language, Reading, Writing, English Grammar, Geography and Arithmetic. The fees, for tuition, will be Ten Dollars per Session; for Latin, English Grammar, Geography or Arithmetic: For Reading and Writing Seven Dollars & Fifty cents per Session. He can accommodate 6 or 8 students with board, at $35 per Session, each boarder furnishing his own bed, bedding and candles. The fees, both for board and tuition, to be paid, one half when the student is sent, the remainder at the expiration of the Session. There will be an examination of the students at the close of each Session. The first Session will commence on the 26th of January and end on the 20th of June; the second

Session will commence on the 1st of July and end on the 20th of December. Those that wish to board with him, are requested to make it known, as speedily as possible, in order that he may make the necessary arrangements for their accommodation. The strictest attention will be paid to the morals of the students entrusted to his care.
JOHN D. TYLER
December 12, 1819

John Duke viewed teaching as the noblest of professions. Classes were given in one room of the cabin while John Duke, his wife and three children occupied the other. It became necessary to build onto the cabin as the school's enrollment increased.[19]

When Harriet died October 18, 1820 at the age of 29, John buried her on a hilltop across from his land. She was buried with relatives in what is now the Minor Family Cemetery located about nine miles north of Clarksville, a quarter mile from where Hampton Station Road enters Highway 79. The cemetery, containing seven graves, was once surrounded by a grove of large Osage orange trees enclosed by a wooden fence. Male Osage orange trees, *Maclura pomifera*, with their thorny branches were intentionally planted at gravesites in the time of the pioneers to protect the graves.

Another source states that before the invention of barbed wire in the 1880s, these trees were trimmed back and used as hedges, hence the nickname hedge apple. "Horse high, bull strong and hog tight" was the saying that accompanied the story of these trees which meant they were too high for a horse to jump, too strong for a bull to push through and woven too tightly for a hog to get past. Each deep green, glossy, lance-shaped leaf has at its base a sharp thorn that is strong enough to pierce and flatten the tire of a tractor.

Harriett's grave when still surrounded by the Osage orange trees in 2006. Since then the trees have been removed. Photos of cemetery by author.

In Memory of Harriett Tyler, Consort of John D. Tyler. Born May 31ST 1791 Obit in 8th 1820 Age 29 Years, 4 months and 20 days

Peace still visits this hill and the pioneers sleep. The occupants of the cemetery are:

Thomas Carr Minor (1757-1819)
Ann Redd Minor (1762-1834) wife of Thomas Minor.
Robert Minor (abt. 1762-1823) possible brother to Thomas.
Frances Minor Gordon (1790-1828) wife of (unknown) Gordon. Daughter of Thomas Carr Minor and Ann Redd Minor.
Harriett Redd Tyler (1791-1820) wife of John Duke Tyler.
Maria Carr Minor Collins (1794-1821) wife of George H. Collins.
Ann Redd Minor Minor (1801-1825) cousin and first wife of Dr. William Tompkins Minor (1797-1854).

From *The History of Redd Family of Virginia*, by J.S Redd of Pacos, Halifax Co. Virginia, it is learned that,

> **The name of Redd is believed to have been originally used as a nickname, having reference to the red hair or ruddy complexion of its first bearers. It is found in ancient English and early American records in the various spellings of Rede, Redde, Reede, Reade,**

[19] This land later became part of the Hinton family farm on the Russellville Road near Spring Creek.

Read, Reide, Reid, Red, Redd and others, of which several of the other forms are more generally used today, but that of Redd is still frequently found in America.

The Redd name is a very uncommon one and there is little doubt that all the families of that name in Virginia and in the other Southern and Western States are descendants of the same ancestor, Sir William Rufus de Redds who came to Virginia from England, with Governor Alexander Spotswood, during the early part of Queen Anne's reign, 1702-1714. From the best authority that can be found, it cannot be doubted that the name Redd or de Redde, as it was originally called, had its origin with a noble house, that of William Rufus, the son of the Conqueror, which latter is known by every school boy as the first of the Norman kings in England, and mounted the throne of England immediately after the famous battle of Hastings, fought in the year 1066. English historians have generally denied that William I or William Rufus was lawfully married. This statement is not true, as there is authority of the highest order to establish the fact that he was married, but not 'in the purple,' as it was then called, which means that he was not married during his reign. He was, however, married before the death of his father, the Conqueror, and had one son. This son was also named William, and accompanied his uncle Robert, Duke of Normandy and his crusading army to Jerusalem during the year 1098, that being known in history as the 'First Crusade.'

Also, from *The Name and Family of Redd*, compiled by the Media Research Bureau, Washington, D.C. it was stated,

The history of the Redds in America is that of a sturdy, self-reliant, resourceful, and courageous race, possessed of physical stamina and perseverance. Other characteristics of the family include generosity, kindliness and sociability.

At Harriett's death, John Duke was left with three small children, all under the age of six. Marcus Marcellus was age 5, Quintus Marcellus, age 3 and Mary Frances (born in Tennessee in 1819). For three more years, he continued his instructions on the land he was renting from James Johnson.

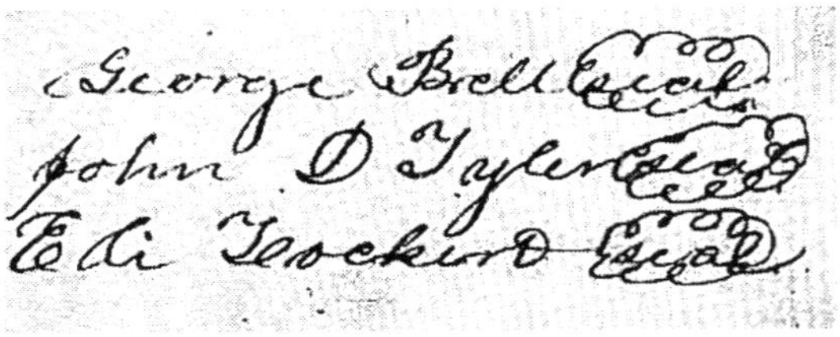

John Duke Tyler's signature along with George Bell and Eli Lockert who were also early settlers in Montgomery County.

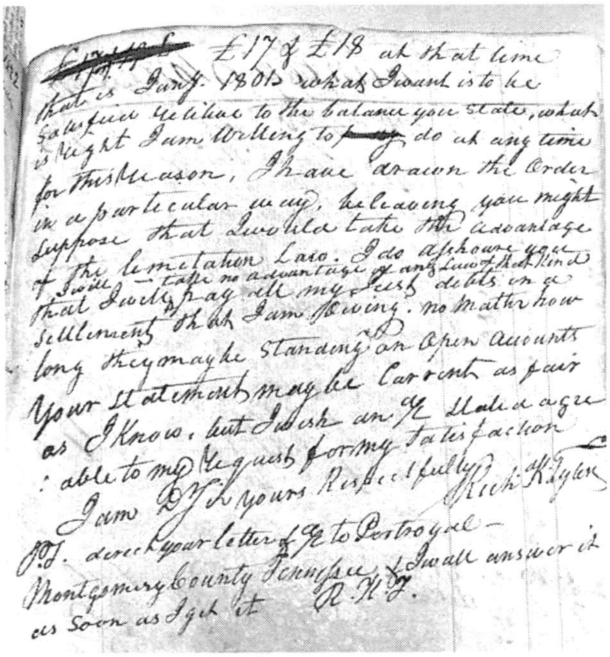

Richard Keeling and Mollie Tyler left Tennessee and moved to Trigg County, Kentucky. In 1846 Mollie passed away and it was not surprising to anyone who knew the couple's devotion to each other that his death should so closely follow her, by just one year. Friends recalled how Richard and Mollie spent many happy times dancing the minuet together.

A legal document signed by Richard Keeling Tyler in 1801. (GF)

Chapter Two: Pine Knots and Black Gumology

On January 15, 1820, two years after the Tylers came over the mountains to settle in what became known as District One, the newly incorporated town of Clarksville elected its first city council: John H. Poston, Frederick Huling, Cave Johnson, Samuel Vance, Peter N. Marr, James A. Marable and James E. Elder. Elder was chosen to be the township's first mayor. By February 15, 1820, they had adopted their first twelve by-laws. Of eleven ordinances, eight related to misconduct which could result in arrest or fines, the twelfth dealt with the appointment of the two-man patrol. Such was Clarksville's first police department! The by-laws were as follows:

(1) Be it ordained that there shall be a patrol to consist of two persons for said town, who shall receive the sum of Fifty Dollars each for their services, and that it shall be the duty of that patrol at least two nights in every week to go to the rounds and to visit in every part of the town twice each night that may be set apart for watching once before the hour of 12 o'clock, and once after—and that it shall be further the duty of the patrol should they discover any Negroes (without a special permit in writing) to inflict upon them a punishment not exceeding ten lashes should they be walking about the streets at an improper or unusual hour, in any kitchen, not belonging to the master of the Negro or his employer, unless they be refractory or insolvent. And that it shall be further the duty of the said patrol should they discover any white persons in company after dark with any slave or slaves or in any Negro kitchen, immediately to arrest the said person and keep him in custody until the next morning and bring him before the Mayor and he shall be fined, therefore, not less than one dollar and not exceeding ten dollars, at the discretion of the Mayor.

(2) And it is further ordained by the Mayor and the Alderman of Clarksville that it shall be the duty of the patrol, if at any time required by the Mayor, to patrol the town not exceeding four nights in the week for which they will receive the sum of fifty cents each.

(3) Be it further ordained by the Mayor and the Alderman of Clarksville that no Negro shall be permitted to come to the town of Clarksville on a Sunday, a holy day or a night without permission from the owner or employer in writing setting forth their business, as also the time they are permitted to remain in town, under penalty of receiving ten lashes to be inflicted by the town constable or patrol.

(4) And be it further ordained by the authority aforesaid, that no person shall hereafter sell to or buy from, or in any manner whatever employ any slave without a permit in writing from the master or owner of the said slave or slaves, under a penalty of five dollars for each offense.

(5) And it is further ordained by the authority aforesaid, that Phillip Johnson be appointed overseer of the streets of the said town for the year 1820, and that it shall be the duty of the said overseer of the streets to work upon said streets at such time and at such places as may be directed by the Mayor and Alderman of Clarksville and further to keep an account of the failure of such persons to work on the streets as are bound so to do, and make a return thereof to the recorder of the town within five days after the time appointed for working on the said streets.

(6) And it is further ordained by the authority aforesaid that all white males from the age of 18 to 50 years and all black males between 15 and 50 years, within the bounds of said town, shall be liable to work on the streets of said town under the said overseer, and in case any persons residing in the bounds of said town failing to attend, or to send, all of his, her, or their hands liable as aforesaid, or to bring such tools as may be directed by the overseer, or refusing to perform a reasonable portion of labor, when they do attend, upon having two days previous notice thereof, shall be fined the sum of one dollar, for each person so failing to attend, or send with such tools as may be directed for the performance of the work.

(7) Be it further ordained by the authority aforesaid, that any person or persons throwing or causing wood or other rubbish to be thrown in the Public Square or on Franklin Street and permitting it to remain there for the space of twelve hours shall be fined the sum of two

dollars for each offense.
(8) Be it further ordained, that no person shall permit their wagon or cart to remain on the Public Square or Franklin Street, nor shall any person linger in the places aforesaid, or feed their teams therein under penalty of one dollar for each offense.
(9) And it is further ordained by the authority aforesaid that any person or persons who shall be guilty of gaming or playing any game of hazard or address for any valuable thing within the bounds of the corporation aforesaid shall be fined for each offense the sum of five dollars, and each house holder permitting these to be carried on at his house shall be fined not less than five dollars and no more than fifty dollars.
(10) Be it further ordained, that no person or person shall make any theatrical exhibition (shows) or exhibition for public amusement of any kind without having first applied to the recorder of the corporation and obtaining a license therefore and paying the recorder the sum of five dollars for the benefit of the corporation under a penalty for a failure, or neglect to do so to twenty-five dollars.
(11) Be it further ordained by the authority aforesaid that the foregoing ordinances be enforced from and after the 15th day of February 1820.
Joel C. Rice (recorder)
For the Corporation of the Town of Clarksville, TN[20]

John Duke's school at this time was exclusively for boys. In the same general area was one open only to girls as announced on March 2, 1821:

Mrs. Killebrew, having had several years' experience in teaching, flatters herself with the hope of success in inspiring her pupils with sentiments of delicacy and correctness; with habits of industry and economy-essential parts of female education. Each young lady must furnish her own trunk and bed etc. The terms will be $100.00 per annum--$25.00 to be paid in advance.

A female boarding school will be opened by Mrs. Mary Jane R. Killebrew, at her residence in Montgomery County on the first Monday in April, for the instruction of young ladies in the following branches:

The English Language	**The Elements of Rhetoric & Composition**
Writing	**Drawing**
Arithmetic	**Painting**
Practical Geometry	**Construction of Maps**
Geography	**Construction of Artificial Flowers**
Astronomy	**Embroidery**
Ancient and Modern History	**Various Kinds of Needlework**

The county was making progress as it looked to improve travel conditions in and around the town. The first bridge to span the Red River connecting Clarksville to New Providence was constructed in 1829. The Tylers would cross this bridge many times when going in to Clarksville. Previously there had been a ferry at the spot and during certain seasons when crops were harvested, the roads leading to the ferry would be inundated with wagons, horses, oxen and people waiting to cross the river. This bridge was built using funds provided by James B. Reynolds, a distinguished and wealthy gentleman, nicknamed the "Irish Count" by those who knew him. When this bridge was condemned as unsafe in 1836, a new bridge was built after a stock company was formed. This was to be a toll bridge. From the record book, it can be seen what goods were being transferred across the river. Corn, bricks, garden produce, tobacco, flax, fruits such as apples, various grains, pigs and cattle were all entered into the toll book. Two, four and six-horse wagons also came across the bridge. By far oxen, two-mule and two-oxen carts outnumbered the other means of transportation. Tolls included:

Foot passenger: 2 cents
Person with mule or horse: 5 cents
Additional horse or mule: 3 cents
Head of cattle: 2 cents

[20] How could John Duke have known then that one of his sons would preside as judge, enforcing city ordinances such as these for 47 years in Clarksville?

Sheep or hog: 1 cent
Two-horse, two-mule, or two-oxen wagon: 25 cents
With additional team to six animals: 30 cents
Every cart ranging from 1 to 6 animals: from 12½ cents to 25 cents
Every two or four-wheeled light carriage with two to four animal teams: 25 cents

By this method, Count Reynolds and later the corporation was paid in full for their investments. On December 9, 1862, during the occupation of Clarksville by Federal troops, that bridge burned down and was subsequently rebuilt. It remained a toll bridge until the early nineteen hundreds when John Duke Tyler's son Charles, acting as County Financial Officer, removed the toll on it and other county bridges.

By 1827, John Duke decided to take a trip by horseback to visit his home state of Virginia. His health had been poor up until this time. His traveling companion was Richard Waller, a close friend. Richard (1782-?), had been born in Spotsylvania County, Virginia to Rev. William Edmund Waller (1747-1830),

The name "Waller" was in origin an English occupational name for a builder of walls, mason.

Richard Waller was the captain of a company in Shelbyville, Kentucky where he was for some years a merchant (Waller & Bolling Holmes). He was in 1816, a stockholder in the Shelbyville Branch Bank of Kentucky. Richard was described as a "very handsome and intelligent gentleman." In 1803 he married Susanna Grigsby. They had the following children:

William Edmund Smith Waller (b. & d. 1806)
Ann Duke Waller (1809-?)
Mildred Smith Waller (1809-1884) would become the wife of John Duke Tyler.
Maria Louisa Waller (? -?)
Emily Burnley Waller (? -?)
Charles Smith Waller (? -1897)
Mary Price Waller (? -?)

Leaving his children with relatives, John Duke and Richard embarked on a trip made, not due to necessity, but for pleasure. Their journey, without being encumbered by wagons and people, lasted two months. While riding to Virginia in all kinds of weather, the men took time to enjoy stops along the way, lingering as long as they wished to "see the sights." After their arrival in Virginia, they spent much of that summer with family and friends, finally returning to Tennessee in the fall. With his health greatly improved, John Duke often recalled that the trip was one of the greatest experiences of his entire life. Richard died in Princeton, Kentucky in 1833.

John Duke had remained a widower for almost ten years but upon his return to Tennessee, he asked his friend for his daughter's hand in marriage. On January 5, 1830 in Princeton, Kentucky John Duke wed twenty-one-year-old Mildred Smith Waller. John Duke was now thirty-six, fifteen years older than his new bride.

During their marriage, Mildred presented her husband with five children. They were John Duke Tyler, Jr., the eldest child (1826-1895), Nannie Waller Tyler (1843-1912), Joseph Addison Tyler (1837-1856), Charles Waller Tyler (1839-1920), and Emmie Tyler (1849-1932). An additional family member was Anna Waller Pettus (1861-1912), one of eight children born to Thomas Franklin Pettus, Sr. (1818-1875), and Martha Alice Cowherd Pettus (1819-1870). Anna was born at the Old Kentucky Landing and was probably related to Mildred Tyler. It appears that the Tylers raised her along with their other children.

Anna's parents. Photo courtesy Jack Pettus.

Thomas F. Pettus, born in Alabama, helped to establish the New Providence Building Association in 1855 and the Montgomery General Insurance and Trust Company in1856. In 1860, Pettus was mayor of New Providence and operated a stemming house there. During the Civil War, he served as a captain in the Confederate Army in Co. H. Mississippi regiment. After the war, Thomas was partners with his brothers in the tobacco commission business and then in July 1869 he was appointed county registrar by the governor. He was also the first vice-president of the tobacco board. At this time the Pettus family including

Anna, lived in New Providence with several of Thomas' relatives. When Anna's parents moved to Mississippi, Anna was given to the Tylers to raise.[21]

After their marriage, John Duke and Mildred, moved to Port Royal where he opened another school. His time in the Port Royal community was short but memorable, for he formed many lasting friendships among the Norfleet, Hopson and Northington families. John Duke taught for one year in the crude cabin before purchasing his father's Hickory Wild farm in January 1831 when his parents moved to Kentucky. Many of the Tylers had settled in counties Trigg, Todd and Christian. John Duke's school therefore was named Hickory Wild Academy.

John Duke Tyler. From the *Nashville Banner.*

The house was a major improvement over his previous home that served as his school. It sat at the top of a ridge overlooking a wide expanse of farmland located in what is now known as the Kirkwood community. The large Federal-style building was a simple frame structure with lap siding, one and half stories high, with four windows on the front of the main floor. In addition, there were two dormer windows on the second floor. The lap siding was made available to settlers as the water-powered sawmills began operation on the Red River near Sulfur Fork.[22] Chimneys were built at both ends of the structure and a gabled portico with four posts with a railing between them decorated the front entrance. A tall set of eight stone steps led down to the front walkway. The foundation of the house was laid with hand-hewn blocks of limestone which measured 8-10 inches thick, 12-inches wide, by 3 feet in length. There was a winding staircase up to the second floor. The school had a basement, which stood above ground level and included front-facing windows to allow for air circulation during hot summer months. Perhaps the Tylers and their children used the basement as their living space, the main floor might have been where the classes were held, and the upper floor with its two windows was where the boarders lived.

As one entered the double front doors of the school, they would be in a spacious entrance hallway. On either side of the hallway were rooms of good proportions. The front entrance hallway served another purpose for whenever there was a death in the family; it was there that people came to view the body during what was called the "laying out." Funeral homes and embalming were not in use at this time.

A photo of Hickory Wild taken in 1910. John Duke ran the school from 1831 until his death in 1860. Courtesy Gene Washer of the *Leaf Chronicle.*

Large trees dotted the hill on which the academy sat providing welcome shade for the numerous picnics and commencement parties held there. John Duke thoroughly reveled in these gatherings as stories abound of the fun enjoyed under those trees. One can imagine John Duke standing high up on the porch, surveying the hillside

---

[21] In 1877, Anna was living in New York. She married Montgomery H. Dingee (1859-1927), of Brooklyn, New York on November 30 1880. His grandfather was Jesse Tyler Dingee, Sr. (1796-1877). She died on January 18, 1912 in Manhattan and her body was delivered to Clarksville on the L & N train. She is buried in the Tyler family plot at Greenwood Cemetery. The Pettus family plot adjoins the Tylers' in Section 6.

[22] The earliest permanent settlers arrived in 1784, making Port Royal an early trading center because of its location at the junction of the Red River and Sulfur Fork.

filled with occupants and filling the air with lively music from his fiddle. [23]

Certainly all of his students were expected to conduct themselves as gentlemen or suffer the consequences. It made no difference to John Duke the parentage, size, age or color of the child. If they required discipline, they would most definitely receive it, usually in the black gum thicket near the school. Here the schoolmaster had cleared away the vegetation in a grove of hickory trees for the special purpose of modifying the negative attitudes or behaviors of any student who was foolish enough to be disobedient. This led to the discussion as to how the academy got its name. One account suggested the name came from the grove of hickory trees. Yet another source insisted that it was black gum switches that were used and this seemed to be the case. Of course for fairness' sake, he gave them about an arm's length distance. Up until this time, the only known use for black gum wood was in making wagon wheels. John Duke thus invented a secondary purpose, which became famous as "black gumology." Translated t means, "loving black gum."

It was said by James Ross, a former student of Tyler's,

> **every student was taught to be honest for honesty's sake. Few men attached less importance to the mere breath of popular applause than he, but character was everything to him. As a rule, he was kind and companionable with his students. I always considered him a superior and in many respect a remarkable man. While all proceeded smoothly in his school he was singularly mild and gentle. When insubordination or defiance made its appearance, which he was quick to observe, and the crisis came, he met it with a nerve that never failed fully to impress all with the knowledge that he was master of the situation.**

Regardless of John Duke's strictness, the school was instrumental in turning out some of the most esteemed lawyers, doctors and bankers in Clarksville. Also it was always remembered that his students dearly loved him and were dedicated to him to the end of his life. He had total control over every aspect of his school, as he did not abide outside interference in decisions and to that end, he never allowed trustees to visit his school.

James Ross was the son of Elder Reuben Ross the well-known pioneer Baptist minister in Tennessee and Kentucky. James was born September 3,1801, in Martin County, North Carolina. He attended the private classical school of John D. Tyler and became a schoolteacher. He once taught at the Masonic College in Clarksville. James died March 14,1879.

Tobacco, known as a "cash crop," was grown at Hickory Wild and later sold in Clarksville, but additional crops were raised to feed his large family, students and slaves. Grains such as corn, wheat or oats could be taken to the Port Royal gristmill in operation since 1809, to be ground. In the late fall, after temperatures were consistently cold enough, hogs would be killed, the meat salted and smoked.

The decade before the Civil War, Tennessee was the largest iron-producing state in the South. It was estimated that 1700 workers were employed at the furnaces. As the slave population increasingly outnumbered the whites in the iron furnace communities, the thought of a possible revolt or uprising caused concern. That manifested into two rebellion scares. To calm the fears of citizens in Clarksville, freed Negroes were ordered to leave town or face being jailed. This fear would last until the 1850s. The first rebellion scare in Montgomery County actually occurred in 1835 and was the catalyst for the general assembly of Tennessee to pass an act making it an offense to "circulate printed matter, make addresses, or preach sermons which fostered discontent or insubordination among slaves." John Duke's part of the county seemed far removed from these troubles and have no proof of him having to deal with insubordinate slaves.

John Duke was involved in raising a cavalry unit, whose purpose is unclear. Perhaps it was related to lingering fears over an insurrection. He ran a notice in the *Clarksville Chronicle* September 22, 1837 issue which read:

Cavalry Notice:

> **A meeting of the officers and privates of the troop of Cavalry lately raised in the 91st Regt. is earnestly requested to be held at the Courthouse in Clarksville on Saturday the 30th inst. for the purpose of making such laws as may be allowed necessary for the government of**

---

[23] In the Montgomery County tax lists of 1836, John Duke is listed as having 320 acres of land at a value of $2,560 and 15 slaves, valued at $9,600.

the troops. A full meeting is most respectfully solicited by
John D. Tyler, Capt. Sept. 22, 1837

Still, he conducted his school with classes beginning early around sunrise and continuing until almost dark. Each day during the school session, the boys were taught in the classical pattern of that time. Certainly Latin and later Greek were emphasized, along with a study of the history of England.

In addition, he taught non-boarding students who would have had to walk or ride to school each day on horseback. They were dismissed ahead of the others to allow them to travel while there was still light.[24] Present-day school children would have a difficult time imagining the length of a typical day of instruction at this schoolmaster's academy.[25]

As an avid reader, John Duke loved discussing and translating the Greek author, Homer, to his students. Often well into the night John Duke would read the classics. Sometimes, his students would catch John Duke awake reading and insisted on staying awake to hear "just a few more stories." He especially enjoyed the writings of Shakespeare and always looked forward to the next opportunity to involve his students in what he considered to be the highest forms of literature.

Modern educational "experts" pride themselves on advocating a teaching method that was long in use at Hickory Wild. John Duke had this method of learning down to an art with quite a unique approach. He would have each student read a few lines, lay the book down and repeat the verses over and over until committed to memory. The catch was this: these lessons were executed at night when there was no natural light and candles were not used as they were considered a luxury. So how was this accomplished? In preparation for the lesson to begin, the schoolmaster had the students go behind the school to collect pine knots. Pine knots are found on dead/rotten trees where the limbs connect with the trunk. Pine knots are known to be as hard as bricks and heavy as lead due to their high resin content. Called "fat wood" in other parts of the country, pine knots are impervious to moisture. When inserted into a fire, they burned giving off blue, green, red and yellow light.

Pine knots. These two were about 14 in. long. From author's collection.

It was during this span of time that the students received "illuminating" lessons. When light was sufficient, the boys hurried to memorize their lines before being cast into darkness once more. If they encountered a block, throwing a pine knot on the fire once more would give them the opportunity to attempt to recover their lesson. By memorizing just a few lines at a time, the end result was accomplished and according to former students, these lessons stayed with them throughout their lives. John Duke used this method as long as he taught school.

John Duke's sister-in-law, Ann had married Thomas Carr Minor. Their son, Charles Minor had a nursery, which boasted several hundred types of trees and shrubs for sale. The nursery began its operation around 1839. A post office named for the nursery was located nearby and opened on February 2nd of that year. Charles passed away on September 15, 1842, leaving his tree nursery business in the hands of his friend, John Duke. The land was located near John Duke's on the Russellville Turnpike. On November 17, John Duke, acting as trustee for Minor's Nursery advertised the nursery trees for sale and planned to sell the tract of five or six hundred acres separately. The property did not sell and so therefore he sold the land at auction on February 25. The terms were 1/3 cash, 1/3 in twelve months and 1/3 in two years.

Diaries are such invaluable sources of information, even when they may seem to be of little importance at the time. When no official weather records were recorded, these personal accounts

[24] As the schoolroom at Hickory Wild could hold up to fifty students, the additional students were "day students" who did not board.
[25] By 1860, students came from every Southern state to be educated there.

suffice. Such is the case of the diary of John Nick Barker. Described as an owner of a large number of slaves, Barker lived from 1793-1873 on a plantation eight miles from Clarksville across the Red River near Dunbar Cave. His diaries contain several references to the Tylers and serve as an important source for daily happenings such as the deaths and births of family and friends in his community. He noted that on February 25, 1843, "the Minors land sold bot (sic) by Tyler $8 per acre."

In town with whispers still circulating about possible slave insurrections, the city revised its city ordinances dated February 6, 1844 to read:

(1) No Negro shall come to Clarksville on the Sabbath Day. If the Constable should find an unusual assemblage of Negroes, he should disperse them and punish them by inflicting ten lashes on each If he deems it necessary.
(2) No Negro shall be allowed to own land. Any merchant or grocer selling, trading or trafficking on the Sabbath Day shall be fined $20.00
(3) Anyone caught buying from or trading with Negroes on the Sabbath will be fined $1.00 for reach offense.
(4) No person shall be allowed to leave his wagon or cart standing on the Public Square or any of the public streets. Cannot ungear team. $1.00 for each offense.
(5) Anyone throwing wood or rubbish on the Public Square[26] or any of the public streets shall be fined $2.00 each day it remains there.
(6) No gaming or playing any game of hazard. Fined $5.00 if one does so. $25.00 if gaming is allowed in someone's house.
(7) No one can exhibit any show or make any theatrical exhibition whereby they receive money, without having first obtained a license from the recorder.
(8) No one shall shoot a pistol in the city or gallop a horse. $1.00 fine for each.
(9) No wagon or cart allowed to run on Sabbath Day unless the mayor or treasurer approves it. $5.00 for each offense. No person shall work or sell intoxicants to slaves on Sabbath Day.
(10) Persons keeping more than one dog shall pay a tax on $1.00 for each additional dog.
(11) White men or free men of color who are caught gambling with slaves shall pay a fine of $10.00 and must answer to the state for such an offense.
(12) Public drunkenness. $5.00 fine.
(13) Any white man or free man of color who shall furnish slaves with food or entertain them in any way for profit fined $5.00.
(14) Unlawful for someone to stop and wash in the Cumberland River in daylight. $21.00.
(15) No boat (steamboat, etc.) shall be allowed to unload on the Sabbath Day without permission from the mayor or treasurer. $50.00.

John Duke, in addition to his teaching, managing his farm and overseeing his slaves, became involved in various other ventures such as serving in the House of Representatives, 25th Assembly from 1843-45, serving as a Presidential elector in 1844 on the Whig ticket of Henry Clay and Theodore Frelinghuysen and representing Montgomery, Stewart and Robertson Counties in the Senate 26th and 27th General Assemblies from 1845-49.

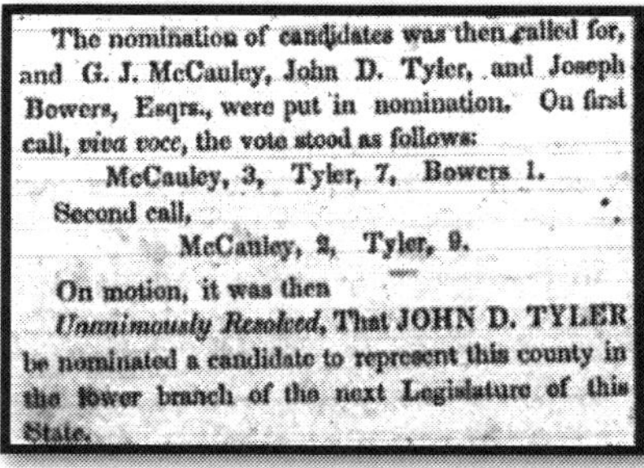
The nomination of candidates was then called for, and G. J. McCauley, John D. Tyler, and Joseph Bowers, Esqrs., were put in nomination. On first call, viva voce, the vote stood as follows:

McCauley, 3, Tyler, 7, Bowers 1.

Second call,

McCauley, 2, Tyler, 9.

On motion, it was then

Unanimously Resolved, That JOHN D. TYLER be nominated a candidate to represent this county in the lower branch of the next Legislature of this State.

On the left: *Clarksville Weekly Chronicle*, April 13, 1843. On the right: April 30, 1844 issue from the *Leaf Chronicle*.

WHIG ELECTORAL TICKET.

FOR THE STATE AT LARGE,
JOHN BELL,
OF DAVIDSON,
GUSTAVUS A. HENRY,
OF MONTGOMERY.

FOR CONGRESSIONAL DISTRICTS,
1st—THOS. A. R. NELSON, of Washington,
2d—ROBERT H. HYNDS, of Jefferson,
3d—JOHN H. CROZIER, of Knox,
4th—THOMAS L. BRANSFORD, of Jackson,
5th—DANIEL L. BARRINGER, of Bedford.
6th—NEIL S. BROWN, of Giles,
7th—ROBERT L. CARUTHERS, of Wilson,
8th—THOMAS R. JENNINGS, of Davidson,
9th—JOHN D. TYLER, of Montgomery,
10th—ROBERTSON TOPP, of Shelby,
11th—WILLIAM T. HASKELL, of Madison.

During one of this first public speeches, the schoolmaster failed miserably as the words stuck in his throat. He admitted that, "every idea he had abandoned him and he was utterly helpless." Not to be discouraged, John Duke summoned up his courage and later was known to be quite an acknowledged speaker. Friends had urged him to run for election, and he felt duty bound to do so since service was one of the virtues he strongly instilled in his students.

---

[26] The first market house was a crude wooden structure replaced later by one larger constructed of bricks.

In the election of 1847, Tyler received 238 more votes than William Rogers in Montgomery County and 422 more votes than Rogers in Robertson County. John Tyler, then serving as the U.S. President shared with John Duke a common fierce dislike of Andrew Jackson.

An interesting ad was placed on January 16, 1848 that shows their involvement with the Minor family.

IT MUST COME

> **I have left in the hands of Quintus M. Tyler, Esq. the notice due Miss Caroline Minor for Negro hire; also the notes given to Capt., John Duke Tyler, Trustee of Charles Minor and transferred it Caroline Minor which, if not paid by the first day of February next will be placed in the hands of an officer for collection.**
> **E. Mason, Agent for Caroline Minor**
> **Jan. 16, 1848.**

J.J. Hooper, a dedicated Whig, known as the "Whig Missionary" of the time, traveled through several counties getting a feel for the leanings of the people in each area. He was happily and "snugly ensconced," as he said at Clarksville's Franklin House, sending a report back to the *Nashville Banner* that printed on May 26, 1852, that he had stayed two nights with the "Grand High Priest" of the party in Montgomery County, John Duke Tyler. He described him as a real man, staunch Whig and stated,

> **I took his dimensions and the measurements of the man is fully square and complete, every way, up and down. He has one of the finest institutions for educating young men in all the country and is making money, but the general impression is that his services would be much more acceptable to the people as a representative from this district in the next Congress of the United States. And I am satisfied that with a Congress of such men as John Duke Tyler, and Fillmore at the head of the government, the South would have nothing to fear.**

And in February 1853 in the *Springfield Intelligencer* came this statement pressuring John Duke to run for re-election as Senator, a position he no longer wanted:

> **He has filled with honor and credit the same station heretofore and would doubtless do so again if called to it by the voice of the people and with an increased degree of ability, derived from past experience in the halls of both branches of our State Legislature. But while others may be, I am very sure that Mr. Tyler is not an aspirant for this station for if so, he might have remained in it as long as he chose and I hope for the reason I will assign that the call will not be accepted.**
>
> **Mr. Tyler is both a gentleman and a scholar and is not without experience in matters of legislation and the duties of public political life. He is courteous and respectful in his bearing and deportment towards all- whether political friends or foes, devoted in his attachments to our common country and her best interest and would labor as constantly as ardently as anyone to advance her general prosperity. He has secured the esteem and admiration of all who know him and, being the enemy of no one, I presume he has no enemy within the extent of the large circle of those who know him and though a consistent Whig in his political opinions, he has never betrayed that rancorous feeling and ambitious spirit which often mark the course of narrow-mindedness towards a political rival. I know of no man amongst us better calculated to conciliate the feelings growing out of the past party strife or would be so generally acceptable and meet the wishes of the people of the district regardless of party nor one whose talents, worth, and influence would be more sensibly felt or highly appreciated in the counsels of the country than his. I therefore suggest to the people of this Congressional District the name of John Duke Tyler of Montgomery as a suitable person to represent them after the next general election in the Congress of the United States.**

But the school teacher was done with politics. Was it the rumors of an impending war that caused him to stay home or the need to see to the management of his large farm, or something else? He did recall with fondness his early years in politics as revealed by one of his students but staying at Hickory Wild in 1853 seemed like the best course to take. John Duke re-opened his school in 1847 after his service in politics and jumped back into the role of schoolmaster. For many years John Duke prospered and added to his land holdings. The 1850 Census showed:

John D. Tyler	**age 55**	**teacher (born in VA) Value of real estate $4,000.**
Mildred Smith Tyler	**age 40**	(wife)
John Duke Tyler, Jr.	**age 19**	(son) called "Duke" to distinguish him from his father
Joseph Addison Tyler	**age 13**	(the "forgotten" son)
Charles Waller Tyler	**age 11**	(son)
Anna D. Waller	**age 9**	(relative of Mildred's)
Emma Tyler	**age 1**	(daughter)
Mary C. Mockbee	**age 21**	(cousin of John Duke Tyler)
Charles W. Bailey	**age 23**	(family friend and doctor)

The boys who were attending Hickory Wild Academy listed in the household during that census were: William Harris age 19, Richard Quarles age 17, Luke Moody age 20, Frank Poston age 20, Thomas Bayless age 19, Frank Smith age 14, Robert Nelson age 16, Lynch Donoho age 18, Sam Wright age 13, James Collins age 21, Thomas Baxter age 13, Samuel Jones age 16, Monroe Moody age 18.

The census also showed that he owned 23 slaves at the time.

2 females	**age 65**	**1 female**	**age 12**
1 female	**age 55**	**1 male**	**age 11**
1 male	**age 44**	**1 male**	**age 9**
1 female	**age 36**	**1 female**	**age 10**
1 female	**age 33**	**1 male**	**age 8**
1 male	**age 21**	**1 female**	**age 7**
1 male	**age 19**	**1 female**	**age 5**
1 female	**age 18**	**1 female**	**age 1**
1 male	**age 17**	**1 male**	**age 1**
2 females	**age 16**	**2 males**	**age 6 mos.**

Prior to the Civil War, Clarksville's main slave market was run by C.H. Peter Marr and his son Duncan. Their slaves were sold from their business on Franklin Street. The Marr slaves were housed in quarters on North Spring Street within sight of the Public Square.

By their ages, it may be guessed that the older ones were inherited and probably house slaves. There are a lot of mouths to feed; not just the Tyler family but also all the boys who boarded at the school and the 23 slaves themselves. The younger male slaves probably worked the crops on the property.

In March 1850, Dr. Charles W. Bailey (1826-1897), came to Hickory Wild to act as the school's physician. Within the same year on November 26, Dr. Bailey married and he and Mrs. Bailey stayed at Hickory Wild until March 1854 when they moved to Trenton, Kentucky. About the same time, Duke Tyler brought his wife, Fredonia "Donie" Smith Tyler (1835-1925) and children to live at Hickory Wild. Their two sons were:

Joseph "Josie" Duke Tyler (1859-1937) an attorney, married Jessie Settle (1865-1951). Their children were:
- **Mildred Emily Tyler (1891-1974)** married Charles Haddox Gill.
- **Joseph Rex Tyler (1894-1959)** married Georgia Crouch.
- **John Duke Tyler (1896-1979)** married Eleanora Hammond.

Jessie and Josie with Mildred and Rex. (GF)

Dr. Burnley Duke Tyler

Burnley Duke Tyler (1863-1930) married Helen Irvine Hollins (1871-1922) and later moved to Todd County, Kentucky. He became a physician, practicing medicine in Guthrie until his death from asthma. Their children were:
- **Donia Jane Tyler (1895-1948)** unmarried.
- **Mary Tyler (1898-1944)** married Reems Dillery.
- **Charles Waller Tyler (1900-1903)** died of tuberculosis of the brain.
- **Nannie Tyler (1907-?)** married Stanley Gambill.
- **Helen Tyler (1909-1974)** married Archie Scott.

In a deed dated July 10, 1854 at 2:00 p.m., Duncan Marr sold a twenty-four-year-old male slave to John Duke Tyler for a sum of one thousand dollars. His reputation as a slave owner was that of a caring master who highly regarded his people and in return, earned their loyalty. Children of such landowners never addressed the older servants by their first names but by such references as "Uncle" or "Aunt" as terms of endearment, for these servants were considered members of the family. Also, a slave usually took the last name of their owner as their own but this might change if the slave was sold to another family. Such was the case of "Aunt Roxy" (1839-1926), once owned by John Duke Tyler who for years after emancipation, worked for his daughter, Nannie Tyler Johnson. Roxy's real name was Mariah and being just a few months younger than Nannie, was a valued playmate to her and would remain with the Tyler family for her entire life.

Nannie Haskins (1846-1930), was the teenage daughter of Dr. Edward B. and Tennessee "Tennie" Haskins. In the 1850s, his office was located on Strawberry Alley across from the courthouse. As the daughter of a physician she would have been privy to much of the news around town. It is fortunate, indeed, that she kept a diary in which she recorded daily events in her life. Her writings are those of a typical young lady, writing about visiting friends and seeking to find normalcy among chaos. This diary has become a valuable resource for details of life in Clarksville during the Federal occupation, especially since publication of the local newspapers was suspended for the duration of the war. She would become friends with the Tylers and would mention them quite often in her diary. In one entry she wrote that James Ross got "the finished part of his education from Captain Tyler and later he established a successful school himself on the principles of his preceptor, whom he ardently admired." She also quoted other sources as saying, "There never have been and never will be again such teachers as Captain Tyler and Jimmie Ross."

Chapter Three: Before the War

Joseph Buckner Killebrew became a valuable resource for information on the Tylers and Hickory Wild. Killebrew was born in Montgomery County in 1831. He provides us with an insight into the Tylers from someone who knew the family on an intimate basis. After losing his mother at age 4, he was passed around from relative-to-relative. He was thoroughly interested in agriculture, geology and education and attended Franklin College in middle Tennessee until he ran out of money. Killebrew wrote of his encounter with the schoolmaster when at a time in his life, it seemed hopeless to complete his education.

> **For a while I was greatly distressed about what course to pursue. One day in the month of January 1852 I was in Clarksville and stepping into a barber shop to have my hair trimmed, I saw a venerable man sitting in a chair, the barber then shaving him. He looked at me for a while and then said, 'Is not your name Killebrew?' I replied, 'It is.' He then said, 'Mr. Killebrew, I have been wanting to see you for some time. You have the reputation of being a fine mathematician. I want you to come to my school, teach mathematics to those who desire to pursue such a course and for this service, I will carry you through a course of Latin and Greek, furnish you a room and board you.'**
>
> **When I comprehended his proposition, I did not hesitate, but accepted it at once. This venerable man was Jno. Duke Tyler, a man known far and wide as a successful classical teacher and as a manager of unruly boys. He had educated my uncle, Joseph Ligon, who was my first teacher.**
>
> **In a few days I entered his school and began in Caesar's Commentaries, although I had read Virgil and Ovid at Franklin College. Mr. Tyler was a thorough believer in laying the groundwork of a language solidly and firmly. The grammar was studied every day and lessons recited in it the first thing in the morning throughout the course. We went through Rudman's Rudiments time and again and he never let a student in Latin be so far advanced as to stop reciting a grammar lesson in the morning. Every sentence that we read had to be parsed word for word and line for line. Every noun and pronoun in the lesson had to be declined and every verb conjugated. It was tedious work, but we became as familiar with these things as we did with the English alphabet. What we read in four days was reviewed on the fifth so when we finished reading a Latin book we almost knew it by heart. The same was true of the Greek books that we read under him. There was one part of these languages that the old gentleman knew nothing about and that was prosody.[27] When afterwards I went to the University of North Carolina I found I was woefully deficient in that part of the Latin and Greek grammars.**
>
> **Every afternoon I would take my class in mathematics and teach them. I had some few scholars that took a decided interest in the study. Mr. Tyler himself started to take a course in algebra with me but gave it up after a while. He never could comprehend the subject of factoring, though he tried hard to do so. His knowledge of mathematics was confined entirely to arithmetic.**
>
> **I spent two years at this school. Mr. Tyler was a thorough gentleman and seemed to enjoy my company very much. Every few evenings after tea he would come to my room and talk for several hours. He was very proud of having represented at one time Montgomery County in the Legislature and he would often begin a narrative by saying, 'When I was in the Legislature.' He was a good, true, honest and honorable man, not broad in his views, but thoroughly trustworthy and consistent. His sense of duty was very high and he was much respected and beloved by all who knew him. He used to tell his students that Geo. W. Boyd,**

---

[27] From the Oxford Languages: In linguistics, prosody is the study of elements of speech that are not individual phonetic segments but which are properties of syllables and larger units of speech, including linguistic functions such as intonation, stress and rhythm.

who became a famous lawyer and myself were the best scholars he ever taught. I think in this his partiality for me obscured his judgment. I do not think, in fact I know, that my knowledge of the classics was not equal to that of my uncle Joseph Ligon or any of his (Mr. Tyler's) three sons, Duke, Joe, and Charlie. I believe that John Keeling, though he did not apply himself was a much better Latin scholar than myself. I applied myself however, with great diligence and learned every lesson thoroughly. I had no time to lose for when I entered his school I was in my twenty-second year. In the period of two years I read in Latin Caesar, Virgil, Ovid, Sallust and Horace and in Greek the Testament, Xenophon and a part of Homer's Iliad. During this time, I taught classes in algebra, geometry, trigonometry and surveying.

J.B. left Tyler's school in 1853. His education was finally completed when George S. Wimberly[28] financed his college expenses at the institution of his choice which was the University of North Carolina at Chapel Hill. He graduated second in his class in 1857. Killebrew went on to be an attorney. Joseph Wimberly, the son of George S. Wimberly was a hard-working but afflicted with rheumatism that caused him to be lame. He later studied Latin and Greek under John D. Tyler and probably would have studied law but his death in 1850 to measles ended that dream. His brothers Tom and George and sisters Louisa and Margaret also succumbed to measles. After college, J.B. Killebrew took charge of the family farm which was within a short distance of John Duke Tyler's. In 1857, he studied law and entered the bar. For a short period, he taught mathematics at the Clarksville Female Academy. Killebrew married Joe Wimberly's sister, Mary Catherine "Kate" Wimberly on December 3, 1857, and they had six children.

Kate Wimberly Killebrew and J.B. Killebrew

John Duke's daughter, Nannie Tyler was listed as having been a "waiter" at their wedding along with Lucy and Lettie Donoho, Emily and Bedie Fort, Mag Wilcox, Thomas Henry, Finis Ewing, Charles G. Smith, Thomas "Tom" Beaumont, W.H. Brierley, J.C. Hester and Robert Johnson. He and "Kate" Wimberly both kept a journal. Killebrew's 900-acre farm in the Rossview community was worked by twenty-two slaves. Killebrew managed to come through the war without debt and with his property intact by carefully avoiding any conflict with either side of the combatants.

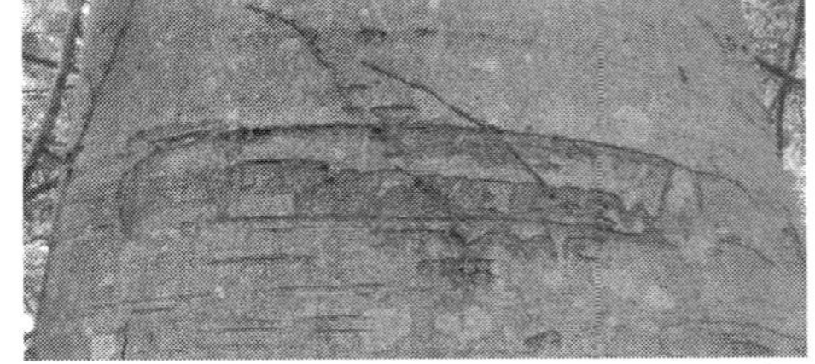

The name "Killebrew" is carved into the trunk of a massive hackberry tree on the road leading to the Wimberly house. The Killebrews' house no longer stands however, the Wimberly house does and is still occupied. Photo by author.

In 1870, J.B. Killebrew became agricultural editor of the *Nashville Union* and began his public campaigning of New South principles: improvement and extension of the system of public education, encouragement of immigration to the South, development of natural resources for industrialization and agricultural improvement. He later became the state's first Commissioner of Agriculture, serving in that capacity until 1880. In 1872, Killebrew published the first issue of the *Rural Sun*, as part of the Bureau of Agriculture, promoting immigration, development of timber and mineral resources and industrialization. In 1894, Killebrew took the position of immigration agent for the Nashville, Chattanooga and St. Louis Railroad until 1904 when he retired to his farm. He was against secession and remained neutral when visited by troops on either side. He educated his slaves in reading, math and writing to prepare them for life once emancipated. During Reconstruction he pushed for an equal education system to all of its citizens and so authored the education reform bill in Tennessee. He published massive volumes of work concerning the

[28] George S. Wimberly was a widower who had married Killebrew's aunt Judith Keesee.

geology of the South, mining, iron deposits, etc. Killebrew died in Nashville on March 17, 1906. On October 18, 1972 a tablet was unveiled at the Ellington Agricultural Center honoring Killebrew for being the First Commissioner Tennessee Department of Agriculture. He was placed in the Tennessee Agricultural Hall of Fame. The tablet was unveiled by James G. Killebrew. And in 2019, a historical marker was placed on the intersection of Killebrew and Rossview Road.

In 1855, the state legislature passed an act that clarified the boundary lines of Clarksville and allowed it forever to be known as the City of Clarksville. This was indeed a milestone in local history, one of which a son of John Duke was to significantly impact. The population of Clarksville at this time was approximately 5,000. The county population was 21,211 of which one fourth was slaves.

By 1856, John Duke's son "Duke" Tyler was twenty-four years old and part of the social "goings on" around Clarksville. An invitation issued January 28th showed how his presence was valued at community functions. The event mentioned was the Grand Washington Ball to be held at the Graysville Inn in Kentucky. This inn was built in 1833 by Hopkinsville mayor John Gray and was later renamed the Stagecoach Inn. It then became a private residence in 1976. The invitation read, "You are earnestly solicited to attend a ball to be given by M.E. Spurrier and lady, at Graysville, Kentucky, on the 22nd of February, 2 o'clock p.m." Duke was listed as a manager of this event along with James C. Johnson, A.G. Wilcox, J.W. Kendall, E.G. Sebree, Horace Marshall, A.L. Johnson, S. Smith, Thomas L. Yancey, John Moore, Frank Duffy, William Tyler, W.B. Taylor, R.Y. Johnson, Charlie Ware, D.C. Farmer, J. Ross Perkins, Dr. R.S. Ware, J.R. Roberts, J.M. Moody and J.A. Grant, promoter. The word "manager," as it is used here, is meant to represent the bachelors who were hosting the ball. An invitation such as this was greatly desired by the young unmarried ladies of Clarksville who dreamed of meeting the "right man."

The second of the insurrection scares came in 1856 causing terror throughout the entire iron district on the Cumberland and Tennessee Rivers. This scare was substantiated when a keg of powder was found under a Negro church at Louisa Furnace in Montgomery County. It was discovered that indeed a concerted rebellion at many of the iron furnaces was planned and a nearby black preacher was inciting a group of slaves to insurrection. When the preacher refused to heed the warnings to stop, he was shot on the spot. A slave at the Cumberland Furnace revealed the plotters' names resulting in the immediate arrest of nearly 80 slaves, some of whom were hanged. This episode resulted in serious financial loss for the iron furnace masters.

On October 8, 1856, Hampton Masonic Lodge No. 257 located at Hampton's Springs was chartered. Two years later on October 23, 1858, Hampton Lodge and Turnersville Lodge No. 137 petitioned for a new lodge to be located at Port Royal to be known as Hampton Lodge No. 137 (retaining the name of one and the number of the other.) The Grand Lodge granted the petition and John Duke Tyler was elected first master.

A carpenter in town known only as "James" was arrested November 25, 1856 for visiting Negro cabins and discussing freedom with them. His bail was $500. The same week, a black man named Kennedy was caught with an "abandoned" white woman in Gallows Hollow. His punishment: "Corrections intended to bring him to a sense of the enormity of his conduct and the difference between white and black were ordered to be administered." And on the same day as the above, a slave boy was whipped in the market having possession of more pistols and other weapons in his trunk than the law allowed.

In Clarksville a vigilante committee was formed to deal with suspect slaves, but on December 17, 1856, the committee adjourned until "there is any necessity." J.B. Killebrew believed the rumors were started by "some hot-headed white men, taking counsel of their fears, imagined that they saw indisputable evidence of an insurrection." The headlines of the December 24, 1856 issue of the *Tobacco Leaf* newspaper in Clarksville read as follows:

More of the Negro Insurrection in Tennessee

Excitement at Dover, Tenn.

The White Population in Arms

Nine Negroes Arrested as Conspirators

Sixty More Imprisoned at the Cumberland Iron Works

Origin of the Plot

Clarksville leaders in a pro-active move, appointed a Committee of Safety for Montgomery County which wrote eight resolutions as precautionary measures. William A. Forbes, who had lived in Richmond following the Nat Turner insurrection, was asked to serve on that committee that adopted the following resolutions:

1st *Resolved:* That we recommend to our city and county authorities to suppress in the future, all assemblages of Negroes under any pretext whatever, at frolics, balls, benevolent societies, or at public worships where Negro preachers officiate as preachers and that our Ministers of the Gospel be requested to suspend absolutely their habit of preaching to the Negroes on occasions separate from their ordinary preaching as Ministers of the Gospel. Our churches are large enough for our whole population, white and black. We deem all such meetings for Negro preaching alone improper; that they degenerate into unlawful assemblages and are otherwise productive of incalculable mischief.

2nd *Resolved:* That the owners of Negroes ought not to give orders for their Negroes to get buggies and carriages for pleasure on the Sabbath or on any occasion whatever, and that it is the sense of this Committee that the owners of livery stables in Clarksville ought not to hire horse and buggies to Negroes even when their masters permit it; for the reason that such indulgence to Negroes promotes insubordination amongst the slaves and stimulates feelings wholly inconsistent with their duty to their masters and the subordinate position that they should occupy in reference to white people.

It is further the sense of this Committee that our merchants and traders ought to abstain absolutely from dealing with the Negroes unless by the express permission of their masters and on no account ought they sell to them fire arms, ammunition, or other weapons, whether with, or without their owner's consent, if any be so indiscreet to grant it.

3rd *Resolved:* That in the opinion of this Committee, the present evils that affect us are mainly to be attributed to the late Presidential canvas, not meaning to cast more blame on this, than on that political party we condemn the public discussion of all questions touching Negro slavery before crowds of people in the hearing of vast multitudes of Negroes. We further think slaveholders are guilty of gross folly when they permit their Negroes to go to barbeques and other public gatherings where public speakers for the one party or the other discuss these delicate subjects of Negro slavery, the true bearing of which they do not comprehend and where they imbibe crude and disjoined notions of freedom which can only imperil the safety of the white and the certain destruction of the black race.

4th *Resolved:* That we call upon our city authorities to take strong measures to prevent Negroes passing to and from the Iron Works, from spending Christmas holidays in our town and especially from staying a single night in the corporation unless their masters reside here. In case, however, such Negroes' wives live in town, he will be permitted to stay here provided he has a pass from his master which is recognized or endorsed by the owner of his wife and that they increase the day and night watch in each ward in the city during this period at the expense of the corporation. We further earnestly recommend to our whole population in the town and county, to abolish the usage of giving to their servants Christmas holidays. It is a usage more honored in the breach than the observance for the reason that it breeds idleness and encourages dissipation amongst the Negroes, impairs their health and corrupts their morals. It would be a blessing to them to be kept constantly employed as a protection against the evils engendered by idleness and a decided comfort to us as affording exemption against the petty larcenies and the bacchanalian broils that always disgrace the Christmas week during which time we hope additional pains will be bestowed by our citizens to prevent Negroes from getting whiskey and that all saloons and liquor shops be closed till after New Year, if not forever.

5th *Resolved:* That, though the Committee may adjourn from day to day, it will not disband till we are sure the community are safe from the troubles that caused our organization to secure this end, we invoke the ard of our city authorities, the strong arm of the law and the sincere cooperation of all good citizens.

6th *Resolved:* That, we advise the people of every civil district in the country to organize a vigilante patrol of 20 men under the command of a captain, who by turns shall patrol their respective districts by day and night until the present excitement is allayed. By these precautionary measures we seek to create no alarm but to allay it and if this advice is followed, all danger will be averted. In caution, there is safety.

7th *Resolved*: For the future, Negroes shall not be permitted to hire their own time, as it is called, under any pretext whatever, or be suffered to remain in town if it is attempted, and we pledge ourselves to enforce the law against all persons who in this respect shall attempt

to evade it. The evils growing out of such practices are too great to be tolerated any longer, nor will it be permitted that captains or other officers of steamboats shall hire Negroes at night about the town to assist in loading and unloading their boat at the wharf or landing except they have the written permission of their masters. The Negroes invariably return to their masters next day, if not drunk, broken down, and unfit for service.

8th *Resolved*: That we recommend in the appointment of patrol in the town and county, the strictest attention be paid to the selection of men of character and prudence and that masters be requested to keep their Negroes upon their own premises as much as possible, till the excitement in the public mind is allayed and this as well prevent the destruction of the slaves by imprudent men as to prevent combination and concert on the part of the slaves, should they entertain any improper design.

Signed, Gustavus A. Henry, Chairman, William M. Stewart, John McKeage, William A. Quarles, William E. Newell, Bryce Stewart, F.A. Hannah, Joshua Elder, James O. Shackelford, Larkin Bradley, George A. Harrel, William Luton, William M. Shelton, Cave Johnson, Sr., Henry F. Beaumont, William A. Forbes, Charles H. Smith, Jo M. Dye.

An article printed in a Nashville newspaper claimed that slaves planned to march on Clarksville on Christmas Day in 1856, with the intention of plundering the city's banks and then taking refuge in free territories in the North. The city council met and agreed that no visiting slave would be permitted to remain in town for more than two hours unless accompanied by a "responsible white person."

Killebrew wrote that many families became so fearful, they armed themselves in preparation for the uprising and enlisted men for protection. Because of this, innocent Negroes were rounded up and whipped until they confessed that they had been discussing such. The whippings were so severe, the slaves to be relieved, would name the names of others without foundation, who were then also punished. Fear of such chastisement kept many slaves at their master's homes, not wanting to go out in public. This reign of terror lasted two to three months. Killebrew likened the whole affair to the Spanish Inquisition. Many blamed the threat on Northern politics as Republican John C. Fremont ran for the presidency and the slaves believed that were Fremont elected, they would all be set free.

Also in 1856, John Duke, Sr. acted as one of the founders of the Bank of America in Clarksville, located on the west side of Public Square between Franklin and Main Streets. The building itself was constructed in 1841 as the Bank of Tennessee, next the Montgomery Savings and Loan and then the Clarksville National Bank. The bank, established by Col. Montgomery Decatur Davie depended completely on its own capital.[29] John F. Barnes was cashier, Charles Hiter succeeded Barnes as cashier, and then Capt. R.Y. Johnson.

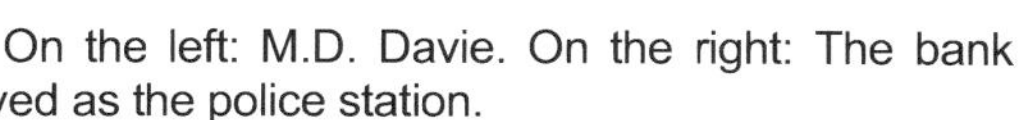

On the left: M.D. Davie. On the right: The bank building when later it served as the police station.

When the cotton crop failed in Arkansas and as the national financial Panic of 1857 shut down many banks in the nation, the Bank of America was forced to close as well. John Duke, along with the other founders of the bank, was faced with disposing of $100 shares of the $100,000 enterprise. This put John Duke, now called "Old Duke" heavily in debt. To cover the expenses, John Duke sold parcels from his 4,000 acres of land.

[29] Of course at this time banks did not have the backing of the FDIC.

A promissory note for $480 signed by John Duke Tyler dated 1841. Courtesy GF.

About a mile and half from Hickory Wild, on the Rossview Road, (off exit 8 and east of Interstate 24), stands a small, perfectly charming country church. When this church was founded in 1850, it was called Union Station but over the years the name changed to White's Chapel and then to the name it bears today, Grace's Chapel Episcopal Church. This building is not the one room church/school constructed of logs that existed during the 1850s when it served the three-fold purpose of a community church, a school and community center.

The Tylers' attendance at the early church cannot be verified due to the lack of roll books. It is within reason to believe that John Duke, with his entrenched Episcopalian upbringing and the church's close proximity to his farm, attended services here with his family.

Most country churches in this area were serviced by circuit riders, preachers who traveled from place to place pastoring several congregations. At first, the tiny church served as an Episcopal mission actually serving all denominations in the area, the work of Rev. Samuel Ringgold of Trinity Church in Clarksville. Of Grace's Chapel a member of the church stated, "What memories cluster about that blessed spot, with its Killebrews and its Rosses and its Marshals." Later in 1866, this building was replaced by another building and then was finally rebuilt again in the 1940s into its present design.

The building itself is indeed small, measuring just forty-five feet by twenty-five feet. It is nestled among the trees at the foot of a slope. The nearby fenced cemetery is full of the graves of the families who worshipped there. Within the boundary of the cemetery are two of the largest eastern hemlock and holly trees in Montgomery County. The boughs of the hemlocks give the impression of protecting the graves in a manner similar to the wings of a mother bird over its nest. This chapel embodies the beloved hymn, "The Church in the Wildwood." In the churchyard are immense oak trees. What happenings they must have witnessed throughout the years! Grace Chapel is on the National Register of Historic Places and still holds Sunday services.

Grace Chapel with an insert of Rev. Ringgold.

When they came of age, each of John Duke's children left Hickory Wild to start their lives. Marcus M. and Richard Keeling, Jr. settled in Kentucky. In 1839 Marcus practiced law with G.C. Boyd in Stewart and Humphreys Counties. Their law office was located in Dover, Tennessee.

LAW NOTICE!

G. C. BOYD & M. M. TYLER, will hereafter practice Law in partnership in Stewart and Humphreys counties, under the firm of *Boyd & Tyler*. All business entrusted to them, shall receive diligent attention. Address Marcus M. Tyler, Dover, Tenn., Mar. 21, 1839.—9t.

Marcus became Grand Master and Grand High Priest of the Grand Masonic Lodge and in January 1844, he re-started the Princeton, Kentucky *Examiner* newspaper which had been out of circulation for a year. Marcus acted as both the editor and publisher of the newspaper. He married 1st Sarah Jane Mims (1819-1850), daughter of Col. S. Mims of Eddyville, Kentucky on May 25, 1842 and 2nd Caroline Hutchinson on November 5, 1851. The 1850 U.S. Census shows him living in Trigg County, Kentucky. In his household were Sarah's relatives:

Robert Livingston Cobb	**age 14**	Sarah's nephew
Irene Cobb	**age 13**	Sarah's niece
Linah M. Cobb	**age 12**	
Byron O. Mimms	**age 11**	

That year Marcus was announced as a candidate for the office of Assistant Clerk of the Senate at the next session of the Kentucky State Legislature. In February 1851 he served as a delegate to represent the Whig party of Trigg County in the convention held in Frankfort. Mention was made of Marcus in the July 6, 1855 issue of the *Louisville Daily Courier* when Marcus was presented a gold chain by the Masonic lodge in Hickman County. In 1858, Marcus was elected County Clerk for Lyon County. He died just a few months later on November 27 in Eddyville, Kentucky at the age of 44 and is buried there in the Riverview Cemetery. His lodge honored him by stating

> **In the death of Brother Tyler, Masonry has lost one of her brightest ornaments, his friends a companion and his family an affectionate husband and parent.**

Whereas there are records of Quintus coming back for visits to his Tennessee relatives, it is quite the opposite for Marcus. In fact, he is not mentioned as ever visiting any of his Tennessee family.

Quintus left home at age twenty and became a salesman at a store in Port Royal and three years later moved to Dover to clerk. He returned to Hickory Wild on January 1, 1840 and "assumed control of his father's business." It is not certain if this business was the school, the farm, or both. Quintus may have simply been helping his father during the time John Duke was involved in politics. He continued there for six years, leaving to teach at the Spring Creek Church for three years. On January 12, 1843, Quintus married Emily "Emma" B[illegible]rnley Waller (1816-1851), daughter of Richard and Eliza Waller and his father's niece. Quintus and Emily moved to Cadiz, Kentucky, in January of 1849 where he taught until June 1860, with the exception of one session when he lost his wife in 1851. He buried her at Hickory Wild. Unfortunately, during their eight-year marriage, they had no children.

Mary Frances Tyler (1819-1892), John Duke and Harriett's daughter married a member of the tobacco board, Henry Hunter Bryan, Jr. (1812-1878), one of nine children born to Henry Hunter Bryan, Sr. (1786-1835), and his first wife, Elizabeth Ann Averitt Bryan (1786-1824), daughter of Jesse Averitt and Mary Grimes Averitt.

Bryan, Sr. was born in Martin County, North Carolina. He attended grammar and high schools there before moving to Tennessee and held several local offices. He was elected to the Sixteenth Congress (March 4, 1819-March 3, 1821) representing the Clarksville District. Elizabeth died in 1824 in Montgomery County. His second wife, Mary Frances[30] raised her children and Henry's from his previous marriage to Elizabeth. Mary Frances and Henry's children were:

John Duke Tyler Bryan (1858-1880) killed in Clarksville.
William P. Bryan (?-?)
J.B. Carter Bryan (?-?)
Henry Hunter Bryan, III (1845-?)

H. H. BRYAN. JESSE A. BRYAN
H. H. BRYAN & SON,
TOBACCO BROKERS.
Clarksville, Tennessee.
Refer to Factors and Brokers of New York and New Orleans.

Leaf Chronicle, January 19, 1876.

John Duke's son, Joseph Addison Tyler, named in honor of his mother's brother, with the same name, died as a result of a freak accident on the morning of July 22, 1856. For some unknown reason he had been sent to the local school run by James Ross. From the Ross family journals, an entry shows that on June 26, 1859, John Duke Tyler paid James Ross $36.00 for "tuition for his ward Joseph A. Tyler nine months ending June 24, 1859 at $4 per month." His death was recorded by J.B. Killebrew: "Jo Tyler was the flower of the Tyler family but in a sportive contest with a fellow student, some years after I left school, he was struck on the chest and died almost immediately." Joseph was buried in the Tyler family cemetery within sight of Hickory Wild but due to the destruction of that cemetery in the 1990s by a developer, his grave will never be located. As was common in those days, because of his tragic death that was

[30] Mary Frances' sister-in-law, Marina Turner Bryan (1811-1890), first married William H. Dortch and had four children by him. She then married Joshua Cobb (1809-1879), and they had 3 children, one of which was Bryce Stewart's second wife.

so painful to his family, he was not talked about. In fact, present day descendants were surprised to learn that he even existed.

At the same time, John Duke's daughter, Nannie was being heavily courted by someone with the initial "W" who, on January 5, 1859, wrote a love poem to her entitled, "Acrostic, Impromptu." Women often kept love letters/poems even after marriage and even from someone she did not marry. This, along with another poem, were found in a tin box owned by Polk Grundy Johnson who she would later marry and kept by Nannie after his death.

Nothing brighter 'neath the skies,
Artless Nannie! Peerless Nannie!
Nature's darling beauty and prize;
Never-ending sweetness lies.
In those loving, star-like eyes,
Enchanting, glorious Nannie!

The metal box belonging to Polk Grundy Johnson. Courtesy GF.

Was the "W" one of the Wallers that the Tylers knew?

The city of Clarksville in 1859 included 5,000 inhabitants, 400 homes, a courthouse, jail, female academy, male academy, public school building, seven churches, a market house and masonic hall. Clarksville was expanding and flourishing and, unknowingly, John Duke was looking at the last months of his life.

With Clarksville's continued growth there was a need for more doctors. It was estimated that there were only seventeen doctors in Clarksville, which meant there was only one doctor for every 200 people. The call was put forth that if two or three more doctors came to town, they would experience a "fine chance for a big fortune!" One man who did indeed come to Clarksville was one of her own native sons, Dr. John Duke Tyler. Tyler moved to Clarksville, boarded at the house of Mrs. Susannah McDaniel, the widow of Dr. George McDaniel and set up his office on Franklin Street opposite the courthouse in January 1859. At the time, he had several years of practice under his belt and was considered "well educated."

The Memphis, Clarksville and Louisville Railroad began its operations in 1859 and was the first to pass through Clarksville that was already a bustling transportation center. This railroad played an all important part in the development of Clarksville as a city and would be a major factor in the War between the States.

The announcement was finally made: the new bridge over the Red River was open to traffic although the bridge was not completely finished that second week of February in 1859. The cover had not been added, but it was not going to hold back all the people wanting to utilize the new bridge into and out of town. While working on the "old" lower Red River Bridge, a worker fell some fifty-eight feet into the chilly water of the river. The man suffered only bruises on his arm and enjoyed a "thorough dunking." The bridge was finally dismantled in 1930 when a new steel and concrete-constructed bridge was built at its side.

The new Red River bridge side-by-side with its 1859 predecessor. Photo courtesy Earl Coppedge.

At least five percent of landowners in Montgomery County owned between 1,000 and 5,000 acres by 1860. Nowhere else in the state was this figure matched. It meant that Clarksville sustained a large slave population to work the immense farms.

Death was to come to John Duke after he returned home one evening in a drenching rain from a ten-mile trip to Clarksville on horseback. He had been ill for five days previous to the trip but caught cold and died on his farm two days later on Sunday, May 20, 1860. As the people of Clarksville heard the news of his death, the courts adjourned and area businesses closed down for the day. John Nick Barker recorded the weather the day Captain Tyler died as fair and windy.

The May 23rd issue of the *Clarksville Jeffersonian* printed proclamation after proclamation in his honor. According to the paper, there was a great outpouring of grief over his death, seen as a true loss for the entire community and even beyond, due to the numerous students he taught over his forty years as a teacher. The *Jeffersonian* stated that:

> **The universal feeling of respect and esteem entertained for Captain Tyler, by all who knew him, is better indicative of many admirable and noble qualities of head and heart that adorned his character than anything we could say; and nothing perhaps can better attest this feeling for him than the sentiments cherished for him by the hundreds of men now scattered throughout nearly every state from Maine to California, who in their youth or early manhood received instruction by his hands.**

The May 25th issue of the *Clarksville Weekly Chronicle* announced the cause of John Duke's death as erysipelas. This disease, also known as St. Anthony's fire, is described as an infection of the skin and underlying tissues caused by Group A streptococci bacteria. The obituary stated that, "He was singularly pure in his private life and his death was mourned by all who knew him. 'Old Duke' as he was familiarly, but not disrespectfully, termed by his 'boys' was their faithful friend and advisor." Of John Duke Tyler, the *Nashville Banner* stated,

> **Mr. Tyler died in May 1860 lamented by everyone, rich and poor, white and black, bond and free. In his own neighborhood he was best beloved and it may be that the termination of his life at the time was a merciful disposition of Providence to relieve him of the darkness and tempest that soon overshadowed the land and destroyed the hopes of all old men in the future. He was a grand old gentleman and his name should be perpetuated and revered in the county in which he did so much good and gave such a splendid example of high citizenship and Christianity.**

Active even to the day of his death, he had been serving as the president of the Montgomery County Agricultural and Mechanics Association. For John Duke: "Disciplina confecta est nam magister quiescit." Translated, it means: "The lessons are over, for the schoolmaster is at rest." "Old Duke" was buried at Hickory Wild near his beloved school in the family cemetery. A tall obelisk marked his grave in the cemetery that was surrounded by an iron fence.

Upon the sudden death of his father Quintus returned once more to Montgomery County. Quintus acted as the administrator of his father's estate along with J.B. Killebrew and in the meantime, taught school. In 1864 he decided to travel which lasted a year perhaps to avoid the ghastly times in the South during the Civil War. Quintus then opened a school in September of 1866 in Garrettsburg, Christian County, Kentucky. Seemingly unable to remain in one location for very long, he left in 1870 and taught a session at Glendale, Logan County. This employment lasted but a year before he came to Canton, Kentucky and partnered in the mercantile business with his half-nephew, Duke Tyler. Here he stayed but 5 years, finding this an unsatisfying venture and so returned to teaching in March of 1878 and continued in this profession until he retired. Quintus never remarried but it is remembered that he certainly enjoyed the presence of women and was the consummate gentleman.

John Duke was extremely and uniquely fortunate to have lost just one of his children during his lifetime. As mentioned above, he was also spared the horror and destruction of the Civil War. To have lived, he would have seen all of his life's works disappear. Several months after John Duke's death, the Civil War began and as other male private schools did, Hickory Wild Academy closed when some of the boys left to fight in the war.

The Census of 1860 lists the following living at Hickory Wild including the names of the new teachers.

Mildred Tyler	**age 51**		**Eliza Tate Knott**	**age 35**	dancing master
Charles Waller Tyler	**age 21**		**Luanna Knott**	**age 8**[31]	
Anna D. Waller	**age 19**		**Mollie B. Knott**	**age 6**	
Emma Tyler	**age 10**		**Walter Tait/Tate**	**age 25**	son of James A. Tait/Tate
James Acree	**age 27**	overseer			

Nannie, John Duke's daughter is not shown in the census: This may have been because Nannie was sent to Clarksville to board and attend the Female Academy on Madison Street. After

---

[31] Luanna/Lou Ann Knott married Walter S. Ramey in 1877. She died in 1890.

all, Nannie was in a school for boys being taught lessons deemed by her father to be beneficial to boys and the concept that girls may not have a need in their world to learn the ancient languages was lost on John Duke, at least for a while. J.B. Killebrew recorded this about Nannie Tyler,

> **Nannie Tyler, the youngest, but one of Mr. Jno. Duke Tyler's children was also a student in 1852-53. Her father put her in Latin when she should have been in the 3rd reader. She had an uphill task and though sprightly, she must have felt deeply mortified to receive the most severe reprimands from her father in the presence of the whole school.[32] She grew up to be a beautiful girl and a great musician. Indeed, I think she excelled any performer I ever heard on the piano, except always the professionals. She married Polk G. Johnson. She now lives in Clarksville, a widow with two children. She was for many years a favorite visitor in our household.**

Being a student at the Female Academy introduced her to so many of the young people her age in Clarksville. She was often mentioned in groups of friends in social outings. Nannie seemed to be a favorite among the students as there were only pleasant comments made about her.

The original Female Academy school building, formally the Allen residence, used as a hospital during the Civil War. By 1888 it was razed and a new building built for the school. (TSLA)

A second love poem dated October 28, 1860 was also in the tin box owned by Polk Grundy Johnson. Again the author is unknown. However, in March of 1863 an acquaintance, Eleanora Willauer (to be mentioned later in this manuscript), recorded in her journal that Polk Grundy Johnson and Nannie were engaged. So before he left for the war, did he propose?

To Wife Nannie

**'Tis night, and countless stars are trembling
In empyrean blue above;
And now my heart, all undissembling,
Beats with holiest human love.**

**Like perfume of the first land blossom,
To the tired bird at sea,
So some trooping to this bosom,
In my sadness, thoughts of thee.**

**I may not tell thee what deep feeling
Trembles on my heart strings now;
Such love as this know no revealing
In the empty, spoken vow.**

**Every thirst of young ambition
That served my heart to noble strife,
Sinks thee with the blest fruition
Of such aim, such hope, in life.**

**Let not let then the dream be broken
That I yet may claim thee mine,
Since love, that never may be spoken
And heart and soul all, all I'm thine.**

---

[32] When she started receiving her education at the Female Academy is not known but perhaps the move was due to the extreme pressure she felt from her father to succeed in Latin.

John Duke's youngest son was Charles Waller Tyler who was born July 11, 1839, in District One of Montgomery County. He began his education under his father at age five. J.B. Killebrew described Charles in his early years, "For many years he did nothing but read novels and lie in bed." By the time Charles was fifteen, he was well-versed in Latin and Greek. After leaving Hickory Wild, Charles furthered his education at Cumberland College in Lebanon, Tennessee. Its School of Law was founded on July 29, 1847, the first in Tennessee and west of the Appalachian Mountains. Students were taught through reading treatises, approximately two hours' worth of recitations each morning and a mandatory moot court program. The cost was $50 a session and a $5 "contingent fee."

Cumberland College School of Law

As Charles left to attend law school, Mildred Tyler was a fifty-one-year-old widow with no sons to help run the farm or the school. It is known that Quintus did return for a short time to help with his father's school as J.B. Killebrew recorded that in 1861, "We took several boarders who attended a school taught by Quintus Tyler at his father's old house."

John Duke's daughter Emmie was born in 1849 at Hickory Wild. It appears, as she grew into adulthood, she determined to dedicate her life to the church. She is never mentioned as having been in the social circles with her sister Nannie nor "paired off" with any particular gentleman. She will be discussed in detail later.

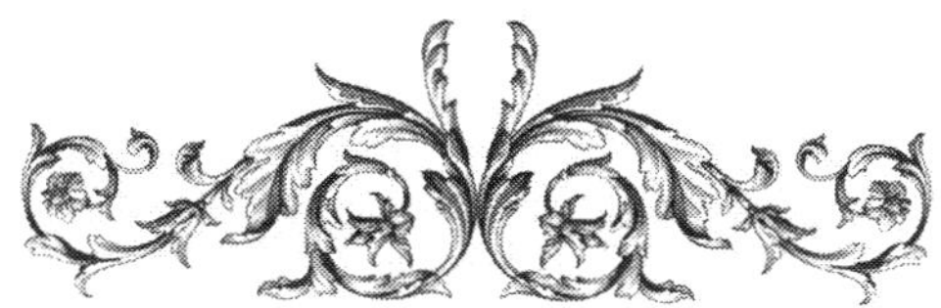

Chapter Four: His Family Left Unprotected

Events were to transpire that would alter the history of the Tyler family as well as the entire South when on May 1, 1861 the *Clarksville Jeffersonian* newspaper ran a notice, which read:

WAR! WAR! WAR!
WANTED!

> **ABLE BODIED MEN FROM EIGHTEEN TO THIRTY-FIVE years of age to enlist in a Cavalry Company. None need apply, but those willing to go into Active Service, such as will hold themselves in readiness to answer the call of the Governor of the State for service at any point. Those desiring to join such a Company can do so by calling upon W.E. Lowe, R.W. Johnson, W.A. Quarles, or A. Robb, Esq. when full particulars will be given.**
> **April 24, 1861**

Charles was still a student at Cumberland College when the Civil War erupted. Montgomery County in June 1861 voted 2,632 to 32 to join the Confederate States of America; within the city the vote was 561 to 1 to join. Later in his life, Tyler commented that so many men from Montgomery County volunteered to serve that the number "exceeded the entire white population subject to military duty."

It was announced on June 21, that Clarksville's post office was under the control of the Confederate States and therefore no more U.S. stamps would be issued. Citizens were informed that in order to send a letter, they should expect to pay postage in money until the new stamps were printed.

Charles left Cumberland College to return home to enlist, adding his name to the roll on July 10, one day before his 22nd birthday. He had only to travel a short distance down the road from Hickory Wild to Hampton's Spring, a staging and training area for Confederate recruits. The campsite was named Camp Quarles after William A. Quarles, a Clarksville attorney who would become a brigadier general.

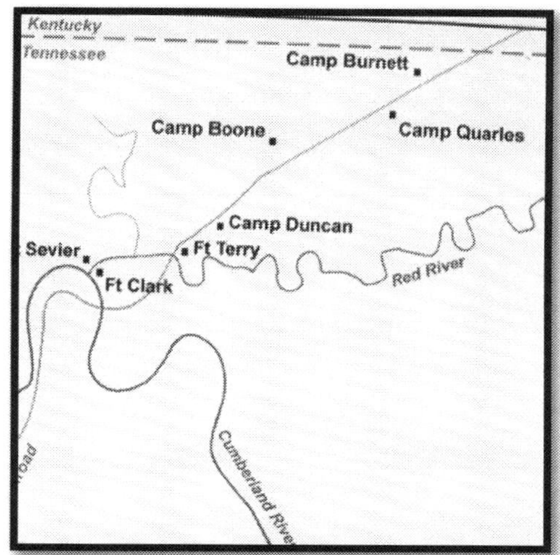

On the left: the camps located in the northern half of Montgomery County. On the right: Gen. W.A. Quarles.

The men drilled daily on the parade ground located one half-mile from the camp. Their tents were pitched comfortably among the shade trees near a refreshing spring. Friends and family members of the enlisted made numerous visits to the camp to bolster their spirits and bring provisions, which were much appreciated. Also, in the same general area was Camp Boone, a mustering site for Kentucky soldiers who could not enlist in their home state due to the fact that Kentucky voted to remain neutral. No doubt, Charles worried how his mother and two sisters would be cared for during his absence.

Where were the final goodbyes said? At the training camp, the door or gate of the soldier's home...where all mothers cling to the last sight of their sons going into battle. They would save the image like a treasure in their hearts where a thousand times over they would revisit that memory in his absence and then perhaps forever, if God forbid he should be taken from her!

In mid-summer of 1861, Clarksville families were encouraged not to curtail their daughters' education "in the midst of these dreadful times" but instead know with certainty that once the war was over, these daughters would be needed to fill the ranks of the Northern women then teaching in Southern female schools. The public was assured that for the two decades following the war, both the demand and salary of teachers would be "immensely large."

The Civil War had been in progress for months and rumors were abundant. Speculation that Lincoln's gunboats could actually reach the Cumberland was fanned by Northern newspapers such as the *Springfield (Ill.) Journal.* The writers of Clarksville's *Chronicle* dismissed the report as ludicrous when they wrote

> **The editor of the *Springfield* (Ill.) *Journal* takes a good deal of pains to prove himself a fool, and has succeeded admirably. He says the gunboats that are built at Cincinnati and Pittsburgh are intended, some of them, to ascend the Cumberland for the purpose of taking Clarksville and Nashville to a point which will enable the abolition army to attach Memphis in the rear. If such be the intention of the Northern Government, the editor is a fool for telling it, but whether it be or not, he is a fool if he does not know that the Tennessee and the Cumberland are not navigable at this season of the year, and that, if navigable, there are batteries on their banks sufficient to sink all the boats that Lincoln can send into them.**
> **July 5, 1861**

By mid-September the *Chronicle* writers continued to squelch fears by reporting that the river level at Dover Shoals was less than four feet doing "away with all danger or hope of a visit to us by Lincoln's gunboats, at least for the present." They listed further reasons why the boats could not reach Clarksville.

> **There are two cannon down about the state line, and two somewhere above. We know not their size, but those who planted them believe they are large enough to take care of themselves, and the general impression is that if the gunboats come up to the battery the guns will certainly go off, and that somebody will be hurt and most likely, the parties who have to foot the bill. Others fear that a Lincoln force may come upon us by the railroad, but they seem to forget that by leaving the draw of the bridge open, the enemy will be precipitated into the river whether they come from one direction or the other. This dead fall ensures the safety of Clarksville, and this assurance may be made doubly sure by informing the enemy that there is a battery on Franklin Street,[33] securely housed to keep it from going off and any amount of minute men in the county, armed by nature, drilled by the same, and organized by accident. Clarksville is in no danger so long as Memphis is safe and its citizens may sleep soundly under the protection of the marvelous consternation of circumstances above mentioned. The eye of sleepless vigilance is upon Memphis.**
> **September 13, 1861**

A Tennessee preacher offered the following prayer: "Oh Lord, do not raise the Cumberland sufficient to bring upon us those d--n Yankee gunboats." In just five short months, Lincoln's gunboats would be anchored in the Cumberland River below Clarksville's Public Square!

On November 7: Clarksville lawyer and politician Gustavus A. Henry while in Hopkinsville reported to A.S. Johnston in Bowling Green about the conditions at Ft. Donelson, where soon Charles Tyler would be stationed:

> **I hope you will not consider me importunate,[34] but the condition of things at Fort Donelson demands immediate attention. There are there about 800 cavalry and 500 infantry, and great want of organization and drill. They have not men enough to form a regiment, and no sort of order prevails. Some of the cavalry might be transferred to Tilghman,[35] and five more companies of infantry ought to be sent there (to Donelson), so as to organize a regiment immediately. Captain Sugg's company, now ready to march, already sworn in and armed, can go to Donelson at any moment. There is another company at Camp Cheatham, Dr. J.B. Walton, commander, could also be transferred there. They have no arms, but are**

---

[33] This was not correct.
[34] Demanding.
[35] Confederate brigadier general Lloyd Tilghman.

> **sworn in the service. Three other companies can be organized in a few days if proper energy is used. The guns at Donelson are wholly unprotected, as they were at the date of my last letter, and will probably remain so till the regiment is organized and someone is in command who will push on the work to completion. Captain Dixon is ready and willing to work, but he is not sustained. I strongly urge that Sugg's and Walton's companies be ordered immediately to Donelson, and the regiment be put in an organized condition as soon as possible. The abatis is finished at Donelson, but no work done to protect the guns. They are in a very exposed condition, for we learn the enemy's gunboats have passed the place on the river where Captain Harrison sunk the barges. They constitute an ineffectual blockade, as our board here are advised.**

On November 8, Capt. Cyrus Sugg's company paraded in Clarksville to the delight of all. The writers of the newspaper described the company as, "one of the finest and most effective looking companies that the war had brought out: being made up, almost without exception, of large, robust, genteel men."

Capt. Cyrus Alexandrian Sugg (1833-1864)[36]

Ten days later Sugg's infantry company, fully armed and equipped, drilled again on the Public Square in front of yet another appreciative crowd. Charles had been at Camp Quarles just two days when the 50th TN received their orders to strike their tents and report to Ft. Donelson. The soldiers left Clarksville the next morning aboard a steamship (probably the *General Anderson*), and arrived four hours later at the fort's landing. Disembarking from the boat, the new troops climbed the muddy hill up to the fort to what would become their home for the next several months.

For a month other units joined them until ten companies made up a regiment. Charles was elected Brevet-Second Lieutenant of Company E of the 50th TN under Capt. Sugg. They wintered at Ft. Donelson where they built small log huts, which Tyler described as "comfortable," receiving from friends in Clarksville "good things by nearly every boat." This included government rations of flour, fresh-cured meats, sugar and the much appreciated supplies of coffee.

Reconstructed log hut at Ft. Donelson. Courtesy Ft. Donelson National Park

Indeed, while the "Clarksville boys" were at Ft. Donelson, the women back home were busy cooking food, collecting blankets and necessities to send by available boats going to the fort for the relief of the soldiers there. Several ladies' groups consolidated into the Soldiers' Aid Society, which met at the courthouse. The officers of the society were: president: Mrs. Gustavus A. Henry (whose husband would serve as a Confederate State Senator); secretary: Mrs. W.B. Munford and treasurer: Mrs. Edward B. Haskins. These ladies worked tirelessly every day to collect or make bed clothing, socks and other items for the troops. There was a Juvenile Relief Society too with president: Nannie Haskins (her daughter); vice president: Dora Judkins; secretary: Sally Lewis and treasurer: Nina Cobb.

Boredom among the routine would have been relieved by board games (checkers, chess, draughts and dominoes), whittling, writing (which was uncensored) and gambling (a forbidden but common activity). Timber was abundant and when completed by both soldiers and slaves, there stood up to 400 log huts for winter quarters in this area. Game was easily available too and off-duty soldiers were successful in both hunting and fishing while garrisoned.

The Tennessee and Kentucky Tylers heard that back in Virginia, former U.S. President John Tyler passed away at age 71. Tyler was the only U.S. President to not be officially recognized in

---

[36] The Suggs lived in District One and knew the Tyler family before the war.

Washington D.C. due to his allegiance to the Confederate States of America. Tyler wanted a simple burial but Confederate President Jefferson Davis arranged a funeral befitting his presidential status, complete with a Confederate flag draped over the coffin. Tyler was buried in Richmond's Hollywood Cemetery in the Presidents' Circle overlooking the James River. Charles Tyler never forgot this kindness rendered to his relative by Davis. In the future, both Micajah Clark and Jefferson Davis would be buried up on the same bluff in Richmond.

President John Tyler

On January 19, 1862, the troops of the 49th and 50th TN marched to Ft. Henry; a distance of thirteen miles, remaining there only ten days before returning to Ft. Donelson. On January 21, the 50th TN Regiment rolls recorded 499 present for duty.

Polk Grundy Johnson was the youngest son of Elizabeth and Cave Johnson, the Postmaster General under President Polk. In fact, he was born on the very day (November 2, 1844), that James K. Polk was elected President. At age sixteen, Polk Grundy joined the Confederate Army and served in the 49th Tennessee Regiment. Regardless of being "just a beardless boy in his teens." Confederate general William A. Quarles appointed Polk as his aid-de-camp. In this important position, Quarles wrote of Polk twenty years after the war, "His conduct did not disappoint my expectations. He was invaluable, polite and affable to and with the men. He proved himself every inch a soldier." Johnson was captured at Ft. Donelson, later exchanged and survived the Battle of Franklin, which virtually wiped out his entire regiment.

Cave Johnson

Polk Grundy Johnson

The troops were sent back to Ft. Henry on February 6 to act as reinforcements in preparation for the upcoming attack by Union boats. The Tennessee River was at flood stage, due to heavy winter rains, they realized would allow the enemy the distinct advantage of firing, not upward, but directly at the fort. Grant captured the fort and then began moving his troops to Ft. Donelson.

Commanded by forty-year veteran, Flag Officer Andrew Hull Foote, the Western Flotilla took full advantage of the conditions rendered to them by Mother Nature. On February 11, there were seven gunboats in all to make the attack upon the vulnerable fort, including four armored: the flag ship *Cincinnati, Carondelet, Lexington* and *St. Louis* as well as three wooden (timberclad) gunboats: The *Essex, Tyler and Conestoga.*

The *Cincinnati, Carondelet, Essex* and *St. Louis* lined up side-by-side and fired in succession while the *Lexington*, *Conestoga* and *Tyler* fired long-range shells at the fort. This sequencing of firing allowed for a systematic reloading period. On deck were thirteen heavy cannons; four guns forward, two aft and the rest on the sides. Meanwhile Ulysses S. Grant and his 15,000 troops awaited 10,000 reinforcements and for both of the water-logged roads to Ft. Donelson to dry before he commenced his attack by land. Confederate forces were ordered back to reinforce Ft. Donelson. Charles recorded the event:

> **We evacuated the fort (Henry) and marched up to Dover, two miles. There we stood shivering in the cold. . . . The enemy's campfires blazed up brightly, all around us, and looked cheerful enough as we stamped our feet in the snow. We expected orders to cut our way through them.**

On February 15, the 49th and 50th TN regiments engaged the Federals advancing on the fort. The next day at 1:30 a.m. Confederate general John B. Floyd held a strategy meeting at his headquarters at the Dover Hotel. Meanwhile, the noise of the battle at Ft. Donelson, a distance of thirty miles, was heard by the citizens in Clarksville. Grasping onto any piece of information from the forts, Clarksville braced for the news of the final outcome, realizing what a defeat there would mean for the city. With rumors of Grant's advancing troops flying about, tempers flared, quarreling over the appropriate course of action. In a classic example of passing the buck, Gen. Floyd, fearing capture and possible imprisonment in the North, turned his command over to General Pillow who feared the same, and so handed the command of the fort over to an ailing Buckner. The two commanders evacuated Donelson, Pillow by small boat, crossing the Cumberland River that night, and Floyd the next morning aboard a steamboat on the Cumberland River, which traveled first to Clarksville then Buckner felt he had no choice but to surrender the fort along with 12,000 men.

Col. Nathan Bedford Forrest argued that the Confederate forces should instead retreat across the Cumberland River. In total frustration at having his plan discounted, Forrest realized he had wasted his breath. In his characteristic commanding style, Forrest told the generals that he had not come to Ft. Donelson to surrender his command; that he would rather have the bones of his troops bleach white on the nearby hills than to have them captured and sent up North to a Federal prison. Pillow then offered that Forrest should be allowed to attempt an escape. Immediately Forrest gathered his field and company officers and advised them of his plans, "Boys, these people are talking about surrender and I am going out of this place before they do or bust hell wide open!" Those with a horse were told to cut their extra blankets to cover the hooves to muffle the sound. In order to ride fast, they had to leave just about everything else behind. Charles considered his options and at about 4:00 a.m. he escaped with 500 of Colonel Forrest's cavalry and 200 stragglers from other companies.[37] In extreme cold and with sleet coming down hard, they marched down Charlotte Road and then across the freezing waters of Lick Creek "about saddle skirt deep." The creek, 100 yards across, was swollen from the backwater of the Cumberland River and was covered by a thin layer of ice along its banks. Forrest asked for a volunteer to test the waters and since no one came forward, Forrest himself plunged into the creek before leading the men across. Those not on horseback had difficulty fording the creek but for those on foot, the crossing must have been excruciating.

The "Breakout"

Years later, Dr. John Reuben Moore (1840-1912), of New Providence and part of the medical corps during the battle, recalled the crossing of Lick Creek. While fighting the waters of the swollen creek, he held on to a horse's tail. He recalled many soldiers who plunged into the creek ahead of the cavalry were trampled and drowned.

Dr. J.R. Moore

Forrest and the evacuees did not encounter one single enemy shot. The men came to Dudley's Hill and then took the road headed to Charlotte in Dickson County, Tennessee on their way to reinforce Nashville. Although not present, Charles described the subsequent surrender of Ft. Donelson:

> **In a short while a courier came from General Buckner to Colonel Sugg with an order to raise a white flag over the fort. Curses both loud and deep followed this intelligence. There was no white flag in the regiment, nobody expecting to need one, but Ordinance Sergeant R.L. Cobb had a white sheet, which was run up at daylight.**

It was from the *Cincinnati* that a boat was sent to secure the surrender. Upon meeting Foote, Buckner told the commodore, "I am glad to have surrendered to so gallant an officer." Foote replied, "You do perfectly right, Sir, in surrendering but you should have blown my boats out of the water before I would have surrendered to you." When Buckner asked Grant for his terms of surrender, Grant replied, "No terms except an unconditional and immediate surrender can be accepted. I propose to move immediately on your works." The Confederate general was astounded at Grant's stern reply. In his message back to Grant, Buckner characterized the terms

[37] Estimates vary on the exact number who were part of the breakout.

as "ungenerous and unchivalrous." By the end of the battle, which lasted from February 13-16, 1862,[38] approximately 1,976 Federal troops were wounded, 507 killed and 208 captured/missing. About 1,127 Confederate troops were wounded, 327 killed and 12,392 captured/missing.

Following Forrest out of Donelson was probably among the first of many decisive moments in Charles Tyler's life. The majority of Tyler's regiment had elected to stay at the fort and therefore had been captured and sent with other regiments to three Union prisoner camps up North: Ft. Warren received the field and staff officers, Johnson's Island in Lake Erie took the line officers, and all noncommissioned officers went to Camp Douglas (Ft. Dearborn) in Chicago.

In Clarksville, the wounded and dying were being transported from the Cumberland River to the Female Academy on Madison Street where they were attended by Blanche Lewis, her mother Margaretta and the Bibb sisters. Initial numbers stood at 180 of those carried into the school, filling the rooms and hallways with moaning, screaming wounded and dying.

P.G. Johnson with other Clarksville boys in a POW camp.

On the night of February 16, Forrest and the troops who followed him reached Cumberland Furnace, Tennessee. Forrest's men were in need of immediate shelter. Having left most of their supplies, including blankets, back at Donelson, many of the men were sick and dying. Many bivouacked on the hillsides and woke up the next morning in sub-zero temperatures with 10 inches of snow covering their bodies. People of the tiny community opened their homes to the men where they received much needed care. Despite the care provided by the local citizens, those who died were interred in the Van Leer Cemetery and elsewhere.

It is well to include here some idea of the type of situation the soldiers faced. Many of the "men" were actually young boys from farming communities who had never really been away from their family farms and certainly had never faced these types of hardships before. Such was it with Charles Tyler. The common belief was that the war would be settled early, perhaps in "one glorious battle" and the boys could simply go back home to raising crops and continuing with their lives. Now sickened from the freezing temperatures and exhausted from the battle and escape, the followers of Forrest were probably in a state of disbelief. Those who could not travel were left behind as Forrest proceeded to Charlotte, then a town of 300 residents. Upon their arrival the next morning, blacksmiths began re-shoeing the horses in need and immediately Forrest began re-equipping his men in preparation for the march towards Nashville at daybreak. In the meantime, some of the soldiers spilled into the court house square saloons to ease the cold and misery and regale the locals with first-hand stories of the Battle at Ft. Donelson. Forrest realized quickly that the men needed to be curbed and rode from saloon to saloon ordering that no more whisky should be sold to his soldiers. One such saloon was inside the Hickerson Hotel and as witnessed by "Uncle" Dan Rook Hickerson, the pouring stopped immediately upon Forrest's order.

The Hickerson Hotel

Despite that, still some of the men were so drunk the next morning they refused to mount their horses to leave but Forrest knew exactly how to cure this situation. Forrest took a company of his men to a hill east of Charlotte and ordered them to fire their guns and give the rebel yell. This had the desired result as those left behind interpreted this that the enemy had come from the nearby

[38] At the time Quintus Tyler was running Hickory Wild he placed a notice in the newspaper on February 14, 1862: "My business is such that I am compelled to postpone the commencement of my school from the second Monday in this month to the first Monday in April."

Cumberland River to cut off Forrest before he reached Nashville. It was stated that in just a blink of an eye, there was not a single man left on the court square. By nightfall, he gathered up the troops and headed towards Nashville, reaching the Harpeth Valley just before nightfall. The mouth of the Harpeth River and Betsytown would become favorite spots of Confederates to ford the Cumberland River during the war.

In the book *Picturesque Clarksville, Past and Present,* W.P. Titus wrote of a "young lady of high standing" who received a permit from a Union colonel at the Federal headquarters downtown to cross over to the south side of the Cumberland River with the intention of visiting a friend. Her real purpose was to get items to "a poor rebel" hiding in the bushes. After crossing the ferry and arriving by horseback, she had on so many smuggled items she had to be carried down from her horse and into a nearby house. In addition to wearing a pair of heavy (three feet long) cavalry boots, she had a bustle of several pounds of powder, numerous pairs of socks and yards of flannel, the amount enough according to Titus, "to start a country store." The young lady was none other than Nannie Tyler delivering "items of comfort" to her brother Charles who had escaped with Forrest from Ft. Donelson. Nannie, as she traveled alone by horseback over country roads was faced with the possibility of arrest, or worse, if the contraband she hid under her skirts was discovered. Due to the suspension of civil government, lawlessness was widespread outside the city boundaries and as an unprotected female, the unthinkable could have occurred. The Federals were more occupied with maintaining control within city limits than out. Charles must have been enormously proud of his sister's courage and cunning but how difficult it also must have been for him to know that his two sisters and mother remained in an area controlled by the enemy. All the while the wait for Nannie's return must have been torturous for her family back at Hickory Wild.

Tyler was not yet under Forrest's command. He hid out at Stephen D. Watkins' house in the coalings where the timber had been cut for the area's iron furnaces. The woods had been replaced by scrub oaks, vines, cedars, wild grasses, etc. Stephen Dupree Watkins (1820-1874), a veteran of the Mexican War and his wife, Mary Baxter Watkins (1823-1908), at great risk to themselves and their property, gave aid and support to the Confederacy during the war. The Baxter Furnace was in Montgomery County as was the Watkins' home that would serve as a refuge for Southern soldiers needing supplies and comfort. Several times, Federals searched their home and, several times, those they hid were captured. They risked much because they had much to lose. Stephen had taken over several furnaces when Mary's father Samuel Baxter passed away. Mary's brother, Robert Baxter, Jr. and his family lived nearby. It was here that Nannie brought him necessary items until he could rejoin his regiment.

Forrest camped his men at the Harpeth River on the Charlotte Pike for the night. Forrest knew it was imperative to protect the capitol city and the Louisville & Nashville Railroad, a vital supply route for the South. The Nashville and Chattanooga Railroad transported Confederate gunpowder and iron supplies brought in from the numerous Western Highland Rim furnaces that were scattered throughout middle and western Tennessee and if captured, would provide arterial openings into the very center of the South.

The next day Forrest and his soldiers arrived in Nashville where they were met with scenes of total chaos. Confederate Gen. Albert S. Johnston, who felt Nashville was indefensible against the advancing Union Army, ordered his army to evacuate the city. Forrest was infuriated by the chaos so began to coordinate the evacuation. Looting had already commenced. At the same time, he ordered his men to locate munitions and to burn whatever military stores could not be saved. The Nashville Armory located on College Hill, just south of town, stored large amounts of arms and ammunition and needed to be destroyed immediately. Realizing that the defense of Nashville was futile and as the Confederate Army was retreating, Forrest provided a rear guard for Hardee's Army of Central Kentucky as it withdrew to Alabama.

So what did this Union victory mean for the South? The Confederacy lost southern Kentucky and much of Middle and West Tennessee. Clarksville's Cumberland River and the larger Tennessee River along with the railroads servicing the region, became instrumental Federal supply lines. And on February 25, Nashville fell to the Union Army and was the first Confederate state capitol to do so. Thus it became a huge supply depot for the Union Army in the western theater. Days earlier, on February 19, the telegraph office in Clarksville received the dreaded, but expected, news that the Yankees were coming! One eyewitness to the scene as the word spread was Joseph B. Killebrew. He described the city as one in a state of total panic. "Everyone seemed to have lost his senses. Men were running their horses up and down the streets shouting to another and acting precisely as their lives were forfeited." Clarksville citizens decided to prevent the liquor in the town from falling into the hands or stomachs of the enemy as to prevent possible outrages. Thus every drop was confiscated and poured out.

A member of Grant's staff wrote after entering the city, "Clarksville was a very pretty place of about 3000 inhabitants when they were at home. The people were in great fear that our army will plunder and destroy their property. The citizens themselves destroyed all the liquor of every kind." This incident would serve as the basis for a major lawsuit in Clarksville twelve years later.

Foote accepted Clarksville's surrender after sending for city leaders to meet with him on the *Conestoga* as he was recovering from wounds he received during the Battle of Ft. Donelson while aboard the ironclad *St. Louis.* With Forts Henry and Donelson captured, Clarksville was occupied by enemy troops. Citizens who had been so confident that with two regiments nearby, they had nothing to worry about were now inundated with troops in their homes, on their farms and on the streets of Clarksville. The city was garrisoned initially by 1,138 Union troops under the command of Gen. William Rosecrans, who was headquartered in Murfreesboro, Tennessee. Clarksville was occupied for several reasons. First as mentioned before, the Cumberland River acted as a main supply route for Federal forces in Tennessee and it was vital that the supply lines be kept open. Secondly, because the river dropped to lower than normal levels, a large number of supply steamers could not make it down to Nashville and therefore had to unload and protect their cargo at Clarksville until the river level rose. The number of stores in Clarksville produced a tempting target for rebel raiders. Thirdly, Clarksville and the surrounding areas would become a hot bed of resistance full of guerillas who were to harass Union forces until and even after the end of the war.

When Clarksville became an occupied city after the fall of Ft. Donelson, the publication of the local newspaper was suspended. The *Clarksville Chronicle* had its printing discontinued from March 14, 1862, until July 14, 1865. The Federals however, published their own paper entitled the *83rd Illinoisan*, "devoted to the Interest of the Regiment and the News in General." Three members of the regiment, George Mitchell, Lem Lusk and Frank Stanley, who had previous printing experience, ran the newspaper using the local presses.

In November, Clarksville citizens began to see black soldiers dressed in the blue uniforms of the Union Army in town. This was unsettling to say the least to those whose hope was that soon the war would end and enemy troops would vacate the city. Reports were given that 2,000 ex-slaves from Kentucky had enlisted in the Union Army in Clarksville. They formed the 16th Infantry and 9th Heavy Artillery. Fort Defiance, along with other area forts, became contraband camps.

Clarksville citizenry consisted of the old, infirmed, women, children and their servants and was defenseless with most of the able men, or those capable of bearing arms, gone with the Confederate Army. There is no record of the Hickory Wild farm being pillaged for food, livestock or any outrage committed in the four year conflict.

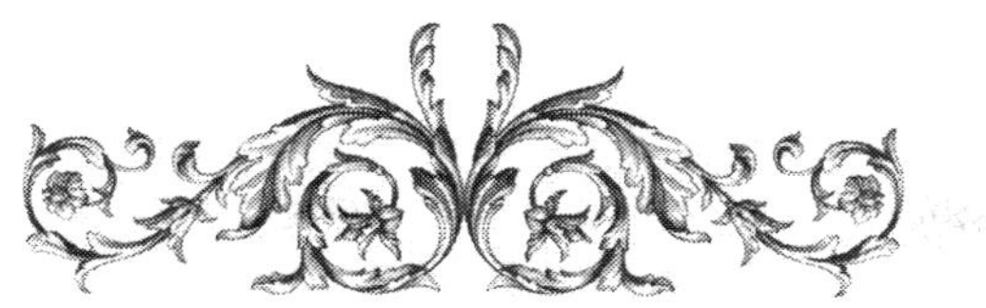

Chapter Five: Charles Tyler in the War

The diary of Nannie Haskins and the journal of eighteen-year-old Eleanora Willauer (1844-1906), grandniece of the iron master Anthony Wayne Van Leer, born in the Cumberland Furnace community, provide information on the Tylers during the war. (Willauer specifically names Charles Tyler and her encounters with him and the guerillas with whom he rode.)

Nannie Haskins

Eleanor Willauer

Eleanora recorded the tumultuous events surrounding her home throughout the Civil War and the encounters she had with the likes of Nathan Bedford Forrest and Thomas Woodward among many others. She also knew many people from Clarksville and included them in her writings. By Nannie Haskins' and Eleanora's entries it seems that Charles' sister, Nannie moved about freely even with the county being occupied by enemy soldiers.

Guerrilla warfare[39] was common around Dickson (then known as Smeedville), and surrounding areas by the summer of 1862 and so a prison was established on the Public Square in Clarksville by the Federal Army. Prisoners were also secured above the law offices of Robb & Bailey on Strawberry Alley. Seven captured guerillas from Dickson County were confined as prisoners and held in Clarksville, charged with being a rebel agent or spy. These men were lucky as in nearby Humphreys County several Confederates were shot or hanged for the same charges.

On June 22, 1862, Charles requested his discharge from the army. The reason was simple and typical of the integrity of this man. He was upset that the troops under his command were expecting to be paid while failing in their duties and he wanted none of it. Brig. Gen. Johnson in Tupelo, Mississippi did grant an honorable discharge to him. One month later on July 28, Charles Tyler sent a letter addressed to the Hon. George W. Randolph, CSA Secretary of War that read:

> **Dear Sir, I am an applicant for the position of Second Lieutenant of the Provisional Army of the Confederate States. This position I formerly held in the 50th Tennessee Regiment which was taken at Fort Donelson: Escaping thence with about twenty men I remained with the army under General A.S. Johnson (sic) and General Beauregard for about two months. When my men, being assigned to the First Kentucky Cavalry Regiment and being unwilling to draw pay for services not rendered, I resigned. Enclosed you will find my discharge signed by General B.R. (Bushrod Rust) Johnson, Commanding General (William Joseph) of Hardee's division. Observing that there is to be a general exchange of prisoners, I desire to be reinstated in my former position. Hoping this application may be granted: I am Sir: Very Respectfully Your Obedient Servant, Charles W. Tyler**

For a short time, Col. Thomas G. Woodward, the "Red Headed Colonel," recaptured Clarksville from August 18-29, 1862. Woodward had been raised in New England and graduated from West Point. He moved to the South where he taught for twelve years in Christian County, Kentucky. He also practiced law at one time in Hopkinsville. Short in stature, (his boots reached up to his knees), with disheveled shoulder length hair, parted in the middle, close-set eyes and an unruly, long mustache, Col. Woodward immediately volunteered to defend the Confederacy when the war broke out. He was among those who escaped Ft. Donelson with Nathan Bedford Forrest

[39] Gen. Robert E. Lee knew the war could not be won by guerrilla warfare and yet the he did not order Forrest to cease his operations. He knew that Forrest would have a morale effect on the enemy.

and later became the leader of the Oak Grove Rangers. Jubilant at the return of the Confederate forces, Nannie Haskins recorded their recapture of Clarksville by writing:

> **They came in on their poor old horses, dirty clothes and all sorts of arms, they had no band at all, not even a bugle or a flag to show to whom they belonged but their old dirty 'grey'—but fight was in 'em and the 'tuck' the place and the 'Feds' with all their blue broadcloth and brass buttons.**

Woodward held Clarksville until September 1862 when they were driven out by Union colonel William Lowe's army sent from Ft. Donelson. Lowe chased Woodward outside of the city limits and insisted upon the surrender of both his forces and the city of Clarksville. To this Woodward replied that, "he held no city and had none to surrender…the city of Clarksville belonged to its citizens." Woodward actually invited Lowe to try to capture him and his men but for whatever reason Lowe decided against it and so the "ragamuffin colonel" and the small group under his command crossed the Red River without being stopped.

Woodward may have given Clarksvillians a temporary respite from Federal occupation but by his actions and the resurgence of citizen pro-South sentiments, the wrath of the North fell upon their heads. Immediately there began a period of "outrages, robberies and insults upon citizens without regard to sex or condition." Federal troops confiscated horses and took off large numbers of Negroes and horses. Livestock was shot or stolen and downtown stores broken into and robbed. Occupants of homes were constantly subjected to Union troops demanding to be fed. Refusal to do so had an immediate consequence: having their homes torched.

Immensely offended by this outrage, citizens authorized Cave Johnson to send a letter of protest to Jefferson Davis. G.W. Randolph, Secretary of War responded to the news by insisting that if colonels Harding and Lowe were to be taken prisoner, they "should not be entitled to the treatment of prisoners of war, and to that if captured, will be treated as felons." A letter dated September 15, was also sent to U.S. Grant, which read:

> **From Sunday noon until Monday noon, a reign of terror, kept alive by every species of outrage was established in this city…. Can you as one of the military chieftains of your proud nation quietly permit its honor to be spotted and tarnished by such acts of robbery and vandalism as we have described?**

Clarksville citizens were appalled when no relief came from these crimes committed upon their persons or property. In later years Charles related that:

> **Though fences were down, and work stock stolen, and slaves for the most part were in the camp of the enemy, the Southern people during the Civil War did always manage to scratch around in fertile places, and produce food enough for themselves and the strangers within their gates, provided these latter were of the right stripe.**

Eleanora's first entry in her journal that mentioned the Tylers included the day she was invited by Mrs. Baxter to visit at Louisa as there were girls coming down from Clarksville.

> **Willauer journal- Tuesday, October 21, 1862: I wonder what kind of girls I shall find them? One of them I have heard is very wild and very beautiful: Nannie Garland. I used to go to school with her but do not remember her. She and Mary Nichol are great friends. Nannie Tyler is very pretty they say. We have had glorious news, if it were only true but there have been so many conflicting reports that we have no hope of getting to the true one. Among other things 'tis reported that the 'Links' are evacuating Nashville. Oh! if it were only true!!! Wouldn't it be glorious!**
>
> **Willauer journal- Friday, November 14 or 15, 1862** [It was the 14th]: **Oh, I have been having such a glorious time ever since I wrote in here last. I did go down to Louisa.[40] Nannie Tyler, darling Nannie Tyler and Beckie, my sweet little sister[41] came up for me. The illustrious Frank Phillips[42] came with them. They took dinner and Van and I went back with them.**

---

[40] Louisa is a nearby community with its own furnace.

[41] Again she is using the word "sister" as an endearment. Eleanora had no sisters.

[42] Later a policeman in Clarksville and involved in one of the city'

Wayne [43] went part of the way and rode with Nan. Phillips rode with me. I do not admire him much and I am glad that I can think Beckie does not either.

Nan [Tyler] came over next day and we had a grand time rarely ever retiring until two or three and riding nearly all day. There was great rivalry as to who should receive the greatest attention from Lieut. Baxter. Nannie distanced us all I think that time. The lieutenant had to return to camp though and we all returned to Louisa and came from there up here. Nan, Beckie, Dora and I came first and the next day or so Florence and Mrs. Watkins and Mrs. Jackson came. We stopped at Hickerson's on the way up and there we met a young man from Woodward's. Mr. Grimes, Nan and I wrote a note just for fun to Lieut. Bill, and Beckie wrote to Charlie Tyler, Nan's brother, [Nannie Tyler's] a captain in Woodward's, sending him a pair of socks.

We all returned to Louisa at the expiration of a week and heard that Woodward's whole command was camped at Antioch only 6 miles from Louisa. It was on Friday, very cold and snowing; we were so glad to hear it and Nannie was so anxious to see her brother that we all jumped on our horses and rode down. We met some of them at Ramey's, a mile from Louisa and one of them rode down to camp with me. Wayne and Collier rode down with us also. We arrived at camp and found Capt. Tyler gone. Lieut. Baxter however, was there and he took us down and we were all introduced to the celebrated Woodward. He had given orders that no man should leave camp but Nannie begged him so hard that he at last promised to let us all have a bean apiece to take home to stay all night.

Willauer journal- Tuesday, November 17, 1862 [If it was Tuesday, the date should have been November 18]**: [Last ?] Wednesday I was left all alone and was just setting down in to the old routine when Saturday just after dinner, Beckie, Dora, Nannie, Mrs. Finley and the often-heard-of Charlie Tyler came. They came back so that Nan could be with Charlie on Sunday. Charlie Tyler asked me to name his horse.**

Saturday, November 23, [it was the 22nd] **1862: Charlie Tyler was here last night. He came in the evening but would not have his horse put up as he only intended staying a short time. He stayed all night and seemed to not be very anxious to go this morning. He likes to hear me sing. Van has gone down to camp. They will not swear him but he will go with them. We have done all we could to prevent him from going and of course there is nothing to be done but let him go.**

Van [44] came up while Capt. Tyler was here. Just before Charlie came in, six or seven of the soldiers came in to hear some music. I did not know them but complied and they departed. I like Capt. Tyler very much. He is handsome. He is about five feet eleven, has brown hair, blue eyes, and good skin; all of his features are exceedingly good, and except that he is too thin a little I think, him so good looking and then he is such a nice fellow, so pleasant in every way, and moral and sincere.

December 6, 1862: Capt. Tyler has been here a time or two. I like him so much.

Tuesday, December 9, 1862: Mr. H. saw Mary Nichol who had just come in from Maury [County]. Van had reached there in safety. Maj. Robertson and Capt. Charlie Tyler had been out there.

Mr. H says Mary N. seems quite fascinated with Capt. Tyler. Selfishness whispers to me, that old "E.W." [herself] would be very sorry to hear that C.W.T. [Charles Waller Tyler] was fascinated with Mary in like style.

Friday, December 12, 1862: Capt. Tyler has left the regiment and gone home. The Yanks are thick and these I am afraid they will get him prisoner as well as the remainder of Woodward's who have gone home over there.

Author Notes: Thomas Baxter at age 16 and William Baxter at age 13 attended Charles Tyler's father's school before the war.

---

[43] Eleanora's brother. Her other brother, William was a Union soldier that died in a POW camp.
[44] Her cousin.

The emancipation proclamation was due to go into effect starting January 1, 1863. Military Governor Andrew Johnson managed to delay the proclamation in Tennessee for two years requiring the state to put it into law. Until then slavery was still in effect in Tennessee. Citizens in Clarksville began encountering black troops on the streets as the city was still under Union occupation. A description of Clarksville then is learned from reading the letters written by Mrs. Sarah Bailey Kennedy to her husband banker, David Newton Kennedy, who for much of the war was not able to return to Clarksville. She wrote on February 2: "Our town looks like desolation itself. All its glory has departed."

Willauer Journal- Saturday, January 3, 1863: Lieut. Wright here last Thursday staid (sic) all night. Does not know anything of Capt. Charlie Tyler; is rather afraid that he is taken prisoner. I do most fervently hope that it is not so. I should be so, so sorry if it were really so. Perhaps if he is free he will be here e'er many days.

Monday, January 5, 1863: I received a letter or rather note from Capt. Tyler, in the care of Katie McCauley, dated yesterday; suppose he must have been there.

January 12, 1863. Monday night: A squad of blue coats passed here today under a flag of truce. The Negroes say, they were going towards Clarksville. Said to Negro that they had been to look for W. Bell, some Morgan men, who are reported to have been [?] and Capt. Tyler, found neither.

Night: Federals reported to be in Franklin, going to Columbia. Capt. Tyler with the command.

Eleanora no longer saw Tyler; this was because he had joined Col. William E. De Moss' 10th TN Cavalry organized in February 1863 when Cox's and Napier's TN Cavalry Battalions were consolidated. Men from Perry, Humphreys, Decatur, Hickman, Davidson, Montgomery and Henry Counties filled its ranks. Tyler was with Longstreet's Corps in East Tennessee in 1863 and with Gen. Hood as Hood advanced into Middle Tennessee in 1864. The 10th TN served in Forrest's, Humes', J.B. Bifle's and Dibrell's Brigades.

Haskins diary- Wednesday, February 25, 1863: Yesterday was a very pretty day. In the afternoon we went down to see Mrs. McKeage but as she was out, we went up to see Nannie Johnson. She is another soft headed girl, but a good one. I like Nannie. I said we went; I meant Mattie Hillman and myself.

Willauer journal- Wednesday, March 11, 1863: Went down Sunday the first with Beckie who came for me to Louisa and spent a week. Mrs. Finley, being here, went also. On getting there found the Watkins family and W. Baxter also Miss Bettie Garland from Clarksville and her Uncle Hick Johnson who was staying there being a captain in the 14th Tenn. Regiment wounded in the foot seven months ago and not yet sufficiently recovered for infantry. Capt. Johnson is a handsome agreeable young man, reported to be engaged to Nannie Tyler. Young 23, 8th of next November, he was taken prisoner just exactly seven months from the day he was wounded. He was wounded on the 9th day of August '62.

J.B. Killebrew's daughter, Mary Catherine, wrote later of the fears she had during this period.

March 1863: Our greatest fear was a constant dread, not knowing at what time we would be driven from our homes, as was the case in many parts of the South. Our fears were groundless for we were not molested personally. We fed both sides whenever they came. We gave to the Southern soldiers freely anything that would be of use to them. Often after the Federals had possession of this country, the Southern soldiers would come in to see their friends and to get supplies. They would hide out during the day and come to the houses at night to get food and other things. At one time, three of the Clarksville boys who were in the Army of Virginia came home on a month's furlough. The Federals had possession of the country and they were afraid to go to their own homes so they spent the month with us resting. Charles Tyler's (now Judge Tyler) mother lived near us. The other two, Hickman Johnson, oldest son of Hon. Cave Johnson, and his cousin, Robert Johnson lived in Clarksville. These visits of the Confederate soldiers increased our fears, for if the

Negroes had betrayed us, they as well as ourselves, would have been arrested and our homes destroyed.

Haskins diary- Sunday, April 26, 1863: And I have seen Col. Brewer, and I am inclined to think him handsome.... The above spoken of man is a colonel (so he says) who was captured a few days ago by the Yankees and brought to Clarksville. Upon trying to make his escape, he was shot and wounded in the shoulder. He is now staying at Mrs. Forbes. It is so seldom that a Confederate soldier is seen that they are making quite a lion of him. Nannie Tyler and Nannie McClure are staying at Mrs. Forbes. Ma, Pa, and I walked up to Mrs. Forbes' this afternoon. Miss Nannie was worse. Pa remained and has just returned (ten o'clock) says she is no better. Poor girl. 'tis sad to one so young dying with consumption; yes 'tis sad to know that soon she will have passed away. There were these Yankees there to see Coln. Brewer. Adjutant Boone and Busby (I don't know any title to put before his surname. Bettie Garland and I were sitting at one end of the porch. Nannie Tyler and Mary Boyd[45] on one side. Emma Robb[46] and Nannie McClure on the other of the steps, when they (the blue coats) came down to leave; of course they bowed.

Mary Boyd (Johnson)

Why was this prisoner taken to the Forbes' house while Nannie had such a contagious disease with Elizabeth struggling to keep her daughter alive? The young man had many visitors come to see him including Union soldiers checking on their prisoner. There was no mention of Will Forbes, the son. His sister was dying and there were enemy soldiers in their house.

On May 7, Barker wrote, "Boy Tyler left for Linksdom." Below this entry Barker wrote of other boys leaving for the North. In a side column he wrote the following, "Lincoln rules here yet, Home Links worst of all. God Almighty hates a traitor I believe." At age 37, it does not appear that Charles Tyler's older brother, Duke Tyler served in the war. Had he argued over the matter of slavery and refused to fight? Duke may have stayed at the farm at least until he left in 1863 to go north. This meant that their widowed mother and two sisters were left unprotected on the farm. It can be assumed that while he was up north, he got his education in law.

Hickory Wild's overseer, James Hardy Acree (1832-1911), was born in Port Royal, Tennessee to Joab Cotton Acree, Sr. (1799-1885), and Sophia Campbell Marshall Acree (1805-1885). On May 22, 1862, Acree left Hickory Wild and joined the 14th Tennessee Regiment that organized at Camp Duncan and spent the majority of the war in Virginia.

James Hardy Acree

After several months of sporadic fighting, the 50th TN again saw heavy combat on September 18, when it reached Gen. Bragg's army on the eve of the battle of Chickamauga near Chattanooga, Tennessee. From September 19-20, 1863 the Battle of Chickamauga was fought and lived up to its Indian name which meant "River of Death." Forrest dismounted his men and led them into the foray as infantry. Over 16,170 Federals troops and 18,454 Confederate troops lost their lives in this engagement. Confederate Maj. William Miller Owen recorded this account of the battle:

Our division, in advancing, passes the spot where Gen. Bragg is seated upon his horse...He looks pale and careworn... The enemy seems to be fighting in detached bodies. Longstreet discovers, with his soldier's eye, a gap in their already confused lines... The men rush over the hastily constructed breastworks with the old time familiar rebel yell; and wheeling then to the right, the columns sweep before it, and pushes along the Chattanooga Road towards Missionary Ridge in pursuit. It is glorious!

---

[45] Mary "Mollie" Boyd would later marry James Hickman Johnson and in 1886, become Clarksville's first female postmaster.

[46] Like Bettie Garland, Emma V. Robb also lost her father Col. Alfred Robb during the war. He received mortal wounds during the Battle of Ft. Donelson. He was the commander of the 49th TN Infantry.

It was during this bloody battle that Thomas Beaumont lost his life and Charles Tyler was wounded. Beaumont's remains were brought back to Clarksville's City Cemetery (now named Riverview Cemetery), in 1865 and buried in the Beaumont family plot.

It is not known where Charles was wounded. No remnant of this injury was evident after the war, nor was any mention of it made.

Next came the Battle of Missionary Ridge on November 25. By the end of these two battles, the 50th TN lost all of its field officers, a great number of its company officers and over half of its men. More specifically, 186 men from the 50th TN began the battle but only 54 survived. It was then necessary to consolidate forces and so it was that the 50th TN joined the 1st and 4th Tennessee regiments. Overall, Charles Tyler described the year 1863 in this way. It was:

> **One of mingled hope and anxiety for the men who fought, and the women who prayed, for the success of the Confederate cause. The overwhelming confidence that followed the early victories of the war had passed away; but the deep despondency that characterized the last months of the conflict had not yet settled upon them. The star of hope was still shining, resolve was unshaken, and faith in the ultimate success of the cause was still strong in the hearts of the Southern people at this time.**

On January 26, 1864 Charles was present for muster roll in Tilton, Georgia, serving at this time as a 3rd lieutenant. The Confederate Army struggled to galvanize its remaining numbers. In late October 1864, Nannie told of how Bettie, Nannie Tyler, Emma Robb, Marion Stewart and Juliet McDaniel were visiting the Louisa Furnace and the group saw Union Gen. Nathaniel Lyon and his men. The war dragged on with no end was in sight.

Charles Tyler probably knew Maj. Thomas W. Lewis of Stewart County before the war, but their paths crossed again as Lewis was serving under Gen. Cerro Gordo Williams after the Battle of Chickamauga. At this time, in 1864, Col. Thomas Woodward had been charged with insubordination and removed from command and Lewis took over.

Maj. Thomas W. Lewis

The surviving members of the 50th TN marched south to Alabama, arriving there on New Year's Day 1865. So decimated was the Southern Army after the Battle of Franklin that it took the 11th, 12th, 13th, 19th, 50th, 51st and 52nd Tennessee regiments grouping together to form one single regiment, then called the 2nd Tennessee. This regiment engaged in further fighting but, as Charles later wrote in his sketch of the 50th TN Infantry,[47] "the most ignorant solider in the army knew that the cause was lost and that every life taken was felt to be a useless sacrifice." From that point on, the regiment simply tried to stay the advance of Sherman and his men.

From February 1863 until January 1865, the institution of slavery in Montgomery County gradually faded into the past. The last legal sale of slaves in Montgomery County was made in January 8, 1861 as part of an estate settlement for Jane Ramey.

On March 24, 1865, the *83rd Illinoisan* newspaper printed this:

> **People of Clarksville! To one and all, we say: The sooner you give a hearty support to the Government of the United States; coming out boldly and proclaiming yourselves upon the side of the Union, the better it will be for you, now and hereafter. The rebellion is dying- almost dead- and if you do not wish to be set aside and your places filled by loyalists from other quarters, fulfill the obligations that you have imposed upon yourselves and assist in restoring the Government, State and Federal, and the good feeling that existed years ago between the different parts of our common country.**

The former slaves seemed incapable of understanding what this newfound freedom meant for them. For a people who never worried about self-responsibility, this came as a shock. The slaves made up their minds about their future, basing their decisions on the former relations they had with their previous owners, what they felt they could take on as a trade, or simply followed along with the other blacks leaving the area. Nannie Haskins described the situation in her diary:

---

[47] Printed in the *Military Annals of Tennessee, Confederate,* published in 1886.

The entire South was prostrate. The happy, carefree slaves of just ten years ago and less are now completely adrift, misled, and confused. Some cling to their old masters and life went on serenely for them. This was particularly true of the domestics, who worshipped their 'white folks' and looked with disdain upon all others as 'poor trash.'

While the regiment was in South Carolina, Maj. Thomas W. Lewis was called by Gen. P.G.T. Beauregard to meet him in Charleston, South Carolina. His only instructions were to bring four handpicked individuals to accompany him to Lexington, Kentucky, for a secret mission. These four were to be of the utmost character and daring. The chosen were: Lt. Frank Buckner, Capt. Since Bell, Lt. Charles W. Tyler and Emmett Gilbert. Before they reached Lexington, they received word that on April 9, 1865 Lee had surrendered. The reason behind the secret mission remains a mystery to this day.[48]

The newspaper carried the dreaded news on April 7, 1865: the intentionally large print announcement of the capture of Richmond, the Confederate capital. The publishers of the paper were exalting in the victory and wanted to rub it in the faces of those who had yet hoped for Lee's army to end the war in favor of the South. The *83rd Illinoisan's* last issue was May 26, 1865.

Two days later, on April 9, the end of the war did indeed come. Polk was the only staff officer present with Gen. William McComb when he surrendered with Robert E. Lee on that fateful day at Appomattox.

The 50th TN laid down its arms for the last time in Greensboro, North Carolna on April 26. From its beginning number of 499 men only 37 from Charles' regiment were alive to answer the final roll call. Charles was later to recall in a book he wrote, the mindset and resilience of those in the South. He stated:

There is a streak of humor running all through the Southern character as plainly discernable to the eye of the moralist as a vein of fine metal in a rock to the skilled mineralist. . . That just home from the war, with their cause utterly lost, and wreck and ruin about them, they were able to extract fun at all from the situation shows the wonderful elasticity of the Southern temper. But they did, and their merriment was honest merriment, while their earnestness of purpose at the same time, and along with it was, unquestionable.

Barely able to comprehend what the end of the war meant for the South, its citizens along with the rest of the nation were stunned to learn of Lincoln's assassination on April 14.[49] This author was not able to locate any written statement made by Charles concerning the death of the President. This was, however, the man who sent troops to invade the South and was responsible for the death of many friends and acquaintances. Lincoln's soldiers laid waste to the town and farm he called home. It is known that Charles saw Lincoln as a man who had broken his promise to the South. And yet Tyler expressed his belief, "No human being on this earth ever did have the right to hold in bondage another human being."

Nannie Haskins reported on April 30, that Dick and Polk Johnson along with Billy Green, William M. Daniel, Bob Moore and others were home paroled from the war. Their homecoming was far different than the jubilant send-off they received years before. For those returning home, a stark reality was awaiting them. Having sacrificed so much, the sons of the South were challenged, beyond their physical and emotional scars, with an additional agony...home was never to be the same again. The psychological effect this had on the veterans was tremendous, some were able to cope, and others were not. Nannie Haskins' own brother, Ben returned from the war with what today we would term PTSD. Her other brother, Robert had died in a Union POW camp.

Charles was paroled from the Confederate Army on May 6, at Paducah, Kentucky, with the rank of captain. Curiously, Charles did not fill out the questionnaire that soldiers were asked to complete before returning home. Killebrew may have the answer to this when he wrote, "When the war broke out he affected to join some of the commands but it is doubtful if he was ever in

---

48 One can guess it had something to do with the Confederate treasury.

49 The man supposedly identified as John Wilkes Booth, President Lincoln's assassin was shot at Garrett's barn on April 26th, by Federal troops in Caroline County, Virginia very close to Charles' ancestral home.

any regular engagements."

The occupation of Clarksville finally ended on May 31, almost two months after the surrender at Appomattox. Federal troops finally evacuated the courthouse and local elections were held for municipal and county offices. In this election, Joshua Cobb was elected mayor.

The three sons of Cave Johnson.

During the spring and summer of 1865, most of the people tried to the best of their ability to return to their normal routines and to start the healing process. Some Southerners were never able to reconcile the loss of the war and the ramifications it had on their entire lives. They seemed better able to accept the physical loss, but what of the spiritual? By far the saddest task of the post war period was awaiting the arrival of the wounded and dead. It would take months or even years for some bodies to arrive home, while others were never recovered. Parents grieved thinking of their loved one lying in an unmarked grave, denied a Christian burial.

As the U.S. government had already made arrangements for Union dead to be collected and reinterred in national cemeteries, the horrific duty of removing and properly burying the Confederate dead was left to ladies' memorial associations across the South or to individual families. The stated reason was that since the South had seceded from the union, the Confederate dead were not citizens and therefore did not deserve burial in national cemeteries. John F. Couts, Clarksville undertaker offered his services for those families wishing to bring their soldier home for burial.

Stories of families on both sides disinheriting their sons for fighting on what they believed to be the wrong side was mentioned by Judge Tyler in later writings about his war experiences. He wrote of Lieut. George W. Pease, a Northerner from Pennsylvania, fighting for the Confederacy, who, after the war, would not be received by his family, save one sister. Pease had served the entire war as a member of the 50th TN showed honor and bravery and yet for ten years after the war and before his death, his family refused to forgive him. Such feelings ran deep in families.

Nannie Haskins and Bettie Garland visited Gen. Quarles and his new wife and the next day she and Bettie went on a picnic at Thomas Sulfur Springs. Gen. McComb was there as well. Nannie Haskins offered McComb to stay at her parents' house which he did. The next day they all rode out to Hampton's Spring. Haskins recalled the visits in her diary, October 9:

> **We went out on Saturday. The first week we were alone. The next Gen. Quarles and lady and Bettie Garland came to the Major's. This was Mrs. Q's (Quarles) first visit. On Sunday the Misses Morris, Mrs. Barker,[50] and Mr. Amos Thomas came to see us. Wednesday we all came to town, Polk Johnson, and Irwin Beaumont came to see us in the evening. Next morning, Bettie, Ritchie, Irwin, and I went in the carriage. Brother rode with the driver. Emma Robb went with Dick and Polk Johnson in their barouche, went out to a very large picnic and bran [51] dance at Hampton's Spring given to the survivors of Quarles, Boone, Burnette, and Woodward. Danced all day. Went home with Nannie Tyler and danced 'till 1 o'clock.**

Being able to move about unencumbered by troops checking for the appropriate passes or papers was a start. The young people seemed to be able to recover better than most. Nannie Haskins wrote about going with her brother Ben and accompanying such friends as Irwin Beaumont, brothers Dick and Polk Johnson, along with Emma Robb out to the country on October 14, to a very large picnic and bran dance at Hampton's Springs. She wrote that they:

> **danced all day. Went home with Nannie Tylor (sic) and danced 'til one o'clock . . . . We had a gay time but the next morning we were fagged out completely. Friday we came into town and went to bed.**

---

[50] Mrs. Barker was Mary Minor Merriwether before her marriage.

[51] This is not a misspelling of the word barn. Bran dances were called such because bran was scattered on the dirt floors of barns to keep the dust down while dancing.

Haskins later recorded in her diary a trip that appears to be rather insignificant, but that was not the case. On Thursday October 28, six months after the Civil War ended, her friend, Nannie Tyler retraced her trip to the south side of the river, this time taking several friends along. Bettie Garland, Emma Robb, Marion Stewart and Juliette McDaniel accompanied Nannie Tyler to the Louisa Furnace to see Stephen and Mary Watkins. This trip was made to personally express her gratitude for hiding out her brother Charles immediately after the surrender of Ft. Donelson.

One year later Eleanora was still recording day-to-day activities.

> **Willauer Journal, Woodland Heights, Nashville, November 5, 1866: Journal – I am at home – came from the furnace a month ago. We came by way of Clarksville – I and Emma and Mrs. Forbes – Bettie was out at Nannie Tyler's.**

In a later entry Haskins recorded that she and Lucy Kerr entertained Messrs. Merritt, Anderson, Lurton and Lucy's brother at her parents' house. She added that they were joined by "Maj. Henry, Nannie Tylor (sic), Maj. Johnson and Emma Robb."[52] She stated, "We had a real party unexpectedly. We danced, played euchre and promenaded by moonlight, being a charming evening." These dances were important to yet unmarried women after the war. Remembering that Montgomery County sent over 2,000 of its male inhabitants to fight in the war and just a handful returned, it was a sobering thought indeed to many a young lady, who feared becoming an old maid. A perfect example of the situation was Nannie Haskins herself. Even though it was declared a love match, she married her mother's cousin, a man old enough to be her father. It also does not appear that Emmie Tyler was being courted by anyone. She never seems to be included in the social circles of her sister Nannie nor are there any suggestions that she may being paired with someone. So, as it is said in the South, "There were slim pickin's."

The honorable Cave Johnson died on November 23, and shortly before his death in a letter to his son, Polk Johnson, dated March 17, 1866, he wrote

> **We should always bear in mind the distinction between the Government and the administration of the government. Our government is the best ever made and its administration for a few years past the worst. We should not therefore destroy or attempt it but by a change of Rulers in the legal mode.**

Nannie Haskins Williams wrote of Cave Johnson in 1896,

> **Mr. Cave Johnson, that grand man, exponent of the purest age of democracy whose cordial home when at home, on the outskirts of town was the rendezvous of political and social friends. I can remember when my father would take me there with him, this warm friend would meet us and taking my right hand, tuck it under his left arm, walk with me into the house, bending forward to address the little girl with the courtesy due a princess.**

---

[52] This is Maj. Thomas F. Henry and if she got the rank correct, Maj. James Hickman Johnson.

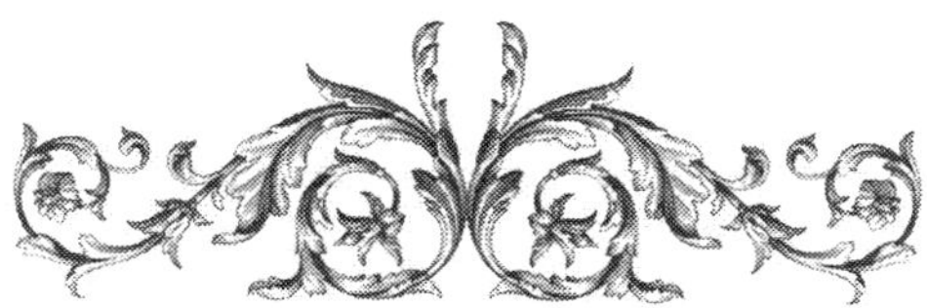

Chapter Six: The Soldier Comes Home

Having lost all of his slaves due to emancipation, Charles' father, John Duke's wealth was decimated. Charles arrived at Hickory Wild just in time to find the family farm being sold at public auction by the sheriff to pay off his father's debts. At the time of the sale, the Tylers' property, in addition to the house/school, there was a smoke house, detached kitchen, carriage house, "comfortable" Negro quarters, stables, two large barns capable of housing 30,000 pounds of tobacco and an orchard with various fruit trees. Many such sales were taking place in Montgomery County and the newspaper was full of these advertised sales for years.

How did the Tylers survive? Again J.B. Killebrew gives us the answer, "When he (Charles) returned he found that his father's estate was bankrupt and there was nothing left but his mother's dowry. He speculated largely for a while in wheat and possibly mules, then studied law and developed a good deal of ability." Indeed, Charles bought a section of the farm on credit, lived for a few years with his widowed mother, sisters Nannie and Emmie, and for a while at least, managed the school. Charles struggled to keep the farm but the inevitable was right in front of him. With no slaves to work the land and but a few students being able to afford the school, time had run out. The decision was made to sell the reminder of the farm and move to town. Charles advertised the sale of their horses, mules, hogs, cattle, sheep and all of the farming equipment. His half-brother Quintus came to help settle the sale scheduled for August 4, 1866.

Chancery Sale of Valuable Farm

Charles (D.) and O. M. Tyler,[53] Adm'rs, vs. Geo. H. Warfield

IN pursuance of an order made in this cause at the April term 1866, I will sell, upon the premises, to the highest bidder at public auction on Saturday, August 4th, next, the tract of land situated in District No. 1 and belonging to the estate of Jno. D. Tyler deceased. Said tract contains 467 acres of valuable farming lands.

Terms, fifteen per centum cash and the balance on a credit of one and two years with interest from date. Notes with good security required and a lien retained until the purchase money is paid. The land will be divided to suit purchasers.

W.T. Shackelford
June 29, 1866

At the same time as Charles' father's land was being sold, Dr. Duke Tyler put up his house and lot for sale on Franklin Street next to Gilbert C. Breed. Duke gave up his medical practice and moved to Kentucky to begin large-scale farming.

Aside from the tangible destruction from the war, the emotional remnants of the Civil War were very much evident. The Ku Klux Klan, the secret society that used violence to intimidate blacks, was engaged in its campaign of terror, cross burnings and lynching's in 1868. At Dunbar Cave and in the basement of Stewart College, the Klan held its meetings. One incident was reported in which a Northern preacher and teacher were ordered to get out of Clarksville. Also the Klan was reported by the Freedman's Bureau in Clarksville to have broken "down the door of a colored man's house and shot at him two or three times." On Strawberry Alley, a barbershop called the Ku Klux Klan opened. Also the Klan utilized various methods to prevent blacks from voting and trying to achieve equality.[54] That year, many of the Confederate dead buried in the Female Academy gardens were disinterred and moved to the City Cemetery to a mass grave. Their names are inscribed on the grave monument.

---

[53] This should read Charles W. and Q.M. Tyler.

[54] The last visit in Clarksville from this group was a peaceful march downtown in the 1980s. This author viewed the figures in their white-hooded outfits in astonishment. The purpose of this march was not clear.

It is interesting to note that an appeal was printed in the April 27, 1868 issue of the *Clarksville Chron*icle asking for money to aid war veteran families from losing their homes to because of security debts. It stated, "With your assistance and that of your friends, their home may be wrested from the gavel of the auctioneer." Funds were to be sent to the Northern Bank[55] in Clarksville. There were three committees appointed: for Clarksville, for New Providence and for the county. Nannie Tyler, in spite of what happened to her family, was listed as being on that committee. The war had changed everything in the South: the economy was devastated and the male population depleted. Farms were lost and families destroyed. Both conditions led to the difficulties at Hickory Wild. Families could no longer pay for the expenses of the Hickory Wild school. This would later impact the decision in later years to allow girls to attend the school.

It was not by accident that on Christmas Day in 1868, President Andrew Johnson proclaimed unconditional pardon and amnesty for those accused of treason against the Union during the Civil War. Everyone involved could breathe a sigh of relief.

The Census of 1870 lists the household of Charles W. Tyler in District One as follows:

Charles W. Tyler	**age 29**	farmer
Mildred S. Tyler	**age 55**	keeping house
Nannie Tyler	**age 27**	no occupation
Emma Tyler	**age 20**	no occupation
Sydney Doak	**age 24**	school teacher

Note: Charles' age here should be 31 and his mother should be 61. The value of the Tyler real estate was listed as $12,000. In 2025, that amount of money would be worth $288,362.75.

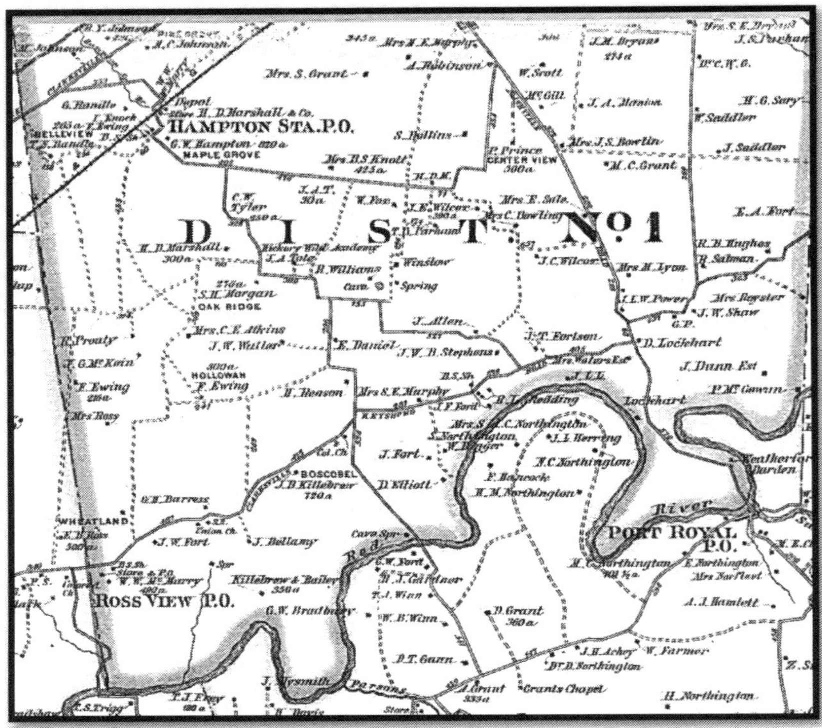

Also listed were the former slaves who resided on the Tyler land:

Minor	**age 65**	farm hand	**Edmund**	**age 14**	farm hand	**Sampson**	**age 2**
Roxy	**age 60**	cook	**Cesar**	**age 12**	at home		
William	**age 31**	farmer	**Henry**	**age 10**	at home		
Joseph	**age 30**		**Claiborn**	**age 6**			
Alice	**age 25**	keeping house	**Bettie**	**age 4**			

[55] The only Clarksville bank solvent after the war.

An unsettling event occurred at Mildred Tyler's house in late February 1871. The question is: where was this house? She was not living at Hickory Wild and had not yet moved to Clarksville. A letter from J.H. Johnson was addressed to her at High Point, a community located above New Providence.

While the house suffered a fire, someone stole a set of diamond earrings and a breast pin worth fifteen hundred dollars. These belonged to her daughter Nannie, highly prized by her as they were from her half-brother Quintus. It was said that because of the differences in their ages, Quintus referred to Nannie and Emmie as his daughters.

Charles continued to manage the school even after he returned to Cumberland College that was in a rebuilding stage since it was burned during the Civil War. By the summer of 1872, he earned his license to practice law, entering into a partnership with Edmund Berry Lurton.[56]

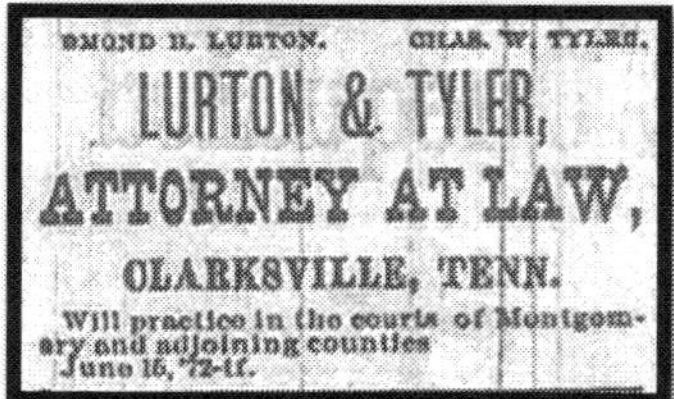
EDMOND B. LURTON. CHAS. W. TYLER.
LURTON & TYLER,
ATTORNEY AT LAW,
CLARKSVILLE, TENN.
Will practice in the courts of Montgomery and adjoining counties
June 15, '72-tf.

Tyler's ad with law partner Edmund B. Lurton. (LC)

Charles was one of 10 men[57] who wrote and published an adamant request for a new jail to be constructed in town. This notice was printed in the October 5, 1872 issue of the *Clarksville Chronicle* after hearing a rousing sermon (printed as well in its entirity), from Rev. Samuel Ringgold at Trinity on September 18. In his sermon, Ringgold gave a very disturbing and raw description of the conditions of the city's present jail so much so that, considering the time period, it was a wonder it was printed in the newspaper. But if the human factor is removed, the only insight into the design of this jail can be realized.

> **The part of the jail appropriated for to the prisoner's use consists of an upper room, large and well-ventilated. This is the parlor chamber of the prison. In this room is an iron cage about ten feet long, eight feet high, just about as large as the cage of a lion and a tiger. Downstairs there are two cells, very dark with no ventilation, no heat and no light except what comes though a small door opening on a dark passage.**

Because of lack of space whenever black prisoners were contained in the same jail cell with white prisoners, it became a clear violation of the Jim Crow Laws and it was incombant to rectify the situation. So decisions needed to be made. In early April a committee appointed by the County Court considered two options: to purchase a new site and build a new jail or repair the old one. Even though the majority favored the first option, upon a motion made by Mayor Joshua Cobb, It was decided to repair the old one. The city appoved renovation of the old jail not to exceed $2500. Some of the expenses incurred in October 1872 with regards to the jail can be seen in the following report:

Hamlett & Welch-work at jail........ $7.00
J. McDonald-shackles for prison..$10.00
Cleaning out jail.........................$65.50
S. Buckley, overseer...................$18.00
Amount for cage at jail............. .$800.00

Tyler had not started his term as judge yet but this situation made an impression on him such that while judge, he always sought to treat prisoners always according to the law but humanely.

At this time, Tyler was still unmarried and enjoyed social events with friends. On December 10, Thomas L. Mabry wrote about a party he attended with Tyler,

> **The elite of the city and country (Will Elliott and myself) were there. The Nashville Band made splendid music and dancing continued until 2 a.m. Capt. Tyler and myself introduced some new fashions in the dances, at which the band seemed quite disgusted, but we have never had the advantages of any dancing master, therefore ought to have been excused, however we conducted much to the amusement of those better skilled in the art.**

---

[56] Lurton built and lived in the lovely house at 625 Madison Street, today known as the "Purple House."

[57] The other men were: Horace H. Lurton, James J. Hamlett, David W. Cooke, J.J. Thomas, David Kincannon, George E. Cooke, S. Brockman, Thomas D. Johnson and John F. Couts.

On January 3, 1873, Mabry wrote of his visit to town seeking to see Mrs. Clay Stacker and Mrs. Lucy Castner but actually getting to spend time with Mildred and Emma Tyler. He wrote,

> **I dined at 4½ at Mrs. Tyler's. They were all very pleasant. Asked about you. Mrs. Tyler said she was really glad you left before the cold spell that she did not think you could have stood it. Miss Emma and I kept up a brilliant conversation, how different when we were young! I like her very much. She is so fat.**

His letter of April 7, 1873 to his mother was written on Lurton and Tyler letterhead,

> **I stayed with Capt. Tyler last night and have just returned from Mrs. Tyler's. . . . Miss Nannie has promised to go out and tarry some with you this spring.**

In July 2, Charles occupied a home on Marion Street that sat on 3½ acres that was owned by Polk G. Johnson. Since the house was up for sale, Charles may have moved to live with the remainder of his family possibly at High Point.

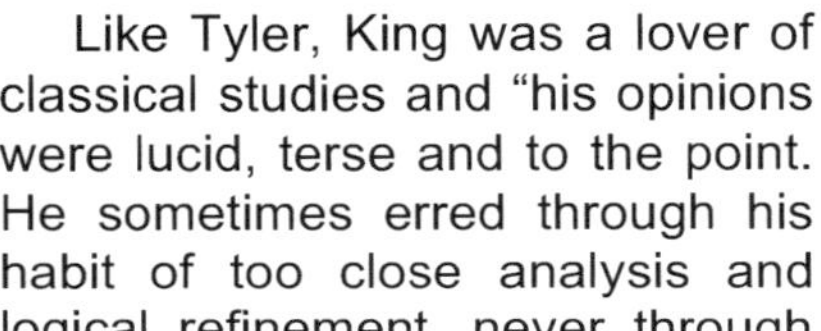

HICKORY WILD ACADEMY.

The second term of this Institute begins 1st Monday in Sept., 1873, and closes June 12, 1874. The course of instruction will embrace the Sciences, Ancient Languages, French, Music, Drawing, Painting, etc.

The principal, assisted by his sister, Mrs. E. S. Knott, and her daughters, proposes, and from the flattering success of the first term expects, to build up a first-class boarding school. The neighborhood is healthful, moral and intelligent. The buildings are commodious and the grounds tasteful. We feel assured young ladies can find no safer and more pleasant retreat while pursuing a thorough course.

TERMS—ONE-HALF IN ADVANCE.

Primary Course	$24 00
Intermediate	30 00
Senior	40 00
Music, with use of Instrument	50 00
Drawing, and Painting in Oil	20 00
French	10 00
Board, including lights, fuel, washing	130 00

No deduction for absence except in cases of protracted illness. For further particulars address the Principal,

J. A. TATE, Guthrie, Ky.

Or any of the following Board of Advisers: Geo. R. Randall, H. D. Marshall, Geo. W. Hampton, S. H. Morgan, Dr. S. W. Dawson, S. P. Hollins, T. G. Parham, F. Ewing, C. W. Tyler, Clarksville, Tenn.; or W. S. Giltner, Pres't Eminence College, Eminence, Ky. [July 23, 73-3m.

Hickory Wild advertisement ca. 1873 showing Charles W. Tyler on the Board of Advisors. (LC)

Tyler's partnership with Lurton lasted but a year before Tyler took over the seat of Criminal Court Judge when Governor J.C. Brown appointed Tyler to fill the unexpired term of Judge Thomas King. King on July 29, died while at Bethesba Springs in Wisconsin seeking a return to health.

Judge Thomas King. (MCA)

Like Tyler, King was a lover of classical studies and "his opinions were lucid, terse and to the point. He sometimes erred through his habit of too close analysis and logical refinement, never through a want of clear understanding of facts or of a wide grasp of legal principles." The following year, Tyler was elected to the office. Politically, Charles' longevity as a judge in Clarksville could be attributed to the loyalty he established with area farmers Tyler had never forgotten his father's struggles to maintain the family farm and understood the difficulties endured by farmers.

The judgeship to which Charles was elected was actually incorporated on February 18, 1858, when the State Legislature authorized the election of a person "learned in the law, to be styled the County Judge." Later the State Legislature Act of July 6, 1870 declared that the County Judge also be the Criminal Court Judge. Additionally, Tyler was to serve as Montgomery County's Financial Officer. Simply put, this put him in an extremely powerful position; one not given to anyone else in the county before or since.

A lawsuit stemming from an event that occurred prior to the occupation of Clarksville by Federal troops was tried in January 1874. Forts Henry and Donelson had just fallen and for Clarksvillians this meant, "The Yankees were coming!" To prevent "spirits" from falling into the hands and mouths of the enemy, citizens decided to the ditch the alcohol to prevent possible outrages. Barrels and barrels of the stuff were smashed and the contents drained into the river. The "celebrated whiskey case" of George Alwell vs. Henry Wisdom, Bryce Stewart, et al. was tried by the Circuit Court with the Honorable J.M. Quarles presiding. The suit was filed to recover losses from the whiskey destroyed by citizens. This suit involved an interesting legal question as to the right to destroy property in view of an approaching army. The local court ruled in favor of the defendants but later the ruling was reversed by the Tennessee Supreme Court. The defendants, Bryce Stewart, Henry Wisdom, and others, were required to pay the plaintiffs, Augustus B. Harrison and George Alwell, a sum of $1,250 for the lost alcohol. A humorous spin was put on the situation as the *Tobacco Leaf* declared "the catfish have been drunk ever since and some people about here frequently get tipsy even now from eating catfish."

In probably the last newspaper article written about Hickory Wild while Charles Tyler was associated with it was one describing a student performance during a Friday evening in late February 1874. The program was intended to raise money to purchase "an organ for the Sunday School." Despite a constant rain, the event was attended by a large crowd from Clarksville who enjoyed seeing each student display his or her particular talent. So well-received were the performances that an encore at a later date was called for due to the weather. The newspaper article stated that, "Hickory Wild is growing and becoming daily more popular. It is situated at old Tyler site, on classic ground and the proprietors are showing that the genius of education has not departed." [58]

In the February 28, issue of the *Clarksville Weekly Chronicle* a letter of thanks was submitted entitled, "Complimentary." The article read

> **We, the undersigned Grand Jurors, empaneled for the January Term 1874 of the Criminal Court for Montgomery County, Tennessee have witnessed with pleasure the dignified and impartial manner with which our Criminal Judge Charles W. Tyler has presided over the deliberations of the Court and the ability with which he has discharged all the duties incumbent upon him; also the energy and ability displayed by our efficient Attorney General Baker D. Johnson, not only in the management of the State's interest in the preparation and trial of causes, but in ferreting out and bringing offenders before the Bar of Justice to answer for their evil deeds; also the indefatigable industry of all the officers of this Court, therefore,**
>
> **Resolved, that we tender to all, Judge, Attorney General, Clerks, Sheriff and Jailor our sincere thanks for the many courtesies shown us during this Court.**
>
> **J.M. Anderson, W. Ferrell, L.W. Crotzer, E.H. Dean, Ransom Morrow,[59] J.H. Meacham, James P. Kelly, J.O.R. Hooper, W.L. Andrews, D.C. Frey, W.H. Mason, W.W. Walker, J.W. Hawks.**

The city was still reeling from the Civil War and in the midst of reconstruction when in May, Clarksville suffered a major flooding of the Cumberland River. The water level rose to such a degree that the buildings and shanties along Front Street were inundated with water. The business sector of town was in no danger, perched high upon the hill, looking down on all the flooding. The city fathers had wisely chosen high ground on which to situate the Public Square. Judge Tyler would have other such disasters with which to contend over the years.

Flood waters along the east bank of the Cumberland River looking south. (MCA)

At Hickory Wild, James A. Tate resolved to take over the school and continue its high standards. Tate was born September 18, 1837 in Todd County, Kentucky. His father was from Virginia, of French descent, and his mother was the daughter of Col. Anthony New, who was a member of Congress from the Eighth Congressional District of Kentucky. J.A. attended school in Elkton, Kentucky and later a boarding school in Montgomery County. Tate finished school at Bethel College of Kentucky. On December 3, 1874 he married Ambie White, the daughter of Rev. John F. White of Trigg County. They had three children, of whom two survived.

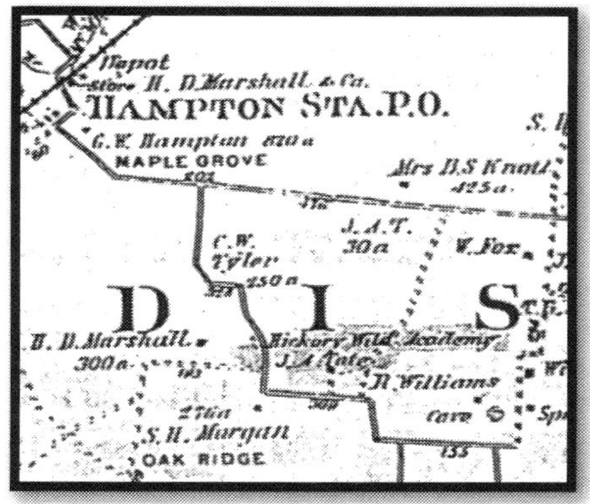

This enlarged District One map shows that Charles W. Tyler still owned 250 acres of his father's farm and the location of the Hickory Wild Academy when it was run by James A. Tate. (CMCPL)

---

[58] There was no mention of the Tylers returning to visit Hickory Wild after it was sold. Charles served on the school's board for a number of years but there was no mention of him actually returning to the school.

[59] In just eleven years, Judge Tyler would send Ransom Morrow's son to the gallows for murder.

The Tates moved to Hickory Wild and operated the school with the help of W.H. Willett for years until the public school system so improved that the number of privately-run schools began to diminish. Under Tate, a neighbor, Mrs. Eliza S. Knott[60] was designated as the principal, assisted by her daughters Mollie and Anna. The Knotts' land adjoined the Tylers. And for the first time in the school's history, it was open to both boys *and* girls.

Eliza J. Knott and one of her daughters (Mollie or Anna), had been praised in the July 30, 1873 *Leaf Chronicle* Hickory Wild ad. It read:

> **Mr. J.A. Tate, principal assisted by Mrs. Eliza Knott and her daughter.[61] All have earned a fair reputation as teachers. We have known Mrs. Knott in that capacity a number of years and no lady has ever given greater general satisfaction. Young ladies attending this school will receive thorough culture and training of intellect and deportment.**

Charles' mother Mildred moved to Clarksville in 1875, along with his unmarried sister, Emmie to a house at 409 Greenwood Avenue that she bought July 3 from the Cave Johnson heirs. This was one of the loveliest streets in Clarksville at that time. Once known as Charlotte Road, this street was sparsely populated with pastures dotting the landscape.

Mildred increased the size of her lot when she bought nearly an additional acre from John Bradley.[62] The house which was built in the mid-1800s had also been owned by Bradley. He had purchased the house from Henry C. Merritt who acquired it from the clerk and master of the county in the case of Dortch and Bradley v. John A. Bailey et al. The brick used on the house came from George Buck who used all his remaining bricks to build the house before getting out of the brick manufacturing business. People in the Greenwood neighborhood could purchase bricks from Buck who, unlike his predecessor, did not have 15-20 workers, "indulging in the most boisterous singing, swearing, etc." and whose teams of mules were run nearly to death each day from early in the morning until late at night. Buck's teams were well cared for, "fat and sleek as a ribbon" and his workmen polite and attentive to the quiet of the neighborhood.

The Tyler house itself is much deeper than it is wide and so gives the impression of not being very large. There does not seem to exist any photos of the house before major structural changes were made. There were once decorative cornices at the roofline and window heads. Upon entering the front door, tall, simple columns separate the twin parlors. The floors are hardwood oak laid at diagonals and each downstairs room with wooden floors, the diagonals ran in different directions. A bookcase for the judge's favorite books was built under the staircase. The parlor to the left had a coal-burning fireplace and tall windows on the front and side of the room. The two front windows were used as walkouts to the front porch. In this parlor sat their piano for this was a family who were musically talented. Leaving the double parlor, a set of double doors opens into the dining room and to the left of this room was the master bedroom. It too had a coal-burning fireplace facing the dining room door. Later, Tyler had a bathroom and a closet added onto this room. After passing through the dining room, one enters a small passageway with a butler's pantry on the left. Straight back was the kitchen, also added on at a later date. The original kitchen was, as a deterrent to fire, detached from the main house. Today, off the side of the kitchen is a lovely screened-in porch, shaded by the large trees in the yard. The ceilings throughout the house are fourteen-feet tall, intended to allow hot air to rise in the hot, muggy summers. The interior walls are solid handmade double brick (two feet thick) and are plastered. The house also has a cellar, so valuable for extra storage room.

After the war, people simply could not afford to send their children to private schools no matter how respected the facility was. Enrollment never recovered to its pre-war numbers. Tate, in dire straits financially, tried to sell the school but no buyers came forth. On June 28, 1877 Tate announced that the sale of Hickory Wild did not take place "owing to the stringency of money matters." He was unable, Tate stated, "to collect old claims of various sorts without a legal process" but due to a successful last term, the school would continue.

---

[60] The Knott and Hollins families were related.

[61] In 1875, both Knott daughters were teaching at the Hickory Wild Academy.

[62] John Bradley also sold bricks; his brickyard was next to the L & N Train Depot on Depot Street. In 1873, he was selling bricks at $6 per thousand. He moved to Kansas and died in 1894.

Next Tate leased the property for a period of time but left when his health began to fail and so around May 17, 1879 he purchased the mineral springs of Montgomery County, known as Idaho Springs. Tate left Dunbar Cave and Idaho Springs after just two years in 1881 to open a school in Scottsville, Kentucky.

Tate and his wife invited the editors of the *Tobacco Leaf* to Hickory Wild, to help celebrate the end of another "successful term" in June 1879.[63] The editors described the trip as

> **a pleasant drive...through as fine a scope of country as one could wish to see. Evidences of thrift are on every hand. Here is a cottage home surrounded with shade trees that nod a friendly invitation to the passerby to stop and rest beneath their spreading branches. There is a wheat field with its golden grain almost ready for the reaper, and then again a field of waving corn that speaks of well-filled barns in the 'sweet bye and bye.' Its next neighbor is a field of tobacco just set, that hints of a puffed up pocket book, provided the August glut of worms and the numerous other ills that this plant is heir to, do not cut down the average too largely. As we neared our destination, the bright lights that adorned the grounds lent an additional charm to the appropriately named spot.**

About 150 young people were in attendance and couples promenaded around the grounds until ice cream and cake were served in the schoolroom at 11 p.m. The evening continued well into the early morning hours.

An ad in the September 6, 1879 edition of the *Clarksville Tobacco Leaf* read, as the academy hung on by a thread:

> **Hickory Wild Male Academy will open its 8th term September 20, to continue nine months. The former principal has associated with him, Prof. W.H. Willett, a graduate of the Lebanon O., Normal School. In addition to our usual Scientific, Literary and Classical Courses, we add the Commercial and Military. Terms-Board and tuition for the term of nine months, from $141 to $153, according to classes. For further particulars, address**
> **J.A. Tate**
> **W.H. Willett,**
> **Principals, Hampton's Station, Tenn.**
> **Sept. 6, 1879**

The *Tobacco Leaf* advertised that the academy would reopen under the direction of Professor Daniel M. Quarles after the buildings had been repaired and put in "first class condition." In late August 1882, Professor Quarles and his family did indeed move to Hickory Wild. He re-opened the school on September 3, 1883. Although it is not known exactly when the academy closed its doors for the last time, it seems to have been around the mid-1880s. For nearly half a century, this school had been recognized for its high standards. Even after the school closed, the community retained the "Hickory Wild neighborhood" name.

Elisha Davis Powell bought the property at auction. Powell was considered by some to be a late arrival to the fertile lands of Montgomery County to farm and raise his family. Born in Halifax County, North Carolina, on February 29, 1848, Elisha eventually moved to Montgomery County. He was first married to lantha Acree and after her death on September 3, 1884, he married Lucy Ellen Clark (1861-1948), thirteen years his junior. Elisha and Lucy had the following children:

Jennie Irene Powell (1887-1965)
Sarah Lucille Powell (1891-1965)
Nellie Rhea Powell (1898-1952)
Homer McFerrin Powell (1899-1965)

Elisha and Lucy Powell from the *Montgomery County Family History Book 2000.*

Elisha made several additions to the old schoolhouse, now his home. The old front porch portico was removed and a roof was extended over the three second-floor windows. Powell also enlarged the front porch to run the entire front length of the house. The back of the house had a

[63] This was an effort to put on a good face, hoping it was enough to get enrollment up.

large porch added as well. As with many houses of that time, cooking was done in a separate kitchen out back.

Sketch of Hickory Wild contributed by Judy Landiss, a Powell descendant.

The late Alma Speth related a story of how she would sit on the back steps of this, her grandparents' house, eating a raw onion and a biscuit. Other family members recalled that Elisha would sit at one end of this long porch in the shade and then move to the other end as the sun moved. It was on this front porch on April 21, 1920 that he had either a heart attack or a stroke and then fell over the railing. They found him later lying in the yard dead.

Mrs. Powell sold the farm in 1930 to Luther Wade. Wade reported that in that year there were at least five graves there in the Tyler family cemetery, probably more. According to cemetery records, the following graves were located at Hickory Wild: Emma B. Tyler. Her tombstone read "Tyler, Emma B., consort of Q.M. Tyler, born December 29,1816- died August 16, 1851." This marker was reported as being broken into pieces and piled against a tree. Also known to have been buried there was Lucy Quintus Tyler. Her marker read: "Tyler, Lucy Q., consort of Richard K. Tyler, Jr., born January 5, 1804, departed this life November 5, 1829, aged 25 years and 10 months; was married December 18, 1823." She was the daughter of Phillip Redd and Elizabeth Temple Redd. Lucy was also a native Virginian having been born in Caroline County.

AT AUCTION

"Hickory Wild"

TO WIND UP ESTATE

THURSDAY

SEPT. 25, 1930--11 A. M.

We will sell the excellent farm known as Hickory Wild, containing [illegible] acres owned by the heirs of the late ELISHA POWELL, located in the First Civil District of Montgomery County, Tennessee, 10 miles East of Clarksville, 1 1-2 miles East from Hampton Station and 5 miles Southwest from Guthrie, Kentucky, on the Cave Springs Pike.

The land lies well and is a splendid type of soil that produces a fine type of tobacco, in fact, will grow any crop in abundance for which this section is adapted. 18 acres of timber.

The improvements which are ideal, consist of one beautiful 8-room bungalow, one 3-room tenant house, 1 large tobacco barn, 1 stock barn, poultry house and many other good outbuildings, all in a splendid state of repair.

This will be an excellent buy for some one. It is just the right size. The land is level and produces well. The location cannot be surpassed anywhere. In a fine community of prosperous farmers. Adjoins the Kirkwood School property and church and the improvements are high class.

Immediately after the sale of the farm we will sell a lot of personal property, consisting of mules, horses, dairy cows, household furniture, cream separator, etc.

BARBECUE DINNER

TERMS EXTREMELY EASY

For Further Information Confer With Mrs. Powell on the Farm, or [illegible]

G. S. MOORE & SON, AGENTS

PHONE 100 SPRINGFIELD, TENNESSEE

The upcoming sale in which the Wade family acquired the property in the September 24, 1930 issue of the *Leaf Chronicle*.

The graves of the descendants of Richard Keeling, Jr. and Lucy Q. Tyler are found in Todd and Trigg Counties. They include: John Duke Tyler (1826-1895), who married Lizzie McAfee Moore (1841-1886), and Helen Mary Harpending (1826-1870).

Luther Wade willed the property to his son Elmer. It remained in his possession until he sold the land to a developer who subdivided it into lots for homes. Today a private home sits in the exact location of the school. Nothing remains of the school but a few of the foundation stones salvaged for use as a border for flower gardens. Also there remains old photos and the remembrance of Hickory Wild through handed-down stories from older people living in the area. Elmer Wade died in 2018.

In 2008, Charlotte Oliver Marshall wrote,

Adjoining our farm was the old Hickory Wild Academy. My brother and I have not forgotten. On the line fence that separated the two farms. Our farm being part of the original John Duke Tyler tract was the family cemetery with dates on the stones back to the early 1800s, with one tomb walled up above ground, another tall obelisk for John Duke that seemed like the Washington monument to my brother and me. There were many less grand tombstones, all protected by a wrought iron fence. On this spot just up from our stable we played and wondered at the silent tombs, knowing somehow that we were on hallowed ground.

As children, we were taught not to step on earth that held sacred bones. Now there is no trace of this family graveyard. No one knows; all is silence; gone where God only knows. Who among us holds this secret of the dead, the destruction of the Tyler cemetery?

I remember well the original Hickory Wild Academy building. There were tall stone steps that led up to the columned porch that boasted two grand doors and led into the front hall. Typically, there were four large rooms downstairs, two on each side of the hall. A stairway in the hall led up to the second story where some boarding students in times past had lived. There was dignified grandeur there; but from the fireplaces in each room, I could imagine the drafts from such large spaces to such small sources of heat.

When I first knew Hickory Wild, it had lost its academy status and had been divided into smaller tracts of land. It was home to a family of Powells, who many old-timers will remember. It was a big family.

During the Great Depression the country side was in economic turmoil and Hickory Wild was sold. The new owners demolished the academy and replaced it with a four-room concrete block house that stood until the farm was sold again to developers. Somewhere in this time frame, the cemetery was destroyed. By whom is the mystery. The old owners knew nothing, the developers knew nothing and all I know is that this valuable piece of history is gone.

Who is honorable enough to step forward and say, 'I know where John Tyler's stone lies.' That would be honor and courage indeed!

May eternal rest be with the Tyler family wherever they are placed away from Hickory Wild, and may unrest be in the hearts of the ones who took away these scenes of my early childhood.

Author Note: A witness described how the developer bulldozed the entire cemetery with the iron fence that surrounded it into a nearby pond. This also included the tall obelisk that marked John Duke's grave. This desecration was a violation of Federal law but happens in so many places.

Chapter Seven: The Johnson and Settle Families

After the Civil War, Polk Grundy Johnson returned to law school, graduated in 1868 and began his law practice with his former commander W.A. Quarles. Curiously Polk married Emma V. Robb, the daughter of Alfred Robb who commanded the 49th Tennessee Regiment. Had Nannie Tyler changed her mind about their engagement? Polk and Emma lost both of their daughters: Mary Elise Johnson (born and died in 1869), and Emma Robb Johnson (1869-1870). Emma passed away at age 26 after four years of marriage in 1872. Nannie accepted Polk Grundy Johnson's proposal in 1875 and moved into their new house on Greenwood Avenue completed in 1877 next to the house occupied by the rest of her family.

The Johnsons' house. Photo by author.

The Johnson's two-story house at 403 Greenwood was grand. G. Tandy Smith, Jr., the architect for the home, designed the dwelling in both a Colonial Revival and Italianate style. At the time of their marriage, Polk was serving as clerk for the Montgomery County Court and did so for the remainder of his life.

This house sits farther back from the street than the Tyler home. Separating the yard from the street is a low curved brick wall. The right side of the home was constructed with a multi-angled pavilion. The windows are arched with stonework window heads and there is a large front porch. A handsome staircase in the center foyer leads to all the different levels of the house. Behind that staircase and connecting to it from the backside of the home is the servant staircase. Once the top floor has been reached, an additional set of steps leads to the roof. Each room exuded a comfortable, welcoming feeling as sunlight steams through the tall windows and French doors.

The Tylers and Johnsons attended the Trinity Episcopal Church located at 317 Franklin Street in downtown Clarksville. It was here that Charles met his future wife, Mary Mildred "Mollie" Settle who attended with her widowed father, William B. Settle, sisters Anna Settle, Beulah Settle and brothers William A. Settle and Matthew Gracey Settle. The entire Settle family had beautiful singing voices. Mollie's sister, Beulah was later hired in the music department at Fairview Academy.

Mollie's father, William B. Settle was born April 2, 1819 in Lynchburg, Virginia and came to Clarksville at age 14. Initially he was trained in the tanning business under Austin Caldwell and clerked for several firms. He then partnered with James Carr in the grocery business. This partnership dissolved and Settle bought out Matill's Confectionary in partnership with George A. Ligon. This business operated for nine years from 1852 until the Civil War.

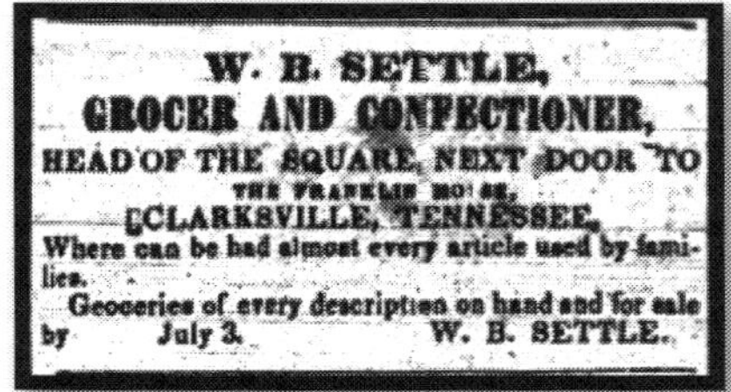

1849 *Leaf Chronicle* ad.

From that point on Settle ran his own business partly with help from his son Billy. In July of 1874, William took a trip to Cincinnati to restock his store. The newspaper teased him by stating

> **With the exception of a trip to New Providence a few years ago, this is the first time he has gone abroad for about twenty-five years. We commend him to the tender mercies of the people of Cincinnati and we hope his only business with the police may be to get them to put him in the right track when he gets lost.**

In the great fire of 1878, Settle was to lose over half his stock in spite of having five wagons ready to load up as soon as it appeared the store was in danger. Too late, the fire swept through his business before he had time to react. He continued to suffer financially as well as in health and his last months were spent dealing with paralysis.

Tragically Mollie mother, Margaret Johnson Settle had a history of mental problems which resulted in her death. The Haskins, whose house was on the corner of Second and College (once known as Washington) Street, lived next door to the Settle family. On July 12, 1864, Nannie reported that Mrs. Settle had just returned home from "the asylum" the day before when she gotten into a pond[64] in an attempt to drown herself. A soldier intervened and saved her life.[65]

On August 3, 1864, Nannie wrote that her mother went over to help Mrs. Settle who had severely attacked her nurse, Mrs. Simpson. She then wrote that Mrs. Settle is "worse every day." Mrs. Settle had, by that time, lost two children, a son, named James Wheatley, who died August 28, 1852 and a daughter, Margaret "Maggie" Izetta, who died at one day over six months on October 12, 1861. The following poem was written for Maggie:

The flowers of fairest beauty rise
To lavish sweetness on the morn,
And 'mong the souls that throng the skies
The brightest are of life's young dawn
Sweet child no sin had touched thy heart,
But fair and pure as heavenly love,
Thy spotless spirit did depart
To join the shining hosts above.

There is no way to know the effects that these two losses had on Mrs. Settle. On Thursday, August 24, 1864, Nannie Haskins noted that when she returned from a visit in the country, she learned of the death of Mollie Settle's mother. She wrote,

> **I did not hear of poor Mrs. Settle's death until she had been buried a week. Poor woman, she hung herself. Mollie Settle and Mary Bailess (sic) were sleeping in the room with her. When they awoke in the morning she was hanging to the door dead. 'Tis sad, sad!**

Large landowner, John Nick Barker also recorded the terrible occurrence in his diary, recording her death as having taken place on August 16. In her entry on September 13, Nannie Haskins wrote,

> **Mr. Settle has broken up housekeeping. Mollie will go to Mrs. Williams' to school.[66] Beulah's (Mollie's sister) with her Grandma. Willie (Mollie's brother) and Mr. S. will board at hotel. Mr. Joe Robbins to take the house. I hope they will be pleasant neighbors.**

Molly's brother, William A. "Billy" or "Willie" Settle (1847-1919), married Anna Wilkinson (1847-1905). Anna was an invalid during much of their married life. Their only child, a daughter, Maggie (1870-1933), would later marry J. Owen McKeage (1870-1945).

Billy Settle

Billy was known to be quite the prankster. Billy, over the years, engaged in several business ventures, one of which was selling ice. It was a seasonal business in 1875; not one of steady income. He also worked as a brick manufacturer. His bricks can still be found all over town and easily identified as each one is stamped with "Settle."

---

[64] This pond was very likely the double pond located near the Settles' house. This pond was described by the press as "the receptacle of many a victim of violence."

[65] It is possible that the asylum mentioned was either the one in Hopkinsville, Kentucky known as the Western Lunatic Asylum or the one in Nashville known as the Tennessee (Central) Hospital for the Insane. Also, there was an asylum located in South Clarksville prior to 1870.

[66] This was the school at White Hall.

Billy's 1903 ad. (LC)

Brick, Brick, Brick.

I manufacture the following kinds of Brick: FACE, BUILDING, CISTERN ARCH and PAVEMENT, and can furnish same in any quantities, at all times. Works on Spring street, office over Clarksville National Bank. Orders solicited. Telephone 140-8 Rings.

W. A. SETTLE.

His brickyard stood at 9 Settle Avenue which was located across from the Smith-Trahern mansion. the Settle Brickyard. By 1913, using three large kilns, it was able to produce 25,000 bricks per day! The bricks themselves were solid, weighed around five pounds apiece and were plainly marked with the Settle name on them. The avenue is gone and nothing remains of the brickyard.

In what was once a private residence in the Ringgold community, Mollie received her education. The girls' school there was called White Hall. This school was established in 1845 by Lucy Williams, the widow of Fielding L. Williams, a tobacconist and owner of the Ringgold Mill, who built the residence in 1839. The school operated through the Civil War years under the guidance of Lucy and her sister, "Mollie" Mary G. Ward. Classes were conducted daily. An advertisement in the August 30,1851 issue of the *Clarksville Jeffersonian* read, "no efforts will be spared to secure to the pupils, refinement of manners and moral culture, as well as the advantage of sound learning." The school year at White Hall was divided into two sessions, lasting 5 months each.

FEMALE SCHOOL AT WHITE HALL,
Montgomery County, Tennessee,
UNDER THE DIRECTION OF
Miss Mary G. Ward.

THE services of Miss Timberlake have been secured, who will take charge of the French and Music department.

The scholastic year is divided into two Sessions, of five months, each, the first commencing on the first Monday in October, and the second on the first Monday in March.

TERMS PER SESSION.

Boarding and Tuition	$50 00
Tuition alone in the common English Branches	10 00
" " Higher	12 00
French	10 00
Ornamental and Fancy Work	5 00
Lessons on the Piano or Guitar, with the use of Instrument,	$25.00

Payable one half at the begining, and the other at the end of each Session.

No deduction made for absence except in case of positive sickness, and then, for no period less than one month. This school is taught in the beautiful and spacious residence, of the late Fielding Williams Esq. Pleasantly situated on the road from Clarksville, to Hopkinsville, six miles from the former place. The boarding department will be under the direction of Mrs. Williams, and no efforts will be spared, to secure to the pupils, refinement of manners and moral culture, as well as the advantage of sound learning.

Pupils must furnish themselves with Towels, and have every article of clothing distinctly marked, with name in full.

Clarksville, Tenn., Aug. 30, 1851-381-4w.

White Hall. (LC)

The first session began on the first Monday in October and the second on the first Monday in March. Tuition was as follows:

Boarding and tuition $50, tuition alone in the common English branches $10, tuition in the higher English $12, French $10, ornamental and fancy work $5, lessons on the piano or guitar, with the use of instruments $25.

The splendid white house constructed of wood instead of brick consists of two stories. The front portico runs the entire length of the front of the house and is supported by six Doric columns. Headlights and sidelights accent the front doorway, illuminating the enormous entry hallway within. Nine shuttered windows are found on the front of the house. The interior includes a two-run staircase leading up to the second story of the residence. This second story served as housing for boarding students. It was listed on the National Register of Historic Places on January 31, 1978 but as of 2025 is in danger of being razed.

A new fascination with the occult called spiritualism was spreading all over the nation in 1874 and Clarksville was caught up in the phenomenon. In a light-hearted article in the *Tobacco Leaf*, a story appeared about a disturbance at the Settles then living at 525 East Commerce Street (also called Mud Alley) near the double pond at what is now the intersection of Franklin and University Avenue.

It was here on September 27, that was supposedly a place where one might expect, "turbulent and unquiet citizens of the other world" to, on occasion, "play ghostly pranks." Mollie's father, brother Billy and probably Mollie's younger sister Beulah, along with several servants are mentioned as having witnessed a six-inch tall butter dish complete with butter and knife moving from one person to the next on the table. The servants became quite alarmed by the specter. The newspaper reporter who got wind of the story, added fuel to the fire by stating that W.A. and Billy were known to be trustworthy citizens and would not simply have made up such a story. Of course, as it turned out, Billy himself had placed the dish over a large beetle that did not appreciate its new circumstances and so made it known by pushing the dish around. It was obvious the newspaper enjoyed its little foray of poking fun at a topic so widely discussed in town.

The two-story brick residence on Commerce Street with two entrances built ca. late 1800s. The second entrance may have been added after it became an apartment house. Billy's daughter, Maggie (1870-1933), who had married J. Owen McKeage (1870-1945), later inherited the house. In its last years, it served as an apartment house. It was later razed. The photo on left was taken in 1965. (MCA)

Judge Tyler had an unusual case in his Criminal Court in February 1875. Sarah Johnson was accused of killing a black woman the previous summer. Described as, "a maiden robust of form and ruddy of complexion and to some eyes, fair of feature, a young woman which stands as firm as a rock and appears ready for any emergency, calm and collected and almost indifferent," but her social standing was "not the best." The murder came after the black woman and her husband were "making a murderous assault with rocks on Miss Johnson's father" and so Sarah came out of the house with a pistol and shot the woman. There was prior animosity between the two as they had, on several occasions, exchanged "sweet-scented names" and this was stated as the reason Sarah had purchased the gun beforehand.

After testimony was given, Johnson was acquitted of the murder. The newspaper gave very little insight into the details as post-war race relations were still strained during this time period. Soon however, those sparks of friction would explode on the city streets of town and have catastrophic repercussions.

Trinity Episcopal Church where the Settles, Johnsons and Tylers attended, was declared structurally unsafe in 1875 and so on April 16, was torn down.[67] The blue-gray stones used for the new building were quarried from the limestone bluffs along the Red River in New Providence and cut into blocks by Irish stonemasons. Four Tiffany stained glass windows were purchased for the church along with a grand pipe organ, once displayed at the Centennial Exposition in Philadelphia. The interior of the church was impressive. Carved woodwork, wooden ceilings, ornate pews and plastered walls culminated into a devoutly spiritual setting. On the front facade of the church is a large stained glass window, which displays stylized leaves of tobacco and corn sprouts. Rev. Mickey Richaud, past rector of the church stated that, "tobacco built Clarksville and tobacco built Trinity Church."

On the left: Trinity's interior. On the right: The church's stain glass window on its front facade. Photo by Chris Smith.

The total cost for the structure came to $40,000. The church's foundation was nearly finished as plans were being made for the new rector, Phillip A. Fitts, to arrive in Clarksville. Fitts was

[67] The present day church's cornerstone was laid on June 30, 1875 and then on December 1, 1881, the beautiful Romanesque Revival Style church was consecrated under the pastorate of Father Phillip Fitts.

"a bright 36-year-old Alabamian of impeccable credentials." He served in the Confederate Army and earned the respect of Charles Tyler, Dr. Charles W. Beaumont, Polk Grundy Johnson and Horace Lurton. The ladies had gussied up the parsonage in preparation for the Reverend and Mrs. Fitts and their large family. Father Fitts was scheduled to preach his first sermon on Halloween Day in 1875. The congregation was excitedly waiting to listen to a man who gave up a promising career in law to save the lost but fate intervened in a most tragic way.

Father Phillip Augustus Fitts, Sr. (1839-1900). Photo courtesy Trinity Church.

In route to Clarksville from Alabama, the Fitts' seven-year-old son died from diphtheria. The Fitts turned around and returned to Alabama to bury their boy. They finally arrived in Clarksville in late November where they were met with open arms and understanding hearts.

Praises were heaped upon Judge Tyler by the *Waverly Journal* who printed a letter of gratitude for serving on the circuit court bench in mid-August 1875 in place of Judge Rice. The writer stated

> **His rulings upon the bench were prompt, accurate and dignifed, bearing the impress of high culture and deep research in the mysteries and science of law- gave universal satisfaction and elicited high enconiums from his legal brethern. Although a stranger to us, save to a few army associates, his deportment- so dignified and affable, irresistably drew our people to appreciate him and now a common desire is expressed to again meet his Honor.**

The city of Clarksville was honored to receive as a guest Jefferson Davis who stopped in Clarksville in October to visit his friend, Micajah Clark on his way to Hopkinsville, Kentucky to address the Christian County Agricultural and Mechanical Association. Clark, a prominent tobacco broker had served as Davis' personal secretary. Born September 4, 1830 in Richmond, Virginia, Clark was the son of one of the most "prominent physicians ever claimed by the Ole Dominion." Micajah Clark was present at Washington, Georgia, when the Confederate cabinet disbanded and at that time was the last acting treasurer of the Confederacy. The two men maintained their strong friendship through the years.

Micajah Clark and wife.

Davis had been born and raised a short distance from Hopkinsville in a community called Fairview. When word got out about Davis' visit to Clarksville, citizens were asked to meet at the Hook and Ladder at 10:00 p.m. to form a procession to the railroad depot to welcome him. At this time the depot was located off Madison Street behind the Wenzler-Darnell house opposite Seventh Street. The procession included the Knights Templar, Knights of Pythias, a band and numerous admirers who marched with torches to the depot to meet the person held in such high esteem by so many Southerners.

When the train arrived at 11:45 p.m., the ex-Confederate President, "amidst deafening cheers, was received by a committee and conducted to a carriage." The procession followed this route: from the depot to Madison Street to Fifth, down Fifth to Franklin, down Franklin to Second, up Second to Madison Street to the residence of Clark which stood opposite Hiter Street.[68] The houses all along the route were beautifully illuminated.

The only known photo of the Clarks' Madison Street home.

At Clark's house, Rev. Achilles Degrasse Sears of the Baptist Church, welcomed Davis with a

---

[68] The house stood in what is now a parking lot to a small shopping area.

speech to which Davis replied, "I did not suppose that but two persons in your city would know of my coming. It awakens such gratitude in my heart which cannot be expressed by words." It would be the first time Davis was able to meet Micajah's wife, Lillie W. Kerr, daughter of M.M. Kerr of Clarksville. They married at Trinity in July 1861. Perhaps Clark showed Davis his two percussion pistols he captured from a member of the 2nd Vermont cavalry during the Dahlgren raid near Richmond, Virginia in March 1864.

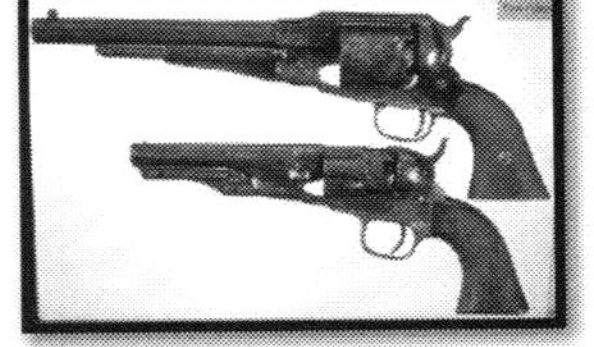

The next morning Davis enjoyed a breakfast given in his honor and then from 10:00 a.m. until 1:00 p.m., he greeted the welcoming citizens. Even the students from schools and the college were introduced to him in groups. Charles Tyler would have been there given that Tyler was trusted by Davis to be considered for some type of secret mission during the war. No doubt the two men visited and perhaps discussed the topic.

Holiday season or not, Tyler still had to decide cases. A week before Christmas Alex Kirby, a black prisoner set fire to the jail. He was sentenced to 5 years in the state penitentiary.

The dark effects of the war still festered in the South and Judge Tyler, recalling coming home to his father's farm being sold for debts, in early February 1876, gave debtors a chance to keep their farms. He offered for those who had lost their lands sold for taxes on the first Monday in January, that if they came immediately and paid just their 1874 taxes plus $3.25 in court costs, they would receive a receipt-paid in full. Six months earlier in September 1875, a notice was printed in the *Leaf Chronicle,* concerning the overdue taxes.

WARNING! TAXES! 1875!

The Assessment for the year 1875 is now on file in the office of the Clerk of the County Court, subject to inspection until the 1st day of October, 1875, at which time all persons considering themselves aggrieved by said assessment shall make their complaint, as under the law they cannot get relief after that time for four years.

The Committee on Assessments will be in session at the Court House, on Friday, Oct. 1, 1875 to hear all complaints and adjust wrong assessments.

By order of C. W. Tyler, County Judge.

PETER ONEAL, Cl'k.

Sept. 11, 1875-3w.

Church was always important to Judge Tyler and in early May he was elected secretary of Trinity and attended, with Polk Grundy Johnson and Horace Lurton, the Episcopal convention at Sewanee later that month. During the time that Trinity was being rebuilt, the Presbyterians began work on their new church. Clarksville was certainly becoming the "city of steeples."

Nannie and Polk lost their first child who was born and died on the same day, August 6. They later had a son, Cave Johnson and a daughter, Mildred Waller Johnson.

Polk and Nannie's baby's grave. Photo by author.

In late September, Judge Tyler had some "substantial and tasty" improvements made to the house on Greenwood. The workmen assured the public that it would be a beautiful house when the work was completed.

In October the Tilden and Hendricks Glee Club consisting of Mollie Settle, Emma Tyler, Ella Munford, Betty and Charlie Symes,[69] William A. Forbes, Jr., Tyler Bryan (the judge's half-nephew), Richard Jackson, G.A. Byers and Dr. Daniel F. Wright loaded into a spring wagon and joined a cavalcade to a barbeque at Wilee's Chapel (built in 1870), on Cooper Creek Road. Polk Grundy Johnson coordinated the big event and had the cortege meet at the Red River Bridge at 8 a.m. and travel on to the church grounds in a procession. In front was the barouche of Gustavus A. Henry, Gen. W.A. Quarles, Polk G. Johnson and Judge Charles G. Smith. Next was the large spring wagon containing the Tilden and Hendricks Glee Club with Mollie Settle, Emmie Tyler, Richard Jackson, Ella Munford, Bettie and Charlie Symes, Will Forbes, George "Newton" Byers and Dr. Wright. Following this wagon was that of the speakers of the day: Maj. Nathan Brandon and A.E. Gardner. The Clarksville brass band marched behind them with an estimated 100 young men on horseback and innumerable carriages following. Upon reaching the center of New Providence, the Glee Club and band entertained the citizens and more joined in the procession.

---

69 Betty and Charles' mother was Emelyne Robertson Symes (1828-1908). Her uncle was James Robertson, the founder of Nashville!

The scene was repeated in Woodlawn and at Ferrell's old store. They traveled fourteen miles to the church where the speeches soon commenced. After Judge Smith, Gustavus A. Henry was said to have given an "exhaustive oration" on the issues in Federal politics. It was also observed that like bees around a flower the

> **cavaliers were caracoling gracefully around the ladies in their various vehicles- these young gentlemen seemed to be inspired to astonishing feats of horsemanship by the smiles of beauty and perhaps by smiling a little themselves.**

Also that month, the democrats of Montgomery County gathered once more at a "jubilee" at Hampton's Springs. Much like its predecessor, this gathering consisted of speeches, speeches, and more speeches by those termed the "Democratic guns of the day." Judge Tyler's part of the program was described this way by the press: "Judge Tyler gives remarkable force and energy to what he says, and never fails to interest his hearers because he himself is interested." Also present was William A. Quarles for whom the camp was originally named. The joy of the occasion was tempered by solemn memories. It was at Hamptons' Spring the newspaper printed that

> **More than once during the day it occurred to us that there were some sad and mournful associations with the ground we occupied. In the beginning of the war it was known as Camp Quarles. We thought of the many, many noble, gallant boys who gathered there and enlisted under the banner of the Lost Cause. All buoyant with hope they went out to the more active scenes of the war when Camp Quarles was left far behind and the kind attentions of the dear ones at home could no longer reach them, what was their after history? How many perished from hunger and cold? How many fell in noble, honorable battle and alas! How few returned to Camp Quarles when the smoke of battle was gone?**

Improvements were made to the train passenger depot off Madison Street in November. The old plank sidewalk that connected Madison Street to the depot was taken up and a solid bed of cinders laid down in its place. The sidewalk had been described as "dilapidated" and citizens embarking or disembarking from the trains could only appreciate the benefits of the new arrangements.

Early Clarksville public schools did not assign grades. They operated on a pass/fail system until 1877. The new concept had to be learned by area instructors so superintendent J.C. Brooks sent Clarksville teachers on a trip to Nashville to insure they understood how the system worked. He also invited the public to visit schools to see on a personal basis what the schools were doing for their children and how it was being done. He ended his public announcement with the statement, "We invite at all times FRIENDLY criticism."

January 1877 proved to be a brutal one weather-wise. The first 10 days of the month the Cumberland River was frozen over. Clarksvillians today would be astonished at such a sight.

Six weeks later on February 27, Charles Tyler and his mother Mildred sold "one lot of ground in District One of Montgomery County containing ten and seven eights acres" to S.H. Morgan. They sold the land to pay a debt of $500 to Morgan. This may have been the property owned by Mildred from her dowry.

In early May, an anonymous person wrote to the paper describing the conditions of the Clarksville jail as

> **a vile, filthy, murderous place, unfit for a kennel for dogs, or a wallow for hogs, with its stinking unhealthy dens filled with vermin, with Negroes and white men crowded together and compelled to eat and sleep together.**

Judge Tyler took it personally and picked the letter apart and defended every charge the writer made. He wrote in his rebuttal to the *Tobacco Leaf*

> **I have no doubt that your correspondent was influenced by an honest desire to call public attention to what he considered a great evil, but his statements are on the whole so inaccurate that I cannot think he was ever, as he claims, an inmate of the jail, or knows anything except from rumor of the subject he writes. If I am mistaken I ask him to publish his name in full in next week's *Tobacco Leaf* and I will have the particulars of his case fully inquired into and the facts published.**

Tyler's sister, Emmie was very active in the Clarksville Reading Club whose purpose was to discuss literature and acquire books, (especially reference books), for a future circulating library. The club was organized in 1877 after attempts by the Trinity Church to form a public library failed to materialize. The meetings were held in private homes such as the home of Mr. and Mrs. Clay Stacker near Madison Street.

. Emmie Tyler. (GF)

A new era of brutality was dawning in the South. Numerous lynchings were reported in surrounding counties. On February 28, 1878 in Montgomery County, a black man, Winston Anderson was arrested for an attempted sexual assault on a neighbor's 14-year-old daughter. He was captured near Adam's Station in Robertson County by a mob led by the girl's father and placed in the Clarksville jail. Anderson was taken out at gunpoint by the mob, described by the jailer to have consisted of forty to fifty men. The jailer himself was thrown in a cell and locked up while the mob took the man to a location 1½ miles out of Clarksville and hanged him from a thorn tree along the Nashville Pike not far from the home of William Daniel. The *Chronicle* reported that, "News of the lynching made it into papers in Atlanta and Memphis, Chicago and Cincinnati. The black community here was outraged, as was the top Montgomery County official, Judge Charles Tyler." This was the first instance of mob violence in Montgomery County. Because of this incident Tyler would later write a book condemning mob violence and lynchings.

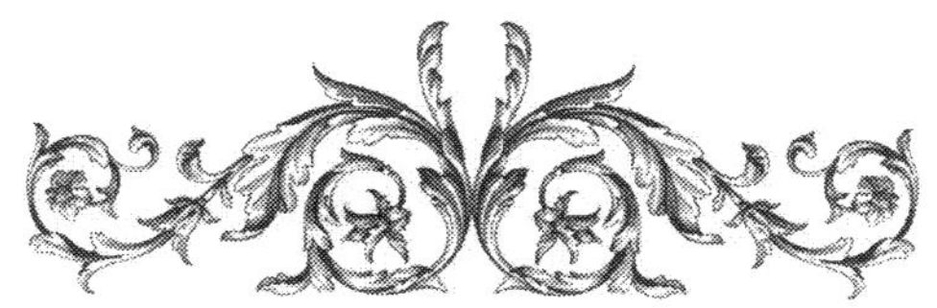

Chapter Eight: The Great Fire and the Judge's New Courthouse

On April 13, 1878, a devastating fire broke out in Clarksville that would forever change the city that just a year before was described as

> **a city of palacial residences, beautiful groves, lovely valleys where the beeches, oaks, and sweet gums. Its streets are many shady retreats of elm and maple, most forest like and its turnpikes and well-metalled and graveled streets afford miles of driving on the turnpikes. But these are not all. Its people genial, hospitable, well informed, moral, temperate, and with these energetic and equal to any business emergency, of a private nature and never wanting in public spirit. With their increaased tobacco trade and their surrounding country producing all products of the soil in profusion...**

After burning all night, the destruction was visible early Sunday morning. Fifteen acres of downtown lay in smoldering ashes. It was suspected that the cause of the fire was arson, related to a disturbance Saturday night in which a black man, Columbus "Lum" Seat, while resisting arrest, was shot and killed by police officer Frank Phillips. Tension quickly began to escalate to the point that, for safety reasons, Sheriff James Mosely had Phillip locked away in the jail to prevent friends of the slain man from retaliating. Even as the county coroner was holding an inquest, a shout of "fire, fire" was heard. The fire appeared to have begun at around 11:30 p.m. in a frame building at the rear of Walter B. Kincannon's Tin and Queensware Store located at 112 and 114 Franklin Street, between First and Second Streets. Dubbed the "commercial artery of Clarksville" by the *Nashville Tennessean,* the flames spread down Franklin Street, aided by a brisk wind from the west that carried hot ashes from one building to the next. So hot was the fire that the burning shingles were described as "shooting through the air like so many sky-rockets." One such rocket passed over Lucy Elder's house, setting fire to a house on Main Street, near the Presbyterian Church. As the winds blew from the west, the buildings on the Public Square were spared.

Lost in the disaster was the Franklin Street courthouse which was built in 1843,[70] livery stables, various businesses, two banks, the Melodeon Hall, Lehman's Saloon, the *Tobacco Leaf* newspaper office and residences including the most eloquent one in downtown Clarksville, that of Mrs. Mary E. Anglen Wheatley on the northwest corner of Third and Franklin. Barely escaping the fire was Trinity Episcopal Church. Remarkably, no one was killed during the fire however, there were some accidents associated with it, as well as a fatality afterwards. While knocking down the back wall of Well's Bakery with an axe, Albert V. Goodpasture was struck by the very axe he was using when an overhanging timber repelled his thrust, causing a severe cut to his head. The one fatality occurred after the fire as a worker on Hodgson's new Marble Works building came back to the site one evening after indulging in some alcohol. For some unknown reason, the worker climbed up the scaffolding onto the rafters and laid down. At some point, he rolled over the side of the plank and fell to his death. The next day's headlines in the *Tobacco Leaf* read:

Clarksville's Great Calamity
FEARFUL LOSS BY FIRE!
Sixty-Three Buildings and Thousands of Dollars in Machinery, Goods, Etc. Destroyed
FIFTEEN ACRES LAID in ASHES SUPPOSED to be the WORK OF AN INCENDIARY

---

[70] Many important legal documents were lost when the courthouse was destroyed so the stress of working without them fell on Judge Tyler.

The total loss of fire was estimated to be $942,000! Some of the losses were printed in the newspaper:

Kincannon, Wood, & Co. loss $56,000, insurance $13,000
***Tobacco Leaf* Office loss $6,000, insurance $3,200**
Polk G. Johnson on C. & M. Office loss $2,000, no insurance
W.J. MacCormac loss on building and stock $16,000, stock of 7000; negatives destroyed, insurance $2,500
John F. Couts loss on stock about $500, fully covered by insurance
Clay Stacker and Rufus Rhodes loss on some law books
W.A. Settle loss on stock and fixtures $700, buildings $1000, insurance $500
George W. Hillman loss $200, insurance $9000
Sam Hodgson loss on buildings, marble yard and furniture $15,000 and Hodgson & Maguire on millinery $10,000-$25,000, insurance on whole $75000
Mrs. Wheatley loss on buildings, furniture, etc. $6,500, insurance $5,000
Mrs. Jennie Johnson loss on buildings $4,000

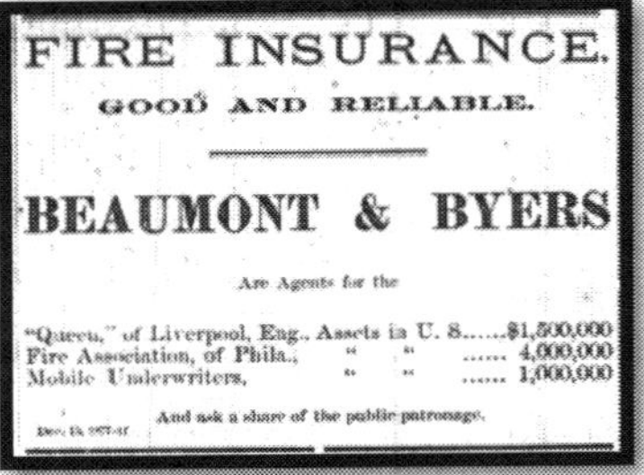

Fire insurance was readily available in Clarksville and many were to regret failing to cover their property. This ad was printed in the *Leaf Chronicle* on April 13, just two days before the fire.

A contributing factor to the spread of the fire was the inability of the city's one fire engine to operate. The engine broke down immediately due to corroded flues, which were full of holes. It was totally worthless to stop the fire from spreading. Clarksville mayor George Ligon telegraphed Nashville for help as the fire spread over the downtown area. Nashville was a mere fifty miles away but the train from Nashville loaded with men and equipment arrived too late to be of any assistance. From that point on for several years the area of downtown from Third Street on the east to Hillman Block, on the west from Franklin Street between Second and Third Street, from Strawberry Alley on the north, to Commerce Street on the south was referred to as the "burnt district of Clarksville."

Clarksville fire engine next to the opera house in the Public Square. Note the *Chronicle* newspaper office on right. (MB)

On April 27, the fire department had the newspaper inform the public that

Our fire engine has been thoroughly repaired by Messrs. Whitfield, Bates & Co. of our foundry and is now in good working order. We hope we will not have occasions to use it soon.

Following the fire, Polk G. Johnson was quoted as saying he was not going "to weep over misfortune but to go to work; that we have to build up the city again and build it up right."

And so it was because of the racial tension that the two local newspapers, the *Tobacco Leaf* and *Clarksville Chronicle* fell silent on the events which led up to the fire but printed instead material related to the reconstruction of the downtown. However, the black school teacher, Mr. Jackson candidly stated that "the great body of his race was misrepresented when they were spoken of as lawless and vindictive; he said that there were lawless white and lawless blacks, but that respectable men of both races condemned them and wanted them punished by due process of law. He added that he would give his best efforts to the investigation of both the matters which had been represented as exciting discord between the races.

As with all disasters, the best side of human nature was seen. Frank and Matt Gracey offered their drays and wagons for two days and nights free of charge to property owners needing to move salvaged items from their buildings. They also generously permitted the use of their telephone "to anyone having business with the agents of the railroad at the depot whether the business has any connection with our house or not."

Some Clarksville college students perpetuated an inappropriate joke in late April when they falsely raised the alarm that there was a fire on campus. For this they received much public condemnation at a time when nerves were already unraveled.

Police officer Phillips was cleared of the charge of murder when he shot and killed Columbus Seat on the night of the fire. The court declared that the act was done in self-defense and Phillips was immediately reinstated as a policeman.

Judge Tyler instructed workmen to gather as much reusable material as possible from the ruins of the old courthouse. He sold the courthouse property, divided into 4 lots for $8,530.16, the iron fencing for $144.50, the stone foundation for $104.00 and the brick to George Edward Cooke for $430.

The fence was later installed in front of the new Clarksville High School, which opened in 1906 on Greenwood Avenue across from the Tyler and Johnson homes. Manufactured by the Champion Iron Works in Kenton, Ohio, the fence was placed on the front and left sides of the school. The portion facing Madison Street later had to be removed when Madison Street was widened and the railroad overpass improved. In the 1960s the rest of the fence was removed. Today pieces of it still can be found throughout town such as between the stone pillar entrances of Riverview Cemetery and a portion connecting the Roxy Theater with the old Brenner's Furniture Store downtown near the "Bursting with Pride" mural on Franklin Street.

On the left: a gate from the old Franklin Street courthouse. This gate was removed later and its whereabouts unknown. On the right: a section of the fence at the entrance of Riverview Cemetery.

A major rebuilding of the burnt district began. Bricks were laid with a combination of lime, sand and water, along with horse or hog hair added as a binder for the mortar. In the South, the saying was that the only thing wasted when hogs were killed was the squeal.

In 1873-1875 John Conroy bought for a very low price, the large limestone bluff on New Providence hill[71] on about 10 acres of land. He built his lime kiln which produced "pure white lime, the best quality of lime now known in the markets of the country." The quick lime was used for mortar to construct the new courthouse. Also, the limestone block foundation of the courthouse was quarried from the property. Conroy later sold the kiln to F.G. Williams for $3,000 cash.

Conroy's lime kiln on the right side of New Providence Boulevard headed north. Photo by author.

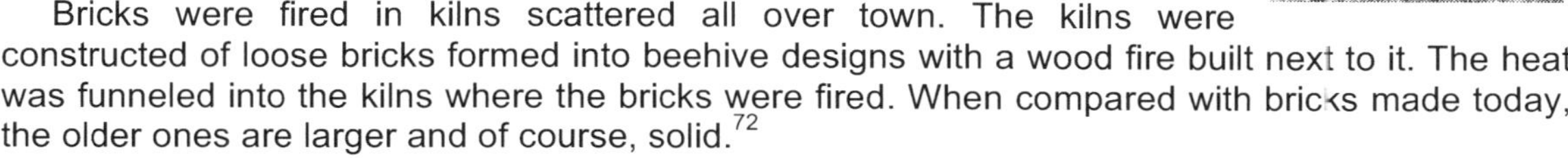

Bricks were fired in kilns scattered all over town. The kilns were constructed of loose bricks formed into beehive designs with a wood fire built next to it. The heat was funneled into the kilns where the bricks were fired. When compared with bricks made today, the older ones are larger and of course, solid.[72]

It was argued by some after the 1999 tornado that the bricks had not been fired long enough during the rebuilding after the great fire. Others blamed the crumbling mortar between the bricks as the culprit for the damage done to the downtown buildings when the tornado passed through. Even the buildings that survived the tornado revealed their weakened state. People currently working in downtown buildings comment that there is continual dust and hog/horse hair on the floor from the old brick walls. Sealing the bricks has been the answer to the problem.

J.R. Hawks, a local bricklayer claimed to be the first to set bricks in place after the fire. He was

[71] In the winter, the kiln can easily be seen from New Providence Boulevard.

[72] The brick manufacturers at this time were George Buck, John Bradley Sr. and Jr., and George Dick.

hired to rebuild the Caldwell and Shelton Livery Stables on the site of their old building. Soon other bricklayers were hired and it was predicted that the "trowel and hammer will be plying their trade with a cheerful activity throughout the burnt district." George Dick's brickyard also stepped up production to help supply much needed bricks to rebuild the downtown. The large Dick family home was located on what was once called the Port Royal Pike. Constructed in the late 1800s, the two-story Italianate style brick house stood for over 100 years. During the Civil War, George served in Woodward's cavalry with Charles Tyler.

A plea for honesty by the first downtown business to perish in the fire was printed in an ad placed in the *Tobacco Leaf* on May 2, 1878. The owners of Kincannon, Wood & Co. announced that all their books and accounts were consumed in the fire to the amount of $15,000 and so requested "all parties knowing themselves to be indebted, to call and pay, as they need the money very much."

Samuel Hodgson

Samuel Hodgson, whose marble works was also a victim of the fire, immediately began rebuilding, allowing space on the second floor for Dr. Thomas Dickson Johnson to use as his office. Dr. Johnson was the brother of Polk Grundy Johnson and the son of Cave Johnson. The building stood at the southwest corner of Legion (once named Strawberry Alley) and North Second Streets, just one block over from the courthouse. The bricks were Ohio Valley pressed bricks originating from Louisville, Kentucky. Additionally, the building had iron cornices, window caps and trimming. The architect for this building, John Andrewartha of Louisville, was also the architect of the Trinity Episcopal Church, Elder's Opera House, as well as other important buildings of Clarksville. While working on these buildings, Andrewartha stayed at the Southern Hotel in the Public Square untouched by the fire. Andrewartha (1839-1916), born in Cornwall, England, began working in the United States in 1865, first based in Louisville, Kentucky, and after 1881 in Austin, Texas.

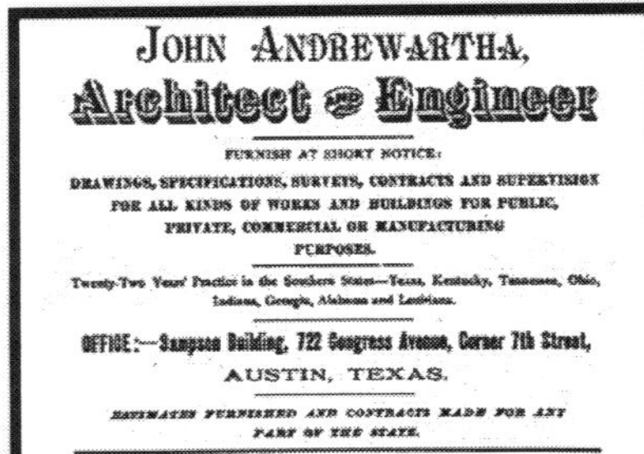

Hodgson was born in England where he learned to sculpt stone. He established the Marble Works in Clarksville in 1842, importing marble from Carrara, Italy and red and gray granite from Aberdeen, Scotland. Numerous examples of Hodgson and his artisans exist around Clarksville.

Citizens living downtown after the great fire were never in the dark as to what the time was at night. From 9 p.m. until midnight, the police rang the market house bell on the hour. Added to that, the courthouse clock chimed at 11 p.m. and midnight also. Then there was John Elder's clock clanging off the hour and just when everyone thought they could settle down, all the clocks in Rohner's Store on the corner of Franklin Street and the Public Square, joined in and punctuated the night. At one time, Clarksville so many bells because George W. Fuller and Otis E. Davidson made a full-time living as bell hangers! Davidson advertised that he had hung bells for Thomas Munford, Dr. C.W. Beaumont, Samuel Hodgson, John F. House, John W. Faxon, Bryce Stewart, Polk Grundy Johnson and Judge Tyler.

Of utmost importance to the city was the need for a new courthouse. The newspaper called upon the courthouse committee to construct a building that "will not only be an ornament to the city but reflect credit upon the pride of the county." The magistrates met to elect a board of commissioners to select a new courthouse site. There were heated debates and lots of suggestions for the new location and local leaders publicly petitioned Judge Tyler "to take some steps or action towards building "a new courthouse and any other business your honor may think proper." At one point it appeared the courthouse would be rebuilt on a vacant lot across from the Methodist Church, then on Franklin Street, but it was strongly argued that this site was too far from the downtown area. The vacated lot on which the old courthouse stood was subdivided into lots fronting Franklin Street. Judge Tyler advertised the lots for sale in the *Clarksville Tobacco Leaf* and they were sold to the highest bidder on May 20. The new owner was allotted one, two, or three years to pay at 6% interest. That buyer was Samuel Hodgson. He was responsible for the construction of the buildings such as the Farmers and Merchants National Bank at 139 Franklin Street (later Joy's Jewelers), Lehman's European Hotel and Saloon (later the location of A.J. Clark's Jewelers) and various other structures on Franklin Street.

During the re-building of the downtown, court was held in the market house on the Public Square. It had been seventy years but A.J. Green remembered it well, the time he served on the jury the first time court was held in the market house with Judge Tyler presiding over the case.

Immediately after the fire Clarksville was inundated with men/boys from surrounding areas seeking "work" and then doing their best not to get too close to it. The local newspaper stated, "Tramps! The town is full of tramps! There is plenty of work they could be put at, cleaning sidewalks. etc. but it takes three honest men to keep one at work." Policeman Frank Phillips charged the tramps with violation of the vagrancy law and ordered them to labor fifteen days on city streets. In November, Phillips had about ten loafers toiling to pay off their fine. When their time was up, the men were ordered to leave town and leave, they did.

Town property owners hurried to find new accommodations to restart their businesses and were just as quick to advertise when they were up and running. One such business, a mainstay in Clarksville for 30 years was the Saddles and Harness Shop of John Young. His advertisement listed:

> **Old reliable, time tried and fire tested harness, saddles, bridles, collars, whips, and trunks. Having passed through the ordeal and emerged from the ruins of the great fire; I am now on the west side of the Public Square adjoining the bank building.**

Sealed Proposals!

Until the 2d Monday in May Next

SEALED PROPOSALS will be received by me from all persons owning lots suitable for the erection of a new Court House building. [illegible] proposal must describe the lot offered, stating the locality, [illegible] of feet front and its depth, the terms and the [illegible] which the owner obligates himself to sell should his bid be accepted by the county.

These bids will be opened by the Commissioners on the second Monday in May.

By order of Court House Commissoners.
CHARLES W. TYLER, Chairman.
May 2 td.

Building Lots!

FOR SALE!

On MONDAY, MAY 20, 1878

the lot upon which the Court House formerly stood will be subdivided into lots fronting 20 feet on Franklin street, and sold to the highest bidder, on one, two and three years' time. Notes bearing interest at six per cent. from date required. Sale subject to the ratification of the Quarterly Court on the first Monday in July next.

By order of Court House Commissioners.
CHARLES W TYLER, Chairman.
May 2, tds.

MacCormac's Galleries made arrangements to use the reception room and yard of Dr. T.E. Cabaniss, a local dentist whose office was located on Third Street near Franklin. Here William J. MacCormac set up a tent which enabled him to continue his photography business. He advertised that he would be "prepared to make pictures in the best style."

The buildings in the fire district were quickly rebuilt with two- to three- story brick structures distinquished by arched windows, metal hood moldings, corbelled brick and metal cornices at the roof line. Even in 2025 some of the buildings still exhibit their original cast iron columns and pilasters on their facades.

Charles Tyler's half-sister Mary's husband Henry H. Bryan and son, John Duke Tyler Bryan, both tobacco brokers, moved their office to a room in the basement of the First National Bank on Franklin Street. Billy Settle bought the lot adjoining McCauley's Drug Store with intentions to build on it while his father opened his family grocery in the room under J.G. Joseph's clothing store. The telegraph company announced that they erected "splendid" new poles to replace those destroyed in the fire.

The large, double pond at the junction of Franklin and Sixth Streets on property owned by Mrs. Susannah McDaniel caused problems when heavy rains fell in May. According to the *Clarksville Weekly Chronicle*, "a thick green scum of cryptogamous vegetation" formed on the surface and so it was declared a health hazard to the public. The term "cryptogamous" must have sounded mysterious and harmful, but great to get a point across, which was the newspaper's intent! Dr. Daniel F. Wright concurred with the newspaper and attempts to improve drainage of the pond commenced.

In his role as criminal judge, Charles was always known to be an independent thinker, often not siding with popular opinion but always proceeding with what he considered to be the best course of action. In his courtroom, there was no gray area. Things were either decisively right or decisively wrong and his judgments were quick as well as final. Like his father before him, Tyler accepted no more interference in his courtroom than his father did in his school. There was no second-guessing or hesitation, he assumed complete authority, had absolutely no tolerance for lawbreakers and did not suffer fools lightly.

Tyler was often sought out for advice as his opinions and thoughts were so well-respected. Idle conversation was not something Charles engaged in. From all indications, his conversations were exceedingly purposeful and insightful. Throughout his life he exuded a distinguished demeanor and even into his old age, was quite a compelling figure. Judge Tyler's eyes were a hazel green, a trait seen in many Tyler family members, including descendants. His entire adult life, Charles had the same slender, lean attributes of his father before him. Photos of the judge in his later life reveal that this never changed, except that his hair turned completely white. He let a lot of criticism roll off his back but when someone chose to publically print it in the newspaper, they were in for it. Tyler let no public criticism of him in the newspaper go unanswered. In his distinct clear-cut albeit overboard manner, he fired back with intensity, the same manner that he employed in the courtroom. Always direct and to the point, the judge would state what had been said of him and then defend himself, point by point, until no doubt was left in the reader's mind that what he had done was not only completely appropriate but indeed the only course of action to take.

J.B. Killebrew stated his opinion about Tyler's overall personality, "Had his probity and fidelity to his friends been equal to his mentality, he would have made a very strong man. With men of high character and strong moral qualities, he is not highly esteemed and yet his power is so pervasive that it is difficult to beat him in a contest in county elections." And amid all the chaos following the fire, it was an election year and so Tyler advertised and once again to no one's surprise, he was re-elected.

COUNTY & CRIMINAL JUDGE.

CHARLES W. TYLER—We are authorized to announce CHARLES W. TYLER as a candidate for re-election to the office of County and Criminal Judge of Montgomery county at the ensuing August election.

Clarksville Weekly Chronicle, June 8, 1878

The decision was made on July 4 to simply put all the suggested sites for the location of the new courthouse to the vote among the magistrates. The lot across from the Methodist Church received two votes, Joshua Cobb's residence and grove opposite the Female Academy on Madison Street between Fifth and Sixth Streets received two votes, the lot on the east side of Public Square between Strawberry Alley and Main Street, received no votes; G.W. Hillman's residence, grove, garden and orchard on Second Street received no votes. Finally, after numerous meetings, the final selection was made amid "fur flying" and Judge Tyler struggling to contain his laughter at the proceedings. Jennie Johnson's lot on Commerce Street between Second and Third Streets won the majority of the votes. The recommendation was ratified and it was declared that the question could NOT be raised again. i.e. the decision was final! The newspaper reporter present recorded that the meeting was a "jolly time." Tyler wisely secured an insurance policy to cover the courthouse in the event of another fire in the amount of $333 for a period of three years.

The insurance agents representing the different companies who had been in Clarksville following the fire to take care of those who had been able to afford coverage on their properties. began to leave town. When able, people wisely signed up for fire insurance.

Clarksvillians waited for the announcement of the design selection with elevated interest. In the end, George W. Bunting (1829-1901), of Indianapolis submitted a design accepted by the courthouse building commissioners with an estimated cost set at fifty thousand dollars. It probably helped that Bunting was a former Confederate colonel in the 1st Mississippi Cavalry. In 1869, he moved north and by 1874 was in Indianapolis with the firm of Bunting and Huebner and later by the mid 1880s, Bunting and Son.

GEORGE W. BUNTING

George W. Bunting

The plans showed a building that was "bold in detail, substantial in construction and dignified in character appearance." When completed, it lived up to its description. A total of three courthouses in the country used the same blueprints as Clarksville's but in 2025, it is the only one that remains.

Beautifully constructed of pressed brick and decorated with limestone trim, the courthouse, combining both Italianate and Victorian elements, stands two and a half stories high. Numerous architectural details were incorporated into its design. Windows are double-headed and Doric and Corinthian style columns decorate the Second and Third Street entrances. The upper panels of the large interior doors had embossed glass with the names of the respective offices on them.

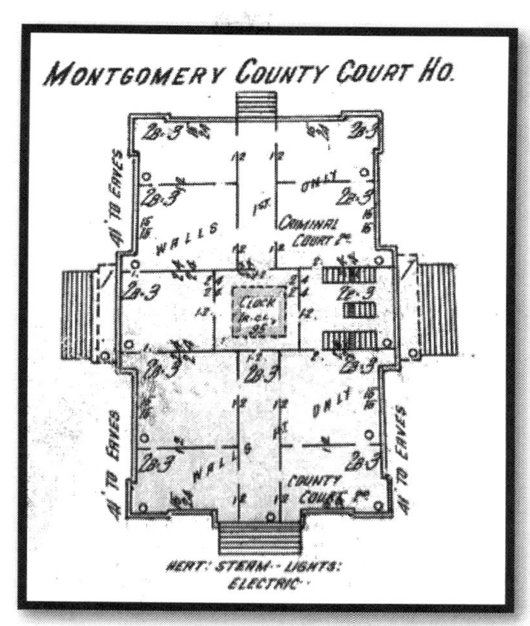

The Sanborn Fire Map of the new courthouse.

The foundation sits upon a tall stone basement which added height and was built with eight spacious rooms for various uses. Four entrances with large halls made up the main floor. A wonderful walnut double staircase winded up to the top floor. The main floor had offices for the County Clerk, County Judge, Trustee, Register, Circuit and Criminal Clerk.

Additionally, the first floor was designed to hold two rooms for the Chancery Clerk, as well as a law library and a room for the Chancery Court. The second floor contained a large courtroom for the Circuit and Criminal Courts, with a jury room and two other rooms for use by the witnesses. There were additional rooms for lawyers and their clients. The large Criminal Court room was furnished with walnut molding and seats for 200. A twenty-four light chandelier hung in this room as well as six sidelights to illuminate the sizable space. It also contained desks that were utilized by the forty-three magistrates of the county. Finally, there was a substantial grand jury room in the back.

The second story landing outside the courtrooms. Judge Tyler would climb these numerous times over the next decades. (MCA)

The office of the Montgomery County Assessor, Highway Department and Trustee Office in 1963. Note the fireplace and radiator that were no longer in use. An electric heater is on the floor in the center of the photograph instead. An air conditioner is seen installed in the left window. The beautiful wood work high on the window frames was recreated when the courthouse was rebuilt after the 1999 tornado. Also note the condition of the furniture still in use probably since the courthouse was remodeled in 1900. (MCA)

Brenda Runyon was a unique individual and because of her determined personality, earned her own separate identity. Not satisfied with simply being "the wife of Dr. Frank Runyon," Brenda paved a path in the business world (usually not accepting of women and their ideas), and opened a door of opportunity that would from then on, never close. She later would be instrumental in organizing the Red Cross in Clarksville during World

War I and played a principal role in starting the public library and the city hospital. Thinking of women who came to town on Saturdays with their families, she convinced Judge Tyler to provide a room for mothers to change their babies, feed them or allow them to rest. Not to show favoritism, Tyler also saw that men were also granted a restroom in the new courthouse.

The splendid tower of the courthouse was constructed with illuminated clock faces on all four sides that contained a 3,000-pound bell. This tower sits upon the steep mansard roof and rises 150 feet above the ground that can be seen for miles in all directions. A soaring eagle acted as a weathervane at the very tip of the tower. The four corners of the courthouse display pyramidal roofs. Decorative ironwork was used for exterior banisters for the exterior steps leading up to the main level. An iron fence was added to the perimeter just to the inside of the sidewalks as well as maple trees planted in two staggered rows in the courtyard. A 75-foot lightning rod was installed to insure against damage from lightning strikes.

On the left: the courthouse tower illuminated. On the right: one of the two goddess statues located on the Second and Third Street pediments on the roof over the entrances. If these were goddess of justice statues, they would be blindfolded, holding a sword in their right hands and scales in their left. A goddess of liberty statue holds a lowered sword in her right hand and a star or some other object like a flame in her left hand. In 1982 an elderly man passing by suggested to two men, one a reporter for the *Leaf* who were craning their necks to see what the statues held in their left hand. The gentleman quipped that it was a hand grenade.

Listed below is the amount of money appropriated and used for the following purpose:

MacCormac & Sweeny contractors	**$13,371.46**	
G.W. Bunting, original architect	**$1679.14**	
C.G. Rosenplanter, architect	**$2,545.00**	
Commissioner's 2½ years' service	**$870.47**	
E. Howard & Co., on bell	**$800.00**	
Freight on bell	**$25.00**	**(to be deducted from clock bill)**
Tarpley & McGuire, on extra painting	**$175.00**	
O'Conner & West, on extra plumbing	**$300.00**	
O'Conner & West, on steam heating	**$500.00**	
Eagle and ball on tower	**$103.60**	
Wm. McCarty, 705 ft. lightning rod	**$264.37**	
Expenses of trip to Cincinnati	**$61.75**	
Expenses of trip to Nashville	**$34.00**	
Sewerage to street and other items	**$59.33**	
Insurance, 8 months to April 28, 1881	**$240.00**	
Paid on Grounds		
For lot of Whitfield	**$3,000.00**	
For lots of Ewing & Bailey	**$1,250.00**	
For interest on Drane lot, 2 yrs.	**$1,880.00**	
Aggregate Amount Paid	**$58,655.46**	

**The cost ran over almost $9,000.

From reading the news, the courthouse could not be built fast enough to deal with all the crimes being committed in town. Today when someone comments on how much safer it was in the good ole days, they should read the surprising number and descriptions of the crimes, including murders, that occurred in Clarksville's past. Crimes committed then were just as cruel and senseless as they are today. Imagine reading the following news report but remember that the date is August 24, 1878:

Drunken fights and street brawls are more frequent in Clarksville now than was ever known before. The calaboose is kept filled to its utmost capacity nearly all the time. Most of these disturbances take place Saturday night and Sunday. Last Saturday night there were six arrests before midnight, and on Sunday, besides the killing of Lawn, there were four street fights. Is it not a fact that there is more crime, especially of the violent sort in hot weather than any other time? Are men not more irritable and petulant in torrid weather than in the milder seasons?

So what firefighting measures did Clarksville have over the years? When one learns of the early firefighting measures in the Public Square during the 1830s, one realizes the absolute futility of extinguishing any fire that might have broken out in the new town. It is known that in 1830, four "substantial yellow poplar ladders, 35 feet in length" were ordered for the city to which the city paid $33.50. It was estimated that a ladder of that height could reach the top portion of almost any existing building at that time. Buckets of water were handed up to men on the ladders. The volunteers also used hooks, which were used to disengage or drag away the burning portions of any structure on fire, hence the name of the Hook and Ladder. By June 1831, a 6000-gallon capacity cistern had been dug at Public Square and a fire captain selected. George G. Gossett was appointed to organize a company of volunteer firefighters as the city lacked funds to pay for such protection. Gossett then required each owner of property on the Public Square to furnish his or her building with two leather fire buckets, each "to be made of leather with the owner's name plainly marked." This would allow the firefighters to return the buckets to their appropriate owners following their use. It was a serious matter not to comply with the order, such that a fine of $2.00 on the square and $1.00 elsewhere was enforced.

In 1859, two fire departments were established: The Independent Deluge Fire Company Number One was located on the south side of Strawberry Alley between First and Second Streets and the Independent Eagle Fire Company Number Two, was located at the market house on the Public Square.

A total of seven ponds were scattered around the town area, which could be depended on for a source of water if the need to fight a fire arose. There was the large double pond, which overlapped the present intersection of Franklin and Sixth Streets, the large Drane pond at the foot of Third Street (which prevented this street from continuing further), Big Beach to the east of Robb Avenue, Little Beach to the north of Big Beach, one on the campus of Stewart College and the one between North Second and North First Streets, covering what is now McClure Street. Both Big and Little Beach were used by locals for ice-skating. Also available in case of a fire was, of course, was the town spring, private cisterns and the two rivers. The locations of the cisterns on the Public Square and elsewhere in town can be seen on the various Sanborn Fire Maps. These can be viewed today in the genealogy department of the public Library.

Naturally there was some finger pointing after the fire. Engineer Jack McNeal stated that he knew the condition of the engine prior to the devastating 1878 fire and had alerted Captain John Young and the officers of the fire company as to its condition several times. However, it was felt that the engine would last until summer when, with less chance of fire, it could be thoroughly repaired and more city money would be available to cover the expenses. The group of volunteer firefighters could not have foreseen such a catastrophe.

From 1878 through 1886, Thomas Hyman acted as the city's first fire chief, succeeded by William Kleeman who served until 1891. Fire chiefs did not receive payment until 1891. The new brick Clarksville fire hall located on South Third Street between Commerce and Madison Streets had three stalls for wagons and a small stable next door for the horses.

The engine being pulled by eight men. This was before horses were brought in.

Perched on top of the fire hall was a wooden tower

whose bell was rung for several reasons. On New Year's Eve, it rang at midnight as did church bells and the bell at the college. When a fire occurred, the bell would ring the number of times to indicate the particular ward in which the fire was located. By this method it would announce to the volunteer firemen where to assemble to meet the regular firemen with the firefighting equipment. There were also times when the bell was rung simply out of jubilation, such as when the end of World War I was announced.[73] Also established was a city fire code with laws that required all new construction be of fireproof materials, such as brick or stone with slate or metal roofs and also be finished front, back and side with firewalls. These parapet walls had to extend above the roof to the height of 24 inches to prevent the spread of fire from windblown wooden shingles.

By May the fire engine had been repaired and by June 27, the fire department had received two dozen leather buckets, two ladders and six fire axes to replace those lost in the fire. In total the fire department had a ladder wagon, a wood burning pumper wagon and a hose wagon. In order to keep the horses ready at a moment's notice to pull these wagons, they were exercised daily for one hour.

The 1878 fire hall on South Third Street. The horses were an absolute blessing. (MCA)

In discussing day-to-day happenings, Clarksvillians had used the phrase, "before the war," or "after the war." Now added to that, was "before the fire" and "after the fire." The *Clarksville Tobacco Leaf*, among the victims of the fire, began publishing from their competitor's office. Using the presses of the *Chronicle*, the writers from the *Tobacco Leaf* expressed their strong belief that Clarksville would rise from the ashes and so stated the prevailing feeling of optimism:

> **One of those terrible calamities that sometimes visit cities and for a time paralyze industry and commerce has fallen to our lot. We meet it with a courage and a heroism that knows not to give up. We are down. But the help of God we won't stay down. Clarksville people are not made of that kind of stuff.**

The history of these two newspapers is of interest. The *Clarksville Chronicle* began its publication in 1808 as the first statewide circulation newspaper. Due to the city's reputation as a major tobacco center, a second newspaper, the *Tobacco Leaf* began printing in 1869. The importance of tobacco to the economy of this area was reflected in the name of this newspaper. Both papers started out as simple four-page manuscripts of advertising and political news but were to evolve into publications featuring local, regional and national news plus political and gossip columns. These two merged as a single newspaper, the *Clarksville Leaf Chronicle* in 1890, later dropping the city's name in 1970 to simply the *Leaf Chronicle*.

The families residing on Greenwood Avenue were not endangered and spared the fire. However, because they were located "so far from town," they did not receive their water from the waterworks on Front Street nor the electric light. Homes belonging to Judge Tyler, Polk Grundy Johnson, Samuel A. Caldwell, Emmett McCulloch, William J. Lynes, Jones Neblett, Dr. Thomas H. Marable and W.H. McReynolds were among those that ran along the avenue. The city folks had what the "Greenwooders" considered to be "metropolitan airs." As one resident said,

> **Well, if we do not have all the privileges enjoyed by the downtowners, we have the**

[73] The location of the fire station was a problem for the First Christian Church on the northeast corner of Madison and Third Streets. Not only were streetcars a noisy interruption of services but also the very sound of them rattled the nerves of horses hitched along the Third Street side of the church. At any time during a service when the alarm bells were rung, men from the congregation would rush outside to settle the horses down as the firefighting equipment bellowed forth from the station.

advantage so to speak, of town and country combined and breathe pure air, drink cistern water, burn coal oil at fifteen cents per gallon, rise our own garden and enjoy more sociability; worship God according to the dictates of our own conscience—all of which we think is good enough for poor folks and but a few Greenwooders feel stuck up about it either.

It was indeed welcome news to city folks when, in September, Mayor George Ligon announced that the plank sidewalks all over town would be replaced. He did, however, ask those who were able to replace the walks in front of their houses with brick to do so. One must remember that city sidewalks at that time were nothing more than two planks laid side-by-side with just enough room between them to allow the runoff of rain or melting snow. Dust was such a health hazard that storeowners were asked to sprinkle the sidewalks in front of their establishments before sweeping.

The market house had various renters throughout its time on the Public Square. Polk Grundy Johnson in September of 1878, used it as a central location to sell large tracts of real estate. It proved to be a good location for its proximity to the rivers and the courthouse. Investors disembarking the riverboats had but to climb the hill to locate Johnson who could explain what tracts of land for farming, business or private homes were available.

In 1878, a person might have to share the road with livestock! One day in October, a young gentleman was minding his own business, riding his mule down a city street when a "thoughtless young hog, in the recklessness peculiar to youth," decided to cross the street just as the mule and its rider were passing by. It was reported that:

They collided. They stumbled. They fell. The juvenile porker escaped unhurt from the debris, and tripped gaily away, laughing in his sleeve, and exclaiming 'veni, vidi, vici.' It is thought the mule will die.

About the same time as Tate was operating Hickory Wild, in town a new school opened. Howell School, a three-story brick building available to students in grades 1-10 was located at 501 Franklin Street on "one of the best sites in the city being on the summit of few eminencies that overlook the rest of the area."[74] It was constructed with two wide staircases, one each for boys and girls and twenty-four windows on each floor to provide the best lighting. In September 1881 it was reported that there were 273 students enrolled. Howell was open for grades 1-10 until Clarksville High School opened in 1906 and then it became a school with grades 1-7 only. Because of his long service to the community in various capacities, the school that once stood on Franklin Street was given Arch Howell's name. Howell served as mayor of Clarksville during Nannie's short life. His name is also found on the front entrance pillars of the Madison Street Methodist Church for his contributions to the establishment of that church.

On the left: Arch Howell. On the right: the original Howell School on Franklin Street. (MCA)

[74] It was from this eminence that Confederate colonel Thomas Woodward positioned one of his "cannons" in a ruse to force U.S. colonel Rodney Mason to surrender Clarksville. His "cannons" were simply logs that he had his men cut, place on wheels and situate them in such a way as to appear to be ready to fire at the college campus where Mason's troops were stationed. Mason succumbed and agreed to surrender.

Part Two

Chapter Nine: The Judge Marries

After moving to town and joining the Episcopal Church, Tyler met his future wife, Mollie Settle. She was everything desirable in a woman: lovely, popular, fashionable, submissive, quiet and gentle. She had a beautiful singing voice and was known as the "sweet song bird of Clarksville." Tyler was smitten and it seems it took him a while to muster the courage to approach her about marriage. He courted her for several years before taking the big step to ask for her hand. In a novel Charles penned years later, he described how a young man in love might propose. It causes the reader to wonder if this was the manner in which he had proposed to Mollie. He wrote:

> **There was a great deal of beating around the bush, discussion of subjects foreign to the matter in hand and then at the most inopportune moment the question was 'popped'. And once popped, there was no checking his impetuosity or the flow of the words that followed. His heart was like a champagne bottle; the stopper once withdrawn, the entire contents had to gush forth in a torrent that could not be stayed.**

MARRIAGE LICENSE.

STATE OF TENNESSEE, MONTGOMERY COUNTY.

To any Minister of the Gospel having the Care of Souls or any Justice of the Peace of said County—Greeting:

You, or either of you, are hereby authorized to solemnize the Rites of Matrimony between C W Tyler and Mary Settle he, the said C W Tyler having given bond and security agreeably to the Act of the General Assembly in such case made and provided.

Given under my hand, at the Clerk's Office, in the City of Clarksville, this 21 day of October 1878

[signature] County Court Clerk.
By C A Bailey D. C.

I CERTIFY, That I solemnized the Rites of Matrimony between C W Tyler and Miss Mollie Settle on the 21 day of October 1878
P A Fitts Pastor Trinity Church

Know all Men, That we, C W Tyler & C A Bailey of the County of Montgomery, and State of Tennessee, are held and firmly bound unto the State of Tennessee, in the sum of TWELVE HUNDRED AND FIFTY DOLLARS, to which payment, well and truly to be made, we bind our heirs, executors and administrators, and each and every one of us and them, both jointly and severally, firmly by these presents.

The Condition of the above Obligation is such, THAT WHEREAS, C W Tyler hath prayed and obtained a License to marry Mollie Settle

Now, if there shall not hereafter appear any lawful cause why the said C W Tyler and Mollie Settle should not be joined together in Holy Matrimony as Husband and Wife, then this obligation to be void and of no effect; otherwise to remain in full force and virtue.

Witness our hands and seals, this 21 day of Octo 1878

C W Tyler [L. S.]
C A Bailey [L. S.]

While Clarksville was in the midst of rebuilding, Charles and Mollie were planning their wedding. The blissful ceremony might not have taken place at all given a near tragic event three months before. Charles Tyler and Burr Coleman, a businessman from New Providence, were returning to Clarksville from the Blooming Grove community on a Monday evening July 31, 1878 when, while trying to cross the swollen creek, their buggy was overcome by the deep waters and began washing downstream. To avoid getting trapped under water with the carriage, the two men jumped into the water and swam to shore.

Happily, Charles on Monday, October 21, married Mary Mildred Settle. The Episcopal Church was still under construction after the great fire and the congregation was temporarily using the Cumberland Presbyterian Church at the corner of Main and Fourth Streets until its new building on Franklin was completed.

The wedding was performed by Father Fitts. Among the small group of intimate friends and family to witness the nuptials was Polk Grundy Johnson and close friend and banker, David Newton Kennedy. The wedding was described as, "quiet and unostentatious, one perfectly in keeping with the lives of both parties." Months prior to the wedding it was said that the judge's face was covered in smiles and blushes which was a sure sign to their friends that the union was imminent. A Kentucky newspaper further quipped that, "the judge had just finished a long suit . . . settled to the advantage of both parties." The *Tobacco Leaf* pronounced the following sentence upon the judge, "a long life of happiness is the award, we trust, of fate, with a unanimous verdict from a jury of his friends 'serve him right.'" Charles was 38 years and Mollie was nearly ten years younger.

After the vows, the couple left immediately on what was termed a "wedding tour." The couple left town on the 7:47 p.m. train headed to Nashville and stayed at the luxurious Maxwell House Hotel. On November 2, the newlywed couple returned home from Nashville. The only known photo of Charles and Mollie as a couple was taken in Nashville, probably on their honeymoon. Seated at a desk in a chair beside Mollie, Charles is wearing a double-breasted long sack suit with a wide lapel. He is wearing a white shirt and a narrow black tie, tied in a bow under a wing collar. He appears to be wearing cufflinks.

The Tylers' wedding day photo. (GF)

The photo shows her to be a lovely lady with dark hair and gentle eyes. She is dressed in a plain dark, short wool overdress that is buttoned tightly down the front of the bodice and finished with wide double V-neck trimmings. The long sleeves are also tight fitting and reveal white undersleeves. The underskirt is of the polonaise style, meaning that the skirt was draped with drawstrings revealing the underskirt. These dresses were made of wool or some other more expensive material. Layers of ruffles and fringe embellish the bottom. The hem of the dress is interesting in that it is made with flounces of knife pleats as well as a wide border of crocheted lace on top of the pleating. She is wearing a bar pin at the high neck of the dress, earrings, a ring on the pointer finger of her left hand and a necklace. Throughout time jewelry has been an important accessory item. Charles L. Cooke's store in Clarksville advertised such jewelry items as "pins, earrings, bracelets, buttons, chains and lockets and rings plain and with diamond, pearl, emerald, amethysts, cameo and turquoise sets." Women of Clarksville visited this store as well as others to purchase such grand embellishments. The Victorian lady would wear lots of jewelry.

Cooke's jewelry store was established by George E. Cooke in 1855. His brother C.L. Cooke joined him in 1859 until 1865 when it became known as the C.L. Cooke Jewelry Store. In 1907 George's son, Charles Edward Cooke took over the store. In 1922 the store was bought by C.E. Sites of Owensboro, Kentucky.

In her hand appears to be a pair of glasses. Clarksville was fortunate indeed to have a skilled watch maker and eye glass maker trained in Basel, Switzerland. Thomas Rohner's business was on Franklin Street.

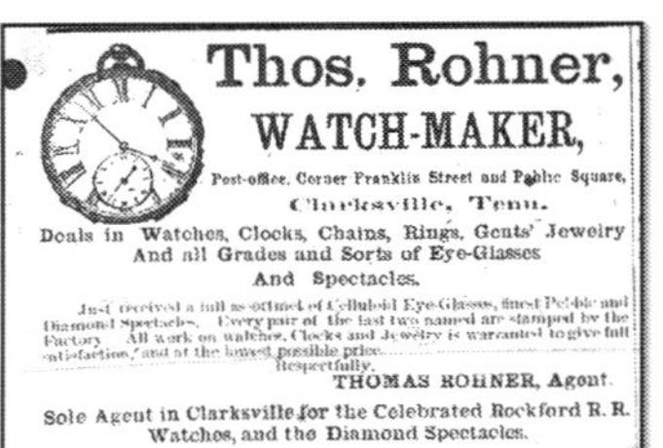

Her hair style was in keeping with the latest style. Fringes (bangs) once thought of as inappropriate was now considered fashionable as were big curls, big braids and long hair. Often women wore their hair in ringlets down the back of their necks. A hairstyle like this takes a lot of hair, so women often had to supplement with false hair pieces. Although women did not wash their hair but once or twice monthly in the 1880s, they did brush their hair quite often. One hundred strokes before going to bed was a common practice. Today in some antique stores, a shopper may come across a round porcelain container with a hole the size of a half dollar in the top. These dishes sat on the dressing or "vanity" tables of the Victorian woman to use as a hair collector. After brushing, the hair would be removed from the brush and stuffed into this container for use later. If the lady's hairstyle called for a fuller appearance, she could use her own hair to tuck in and about her hair. Women also collected hair from hair brushes for making mourning hair art, to add volume to their hairstyles or even to fill pincushions. The coiffure might also include chignons, braids, or plaits (the term the Victorians used) and loops. The more elaborate the better, however time often dictated how elaborate these styles were. Ladies' hairstyles of the 1860s had been worn parted in the middle and pulled back giving a severe appearance. Women were able to curl their hair using a heated tong (curling iron) after its invention by a Parisian hairdresser in the 1870s. The iron resembled modern day ones with a single exception. Before wrapping the hair around the rod, the end of the iron was heated over an open flame sometimes to the point that quite often while curling, the hair was singed or even burned off. If a lady could afford such an expense, there were hair saloons available. On Franklin Street adjoining Lehman's European Hotel and Saloon, Adeline "Addie" Buck ran her Ladies Hair Dressing establishment. She purchased an ad that ran in the *Leaf Chronicle*, which read:

> **Braids, clubs, puffs, frizzes, crimps, etc. in the best of styles; watch guards, hair jewelry, and all kinds of beautiful flowers. Hair combings stranded out-roots all turned one way-and made up in elegant style. Hair dressed for picture taking, in any style desired and all orders for shingling children's hair or shampooing ladies' heads at residence will be promptly attended to.**

William Buck operated a "fashionable" barbershop on the second floor of his wife's hair dressing shop. He advertised, "only competent and polite barbers were employed." Both she and her husband were examples of successful black entrepreneurs in Clarksville.

The detested hoop skirt was long gone from women's closets but in came another aggravation. The newest in fashion in 1887 was the bustle and men definitely had their opinion on them. Even the newspaper chimed in on their dislike. The reporter wrote,

> **During the last few days I have been expecting to see cards in front of the dry goods store bearing inscriptions like this: 'Dynamite bomb bustles, fully warranted to blow up when the string is pulled by the wearer;' but I am glad to observe that none of our dealers in fabrics intend handling these newly invented infernal machines. If any of the Clarksville ladies send away and get them, I intend on staying away from church and the theatre and I declare that I will not go to a single dance during the coming 'mazy' season.**

The *Tobacco Leaf* teasingly suggested that the "wrong doers of Clarksville" had better not depend on the judge's heart being softened by his recent marriage. Another article reported that marriage had done him a lot of good and he was receiving a multitude of good wishes. When the reporter met the judge on the street three weeks later and before he could utter a word of congratulations, the judge oddly exclaimed, "Yes sir; yes, sir, thank you; I am feeling much better now, much better."

After their marriage, Charles and Mollie joined his mother Mildred and sister Emmie at the house on Greenwood Avenue. It seems that every man in high position needs a competent woman upon which to rely and most assuredly, Mollie was a lady of integrity whose benevolent spirit was well documented. Not only a Victorian, but the wife of a judge, Mollie was expected to follow the rules of decorum. Such adjectives as respectability, comfort, appearance and propriety were the operative words. Mollie was expected to help maintain the home to reflect the personality of her husband. It was to be kept as a place of refuge for him and to enhance his public standing. Mollie was also judged on the appearance of the yard and gardens which must, at all times, be well maintained. Her training for this role had begun early in life; femininity was constantly emphasized.

Mollie's schooling at White Hall had prepared her in all the social graces and those of household duties. She was also required to be a wise steward of the family income. Frivolous spending was unacceptable and certainly would be frowned upon. After all, she was married to the county financial officer!

Clutter and excess was the rule for the Victorians and it showed in their homes. Knick-knacks would be everywhere, on every available shelf, on any table or piano top. Victorians felt that a bare room showed a lack of taste. Walls were covered in patterned wallpaper and hung with framed photos, paintings and art. Did Mollie adhere to this, or was there a sparsity of items decorating each room?

Charles, on the other hand, did not have the restrictions placed upon him such as those on his wife. Although contradictory, the Victorian man was expected to be an absolute gentleman in front of ladies but also to be a "man of the world" among men. To be out of control or to show poor manners publicly was not in keeping with being well bred and raised.

Charles was not only the law in town but also at home; he was seen as the head of the household since it was his responsibility to provide the living for the family. Judge Tyler also saw it as his duty to protect the female family members and to shield his delicate women from "the harsh realities of a man's world."

Mollie and Charles Tyler. (GF)

The woman's routine for dressing daily was an exercise in layering. The Victorian woman would have worn drawers, a bodice, a corset, one or more petticoats and finally the dress, which in itself might have been layered. Ribbons, flounces, pleats, laces, ruffles, beads, braid and oh so many buttons were the sown on their dresses. Often the woman required help to dress, especially if she was tight lacing her corset or trying to button the back of the dress. Someone who fussed about the time his wife took to dress said that, "planning the Parthenon probably took less time than his wife's daily toilette." Certainly dressing was overdone which was the manner of the Victorian.

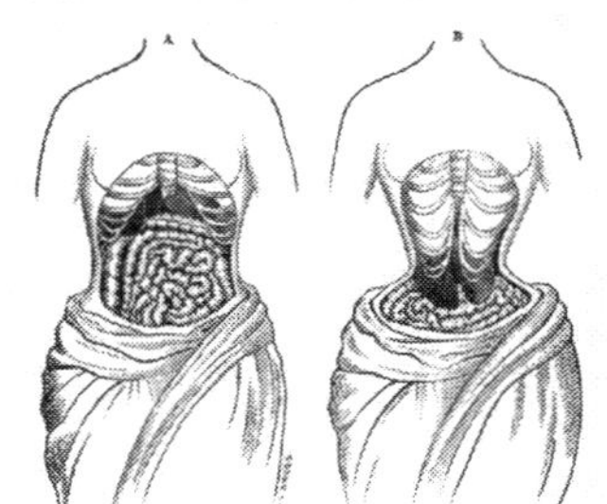

What corseting does to the female anatomy. No wonder women needed fainting couches and smelling salts. Sketch from Kristina Kilgore.

Dress styles included a cushion called a bustle, which was worn at the back waistline. Its purpose was to call attention to the back of the dress. Corsets were essential garments, tightly laced to give waistlines the smallest possible dimensions. A 19-inch waistline was considered to be appropriate. To give the reader the idea of the size of a nineteen-inch waist, imagine the circumference of a saucer; the waist would be smaller than even that! No wonder women of this era needed fainting couches! It has been a cause of argument for years, the effect that corseting had on the women of that time period. Some critics went so far as to say that wearing a corset is "a crime like self-murder. Because of vanity, corsets lay their victims in the grave... loaded with guilt."

Throughout history, blame for numerous ailments and diseases has been placed directly on the doorstep of corsetry. Such examples include deformities of the spine, miscarriages, circulatory diseases, birth defects, displacement of internal organs, cancer, curvature of the spine, broken ribs and puncture wounds. While this list seems long, according to a book written in 1874 by Luke Limner, entitled, *Madre Natura Versus the Moloch of Fashion*, there were as many as ninety-seven "diseases produced by stays and corsets according to the testimony of eminent medical men." One disease on the list was apoplexy, the condition of paralysis due to a stroke.... the prescribed cause of Mollie Tyler's death in 1900. The argument was that if the ribs were constricted, so also would be the diaphragm. If the diaphragm was constricted, breathing would be inhibited and therefore circulation would be reduced and if circulation was reduced, a stroke could occur. However, there is no hard medical evidence to support this. Valerie Steele, author of the book*, The Corset: A Cultural History*, maintains that although tight lacing did affect a lady's comfort, its long-term use could not be linked to any life threatening condition. The *Leaf Chronicle* January 28 issue of 1884 advertised corsets for sale. It read, "We have a large stock of patent Roman, French and sateen corsets. Come and see our 65-cent corset, best value in the city for the money. Coulter Bros." Corsets were routinely made of linen, reinforced with either steel or whalebone. Whalebone was lighter in weight than steel and also afforded more flexibility. In the book, *Vintage Clothing, 1880-1960*, the question arose as to, "who suffered more from this fashion, the Wright Whale which almost became extinct or the woman who wore the corset."

Undergarments such as drawers were essentials to cover the "lower area" under a lady's dress. A drawstring was used at the top, which allowed for expansion. These long underpants were usually made out of cotton or muslin and often embellished with ribbons and lace trimmings. Mollie would have worn a lot of black, which was in fashion, along with the necessary gloves and hats. In 1880, Rice, Broaddus & Co. advertised "Black Dress Goods" as their specialty items that season including "black cashmeres, Henrietta cloth and Barite, which is the best black goods known."

Dresses were floor length and long sleeves were worn even on a hot summer day. No respectable woman would have allowed her arms or neck to be exposed during the day. Dresses made of lightweight material such as cotton were worn at home, although a lady might have to make several dress changes according to the activities of the day. However, the number of dresses owned by a lady of this time would probably be limited to four or five. The underskirt usually would be made of a less expensive material such as cotton since it would be the material coming in contact with the dusty or muddy streets and sidewalks.

For a special occasion such as a formal dinner or ball at the Tobacco Exchange or Washington Hotel, Mollie would change into a more elaborate dress. It was considered to be sociably correct in the evening for a lady to show her neck, arms and top of the bust. The materials used for these dresses were taffeta, or brocades, as silk was very difficult to come by and considered to be extremely expensive.

A lady's overskirt and skirt bottom might be pleated. The folds of the overskirt would cover the bottom edge of the bodice and the dress would be laced up the back with ribbons and secured with eyelets. No matter what a lady wore, she always had a cotton chemise under her dress. To be practical, and Victorian women were most definitely practical, this article of clothing would be white since repeated washings, often with bleach, made dying the material pointless.

"Ready-made" clothing was becoming more available in stores as they competed to offer the latest styles from New York or what was being seen in Paris. Clarksville storeowners made several trips a year to New York to purchase the newest trends. These buying trips were routinely announced in both city newspapers and the ladies of Clarksville waited in excited anticipation of the storeowners' return to make their purchases.

Samuel Hodgson's wife, Julia made yearly trips to New York to purchase goods for her store located on Franklin Street. On October 16, 1880 her newspaper ad stated

> **Mrs. Hodgson is again in the field with inexhaustible array of female paraphernalia, irresistible to the feminine fancy when spread on the counter and to the masculine heart when well-disposed for adorning the female of the species. Ladies visit her establishment and be ready for the gentlemen when they visit you.**

A shawl was an important accessory in the 1880s as it was one of the most feminine pieces in a lady's wardrobe. It could be draped and used to accent or enhance the appearance. At that time, the most popular pattern for shawls were those done in the beautiful swirled paisley. Some shawls had heavy fringes and bright colors which were not allowed on the dresses themselves, so in effect, they accomplished the same function as jewelry.

Bonnets and hats were essential and usually fashioned with ribbons to allow them to be tied under the chin, to secure them in case of a breeze or during a buggy ride. These were always worn during the day outside and varied according to the occasion. The adornment on hats included ribbons, feathers, bows and silk flowers. During the 1880s hats were worn on the crown of the head, not tipped towards the front as had been seen in the 1870s. This was to accommodate the changing hairstyles.

During the 1880s, makeup was considered to be improper. Rouge was definitely considered taboo at this time. Accordingly, women tended to look pale or lifeless, especially in photographs. Mollie was much too proper and practical a lady to even consider wearing makeup. Dress styles and parasols assured that a woman's skin would receive no tanning from the sun, thus adding to the light skin pallor. Parasols were large and domed shaped and to accommodate the bustle style dresses; some umbrellas were specially designed lopsided! The handles of the umbrellas were very decorative and the umbrella itself would have laced or frilled edging, often made with materials to match the dress. Similarly handbags were often made of material that matched the dress being worn and in the 1880s, clasps on bags began appearing. These were made of tortoiseshell or steel. Ladies' bags always contained handkerchiefs (unless she was Scarlet O'Hara). For day use, handkerchiefs were fashioned with colored borders or embroidered corners. Fans also re-emerged in popularity in the 1880s. Given his position in the town, it is very likely that Judge Tyler wore a wool suit, white shirt, tie and vest every day and would never be seen outside the house without a hat. Shirts had long tails since underwear was not usually worn and the wool in the trousers could cause discomfort. It was totally improper for a man to be seen in "bare shirtsleeves" by anyone other than his wife or close family.

Rice, Broaddus and Company store in Clarksville advertised "the best $1.00 shirt made in the United States." Creases were not used in the trousers. Suspenders were necessary because belts were not used and zippers, not yet invented, meant that pants featured button flies. Hats, which were made of beaver or silk, were essential items in a man's wardrobe. They would be black, tan, or gray. The vest or waistcoats as they were called, remained a staple of a man's wardrobe. Detachable white collars and cuffs became more affordable and since they were the only part of a shirt that really showed, they were keep in the best condition while the dirty shirt could wait until laundry day. The collars could be of two types: the stiff standing collar or the folding kind. These were purchased as a separate item from the shirts themselves. Bowties were of the "four in hand," ascot, the English square, silk puff and silk imperial type. They were popular due to their availability in abundant designs and patterns, as were "teck" ties, with their convenient pre-tied straps. The long sack coat was falling out of fashion during this time. The new style included shorter, more narrowly fitted coats designed to close high on the neck, almost to the point of covering the tie. A vest was always worn with the suit where the gentlemen's pocket watch was tucked away.

A man in the 1880s would also accessorize by using fobs and canes. From the will of Judge Tyler's daughter Em, we know that he owned a gold-handled cane. From entries in the *Virginia Will Books*, it is known that Charles' grandfather, Richard Keeling Tyler, inherited a silver watch from an aunt that he brought with him over the mountains into Tennessee.

Men wore their hair short with no side burns. Judge Tyler sported a well-manicured mustache, which was in favor in the 1880s and he kept a full head of hair until the day of his death. Once Charles wrote a description of a typical Virginia gentleman. He could have just as well been describing himself when he stated, "hospitable to a fault, full of self-assertion, polite at all times to high and low."

The late, retired high school teacher, Marie Riggins remembered Judge Tyler from her youth when her father, Wesley Warner Riggins, was a magistrate. In fact, she remembered that as a young girl, she had even sat in Judge Tyler's lap! She said, "my impression of Judge Tyler was that he was a well-educated person for that time." She continued by saying, "There were some things that he was very courteous about, very polite."

W.W. Riggins

With a twinkle in her eye she also related that, "I think he and my father kind of enjoyed some interesting arguments, but they were polite, oh they had to be polite! When Judge Tyler talked about things, he had a way of his eyes sort of snapping. Some people may not have liked Judge Tyler, but they always respected him!"[75] When others described Judge Tyler, these words were written: "simple in his tastes and democratic in his whole life. He knew no class-mankind was a brotherhood to him. He was a generous man, but never let his left hand know what he gave with his right."

It was business as usual. After a jailbreak in January of 1879, prisoners were confined to the jail "dungeon" whose floors were made of heavy oak logs covered with two-inch thick planks. But on March 14, 1879, prisoners again tried to make their way out of the old calaboose by a very unique method. Using the matches (what a brilliant idea to give prisoners matches!) given the

[75] One such clashing of opinions between Riggins and Tyler was the argument over highway bonds in July of 1917.

prisoners with which to light their pipes, the convicts burned the logs a little bit at a time. They were able to conceal their work by not producing too much smoke at a time. After spending three weeks on their project and burning an opening almost large enough to squeeze through, the men were caught.

Problems arose requiring Judge Tyler's attention such as difficulties involving the L & N Railroad. Former Clarksville Mayor Joshua Cobb, for whom the elementary school on Franklin Street was later named, died Monday, April 7, 1879 a few minutes after 12:00 noon while forcibly stating his case on the matter of the railroad in front of Judge Tyler at the temporary courthouse on the corner of Commerce and Second Streets. Cobb unfortunately would not be alive to witness one of the county's most historic events to date.

Joshua Cobb. From Titus' *Picturesque Clarksville.*

At the time, Cobb was serving the county as a magistrate. Both Tyler and Cobb were strong-minded personalities and for various reasons, did not get along. Cobb argued that Tyler had overstepped his authority by agreeing to a compromise with the L & N Railroad without consulting the magistrates. The next day's newspaper, instead of an article detailing the meeting, sadly printed a eulogy for Cobb. The newspaper obviously did not know that Cobb's wife, Marina was a distant relative of the judge.

Without a doubt, the crowning architectural achievement of Clarksville is the courthouse. It was said to have been the "handsomest in the state and one of the handsomest in the South." The ceremony to place the cornerstone for the new courthouse was held on Friday, May 16, 1879. Billed as Clarksville's most historic event, citizens were encouraged to participate and celebrate the occasion. Owners of all public buildings and private residences were asked to decorate to the fullest and members of secret societies, benevolent societies and organizations of all types were asked to be a part of the celebration. During the ceremony, Judge Tyler placed numerous items within a tin box to be inserted within the corner stone. What irony that the tin box used for the cornerstone was purchased from the very same store in which the great fire began: Kincannon, Wood, & Company! The box cost all of one dollar and was to prove a poor choice later when, under the circumstances of another disaster years later, it was removed in a disintegrated state from the cornerstone.

On a pleasant day in May of 1879 the residents between Second and Madison Streets and the Red River Bridge apparently let their mules out to graze. The mules instead decided to roam the public streets and earlier in the month, one man claimed a "gang" of fifteen mules accosted him while driving home from church by horse and carriage.

On June 18, 1879, at 11:00 p.m., jailer George Harris, once again caught prisoners in the act of trying to escape. At the time of the discovery, a large plank from the floor had been torn up. The prisoners managed to dig a hole beneath the rotting logs under the plank floor. Harris called in the police and directed that they be "ironed" to prevent further attempts. These incidences underscored the immediate need for a new Clarksville calaboose.

The newspaper announced in June 1879 that Judge Tyler had devised a new plan to summon jurors for his Criminal Court. The juries would be selected from the various civil districts of Montgomery County. An officer of the court would simply travel to the different districts to hand out the summons for the jury selection. This would give residents time to rearrange their schedules in order to be available for their court date. Also they knew that once they had served that term, they would not be asked again for the same term. This was to stop any confusion about when each person was to report for duty and, according to the paper, "those who have not been summoned as jurors, but put off their intended trips to town on business because they fear they may be snatched up and put into the jury box, may now come with impunity. So come along and attend to your business here-you will not be molested." This referred to Tyler's previous method of standing on the courthouse steps and when spotting someone to serve, he yelled at them to come on to the courthouse, no if, ands or buts. So the men kept a wide berth of the courthouse on court days. Tyler described what he believed to be ideal characteristics of a juror:

> **In Tennessee to be a competent juror, one's mind at the outset of the investigation must be like a sheet of blank paper, upon which lawyers, witnesses and the court will inscribe matter for subsequent consideration. The best juror in the world, one would think, would be an intelligent, fair-minded man who had formed perhaps an offhand opinion from newspaper reading and promiscuous talk, but who stood ready to discard such opinion and give the accused a fair hearing on the law and evidence.**

The Clarksville (later Bailey Cobb) Elementary School for blacks was completed in 1879. Prior to this site being used for a school, it was the cemetery for the Trinity Episcopal Church. The four-acre lot between Franklin and Main Streets, opposite Tenth Street, was purchased from John Poston in 1840. It served as the church cemetery until the 1870s when it became evident that future expansion was impossible. During the Civil War, headstones and monuments had been destroyed or defaced and the fencing around the cemetery torn down. Since every burial lot had been purchased, no further income to support the upkeep of the cemetery would be forthcoming. The church leaders decided to remove the bodies to the new Greenwood Cemetery or the City Cemetery where the graves would be better maintained. The land, which was the cemetery lot, was deeded to fellow church member, George Edward Cooke, as compensation for the removal of the headstones and bodies.

George E. Cooke

Not forgetting the black population, on June 6, 1879, Judge Tyler asked that a committee be appointed by the County Court to buy land for a black graveyard within the city. Also that year, while passing under the Madison Street bridge, a train ignited the wooden supports. The bridge caught fire but, due to its early detection and subsequent extinguishing, there was very little damage. However, while inspecting the burn damage, authorities found the wooden supports to be in a rotted state. The fire was a blessing in disguise since it alerted citizens to the poor condition of the bridge. Repairs were done and saved possible injury or death from the bridge collapsing. For a couple of days, Judge Tyler would have had to find some other way to get home.

It was reported that engineer Jack McNeil kept the fire engine as "bright and shining as a silver dollar, with plenty of fuel on hand" and that he slept in the engine house every night, although he was not duty-bound to do so. No doubt Mr. McNeil never wanted to find himself facing another horrible episode as the one that occurred in 1878.

Interesting Note: The great fire of 1878 that began in the back of David Kincannon's store perhaps inspired him to become the Chief of the Fire Department!

David Kincannon

Chapter Ten: Their Dark Days

Statistics show that Clarksville's 1880 population was as follows: white, 14,786; black, 13,694; Indian, 1; males, 14,103; females, 14,378; over twenty-one years of age, 6,386. Clarksville's real estate was assessed as $3,997,880 and personal property, $522,745. The monies collected from taxation were as follows: state tax, $13,050; county, $35,652; and city, $20,006.

The New Year, which also happened to be a Leap Year, was celebrated by yet unmarried revelers at a grand ball at G.A. Henry's house on January 8, 1880. This event was fashioned after a party given by Andrew Jackson many years ago when the "usual orders of things are reversed and woman comes to the front, makes terms to the boys which they are bound to accept and foots the bills." The celebration began at 9 p.m. in the parlors of the house where splendor and fashion were on display. Ladies from Memphis and Nashville, adjoining states and counties were there with their chosen ones. Dancing commenced until 1 a.m. when supper was served on a table filled with delicious offerings. One hour later, the dancing resumed until nearly morning. The couples included among the many were

Mr. Lelia Robb and Miss Jake Rudolph Note the "reversal"
Mr. Minnie Robb and Miss Richard Lockert
Mr. Bettie Garland and Miss C.D. Bailey
Mr. Emmie Tyler and Miss Charlie Cooke
Mr. May Byers and Miss G.N. Byers
The chaperones were Elizabeth Forbes, Mrs. Mollie Tyler, Mrs. Tom Henry, Mrs. Byers, Mrs. Bettie Drane, Mrs. Drane, Mrs. Charles W. Beaumont, and others.

The streets of the 1880 Clarksville era were, of course, unpaved and consisted of dirt lanes since it would be years before the first automobiles would make their appearance, but there were sidewalks extending all over town. Dust was still an issue and so later an official street sprinkler was hired. Where streets intersected, stepping stones, projecting several inches above the surface of the crushed stones, were placed to prevent pedestrians, especially women from stepping in mud and mire in the winter while crossing the streets.

In early May, Mollie was to lose her father William B. Settle. Mr. Settle had been in the grocery business with James D. Carr. He was initially buried at the Trinity Cemetery on Franklin Street but was moved to Riverview at the closing of the church cemetery. Three months after William Settle's death, Charles took Mollie and her sister Beulah, along with his sister Emmie, to Niagara Falls and the Great Lakes for a rare vacation. They also visited relatives who lived in New York. At this time Charles and Mollie would have been expecting their first child… Nannie.

Clarksville's "country friends" were asked via the local newspaper, not to hitch their horses/wagons to city trees. A new ordinance in 1880, approved by the mayor and city council, was meant to encourage and protect the planting of shade trees along the streets. The trees provided respite from hot, sunny days as folks were accustomed to in the South. However, it was mentioned that violation of the ordinance was a fineable offense, the police would enforce it, and the country people should support it.

The Montgomery County Courthouse Commission on May 15, agreed that the new bell for the courthouse be engraved with an inscription reading, "Let my tones ever sound above justice, mercy and brotherly love." The commission consisted of Tyler, chairman, C.G. Smith, treasurer; G.H. Slaughter, secretary; Griffin Organ and W.S. Mallory.

The 1880 Census of Montgomery County lists the household of Judge Tyler as follows:

C.W. Tyler	**age 39**
Mollie Tyler (wife)	**age 31**
Emmie Tyler (sister)	**age 28**

Tyler Bryan (boarder, bank clerk) **age 22**

Tyler Bryan was born in 1858 and was Charles W. Tyler's half-sister Mary's son. Judge Tyler and his half-nephew were close and Charles probably regarded Tyler as more of a son.

After the great fire and its busy aftermath, everyone needed a good laugh and one has to believe the judge took part in the enjoyment of reading the latest news. Just two days before Independence Day in 1880, the *Clarksville Semi-Weekly Tobacco Leaf* was proud to announce a new song available for sale in Clarksville entitled: "Squeeze Me 'Till My Corset Cracks."

Tyler's request for a black cemetery was realized. The Olive Hill, later Mt. Olive Cemetery was dedicated on July 3. The cemetery is located between Cumberland Drive and Rollins Road. The day included a barbeque and speeches by Rev. C.O.H. Thomas and Elder D. Jones

The summer of 1880 was getting hot, but it had nothing whatsoever to do with the weather. The common practice of carrying concealed weapons with the addition of a drink or two...or three was culminating in a cutting or shooting affray every week. Men "armed to the teeth" often came into town to wet their whistles but afterwards felt the need to assault someone with either their gun or knife. On July 7, some men got into a row on Franklin Street and threatened the lives of bystanders on that crowded street when shots were fired. Yet another altercation occurred between George Washington (yes, that was his name), Press Ellison and Charlie Martin. Washington, forgetting the story of the real first President and his little hatchet, "used his knife rather extensively" on the two men on a Saturday night that summer. This got him hauled off to jail immediately to await trial. But the public had enough. Citizens rallied to condemn the practice of carrying guns and ask that lawmakers do their part to bring such offenders to justice. Judge Tyler himself, made a practice of having all men unload their weapons into a basket by the door before entering his courtroom. Stories abound however, that he kept one for himself in the top drawer of his judge's bench for restoring order if need be.

The criminal courtroom. (MCA)

On August 13, the *Tobacco Leaf* advertised the opening of the fall term of Clarksville High School, located then on Main Street. The high school was open to both males and females with D.M. Quarles (formally of Hickory Wild) acting as principal and Mrs. L.M. Humphries and Professor H.J. Fusch serving as assistant principals. It stated that Prof. Fusch would teach mathematics and modern languages and that the principal himself would teach:

> **Greek, Latin, English language, and Literature. The course will embrace Latin, Greek, German, French, Spanish, Mathematics, the sciences and especially the English language, literature and History. Music will be taught by the best teachers. Painting and drawing also, should a class be formed large enough to justify it. Fees-for five months' term $25, $20, and $15, according to grade of scholar. *No Contingent Fee.* No extra fees except for Music or in the Art Department. Ample arrangements for boarders at moderate rates. The Fall Term will begin September 1, 1881.**

In mid-August there were complaints in South Clarksville of nightly episodes of pistol firing, yelling and "hideous noises" all disturbing the good citizens of the area. Just a few days later there occurred an altercation on Franklin Street between William A. Forbes, son of Col. W.A. Forbes and G.N. Byers. Words were passed and Forbes, known to be quick-tempered, pulled put his pistol. Byers tried to yank the gun from Forbes' hand, causing it to discharge, striking Forbes in the hand and himself in the arm. Once tempers cooled, both parties seemed truly sorry things had progressed to violence. This shooting was of course used as the perfect example by the newspaper of why concealed weapons should be outlawed.

Judge Tyler remained a popular choice as a guest speaker and honored many such engagements. On October 27, he spoke at Vernon Furnace. The newspaper declined to ask people to attend because, "Judge Tyler is so well known in this county and has opinions so well respected," there was no need. The article added that "he always speaks to the point." This area as well was so familiar to him during his time with Forrest, in and around the iron furnaces in southern Montgomery County and northern Dickson County. What memories must have been stirred when he returned.

The friendly and sometimes quite amusing competition between the city's newspapers was evidenced in November during the time of the courthouse's rebuilding. In one article, the *Semi-Weekly* stated that the measurement of the courthouse eagle was 12 feet from tip to tip and the ball upon which it was to stand at 8 foot. The *Weekly Chronicle*, responded by saying their measurement was "magnificent" and that the eagle was actually just 5 feet, 6 inches and the ball, 1 foot, 6 inches. Not to be outdone, the *Semi-Weekly* came back with the assertion that they stood by their measurements and that "if the *Chronicle* man don't (sic) believe it, he can just crawl up to the top of the cupola and take the exact measurement."

The iron work needed to finish the cupola of the courthouse had finally arrived and at the same time during the last week in November, so had the "heating apparatus." Workmen were busy plastering the walls and completing the install of the staircases. As the flooring was being laid everyone hoped the completion would be soon.

The Tylers excitedly anticipated the arrival of their first child. Unfortunately, Mollie's pregnancy was not peaceful at all but several tense, traumatizing events occurred while she was expecting Nannie.

John Tyler Bryan came to Clarksville from New Orleans to care for his mother following his father's death in 1878. Bryan had been a successful businessman in Clarksville, at one time, serving as a bank bookkeeper in town. After leaving his job at the bank, he became a traveling salesman for Middleton, Barrett & Bourne, a clothing store in Louisville, Kentucky. The unimaginable occurred when Charles Tyler's half-niece, John Duke Tyler Bryan's sister, was sexually assaulted by Robert West Beaumont (1863-1925),[76] the grandson of Rev. Henry S. Beaumont and the son of Dr. Charles W. Beaumont and Sarah West Beaumont. West Beaumont was an agent for J. Winter & Co. in Louisville. Knowing how this act by his grandson would have devastated the preacher/tobacconist, it was fortunate that Rev. Beaumont had passed so many years before.

On the left: Rev. Henry F. Beaumont and on the right: his son, Dr. C.W. Beaumont.

On Wednesday, November 3, Beaumont had gone to the passenger depot off Madison Street to take the train back to Louisville and Bryan having heard of his intention arrived at the depot before Beaumont. Bryan, the outraged brother, confronted Beaumont at 4 p.m. armed and ready to defend his sister's honor. As soon as Bryan spotted Beaumont, he shot his pistol but missed Beaumont. Beaumont returned fire, first striking Bryan in the scalp.[77] Bryan fired twice more, missing Beaumont but Beaumont's final shot struck Bryan just below his right eye and lodged in his neck.

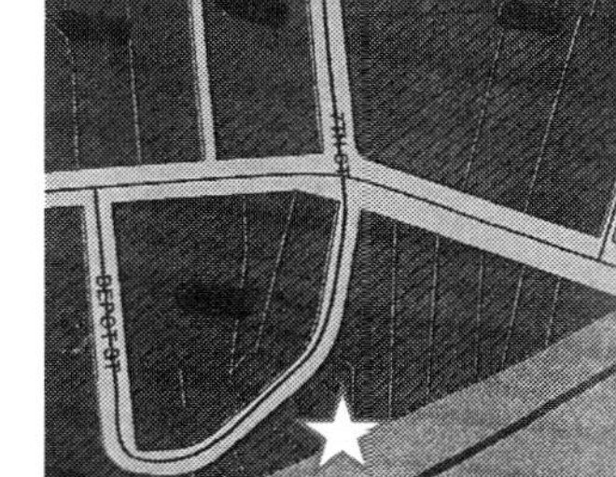

The location of the train depot shooting.

[76] He died on March 1, 1925, in Waxahachie, Texas at the age of 71, and was buried there.

[77] It was common for men to carry guns even this long after the Civil War but also Beaumont carried because months prior to the fatal shooting, Bryan had shot West Beaumont in the leg. Apparently there was already serious trouble between the two men before the assault of Bryan's sister.

Beaumont gave himself up to the police and placed in jail with a one-thousand-dollar bond. He was able to give the bond and later came before a magistrate and was acquitted on self-defense. Bryan was carried to his uncle Charles' house on Greenwood. The *Tennessean* mistakenly stated that "Bryan's wounds were at first considered dangerous but he is doing very well and at the present writing will no doubt recover." By Friday, young Bryan was experiencing violent delirium until nearly 4:30 a.m. Saturday morning. He lingered just two and a half hours more before succumbing to the injury. Imagine the Tylers' horror at this incident and the disturbance it caused in their household! At this time Mollie was 5 months into her first pregnancy with Nannie. Judge Tyler was, of course, much attached to this relative who had stayed with him and his family while working in Clarksville. The *Clarksville Weekly Chronicle* as described young Bryan as:

> **a youth of gentle and amiable disposition, very popular with his friends, and by nature adverse from such deeds as that into which he was impelled by (as we see it) a mistaken sense of honor. If he was in error, he atoned for it by his death.**

The newspaper stated that Bryan was buried at Greenwood Cemetery on November 7, with Father Fitts conducting the service. The memorial printed in the November 13 issue of the paper alluded to "The Legion of Honor" marked on his cross. This is a mystery as Greenwood shows no record of him being interred there! [78]

Killebrew recorded the confrontation between Judge Tyler and Dr. Beaumont,

> **One of Beaumont's sons killed a young Bryan, the brother of the scandalized girl. Then Tyler, smarting under the double grievance, in a drunken spree shot at Dr. Beaumont in the night while he was standing in his own door. Tyler at the time was not only the judge of the County Court but was the criminal judge likewise. He was never brought to trial because he would not exchange circuits with any other criminal judge. He is a man of weight, unquestioned ability and takes responsibility without fear of consequences. He has great sustained energy and is rarely defeated in questions in which the county is interested.**

The Beaumont house on the corner of Second Street and Munford Avenue where Tyler took a shot at Dr. Charles W. Beaumont. (MCA)

The facts are these: Just the night before the shooting, at around 11:00 p.m., West's father, Dr. Charles W. Beaumont was fired upon three times while standing on the front porch of his residence near Munford Avenue at 422 South Second Street.[79] Beaumont stated he had intended to go to the post office on the Public Square when he was fired upon. The shot, he thought, came from the alley between his and Mrs. Munford's house.

Searching for the person responsible, a second shot rang out and then he heard someone yell, "God d___ you, come out here," to which he responded, "wait a minute and I will come out" as he turned to unlock his door to get his pistol. At that moment a third shot was fired, coming from the corner of Second Street and the alley. Beaumont had second thoughts of confronting his intended assailant because of possibly endangering his family. At the time he claimed he was not sure who his would-be assailant was. Of course he knew it was Judge Tyler and why he came to his house. Tyler would later be charged with attempted murder. Was Tyler drunk at the time? It was possible for two reasons: a seasoned war veteran would not have missed a shot at that short distance. Also he may have been drunk enough to forget his strong opposition to vigilante justice. If Tyler really wanted to kill Charles Beaumont, he would have gone to his house sober. To judge

---

[78] On Saturday, March 11, 1881 in the *Clarksville Weekly Chronicle*, Polk G. Johnson posted a note of recognition of the payment of a life insurance policy on the life of Tyler Bryan in the amount of $1000. Johnson who was acting as the administrax of Tyler Bryan, acknowledged the quick payment by the Mutual Benefit Life Insurance Company of New Jersey.

[79] In the last week of October 1885 C.W. Beaumont sold this house to Dr. and Mrs. Jessie R. Wilson for $5,000, stating the house was too large for his family of three. Dr. Wilson was the professor of Theology at Southwestern Presbyterian College. Their son, President Woodrow Wilson never lived in this house, however, he did make the trip to Clarksville in 1888 after the death of his mother.

him may not be appropriate here: these were different times and a matter of such a serious nature still was handled by family members and usually condoned by the public.

Rumors were flying that because of the shooting, Beaumont would move out-of-town but he and his wife stayed however, West moved to St. Louis. Dr. Beaumont died in 1902 in Franklin, Tennessee of heart failure and was buried at Greenwood. It appears that West did not come home for the funeral.

Although not connected to this situation, another tragedy occurred involving an older brother of West Beaumont twenty-two years later in Nashville on July 19, 1902. In a bizarre suicidal plan, Henry F. Beaumont approached a policeman with a butcher knife, forcing the policeman to shoot him twice. Before dying Henry admitted to some "unforgivable sin that he had committed." Whatever sin he felt he had committed, it certainly weighed upon his mind that his grandfather, Henry Beaumont, for whom he was named, was a preacher. Family members were to publicly state that the oppressive summer heat caused his bizarre behavior prior to his death. Henry also left suicide notes exonerating the policemen, saying that he wanted to die but had not wanted to kill himself. He left behind a wife in ill health and four children. Beaumont formally lived and was educated in Montgomery County and was at the time of his death, a traveling salesman for Nashville Tobacco Works. He was buried at Mt. Olivet Cemetery in Nashville.

A cry for a new jail was heard once more around town in early February. The new courthouse on Franklin Street was nearing its completion and it was suggested by the press that it would be proper and timely to build a new jail closer to the courthouse.

In what could be termed Judge Tyler's most challenging professional episode to date came in mid-March. Rufus Napoleon Rhodes, a representative in the Tennessee House of Legislatures, introduced a bill that called for the Criminal Court and County Judgeship to be abolished and brought a petition signed by 864 citizens from all backgrounds including lawyers, bankers, farmers and merchants. He filed six charges of articles of impeachment against Judge Tyler. Of course there was stiff opposition to the bill from Tyler's supporters in Clarksville. It was claimed that the magistrates who opposed the bill were paid between $50-$150 by Tyler. Rhodes charged Tyler with high crimes and misdemeanors to include:

First: drunkenness
Second: drunkenness in office, materially interfering with an intelligent discharge of official duty
Third: misapplication of the county money
Fourth: misappropriation to self of the county money
Fifth: neglect of official duty
Sixth: an attempt to commit an assassination in the nighttime by lying in wait and shooting at a citizen (C.W. Beaumont) in his own house.

"We respectively pray your honorable body to take such steps as may satisfy you of the probable truth of the charges to the end that order may be taken for his due impeachment as provided by the Constitution and Laws of the State." On March 17, Alex Bagwell, state representative from Montgomery County, read the following letter from Judge Tyler:

> **Dr. Sir:**
>
> **On yesterday, as I am informed, Representative Rhodes introduced into the House of which you are a member, a resolution which provides for the appointment of a committee to investigate charges then and there made, with a view to my impeachment. Will you do me the kindness to call up the resolution at your earliest opportunity, and ask that the same be adopted and the committee be appointed charged with the full investigation of said charges? By so doing you will greatly oblige.**
>
> **Yours Respectfully,**
> **Charles W. Tyler**

The rules were then suspended and the resolution was adopted and the letter of Judge Tyler was ordered to be included in the minutes of the meeting.

Rhodes (1856-1910), was born in Mississippi but later moved to Clarksville His mother taught school from their home on Main Street. This young politician was described by Nannie Haskins as "tremendously magnetic and popular." Later in his life it is said that he amassed a considerable fortune. He married the daughter of wealthy tobacconist, Christopher, "Kit" Smith" and Lucy Smith who lived in their antebellum mansion on the east bank of the Cumberland River.[80]

Interestingly, the name at the top of the list of 16 complainants was that of Charles W. Beaumont. Along with Beaumont were the following names: John S. Neblett, Sterling Beaumont, (C.W. Beaumont's brother), Henry Frech, John J. West (C.W. Beaumont's brother-in-law for whom John Wes t Beaumont was named and who was acting as the Public Administrator for Montgomery County), Archer Howell, R. Tompkins, William H. Crouch, Henry C. Merritt, J.J. Crusman, Gilbert Bailey Wilson, David Kincannon, Thomas L. Yancey, (who ran unsuccessfully against Tyler in a very emotional and heated election for the judgeship in the 1878), Bailey W. Macrae, F.G. Irwin and R.H. Williams.

R.N. Rhodes, the man who tried unsuccessfully to bring Tyler down.

The date these charges were filed was March 16, 1881...the day of Nannie's birth. During this difficult episode, Charles' older brother, Dr. John Duke Tyler attended to Mollie.

On March 23, the investigation against Tyler by a committee appointed by the House of Representatives began in Nashville. The hearings were held in the law office of H.H. Harrison on Cedar Street. It came as no surprise that T.L. Yancey served as the attorney for the prosecution. He presented the charges of:

NEGLECT OF DUTY

1. Tyler demanded and received of Robert D. Moseley, County Trustee, the railroad tax, instead of having it paid into the First National Bank as required by law. See Acts of 1850-60, p. 306 and acts of 1865-66, page 213.

2. He refused to give County Trustee a warrant requiring him to pay said fund into said bank but required that it should be paid to him.

3. When Neblett paid said fund into said bank, Tyler endeavored to use and pay the same to other purpose than the railroad debt of the county, willfully and knowingly in violation of the law.

4. That Tyler has permitted interest on the county bonds to go unpaid although there has been sufficient money in said bank to pay the whole of the accrued interest, he having refused to issue warrants for that purpose as the law required.

5. That said Tyler has habitually and willfully failed and refused to hold the County Court and perform his duty as judge thereof to the injury of those having business in said court.

6. That he unlawfully took and received from Peter O'Neal, Clerk of the County Court of Montgomery County about $1,000 annually for four years being the county's revenue proper and he unlawfully attempted to get the county revenue collected by the present clerk into his hand.

7. That said Tyler unlawfully demanded and received from R.D. Moseley the present clerk of said County Court about $4,000.

SPECIFICATIONS OF MISAPPROPRIATIONS MADE WITHIN FIVE YEARS BY C.W. TYLER AS COUNTY JUDGE:

1. That C.W. Tyler being a judge could not have or take any fee or prerequisites or moneys except his salary and that he appropriated to himself three percent of all railroad moneys that have come into his hands wrongfully and without authority of law, yearly from $600 to $1500.

2. That said Tyler assuming to be above law willfully and knowingly paid R.D. Moseley, Trustee $3000 out of the county treasury without authority of law and without appropriation by the Quarterly Court.

3. That he paid I.S. Neblett $1500 out of the county treasury in 1878 in violation of law and without appropriation by the Quarterly Court.

4. That he has for two years paid R.H. Burney, Attorney General of the State for Montgomery County $600 per annum out of the county treasury without authority and in violation of the law and public policy of the state.

5. That he has paid and presented Ed C. Campbell $50 out of the county treasury without authority of law or conscience.

[80] The house is known as the Smith-Trahern mansion.

6. That he unlawfully presented and paid to L.G. Munford $200 out of the county treasury.
7. That said Tyler without authority of law or appropriation of the Quarterly Court paid to Griffin Organ $175 out of said county treasury.
8. That he paid J.M. Anderson out of said treasury without authority of law and without appropriation of said Quarterly Court.
9. That he paid Jesse Bryan[81] $200 out of said treasury without appropriation.
10. That he unlawfully paid J.D. Bailey $600 out of said treasury without appropriation and other moneys wrongfully out of the courthouse fund.
**Judge Tyler himself participated in the questioning of the witnesses! Imagine how intimidating it would be to these accusers to be face-to-face with Tyler, the man they sought to remove from office.

There was an immediate reaction from Judge Tyler's friends concerning the charges and his supporters back in Clarksville were appalled at what they perceived as an attack by the *Nashville Banner* on Judge Tyler's character. This paper was covering the trial daily and reporting the story to the *Clarksville Tobacco Leaf*. Tyler's friends claimed that the charges were "trumped up for the purpose of influencing legislative action" upon the bill proposed by Rhodes to abolish his court. These supporters called for a committee to investigate the matter and added that "the Judge is willing and more than willing to meet his accusers face to face at any time."

During the actual investigation, Judge Tyler stayed at the Maxwell House in Nashville, the same hotel where he and Mollie had spent their honeymoon.

Nashville Tennessee Maxwell House Hotel. Circa: 1890-1910. Located on the northeast corner of Fourth Avenue North and Church Street. The hotel operated from 1869 until 1961 when it burned on Christmas night. Photo Courtesy Metropolitan Government Archives of Nashville and Davidson County

There he prepared his defense with his legal advisors. The actual examination of the charges lasted from March 21 to the 25 with Judge W.A. Milliken acting as Tyler's defense lawyer. After examining evidence and hearing from witnesses, the five-member committee appointed to investigate the charges against Judge Tyler unanimously decided that no such case against him warranted the articles of impeachment. The chairman of the committee, W.C. Houston stated:

> **Upon the whole case made by the prosecution the committee is unanimously of the opinion and instructs me to report, that no such case has been made against Judge Tyler as warrants the bringing of articles of impeachment against him and the committee asked to be discharged from further consideration of the matter.**

The committee then presented their bill of expenses for the investigation:

Expenses of witnesses: $159.50
Expenses of reporters: $16.40
Mileage: $12.40

As for the attempted murder charge- given the circumstances, the charge was quietly dropped. One can guess the reaction to the decision on both sides. Tyler's opponents failed in their attempt to charge a man with corruption who was innately opposed to corruption. One has only to remember how he was raised and who his father was to recall that "black gumology" was dispensed to anyone who proved to be dishonest. That policy was most certainly used on John Duke's children as well as his students. Charles was exonerated and able to enjoy with his wife the welcome addition of a beautiful daughter into their lives.

[81] Tyler's other half-nephew and brother to Tyler Bryan.

Chapter Eleven: Nannie's Hometown and the World in Which She Lived

Around the time of Nannie's birth, the Russian composer Tchaikovsky was becoming an international phenomenon. He had already composed his "Romeo and Juliet" Fantasy Overture and his best known opera "Eugene Onegin," as well as his Piano Concerto #1 and #2. As music was such an integral a part of the Tyler and Settle families, one has to believe that music in Nannie's life was equally important. As music was such an integral a part of the Tyler and Settle families, one has to believe that music in Nannie's life was equally important. The Tylers owned a piano even though such a purchase would definitely be considered a luxury, but appreciated and well-used.

Nationally, the Statue of Liberty was nearing its completion in New York City Harbor; Sitting Bull surrendered at Ft. Buford on July 18, 1881; the Buffalo Bill Wild West Show opened its first performance on July 4, 1883 as it began touring. Helen Keller was born in 1880 and in just two years would lose her sight to scarlet fever. The Brooklyn Bridge, the longest suspension bridge in the world was completed in 1883. By 1884 some 50,000 Americans owned a bicycle. Many parlors around the country bragged of a new invention called the stereoscope and William H. Vanderbilt was making his millions building railroads.

In 1880, the U.S. could boast of 50 million people, most of whom still lived in small towns or on farms. Urbanization was becoming part of the American way of life. Larger towns struggled with labor problems. American newspapers began advertising articles for sale such as clothes, furniture and food. Over 789,000 immigrants had come from Europe to America by 1882, most by way of the faster and more comfortable steamships. A new enterprise, Dow, Jones & Company, the financial news service was established in 1882. In 1883, with the passage of the Pendleton Act, came the Civil Service Commission.

President James A. Garfield was sworn into office in 1881 and died six months later from an assassin's bullet. Famous bandleader John Philip Souza wrote the inaugural march for Garfield and then was asked to write his funeral march. Nannie's parents had now lived through the assassination of two American presidents. Her father was to live through one more after Nannie's death.

The world of medicine was experiencing exciting advancements. Beyond just checking the eyes, ears, mouth and throats, doctors were delving into new realms of treatments. By 1880, there were 100 medical schools in the nation. The training of doctors became more structured since beforehand numerous doctors had no formal schooling or training at all!

There was more emphasis on scientific inquiry, which meant that doctors did not simply treat the various illnesses, but actually began to investigate the causes behind them. Doctors became respected once again after an extended period in which they were viewed as much of a threat to the patient as the actual disease itself. A popular verse exemplifies this: "Cholera may come now and then, but doctors are always with us."

The local newspapers were full of advertisements of cures for "women's problems," kidney ailments, "torpid livers," poor blood and every ache and pain imaginable. One such product called Ragland's Lightning Relief claimed to stop pain. Tutt's Pills for practically all adverse medical conditions claimed to be "the greatest medical triumph of the age!" But in the 1880s, aspirin was not available yet.

The *Weekly Chronicle* newspaper ran an article in the November 6, 1880 issue, entitled, "Treatment for Diphtheria." In the article, a doctor named J.J. Brown claimed to have a treatment for diphtheria and staked his reputation of thirty years on it. The remedy described is indicative of the lack of the understanding of bacteriology of that day and time. It prescribed the use of:

> **a formula of extracts of verat, viride, aconite and gelsemin; charcoal and sulfur; oil of glycerin (sic), and turpentine to remove the charcoal and sulphur; guinine. Local application-warm salt water locally applied to the throat, with flannel. Gargle with salt, vinegar or with a spray. Keep the room light and temperature not above 70 degrees. Treat early and keep the child from all excitement and company; patient must be continually in bed, and continue there several days after apparently well.**

Just four years before Nannie was born, a German scientist Robert Koch proved that bacteria actually caused some diseases. Anthrax and later, cholera were such examples. This was the beginning of an entire new field of science, one that was to totally affect surgical methods and initiate what we now know to be antiseptic medicine.

Finally, medical doctors began accepting science-based techniques and so required the latest equipment and drugs. A 1880s doctor's bag may have contained salicylic acid (later to become the main ingredient in aspirin) for the reduction of fever, opium, digitalis, mercury, sulphur pills and quinine. Doctors might also have carried a stethoscope and an ophthalmoscope. Increasingly, doctors used the measurements of pulse, temperature and blood pressure to diagnose illnesses.

In the years following the Civil War, the first drug addiction epidemic in the United States occurred. A generation of veterans became addicted to morphine, once called G.O.M. or "God's Own Medicine" during and after the war. With the advent of the syringe in the late 1860s, morphine could be injected directly into the bloodstream to hasten the relief of pain. Taking morphine by mouth could take upwards of twenty minutes before taking affect. Feelings of ecstasy would be replaced with deep depression and a craving for more morphine. Laudanum, a derivative of morphine, in the 1880s was cheaper than beer. This drug was so powerful the dosage was dispensed by drops.

Advertised cure-all's, elixirs and tonics often contained a large percentage of morphine. In addition to war veterans, women and children became addicted after taking these products. At the end of the day, mothers would give a dose to their babies to help them sleep and then would dispense some for themselves for the same reason. Since drugs were not regulated at this time and because there were no so called "illegal drugs," morphine and the syringes could be purchased through mail order catalogs. The little brown package delivered by mail during the post-Civil War years contained what we recognize today as highly illegal drugs and drug paraphernalia. Years later when the federal government required labeling the ingredients on food and drug products, many of these "medicines" disappeared from the market.

Clarksville doctors were always looking to purchase the best medicines for their patients. In October 1845, druggist Townsend A. Thomas sent in an ad to the newspaper in which he promised to furnish local physicians with "genuine medicines" which would be prepared carefully and with dispatch. The ad also promised that the store could fix a medicine chest for steamboats, hotels and planters "put up at short notice." He also included the fact that his establishment had "leeches on hand." Surely he caught the pun later! It gets worse. Immediately below this ad was yet another in which he states," If you have a taste for a tip top article of the weed, call at the drugstore of T.A. Thomas."[82] *Note: the weed he was talking about is of course, not the "weed" of today.

Dental care meant using toothpaste made with soap, baking soda, charcoal, cleansers or even chalk. Nitrous oxide, "laughing gas" and ether were introduced by Horace Wells and W.T.G. Morton in the 1840s as the first anesthetic for tooth extractions. A Clarksville dentist in 1878 advertised ether for dental extractions. An advertised product that did not stay on the market long was that of a teething aid called Teethina. This 1880 medication was supposedly able to "make teething easier, regulate the bowels, remove and prevent worms and cure 'cruptions' and sores. It also stated that, "thousands of children may be saved every year by using these powders." It is hard to imagine that people believed these outrageous advertisements.

---

[82] In 1847, T.A. partnered with his brother E.R.W. Thomas and established the drug firm of Thomas Bros. located first on the corner of Strawberry Alley and the Public Square. The store was later located in the Elder Block.

Before meat was federally inspected, tapeworms were a danger. The common remedy for a person with this parasite was to have the person abstain from eating or drinking for several days. Afterwards, a cup of warm milk was held under the nose and the person was told to inhale deeply. The tapeworm would then exit the nose to get to the milk. Another suggested method to rid the body of parasitic worms was to eat the head of garlic every day until they were gone. This amazing ad ran in an 1869 issue of the *Clarksville Weekly Chronicle.*

Hurley's Popular Worm Candy

> **As this is really a specific for worms and the best and most palatable form to give to children, it is not surprising that it is fast taking the place of all other preparations for worms—it being perfectly tasteless, any child will take it.**
> **James Ruddle & Co. Proprietors**

With fireplaces and wood-burning cook stoves in homes so prevalent, burns were a common occurrence. These were treated with a mixture of lard and flour or the scrapings from a raw white potato. Also mixing castor oil and egg whites were applied to the burned area. One unimaginable method of treatment was to place hot coals on the burn and pour water over it to "draw the fire" out of the burn.

A common complaint was chest congestion that ranged anywhere from a cold to tuberculosis. The remedy used was a poultice of kerosene, turpentine and lard. A wool cloth soaked in the mixture would be applied to the chest. The purpose of the lard was to prevent the kerosene and turpentine from blistering the skin. In addition to "keeping house," women also served as the family doctor, using remedies passed down from generation to generation. These remedies came in the form of herbs or concoctions made in the kitchen such as using sugar in combination with turpentine or kerosene and sugar to treat abrasions and cuts. Sassafras tea,[83] made from the root of the tree was commonly used to clean the blood. Cough medicine was made by boiling the bark from a cherry tree. Placing spider webs over the wound could stop bleeding from a cut. To obtain relief from arthritis, a tea was made from alfalfa leaves or seeds.

By 1900 the average lifespan of adult males was forty-six and adult females, forty-eight. Several reasons contributed to these abbreviated life spans such as poor sanitation, pollution, inadequate bathroom facilities and ignorance of germ transmission. Public spitting was so commonplace that spittoons graced stores, railroad stations, banks and other public places. Adults rarely lived to an age to be ravaged by diseases of the elderly such as heart attacks, Alzheimer's disease, coronary disease, arthritis, etc. So many died from manageable diseases and illnesses, which today are easily treated or cured. Today, dying from the flu or from a simple infection in the U.S. is rare. For thousands of years, the threat of death was never far off.

There came a practice that today would seem strange. Records from the past show that a practice of naming two children in the family the same name was common. This was done when a child was born, named and died before one year of age and so a later child would be given the same name. It was also common that when a child died, little to no mention of that child was found in written form or even spoken about. In 1885, a Clarksville woman gave birth to twin girls in which one of the girls died. Eighty years later the surviving twin was told of the sister she never knew she had; a secret her parents had kept from her all her life. It was devastating to the lady.[84]

Thirty years before Nannie was born, the mortality rate of children five years of age and younger was estimated to be as high as 21%. Among children from birth to five years, the leading causes of death in order were: cholera, diphtheria, unknown reasons, scarlet fever, croup, fever, pneumonia, whooping cough, worms, external causes, teething, convulsions, typhoid fever, measles, smallpox, bronchitis and enteritis. With such statistics, parents lived in constant fear of losing one or more of their children. Death was lurking at any given moment to strike down a loved one. Even the remedy for treating a disease would, itself, led to death. For example, when a baby was teething, a doctor might prescribe using leeches placed behind a child's ears to draw blood or perhaps the gums themselves would be cut to allow the new tooth to emerge. There was

---

[83] Oil taken from sassafras is now listed as a carcinogen by the FDA.

[84] This lady was the author's grandmother. The author was present when her grandmother was told of the baby and saw the effects it had on her health. The family even moved to a different house after the boy died.

a popular nursery rhyme with a death-related message, that had as its first known, or recognized date of existence in the early 1880s called "Ring Around the Rosie." This seemingly cute nursery rhyme has a dark origin. The Black Death in the years 1347-50 and the great London Plague of 1665 were two horrendous diseases to strike Europe during the Middle Ages, killing as many as one-third of the population. It is a mystery to this day why a song about these tragic events resurfaced almost 215 years later in the 1880s only to be sung by children at play.[85] According to Jon Schladweiler, a historic researcher, the rhyme reads and can be interpreted as follows:

> **"Ring around the rosie,**
> [refers to the rosie-red (or purplish) round rash marks on the skin-one of the first signs a person had the plague]
> **A pocket full of posies;** [one of the superstitious ways used by people in the Middle Ages to try to fend off the plague was to stuff their pockets with posies to cover the stench of death]
> **Atischoo, atischoo,**
> [Sneezing was also an early sign of the plague if it was a pneumonic plague; however not all types of plagues involved sneezing]
> or, **Ashes, ashes**
> [The dead were often cremated]
> **We all fall down."**
> [most of the people stricken with the plague died]

The popular children's books in the 1880s included *The Five Peppers*, by Margaret Sidney and *Little Women* and *Little Men*, by Louisa May Alcott. Kate Greenaway's book, *Little Lord Fauntleroy*, became so popular in the 1880s that is influenced children's fashion, especially little boys' wear. One can imagine that Nannie was read to quite often, given her ancestors' well-educated backgrounds.

As with any child, toys and playtime were important during the early years. Attitudes towards children had changed dramatically by the 1880s; they were allowed more opportunities to play. No longer did parents believe that children needed to attend to chores as much due to the ideas that playtime actually contributed to learning future roles. A little girl during the 1880s played with miniatures of household items that her mother used, such as tea sets, stoves, irons and sewing machines to help her learn how to manage her own house when she grew up. Most toy appliances were manufactured in cast iron.

Doll styles and types varied. Before, little girls had played with cornhusk dolls. This changed when the new types of porcelain dolls were imported from Germany and France. Some were manufactured with jointed bodies, or if money was restrictive, a parent might buy doll heads made of paper-mache, bisque or even wax. These could be purchased for just a few pennies and then the body could be finished with soft material. Some dolls came complete with wardrobes with all the accessories and house furnishings that could be imagined. Regardless, each toy had an intended educational purpose that would help prepare the girl for her future role as a wife and mother. Mourning dolls were created so that a mother could teach her daughters the reality of losing a child. Some store-bought dolls even came with their own caskets.

Mourning dolls.

Parlor games became popular as did "dissected (jigsaw) puzzles." These puzzles were usually educational as well. Children may, for example, piece together maps of the states. Card playing was not encouraged due to the belief that it might lead to gambling later in life. The preferred choice of activities included reading, walking, visiting and writing. Boxes of stationary and writing pens were greatly desired gift items of the day. Nonfiction books were deemed more suitable than fiction, again because parents believed their child would learn more from nonfiction types. Using their imagination was a favorite pastime of children as well as "dress up" for little girls who loved donning their mother's hats and shoes. Having their child master at least one

[85] In the 1960s this author sang this song with her friends on the playground at Moore School, of course not realizing its meaning either.

musical instrument was also desired by parents.

Nannie lived her short life in a city with much history. Clarksville is built on a series of seven hills like Rome. The site was chosen for a town due to the confluence of the Red and Cumberland Rivers. Named in honor of Gen. George Rogers Clark, the famous frontiersman and Indian fighter.[86] Clarksville's first settlement dates back to 1784.

The county name honors John Montgomery, Revolutionary War officer, sheriff of the Cumberland District, justice of the peace in Tennessee County, (North Carolina), commander of the troops during the Nickajack expedition and founder of Clarksville (with Martin Armstrong). This is the county to which Nannie's ancestors would come from Virginia, set down roots and directly affect its history for the next 100 years.

After the Battle of Kings Mountain, the momentous fight that turned the Revolutionary War in favor of the colonists, the captured Loyalist prisoners were handed over to Col. Armstrong[87] who released them. Upon learning of this outrage, the North Carolina legislature strongly admonished Armstrong since they no longer had a large number of prisoners to exchange for Patriot prisoners in the hands of the British in Charlestown. The Patriots had to fight these same men again in a later battle. After the war, Armstrong was commissioned as a surveyor. His scandalous acts became known as the Glasgow Land Fraud and he was removed by President Andrew Jackson as a surveyor.

John Montgomery wrote that the location was good when he, "discovered in the rugged hills that lie in the fork" of the Cumberland and Red[88] "a superior site for the location of a town." Additionally, the site had "the advantages of two rivers, good landings, . . . a gushing spring of pure water" and high ground above the spring as protection from Indians. This spring served as the city's first source of drinking water. This spring was so vital to the settlers that regulations were written which forbade the washing of clothes or the placing of milk, meat and other food items in its waters. Today, the spring is capped off and the only indication of its location is a historic marker below the police department building on Commerce Street. The spring once ran under the foundry of Whitfield, Bradley and Company in the early 1860s where some of the cannons and cannonballs for the Confederacy were manufactured. Later in the 1880s under a new partnership, it became Whitfield, Bates Foundry.

The public spring was on Lot #74, on the northeast corner of Spring and Commerce Streets. Photo by author.

The city's birth began with the 640 acres originally belonging to Col. Montgomery. Armstrong and Montgomery surveyed what is now the downtown area of Clarksville. The first tree to be cut was felled on his property in 1784. Clarksville soon had its "public lot," later to be called the Public Square. Over the years this "square" actually took on the shape of a rectangle.

Armstrong's plan for the town consisted of 20 'squares' of 140 lots and 44 out lots. He chose the names of the streets himself. The north and south streets starting at the Cumberland River were: Water, Spring, First, Second and Third. The streets running east-west beginning at the south were Commerce, Franklin, Main, Washington and Jefferson.[89] In total, the 44 lots sold for 10 pounds each in North Carolina currency.

In the October 14, 1820 issue of *The Gazette* there was an ad for: "Town Lot in Clarksville. All the land is well watered. A.M. Shelby."

---

[86] George Rogers Clark's childhood home was Caroline County, Virginia. Nannie's ancestors lived there as well and may have known George and his famous brother William of the Lewis and Clark expedition!

[87] Col. Martin R. Armstrong (1739-1808), DID NOT participate in the battle but was at home in Surry County.

[88] From the earliest pioneer days, the bluff where the Red River flows into the Cumberland was known as Red Paint Hill.

[89] Today Washington Street is College Street.

Ten years after Montgomery assisted in surveying the town, he was killed near Eddyville, Kentucky by Native Americans. A bronze statue honoring him stands at the corner of Franklin and First Streets. In 1796 Clarksville became the county seat of Montgomery County, named in his honor. This occurred after North Carolina ceded Tennessee County to the "territory South of the River Ohio" in 1790. Therefore, Tennessee County was abolished and gave up its name to the entire state and the new counties of Montgomery and Robertson were formed. The name Tennessee comes one of the Cherokee villages "Tanasi" attacked and destroyed by the Sevier brothers (John and Valentine), James Robertson and others during the famous Nickajack Expedition.

The Cumberland River itself has its origins in Harlan County, Kentucky. It moves westerly across southeastern Kentucky and the northern middle portion of Tennessee. From there it turns northward and flows across western Kentucky and meets the Ohio River near Smithland. The much smaller Red River begins in Sumner County, Tennessee flowing northwesterly across northeast Robertson County and into Kentucky. It then flows back into Tennessee and across Robertson and Montgomery counties in a westerly flow until it joins the Cumberland River in Clarksville.

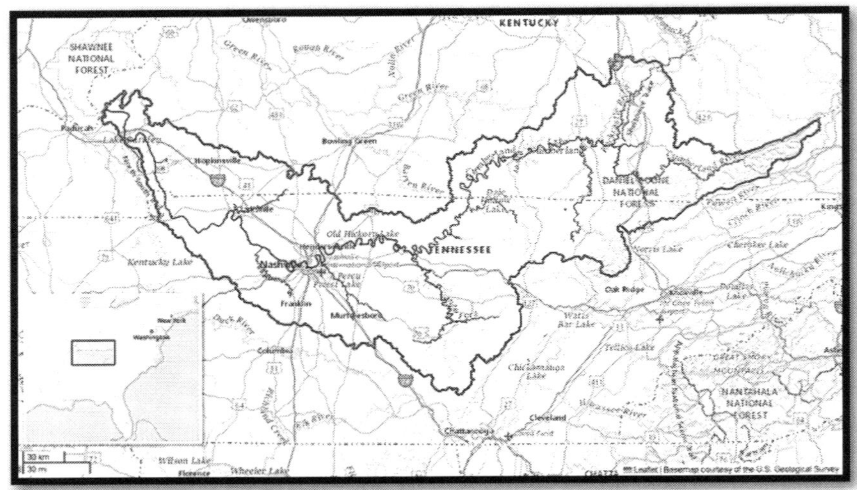

Map of the Cumberland River by Wikipedia

Montgomery County is unique in that it sits on a cavernous system of limestone labyrinths upon which is a deposit of heavy red clay. Because of the forested conditions, there is also a layer of varying depths of vegetable humus, perfect growing conditions for tobacco, wheat, flax and other crops. Rain leeches through the limestone and forms underground springs. The entire area is spotted with sinkholes, which, on occasion, collapse causing problems. Area farmers lose cattle and usable acreage to these sinkholes. The Austin Peay State University Woodard Library is located on an old sinkhole and another sits just in front of the library. Many other sinkholes in the downtown area have been filled in over the years.

The county's numerous caves include Dunbar, Bellamy, Boone, Coleman, Durham, Killebrew and Woodson. Dunbar, the most well-known, is termed a "blowing cave" due to the air rushing out from its mouth. To the north, Kentucky has its well-known Mammoth Cave, which exists because of the same geological formations. One of these caves would be part of a horrific event that required Judge Tyler to send a man to the gallows.

Tobacco had taken hold in Clarksville even before the city existed, as settlers, like Nannie's ancestors, came into the area, bringing with them the seeds from their former farms in Virginia and North Carolina. Also, the settlers brought with them the knowledge of growing, tending and curing the tobacco. The nitrogen-rich soil of Montgomery County assured the success of this crop. At first, tobacco was grown in small family patches and then as the demand for greater quantities came, tobacco installed itself as the area's cash crop. The tobacco trade impacted Clarksville in another important way. It made Clarksville quite the cosmopolitan town! Tobacconists from all over the world came to Clarksville to conduct their business. Some stayed for part of the year and then returned home. Others came and eventually decided to make Clarksville their permanent home. Such names as Hach, Dunzelmann, Kropp and others now are part of the history of the city. Not only did Clarksville take on an "international flavor" due to the foreign tobacconists but also businessmen from such countries as Switzerland, Germany, Scotland, Ireland, Bavaria and England brought their trade to town and set up shop keeping on many of Clarksville's downtown streets. Their presence truly enriched the county's personality.

Rachel Whitfield Herring was born to Bryan Whitfield in District 6 on November 5, 1795. She recalled when in 1807 or '08, a log house belonging to James Saunders stood at the town spring and a larger, better constructed house belonging to Amos Bird stood just below the spring. Bird ran a barge to Nashville carrying goods to trade. At that time, a man named Zack Dennis lived in a log house further down the river where the gas works stood. John Sanders who served as the Montgomery County Sheriff from 1801-1802 was the first boy born in Clarksville to live to adulthood.

The Public Square is situated on the fourth hill above the Cumberland River. Before Nannie's time, Elder Reuben Ross, pioneer Baptist minister in the Cumberland settlements in Tennessee and Kentucky, visited Clarksville and described the early Public Square as the place for men to "settle accounts, swap horses, drink whiskey, listen to lawyers and candidates, hear the news and see something of the world." Horse racing, cock fighting, boxing, fiddling and dancing were also conducted here. Luckily, the square later became more woman-friendly. It was recorded that in 1818 one mare and colt sold for $7.00 at the same time another mare and colt sold for $25. Still, one three-year-old horse was gotten for $15. By the 1830s, horse racing became widely popular in Montgomery County.

Ross in 1831 was the pastor of the Spring Creek Baptist Church. For one Sunday each month he would preach at the courthouse on the square and later at the one on Franklin Street until his death on January 28, 1860.

Cave Johnson, a Democrat, debated his opponent Gustavus A. Henry, a Whig, in the Public Square in 1843. Politics in those days were hotly argued and so these political forays brought large crowds of spectators to the square. It was not uncommon for fights to break out among the crowds when tempers got out of control.

G.A. Henry

There is much discussion about how many courthouses Montgomery County actually had. The problem lies with insufficient records and the loss of records over time. The same problem faces those trying to verify the sites of the different city jails. While still part of North Carolina, the court in Clarksville met in homes or places of business. The earliest recorded session was at the home of Isaac Titsworth whose land was situated in the area of the Sulphur Fork of the Red River and next at the home of William Grimes. This of course is not considered a true courthouse. However, it was there that the court ordered jurors to meet on the third Monday in July 1789.

Most sources can identify four courthouses in what is now Montgomery County, Tennessee. When the first legislature of the State of Tennessee met in its first session in 1796 in Knoxville it authorized the appointment of commissioners to contract to build a courthouse, prison and stocks in Clarksville. These were paid by the sheriff collecting a county tax: White poll, 12½ cents; black poll, 25 cents; 100-acre land, 12½ cents; town lot, 25 cents; stud horse, $1. The legislature appointed the following men as commissioners: Francis Prince, Robert Dunning, Robert Edmondson, Hayden Wells[90] and Joseph Neville, Sr. (Neville was appointed the county's first sheriff for two years on July 25, 1796). They were directed to erect a courthouse of logs on Lot #13, on the southwest side of Spring Street between Main and Washington Streets. When the structure was finished, it was quite rustic. It was found to be "with the most primitive conveniences; they had not so much as seats for the jurors to sit on until 1793 when the court

[90] Wells was a surveyor and millwright and, according to Clara Hamlett Robertson, a descendant, present at the founding of Nashville in 1779.

ordered James Adams to make them. Adams built this log courthouse close to the Cumberland River, adjoining his home as directed.

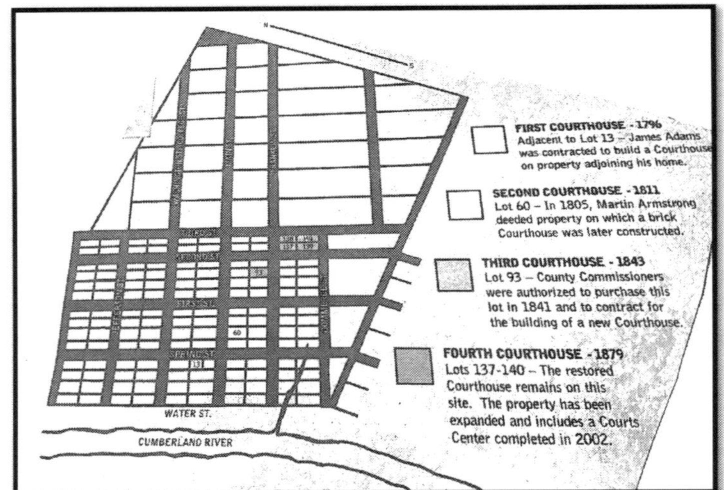

1811: The second courthouse was located on Lot # 60 at the northern end of the Public Square, deeded by Martin Armstrong in 1805. The courthouse was begun in 1807 by Colmore Duvall (1790-1824)[91] and was also used as a meeting place for public gatherings. Only the sheriff or his deputies could ring the courthouse bell for the opening or closing of the court sessions. There is no mention of where the bell was located. The bell was also rung in the event of auction sales of property to cover taxes not paid. When the County Court convened in the early 1800s, the sheriff stood by the door and announced to all, "Oh yes! Oh yes! God save the state and their worshipped court." He might have asked for prayers on a better-designed courthouse. It took 4 years and $9,500 to build and it became the albatross of the Public Square. It was a two-story, 44 ft. square, 36 ft.-tall brick structure, which sat upon a stone foundation. The entire first floor was a single room, which was utilized as the courtroom. Its ceiling was 18 ft. high. The second floor was divided into five rooms with a 12 ft. ceiling and was used as offices. Here were held court sessions, city official meetings, public auctions of property, city and county elections and church services. It is recorded that the first session was held here on January 1, 1811. Although impressed that the new courthouse was constructed of bricks, the complaints were that the building was "too big, too tall, too expensive for our needs and cost way too much to build. And the building covers most of the lot, leaves little room for wagons, horses, etc. and parking has to be at the livery stable.... why would one pay too much to park and have to walk too far?"

The design flaw on the brand new courthouse was the dangerously steep roof. The high pitch of the roof actually came to a sharp point at the very top. The positioning of the four chimneys at each corner of the building was, in itself, a poor design. It is not known what material covered this roof, but whatever was used to keep the rain out was not very effective. Repairs to the roof were nearly impossible since no workman was willing to risk falling off. The county managed to utilize the building for thirty-three years. Finally, enough was enough; it was time to relieve the county of this burden and the committee formed for the purpose of selling the courthouse. They placed an ad in the newspaper listing the courthouse for sale. It read:

> **In obedience to an order of the Montgomery City Court, the undersigned will, on the 6th day of March next, being the first day of the meeting of the Circuit and County Courts, sell the old Court House Building to the highest bidder on a credit of one, two, and three years. Said sale will be at the old courthouse door and the purchaser will be required to give bond with good, ample and sufficient security for the payment of the purchase money.**
> **P. Priestley, Nace F. Trice, A.G. Wheatley, James Reasons, Thomas Raimey**

A sketch of the 1811 Montgomery County Courthouse by Kevin Bonner.

[91] Duvall was born in Prince George's County, Maryland, to Samuel Duvall (1740-1804), and Mary Higgins Withers Duvall (1811-1885). He married Elizabeth Peach and the couple had three children.

On the corner of Commerce and Fifth Streets is this concrete post. It is possible there were more markers like this placed at several locations with the same message to inform people coming into town.

Thirty-three years later, on March 8 at the very door of the courthouse, John D. Everett paid just $352 at auction for the $9,500 courthouse with a roof no one dared to repair. The large brick market house would be built on this spot at a later time.

Today, in the center of the Public Square in the grassy area, several monuments stand. One made of limestone displays a plaque that reads:

> **This stone commemorates the first court house**
> **a rude log house on Public Square 1788-1811**
> **The old stockade southwest from this point**
> **erected by the Captain William Edmiston**
> **Daughters of the American Revolution 1933**

****This marker simply marks the general location in the center of the Public Square but not necessarily its precise location.

The courthouse served multiple purposes during its early years. The *Clarksville Gazette* newspaper in 1820 advertised numerous sales conducted by Sheriff John Neblett at the courthouse. Certainly people knew that the bell would be rung if there were a fire in town. There were no denominational churches in Clarksville in 1811 and so all people worshiped in this building. Up until the day individual church buildings were erected, there did not exist a consistent weekly Sunday church. Itinerant preachers riding from town to town would occasionally stop in Clarksville to teach from the Good Book. Arriving at the Public Square, he would tie up his horse and take the judge's chair in the courthouse, waiting for the resounding bell to announce that preaching was about to commence.[92]

Clarksville was incorporated as a town by the 13th General Assembly of the State of Tennessee on October 23, 1819, and therefore required the necessary officials to act as a governing body. Sheriff John Neblett ensured the elections were held to fill the office of seven aldermen and in January of 1820, he announced,

> **Whereas I, John Neblett, having held an election for aldermen of the town of Clarksville on the second Monday in January 1820, agreeable to the acting of assembly in such case provided at which election Samuel Vance, John H. Poston, Frederick Huling, Peter N. Marr, Cave Johnson, John H. Marable and James Elder being the seven highest in vote were duly elected. Whereas I certify that said persons are duly elected aldermen for the Town of Clarksville for the year 1820.**

On January 15, 1820, seven elected aldermen met to elect a mayor. James E. Elder was chosen to be the township's first mayor serving three terms of one year each. By February, the aldermen had established the first twelve by-laws; the twelfth dealing with the appointment of the two-man patrol. Nobel Ogburn and John P. { ? torn page} were appointed if needed by the mayor (James Elder) or 12 aldermen. They worked no more than 4 nights a week; pay was $50 per year for them to visit "every part of town, once before and once after midnight. Next, as the town grew, it was necessary for every adult male to volunteer for patrol duty. Three were to serve each week. One person who was not at all pleased with the courthouse's location was James Elder's wife, Lucinda. She was Clarksville's earliest trendsetter/influencer. Her beloved strawberry patch stood

[92] The year 1811 was visited by the appearance of Halley's comet also, on December 16, 1811 at about 2:15 a.m. the terrifying New Madrid earthquake shook Tennessee and surrounding states. The 7.2-8.1 earthquake was followed by more quakes and aftershocks. On January 23, 1812 another quake measuring 7.8 occurred but the strongest one on February 7, 1812 measured 8.8 on the Richter Scale. Reelfoot Lake was formed during this time. The earthquake's epicenter was just a couple of hundred miles from Montgomery County.

in the way of the new proposed tree-lined street to accommodate the courthouse. Lucinda was absolutely beside herself. This was the garden where her prized fruit that was used for her all-important strawberry and cream gatherings were grown. Despite her rantings and ravings, the street was constructed and appropriately named Strawberry Alley.

1842: The third courthouse was at the north end of Franklin Street between First and Second Streets on lot #93 owned by Zachariah Grant. The lot extended from Franklin Street to Strawberry Alley. This courthouse was a two-story brick building constructed on a stone foundation. Four stone steps led from the sidewalk to its entry walk and then nine steps up to the doorway. An ornamental iron fence ran along the front of the lot and iron rails were placed on either side of the nine steps. The second story of the courthouse was designed for offices. The only known photo of the courthouse was after the 1878 fire.

In January 1842 the courthouse was officially open. In 1844 the court authorized the sheriff Samuel McFall, to remove the bell from the previous courthouse to the new one as it was his duty since he was the only one allowed to ring this bell. The bell had, in effect, been forgotten amid all the excitement over the new courthouse and no provisions were made for its placement. McFall was to "construct a suitable house to contain the bell" therefore it was placed in the tower of its own separate building.

Upset that repairs were already necessary the next year to fix the leaking roof, it was ordered by the court that repairs be made but using no more than ten shingles. By 1846 internal improvements were necessary and doors were rearranged. Also that year, the Clarksville Female Academy was chartered.

The fire destroyed this courthouse but fortunately most of the important papers and records managed to be saved. Courthouse business had to be conducted in the market house until after the five lots were purchased and business moved to the old Baptist church on the southeast corner of the new site. It was repaired and used as the courthouse until a new one could be built.

1879: The present courthouse is bounded by Second, Third and Commerce Streets. George W. Bunting of Indianapolis was the original architect however, C.G. Rosenplanter of Louisville and Memphis took over supervising the work until it was completed. McCormac & Sweeny were the contractors out of Columbus, Indiana. Constructed of pressed brick with stone embellishments this new courthouse stood on a stone foundation. The partially underground basement was divided into eight large rooms as was the main floor above. The top floor was divided into rooms that served the court. The interior was lighted with gas. The bell placed in the clock tower weighed 3,000 lbs., its tones said to be "sweet, clear and musical and can be heard a considerable distance." The grounds were beautiful landscaped and once more an ornamental iron fence encircled the grounds. Gates were placed at each entrance: the main entrances were on the east and west sides and two more at the north and south ends.

Until the 2d Monday in May Next

SEALED PROPOSALS will be received by me from all persons owning lots suitable for the erection of a new Court House building. Each proposal must describe the lot offered, stating the locality, the number of feet front and in depth, the terms and the price at which the owner obligates himself to sell should his bid be accepted by the county.

These bids will be opened by the Commissioners on the 2d Monday in May.

By order of Court House Commissioners.
CHARLES W. TYLER, Chairman.
April 25 1878-td

*Another source states there were six courthouses. See "Montgomery County, TN Courthouses," by Irene M. Griffey, printed: 2003. The difficulty lies with the words "used as" versus "built as/for." Are cabins/buildings built for other uses but also utilized as courthouses to be counted?

The different locations of city/county jails in Clarksville from the city's beginnings are as follows:

(1796) Lot #13 This crude jail housed prisoners from both the town and country. It was desired that no man be imprisoned for a long length of time as the city leaders felt he should be back at his employment which better served the economy. Ten lashings were the usual punishment for law breakers. The official gallows of 1820 was described as being

erected to the rear of the front portion of the city jail in the alleyway between the river and the back of the jail at Public Square. The platform of the gallows was 6½ feet wide and 18 feet long built between the two walls so as not to be be viewed externally and was raised 16 feet from the ground. An under platform was erected about 8 feet below the upper one and the feet of the party executed were therefore about two feet from the floor thus formed when the drop had been made.

(1822) Lot #49 on corner of Main and Spring Streets. As shown in the property transfer records, Cave Johnson deeded lot #49 at the corner of Main and Spring Streets (Public Square) for one hundred and twenty-five dollars.

(1859-1891) West side of Spring between Franklin and Main Streets. where once stood the Illinois Central Freight Depot. The jail sat on the slope below the Public Square and had adjoining buildings as seen on the Sanborn Map.

A rare photograph of Clarksville's 3rd Jail located on the west side of Spring Street looking towards the Cumberland River. It was here that William Morrow was hanged in 1885. (TSLA).

The building was described in this way,

The new county jail was designed by Rosenplanter. The three-story building contained twelve rooms and four cells. The first floor housed four dungeons walled with stone two feet thick. Above that were walls of George Buck's best brick; the cupola rose nearly 25 feet above the jail and had a weathervane at its apex. Once again E. Gaisser & Son won the contract to build iron cages for the jail that occupied the third floor. In the center of the large room the Gaissers installed a thirty by forty-foot cage. The cage was divided into four parts for separation and security of prisoners. Four layers of flooring prevented escape by that route.

Judge Tyler sent in a notice to the newspaper that he wrote on July 1, 1885, praising the work that Gaisser & Son did on the new steel cages for the jail "at reasonable prices."

C.H. Morrison was the jailer of the new building. In 1903, the old jail was sold to the Illinois Central Railroad.

(1891-1896) North center of the Public Square in the old market house. The police chief was Alex Stafford. The two-story brick and stone market house was constructed as a long building with two short center wings on the front and backsides and a six-sided cupola on the tin roof. The second story was used as a recorder's office and as a town hall for city council meetings. The police used a corner of the first floor for their headquarters. The jail was also located on the first floor. The long hallway was used for the market place. In its last years, an electric light was mounted in the cupola. When the market house was torn down, the police headquarters and jail moved temporarily to the old National Bank building.

(1896-1913) The old bank/police station building was remodeled and used for the city court and quarters for the police force for about 20 years. Its bell was rung at 9 p.m. each night to announce that it was curfew time. A notice to the young people in the February 13, 1905 *Leaf* stated, "Boys, put your banana peels in the trash barrel and keep your ear open for the curfew bell. When the clock strikes nine it is time to scamper."

(1907)[93] At the corner of Sullivan and Commerce Street. Built to hold 75 prisoners. It was a two-story building with a residence for the sheriff attached. He was given five rooms, a bath and closets for his family. The building fronted on Commerce Street and was built with a basement. The jail proper was in the rear. It was built with 8 cells rooms, 10 cages designed to hold black

---

93 At this point in time there is a separation of city and county jails.

and white prisoners separately. Also separate rooms for youths and lunatics were included. The first floor had cell rooms with cages. This jail had numerous break outs during its use.

(1914-1969) 115 Public Square. Beginning on April 8, 1914, the erection of new city hall and jail on the site of the old bank/police station building was begun. G. Tandy Smith was the architect of the building that fronted 63 feet and extended back 102 feet. The city court and jail was housed in this building. The front façade was done in the Victorian Romanesque style with red pressed brick and white mortar joints. Bowling Green stone was built into the front and the main entrance was surrounded by ornamental plaster trim [94] The first and second floor front windows are separated by terra-cotta medallion panels. Each window is capped by an arch.

There still remained, at that time, alleyways on either side of the building.[95] The south alleyway was extremely narrow but the north side alley allowed room for a car to pass. Carney Baggett, the jailer in the 1940s-50s used the alley to pull his car around back of the jail and park in a shed. The alley also connected with a small road that ran behind the buildings next to and including the Poston Building. The police offices moved temporarily to W.J. Manning's office until the new city hall with its jail was completed. In the meantime, the city prisoners were housed in the county jail. Its bell was removed and moved to the new city hall but as it had no placed to be hung, it was simply left on the city hall's roof and forgotten.

An aerial photo of the city hall with an alley on both its south and north sides.

The second floor was constructed as offices for the mayor, the city engineer and council chamber. The 500-lb. bell for the city hall was cast in Louisville by the Kaye & Co. Foundry in 1891. The bell was forgotten and during a later renovation of the building, it was discovered on the roof.[96] Calvin Louie, Sr. (!905-1990), the jailer was supervising an inmate work detail on the building tearing off the old roof that was then nothing but tar paper when the bell was discovered.

In preparation for the country's bicentennial it was decided that the bell should be included in the celebration. The historic bell, donated by the family of Mary Jo Dozier, a long-term city councilwoman, was displayed in the gazebo on the Public Square. The gazebo was destroyed years later when a driver lost control of his car. A new gazebo was rebuilt on the corner of Franklin and South First Streets without the bell.

The bell in 1975 in the Public Square gazebo. (LC)

The contracted cost for this building was $12,000. The basement contained the cells for male and female inmates. Living accommodations for the jail keeper were on the top floor. The chief was J.E. Robinson who served in that capacity for decades.

The *Chronicle* praised the appearance of the new building,

> **The new city hall is rapidly assuming the appearance of handsome building as day by day its walls have grown taller and**

[94] In 2024 the old plaster trim was removed having pulled away from the brick front. It was replaced in 2025 with 26 aluminum plates to resemble the original plaster design.

[95] In later years a very narrow building was added to the south side of the city hall that connected it to the block of present-day office buildings.

[96] This must mean that the bell was used in the 3rd jail and moved to the city hall when built but because there was no structure from which to hang it, the bell was simply left on the roof.

now when the brick work is nearing completion, many complimentary expressions are heard relative to the improved appearance given the Public Square. In fact, it seems the once business section of the city is again coming into her own and as soon as the city dads convert this almost forsaken spot into a beautiful park all will rejoice that the city hall was built where it was located.

The building was listed on the National Register of Historic Places in 1976 as a contributing resource to the Clarksville Architectural District.

On the left: The change in bricks and window headings on the north side reveal the modifications made in 1914 to enlarge the building. On the right: An early photograph of the city hall. The center roof pediment displayed a center spread eagle. (The eagle was removed during a later remodel). Note the small windows for the prisoners at the sidewalk level on the right side. The small openings on the left side was for the coal chute.

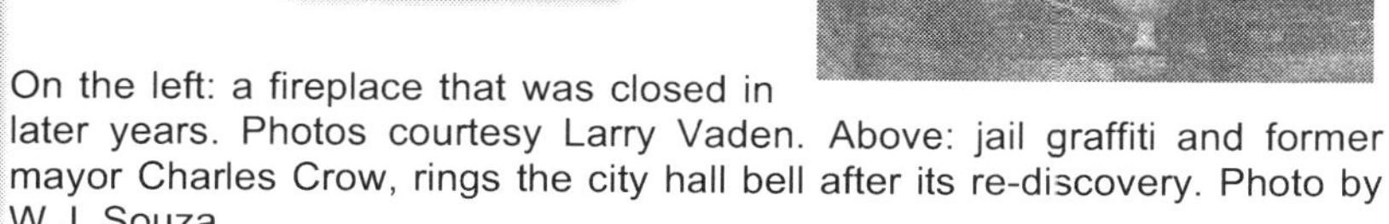

On the left: a fireplace that was closed in later years. Photos courtesy Larry Vaden. Above: jail graffiti and former mayor Charles Crow, rings the city hall bell after its re-discovery. Photo by W.J. Souza.

The Public Square shown: the city hall, Bicentennial gazebo with the bell, the granite two layered drinking fountain and stone depicting the general location of the first courthouse.

Clarksville's current jail complex at 116 Commerce Street.

The Location of Jails in the Public Square Area

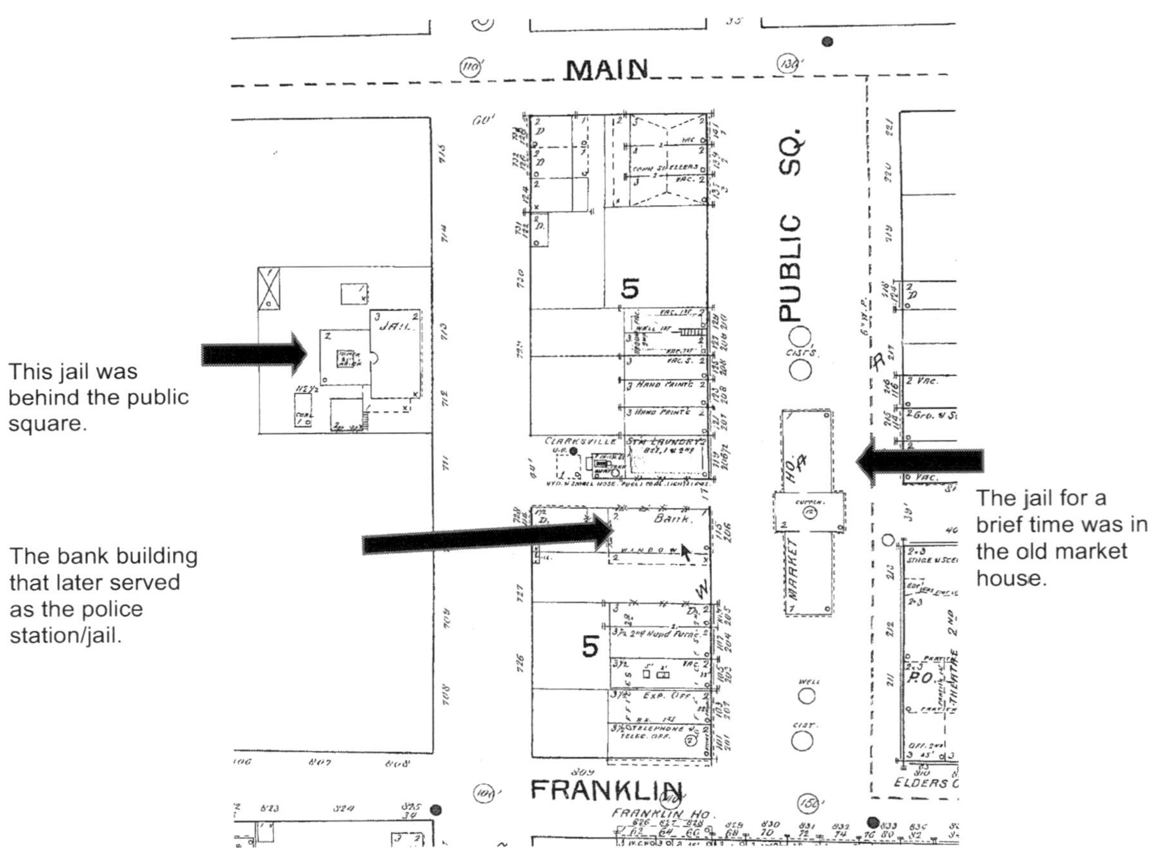

This jail was behind the public square.

The bank building that later served as the police station/jail.

The jail for a brief time was in the old market house.

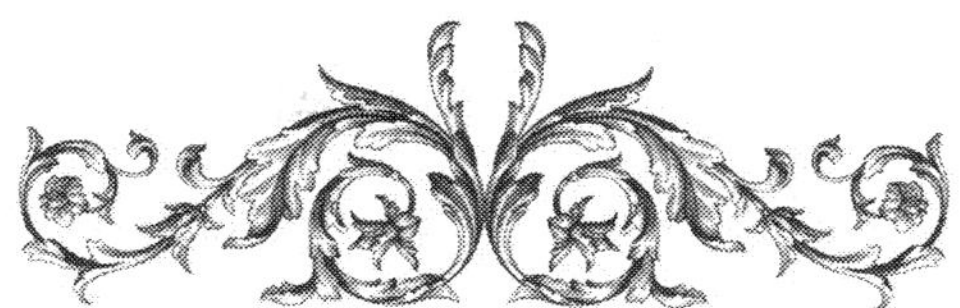

Chapter Twelve: Nannie's Life at Home

Victorian morals dictated that women not display their pregnancy, as this was considered unseemly. They were to wear loose fitting clothing that covered their ever-expanding abdomens; tight form-fitting clothing was forbidden. Corsets were to be left unworn as this was advised by doctors to be best for the baby. Women who were pregnant were to go into confinement which meant they spent their pregnancy at home unseen by the public. Words like "pregnant" and "pregnancy" were considered too sensitive to be used in everyday conversation. Instead "expecting," "in a family way," "with child," or "in a delicate condition" were used instead.

1882 Silk maternity dress. (Image via Met Museum)

The expectant mother's hair could remain undressed or left loose and her comfort during confinement was managed by female family members and midwives. Sometime a doctor may be called in from time to time just to check on the woman. Also during this time period, there were printed motherhood and maternity guides available produced by hospitals, religious organizations and "advice experts."

What should have been the most joyful day in the lives of Charles and Mollie was marred forever by the ugliness of politics as he was struggling to defend his political life. Mollie must have suffered such anguish during the birth worrying about the impeachment charges facing her husband.

We have no idea if Mollie's labor was long, easy or difficult. These things were simply not discussed but once the birth was over, women were to follow strict instructions for the first nine days. The mother was usually changed into a clean nightgown and kept quiet for a few hours in order to rest. They were to remain in bed for nine days to ensure they were given time to recover and usually in a darkened room away from light. Conversations were to be kept to a minimum and the baby should be in the total care of the mother if possible. A mother's temperament was believed to affect the baby and so the mother was to remain in the best humor. Elizabeth Scovil, an author on Victorian pregnancy and motherhood in the late 1880s wrote,

> **Excitement is dangerous and no visitors must be permitted to enter the room, nor should conversation be allowed, even if she wishes to talk. Neglect of this precaution may cause serious disaster, even when all seems to be going so well.**

From the beginning, the couple's hearts were captured by "our little darling"- the very words would be used later to immortalize Nannie on her monument. Nannie lived her entire life in her grandmother's house and from all indications, it would seem that Nannie lived happily surrounded by the love of her family. Unfortunately, not much is known about Nannie in the few years that encompassed her life. What foods did she like, what games did she enjoy and by what names did she call her parents? What was her favorite toy? Did she have a pet? So many things we yearn to know but probably never will. But with her father serving such an elevated position in the town, it would be quite easy to believe that Nannie had a busy, interesting life. Her family certainly would have been at the epicenter of all the happenings of Clarksville. Nannie came into the world while Clarksville was in the middle of a major re-build following the great fire.

Certainly, it is well known that her parents adored Nannie. Her portrait shows her to have been a perfectly lovely looking child with a round face and soft eyes. Nannie was not just any child living in Clarksville; she was the daughter of Charles Waller Tyler, Montgomery County Criminal/Circuit Court Judge and County Financial Officer. Her father's reputation in Montgomery County was legendary.

Judge Tyler's house on Greenwood. Its appearance had been changed years after the last of the Tylers lived there. Photo by author.

Mollie would have dressed their baby girl in a white gown that extended below her feet to help keep her warm. When Nannie began walking she would have worn simple dresses, as she was not old enough to start wearing the more elaborate dresses of older girls, which mimicked their mother's. Often the skirts were made with drawstrings and wide hems to prolong the use of the dress and also to make passing it down to younger siblings easier. The Victorian woman was ever mindful of extending the life of her family's clothes. The age of a little girl could easily be guessed by the length of her skirt. She would wear a dress to just below the knees up until she was twelve, next calf-length skirts until age fourteen. By age sixteen, the skirt would reach down to her ankles and finally, from age seventeen and up, she wore the full-length skirt, identical to her mother's. Unfortunately, Nannie would not live to be an adult. When playing, little girls under age five wore an apron or a pinafore over their dresses. Ribbons not only adorned the dresses but were worn in the hair as well.

The Tylers desired that their daughter be raised in the Episcopal Church. During services, Nannie would have been surrounded by its elaborate, new interior. It is very probable that as she sat there with her family, she would gaze up at the ethereal light pouring through the four stunning Tiffany stained glass windows. The Mohler organ, it was said, resonated music such as only could be imagined when played by the church organist and choir director Professor William Emery, who served from 1881 until 1928. Nannie would have enjoyed her mother's tremendous singing voice during the services.

On any Sunday afternoon the family would have gone home after church to enjoy a large meal and then spend the afternoon "sitting and resting for a spell" on the porch or visiting neighbors and relatives. As strict Episcopalians, Sunday was truly a day of rest. Porches were gathering places for family, friends and people just passing by. It was a place of respite at the end of the day, allowing one to analyze problems and settle down for the evening's rest.

Baths were still, except for the wealthy, taken in wooden, tin or zinc-lined bathing tubs, filled with water heated on the stove. Hygiene was not as it is today, as people took baths only once or twice a month. People bathed so seldom because of a well-circulated belief that a person's natural oils would protect them from germs that might enter their pores. In earlier times in Clarksville, there was a "fashionable" barber at #3 Strawberry Alley near the Public Square who also advertised his business as a "bathing establishment with warm and cold baths at all hours." Outhouses were the norm, since indoor plumbing was not yet widely used in homes.

Nannie, if she was like most children, enjoyed story-telling. Her father's older half-brother, Quintus Tyler, visited quite often. One can but hope that the opportunity arose where Quintus was able to tell Nannie about the Tyler family crossing the mountains in old wagons and settling in Tennessee. Perhaps he told Nannie stories of her ancestors and about her grandfather John Duke, the schoolmaster. Family stories were more often than not "handed down" orally and considered treasures to be remembered from one generation to the next.

Most little girls were taught to sew by age four. If a grandmother lived in the home, it usually fell to her to teach the little ones how to sew dresses for their dolls, make aprons or mend clothes. The grandparents also played a large role in teaching the children in matters of religion. They often read from the Bible and taught the grandchildren to recite scriptures. The extended family worked well during these times because everyone had a role to play and understood what it was. While

Nannie's mother would have been immersed in the running of the household, Nannie's grandmother would have seen to the aforementioned activities.

As a good mother, Mollie would be very conscious of training children in proper table manners. It was common that while the adults would eat in the dining room, children ate in the kitchen. Of course, the adage was that "children were to be seen and not heard." Did the Tylers follow this practice or allow their daughters to join them at meals with the adults? Family meals were important to the structured life of the late 1880s. An article in the *Clarksville Tobacco Leaf* dated February 7, 1878 details why.

Be Agreeable

> **Everyone can do something to add to the social life at the table. If one cannot talk, he can listen or ask questions and draw out others who can talk. Good listeners are as necessary as good talkers. Never argue at the table but tell pleasant stories, relate or read anecdotes and look out for the good of all. Sometimes a single anecdote from a paper starts a conversation that lasts during the meal time.**
>
> **A family table ought to be bright and cheerful, a sort of domestic altar, on which everyone casts down his or her offering great or small, of pleasantness and peace, where, for at least a brief space of the day, all stormy tempers are hushed; everyone being glad and content to sit down at the same board and eat the same bread and salt. Making it, whether it was a rich repast or a dinner of herbs, equally joyful, almost a sacramental meal.**

Charles was the only male presence in a family of five females. What a reversal after having grown up surrounded by dozens of boys at his father's school. In addition to his wife, sister and mother all residing in the same household, Charles' sister, Nannie lived just next door, as she was the second wife of Polk Grundy Johnson. Totally outnumbered and probably desirous of quiet times, Charles recounted that, "when were three women ever thrown together in this world who didn't find plenty to talk about?"

If a lady needed house servants to help with the weekly laundry, there were washerwomen available for hire in town, or they could be paid to come to the house. Laundry day was exactly that, an all-day affair in which the bed sheets, linens and clothes were gathered up and sorted. The dirty laundry would have been soaked in a tub of very hot water and then rubbed with bars of soap, usually lye. This soap was used not only for laundry, but dishwashing, cleaning floors, windows and bathing as well. Anyone who has ever used lye soap can tell you that it was so strong it would "take the skin right off of you." Lye could be purchased from the store in cans or it could be extracted the old way at home by pouring water through a hopper of wood ashes. Grease from cooking would be saved as an ingredient, along with water, all mixed together in a big black iron kettle. The mixture was poured into dishpans to harden. The hardened soap was then cut into bars and wrapped with paper or cloth and stored away.

Washing was usually done outside. The term "wash day" was exactly like for it took much of the day to hand wash and hang laundry. With the long skirts that women wore, imagine the amount of scrubbing it took to remove all the filth that they came in contact with. Large kettles were normally used, sitting on bricks in the driveway or yard, away from the house and outbuildings. The fire underneath heated the water in order to boil the laundry. Think of the task of scrubbing clothes and linens on a washboard along with the wear and tear this had on skin and fabrics. There were separate tubs for scrubbing, rinsing, bluing and starching.[97] Bleach was often used on white fabrics to make them appear as clean as possible. Finally, the laundry was rinsed, wrung out and hung on a clothesline to dry. In the winter, a makeshift clothesline could be suspended in the kitchen by the fire or stove to dry the clothes. The job was only half completed because, of course, the clothes also had to be ironed. This was done with an iron that was either heated in the fireplace or on top of the stove. The expression of "slaving over a hot iron" was an apt description. These indeed were heavy as they were made from solid cast iron.[98] Today, if clothes are torn or worn out, more often than not they are simply thrown away. During Nannie's life, clothes would be mended or in the case of knitted items, darned. Buttons taken off garments

[97] Bluing was the process of adding a blue dye to whiten the fabric.
[98] So heavy were these irons that today people buy them at antique stores to use as doorstops.

were always saved in a "button box" and scraps of material were salvaged to make quilts. Nothing was ever discarded. Even strips of cloth could be sewn to together and then braided into rugs.

Recycling and repurposing was a concept that Victorians understood well before the terms became by-words. When someone outgrew a sweater and there were no younger siblings, sweaters would be unraveled and knitted again to the correct size!

In the South on many typical hot, sultry summer nights, lightning bugs magically appear. At first just a few make themselves known and then the miraculous entities of cold light twinkle in mass among the dark yards. They seem in no hurry to find their place of rest as though they believe themselves allowed the entire night to frolic. One can hope Nannie experienced the delight of every child in the South who ever captured lightening bugs in a jar, realizing God's gifts that special, must be released again to the night. Crickets singing through much of the early evening provide the background melody for the close of another day.

Add to this spectacle the distinctive smell of maple tree leaves permeating the saturated air and cicadas vocalizing their shrieks as they fly from tree to tree before deciding where to pass the night. Croaking male frogs announce their presence to their female counterparts and remind children to anticipate the discovery of tadpoles in area ponds.

The heavy sweet scent of honeysuckle vine on some wild hedge is forever a welcome announcement of summer. The glorious appearance of butterflies enhances the splendor of spring flower gardens. Swallowtails, yellow sulfurs and monarchs flutter about and ladybugs with their dainty black polka dots on cherry red backs perpetually busy themselves striding up the blades of plants with no real destination in mind. Dandelions with their delicate white heads of seeds attached to parachutes are such fun to pick and blow the seeds into the air after making a wish.

Upon waking in the spring and summer mornings, did Nannie hear the sorrowful "boo who, who, who" call of the mourning dove? Outside, did she notice the twirling whirligigs of maple tree seeds showering the ground at every stirring breeze? One wonders if Nannie had a favorite flower. It is hoped that perhaps Nannie's grandmother or aunts might have taken her out into the yard to discover such wonders. Thundershowers accompanied by lightening streaking across the skies would enliven a child's day or night. In the South, these storms can be as strong as to shake an entire house. Would these storms frighten Nannie or would she just take them in stride? The blessing to come afterwards often includes gorgeous rainbows and air as fresh as can be imagined! In the spring and summer, the windows of Nannie's house would have been left open all day to cool down the inside. Even at night with the windows open, the house could be quite uncomfortable, a situation rarely known by children today who enjoy air-conditioned schools, cars, homes and shopping malls. It should be remembered as well that with windows left open, insects were free to enter the house . . . even the nocturnal bats might pay a visit.

Fall in the South is a splendid time of year when the chlorophyll drains from the leaves, exposing wonderful hues of red, yellow and orange. Yards fill with the multicolored leaves. Of course, what child does not delight in piling up the leaves just to run, jump into the center and toss them into the air. And no child can resist scraping the frost off a windowpane on the chilly mornings that follow.

Squirrels frantically rush to gather acorns and bury their little treasure troves in anticipation of winter. These are daring creatures when leaping from branch to branch high up in the trees, however, they lack long-term memories. Squirrels fail to locate many of their stashes of nuts later and therefore are responsible for adding to the tree population. Still, up and down the trees they scurry, carrying leaves and twigs to build their warm nests before the weather changes. Judge Tyler once wrote of a typical November morning as:

> **just a little chilly, but the air was crisp and invigorating. A mouthful of it was a splendid tonic and sent the blood dancing through the veins and pleasant fancies leaping about in the brain. Ah, the late-rising man never knows what a grand stimulant the Almighty prepares for him in the fresh atmosphere that begirts the earth.**

For the farming community, as most of Clarksville was, it also meant that work would be slowing down as the harvest commenced. There is an indescribable feeling of satisfaction knowing the crops were all in, the fruits and vegetables canned and the meat salted or smoked. This was the time of year when the dark-fired tobacco barns wafted their heady, smoky scent over the countryside. Excluding the tobacco farmer whose crop took 13 months to bring to fruition, the farmer could now take his rest, as would his fields, which had once again sustained his family. And if, of course they raised livestock, their work was never-ending. Farmers have a special kinship with the Earth that is missed by those in other professions. Charles Tyler must have recalled on numerous occasions the struggles his ancestors faced while working their land.

In the 1880s, sustained low winter temperatures permitted ice-skating on area ponds! Of course there were no scientific weather predictions possible so locals relied upon "old timey" methods. They simply checked nature signs such as woolly bear worms, the thickness of cornhusks, the height of hornet nests in trees and the insides of persimmon seeds to predict the severity of the oncoming winter. Woolly worms are actually the caterpillars of the North American moth. The body is divided into 13 segments varying between black and reddish brown. On each end of the caterpillar, the bands are black with the ones in the middle showing a brownish-red coloration. The old timers predicted that a wide band in the middle showed a mild winter whereas a narrow band meant a hard winter. Using persimmon seeds to predict weather involved

collecting the seeds and soaking them in water overnight. The seed would then be cut open to expose the kernel, which appeared to be shaped either like a spoon, fork, or knife. According to old timers, the different shapes would predict if a winter would be normal, cold or mild! The image of a spoon meant there would be a lot of wet, heavy snow, the image of a fork meant a mild winter with light, powdery snow and a knife meant that there will be cold, cutting winds. During the cold months, quilts were removed from storage, aired out and placed in layers on top of the beds for added warmth. The high ceilings in homes, which were a benefit during the summer months, were a hindrance in winter in maintaining warmth. Regardless of the season, life in Clarksville moved on at its own particular pace with its own particular purpose.

Ah, the 1880s kitchen; what was it like? Cooking meals would have added to the heat inside the house, so whenever possible, Southern homes had detached kitchens or kitchens situated to the rear of the house. Meals were served three times a day; there was breakfast, dinner and supper. Such terms as "noon day luncheon" or "evening dinner" were not used as a matter of speech. In a Southern 1880s home, dinner would have been simple. The vegetables served consisted of mostly cabbage, corn, green beans and potatoes, but tomatoes were used once their reputation of being poisonous was dispelled. Southern meals might also include a "mess of turnip greens." Local slaughterhouses provided the meats for the city table. However, even some "city folks" raised chickens in their fenced-in back yards. Country people relied on their own cows, chickens and hogs to slaughter. No Southern meal would be complete without some type of bread such as biscuits or cornbread. The drink of choice was coffee or tea.

Desserts included cobblers, cakes, pies and a favorite of Southern families: fried pies. In the summer and fall there were always orchard fruits, berries and vegetables to be "put up" (canned) in preparation for winter. Cooking was done on a wood stove that, in itself, produced an inviting, pleasant odor. Lots of chopped wood needed to be stacked in a woodshed or near the kitchen door to re-supply the stove as cooking commenced. Wonderful aromas filled the house from the stove and the goodies prepared upon the heating plates. Ask anyone what he or she remembers and misses most about their growing up years at home and they will tell you it was simply the cooking! The Tylers maintained a cook to prepare their meals. It was a source of pride to a family, if their cook was known to be especially talented. Jealousy arose among families over having "the best cook in town." Sometimes these cooks were enticed by a higher salary to come work for someone else.

A new innovation was being introduced at this time on grocery shelves: canned fruits and meats.[99] The *Tobacco Leaf* newspaper January 25 issue advertised plum pudding in cans. Grocery goods prices of the 1880s were quite interesting. They included:

[99] The first useable can opener was invented in 1870 by William Lyman.

Bacon-clear sides, 8c, clear rib side, 7 ½c, shoulders, 7c
Sugar-standard crushed, 10c to 11c; powdered, 10 to11c; granulated 10¼ to 11c
Coffee-choice, 15½c to 16c, prime, 14½ to 15c; good, 12¾ to 13½c
Soap-per box, White Russian, $4.80, Blue India 1 lb. bars, $3.25; Kirk's Olive, $2.90, Irish, $3.50
Candles-full weight, 13 ½ c to 14c.
Snuff-1-ounce cans, $4.00; 2-ounce cans, $6.75; 1-ounce packs, $3.25; 2-ounce packs, $6.25
Eggs-10c per dozen
Turkeys-50c to $1.00
Dried apples-2 to 3c per lb.
Dried peaches-quarters, 3½, halves 4c per lb.
Beeswax-18 to 20c per pound
Cotton rags-clean, 2c per lb.
Wool-unwashed, 29 to 25c; tub-washed, free of burs, 35 to 37c
Oysters-per dozen, 1 lb. cans, FW, $1.25; 2 lb. FW, $1.85; 1lb. LW, $1.00; 2 lb. LW, $1.40

While her mother saw to the household duties, Nannie had the opportunity to play. Outside play was such fun, even at night. Nannie's aunt, for whom she was named, lived next door and had a wonderfully large front and back yard that was perfect for running and playing. Nannie was fortunate to have her two older cousins, Cave, born August 11, 1877 and Mildred Johnson, born January 8, 1880, as playmates. These children had so many possibilities to explore in their outside world. Their imaginations would have been ignited at all the mysterious sights and sounds that introduce themselves outdoors.

There is still today a stone pathway that runs between the Johnson and Tyler houses, evidence of the connectedness of these two families. How many times did the Tyler and Johnson families use this pathway to visit, exchange news, or for the children to play? The pathway is well-worn as a testament to its continuous use.

A rare photo of Cave Johnson (on the left) with J.R. Harper playing cards. circa 1900. On the back is handwritten note by Cave Johnson: "Dear Sew, please ask your father if he recognizes the four aces which I hold. Yours Sincerely, Cave Johnson of Tennessee". Harper would live to be connected with city government for the rest of his life. (MCA)

It is said that in the old days, life moved much slower. The world that Nannie knew allowed for people to really know one another. It certainly was one in which she was surrounded by a loving family and a father who would have done anything to protect her, at least, within his ability.

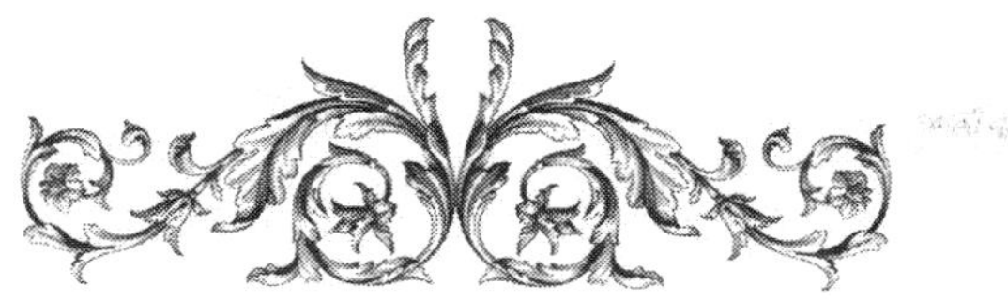

Chapter Thirteen: Nannie's Visits Downtown

A variety of sights and sounds in town that Nannie was to encounter in her short lifetime were the dusty streets, smell of horses and buggies and the odor of gas lamps as she walked the downtown sidewalks with her family. Church bells and train whistles, as well as people conversing on city street corners would be part of her life. There were no wide screen TV's, cell phones, electronic devices, computers...and yet no cures for so many diseases that are easily dispensed of today such as the one that would take Nannie's life.

If a parade, circus, or carnival took place in Clarksville, the Public Square was where to go to catch the exciting event. In the fall of 1882 alone, three circus groups, including Cole's, Sell's Brothers and Forepaugh's, performed in Clarksville. Crowds of spectators lined the sidewalks, straining for the best views of the festivities. People also filled the balconies and windows of the Public Square buildings and even stood on the roofs.

A circus in the Public Square. (MCA)

Pennies and nickels were hoarded for weeks prior to the arrival of the yearly carnival to pay for the rides and sideshows. A plank fence, allowing enough walking space in front of businesses, cordoned off the entire perimeter of Public Square each year. Events such as these were the exciting portions of a child's life especially one as young as Nannie.

Walking in the Public Square there would be the hustle and bustle of tobacco business being conducted in the tobacco exchange building. Situated at the northwest corner of the Public Square stood the very center of tobacco business in Clarksville. The main building was and towered four stories high from the basement up to the distinctive cupola. The two-story rear building had a mansard roof that allowed for the inclusion of a skylight that illuminatec the salesroom. The Tobacco Board of Trade made use of some of the offices and salerooms. A restaurant run by Frank Byers and Charlie Lehman was located on the first basement level.

The imposing tobacco exchange building that cost approximately $20,000. The exchange building was later sold to the Tennessee Central Railroad and served as its offices for many years until it was razed in 1932.[100] (TSLA)

The first and second floor of the main building contained offices that could be rented out to local business men. Social events were held on the third floor that featured handsome chandeliers. Water fixtures and steam heating were conveniences enjoyed by everyone. This mammoth

[100] The Doubletree Hotel now occupies the former site of the tobacco exchange.

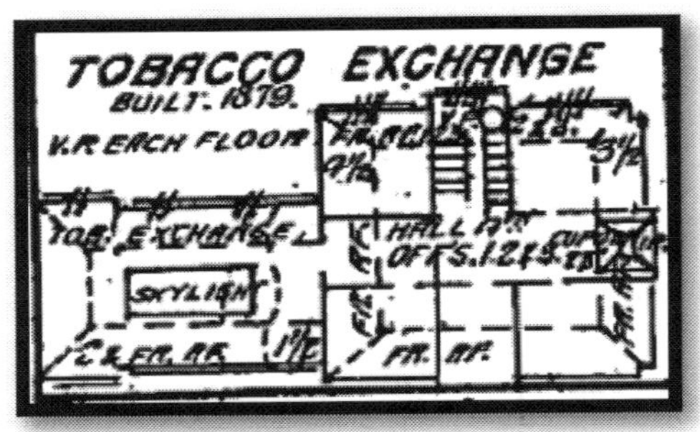

nineteen-room structure was completed just two years before Nannie's birth with exchange business beginning in 1880. Two of the rooms were supplied with fire and burglar-proof vaults making them ideal for banking purposes. It had a fine hall fifty feet square used for multiple purposes. A telephone was installed for use by the members and tenants with speaking tubes that ran to the lower floors. Remembering the great fire, a deep cistern was dug in the yard.

The cupola on top of the building was designed not just as an architectural feature but also as a vent to cool the inside during hot days. At its very top sat an ornate weathervane. Business was conducted with Great Britain, France, Spain, Italy, Denmark, Belgium, Holland, Switzerland, Russia, Austria and South Africa. Alfred Clebsch, the prominent tobacco broker from Bremen, Germany was instrumental in promoting the need for the tobacco exchange building. Also contributing to the overseas trade with Germany was Archer Howell.

The salesroom with a skylight. From author's collection.

Local tobacco sellers would congregate to display their tobacco samples in the salesroom for the best inspection conditions. Here the sellers would barter over prices. Tobacco was such an important part of Clarksville's existence that the newspaper ran a column exclusively on tobacco in every issue!

On the right: The so-called "farmers' gallery." Note the balcony that overlooked the room. The light in the room was provided by two large gas-powered chandeliers and expansive windows. The balcony had its own chandelier. The two back doors were ornamented with pediments. There are divided louvered shutters on the windows. (MCA)

The *Nashville Tennessean* declared the exchange in Clarksville "the handsomest trade building in the state perhaps with the exception of the Cotton Exchange in Memphis."

In the fall, it is also possible that Nannie might have looked down from the Public Square at the meandering river once called the Warioto by the Indians and seen horse or mule-drawn wagons hauling tobacco on Front Street towards the vast Grange or Elephant tobacco warehouses. The economy of Clarksville was directly connected to the sale of its dark fired tobacco and evidence of this would have been seen all over town, especially as the downtown area was expanding and experiencing such tremendous growth.

In 2023, when the level of the Cumberland was at its lowest, the old cobblestone wharf and a heavy iron ring embedded in concrete was exposed at the Clarksville wharf. This embedded ring served as the means to anchor a vessel to the shore. These were nicknamed "deadman anchors" because they were buried in the ground. This particular one may have been used by the Gracey's wharf boat or the City Ferry.

Deadman anchor. Photo by author.

The Cumberland River had several landings for the export of Clarksville tobacco. Today Trice's Landing, looks much as it did when the men on the steamboats loaded hogsheads of dark fired tobacco unto their decks. This landing is found below Ft. Defiance and was the spot were Federals troops disembarked from their gunboats before taking the deserted fort during the Civil War. Other landings include Linwood, (New) York and the Clarksville Landing

It would have been a sight to see on April 19, 1883 when the *Hot Spur* towboat came down the Cumberland towing the new mammoth wharf boat for Gracey & Bro. The boat was "40 feet over all, 160 feet long and had a capacity of almost 5000 sacks of corn or 350 hogsheads of tobacco." Frank P. Gracey, owner of the boat stated facetiously, "The old wharf boat has hatched and the *Julien Gracey*[101] is setting."

The wharf boat is shown in the foreground. (MCA)

The banks of the river were often lined with steamboats and paddle wheelers unloading passengers. Buggies filled with people would have come up the steep Main Street hill by the exchange building into Public Square from the river boats to either the Franklin House Hotel at the south end of the square or the Washington Hotel at the north end. The Washington Hotel (once known as the Southern Hotel or Moore's Hotel) was built as a three-story brick structure.

From left to right in the photo: the tobacco exchange building and the Washington Hotel. (MCA)

During its day, this hotel was the location for many grand balls or galas. An invitation to one of these exciting gatherings was greatly desired by every unmarried young lady in Clarksville. Dances at that time were very social functions and important in the lives of those seeking permanent companionship. There were three classes of such affairs: one in which a dollar was paid as the entrance fee (these were open to anyone), one for three dollars a couple (evening dress was not required), and one for five dollars' entrance for gentlemen in claw hammer coats and ladies in "rustling silk crinolines." Following a fire, its top two stories were removed and the building served as the tobacco warehouse for Adolph Hach and other business until it was demolished in the 1970s.

The Franklin House, built on the southwestern corner of Public Square, was known for its hospitality, great food and NO ALCOHOL policy. The proprietor, Billy Bringhurst and his wife Sally

[101] The *Julien Gracey,* a shallow-draft, sternwheel packet named after Frank Patton Gracey's son, was built in 1880. It navigated the Red River primarily between Clarksville and Port Royal as it was designed for use in local river trade. The line, established by Frank and Matt Gracey, dealt in coal, hay, corn, salt, and lumber. On one occasion it would be used for a much different purpose...

raised their ten children in the hotel and so removed the bar when they purchased it.

Constructed out of red brick, the interior was supported with huge poplar beams and joists secured with impressive wooden pegs. Summer patrons sought out cool breezes off the river from the tiered balconies facing Public Square, which also afforded grandiose views of the Cumberland River and surrounding valley. This three-story structure was filled with river pilots, salesmen, steamboat captains and out-of-town visitors. Salesmen or "drummers" made this hotel their “home base” from which they would rent a carriage or wagon, traverse the countryside to fill orders for their products and then in later years, telephone their requests in to the home office.

The Franklin House known for serving the best food in town.

Competition was fierce between these hotels, each boasting of better accommodations, food and service. Anyone who stayed at these hotels would, without fail, find their names printed on the front page of the *Tobacco Leaf* newspaper, along with the reason for their visit and who they visited while in Clarksville. The owners of these hotels enjoyed feeling as though they served the best clientele.

In later years a large concrete sidewalk was poured in front of the hotel with steps leading down the hillside to the Tennessee Central Railroad Freight Depot on Spring Street. The hotel continued to conduct business until Sunday, October 5, 1952 when a sensational fire caused its destruction. From 7 a.m. when the blaze began until 8 a.m. the next day, firemen, intent on its containment, battled the fire. The fire was such a danger to surrounding buildings that men from the Clarksville Base came to assist with fighting the fire. This, the longest fire ever fought in Clarksville, brought many to tears, whose fondest memories were linked to events held in the hotel.

Situated near the center of Public Square stood the large, two-story brick market house constructed as a long building with two short center wings on the front and backsides and a six-sided cupola on the roof. It replaced a crude wooden one built during the city's early days. On the ground floor farmers were allowed to sell their produce while the second story was used as a Town Hall for City Council meetings. To read the newspapers of the day, it would seem that citizens were sorry that this unpopular building was not brought down by the great fire.

An explanation was demanded by the public for the necessity of ringing the market house bell on the hour, every hour from 9 p.m. until day break each day of the week. It was claimed that the bell pealed forth “deafening sounds” that awoke every guest in both of the Clarksville hotels. If, the intent was to awake everyone in town, they stated, it “succeeded admirably.” Still, they pleaded for “a night of unbroken slumber.” Even during the Federal occupation of Clarksville, the bell was a vexation for on numerous occasions it was rung out of mischief by “small black children.” In later years, this building became such an eyesore to the Public Square; it was razed.

The Poston Building, located on the northwest corner is one of the few buildings on Public Square still standing today from Nannie’s lifetime. John Poston built it as a Federal Style commercial building in 1843. Tennessee limestone blocks serve as the foundation for this structure and the roof has a stepped parapet end wall. The building actually housed three separate businesses, one of which was a cabinet store, specializing in furniture and caskets. Each unit had its own recessed doorway and stairway to the second floor and to the basement. Exterior doors are double leaf, multi-light with transoms. Interior doors connect the three units. The 9/9 windows facing the square are double hung with wooden lintels and sills. There are five fireplaces and the walls are plastered. The undertaking establishment owned by the Couts family operated there for years. Embalming was not practiced until years later at the end of the Civil War. When a casket was required, the family could simply request one of the three sizes, child, youth, or adult and it would be delivered to the home or another location. The steep incline of Main Street separated this building from the tobacco exchange. Still legible today on this side of the building facing Main Street and visible from the Cumberland River once used to attract “river trade” is a painted advertisement.

The Poston Building, the oldest business building still standing in Clarksville. (MCA)

It is amazing that over so many years, this sign has withstood all the elements of weathering. The concoction that made up the background pigment included a lamp black powder mixed with clear varnish and minerals spirits. The other colors that were used were prepared in the same manner with a little Japan Dryer mixed in.[102] It reads:

1845
J.F. Couts' Son Furniture and Undertaking
In rain or shine, just as fine
Uneeda Biscuit
5c a package

Up the hill from the Franklin House at the south end of Public Square was the Heimansohn Building, built in the 1840s. Its construction was similar to the Poston block, however this building stood a story higher and twenty feet longer than the Poston block. Both buildings were labeled as Philadelphia architecture due to their resemblance to business houses found in that famous city. Through the years, this three-story red brick building served as the telegraph office and local newspaper office until being purchased in 1896 by Lui Heimansohn to use as a warehouse for hides, beeswax, wool and furs. For one hundred years it retained the name until the business was relocated to another site.

Elder's Opera House, another impressive building, stood on the southeast corner of the Public Square where memorable dramatic and musical performances were held. This structure replaced the old Melodeon Hall destroyed in the 1878 fire. It was described as an "immense building of great strength supported by iron columns, large stone and brick pillars and powerful wood joists and raftering."

The opera house print from *Picturesque Clarksville* and a diagram of its interior from a Sanborn Fire Map.

The brick structure was 135 feet long, 80 feet across and occupied the entire block from Franklin Street to Legion Street. Originally opened in 1879, the interior of the building was completely remodeled eight years later to include a parquet, dress circle and gallery. In addition, the opera house added four proscenium private boxes, in two tiers, which were richly furnished. Approximately 800 people could then attend the opera house performances in much more comfortable conditions. Parents would bring their children to enjoy a minstrel show, musical, or comedy show.

The western half of the first floor of the opera house was built to serve as the post office that shared the first floor with various other businesses. Before Cave Johnson, as U.S. Postmaster General, introduced the adhesive postage stamp, delivery was paid for by the person *receiving* the mail. Therefore, the only way for the post office to be paid was for citizens to come pick up and pay for their mail. If, after a few days, a person's mail had not been picked up, he or she could expect to see their name listed in the paper with a warning that after a designated time period, it would be destroyed. It was not until 1890 that Clarksville enjoyed its first delivery of city mail. Elder's Agricultural and Hardware Business occupied the second floor. Here, buggies,

[102] Japan Dryer is used to speed the drying time for oil-based paints, enamels and varnish. These can no longer be used as they have been found to be carcinogenic.

wagons and plows were stored. The rest of the second and the entire third floor were reserved for the opera house.[103] At times, the opera house would even be utilized as a skating rink and for just 50 cents couples would be admitted and given skates to enjoy an evening of fun. The rink opened on April 12, 1906.

Just across Franklin Street from the opera house was McComb, Hurst and Company, a store that advertised, "gum drops, decorated creams, assorted jelly, rock candy and a very large assortment of prize candies and gift goods." The store also carried "all sorts of chewing gums." What a temptation for any child to have to walk by that store and not beg for a sample! John Hurst, a Civil War veteran and friend of the Tylers' lived in a house on Madison Street. Judge Tyler would have passed his house twice daily on his way to and from the courthouse and church on weekends.

Walter McComb and John Hurst.

During the workday and Saturdays in downtown Clarksville, the sidewalks would be full of people conducting their day-to-day business, especially on such bustling streets as Madison, Franklin and Commerce. Sidewalks in the 1880s were illuminated by gas, a recent but definite improvement over the old, very inefficient, quick burning oil lamps that did not produce substantial lighting at all and had to be hand-lit each night by a single man who served as the lamplighter for the entire town.

It was a time when men tipped their hats to women on the street and stood aside to let them enter a store first. Most definitely, foul language would not be spoken around women or children. Women were considered delicate creatures that needed protection from the unpleasant aspects of life and were perceived as being incapable of making decisions for themselves.

The downtown was also a mixture of smells. Meat markets with their offerings of beef and pork hanging on hooks or stacked like chords of wood inside the doors of stores, bakeries with tantalizing aromas, tobacco warehouses and the not-so-pleasant remnants of horse and mule traffic.

Kleeman and Co. Meat Market on Franklin Street. Note the stacked hog carcasses on the left of the photo. (MCA)

The time in which Nannie was born was well past the days of the pioneers but still very much in the minds of the citizens. Just by looking across the river to the bluffs at the confluence of the Red and Cumberland Rivers was the land upon which the most horrific of massacres took place. The story of the tragedy of Valentine Sevier and his family were told in the homes, on the porches and in the school rooms of the town.

Fiederling's Cigar Store Indian

Fiederling's Cigar Store Indian. (MCA)[104]

By walking down Franklin Street one would have encountered the life-sized wooden Indian in front of Frank Fiederling's Cigar and Tobacco Store, Children were reputed to be easily drawn to the statue since it appeared that any second the Indian could come alive. For indeed it was the Native Americans who introduced this crop to the new comers to the continent. This plant that would place Clarksville, Tennessee on the map as the dark-fired capital of the world!

[103] During a remodel in 1888, the First Christian Church then located on Madison and Third Streets used the seats from the opera house for services until their new pews could be installed.

[104] The statue was sold years later by Phila Hach to a collector up north.

The wooden Indian stood with feathered headdress and raised tomahawk at the entrance of the business. Fiederling purchased the Indian for $45.00 in Paducah, Kentucky at a bankruptcy sale. Its original price had been $145.00. The statue was carved from soft pine and painted vibrant colors to act as a sentinel at the storefront. In the head of the statue, a hole was bored where oil would be poured on occasion to act as a preservative and as a way to prevent cracking, as pine often does. This store was frequented by men, but rarely visited by women until the holiday season rolled around when cigars were purchased as gifts. Frank took great pride in the quality of the cigars sold in his store. He and his wife Hannah, as many storeowners did, lived in an apartment above. On March 20, 1880, just about one year prior to Nannie's birth, Fiederling introduced Clarksville's first hand-rolled cigar.

It is known that on one visit to downtown Nannie's parents took her for a very special photo session at MacCormac's Photo Galleries across from Fiederling's. William J. MacCormac,[105] a transplanted Scot from Edinburgh, was a favorite among children who affectionately called him "Mac." Unable to have children of his own, Mac doted on those who walked up the steep stairs to his studio on the second floor of the Lieber Trade Palace, a store of dry goods and clothing. His studio was originally located in the Public Square. MacCormac's new gallery was 125 deep and furnished in:

> **elegant style . . . with all the necessary work rooms, parlor or display room, dressing room, etc. The picture gallery is beautifully finished and is very attractive, having a remarkable skylight and handsome walnut and pine trimmings, and with all warmed by a hot air furnace, which heats the whole building, something rarely found in photo galleries.**

Nannie was dressed in a two-piece outfit of crème or white batiste. She wore a sleeved, layered collar decorated with daisies over the bodice, which was hooked in the back. The sleeves of the collar were scalloped and included ribbons, probably of velvet to match the one in her hair, as was the custom of the day.

On the left: Nannie's photograph taken one year before her death. (GF) On the right: W.J. MacCormac in his kilt.

Next to Nannie in the photo is a stuffed toy (a kitten); one has to wonder if it was a favorite of hers. She is standing on straw that was added to hide the base of the stand that was attached to Nannie to help keep her as still as possible. Nannie's photo would serve a very tragic function later.

On the front of her bodice were vertical French pleats. The skirt, also made of batiste, shows faggoting, in which a ribbon would have been woven in through the openings until it encircled the skirt. There was some cut work and scalloping at the hem of the skirt. To achieve the ruffling of the bodice, horsehair braiding was used. To add versatility to her clothes, Nannie's mother would have had several collars made of different colors that could be worn over the same outfit. Nannie wore knee stockings and shoes with buckles. A pin adorned her collar at the top and a bracelet is seen on each of her arms. The pin was indeed special for it was a pin created for Mildred Tyler at Tiffany's in New York and presented to her by her son-in-law, Polk Grundy Johnson. The bar pin has the words "Mother" spelled out in sixty small pearls, set in gold.

[105] Even though MacCormac was not in favor of succession he personally raised money to clothe the local Confederate troops.

MacCormac's Gallery was on the second floor of Lieber's Trade Palace.[106] Note the slanted skylight. In this print the staircase is shown incorrectly on the wrong side of the Trade Palace. From *Picturesque Clarksville.*

Often it is asked why people never smiled in the photographs during the 1800s. Some of the answers offered include the fact that many people simply had bad teeth, as dental hygiene was not widely practiced. It has also been suggested that it was not customary to smile. A practical reason was that photographing a person required up to 30 minutes of exposure time before closing the shutter. This meant the person had to remain perfectly still for that length of time and obviously it was much easier to have a straight face than to maintain a smile for half an hour. Photographers also employed a brace that would fit around a person's neck and waist to reduce movement.

The apparatus for steadying someone being photographed.

Additionally, the brace could be attached to a chair when needed. Studios of the time might have had a half-dozen of these in case they were needed for a group or family photo. Each person would have one placed at the back of their head. By posing the person/persons being photographed, either standing or sitting, the brace would be adjusted to the appropriate height. The fork of the brace would be pressed against the head just behind, and hidden by the ears. The person is instructed to lean into it and remain still while the photographer focuses the camera and loads the plate for exposure and then for the endurance of the exposure itself. Blinking during the 30-minute exposure meant that eyes were usually blurred. The photographer later simply penciled in the eyes. To a child, 30 minutes must have seemed to last forever but her photo turned out beautifully clear.

Nannie certainly would have seen her father's new courthouse located in between Second and Third Streets. This splendid building was impressive both in its size and design. No doubt the judge was quite proud of it due all the effort he put into its completion. One has to wonder if Nannie was ever allowed to visit her father's courtroom.

Commerce Street businesses included buggy and wagon manufacturers, livery stables, horse-shoeing establishments and the all-important foundry. Henry Pitt Dorris began the construction of a foundry on Commerce Street in the winter of 1853 and on August 29, 1853, the foundry was open for business. John P.Y. Whitfield who became his assistant later bought the foundry in 1858 that became known as Whitfield, Bradley & Co.

Six months after Nannie's birth, the Clarksville Ice Factory began its business in Clarksville. It advertised that its ice came from pure distilled spring water. The price was listed as 50 cents per hundred, (there is no unit of measurement noted in the advertisement), so ice was available if the Tylers chose to use it.

Large residences were springing up along Madison Street, as Clarksville merchants and bankers were prospering from the tobacco trade and could afford stately family homes. These residences had ornamental iron or plank fencing as a means to protect property from runaway horses and keep drunks from coming into the yards. It was not advisable for parents to allow their children to play on the sidewalks as runaways were common occurrences, with injury or death a real danger.

Along these streets Nannie would have witnessed some of Clarksville's crowning architectural achievements. One such example was that of the new Madison Street Methodist Church, an impressive structure with two asymmetrical gothic revival towers (145 and 120 feet tall). When

[106] Today the Lieber Trade Palace building houses the Franklin Street Blackhorse Pub.

the church's 1,000-pound bell was installed in the left spire in 1883, its resounding call was heard all over town and would have easily been heard at Nannie's house.

Clarksville's Madison Street Methodist Church. (MCA)

By 1881, more and more business owners opened their own individual markets along Franklin Street thus eliminating the need for a centralized market house. However, as time would show, the market house would remain on the Public Square well beyond its usefulness.

During the second week of July in 1881, telephone poles arrived in Clarksville. It was estimated that by the first week of September, twenty-five to thirty businesses and several private homes would have telephone service. Those who had not signed the contract for the service were encouraged to do so. It is not known when the Tylers may have gotten a telephone but with his position, it is easy to think it would become a vital convenience for the judge to use; or maybe constant nuisance.

RESIDENCE TELEPHONES
Each on a Private Line,
$1.50 per Month or 5c per Day
HOME TELEPHONE CO.

The telephone was not only a business venture, but also termed "an admirable thing for bashful young men and timid old bachelors to have a telephone attached to their girl's ear as a love-making machine!" The telegraph operator, Ed Pearce, John Henry Pearce's brother, managed the telephone lines and hired a number of boys and girls to help in the office. The early lines from Clarksville led to Nashville, Hopkinsville and Russellville, Kentucky. Let the gossip begin!

The people of Clarksville were excited about the new Louisville & Nashville Train Station on Commerce Street which began construction in September 1881. The station was but a short distance from the Tyler home. Already familiar with his previous achievements such as the courthouse, tobacco exchange and the Immaculate Conception Church, architect C.G. Rosenplanter was hired to design the station and Barksdale, Clark & Co. Contractors, to build it.

The L & N train station (MCA)

The station has been through several renovations during the decades, including an extensive one in 1916. Thousands of passengers passed through the station until it closed in 1966. The railroad maintained ownership of the station and used it for other purposes for several years until the City of Clarksville purchased it in 1982. In 1996 the building was renovated again as part of Montgomery County's celebration of Tennessee's Bicentennial. Maintained for years by the Montgomery County Historical Society, the city has taken it over once more to serve as a venue for events. Before its re-opening in April of 2025, the butterfly shed was renovated and inter or improvements made such as a remodel of the kitchen and bathrooms.

When a little older, Nannie probably met many of these businessmen. She also may have witnessed her father's involvement in various ceremonies and gatherings, even though at her young age had no real understanding of his importance in the community. By some newspaper accounts, it seems that Nannie was quite well known herself around town as a child doted on by whoever met her. Certainly Judge Tyler and his wife would have been proud parents.

Six months after Nannie's birth on September 21, 1881 Clarksville businessmen sent samples of their products to be displayed at the Atlanta exposition. They included:

Micajah H. Clark & Bro.: thirty-three samples of tobacco
Meriwether & Patch: a dozen plows, cotton scraper, straw cutter and white oak timber
G.B. Wilson: several packages of lumber
F.G. Williams: a box of Arlington lime
Squire J.M. Anderson: a box of yellow Willis corn
P.H. Porter: a bottle of grape wine
John R. Martin: two grapevine walking canes
Sam Hodgson: a small specimen of marble from Toomb's quarry on the Cumberland River
F.P. Gracey & Bro: five specimens of hematite

It was lamented by the newspaper that none of the millers of wheat and flour sent anything at all in for the exposition.

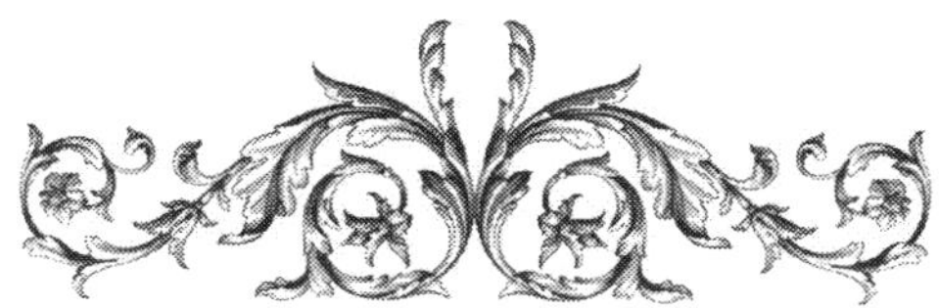

Chapter Fourteen: Clarksville's Last Legal Hanging

The judge had his daily duties and sometime his day might be met with some unexpected event. On October 11, 1881, there was great concern that there was going to be a repeat of events that led up to the fire of 1878. Clarksville was still recovering from the horrific event when a similar occurrence happened very close to the site of where the previous fire began. Officer Frank Phillips confronted two black men on First Street half-way between Commerce and Franklin Streets at 3:30 am. When the men ran and Phillips ordered the one with some unknown object in his arms to stop, the man pulled out a gun. Phillips fired first and then a second shot. The following morning it was discovered that J.J. Crusman's grocery store on the corner of First and Franklin Streets had been robbed. The next morning the money tray was found near the freight depot in the direction the man fled and along with it splattered blood. Judge Tyler had to breathe a sigh of relief that nothing else occurred.

Another fire that might have had spelled a major loss personally for Judge Tyler was one that occurred in his own home at 6:30 p.m. on Thursday, December 8. The fire bells throughout town summoned the entire fire department. They turned around as they reached the academy when they received word that the fire was already extinguished with a water hose. The fire got out of hand while the judge was burning some newspapers and clothing hanging nearby ignited.

On January 21-22, 1882, the Cumberland River overran its banks and flooded low-lying areas making the city an island with all ways into and out-of-town completely cut off. None of the ferries could run and the upper and lower Red River bridges were surrounded by water forcing people to be taken across river in flat boats or skiffs. All of Front Street was under water and the tobacco warehouses and factories along the banks of the Cumberland suffered with several feet of water. People witnessed large amounts of timber and sawed logs floating by as well as an occasional house. One eyewitness to objects being carried down the Cumberland included a fodder stock floating past with a red cow happily chewing away oblivious to its situation.

Front Street covered in water. (MCA)

It was after this flood that the main support of the L & N Railroad bridge was painted marking the level of the river in feet similar to that of one of the bridges in Nashville. Also it was suggested that the buildings adjacent to the river be marked with the river's level in order to record flood levels.

The center pier of the L & N bridge painted with gauges that not only shows the river level but also indicates the clearance underneath the bridge, i.e. the distance between the water and the bottom of the trusses. Photo by author.

Quintus Tyler, who then was a teacher living in Canton, Kentucky, came for a visit to Clarksville in July 1882. He spent his entire summer visiting friends and family, along with former students having taught in Montgomery County years earlier. He stayed with his half-sister Nannie Johnson until he returned home in October. A year later, in August 1883, he returned to Clarksville to attend the Farmers' Reunion held at Dunbar Cave.

People would say that Quintus Tyler had no superior as a teacher except his own father John Duke Tyler. At this reunion, remembrances included that of "hickory oil and black gum tea" and how the rod in Professor Tyler's hands caused "more fear and trembling than the gentleman with the cloven foot." It was also said that even at __ years old, "he still has an eye—yes, two eyes for a pretty woman and a warm heart for his many friends."

In the end Quintus taught for over fifty years, and was known to be "as modest as a woman, never using a word among gentlemen that could not be repeated in the most refined and delicate female and he was never heard to utter an oath of a profane expression. He never used ardent spirits except by order of his physician and then with reluctance."

Quintus made a practice of giving his students a book on literature as a gift. The late Jack Marshall and his wife, Charlotte O. Marshall, owned one such book. Mr. Marshall's grandfather, James Carter Marshall, a former student of Quintus, received his gold embossed leather book in 1865, signed and inscribed with a Latin verse that read, "Si vis vis dactus esse; utere diligentia." Translated it means, "If you wish to be learned, use diligence." At the top of the page is written "Tibi bene ex animo volo" which means, "I wish you well from my heart." The book was entitled, *Melodies, National Airs, Miscellaneous Poems and the Ode of Anacreon* by Thomas Moore. Quintus had beautiful penmanship and the Latin verses, which he included in his signed text, revealed his trademark intelligence. Truly, this was a son of John Duke Tyler.

The late Hazel Goodlett had a copy of the *Ladies' National Magazine* printed in 1848 and within it there is an article reviewing a new book just published entitled, *Wuthering Heights*. The review stated that the book was not worth reading because it was too coarse. The magazine was given to Mattie Bryan Haynes, by her cousin Quintus Tyler. He urged her, "Read it Mattie, you will find it interesting." with the following inscription:

Miss Mattie Bryan Haynes

> **Accept this magazine as a Christmas gift and also as a token the esteem and love of your cousin. Quint. M. Tyler**

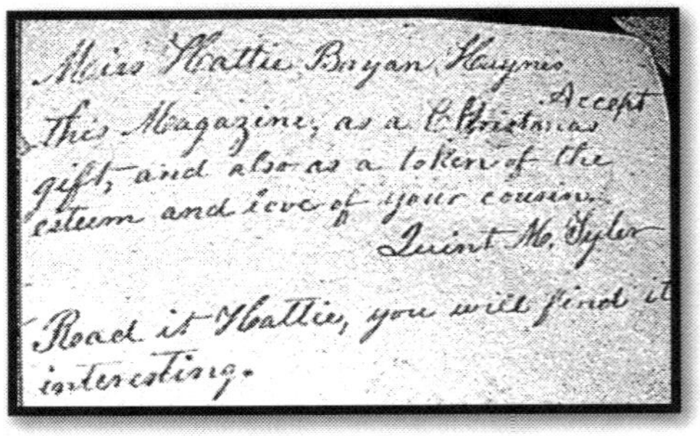

The inscription. (GF)

The Tylers were like other families of the time who traveled from family member to family member to visit. Families kept in contact with each other face-to-face in those days, maintaining strong bonds. In the South, it was very common for family and friends to visit for a "day or so," "a while" (several weeks), "a season or two" (a couple of years), or they might just "stay on" (take up permanent residence). Southern hospitality provided for extended families and older members of the family were assured they would be cared for until their deaths.

If anyone in the South wished to insult a particular thing or situation, all that was needed was to make a comparison between it and some selected portion of the Civil War. Such was the case for the much unloved fire engine in July 1882. Still unsatisfied with the local fire department one local eyewitness to the engine's faults was quoted as saying that

> **While the fire engine was blowing and fizzing with all its might and throwing nothing but wind, that it was like a company of home guards during the *late unpleasantness*- It was h--- on dress parade, but not worth a continental for regular duty.**

On October 5, a small water pipe burst on the upper story of the jail, causing the prisoners to raise an absolute uproar. At this time the jail was located inside the market house. To summon the jailer, the market house bell was rung, which of course stirred up more alarm and considerable excitement. People began rushing to the jail from all around downtown Clarksville. It must have been quite a scene; women running while holding their skirts and men riding on horseback to see what all the commotion was about. After all was said and done, the pipe was fixed and the matter was later termed "trivial." The prisoners did not seem to appreciate their free shower one bit!

Amid complaints and cries for a new jail, Tyler was determined to simply make improvements to the interior of the jail. The management of the jail was revised as well. The renovations included additional room for forty prisoners, doubling the space before. "Better class" prisoners were housed in four rooms separate from the "desperate criminals." Their accommodations included a large steel cage, located on the upper story of the jail. Each room had running water, lights and steam heat.

Clarksville had an expert jail cage manufacturer in Englebert Gaisser & Son. Tyler picked this business to outfit the jail with their cells and highly endorsed their work. He wrote,

> **We take pleasure in certifying that Messrs. Gaisser & Son, who did the iron work for the new jail in this county are reliable and competent workmen and they have done us an excellent job at reasonable prices. Gaisser & Son obtained the contract for the steel cages over several bidders from Louisville, St. Louis and elsewhere and their work has been satisfactory in every way.**

A steel jail cage.

The members of the jail commission who served with Judge Tyler included James H. Achy, G.W. Armstrong and H.R. Rogers. Together the commission members oversaw the purchase of all food, clothing, medicine and other necessities for the prisoners and thus the Clarksville jail was praised as one of the best-managed, most humane jails in Tennessee.

Next came a murder trial that would last for months and end in the first legal hanging in Clarksville of a white man. The murder took place in August 1883, in the Blooming Grove community, located between the Dover Road and the Cumberland River. James William "Bill" Morrow (1851-1885), shot Dick Overton, a black tenant of Morrow's father and threw his body into a 25-foot pit known as "Hell's Hole." This pit is actually a part of Bellamy Cave, named after Morrow's brother-in-law, Dr. Peter F. Bellamy. This was a horrible crime and the body might have never been discovered eight months later except the victim's shirt hung on a rock. A man living in the same community knew who killed Overton went to Maj. Tom Lewis, who lived nearby, told him the details and asked for advice. Lewis told him to go to Clarksville to see the attorney general and tell all he knew.

Bill Morrow. Photo courtesy Ancestry.com.

William was the son of Ransom (1818-1899), and Almeda Caudle Morrow (1823-1902). William's first wife was Delilah Ann Allen-Morrow (1850-1879). By her, he had four children: Wilton Hugh Morrow (1873-1901), Ellen N. Morrow (1875-?), John D. Morrow (1877-?), and Charles Chilton "Charlie" Morrow (1876-1964). William's second wife was Elizabeth Jane Hembrick Morrow Vaughan[107] (1861-1930), and their children were Mary Almeda Morrow Bryant (1880-1941), Sarah Leticia "Lettie" Morrow Bowers (1882-1942), and William Jackson Morrow (1884-1954).

Incredibly, Morrow had murdered another black tenant named Jim Brown just three and one half years earlier in February 1879, using the same motive as Dick Overton's killing. Morrow claimed the men had tried to commit an outrage first upon his sister, Alice Almeda Morrow, (1852-1924), in the first case and then upon his daughter, in the second case. In the first trial, he was acquitted due to "reasonable doubt" but Judge Tyler and the jury had had enough and were not letting Morrow off the hook the second time. Dr. Bellamy did not take part on the killings, but he allegedly ordered the murders and helped cover them up. The trial was laborious and sensationalized in the press.

[107] Eliza Morrow remarried after the death of her husband Bill Morrow; her last name was Vaughn.

The strain of the trial was likely the reason that the judge left for a 10-day trip to Florida. He returned to Clarksville on November 20. The weight of the stressful proceedings and its surety that the man would hang would cause anyone to feel a need to simply get away from everything associated with the trial. But it was officially stated that he was on a "prospecting tour." Humor was often incorporated into the news of the day and to inject lightheartedness, the newspaper reported a mathematical problem to be solved by the public. The problem was:

> **Polk Grundy Johnson, Judge Charles W. Tyler, and John J. West went squirrel hunting on Friday, September 21, 1883. West killed seven more squirrels than did Johnson, while Johnson killed three more than Tyler. How many did the party bring home? Hint: Judge Tyler holds the only key to the solution of this problem.**

A short time following the Overton murder there was another killing. This one involved someone Judge Tyler knew well. During the night of November 19, 1883, Jefferson J. Garrott, a Confederate veteran and well-respected tobacco farmer of an eight hundred-acre farm on the Dover Road heard a burglar entering his bedroom window. Garrott had already led an interesting life. He served in the Confederacy in Co. F, 7th Kentucky, later commissioned as a captain in 1862. Garrott was wounded five times during the Civil War. He saw action at Shiloh, Vicksburg, Port Hudson and Baton Rouge and during his last year in the war, he served in the cavalry under Nathan Bedford Forrest. Garrott and Charles Tyler would have fought together at Shiloh. Following the war, he became a successful mercantile businessman in the New Providence area. This he did for eight years until he engaged in the tobacco commercial business in New York. Later, he returned to Montgomery County and turned his attention to farming.

Garrott grabbed a shotgun from the hall and fired a shot that hit the intruder who answered with two shots of his own, one entering Garrott's left lung. A struggle ensued over control of the intruder's gun in which Garrott was aided by his wife, Nannie.[108] At one point, he had the muzzle of the pistol against the thief's breast and Garrott called for his wife, Nannie, to pull the trigger. Meanwhile, the robber yelled for "Frank" to come to his aid. The struggle was so forceful that the pistol broke in two, useless to either party. Garrott grabbed him by the throat while his good wife beat him with the fireplace shovel until they both fell to the floor. With Garrott bleeding from his wound, the robber crawled under the Garrotts' bed. With one last Herculean effort, Garrott grabbed the man and, with Nannie's help, threw him out the window. The only other occupant in the house was their cook, a black lady who refused to come out of her room.

In order to get help for her husband Mrs. Garrott, barefooted and dressed only in her nightgown, ran to the nearest house which belonged to John Tandy, one half-mile away, Tandy went immediately to the Garrotts' house after sending for Dr. E.J. Neville of New Providence and Drs. Charles W. Bailey and Charles W. Beaumont of Clarksville. Fortunately, although Garrott's wound was very grave, it was not fatal.

Upon later investigation, a 38-caliber pistol with two chambers empty was found on the floor of the Garrotts' bedroom. A hat was found in the bedroom and another on the porch under the window. It appeared the thieves intended to use two 2½ ft. long clubs in their attack, taken from the woodpile. The clubs were found on the porch as well. The next discovery was grimmer; the burglar's body was discovered after the sun rose, twenty-five steps from the corner of the porch where he was shot.

The man was lying on his left side in a fetal position, legs drawn up with one arm across his chest. The other arm appeared to be clutching something, as it lay straight out. All of the shot from Garrott's gun lodged in the lower part of his neck. In the man's pockets were tools of all kinds used for burglarizing. The headline of the *Clarksville Semi-Weekly Tobacco Leaf* covering the attack read:

A DEADLY FIGHT
Tramps Attack the House of a Quiet Citizen,
Break in his Window and Assault and Desperately Wound Him
One of Their Numbers Shot to Death

---

[108] Garrott's wife was Nannie P. Grinstead from Kentucky whom he married on January 4, 1870. Her mother was the sister of Thomas Franklin Pettus.

It was necessary to identify the body to determine who he was as well as his accomplice but this was one of the dilemmas of the case. One person identified him as William Taylor. Others said that he was someone registered at the Franklin Hotel as Samuel Patterson of Louisville. William J. MacCormac photographed the body and the picture was circulated in the local newspaper that stated the body was "exposed to the gaze of the public in Gill's Livery Stable." The man was described in the newspaper as:

> **dressed in a suit of brown with small red dots in it. The suit was in fair condition and was worth when new probably twenty-five dollars. He was apparently about thirty-five years of age (paper is creased) in height and well built, weighing probably 165 pounds. His hair was very dark, almost black, and inclined to curl; brown eyes expressing intelligence and determination; square well-shaped mouth, and short moderately thick blond mustache; head large, features symmetrical, face rather long than round. He had been in more than one bout, as scars on his person showed. Just under the hair over the left eye, running back from the forehead, was a scar about two inches in length that had been made by some ragged instrument; on the forehead over the right eye was another scar, on the left side of the neck under the ear was another ugly one, and still another under the chin. On one side of the left leg below the knee were scars evidently made by a pistol ball passing through.**

On the left: The unknown assailant whose body was discovered in the Garrotts' yard. The photo was taken by W.J. MacCormac. On the right: The sensational headlines for one of the most bizarre cases ever brought before Judge Tyler. (LC).

AN AWFUL AFFAIR.

Attempted Burglary and Assassination.

Two Unknown Men Enter a Residence At Night.

One of the Burglars Killed and Mr. J. J. Garrott Badly Wounded.

Great excitement prevailed in Clarksville Tuesday morning when the news was circulated that Mr. J. J. Garrott had been badly wounded during the previous night by some desperate burglars, who entered his house, and that one of the burglars had been found dead in Mr. Garrott's yard. Everybody was anx-

Confusing the matter even more was the testimony from the Garrotts' cook who claimed to have seen four or five men in the yard that night. She insisted they all ran away after the first shot was fired. As the men ran from the yard, she stated they fired several shots in the distance. The newspaper dismissed this as an overactive imagination. Finally, a suspect, Benjamin Franklin Thaxton was arrested on November 24 in Russellville, Kentucky. In addition, within the surrounding area all "other tramps who could not give account of themselves" the night of the attempted murder were duly arrested as well. Thaxton was accused of attempted murder and robbery upon Garrott. The prosecution used testimony from Thaxton's wife, Purity Hooser Thaxton, who claimed that Ben was "a consummate villain and ought to be hung on general principles."

This attempted robbery was thought to have been precipitated by Garrott's purchase of a small iron safe in Clarksville. It was believed that the assailants probably witnessed him taking the safe home, believing it to be used to store large amounts of money, as Garrott was known to be a wealthy man. Then an amazing thing occurred, Taylor turned up alive and well in Russellville, Kentucky! Thaxton however fought against his arrest with an alibi and was released. Again and again he was arrested, then released. Finally, Chief of Police Matt Carcuff succeeded in getting Thaxton to the jail in Clarksville, believing he had enough circumstantial evidence put Thaxton before the court.

On the day of the examination before Judge Tyler to determine whether a trial was warranted, the courtroom was so crowded and full of excitement it took several minutes before proceedings could commence. Tyler ordered the room cleared of all except the lawyers in the case and the newspaper reporters. He then stationed officers at the openings to keep the crowd back behind the railing. During testimonies, two ladies of questionable reputations testified they saw powder burns on Thaxton's vest and heard him talk about the shooting.

When Garrott was physically able to testify, he told of how he was bitten by the thief and by the marks on his hand he could determine that the man had a tooth missing on his left side. Thaxton was missing a tooth on that side of his mouth. The body was finally identified as that of

Samuel Patterson; another man, Lewis Lowe, was arrested and later indicted for the crime against Garrott. In late January 1884, Judge Tyler threw the case out for lack of evidence and Thaxton determined to sue the State of Tennessee for what he called his unlawful arrest and malicious prosecution. He believed himself to be damaged in the amount of $5,000.[109] At his death on December 22, 1924, Garrott was called Montgomery County's oldest Civil War veteran.

Prayers were on everyone's lips when in January 1884 smallpox posed a possible threat to the people of Montgomery County as cases began cropping up in surrounding counties. Judge Tyler immediately carried out the orders of the State Board of Health by requiring the citizens of Montgomery County to be vaccinated against the disease. To offset any financial difficulties some families might experience, he directed that the vaccine be offered free. Those who could pay were charged $1 each for the shot. Dr. C.N. Carney began administering the vaccine at his office at the corner of Hiter and Franklin Streets, along with Dr. Charles W. Bailey. Judge Tyler emphasized the need for everyone to be vaccinated saying that, "the man who fails to take this precautionary step subjects himself and his friends to one of the greatest dangers that ever threatened our section." Besides, he had his family to think of and protecting them was certainly on his mind.

On January 25, his mother, Mildred Smith Tyler passed away from pneumonia outliving her husband by 24 years. The *Clarksville Weekly Chronicle* described her as an "estimable and faithful wife." Mildred was not buried next to her husband at Hickory Wild but in the Greenwood Cemetery. Her tombstone is a large five-foot stone cross inscribed, "Our Mother" and "Thy Will Be Done" on one side and a verse from a hymn on another.

Nannie, as a young child, had no perception of the meaning of death, only an awareness of the absence of the loved one. For Nannie, this sweet endearing lady had been a second mother to her. Mildred Tyler must have been quite a formidable woman. Charles verified in written descriptions of what a Christian lady his mother was and her profound love of the Bible.

The next month Clarksville experienced its most severe tornado to date. It struck at 12:00 noon on Tuesday, February 19, as it entered the downtown area at the southwestern edge and preceded northeasterly passing entirely over Clarksville, causing major damages to businesses and homes along the way. Three of the four pinnacles on the corners of the courthouse were blown off. Eerily, another tornado in 1999 would take nearly the same exact path.

Mollie was pleased to entertain her sister Beulah for several days in mid-April 1884 who at the time was living in Fairview, Kentucky. The sisters shared a deep bond from the loss of their mother's unseemly death when both girls were young.

During May, Judge Tyler laid down the law on anyone who sold liquor on Sunday. The grand jury indicted two saloon keepers for violating the law and were therefore fined $50 and costs for each. J.W. Tutt and Charlie Lehman were strongly warned and Tyler made it known that if any other parties were brought before him for either buying or selling liquor on Sunday he would, if found guilty, fine them to the full extent of the law and send them to prison also.

On June 4, just three months short of three-years-old, Nannie became a big sister to Emma or Em for short, named for her father's younger sister. For any little girl, this must have been such an exciting time. Nannie would have enjoyed helping her mother take care of this new member of the Tyler family.

It came as no surprise when, in August, Judge Tyler's name was put in nomination by Herbert Nordel Leech to represent Montgomery County in Congress. Leech empathically stated that, "the New South needed to be represented by men new in the sense that the South was new and that Tyler was large enough in every sense of the word to represent Montgomery County in Congress, a man of practical and broad views."

---

[109] The consensus of the Clarksville public was that Judge Tyler had been correct to throw the case out. The *Clarksville Weekly Chronicle* dated February 9, 1884, reacted to the news of Thaxton's possible suit by stating

> **If Mr. Thaxton knows any means by which he can bring suit against this sovereign state, there are several parties in New York and elsewhere who will doubtless like to have him explain the process.**

After several months however, Tyler withdrew his name from nomination. Perhaps like his father, he did not have a politician's heart and he recalled how his father disliked being away from home. Maybe he felt residual guilt at going off to fight in the war leaving his widowed mother to run the farm and he did not want to leave Mollie. It also could have been that he felt duty-bound to the people of Montgomery County to remain serving in the capacity as judge. According to one supporter, the judge declined because Tyler wanted to, "render to his county his best, his most faithful service. Montgomery County cannot say that he lived in vain, or that he did not give to his county the full measure of his ability."

Morrow jailed for over a year on Spring Street and getting unnerved supposedly told an officer that he wanted to go before Judge Tyler and reveal the whole matter of the murder but was told a confession would do him no good and that Tyler would not listen to it. On Monday, December 22, 1884 Tyler sentenced Bill Morrow to be hung on January 20, 1885 for murdering Dick Overton. He sentenced Ransom Morrow, Peter F. Bellamy and Bill Morrow to life in prison for the murder of Jim Brown. Appeals were sent to the State Supreme Court.

Polk G. Johnson and Michael Savage served as counsel for Morrow and did what they could to get his sentence commuted to life in prison. A petition with 1500 signatures asking that Morrow's sentence be commuted was sent to Tennessee governor William B. Bates in April. After a stay of sixty days, granted by Gov. Bates, the date of execution was set. As past public executions were not only common but considered a deterrent to those thinking of committing crimes, the tide had turned and now they were viewed as barbaric. The newspaper applauded Judge Tyler and Sheriff Collier for their decision to follow the new law concerning executions and declaring the hanging of Morrow was to be private. The reporter stated

> **The old idea that public hanging induced a wholesome fear of the law, however expedient the sight might be, has been superseded and rightly we believe. It is a morbid and unhealthy feeling that one should wish to see a human being ushered into eternity from the gallows' trap and we are glad that the law does not now allow it.**

A letter printed years before in the March 1881 *Tobacco Leaf* expressed a man's astonishment of people's behavior towards condemned prisoners before their hanging at Gallows Hollow. He mentioned that women bring them flowers and priests rush to their sides. With people dying all the time he wonders why these "monsters" get the sympathy from the public. He states, "Can a man who has crept up to the gallows through common sewers at the last moment, just before the last efforts to obtain pardon, suddenly blossom out into fervent religious life! I don't believe it!"

An often repeated myth involving Judge Tyler's daughter Nannie was one that had her begging her father not to execute Morrow. Nannie was too young to understand about hangings and certainly her father would have never discussed a murder case in her presence.

The Morrow case was so sensationalized in the press, it even went as far as to describe what Morrow ate and how he slept during his last several days. Any unauthorized attempt to view the hanging was futile since the area was completely enclosed. The scaffold was built in the narrow alley between the two buildings of the jail complex and the only open space, which faced towards the river, was blocked off by a tall plank fence. A two-by-four beam was secured between the two walls and a rope of "three quarters sea grass, twenty-one feet long" was brought from Nashville specifically for this execution.

The platform itself was eighteen feet high by six and one-half foot wide. After its construction it was realized that the platform was too tall. If left at that height, after the hanging, Morrow's body would be suspended ten feet above the ground. This error was quickly corrected. Upon Morrow's request none of his remaining five children were allowed to visit him before he was executed. A large crowd of interested persons assembled on the hill in front of the jail. Fearing the crowd might try to administer justice themselves, twelve men armed with double barrel shotguns stationed themselves in front and to the rear of the jail two hours before the scheduled hanging. At two o'clock on June 19, 1885. the prisoner was led to the platform. Dressed in a black suit and blackened boots, (his burial clothes), he listened as Rev. Sears led a solemn prayer. The condemned prisoner who, before having his arms and legs secured and a black hood placed over his head, shook the hand of several witnesses. The noose was placed around Morrow's neck and at 2:14 p.m. the trigger was sprung. Morrow fell through the trap and into eternity. His neck was dislocated but a pulse was felt for seventeen minutes. No struggle ensued nor any motion was indeed, made by Morrow. One half-minute later, Morrow was declared dead by Dr. Daniel F. Wright who prepared a written report to be sent to Judge Tyler, stating that he was sure the death was instantaneous and painless.[110]

Sketch by John Cook printed in the Cumberland Lore of the *Leaf Chronicle* on March 12, 1985, on the 100th anniversary of the hanging.

Attorney Michael Savage. From *Picturesque Clarksville.*

William Morrow was hanged in the presence of approximately 25 persons with "passes" to witness the execution. Besides members of the immediate family and one or two very intimate friends were the jailer, William Rollow, the Achilles Degrasse Sears of the First Baptist Church, Michael Savage and Polk Grundy Johnson. One can imagine that as Rollow was responsible for Morrow while Morrow awaited his fate in the jail that the two had long conversations together and may have even become friends. The one person absent from witnessing the hanging was Judge Tyler himself. He had witnessed enough killing during the Civil War, enough to have his fill of it. What went through the judge's mind on that day will never be known but one wonders how he spent the day knowing his judgment would terminate a man's life? In the end, Judge Tyler and the court jury put an end to a dark episode in the county's history.

The alley where Morrow was hanged. Sanborn Fire Map

How death comes to the victim is in this way. Not in every instance is the neck automatically broken. The noose itself constricts the carotid artery whereby the condemned begins to lose consciousness. Whether or not the neck breaks does not affect the time for the heart to stop, which can be as long as twenty minutes as it was in the case of Morrow. Certainly this does not support the stories that hangings meant immediate death. Also, accounts abound where many such executions were bungled.

After his body was taken down, according to Morrow's wishes, it was placed in a coffin and transported aboard the *Julien Gracey* up the Cumberland River to Blooming Grove Creek and then transported to his house so that his wife and children could view his remains.

On the left: The *Julien Gracey* (MCA). On the right: The Morrow house. Photo by author.

Rollow accompanied the body aboard the steamer. Morrow's last request was to be buried the next day at the Blooming Grove Baptist Church by the side of his first wife, with room on the other side for his second and present wife. This was not allowed by the church and attempts to locate his grave in the church cemetery have been unsuccessful. Additionally, the

110 According to some sources, Maj. Thomas Lewis bought the rope used in the Morrow hanging at the request of Judge Tyler. The murders took place very near to Lewis' property and it is certain Lewis knew the Morrow family.

church cemetery records do not show him being buried there. This is explained by the newspaper article covering his death, which stated that he was buried at his house. The limestone bluff just opposite and slightly down from the Morrow place is the ridge upon which the Bellamy Cave can be found. Really nothing more than a "bottomless" hole in the ground, previous owners cordoned it off to prevent cattle from falling into the abyss. The cave, first exposed many years previous when the bottom of a sinkhole collapsed, can be accessed by a careful descent down stone steps carved into the side. This cave was mined heavily at one time for nitrite. Once inside, the cave splits in two. The route to the right leads to Hell's Hole where the body of Overton was discovered. Today, in addition to the fence, there is a gate over the mouth of the cave and posted signs warning people to stay out.

Locals, along with some of this author's family members also state that in addition to the aforementioned murders, Morrow allegedly enticed several peddlers to come to his house, murdered and robbed them and tossed their bodies into Hell's Hole. His wife and two daughters would see the peddlers there at night but not in the morning. At dark, they were told to go to their rooms, stay there and to "mind their own business no matter what they heard." Afterwards they would hear a commotion and it was then that the alleged murder took place. There are accounts to this day of bloodstains soaked into the floorboards of the house. Morrow allegedly would then throw the body into a cart; ride down the hill, across the field and creek, down the road three quarters of a mile and up to Bellamy's Cave to dispose of the body. This author heard this story while staying with a cousin at her house in the 1960s not far from the Morrows' house. This story was substantiated earlier in the newspaper on the June 6, 1884 issue of the *Semi-Weekly Tobacco Leaf* when the reporter wrote

> **There is no recounting the crimes that have been committed in that section during the last fifteen to twenty years, that have been kept smothered up or that were done so mysteriously that no clue to the perpetrators could be had. Strangers passing through have been missed and no further account of them was had. Some years ago the dead body of a peddler was found in the neighborhood and the verdict of the coroner's jury as it now appears on records in the courthouse is to the effect that an unknown man came to his death from an unknown cause.**

In recent years the cave and the thirty-four adjoining acres were purchased by the Nature Conservatory, which recognized the cave as a vital bat nursery. Blind crayfish and a rare beetle called Coleman Cave Beetle are found here. Studies of the gray bats in Bellamy Cave reveal that in the mid 1970s, the bat population was reduced to just 65 due to human activities. The population has recovered tremendously and now it is estimated that 91,000 gray bats use the cave for their home. Again, this author's cousin recalled instances of seeing bats come out of that cave at dusk in such numbers that it darkened the sky.

As stated earlier, Morrow was the first white man to be hung in Montgomery County but what of any earlier hangings? As with any town at the same time, hangings were carried out as a punishment for crimes such as murder and rape. There were several sites in Clarksville in which the hangings were carried out.

The first recorded murder trial to take place in Montgomery County was that of slave owner, a Mr. Minott. A rebellious slave named Moses Penrice had just been sold to Minott, when he picked up a gun behind a log, shot and killed Minott. Penrice was beaten nearly to death by the guards who came with Minott to get Penrice. The judge pronounced the sentence upon Penrice that he was to be hung by the neck until "you are dead, dead, dead!" This was March 30, 1807, long before the Tylers moved to "the flat land between Franklin and Main Streets and hang him." The site of the execution was behind the residence of Matt Gracey. Then his head was to be "cut off and placed on a pole on the corner of Main and Fourth Streets until the sun had rotted the flesh off the head and the skull bleached white." It was reported that the sheriff carried out the sentence immediately. So why place the head on a pole at this particular location? One theory put forth is that at that time, Fourth Street was the so-called "outskirts" of town. People coming into town from that direction would enter Clarksville by Main Street. This was the judge's method of warning to anyone who entertained thoughts of law-breaking in his town. Penrice's head stayed on the pole but one day.

Sheriff Cocke (1772-1854), carried out the first recorded hanging in the county.

Henry Lyle, who in 1885 was a young man, twenty years after Moses Penrice was hanged remembered that they used an oxcart, not a wagon, for the hanging. He described the wheels of the cart as having no iron on them except the tires and the hubs were made of black tupelo sour gum *Nyssa sylvatica*, a very sturdy wood. These trees he said grew in the Dismal Swamp (of North Carolina), and were brought here when people emigrated from that state.

The Watchman.

Clarksville, June 1, 1821.

On Thursday, the 24th ult. a special court was held in this place, fo the trial of two slaves, the property of Mr. William Sullivan, of this county, charged with having occasioned the death of Mrs. Elizabeth Crockett, by poison. The court and jury were occupied until about eleven o'clock, on Thursday night, with the examination of the case of TRAVIS, when, for the want of sufficient proof, he was acquitted.

On the succeeding day came on the trial of the other slave, KINCHEN, the son of Treavis; and after a patient and full investigation of the case, he was found *guilty*. We learn that the sentence of Death, pronounced on him by the court, is to be carried into execution, on Friday next, the 8th inst.

Another source states that indeed in 1826, there was only one vehicle in town, that of an old one-ox cart that was used to haul prisoners off to the gallows to meet their Maker. The cart was removed from under the poor soul, left to hang until dead and then when it was all over, removed to their plot of earth.

On June 8, 1821, in a heavy downpour, a large crowd watched as another hanging took place. William Sullivan had two slaves named Travis and his son Kinchen. They were both accused of poisoning Elizabeth Crockett. Travis was acquitted but his son was not, and despite the rain, was hanged publicly. It is not certain where this hanging took place.

Another such site for hangings was Gallows Hollow near Front Street. In the hollow, there stood a large sugar maple tree about "400 yards below the old L & N freight depot" and some distance to the rear of the Capt. James C. Kendrick residence." The natural valley provided a type of amphitheater allowing excellent viewing of the proceedings from all directions. In later years, actual wooden gallows may have been constructed.

List of Clarksville Hangings

Name	Crime	Date	Location
Moses Penrice (slave)	Murder of Mr. Minott	March 30, 1807	In the flat between Franklin and Main Streets, rear of Matt Gracey's property
Kinchen (slave)	Poisoning Elizabeth Crockett	June 8, 1821	At City Jail behind Public Square
Unknown: slave	(Unsubstantiated)	1837	Gallows Hollow
Arbert (slave)	Attempted rape	June 10, 1851	Gallows Hollow
Jesse Trigg	Murder of his master, Hampton Trigg	1855	At Double Pond on Franklin Street
Ben Harbert (free black)	Murder of "Aunt Hannah" in 1853	March 7, 1856	Gallows Hollow
Elias Adams	Rape of Mrs. Bristow	April 7, 1855	Gallows Hollow*
William Gray (slave)	Murder of Joseph Harris	February 20, 1858	Illegal (?) hanging somewhere in New Providence
Winston Anderson	Attempted rape	March 1878	Illegal hanging on Nashville Pike in Wm. Daniel's field
William Morrow	Murder of Dick Overton	June 19, 1885	At City Jail on Spring Street

A map of the city of Clarksville in 1870 shows eight houses standing in Gallows Hollow. A small road ran midway through the valley and on the upper side of it were additional houses. The street now called Crossland Avenue did not exist at that time. When, in later years, Crossland joined with High Street to connect with Front Street, the entire street took on the name of Crossland Avenue. One story states that when the hollow was first used as a "hanging place," a large boulder sufficed as a scaffold. The noose was thrown over the limb of a nearby tree and the prisoner was given a little push or the cart that transported him to the spot was pulled forward. Later a proper scaffold was constructed at the south end of Academy Avenue viaduct. The scaffold consisted of four stone or concrete bases for cedar posts. It measured four feet wide by about six feet long. Eighty-two years later, the remains of the scaffold were unearthed as workmen excavated for the new

Clarksville Distributing Company on Cumberland Drive on March 20, 1938. Buried eight feet underground, the ends of two of the cedar posts were still intact in two of the bases. Gus Thomas, who was eighty years old at the time, positively identified the foundation of the old scaffold and remembered his mother, Mrs. Winnifred Covington Thomas, who died forty years' prior, telling stories of how she, as a young woman witnessed while situated high up in a tree, two of the hangings from that gallows. This would have been Jesse Trigg and Ben Harbert in 1856. Thomas recalled how his mother described seeing the condemned man ride atop his own coffin in a dump cart to the gallows. This was verified by Florence F. Bates who ran the foundry Whitfield, Bates & Co. He stated, "Ben was driven by wagon sitting on his coffin down Greenwood Avenue "as far as the Shea[111] place then down near the Tennessee Central Railroad trestle."

Gallows Hollow. Courtesy Google maps.

In so many ways, for so many years, Gallows Hollow was a forgotten place, sad, remote and despised. Poor, but honest people under deplorable circumstances managed to make this a kind of neighborhood. The valley was crisscrossed with pathways and footbridges over Spring Branch Creek. The creek ran through its entire length to the river. Indeed, whenever the river floods, the water habitually backs up into the valley and while occupied, the water made life for the unfortunates even harder. The valley was choked with wildness and a sense of gloom permeated the air. This was indeed land that no one seemingly cared about, but good enough in which to hang condemned prisoners. The only sign that shows the name of the valley as the name of Gallows Hollow is on the pumping station on Riverside Drive. The construction of South Second Street extension in the 1960s across Gallows Hollow bisected the valley.

S. Second Street extension under construction. (LC)

[111] Jane Shea was a widow who lived alone on Spring Street near the freight depot.

The western end of the hollow was made into a playground: Valleybrook Park. Over the years, the playground has been managed by the city and it offers picnic sites and paths within its boundaries. The tornado of 1999 leveled many of the trees that since have been replaced and the shade they offer is most welcome in the summer months.

Through the years, the houses built in this hollow were condemned as part of the Urban Renewal Project and demolished in the late 1960s, early 1970s. In 2023 the entire hollow was bulldozed and the aged walnut trees cut down to build a new development called Judy's Hope. Its mission is to instill hope in the lives of women and children who need a helping hand to secure employment, permanent housing and renewal in living their best lives. The neighborhood immediately north of the valley neighborhood known as Dog Hill is now a registered historic architectural district. The former home of Gen. W.A. Quarles is located at the top of the hill.

Named for the many dogs that would howl at the whistles of passing trains and steamboats down on the river, the houses display cottage and Victorian styles. At the end of First Street was a set of limestone steps leading to a short path in a wooded area on the slope above the railroad tracks. There was a large wooden staircase leading down to the tracks, which would have to be crossed before descending into the park. At one time, an elevated railroad trestle (between 80-100 feet high), crossed the western end of the valley.

The hanging of Elias Adams, convicted of rape, on Saturday, April 7, 1855, was reputed to have attracted a large "gaping and horror seeking" crowd to Gallows Hollow. Curiosity seekers came to Clarksville by every possible method even, according to the newspaper, with three people astride a single horse. It took fifty armed guards, along with the sheriff and deputies to protect the prisoner as they removed him from the jail at about eleven o'clock. The *Clarksville Jeffersonian* recorded what occurred next:

> **Owing to the almost inaccessible nature of the place selected for the execution, the procession was compelled to make a wide detour to reach it. In the meantime, the majority of the crowd took a 'short cut' over the hills and arrived in advance.**

The large crowd caused concern as Adams rode in a cart down into the hollow. Before his arrival, the impatient crowds found diversions such as fistfights to occupy themselves until the execution time. Described as dejected and in despair, the prisoner spent half an hour talking with his friends, persistently maintaining his innocence. With the rope thrown over the beam of the gallows, wound around his neck and with the cap pulled over his eyes, he fell backward into the cart. Elias was helped to his feet once more and could have fallen a second time if the cart had not been removed from under him. Eleven months later on March 7, 1856, Ben Harbert, a mulatto, took his turn on the gallows there. Hangings in those days were used as a means of crime deterrent, intended for public viewing to discourage anyone from entertaining ideas of thievery or murder.

Harbert was quite the slippery character, arrested for the murder of a slave named Hannah in 1853, Harbert confessed to the crime but came close to being acquitted. On the second conviction, his case was appealed to the Tennessee Supreme Court, where the sentence was reversed. He then faced a new trial. Before this trial, he escaped not once but twice. He managed to delay the final outcome for two years and then his time was finally up. Because of the cold blooded manner in which he committed the crime and also due to the way he seemed indifferent to his sentence of hanging, droves of spectators turned out for the hanging. The paper reported that, "from an early hour, a perfect tide of curious, horror-seeking mortals, about half of whom were Negroes, poured out of every road and by-way into town." Between 11 a.m. and noon, Harbert was taken from the jail with an enormous group of citizens accompanying him to Gallows

Hollow. Before the execution commenced, the Rev. J.B. Jackson addressed the crowd stating that Harbert had indeed repented of the crime and "seemed to place full reliance in the hope of a glorious immortality beyond the grave." Harbert then addressed the crowd himself confessing once more to the killing which he committed "while he was fired with liquor" and supporting the sentence to be carried out. He laid the blame of his crime upon his drinking. After some final farewells to friends, he allowed his hands tied and the cap placed over his eyes. The cart upon which he stood started forward leaving Harbert swinging. After seven minutes, he drew his last breath. But this was not the end to the happenings at Gallows Hollow that day. Immediately after the execution, two large sized "ladies" got themselves into what the newspaper termed, "an entirely new feature of fights in this vicinity." After some nasty remarks towards each other, the crowd formed a ring to allow the two "nymphs de pave"[112] to have at it. Hair pulling, tugs of war and various other exertions resulted in torn garments, smashed bonnets and injured pride. Finally, they both gave up, simply worn out from the fight. Both pled guilty when brought before Justice Bailey and after paying their fines, they left to "bind up their wounds and repair their damaged beauty."

Another public hanging took place at the double pond at the corner of Franklin and Sixth Streets. Jesse Trigg was convicted in 1855 of the murder of his master, Hampton Trigg. City officials announced that each black person in the county was to be given a holiday and was required to attend the execution, "that his fate might be an example to all others." It is possible that there were two additional hangings in Gallows Hollow at an earlier date but this is unconfirmed.

A dispute over jurisdiction figured into the hanging of a black man for the axe murder of Joseph H. Harris. On February 19, 1858, Harris' stemmery (where the tobacco leaves were stripped off their stalks), in New Providence was found to be on fire. When Harris' brother came to the business, he found Joseph dead, his head split by an axe. Suspicions led them to one of Harris' workers, William Gray, who had been fired that day for thievery. The accused was placed in the Clarksville jail where, the next day, some citizens of New Providence, (an incorporated town), stated that their town had jurisdiction over the prisoner. He was then taken back to New Providence, tried by a twelve-man "committee" and sentenced to be hanged. Immediately they threw the rope around the prisoner's neck and over the limb of a tree and pushed the bench away. By grabbing unto the rope, the man managed to save his neck but not before he made a full confession to the murder of his employer. He further stated that he struck his employer in the head several times but did not push him into the fireplace; Harris had simply fallen there himself. The mind of the "jury" was already made up and this time the hanging resulted in the prisoner's death. Barker recorded the event in his diary, "Harris of New Providence killed by his Negro and Negro hung today." It has been argued for years whether this act was a legal hanging or a lynching.

Snow fell in amounts never heard of before in February 1885. Twenty-three inches enveloped Clarksville and life took on a quiet period of indoor activities. Sledding was a popular past time for many children on the city's steep hills.

An upsetting event during this time was when W.A. Settle's coal oil storeroom burned with 66 bbls. of oil the last Friday in May of 1885. Mollie knew the stress that this unfortunate fire had on her brother's finances but she was not in a position to do anything about it.

Seeking a local destination for a family retreat, Judge Tyler purchased a lot "in the valley" below Dunbar Cave in August 1885, and had a three-room cottage built there for the use of his family. The land was once owned by James A. Tate, who purchased and ran the Tyler's Hickory Wild Academy so many years before. The Tylers joined other investors who were buying the lots as a vacation spot to use whenever they wished to remove themselves from town to relax. On Monday, August 17, Judge Tyler took his family to stay at the cottage near the cave.

Adolph Hach was to purchase one of the cabins in later years and during Prohibition, he installed a trap door in the floor of a closet in the back which led down to where he kept his moonshine still. One of the rooms in the cabin still retains the 4-inch wide floorboards. The ceiling is high foot high which is very unusual. The entire cabin has been beautifully restored by owner

---

112 The French word for streetwalkers.

Merry Appleton who had the old mud between the logs removed and replaced with cement. She personally sanded down the logs inside the cabin and added several layers of varnish which not only preserved the logs but also made it possible to clean the walls The log cabin built by individual families in the 1880s predated the cottages.

The Adolph Hach cabin. Photo by author.

It was fortuitous that Tyler had withdrawn his name from Congressional nomination the year before because Mollie would need her husband by her side when every parent's worst nightmare struck at the house on Greenwood Avenue. One might wonder if during this trip Nannie contracted diphtheria perhaps by entering the lake and swallowing some of the water that may have been contaminated with the bacteria that causes the disease. If there was contaminated water there, it is fortunate the Em was too small to get near the water. The incubation period for diphtheria is usually 2-5 days but may take as long as up to 10 days. As it was September 9, that Nannie passed away, it looks as though she became infected later perhaps by coming in contact with someone who was contagious. The Tylers' house is 0.7-mile distance from the courthouse in which the judge spent so many of his years and 1.3 miles from where he would have to take Nannie to her final resting place in Greenwood Cemetery. The specter of death visited the Tylers' house four times in a short six-year period.

Chapter Fifteen: Life Without Their "Precious Little Darling"

At Length

Her final summer was it,
And yet we guessed it not;
If tenderer industriousness
Pervaded her, we thought

A further force of life
Developed from within,--
When Death lit all the shortness up,
And made the hurry plain.

We wondered at our blindness,--
When nothing was to see
But her Carrara guide post, --
At our stupidity,

When duller than our dullness,
The busy darling lay,
So busy was she finishing,
So leisurely were we!

--Emily Dickinson

Everything in the Tylers' world was about to change with a horrible finality. On Wednesday, September 9, 1885, at 7:00 a.m., little Nannie succumbed to a dreaded disease. She was 4 years, 5 months and 24 days old. The disease was diphtheria. Imagine the scene at the Tyler house: concerned and distraught family members hovering around her bedside, unable to relieve her suffering as her air passages slowly closed. As is well-known, the judge was inconsolable. Without a doubt, of all the tribulations faced by the Tylers through the Civil War, the great fire of 1878, the impeachment charges and the deaths of numerous family members, this had to be the lowest point of their lives. Charles and Mollie had to be absolutely terrified that they might also lose Em.

Diphtheria is a very contagious infection that primarily attacks the throat and nose. Occasionally it can also affect the nerves and heart. Although it is not known how Nannie contracted the disease, its spread is usually by person to person contact, either by breathing in diphtheria bacteria that has been coughed or sneezed or by coming in close contact with discharges from an infected person's skin, nose, mouth, or throat. The bacteria responsible for diphtheria was isolated in 1884 by Robert Koch; however, it was additional ten years before he and Louis Pasteur developed an antitoxin vaccine. Immediately there was great public pressure placed on the Boards of Health to push doctors into using this new antitoxin. Between 150,000 and 200,000 cases of diphtheria occurred in the U.S. before 1920.[113]

Obituaries in both Clarksville newspapers showed that Nannie was among several children during that time to die from diphtheria.[114] Regardless of how she contracted the disease, her death was a most horrible one. Early symptoms begin with a sore throat and low-grade fever. It progresses when a membrane forms over the throat and tonsils, making swallowing difficult. The lymph glands and adjacent tissues on both side of the throat begin to swell to an enormous size. The toxins from the disease would, after a time, spread throughout her body and damage the heart muscles and possibly paralyze the diaphragm. Eventually the ever-increasing throat membrane blocks the airway. Death could come as a result of any or all of these. Once considered one of the most common causes of death in children, today diphtheria is prevented by the DTP vaccine. No such vaccine existed at the time of Nannie's death.

Several doctors lived on Greenwood at this time such as Dr. Thomas Dickson Johnson. Perhaps he was summoned to the Tyler's house or Charles may have called in his close friend, Dr. Charles W. Bailey. In Clarksville in the 1880s, the sick were cared for at home; a hospital was not available in which to take Nannie.

The *Clarksville Semi-Weekly Tobacco Leaf* newspaper ran this notice on September 11, 1885:

> **The friends of Judge and Mrs. C.W. Tyler greatly sympathize with them in the loss of their bright and lovable little daughter Nannie who died on Wednesday morning at an early hour of diphtheria. Nannie lacked a few days of being four years and six months old, a most interesting age, and few met the guileless little one who did not feel the power to charm.**

The September 12, 1885 edition of the *Clarksville Weekly Chronicle* obituary read:

Death of Little Nannie Tyler

> **Every sympathetic heart in Clarksville has been touched to the core by the death of little Nannie Tyler, the daughter of C.W. and Mrs. Tyler. The sad event occurred at the family residence on Greenwood Avenue at 7:00 Wednesday morning, the 9th inst. Little Nannie had lived 4 years, 5 months, and 24 days. She was exceptionally bright and pretty and was loved and petted by all who knew her. There is no visitation of the grim destroyer more heart rendering than that, which tears from the arms of doting parents, a lovely child like this, and there is no time when the promise of a blessed immortality gives greater comfort. Death loses its sting and the grave gives up its victory when the lost one is found again in the bright land of the hereafter.**

Father Fitts, who had baptized Nannie, conducted the funeral service for Nannie. The Tylers' grief was new and raw and the Fitts' reawakened. The Tylers were consoled by a family who

---

[113] In stark contrast, by 1970, there were less than ten cases per year! Today, around the world, diphtheria and smallpox have been nearly eradicated.

[114] Just a few years before Nannie was born, a local family lost *all four* of its children to this same disease!

knew the agony of losing a child to a disease so cruel in its completion.

Clothing styles for the American woman of the 1880s were greatly influenced by Queen Victoria of England, the so-called the Victorian Age. After the death of her consort Prince Albert, the queen spent the remaining years of her life in mourning. Fashion followed her example and so dress colors were dark and subdued. Mourning jewelry was marketed at this time where rings of black jet were worn usually with a skull or the initials of the deceased carved into it. Lockets with hair from the deceased were also worn in memory of the lost loved one. Mollie would have donned the appropriate mourning clothes but would not go with the rest of the family to the cemetery. Women did not attend burials at this time but stayed at home to supervise the preparation of food for those returning from the burial. She and Emmie would have been busy opening the shutters, raising the blinds, rearranging the furniture and restarting all the house clocks. Flowers, which would have been used liberally in the 1880s and 1890s, would be taken outside. Everyone who attended the funeral and/or burial would be invited back to the house. It was tradition that no trace of death was to remain in the home after the burial was completed. Lastly, the little white ribbon, signifying the death of a child, which would have been tied to the front door of the Tylers' house, would be removed.

The Poston Building where Charles Tyler's cousin, Mary Mockbee's husband Henry, worked as a carpenter, was called upon the day Nannie died. Caskets were built as part of their furniture business and were stored in the basement accessed through the door seen at the bottom of the photo.

The Poston Building with the basement door where the burial cases were stored. (MCA)

In 1858 John F. Couts, the undertaker located on Public Square, had advertised a "newly invented burial case." The advertisement stated that, the case was "air tight, preventing contagion and slowing the process of decomposition for a long time." It further explained that "the case permits a view of the entire body after it is enclosed, the top being composed of beautiful French glass. The glass is divided into three sections, between two of which is inserted the name plate." Each section, according to the ad, could be covered independently with a decorative cap. It was told that Nannie was buried in a metal casket that contained a glass window. The only method to find if this is indeed correct will probably never be allowed nor should it be.

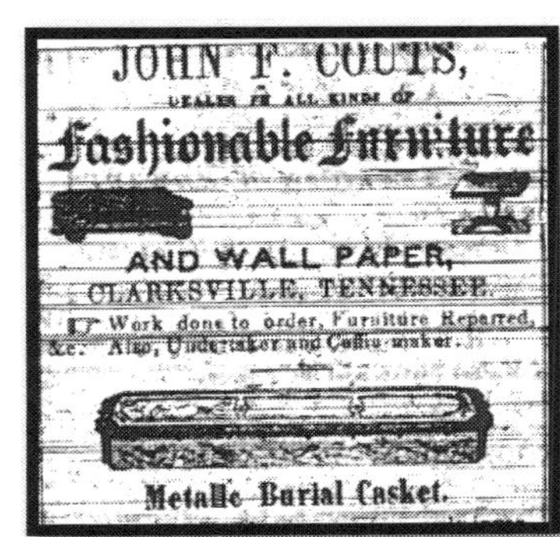

This type burial case was available in Clarksville and may have been the type selected in which to bury Nannie. (LC)

It was decided to use the photo taken at MacCormac's Gallery for the carving of a statue for Nannie's grave. The cost of the statue was substantial even in 1885.[115] Even though Nannie's father was a judge, in those days, they were not paid what they are today. Judge Tyler and Mollie were not wealthy people but were determined to memorialize their daughter, whatever the cost. When finally, the statue was delivered to Clarksville, it was true to the smallest detail, even to the buckled shoes, the bar pin on the collar and the ribbon in her hair. On the left side of the pedestal are the words, "Safe in the arms of Jesus;" on the right, 'Daughter of Charles W. & Mollie Tyler, born Mar. 16, 1881, died Sept. 9, 1885," on the back, "Our little darling" and on the front, "Nannie." On top of her grave is a slab of marble with the words, "Little Nannie Tyler."

---

[115] Today the cost for the same statue, according to the Greenwood Monument Company, would be about $10,000!

Some deviations from the photo were made. Instead of facing forward, the statue was carved to look down at her own grave. The statue's left hand is resting on a pedestal of stones while the right arm is outstretched.

Allison Grace Lewis standing next to Nannie's statue with the rose in the statue's hand. The date is unknown but with Mollie's stone visible, it was after August 1900. (MCA)

Marie Riggins once warned that there were many fables in Clarksville's history and probably no more so than those that surrounded Nannie's death and burial. It has been written and rewritten that she died of pneumonia; this is incorrect. The descendants of the Tylers adamantly state that the cause of Nannie's death was diphtheria and use the family photo album to prove it. On the page with Nannie's photo, it is written that she died from diphtheria. According to the newspaper, the internment took place in Greenwood Cemetery that same Wednesday afternoon, with services conducted by Rev. P.A. Fitts.

The most repeated story was that her photograph was sent to Italy in order for her statue to be carved. But did this really happen? Is it possible that just because the statue was carved from Italian Carrera marble that the story of it being created in Italy arose? There is an article that disputes this story taken for so long as fact: In the June 20, 1886 issue of the Louisville, Kentucky *Courier-Journal*:

Another Specimen of Fine Art in Marble to the Credit of a Louisville House, J.S. Clark & Co.

A special letter from Clarksville, Tenn., to the editor of the *Nashville American* which was published recently in that paper. Referring to a beautiful statue of Judge Charles W. Tyler's daughter, furnished by J.S. Clark & Co. of this city say, 'A description the Tyler statue may not be out of place. The design is the exact likeness made from a photograph taken one year before the child's death. There is a delicacy of expression in the face that is incomprehensible, bringing out every line of the features, showing the very life of the child on marble. Even her pretty little teeth show between the parting lips just enough to give a half-smiling expression to the statue. The child wears a white dress, short sleeves, bows on shoulders. The dress is exquisitely trimmed with Hamburg embroidery and fine lace. All the dimples in the arms, folds and creases in the dress, the delicate embroidery, etc., are all brought out perfectly, showing the pretty dress as it appeared on Nannie in life; the little slippers with bows and the little stockings with wrinkles are here and the breast pin that fastened the dress in front, the hair as it was banged in front and dropping in ringlets on her snow-white neck, all add beauty to the life-like expression. The family are pleased beyond expression.' The above is one among many such letters this firm receives in reference to their monuments and statuary.

Another Specimen of Fine Art in Marble, to the Credit of a Louisville House, J. S. Clark & Co.

A special letter from Clarksville, Tenn., to the editor of the Nashville American, which was published recently in that paper, referring to a beautiful statue of Judge Charles W. Tyler's daughter, furnished by J. S. Clark & Co., of this city, says: "A description of the Tyler statue may not be out of place. The design is an exact likeness make from a photograph taken one year before the child's death. There is a delicacy of expression in the face that is incomprehensible, bringing out every line of the features, showing the very life of the child on marble. Even her pretty little teeth show between the parting lips just enough to give a half-smiling expression to the statue. The child wears a white dress, short sleeves, bows on shoulders. The dress is exquisitely trimmed with Hamburg embroidery and fine laces. All the dimples in the arms, folds and creases in the dress, the delicate embroidery, etc., are all brought out perfectly, showing the pretty dress as it appeared on Nannie in life; the little slippers with bows, and the little stockings with wrinkles are here, and the breastpin that fastened the dress in front, the hair as it was banged in front and dropping in ringlets on her snow-white neck, all add beauty to the life-like expression. The family are pleased beyond expression."

The above is one among many such letters this firm receives in reference to their monuments and statuary.

MONUMENTS.

MONUMENTS.

We are now receiving new Monuments of the very finest GRANITES, in

NEW and ARTISTIC DESIGNS,

and perfect proportion, which we will sell below competition.

J. S. CLARK & CO.

1887 ad in the *Lousiville Courier Journal.*

Now, at last, we know the truth.

In October of 1884, J.S. Clark & Co.[116] located on Green Street between Second and Third received 7 cases of Carrara marble. Perhaps this was the shipment of marble that was used in creating Nannie's statue. By November of 1886, their shipment from Italy had increased to 17 cases of Carrara marble.

[116] John S. Clark was also a tobacco broker.

This company was so respected that in 1891, they were awarded the contract to carve the Alamo cenotaph that was erected that year in Austin, Texas.

It is an interesting note that the company, according to their advertisement in 1889, did not advocate epitaphs on monuments as, "they are entirely inadequate to express bereavement at the death of a relative or friend." However, they still provided a booklet that contained about 500 of "the choicest and briefest suggestions, together with Hebrew, old English and several other alphabets, which renders it a very convenient reference book that will meet the needs of many." In spite of their advice, Nannie's statue has the epitaph, "Our Little Darling."

With Samuel Hodgson, the well-respected monument carver in Clarksville, why would the Tylers choose to order the statue from someone else? Was it a matter of cost, was Hodgson too busy or was there a personal issue between the judge and Hodgson?

Another one of the stories surrounding this child's death was that the judge's grief was so severe that for a while he refused to consent to their daughter's burial. The newspaper obituaries, the parish records and the Greenwood Cemetery records all show that Nannie was buried the very afternoon of her death. However, there is one curious item. The parish records show a mark over on the day entered for the burial day! They show an "S" followed by an "a" which is written over as Wednesday. So did the burial actually take place days later on Saturday? Was this simply a mistake or was the day intentionally changed?

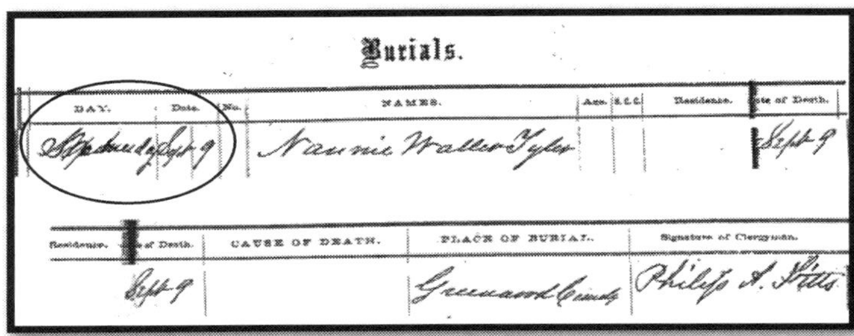

Burials.

DAY.	Date.	No.	NAMES.	Age. &c.	Residence.	Date of Death.
Wednesday	Sept 9		Nannie Waller Tyler			Sept 9

Residence.	Date of Death.	CAUSE OF DEATH.	PLACE OF BURIAL.	Signature of Clergyman.
	Sept 9		Greenwood Cemty	Philip A. Pitts

The burial record from Trinity Church showing the questionable date change.

In looking through all the other records, no other such correction is found. Same day or next day burials were necessary because diphtheria was such a contagious disease. So, was there a delay in the burial?

Flowers were and still are often placed in the statue's hand. Louise Podell, a Tyler family descendant also heard that when Nannie died, Judge Tyler had Nannie buried in a casket with a window and that the grave was dug to where he could look down in the ground and see her face through the glass. Mrs. Podell discounted the story as just that because she reasoned that six feet down there would not be enough light to be able to see anything. But there was a story that Nannie had always been afraid of the dark. Could the hole have been designed for light to reach her?

People alive in the 1990s recalled that the Tylers placed a glass case containing Nannie's toys on her grave and that in the 1940s the case was broken into and the toys removed. This story cannot be substantiated however it is difficult to believe that a glass case could sit undisturbed for nearly 100 years. Such were the rumors, stories and fables often passed down as fact concerning Nannie.

According to Allene Duke Barbee Carneal, another Tyler descendant, the episode in *Gone with the Wind* surrounding Bonnie Butler's death and Rhett's immense grief over losing her was, without question, taken from Judge Tyler's reaction to Nannie's death.

Is it possible Margaret Mitchell had some acquaintances in Clarksville and may have heard the account of Nannie's death from them and then included it in her book published in 1936? This author visited the Margaret Mitchell House Museum and the Keenan Archives in Atlanta, Georgia. The personnel in both locations worked for days to establish a relationship between Miss Mitchell and Montgomery County, Tennessee. They could not substantiate the story after pouring over letters, manuscripts and etc., which were held in each of their collections. Maybe someday a connection will be discovered.

Charles and Mollie were devastated by their daughter's death. For the judge himself, it must have been one of the few times in his life when he found himself in a situation he could not control. Sworn to protect and uphold the law was a large part of who Charles Tyler was. The inability to protect his own little girl and keep her from dying had to have stirred feelings of helplessness he had never experienced before. He wrote about the experience of watching a loved one die twenty-six years later.

> **How earnestly, how desperately we poor human creatures often strive in this grievous world to ward off the Spector, death. Hovering about the loved one descending into the shadow we embrace eagerly every expedient that may be suggested to repel the unwelcome visitor who stands without. On bended knee we send supplications to the Almighty. To the very last we hope. Then the blow falls...we lay our loved ones beneath the sod, we shed bitter tears above them, and then—move on with the caravan. It must be so...hope points us to another life where yet again we may see them face-to-face.**

Sometimes it is difficult to understand how life can continually batter the human spirit year after year. The loss of a child, as anyone can tell you, is the worst suffering anyone has to endure. Charles and Mollie relied upon their stalwart religious beliefs to help them through the horrors of their daughter's loss. The Tylers knew they had to face life without their blessed daughter but their hope, according to their beliefs, was that they would all be reunited in the hereafter, and that hope sustained them.

People in town were becoming greatly concerned about the number of deaths associated with diphtheria. Ten days after Nannie's death, an article appeared in the *Leaf Chronicle* that read:

> **There is considerable alarm about diphtheria in Clarksville and a number of people have carried their children out of the city. The disease is by no means epidemic but the type that prevails is virulent and the cases that have occurred have nearly all been fatal. From careful inquiry among the physicians, and undertakers, we find that there have not been more than a dozen cases in Clarksville this season, and there are only two or three here at present. The fact that the disease is here in such a fatal form, and the uncertainty of who will be its next victim causes the alarm.**

Nine days after his daughter's death, the *Tobacco Leaf* reported that Judge Tyler was at Hurricane Springs. This retreat was situated on a bend of the Cumberland Mountains near Tullahoma, Tennessee. It was widely advertised as the best place around to "take the cure" or relax. The newspaper ad for Hurricane Springs read:

> **Open June 1, with facilities greatly increased for making a visit to these springs enjoyable. IT WILL CURE YOU. So come and try the best water known to the world for the cure of chronic Diarrhea, Dysentery, Dyspepsia, Piles and all diseases of the Stomach, Liver, Bowels and Kidneys. Send for circulars explaining analysis, etc. Excursion routes can be had over all railroads from principal points South, East and West.**

In addition to the "curative properties" of the waters there, the management of Hurricane Springs offered amusements such as card playing, target shooting, dancing and rolling ten pins. Tyler was either needing to get out-of-town to grieve or it may have simply been the need to get relief from rheumatism, a disease that he would have to endure for the remainder of his life.

Men do not grieve in the same way as women. Women are allowed to show their emotions and seek solace from friends by speaking of their loss. Men internalize their feelings and do not share their loss with others. In his position as a judge, his demeanor was that of always being in control and handling situations in a restrained manner. In Clarksville, he was constantly surrounded by people offering condolences and this had to be extremely difficult to handle. A time of reflection was also something he needed. If he was like others who had suffered a similar loss, he probably asked himself a thousand times what he could have done to have spared his little daughter her fate. It would be perfectly normal to experience a feeling of guilt. Charles made the trip alone; Mollie stayed in Clarksville caring for their baby Em. The effects of Nannie's death on the Tylers can only be imagined. Mollie would need to focus more on their remaining child Em along with the day-to-day activities of life. Certainly one can believe that she and Charles leaned more on their faith to sustain them. As any grieving parent can attest, the best therapy is to stay busy. Charles had the advantage in that his job removed him from the house. Parents may put away the physical reminders, the toys, clothes, etc... but the memories will be there along with the void left in their hearts.

Just three months after Nannie's death on December 15, the long-awaited celebration of the Clarksville Street Railway Company first day of operations took placed as the first mule-drawn cars appeared on the streets. The mule teams were rotated every two and a half hours to rest the animals. The route began at Public Square and continued one-mile down Franklin to Tenth Street where it reached the L & N Railroad Depot. Those riding the streetcar[117] paid the conductor when they boarded.

Clarksville mule-drawn streetcar. (MCA)

The new year of 1886 began as one of the coldest in anyone's memory. Temperatures of 19 below zero were recorded and people and animals suffered through the winter. On January 11, the passenger trains stalled at the freight yards and all on board had to suffer through the night.

Imagine having a dance today in the courthouse. In the late 1880s such was the case as the Cotillion, Elegante and Euchre Clubs all held their big social event of the year at the seat of county justice. On occasion, Mollie Tyler would also act as a chaperone for these dances. On January 30, 1886, the newspaper printed the names of those who attended one such dance.

The List of Couples Included:
Charles G. Smith, Jr. and Miss Eva Saunders
George M. Bell and Miss Susie Barker
Louis G. Munford and Miss Frances Barker
Captain E.M. Howard and Miss Lou Redd
Charles Beaumont and Miss Lucy Morris
William McCauley and Miss Lizzie Moseley
Michael Savage and Miss Jennie Anglen
Morris Clark and Miss Ellen Henry

Chaperones:
Mrs. W.J. Ely and Mrs. William A. Quarles

Singles Who Attended:
Robert Henry, Cook Roach, John Otley

Comic relief sometimes occurred in the courtroom. A language barrier provided some fun in late January when the first case on the docket that day involved a theft at Sam Lung's laundry. A black boy was charged with stealing shirts. During the trial, Lung from China who spoke very poor English, had a black man interpret for him but, of course, the man spoke no Chinese. So with some waving of arms and facial expressions, the two men communicated well enough to the lawyers and the boy was sentenced to six months in the county workhouse.

Judge Tyler made his opinion publically known in the second week of April, when he clashed with Dr. Daniel Wright over the matter of the Legislative Act of 1885 and the State Board of Health. Tyler stated that,

> **The Act of 1885 makes the person acting as physician (of the jail) the health officer of the county and I can see no reason for the election of another jail physician when one is already acting elected by the jail commissioners.**

Wright's reply was,

> **In organizing the State Board of Health great care was taken to establish it independent and separate from all other administrative departments, whether political, legal or financial and the law of 1885, establishing county boards, if thoughtfully read, will be seen to have been established on a similar principle. By its provisions the health officer who is also chairman of the county board of health, will take his position at the board on equal terms with his colleagues as firmly seated there as the county judge and the county court clerk. This is what Tyler does not like, he does not desire anyone in this county not dependent upon himself but prefers a person removable at his pleasure and dependent upon him for all authority.... It is with no disrespect to our county judge that I express the opinion that the law has judged more wisely in this matter than he has.**

Always problems within town surfaced. There was a bridge over Gallows Hollow on Front

[117] The terms trolley and streetcar are often used interchangeably.

Street a short distance from John T. Johnson's sawmill (Star Saw Mill), that caved in during the third week of April, due to overflow from the Cumberland River into the Spring Branch Creek. The bridge was described as having a "stone arch over the hollow and stone walls on either side with a dirt fill in-between the walls." Until they could repair the bridge, a wooden one was to be built until permanent repairs could be done.

In July 1886, the first electricity was supplied to houses in Clarksville provided by the Clarksville Electric Light Company, co-owned by Clay Stacker and Mollie's brother, Billy Settle. This new business was located at the corner of Main and North First Street. It was powered by an engine at Anchor Mills (a business on Strawberry Alley located at the rear of Settle's store.)

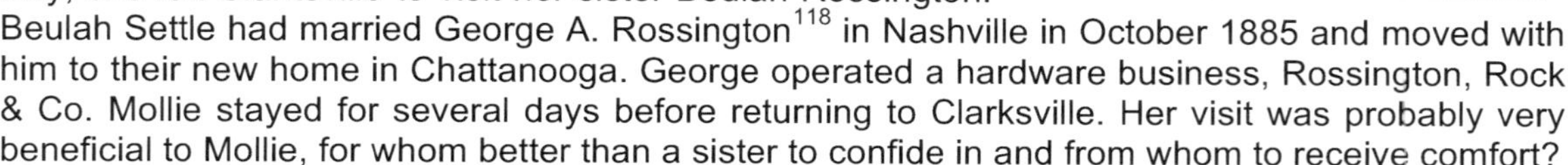

Clarksville Electric Station building years after it was vacated. (MCA)

Mollie took the opportunity to get away from town when in July, she left Clarksville to visit her sister Beulah Rossington. Beulah Settle had married George A. Rossington[118] in Nashville in October 1885 and moved with him to their new home in Chattanooga. George operated a hardware business, Rossington, Rock & Co. Mollie stayed for several days before returning to Clarksville. Her visit was probably very beneficial to Mollie, for whom better than a sister to confide in and from whom to receive comfort?

As everyone knows, life continues even after a personal tragedy. In the city of Clarksville, diversions from serious matter came about in the form of a new sport taking the country by storm: baseball! Within ½ mile of the Tyler's house was Baseball Hill. This area sits at the intersection of Crossland and Cumberland Drives and included Elder, Washington and Martin Streets. It was devoid of trees and buildings and the perfect spot to catch a strong breeze coming off the Cumberland River in which to fly one's kite. This hill was also where circuses might set up. and the already favored game of baseball would be played.

During the summer of 1886, several baseball teams were playing in Clarksville. Two teams, named the Clarks and the Tylers played a game July 6, with the Clarks winning 22 to 10. The Clark "boys" included Pat Ahern, Peter Slattery, James Slattery, Bell Woods, Ed Moore, H. Beaty, Percy Jackson, Albert Rohner and James Moss. The Tyler team included A. Kleeman, Will Moore, L. Beach, H. Atkins, Ernest Elder, W. Gilbert, Irwin McMannus, K. Saunders and Harvey Page. In this game the "little boys" had won handily over the "big boys."

Charles would have been especially interested in the invention of a local farmer during the summer of 1886 when Asahel Huntington Patch patented the Black Hawk corn sheller. The Black Hawk continued to be produced until 1954 and won international acclaim. Patch's gristmill, factory and farm were located on the site of the present-day Austin Peay State University's campus.

Cave Johnson's daughter-in-law, Mary Boyd Johnson was appointed by President Harrison shortly after his inauguration to serve as Clarksville's first female postmaster. Not completely sure the transition would be smooth and without resistance, Judge Tyler and Polk G. Johnson, accompanied Mary to take charge of the post office. The changeover took place at 7:30 p.m. on August 31. Expecting their arrival was the deputy postmaster Dr. Elmer Green. Polk handed Green the formal order from the President suspending him. Next Mrs. Johnson presented Green with an order also from the President to hand over to her the post office with all its effects, which the feeble Dr. Green did "in the most graceful manner." Tom Gilbert and John A. Gholson served as clerks under Johnson.

Complaints, complaints, complaints! The newspaper bemoaned street conditions once more on Saturday, November 6, 1886,

> **Why do the city fathers let mud and water stand ankle deep on the sidewalks on Main Street from the corner of Tom Hyman's lot to the Public School lot when three loads of cinders would let the pedestrians, like the children of Israel, pass over dry sod.**

[118] The Rossington brothers were: F.M. of New Providence, Robert B. of Clarksville, A.W. of Paducah, W.D. of New Providence and George A. of Chattanooga. Robert B. married the daughter of John Kimble Smith.

In November, Jefferson Davis again visited Clarksville on his way to Fairview and stayed once more at the residence of Micajah Clark. While at the Clark home, Davis wrote the following in the guest book, which recorded his visit, "May God's blessing rest upon the friends whose fidelity was most expressed in my adversity." He further stated, "Col. Clark was tried and true, faithful to the bitter end." It is not clear at which visit the following incident took place, but during one of the dinners held at the Clark home in Davis' honor, the former President spilled some wine on the tablecloth. He requested some salt to remove the stain but was refused. Clark informed Davis that, "This cloth with this stain will be one of our most prized treasured possessions." The reason for his visit back to his former home in Fairview, Kentucky was a request by the citizens that he should be present at the dedication ceremony of their new Baptist Church on the land donated by Davis. An engraved slab of Tennessee marble, completed by Clarksville's Samuel Hodgson, was placed in the wall of the auditorium of the church. The inscription read, "Jefferson Davis, of Mississippi was born June 3, 1808 on the site of this church. He made a gift of this lot March 10, 1886 to Bethel Baptist Church as a thank offering to God."

Today the Jefferson Davis Monument, designed much like the Washington Monument in D.C., stands near his birthplace and can be seen for miles over the flat Kentucky farmlands. The monument was finally completed in 1924 and the dedication ceremony was held June 7, 1924. Indeed, Micajah Clark never forgot his deep friendship with Davis for it was he, his brother, Lewis Rogers Clark and eight others who purchased the twenty acres of land upon which the monument sits.

Sadly, the Tylers were to experience more grief as they lost their youngest child on December 7. This child was either miscarried or died at birth. The cemetery records simply list the baby as "child of Judge Tyler." In the cemetery next to Nannie's grave there appeared to be an empty space. Could the child be buried in this spot? And if Nannie was buried in a metal casket, could this child be as well? A call to a city department brought a worker to the site with an underground utilities detector, much stronger than an ordinary metal detector. When the device was waved over the space, a loud high-pitched sound emanated from the ground and the man commented that whatever was down there had to be the size of a cannon to give off so strong a signal. Thus the baby's grave was located. This author had a simple headstone placed next to Nannie to mark its location. The stone simply reads, "Tyler Baby." Sceptics abound but an "old time" tool that has been used to locate water can also be used to locate graves. The real mystery is how it can also indicate the sex of the person buried. Dowsing or divining rods are L-shaped metal rods are held at a 45-degree angle above a gravesite. If the rods cross, it is an indicator of a male; if the rods separate or opens up, it is a female. In the case of the Tyler baby, the rods cross. So indeed, was this precious child a baby boy lost in death to pass down the Tyler name?

On December 12, Judge Tyler heard complaints from steamboat captains about the one thousand or more witnesses to 34 baptisms in the Cumberland River.

The baptisms in the Cumberland River. (MCA)

The problem was that the enormous crowd in front of the ferry landing was blocking the boats from mooring. The baptisms were conducted by Elder Houston Metcalf, the preacher at St. Joseph's Church. The baptisms continued though as in May 15, 1887, 18 converts were baptized in the same location by Rev. A.J. Stokes of the Baptist church. A witness to the baptisms said,

> **I shall never forget the appealing and rich harmonious singing of these deeply religious folk. After a sermon elders would proceed into the river until the right depth was found, usually waist deep, and the preacher would join them. The one to be baptized would be led into their midst, quickly submerged backwards and lifted out again. The convert would run to the river bank where he would be received with open arms by family and friends. The**

seriousness and simplicity of these formalities was highly impressive, the religious zeal contagious.[119]

In 1887, the court charged the following for violation of the law:

Misconduct in office: one cent and cost of prosecution
Keeping a bucket shop: one cent and cost of prosecution[120]
Resisting officer: one cent
Larceny: one year in penitentiary
Maltreatment of wife: three months in county jail and cost of prosecution

Quintus came to Clarksville from his home in Canton, Kentucky on January 19, 1887. His intention was to stay with his sister, Nannie Johnson for ten days while being treated by Dr. T.D. Johnson. The *Semi-Weekly Tobacco Leaf Chronicle* stated that

'Mars' Quint is always welcomed to Clarksville and the longer he stays, the better pleased are his many students. He has whipped more boys and is beloved by more former pupils than any man in this neck of the woods. It is refreshing to hear him relate his experience with boys who 'could not be whipped by any other teacher.'

The old Virginia school master, Peter Nelson had used this method of discipline as had Quintus' father John Duke Tyler. Yet they each earned the respect of their students who were sent out into the world becoming contributing members of society.

On February 28, Judge Tyler and Mollie traveled to Florida. On their way back to Clarksville, the couple stayed for a few hours in Jacksonville where a newspaper reporter for the Jacksonville *Florida Herald* met them and made a prediction, "Judge Tyler is among the most distinguished young jurists of Tennessee and is destined someday to hold high positions in the council of the nation." They returned to Clarksville via Aniston, Alabama.

Three years after her death, the Chancel of the Episcopal Church received as a gift a large bronze cross as a memorial to Mildred by her daughters, Nannie and Emmie. The cross sits on a walnut base. In the center of the cross is a raised figure of the Paschal Lamb and at the top of the upright portion are two Sardonyx stones, set in silver. Another such stone is set in each arm of the cross. On Good Friday, April 8, the cross was publicly consecrated and placed in the Chancel. The inscription read:

In Memoriam,
Mrs. Mildred S. Tyler
Born Nov. 23rd 1809
Entered into Rest January 25th 1884
Numbered with Thy Saints

Mildred's tombstone. Photo by author.

Emmie inherited her mother's pin created for Mildred at Tiffany's in New York and presented to her by her son-in-law, Polk Grundy Johnson. A strand of Mildred's hair was at one time placed in the back of the pin but over time was removed and at some point, Emmie had her name engraved on the back. It is almost certain that it was her most prized possession.

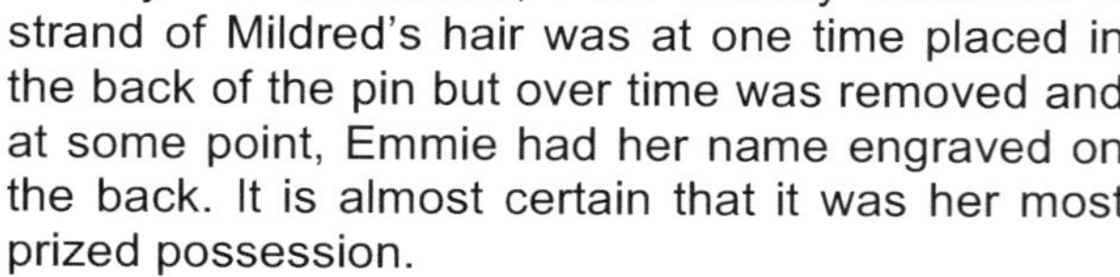

Emmie wearing the pin made for her mother Mildred. Polk Grundy Johnson purchased it at Tiffany's in New York and presented it to his mother-in-law. (GF).

Godey's Lady's Book of 1855 praised the insertion of a loved one's hair into a jewelry piece

Hair is at once the most delicate and lasting of our materials and survives us like love. It is so light, so gentle, so escaping from the idea of death, that with a lock of hair belonging to a child or friend we may almost look up to

---

[119] As late as 1922, baptisms were still being held in the Cumberland River near the City Ferry.
[120] The term "bucket shop" refers to any type of fraudulent business.

heaven and compare notes with angelic nature, may almost say, 'I have a piece of thee here, not unworthy of thy being now.'

One can only imagine what it was like to be Judge Tyler, a man who was a powerhouse for decades in Montgomery County. As judge, he was charged with matters of life and death; as county financial officer, he watched over every cent spent by the county. The stress must have been substantial. In addition to his family, he relied on close friends for support, but there was yet another person upon whom the Judge depended. That person was William Daniel, known to everyone as Uncle Billy who was elected custodian for the new courthouse by the committee appointed by the County Court on Monday, October 3, 1881. Of Billy it was said, "The committee could not have found a better janitor anywhere than Uncle Billy will make. The fact is, the courts of the county could not get along at all without the services of Uncle Billy and the courthouse would look lonesome and deserted without his presence." When death claimed "Uncle Billy' in April 1887, Judge Tyler, Polk Grundy Johnson, Clerk and Master of the Chancery Court and his Deputies: Alexander H. Gholson and Quintus Cincinnatus Atkinson, Robert D. Moseley, County Court Clerk and J.M. Rogers, County Register attended a funeral held at St. Peter A.M.E. Church[121] to pay their respects to a man they held in high esteem.

"Uncle Billy" Daniel is pictured in front and Alex McKinnon who replaced Daniel is in the back. (MCA)

Clarksville's largest and most modern hotel, the Arlington opened in 1887, a few years after Nannie's passing. The four-story structure, located at 122 South Second Street faced the courthouse. Its central location, modern conveniences and the fact that the streetcars passed every 15 minutes to the railroad depot made the Arlington a bona fide rival to the other hotels. This competition between hotels was evident as porters riding on the streetcars met passengers at the train depot. Passing in front of the new hotel, the porter would yell, "All out for the Arlington. It has steam heat!" To which the porter from the Franklin House would retort, "Keep your seats for the Franklin House. You can't eat steam heat!"

The new Arlington Hotel on Second Street. (MCA)

Although not argued in his court, Tyler had to be amused at a suit filed in the Circuit Court in early May, in which a man named Dickerson accused Walter Kincannon of selling him a horse that was "addicted to running away."

Following the lead of the parent organization in Nashville, the old Confederate soldiers of Clarksville organized their surviving members into a bivouac, writing a constitution, by-laws and designing their badge. The purpose of the bivouac was plainly stated. It:

shall be strictly social, historical, and benevolent, and its labors shall be directed to cultivating the ties of friendship between all the survivors of the armies and navies of the late Confederate states, to keep fresh the memories of our comrades who gave up their lives for the cause they deemed right, in battle or in other fields of service, or who have died since the war; to the perpetuation of the records of their deeds and heroism; in the collection and disposition in the manner they judge best, of all material of value for future historians; to aiding, assisting, and relieving, to the extent of their ability, all members, their widows and orphans, in extreme cases of sickness and want, and to providing burial for them when necessary.

This group was named in honor of Col. W.A. Forbes. The organization of the Forbes Bivouac was due to the efforts of Polk Grundy Johnson, who was unanimously voted its first president. In

[121] St. Peter, built in 1878, is the oldest black church in Clarksville and is located on Franklin Street.

the beginning, the chapter listed twelve members. Eventually one hundred and ninety members were signed. Charles was accepted as the thirty-eighth member. Tyler's application revealed that he was recommended by W.H. Brickman and Frank P. Gracey. His acceptance for membership was signed by the same as well as Polk G. Johnson, J.J. Crusman and C.H. Bailey on January 30, 1888. The bottom portion of the application allowed for remarks. Tyler wrote:

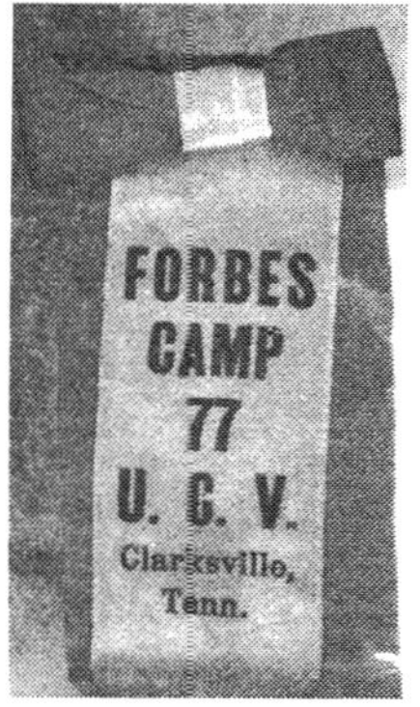

> **Escaped from Donelson after surrender: raised a battalion of cavalry. Remained with 10th Tennessee until after consolidation in winter of 1864. Commissioned to raise battalion of cavalry and (illegible) by Joe Wheeler to (illegible) to find Hylan B. Lyon at Paris, Tennessee. Unionville (illegible) officer (illegible) raid into KY in 1865 and surrendered with portion of his command to General Solomon Meredith at Paducah, Ky. May 6, 1865.**
> **C.W. Tyler**

Each meeting seemed to serve as a reaffirmation that what the Confederate Army tried to accomplish was a righteous and true cause, worthy of the sacrifice of the lives of Southerners young and old. The records kept by the bivouac show that yearly dues were collected. In each instance, Judge Tyler's contribution well exceeded the others listed on the rolls. It is recorded that he attended all of its meetings and never failed to take part in all of its endeavors. The Tylers' type of giving was evident, not only with the bivouac but with church and community projects as well.

Decoration Day was an organized yearly event held the third Thursday in May in which flowers were laid upon the Civil War veterans' graves. The banks and downtown merchants would close at noon and the day was declared a general holiday to allow citizens to participate. The ladies of Clarksville were requested to deliver flowers for the occasion because, as was stressed, it was the "duty that every loyal citizen of the South owes to the memory of Confederate soldiers who fell in battle." During the ceremony Mollie sang stirring hymns, and it is remembered that the surviving veterans who attended these services were brought to tears by the sound of her voice. Charles gave speeches at the cemetery. Years later, this event was re-named Memorial Day.

Young girls such as these were called upon to lay the flowers on the Confederate graves as a way to teach them to forever revere the memories of the dead soldiers. On the the right side of the photo is the monument of Nannie's grandmother and her own statue. (CV)

Elder's Opera House was undergoing major interior renovations in July 1887 that included enlarging the stage by adding 10-12 feet to its depth in front of the parquet. This was a great benefit to both the actors and the orchestra. An elevated dress circle that sloped towards the front, ran around the end of their building opposite the stage was constructed. Cosmetic improvements were made that when done, the opera was described as "altogether a convenient, tasteful and comfortable hall and quite an improvement on the former arrangement."

Quintus Tyler felt that there was improvement in his health while staying with his half-sister, Nannie Johnson at her house since mid-July. He planned to return to Canton to resume his teaching duties by October 1. Well-wishers applauded the news and hoped the gentleman would be around for many more years. It was said of him, "Mr. Tyler is one of the best teachers in the state and his permanent disqualifications to teach on account of feeble health would be a misfortune to his school and to the public." This, however was not to be.

It looked like a busy end of the year for Judge Tyler. On October 3, 1887 John T. Nolen was shot by one of his workers, Harpeth Jordan, in his blacksmith shop in Bryant Hollow (20th District) for the purpose of robbing him. Both he and another worker, Allen McCollum were arrested.

McCullom turned state's evidence. The case of Harpeth Jordan was given to the jury and a verdict of "guilty of murder in the first degree" was brought in. Judge Tyler sentenced Jordan to be hanged on Friday, January 11, 1889. An appeal was filed with the Tennessee Supreme Court and his sentence was commuted.

In mid-October 1887, the newspaper reported the high number of prisoners contained in "Rollow Castle"[122] with the headlines, "Blade and Bullet." There were 38 prisoners from in and around Clarksville. Seven were charged with murder, (one of these for chloroforming his wife), eleven for theft, five for assault with intent to kill, three disturbing the peace, two wife whippers, two robbers, three lunatics, one abduction, (stealing his wife's sister and running away with her), one for bringing stolen property into the state, one for carrying a concealed weapon and one pauper. The newspaper offered its solution for decreasing the population, "Out of the seven murderers, society would be benefitted by the hanging of at least four because only such punishment will be of service on the morals of other people with bloodthirsty principles. Let the work begin as soon as possible." How many Tyler put in the jail population was not stated.

Quintus Tyler succumbed to an unnamed malady. He spent much of his final months at the Johnson home. Nannie and Polk tenderly cared for the old gentleman until it became necessary to move him to the John N. Norton Infirmary in Louisville, Kentucky.

Quintus's mind was affected by his illness and he became confused, often calling the two attending nurses by the names of his half-sisters, Nannie and Emmie. Records show that he was attended by Polk's brother, Dr. T.D. Johnson 14 times between February 24, 1888 and the date of his death. His bill came to $35 which was paid by Charles. Also Charles paid J.J. Hamlett for 42 nights at $2 to stay with Quintus. In April, Quintus was administered morphine twice. Polk stayed with him continuously though the last twelve hours of his life and commented that Quintus's passing was so subtle that it was barely noticeable. Quintus died around 8:00 p.m. on June 8.

His body was taken back home to Clarksville by train where it was claimed by the Knights Templar, of which he was a member. His remains were then taken to Trinity, where just two years previous, he had become confirmed. Hundreds turned out for the funeral services. Charles paid the funeral expenses:

For hearse to depot and for hearse to cemetery $15
5 hacks $20
Sod for grave $1
Paid September 1st $36 **Note: this was nearly three months after Quintus passed away.

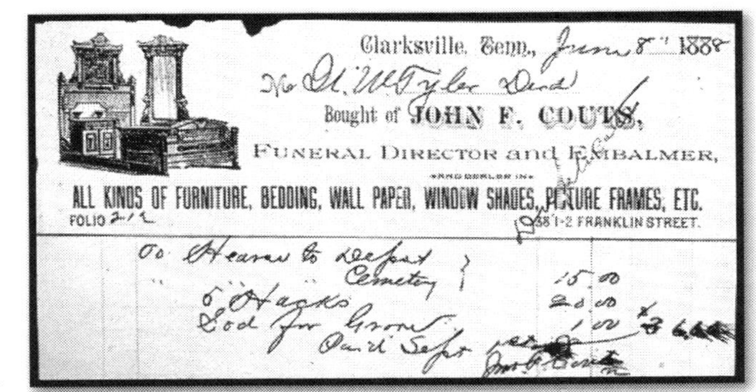
Clarksville, Tenn., June 8th 1888
Bought of JOHN F. COUTS,
FUNERAL DIRECTOR and EMBALMER,
AND DEALER IN
ALL KINDS OF FURNITURE, BEDDING, WALL PAPER, WINDOW SHADES, PICTURE FRAMES, ETC.
FOLIO 212
138 1-2 FRANKLIN STREET.

To Hearse to Depot / Cemetery	15 00
5 Hacks	20 00
Sod for Grave	1 00

Quintus was laid to rest next to his step-mother, Mildred S. Tyler in Greenwood's Section Six. His passing was especially hard for Nannie and Emmie, because of the large age difference between them; they considered Quintus more of a father figure than that of a half-brother. In addition to fifty years of teaching he was a member of Cadiz Lodge, No. 121, A. F. & A. M., Swigert Chapter, No. 40, Eddyville Council and Paducah Commandery, No. 11, Knights Templar; he had been a member of the Masonic fraternity since 1845; had been representative to the Grand Lodge, and had served as Grand Marshal of the State. Quintus had also been a member of the Masonic Lodge. Sometime during his industrious life, he also had taken time to write a brief manuscript detailing the Tyler family history. This manuscript has become a very important source of information on the Tyler family. His reputation as a revered school master probably overshadowed the long, forgotten fact that as a child, he was among those very early settlers that came over the mountain to settle in the fertile farmlands of Montgomery County.

[122] Named after the jailer, William Rollow.

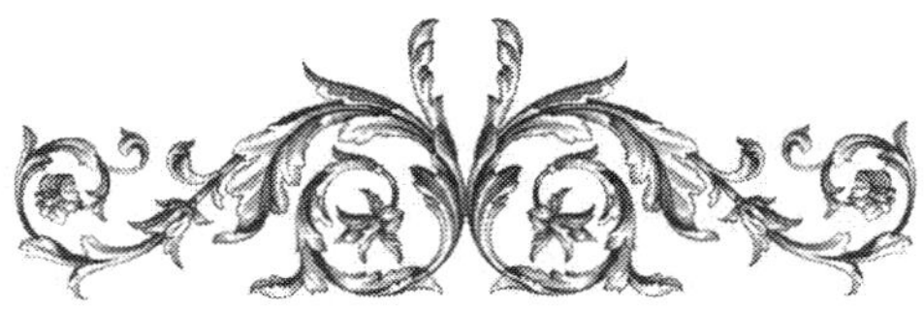

Chapter Sixteen: Court and Residual War Business

One thing for which Judge Tyler was known was his seriousness when it came to his court house. An unnamed man came to see the judge Friday November 16' 1888 with a strange request: he wanted permission to use the courthouse to deliver a lecture on LOVE. It was said that the judge scanned his eagle eye over the applicant and decided quickly that there was no way, under any circumstance the man was going to use his courthouse for such an absurd purpose.

The County Court met in its regular sessions on the first Monday in January, April, July and October. These were considered the four most important days of the year because everyone turned out even "people from across the rivers." What drew the crowds? It was because they were horse and mule trading days. There was excitement when those mules and horses numbering in the hundreds poured into town around the market house on the Public Square or at the vacant lots on Commerce Street behind C.P. Warfield's tobacco warehouse.

On January 16, 1889 Clarksville celebrated her 105th anniversary as a city and could boast of a population of 8,000. There were 5 banks, a water works, streetcars, ice factory, telephones, gas works, the Female Academy, a prep school for boys, electric lights, modern churches, 8 flouring mills, saw mills, 2 planing mills and two iron foundries. J.B. Killebrew was sent by the city to New York to attract northern investment money for the development of the local iron industry as iron ore was in great abundance less than 10 miles from Clarksville and was of a superior grade. Limestone and coke for the manufacture of pig iron was cheap.

The officers of the court then were: Chancery Court: Hon. G.E. Seay (Chancellor), Polk Grundy Johnson (Clerk and Master) Circuit Court: Hon. Arthur H. Munford (Judge), Charles H. Bailey (Clerk), Criminal Court: Tyler (Judge), Robert Darvin Moseley (Clerk), Thomas J. Munford (Registrar), George Warfield (County Trustee), Charles Staton (Sheriff), Cord Cooper and S.D. Tinsley (Deputy Sheriffs), Dorrell Suiter (Chain Gang Boss), Burnett Howell (Turnkey), Alex Stafford (Chief of Police) and his officers were Patrick Ginley and Sam Wilcox.

The Clarksville bar included Henry C. Merritt, Smith and Gholson (Charles G. Smith and Alex R. Gholson), West and Burney (John West and J. Robert Burney), A. Sears Major; G.L. "Pack" Pitt, Leech and Savage (Herbert N. Leech and Michael Savage), Henry W. Watts (New Providence), Albert V. Goodpasture (St. Bethlehem), Col. John F. House and Col. Thomas Yancey.

While the great fire of 1878 may have still been talked about for years, a new topic of conversation filled the businesses and homes in town in late May 1889. It was Judge Tyler vs. Sheriff Charles W. Staton[123] at odds over an incident and the following actions of both men that had tongues wagging. Weeks prior a man named Vanvavry, a travelling tinker, had been arrested, tried and convicted of carrying a concealed weapon and threatening to shoot several blacks. What began as a simple arrest turned into a power struggle between two strongly determined men. The newspaper headline read: "Judge Tyler and Sheriff Staton at Loggerheads."

On Thursday May 16, Tyler had Vanvavry brought before him and ordered his release to Staton's shock who declared he arrested him as ordered and as the man had not paid the court $50 and costs, he would remain in jail. The very next day Tyler again ordered the man released and when Staton refused and proceeded to handcuff the prisoner, Tyler charged Staton $100 for contempt and stated that if an officer of the court were present, he would order Staton to jail.

---

[123] Charles Wesley Staton was in Co. A, 2nd KY (Woodward's) and N.B. Forrest's cavalry so he and Tyler knew each other for many years before this falling out.

Ignoring the judge, Staton took Vanvavry back to jail.

Charles Wesley Staton. Sixth District magistrate and later constable, Montgomery County Deputy Sheriff, Sheriff and Circuit Court Clerk. (MCA)

It was not over yet in fact; things were about to get really ugly. On Saturday May 18 the jail commissioners met and decided to press charges against Staton for allegedly neglecting the county prisoners locked up in his jail. The *Clarksville Democrat* newspaper even accused Staton of starving the chain gang. The lawsuits began. Staton was suspended and Sam Wilcox, the jailer, was elected to replace Staton upon further investigation. Staton refused to turn over the jail keys. Instead of handing the keys over to Wilcox, Staton gave them to his deputy and brother, John Staton and then filed a suit against the *Democrat* for $5,000 for malicious slander. Tyler went before Esquire Samuel A. Caldwell and swore out a warrant for John Staton's arrest for assuming official authority of the jail, retaining possession of the jail keys and interfering with the order of the court. He was arrested and thrown in his own jail in lieu of the $100 contempt fine ordered the day previous. Staton bonded out still retaining the keys and assuming charge of the jail. On Monday, John Staton was brought before C.D. Bailey for trial with the courtroom filled to the brim with spectators.

Squire Samuel A. Caldwell.[124] (MCA)

Norman Smith, Jr. had the first of the new style bicycles in Clarksville in 1889. Because its back wheel was the same size as its front, the bike was named "the Safety". Instead of the large high wheel in the front and much smaller one in the back, this bicycle was considered much safer and with a smoother ride.

Amid all the jail discord, on May 25, there was a meeting at courthouse to discuss a Confederate monument for Clarksville. The newly unveiled Confederate monument at Mt. Olivet Cemetery in Nashville spurred Clarksvillians to desire a monument of their own. The question arose as to where should the monument be erected. The proposed locations were either in the courthouse yard or in Greenwood Cemetery.

In the meantime, Vanvavry brought suit against C.W. Staton for $10.000 for illegal detention in the Clarksville jail. On May 28, the case was heard before the Tennessee Supreme Court in Jackson, Tennessee. On June 8, the Clerk of the Supreme Court issued a mandamus[125] to Judge Tyler directing him to sign the bill of exceptions presented to him by C.W. Staton at once or to appear before the Supreme Court the first Monday in December 1889 to show why he refused to sign. The writ was served on Tyler on June 10.

The same day, "A Citizen" fanned the flames of discord when he wrote in the *Leaf* that Staton's attorneys, Savage, Leech and others should be thrown in prison for daring to dispute Tyler's authority and called Staton an upstart. He further stated that the Supreme Court was meddling in Tyler's affairs but that "our judge is above the law and its decrees also. Such conduct on the part of those curious, sore-headed attorneys and sheriffs is ludicrous. The judge in his supreme power should have their combs and gills removed without delay or put the whole of them on the chain gang."

In May, the popular store of Keesee and Northington were the first in town to use a cash register and Mr. Northington stated that, "If one's cash gets out of balance while using this register, the blame is at once known to be the man's and not the machine. It did the work of a man without the possibility of mistakes." This store sold everything from fertilizer, garden seeds, hams, turkey, and bacon. At Christmas, people purchased raisins, currants, figs, fine candy, nuts

---

[124] In April of 1887, Judge and Mrs. Tyler attended the wedding of Caldwell's daughter, Lucy to John Clements who worked for John Hurst. The Tylers gifted the couple an "ornamental table" and an "elegant peach blow water set."

[125] A (writ of) mandamus is an order from a court to an inferior government official ordering the government official to properly fulfill their official duties or correct an abuse of discretion.

and coconuts.

On July 5, the Confederate Monument committee met to discuss the location for the Confederate Monument. It was argued by S.A. Caldwell that the country people wanted it place in the courtyard because "many of them would not see it if it was located in the Greenwood Cemetery." After much discussion however, the decision was made to erect the monument in the epicenter of Greenwood. This was Judge Tyler's choice of location.

The Staton affair was still ongoing and on July 12, the newspaper printed their hopes for "a truce will be patched up until the decision of the courts has arrived at and the unseemly wrangles of the warring factions will now cease." But then it got messier as there were heated discussions over the chain gang and who was in charge of it. It was still not over.

Mildred Tyler's house at 409 Greenwood was deeded on July 17 to Charles. Mildred's will was never probated, because as was said, "the family knew its contents," or did they? Did Charles let his sisters know the contents of her will or keep it to himself? Some claim it was not probated in order to save money.

On July 23, Polk left for New York expecting to be gone for two or three weeks. He died there on July 28, 1889 at the Hoffman House of Bright's disease while prosecuting a lawsuit. His burial was in Greenwood Cemetery next to his father. On one side of his monument is the uncommon inscription: "What I do thou knowest not now but thou shalt know hereafter."

The *Clarksville Semi-Weekly Tobacco Leaf* printed the following along with the announcement of his death on the 30th:

> **It is not hyperbole to say that this announcement fell upon this people like a pall of sorrow, for there was not a heart in this community, friend or foe to Polk G. Johnson, who did not feel a pang of sorrow that he had passed away. To some the unutterable anguish that it caused is beyond the power of tongue to express or pen to picture. Even his enemies (if he had them) felt that one of nature's noblemen, one who scorned the arts of the trickster, a noble, manly man, had passed away.**
>
> **Capt. Johnson died at the Hoffman House, New York, whither he went just one week before on important legal business. His remains have been shipped from New York and are expected to arrive on the 8:20 train this evening. His body will be met at Guthrie by sixteen members of Forbes Bivouac, appointed a guard of honor and conveyed to the city. His funeral will take place at Trinity Church tomorrow morning at 10:00, his old pastor, Dr. P.A. Fitts, of Anniston, Alabama; and Dr. W.M. Pettis officiating. Burial at Greenwood Cemetery by Forbes Bivouac.**

Johnson in 1883. (CV)

Nannie Tyler Johnson was now a widow and the fact that her brother and sister lived next door had to be a comfort to her. But how could she know that in just a short time, she would lose both her children as well?

A prisoner, J.L. Allen on December 19, held at the jail broke out and during his escape he broke his leg.[126] Allen jumped from the third story window of the jail after hearing Staton' young daughter saying her father was going away that night. Allen thinking a mob might try to break him out of jail for his horse stealing made his escape. He was re-arrested after being seen by a doctor.

Very discreetly the newspaper included the brief announcement on the same day as the report of the prisoner breakout that: "State for use of Vanvavry against C.W. Staton et als, affirmed. (This opinion sustained the decision of the lower court that Staton was not liable for damages in holding Vanvavry). Slowly cooler heads prevailed and the matter no longer appeared in the newspapers if not heard on the streets of town. In January 1890 Staton ran for re-election and was credited by the *Leaf* as "a courageous, prudent officer whose ambition was to discharge his duty as it appeared to him." He was re-elected.

The courthouse was in the news as dissatisfaction about the courthouse's appearance was making its rounds about town. It was pointed out that the courthouse was "unpainted and unkempt." Five years later that the ceiling over the circuit courthouse collapsed dropping its heavy

[126] The jailer's family occupied the downstairs at the jail.

timbers and debris inside the room. Another five years passed when in 1900 the wooden staircases required propping up and it was known that the clock tower vibrated in the wind. These problems were resolved by an unseen calamity soon to take place.

At this time there were two bridges across the Red River: The New Providence Bridge and the Russellville Pike Bridge which were both toll bridges. J.H. Ballantine, an old Confederate veteran with his wooden leg ran the New Providence Bridge toll house and William Buck Collier, who was as deaf as a doorknob, was the keeper of the Russellville Pike Bridge. Judge Tyler was concerned for farmers who had to pay to bring their goods into to sell. This problem was on his radar to correct if not immediately, then sometime in the future.

Judge Tyler and the 1890 magistrates on the courthouse steps. **Row 1**: 1st from left Burrell Joe Corban #19; 3rd from left John Shelby; 4th from left Baxter Watkins; 8th from left Joe Trotter (Southside); **Row 2:** 1st from left Sam Powers (Palmyra); 3rd from right Brad Martin (Dotsonville) #21; **Row 3**: 2nd from right James L. Nesbitt (Shiloh); **Row 4:** 1st from right: Edmund Brewer (Oak Plains) #10; 2nd from left Wes Smith, 2nd from right Dave T. Foust (Sango) #10; 4th from left Charles W. Tyler, Judge. (MCA)

The Greenwood Avenue summer car. (MCA)

In 1890, records show that the Greenwood Avenue Street Railroad Company had two open summer cars and one closed car. These cars were used quite regularly to transport visitors to Greenwood Cemetery.

Who in their right mind would steal a horse from the county's Criminal Judge, much less one with the reputation of Judge Tyler? Sam Anderson, Jr., a young black man who worked for the judge was seen riding his horse around town on April 1, 1890. When Sheriff Alex C. Stafford arrested Anderson that night, he claimed the horse was stolen from him while he was in Shufftown. He then changed his story and said that he had bought a horse, traded it for another horse and then traded it once again for another from some gypsies that were over by the Greenwood Cemetery. Explanations over, Anderson was charged with horse stealing.

Sheriff Stafford (top left) and his police department. Captains A.C. Stafford, Marable, Nilker and Robert L. Black, taken in 1891 Stafford served as Sheriff of Mont. Co. from 1898-1904 Black served as Sheriff of Mont. Co. from 1910-1914. (MCA)

The city and the Electric Light Company finally came to terms and ended a long, drawn-out dispute. In the second week of April, the company chose to accept the city's terms and closed the contract for lighting the town. The Board of Mayor and Aldermen met on Thursday night, April 10 and passed the ordinance unanimously. The terms were:

-The company shall furnish the city with twenty-five lights of 2,000 candle power at a rate of $7 per month per light.

-the city retains the privilege of taking any number of lights it sees proper up to thirty lights.
-the company binds itself to raise fifteen lights to a height of thirty-five feet from the ground and to move six lights at their own expense to any point the committee on lights designate.

Charles Tyler had bigger problems with which to contend and sometimes those problems followed the judge home. Being pre-warned, Tyler was rocking in a chair on his front porch, when a group of his opponents assembled in front of his house. Did he send his family down to the cellar for safety in case there was trouble? They began shouting at him to which he raised the shotgun resting in his lap and responded by saying, "The first one through the gate is a dead man!" The crowd immediately dispersed. At home or in his courtroom, Judge Tyler was a person to be reckoned with.

On September 4, Judge Tyler requested the city council order the Forbes' pond be drained. During such cold winters as back in 1885, people ice skated on it. Henry Percival Wisdom nearly lost his life when he skated backwards into a hole that had been cut into the ice. The wheels of government turn ever so slow but finally on January 9, 1891, Tyler had a work force out at the pond. They dug a drainage ditch through the western bank of the pond and the water poured out past Neal's factory into the Cumberland. As usual, a crowd gathered by the pond from the beginning of the work to catch fish and present their expert opinion on how best to complete the task. It took the entire day to release all the water.

A celebration of the new fire hall located on Third Street was held in the Public Square on October 3, 1890. The celebration included a parade with all of the fire engines, all the chiefs and firemen.

The market house at the center of the Public Square. To its left is Elder's Opera House. The police station is also seen with its columns on the right. (TSLA)

The name "Queen City of the Cumberland" was coined on October 31, by an unnamed *Leaf Chronicle* writer. He wrote, "Call it what you will, solid growth, enterprise or advertising, Clarksville is a basis of solid prosperity and is growing rapidly; none of your sickly spasmodic, colicky swells; but rapid solid growth and people are finding in it out. Everyone is talking Clarksville, her enterprise and get-there spirit; people who know the location and surroundings know that the city is building on a solid basis for untold prosperity and are inspired with confidence in the future of the Queen City of the Cumberland." The name caught on, was highly approved by Clarksvillians and is still used today. Everyone it seemed wanted to use the name: businesses like Queen City Electric Light and Power Company, Queen City Warehouse, a baseball team (Queen City Grays), and even products such as Queen City linens. From that day, one after another reporter called the city by that name and even in the 1920s the *Leaf Chronicle* printed that name in the upper right hand corner of its front page for years.

As happens in families, Elizabeth Forbes, widow of Col. William A. Forbes was sued in October 1890 by her sister-in-law Nannie Tyler Johnson as executrix of the will of her late husband, who was also Elizabeth's half-brother. After his death and in reviewing his finances, Nannie Johnson discovered that Polk had been giving Elizabeth large sums of money for quite some time. Polk had been managing her finances as senility had caused Elizabeth to be incapable of doing so. Nannie claimed that Elizabeth owed the estate approximately $6,000. Sadly, the issue would be passed down for Elizabeth's daughter Bettie to resolve. Elizabeth was an invalid for two years until a brain hemorrhage quickly ended her life at 11:00 p.m. on November 14, 1891 at the age of 72. Her death notice in *The Tennessean* reported that she had been paralyzed "for a long time."

Faithful friends attended her in her failing health and on November 17, her remains were escorted from her home by Forbes Bivouac. The funeral service was held at Trinity and despite a steady rain, there was a long procession that followed her remains to Greenwood Cemetery. Her kinsman, John Hickman of Nashville officiated at the graveside service after which Elizabeth was buried beside her first husband, Hugh Garland and her daughter Nannie[127] in the Johnson family plot.

On the left: The Forbes home on North Second Street. The home is still standing in 2024. On the right: Col. W.A. Forbes.

Bettie had lived and grown up in the Forbes house built in 1861 at 607 North Second Street by her stepfather, William Archibald Forbes (1824-1862), and mother Mary Elizabeth Brunson Garland Forbes (1821-1891). Forbes and Mary wed in 1853 and bought land from Gustavus A. Henry upon which to build the house. Forbes taught Pure and Mixed Mathematics and Natural History at Stewart College, was a trustee and chair of the math department as well as serving as the Clarksville City Engineer and a partner in Forbes and Pritchett Stemmeries, a tobacco business. As colonel of the 14th TN during the Civil War, he was killed in the last minutes of the Second Battle of Manassas on August 30, 1862.

Elizabeth's stepfather, Cave Johnson, stayed with her family during the war. After Elizabeth died, her daughter by her first husband, Bettie Garland, was appointed administrator of her mother's estate in September 1892, but due to Nannie Johnson's lawsuit in the Chancery Court, Bettie was forced to sell her home. Elizabeth and William Forbes had a son, named after the father, who was probably living on his own at the time of the lawsuit. Bettie was forced to leave the house that had been her home for so many years and with it the memories of her family. The lawsuit would take years to settle.

Finally, it was done. Tyler had to be sick and tired of hearing about that obstruction to the streetcar line. The pond at the intersection of Sixth and Franklin Streets was known as the "double pond" because of its size and the fact that it cut Franklin Street in half. It extended from the Conroy and Faxon properties on the south to the Wood property on the north. The pond was responsible for a really big headache: the reason the Main Street of town was named Franklin instead of Main Street.[128] The McDaniels owned the property that sat right in the middle of what is now the intersection of University Avenue (formally Sixth Street) and Franklin Street. One of the "city fathers" decided that the main street of Clarksville could not dead end at a large pond and so designated the next street over as Main Street with the intention of switching the names back after the pond was eliminated. It took many decades of trial and error and loads of dirt to fill it in but by the summer of 1891, it was done and the trolley rout was extended down Franklin Street. However, by then it was too inconvenient and confusing to switch the names of the two streets.

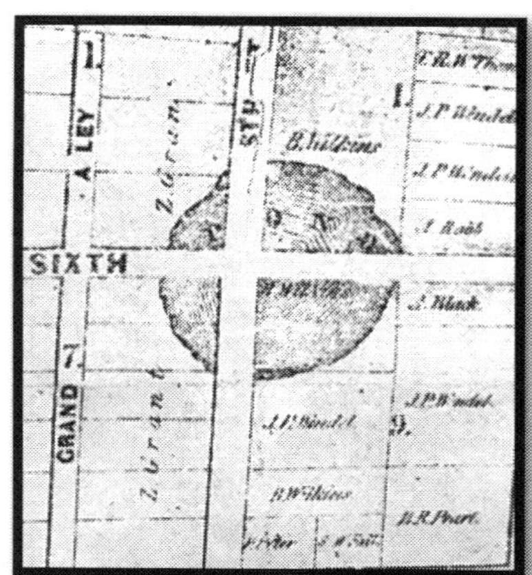

The infamous and troublesome double pond at the interesection of Sixth Street (University Avenue) and Franklin Street. (CMCPL)

Citizens on both sides of the Cumberland River were determined in the spring of 1891 to get the county to cough up the money to build a much-needed bridge on the south side of the river. The *Leaf Chronicle* did

---

[127] Nannie Garland died of tuberculosis on May 7, 1863.
[128] It took decades but the pond was finally filled in during the summer of 1891.

its part on the city side of the river to do the "kicking, cuffing and praying" but left it up to their Southern ally, the Yellow Creek correspondent, to do "the cussing" to get the court to build the bridge. Decriers said, "It's an imposition and the meanest kind of slavery that the people of the Southside should be kept poor all their lives paying ferriage to get to Clarksville that the next generation may enjoy the fruits of their hard earnings." The *Chronicle* cited that the people of the Southside were paying $10,000 per year in tolls just to be able to cross the river to do business in town. So they suggested those citizens, "raise Cain, make things hot and put their demands in unmistaken form and they will get a bridge over the Cumberland within the next year!" Still, it would be years before they were able to have their bridge built. The 1891 City Directory listed four ferries in operation: Searcy's Ferry, Edmondson's Ferry, Seven Mile Ferry and Moseley's Ferry.[129]

Edmondson's Ferry. Note the small paddlewheel at the back of the ferry. This ferry was equipped with an 11 horsepower Ferro engine. (MCA)

To honor the Confederate veterans which were decreasing in numbers rapidly, a committee met on October 13, to decide how to honor the former soldiers. It was concluded that

> **A monument should be raised worthy of this section and of yourselves and using the words of an address already issued to you from Forbes Bivouac, 'It should not only be an enduring testimony of our love, affections, and grateful remembrance of their unselfish devotion and glorious death but one that will be an object lesson to our children which will incite them to learn the true causes that led to that fearful struggle and the reasons that prompted our people to peril their fortunes and sacrifice their lives.'**

Tyler wrote of the need for such a tribute:

> **When the war closed, bringing disaster to the cause for which these brave men contended, the solemn duty remained to erect a monument to their memory to transmit to posterity the fact that they braved dangers, hardships, and suffered and died at their country's behest; that their cause was our cause, and their heroism, courage and sacrifices a rich legacy to our children.**

The members of the original monument committee were: Frank P. Gracey, David Newton Kennedy, Micajah Henry Clark, Rev. Achilles Degrasse Sears (Forbes' Bivouac's first chaplain), Polk Grundy Johnson, Thomas H. Smith, Charles Gholson Smith, Charles H. Bailey, James J. Crusman, William Madison Daniel, Simon Bloch, William Spencer Poindexter, Bailey Washington Macrae and Charles W. Tyler. The officers chosen were Frank P. Gracey-president, David N. Kennedy-vice-president and William S. Poindexter-treasurer.

Unfortunately, six of the original members of the monument committee passed away before the monument became a reality including Sears, Polk G. Johnson, Thomas H. Smith, Poindexter, C.G. Smith and Bloch. The following were selected to fill their positions: Robert Harris Burney, Samuel A. Caldwell, Thomas D. Luckett, Norfleet Lynn Carney, Butler Boyd and William M. Pettus. Later, Bailey, M. Barksdale, Robert Linah Cobb, Alexander David and James T. Kennedy were added to the committee. The campaign was begun and quickly accomplished through the efforts of several ladies and men's groups as well as supplements from Forbes' Bivouac. The contract to erect a fitting permanent monument was issued the following year. One setback was when the Confederate Orphans' Home was no longer needed, the property was sold with the intention of applying the funds to the purchase of the Confederate monument. However, due to a failure to get permission from the subscribers of the original Orphans' Home fund to donate the money from the sale of the property to the monument, the funds were instead turned over to the State Treasury. Determined individuals would not let this setback deter them from accomplishing their goal. When the Hook and Ladder Company failed, it was agreed to donate the money raised

---

[129] The directory also lists twelve landings between Clarksville and Ashland City at that time.

to the new Memorial Association which had been formed in 1889.

In stepped the Soldiers' Aid Society, along with children whose enthusiasm helped to raise funds. The society's committee consisted of Mrs. Gustavus A. Henry-president, Mrs. Edward B. Haskins-treasurer, Mrs. Amanda Munford-secretary and Mrs. Galbraith-recording secretary. The vice-presidents included: Mrs. William M. Finley, Mrs. Jacob G. Hornberger and Mrs. A.D. Sears.

Soldiers' Aid Society members in front of the Confederate Monument. (MCA)

Wives of the association members and Forbes Bivouac who contributed in the work included Mrs. Micajah H. Clark, Mrs. James H. Wells, Mrs. J.W. Graham, Mrs. James L. Lockert and Mrs. W.A. Shelby.

On October 15, a reunion was held in Clarksville complete with a parade through downtown in which several of the surviving veterans marched. The parade included local marching bands and policemen on horseback. It was estimated that over 7,500 people turned out for this event.

Because of Judge Tyler's involvement with this reunion and so many more, he became a sort of tourist advocate for the county and not just reunions but fairs, conventions, expositions and etc. If a pamphlet was requested to espouse the positive aspects of the county, Tyler was the one to write it; if county exhibits were needed anywhere in the state, Tyler collected the items and housed them in his office and if meetings were needed to organize an event, the participants met in Tyler's office.

During Christmas of 1891, Mollie fell ill with what was called grippe. Today it is known as the flu. Mollie recovered from the virus that was considered very dangerous and life threatening.

As usual, a local newspaper reporter announced the docket for that month's court. They added that, "evil doers and transgressors of the law had better hide out" because Judge Tyler was presiding.

One particular accident that led to a fireman being injured occurred in January of 1892, after extinguishing a fire on Spring Street. Once the fire engine was returned to the station, City Marshall Clay Stacker, Jr. suffered an accident when one of the fire hoses smashed his right hand against a wall. His fingers were badly lacerated and after he was carried to his home on Seventh Street, doctors Herring and Johnson who attended him had to amputate Stacker's little finger.

Charles received word that his half-sister, Mary F. Tyler Bryan, died March 8, in Galveston, Texas where two of her four children resided. She had been married to Henry H. Bryan, the tobacconist who passed away in 1878. Thus, now all of John Duke's children by his first wife Harriett were gone.

The court dockets were filled with the usual expected occurrences, until the middle of March when Judge Tyler was presented with a different sort of problem. A tiny baby girl estimated to be about ten-days-old was left at midnight in a box at the gate of a woman's cabin in the Rossview community. The woman turned the baby over to Judge Tyler who decided to give the girl to the Catholic sisters to raise. The nuns lived at the Sisters of Charity House, a parochial school located at the corner of Franklin and Seventh Streets. Nine years later he would place an ad in the newspaper to find a loving home for an orphaned three-year-old girl. Memories of Nannie were likely awakened in the judge and it is certain he made sure these little girls were well taken care of.

Two men were arrested by Sheriff Staton[130] on March 21, for the murder of the black dwarf, Adee Hickman. The murder occurred outside of Billy Settle's Electric Light Company on the corner of North First and Main Streets on March 12. H.F. Goosetree and James Rosser, both employees of the company were taken into custody.

Sheriff Staton. (MCA)

During the trial on the 22nd, Rosser turned state's evidence against Goosetree giving very damning testimony against him for killing the dwarf nicknamed "Hades" due, it was said to his "unadulterated meanness." Just the year before in February 1891, Hickman was arrested and charged with using profane language on the street, the charge was dismissed with a warning.

Squire Caldwell heard the case. The sequence of the murder was this: The two men turned off electricity to the city street lights at midnight as was routinely done and shortly thereafter in the dark, Rosser heard Goosetree arguing with someone. Later, Hickman was discovered lying in the street by Lee McNeal, a black barber who was headed home. He overheard a disturbance nearby but thought nothing of it until he found Hickman. McNeal thought Hickman was drunk but still alerted Officer Stafford at the police station who went to the intersection and, also thinking Hickman drunk, moved him to the porch opposite the electric light station. Someone reported Hickman dead and Stafford returned and examined him to find he had a crushed skull. After the coroner examined the dwarf, an inquest was held with no results. Hickman's body was turned over to Henry Roberts, the black undertaker, for internment. However, other people's testimony did not support Rosser and Goosetree was released. The murder was never solved nor did it seem that any real search for the killer was ever conducted.

By way of the newspapers, competitive bids were solicited for the creation of the Confederate Monument and on April 11, the committee, consisting of Tyler, Bailey, Macrae, Pettus, Crusman, Clark and Kennedy met once more to view the various designs and award the contract. The committee had much from which to choose: twelve different monument companies competed for the contract and sixteen different designs were put forth. The committee took an entire day to finalize their choice which was to award the contract to George H. Mitchell & Co. of Chicago at an agreed price of $7,500. Concurrently, the full committee met and ratified the final choice of the design committee and the date of the unveiling was set for October 25, 1893.

The selected design. Note the lower statues facing the front. This was changed. Also note the bottom statement: "Work erected in any part of the country by the most experienced men." This statement will turn out to be a rather humorous one given the day of Clarksville's arrival.

Mollie Tyler consistently immersed herself in church work. She, along with her brother Billy and sister-in-law Emmie Tyler, were among the collected voices in the choir for a very special Easter at Trinity Church on Sunday, April 18. Molly herself had begun the choir. The building was filled to capacity so that extra chairs were brought in. All denominations attended the service held at 11:00 a.m.

[130] On January 31, 1902 Staton would pass away at age 56 from pneumonia.

The next day, the *Leaf Chronicle* announced there was a "spook" in District Nine. After the death and burial of a black man in December, the undertaker, A.H. Seay, who fashioned the pauper's coffin for the deceased, came to Clarksville to get paid for his services, regardless of numerous reports that the dead man was up and walking around. Seay insisted that he had given the remains an appropriate Christian burial that was witnessed by many friends at the graveside service. Seay approached Judge Tyler to ask him what should be done about the matter. In his characteristic sharp wit, Judge Tyler responded that if the man "had died and been buried, it was his duty as a pauper to stay dead, and if he returned in contempt of the court, it was the duty of the citizens to arrest the spook and bury him again." Still unsure about how to handle the matter, Seay left stating that he would obey the judge's order but "did not know how they were to keep him under."

Within a week, the judge encountered another strange event, this time in his own office. A misguided boy released earlier by the judge for begging, stealing and suspected insanity turned up in Tyler's office after being arrested again by the city police. They took the boy before Squire Smith who decided that he had no jurisdiction in the case; therefore, the police simply released him at the courthouse entrance, ordering him to leave. Instead, the youth ambled into the judge's office, removed his shoes and made himself at home, warming himself by the fire. Judge Tyler came in sometime later, startled to discover his office occupied. Tyler was beside himself. The audacity, the sheer nerve of this kid sitting at his desk! There was going to be bloodshed! Tyler had the sheriff remove the invader and became incensed when he learned that the police themselves had left him there. Before the judge could issue a warrant for the arrest of the two policemen, the janitor of the courthouse, Alex McKennon the custodian, appeared, pleaded the policemen's case and "smoothed down the ruffled feathers of his honor."

With the recent improvements made in the 1890s on the Charlotte Road (now Greenwood Avenue), the connection with the south side of the river was causing a boom in commercial travel. There was even more reason to celebrate at the news of a new ferryboat being put in by Jones D. Neblett in June of 1892.

Clarksville Civil War veteran groups had held meetings and reunions for years but the Tennessee State Association of Confederate Veterans held in Franklin, Tennessee on September 14-15, 1892, was one which would last in their memories for the remainder of their lives. The reunion was held in the grove at Col. McGavock's on ground through which Gen. William A. Quarles' Brigade passed when the charge was made on the Federal works that day, in the Battle of Franklin on November 30, 1864. To these men, they were standing on sacred ground for here, friends and brothers died or were wounded and left on the field to suffer an agonizingly cold night until their removal the following day. The featured speaker that day was Captain Edmund D. Baxter, Baxter's Company, TN Light Artillery. It was reported that Baxter's speech drew repeated rounds of enthusiastic applause.

On Thursday morning after business was concluded, the old soldiers were treated to a concert held at the Franklin courthouse. A choral group from Franklin entertained the group with "The Conquered Banner," "The Grave of the Tennessee Volunteers" and "Tenting on the Old Camp Ground." Each of these brought "tears like rain" from the veterans' eyes. The war had been over for 27 years but for many it would seem like yesterday. Following the concert, a banquet was presented downstairs at the courthouse, tables laden with bountiful food and the men recalled the parched corn ration they subsisted on during the time before the battle in Franklin.

The veterans marched four blocks from town to the grove in a parade complete with floats, buggies, carriages, costumed ladies with their escorts. Once at the grove, honored guests presented speeches. There were warm embraces as former comrades recognized the faces of those, who like themselves had been among the fortunate. Col. John R. McGavock was immortalized for the role he and his wife, Carrie played in their service tending the wounded and removing the dead off the battlefield to a plot of their land near the McGavock plantation house as an eternal resting place. The newly-elected President of the United Confederate Veterans attached a badge of the order to the colonel's coat which again brought such emotion from everyone present. Yet another banquet was served, this time from twenty-four tables, each one hundred yards long with hams, barbeque, pickles, bread, pies and etc. An estimated 10,000 people were there for the meal. Afterwards many visited the old cemetery seeking the names of comrades or loved ones who fell that day. However, the most significant locale visited was the actual battleground itself, marked by flags showing the line of the works, the position of different brigades and the place where generals Cleburne, Strahl, Adams and others fell. For the men of the 49th Tennessee standing on the site of the old gin house was the most memorable point of the reunion. A monument, fifteen feet high reading, "Center of Quarles' Brigade, Nov. 30, '64" marked the spot.

Some of the Clarksville delegates were so moved by the festivities, they delayed their return home to Clarksville. Frank Beaumont, representing the Alfred Robb Bivouac, who intended to stay one day, remained all week before leaving the good citizens of Franklin who had opened their homes and hearts to all the boys in grey who came to reminisce and pay respects. Five years passed before enough funds were collected by the United Daughters of the Confederacy to raise the Confederate Monument on the Public Square in Franklin on the twenty-fifth anniversary of the Battle (November 30th).

Reunions such as these provided opportunities for veterans to gather together to relive their shared memories, find peace in their decisions to fight, to commemorate fallen comrades and note heroic acts. These were times of healing and bonding. Reunions were numerous through the years until no living veteran existed and the gatherings became a venue for their offspring. Some reunions were organized as truly separate entities of Confederate or Union groups but also from time to time met as Blue and Gray affairs whereby veterans from both sides attended.

It was reported in the November 4 issue of the *Daily Tobacco Leaf Chronicle* that merchants in the fire district of downtown Clarksville were prohibited by a new City Council ordinance against burning combustible material on the streets. Anyone violating this law would have to pay a fine of between five and twenty-five dollars. It had been a common practice for merchants to eliminate their trash by piling in front of their store and burning it until it turned to ash. The most notable burning was the conflagration of the Franklin House's guest ledgers by Billy Bringhurst's daughters in their quest to clean out the hotel's cluttered basement. Too late, they realized they had "burned history" when they spotted the name of Andrew Jackson, June12, 1828 among others turning into blackened soot in the street at the hotel's front.

Frustration over convictions handed out by Judge Tyler that were later overturned was the focus of an article in the December 10 issue of the *Daily Tobacco Leaf.*

It's Hard to Do

Something About the Murder Trials of Montgomery County

Within the past few years Montgomery County has had a remarkable experience with murder cases. If the *Leaf Chronicle* mistakes not, Judge Tyler has sentenced some five or six men to hang since he has been on the bench and only one of them was ever executed. That one was Bill Morrow....

Some of the murder cases since the Morrow trials have attracted every little interest, many of then having been almost forgotten. Just a few of them here may be recalled to show how hard it is to hang a man:

1). Harper Jordan killed John Nolen convicted on third trial by jury: appealed and overturned by the Tennessee Supreme Court on insufficient evidence and freed.
2). Finney Saunders killed his wife: conviction overturned and freed.
3). John Gilmer convicted of murder: sent to penitentiary.
4). Later in 1909 Tyler sentenced Marcellus Rhinehart to hang for the murder of Rufus Hunter. He was convicted but on appeal was sentenced to life in prison.

With two rivers and plenty of ponds, drowning was a not-so-rare occurrence in Montgomery County. Whenever drowning victims' bodies in the rivers could not be located, it was Judge Tyler that could give the order for dynamite to be used to help bring bodies to the surface of the water. This occurred in both 1893 and 1909.

Judge Tyler sent one man and two women to the big house on May 23, 1893 for larceny. Matt Stewart, Ada Mallory and Mollie Gentry were given three years at the state pen. The newspaper stated, "Mollie is the damsel who touched a torch to Col. Young's[131] tenement house out of

[131] Col. William F. Young, Confederate veteran.

jealousy for the woman who was occupying it." Ada was a repeat offender and well-known to the police. Just three years later she was convicted again of the same crime.

More and more young people were showing interest in bicycles so much so that bicycle races were being organized in town.[132] In late May 1893, Morton Turnley jumped on the bandwagon and started a fund to raise money to purchase medals for the winners of the upcoming races.

In mid-June, Gossett Bros.[133] received a shipment of bicycles at the furniture store on Franklin Street and one in particular caught the eye of the enthusiast, a Victor, Model D, 35-pounder with the new pneumatic tires. He bragged that it was the first of this type to be received in Clarksville. The bicycles were priced at $165 and, so far that summer Gossett stated he had already sold fourteen. Those who used horses saw the streets as theirs because they were there first, while the drivers of the streetcars viewed the horses as impediments and nobody liked the bicycles!

Clarksville bicycle enthusiasts. Photo from author's personal collection.

A famous nationally known murder had occurred on August 4, 1892 and the trial ended on June 20, 1893 with a not guilty verdict for Lizzie Borden in Falls River, Massachusetts. The murder of Lizzie's father and stepmother had been discussed in Clarksville from the very beginning and continued even past the verdict. Folks around Clarksville as they did all over the country, argued for or against the guilt of the spinster and solved the crime in their own minds. A woman being charged with the murder of her very own father certainly had everyone's tongue a'waggin and Judge Tyler, of course, had his own opinion on the matter. This trial was of particular interest to the judge for what if she had been convicted of these murders? Would they have executed her, a woman seen as harmless and shy? By the end of his career, Judge Tyler never had to pronounce a death sentence on a woman while he sat on the bench.

While discussing the outcome of the trial with a newspaper reporter, Judge Tyler referred back to a murder which had occurred in Clarksville fifteen years' prior at the Southern Hotel. The Emily Draudt murder also ended in an acquittal but for the man accused of murdering a young girl he had "ruined" and run off with.

Judge Tyler believed that a person's guilt or innocence could be easily determined by observing the accused immediately after a crime was committed and that in the case of Lizzie Borden, he said he would have had a better opinion of her guilt or innocence had he been able to watch the sincerity of her grief the morning of the crime.

In the case of the man who allegedly murdered Emily Draudt, Rev. A.D. Sears had arrived at the murder scene soon after and studied the man's emotions. He told the judge, "That man was guilty. I watched him closely in the hotel and I tell you his grief was feigned. There was not that real earnestness in the fellow that will impress the close observer favorably in such cases and I am as firmly convinced of the man's guilt as I would be had I witnessed the deed." Tyler agreed with him but explained that observations alone were not enough to convict someone. To this Sears, who believed the man should have been hanged, consoled himself with the firm belief that the man would get his final reward in the end.

The unveiling day of the Confederate Monument was set, but where was the monument? On September 8, 1893, the newspaper announced that the bronze statue of William Rufus Bringhurst was shipped and on its way to Clarksville with the stone monument to follow shortly after. When the monument arrived by train from Chicago, seemingly everything was ahead of schedule the first week in October when a serious problem arose with the unveiling just three weeks away:

[132] Professor William Emery owned the first bicycle in Clarksville.

[133] In September of 1891, C.A. Gossett's store and surrounding buildings were lost to a major fire.

there was no wagon substantial enough to transport the monument to the cemetery. The monument company representative was under the assumption that the cemetery was close to the depot and that a wagon would not be needed. Finding this not to be the case, the man returned to Chicago to acquire such a wagon to move the 8-ton base. He assured city officials that the monument would be erected before the ceremony on the 25th, unless rain delayed the work. It was a tense period of uncertainty for everyone who had labored for the project and the monument came close to missing its own unveiling.

The impressive Confederate monument made of Vermont granite was placed in the center front part of Greenwood Cemetery next to the section where Nannie was buried. The monument features a 9-foot bronze figure of a Confederate infantryman at its top, as well as 7-foot granite statues on either side at the base of a cavalryman and artilleryman. The likenesses for the statues were taken from a photo of William "Billy" Robert Bringhurst, infantry, Charles H. Bailey, artillery and Clay Stacker, cavalry, all Confederate volunteers. The monument stands 48 feet, 3 inches tall and measures 9 ft. X 13 ft. at its base. It is interesting to note here that the original design had the two lower figures facing forward; when the monument was completed, the figures were turned to face to the sides. The inscription on the front side of the base reads:

IN HONOR OF THE HEROES WHO FELL IN THE ARMY
OF THE CONFEDERATE STATES

And on the reverse side of the base:

THROUGH ADVERSE FORTUNE DENIED FINAL VICTORY
TO THEIR UNDAUNTED COURAGE, HISTORY PRE-SERVES
THEIR FAME, MADE GLORIOUS FOREVER. 1861-1865

Charles Henry Bailey
Artillery

William R. Bringhurst
Infantry

Clay Stacker
Cavalry

The regiments from the Clarksville area included the 14th, the 49th, the 50th and Co. E of the 10th TN Infantry. It is important to note that the 14th TN had more men from Clarksville and Montgomery County than any other regiment in service of the Confederacy. The regiment began with 1,100 in 1861; at the war's end, there remained but a remnant of survivors.

There was excitement the day before the unveiling of the Confederate Monument at 10 a.m. in Judge Tyler's courthouse office. A special delivery of flowers was sent to him from New York. The anonymous sender wanted the flowers to be used in the unveiling ceremony. The long-awaited unveiling of the monument occurred on Wednesday, October 25, 1893. Prior to the solemn ceremony there was a parade from the courthouse to Greenwood Cemetery which began at 11:00 a.m. Thirteen young girls drew for the honor of representing one of the Confederate states to be shown on the float. Of course, each one wanted Tennessee. Miss Robbie Luckett drew the popular home state and the rest was as follows:

Alabama: Miss Mary Keith
Arkansas: Miss Mary Anderson, daughter of Frank O. Anderson
Florida: Miss Fannie Shelby, daughter of William A. Shelby
Georgia: Miss Lucy Bailey, daughter of Charles H. Bailey
Kentucky: Miss Josie Munford
Louisiana: Miss Anne Belle Bringhurst, daughter of Billy Bringhurst
Mississippi: Miss Sara Johnson
Missouri: Miss Mildred Johnson, daughter of Polk Grundy Johnson

North Carolina: Miss Sara Burney, daughter of R.H. Burney
South Carolina: Miss Fannie Herndon, daughter of Thomas Herndon
Texas: Miss Emma Tyler, daughter of Judge Charles Tyler
Virginia: Miss Beulah McCauley, daughter of William H. McCauley

Each of the girls carried baskets of flowers for the ceremony at Greenwood prepared by the ladies. A badge with their state's name was attached to the basket. It was estimated that there were two thousand people in the parade alone including students from seventeen states, 150 students from Stewart College along with all the professors led by Dr. Summey. The ceremony was one Clarksville would talk about for years. Then came the actual unveiling: The newspaper reporter described the event:

> **At the conclusion of Mr. Kennedy's remarks, little Hope Gracey, accompanied by her father Julien Gracey and grandfather, Captain F.P. Gracey, made her appearance at the base of the monument. This feature of the program unfortunately was not fully successful, owing to the breaking of the cord containing the drapery. After some delay, however, the unveiling was partially successful.**

Mollie called attention to an interesting point in the unveiling ceremony when Hope Gracey struggled to get the drapes to fall. At the moment the crowd began to sing "Dixie," the drapes finally gave way and fell to the base of the monument. Mollie believed that to have some sort of meaning. In Charles Tyler's obituary years later, he was credited with the completion of the monument, "To him more than any other one man is due the Confederate Monument in Greenwood Cemetery." Since the day of the dedication and unveiling, the monument serves as the epicenter of the cemetery.

The earliest known photo of the monument at Greenwood Cemetery. (MCA)

Part Three

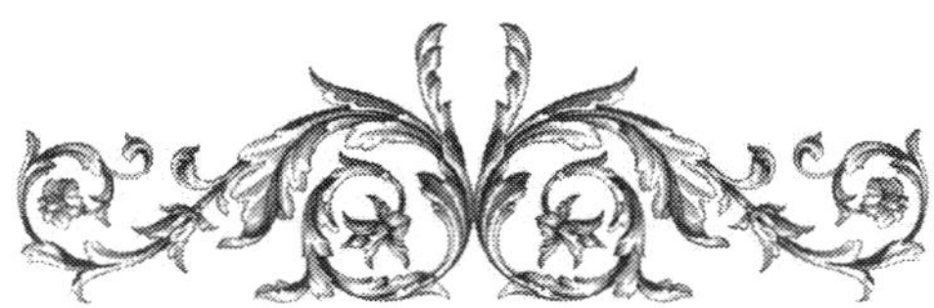

Chapter Seventeen: A Time of Progress

In 1894, Judge Tyler's name was proposed for a seat on the U.S. District Court vacated by Judge D.M. Key. The *Clarksville Daily Tobacco Leaf* newspaper showed their support by writing that they would

> **rather see him appointed than any man in the state. He has been judge of the Criminal Court of this county for many years and has made a most excellent judge. He is eminently qualified for the duties that would devolve upon him and would fill Judge Key's position with ability and fairness. While he is an able, impartial presiding officer of a court, he is a Democrat of the straight type. He had been prominently connected with every battle of the party since he grew to manhood and knows no such word as compromise when dealing with enemies of his party. His appointment would give his friends here much pleasure.**

In the March 3rd issue of the *Leaf Chronicle*, the writer reported that the December *Southern Magazine* printed two of Judge Tyler's short stories. "The Miracle at Mrs. Smiley's" and "Gone to Coopertown" were praised by the magazine as "so simply sketched yet with such ease that it excited the admiration of all who read it."

Finally, the lawsuit over between Bettie Garland and Nannie Johnson was over. Nannie purchased the house and lot at the court sale held in April 1894 for $4,750 and then sold the house and lot in 1899 to Thomas Lawson Mabry (1847-1902), and Elizabeth "Betty" Dabney Mabry (1858-1938), for the same price she paid for the house in 1894. The deed to the property was not recorded until five years later when the total balance of the debts against the estate were paid. After both parents died, their daughter, Malinda Mabry Macon, bought the house from the estate and converted it to apartments. The house was purchased and completely renovated by Don and Patsy Sharpe.

The courthouse yard was in great shape, green and lush and Judge Tyler wanted it to stay that way. When W.D. Turnley wanted to have a gathering in the yard for a local temperance meeting, his request was refused by Tyler. Turnley argued that the yard had been used by other groups and so assumed that his meeting could be held there as well. Tyler explained that indeed other groups had sought to use the yard for meetings but their requests had been denied also. Tyler gave examples such as the exercises of the Jeff Davis Day being refused and several political gatherings too. Instead Tyler arranged for the group to meet inside the courthouse in the county courtroom and supplied the crowd "with plenty of good, pure, straight water and anything else they wanted."

During the July term to show their respect and gratitude for his twenty-one years of service to Montgomery County, a special committee appointed by the County Court presented Judge Tyler with a gold-handled cane. In the resolution read by the committee, Tyler was cited for his dedication in nearly eliminating the debts of the county incurred before the Civil War and for his work in building the "finest courthouse in the state." In his reply, Tyler placed the credit on the shoulders of citizens who "cheerfully paid their taxes." It was noted that Tyler was ill at the time of the presentation.

On September 30, two of the courthouse ceilings collapsed. It goes without saying that this was totally unacceptable to Judge Tyler and the commissioners who approved the building of this courthouse. Architect Gamaliel B. Wilson was hired to clean up the mess, make the repairs and get the courthouse back in order. The total cost for repairs to the ceilings, boxing the roof, installing a new chandelier and repairing another, along with replacing an iron railing, cleaning the stove, painting and purchasing new furniture for the register's office and library came to $7,358.56.

Judge Tyler had a murder case to hear in September-October 1894 in which a white man, Bill Durham, was accused of poisoning a black man, Sam Price who worked on Tom Tinsley's land in Collinsville. In the end, the jury decided Sam's wife had poisoned her husband with strychnine and Durham was acquitted.

On October 1, the first Board of Directors for the new library met consisting of: Mrs. Clay Stacker-president, Rev. A.M. Growden-secretary and treasurer, Mrs. Lizzie Elliott, Miss Mattie Beach and Judge Tyler.

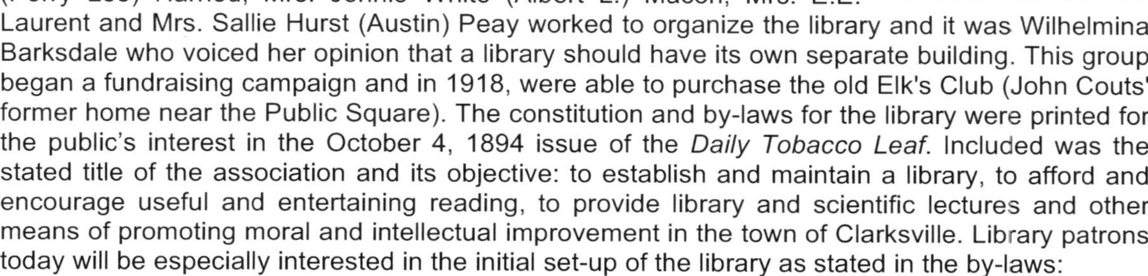

Mrs. Clay Stacker, beautiful, generous and committed to the library.

It is appropriate that Judge Tyler be known as the "Father of the Clarksville-Montgomery County Public Library" due to the 1894 organization of the library association under his leadership. The love of books and reading was instilled in him from early childhood.

A women's group that included Mrs. Brenda Runyon, Mrs. Myra Gill (Perry Lee) Harned, Mrs. Jennie White (Albert L.) Macon, Mrs. E.E. Laurent and Mrs. Sallie Hurst (Austin) Peay worked to organize the library and it was Wilhelmina Barksdale who voiced her opinion that a library should have its own separate building. This group began a fundraising campaign and in 1918, were able to purchase the old Elk's Club (John Couts' former home near the Public Square). The constitution and by-laws for the library were printed for the public's interest in the October 4, 1894 issue of the *Daily Tobacco Leaf*. Included was the stated title of the association and its objective: to establish and maintain a library, to afford and encourage useful and entertaining reading, to provide library and scientific lectures and other means of promoting moral and intellectual improvement in the town of Clarksville. Library patrons today will be especially interested in the initial set-up of the library as stated in the by-laws:

-The library shall be open on Tuesdays and Saturday from 8 to 5 p.m. Books lost or injured shall be paid for according to the assessment of Board of Directors.
-Only one book or volume of a set may be drawn at one time. The librarian shall number and register the books and keep account with each number.
-No book shall be received without the approval of the Board of Directors.
-It shall be the duty of the librarian to notify members of the expiration of their subscription and solicit a renewal.
-Members may keep books two weeks. For each additional week, not exceeding four, a penalty of 5 cents a week shall be attached. Any person failing to return a book within six weeks or without paying value of same, with penalty, if any, shall be deprived of all privileges of the association for one year unless reinstated by the board.

Rev. Growden acted as librarian until Miss Sina Harvey was elected by the board. Her salary was $50 per annum, payable monthly. She served from 1894-1899 and next Lena Beach became the librarian. Mrs. Beach served for twenty-four years from 1899-1923.

Judge Tyler stated, "I believe we are doing a good work in guiding the taste of the reading public into pure literary fields."[134] This organization purchased over 500 books, which were held in the courthouse library until a new library could become a reality.

Three years later a reporter for the *Leaf Chronicle* interviewed the judge for a special article on the operations of the library. Judge Tyler proudly estimated the holdings of the library at a little over 1500 volumes. He went further to say that the library was financed entirely on membership fees, which included lifetime memberships for $3 and annual memberships for $1. This provided a revenue of between $200-$300 a year. In addition, the library received donations of books and money from "public-spirited people." He clarified that all of the money went towards the purchase of books, except for the $5 monthly salary for the librarian.

---

[134] The judge would be pleased to learn that a new library to be built in the northern part of the county is underway in 2025.

On the left: the courthouse library in Judge Tyler's office with bookcases from floor to ceiling. The lady pictured here may have been the librarian, Sina Harvey. Judge Tyler is seen sitting at his desk. (MCA) Below: one of the desks from the courthouse library. It is now in the reading room of the present-day public library. Photo by author.

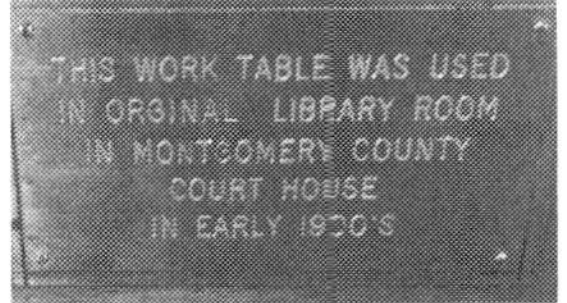

Mollie and Em attended a reception for Mr. and Mrs. Frank Snadon on December 12, at the Tip Top mansion on Madison Street. The reception was organized by Mattie Williams Dunlop who was the daughter of the mansion's owner, J.L. Williams. The reception was attended by a mass of friends. The Clarksville orchestra provided the musical background and decorations were said to be such that they "made an artful argument in the question so long mooted between the beauties of nature and art." Each of Mollie's siblings were present for the occasion. Very seldom did Judge Tyler accompany his wife to social events but instead knew she would be in the company of friends and family in every outing.

In 1894, M.V. Ingram, newspaper editor, published his book, *An Authenticated History of the Famous Bell Witch*. Hickory Wild was just miles from where all the mysterious happenings occurred. Judge Tyler recorded this story in reference to his notable father and this famous entity of Robertson County, Tennessee. He wrote

> **Yes, I have heard my father tell many wonderful things that occurred at Bell's about the time he moved to this county from Virginia. I remember that he said reports concerning the mysterious affair reached Virginia before he left that state, and his friends laughed and ridiculed him for moving to a haunted country. But of course he paid no attention to such jeers and jests, for he did not believe the story. But when he arrived here, which was in the fall of 1818, he found great excitement prevailing all over the country and he joined with the others, visiting the place to investigate the cause. I shall not undertake to detail any statements that my father made in regard to what he saw and heard on these occasions; but you can refer to me for the fact that he did state that he investigated the matter to his full satisfaction; having entered upon the investigation deeply impressed that the demonstrations were not made by members of the family, and he pursued his inquiry along this line, making every test possible, and became thoroughly convinced that no member of the family had anything to do with it, and further than that, the mystery to him was never solved.**

No one at the time would ever question John Duke Tyler's credibility. It seems that he, as well as all others who visited the Bells, were convinced that something beyond the realm of this world was in control of the happenings on that farm.

In his typical style, Judge Tyler, in a letter published in the *Weekly Chronicle* on January 11, 1895 spoke on highway projects stating that Montgomery County should, "continue the policy already mapped out by the court. We should accomplish each year as much as we can in the way of improving our highways using our surplus for this purpose from time to time and employing county convicts on the public roads." He advocated strongly for free bridges, "The people of Montgomery County had paid a railroad tax for many years and have done their duty. They have earned a rest and, in my judgment, ought to have it."

Em Tyler entered school at the Female Academy in "Miss Bryan's kindergarten class" where in February of 1895, Em displayed her emerging talent in performing during public exercises. She read two selections honoring George Washington in special commemoration of his birthday 163 years prior. Miss Sarah Hornbrook and Mrs. E.G. Buford had charge of the kindergarten. The year previous, Miss Bryan's primary and kindergarten school was held at the "old Cobb home"[135] on Madison Street.

A momentous occasion occurred when the city decided to do away with the mules to pull the streetcars and go electric. Many town folks were not happy at all over this planned change, especially the store owners. To lay down the rails, the streets would have to be torn up producing more dust with which to contend. People were suspicious of electricity still and therefore feared the overhead electrical wires that carried the electricity to the streetcar's motor. This fear was underscored when on September 4, 1896, the Franklin Street car's wire came in contact with the low-hanging electric light wire that ran into Gerhart's Dry Goods Store. A stream of fire was sent along the frayed wire. An alarm was quickly raised and the fire was extinguished quickly. This fortunately occurred at 5 p.m. and not during the night or the consequences might have been disastrous.

The new electric lines being installed on the north side of Franklin Street. The First National Bank is seen in the back. (TSLA)

The streetcars had their own garage on Commerce Street next to the L & N Train Station. Its location was convenient as the trolleys would be used to transport passengers to and from the train station. The city owned both summer cars and winter cars. In order to heat the car in the winter, a coal stove was set up in the center of the car. Seating capacity was between 25-30 people with standing room available in the aisles. The wooden seats were smartly designed where the back of each could be moved forward or backward to accommodate facing the direction the car was moving. From early morning until 10:00 p.m., the streetcars ran every half hour and the cost of the ride was just 5 cents. While the motormen drove the car, they also were vigilant for hazards on the rails and for collisions with other vehicles and people

Franklin Street electric trolley. Note all the electric poles. (MCA)

The controls were located at each end of the car which directed its movement at speeds reaching between 15-25 mph depending on how busy the city streets were. The trolley system ceased operations in 1928. The old trolleys sat unused at their former garage on Tenth Street until removed and dismantled.

Next began the most difficult decade in the career of Judge Tyler: the terror of the "Black Patch" or "Tobacco Wars." Because tobacco was the area's main cash crop, the conflict affected nearly every family in northern Middle Tennessee and Western Kentucky. The problem started when three major tobacco companies formed a trust called the American Tobacco Company (ATC) forcing tobacco prices to fall dramatically. In addition, a federal tax was levied against the growers, which inhibited individual sales. Congress did not seem to listen to the farmers' outcry against what they saw as an unfair tax since no other crop was being taxed.

The trouble began in Montgomery County when, on May 23, 1895 the plant beds owned by W. Jerles of St. Bethlehem were destroyed and on the same night,

> **About twenty-five men are said to have called upon D. Johnson and James Moore, colored sharecroppers on N.O. Lovelace's farm in the Spring Creek neighborhood and told them it would be useless to try to raise a crop of tobacco outside the Association. The**

[135] Joshua Cobb's former home.

croppers, it is said became frightened and went to Mr. Lovelace and insisted upon joining. Mr. Lovelace accordingly became a member of the Association today.

Several notable street improvement proposals were accepted by the city council on June 10, 1895. All pavements on Madison Street from Third to Fifth Streets on both sides of Madison were to be made to conform to the line of pavements, eight feet wide.

Other projects were underway: a load of lumber was ordered for the city bridge and a committee was appointed by the city council to determine the price of the lot near the bridge and also the cost of building a cottage for the bridge-keeper. It was during this meeting that the Miller Paving Co. of Memphis was given permission to purchase ten loads of the city's bottom gravel to construct a pavement around the Confederate Monument in Greenwood Cemetery.

In July 1895, the County Court appropriated $100 to the library and furnished the room with chairs, tables and book cases. Judge Tyler who was publically recognized in the *Chronicle* for his efforts,

The Library Association is greatly indebted to Judge Tyler for his untiring efforts on behalf of this highly commendable literary movement in our community for he has left nothing in his power undone that could promote its well-being.

The chain gang was working for a couple of weeks in District Eleven in mid-summer of 1895 on a new road near the James Wilkerson place. The gang's tents were pitched in a grove of shade trees on his property. The prisoners were pleasantly surprised when Wilkerson and his wife pulled up in a wagon and handed over a two-gallon freezer of ice cream and some cakes to boot!

Judge Tyler's cousin, Judge John D. Tyler died at his home on Walnut Street in Hopkinsville, Kentucky on August 13 at age 68 after a long illness. He was educated at Princeton, Kentucky and began the practice of law in 1847, but soon left his law practice and instead farmed a large tract of land in Christian County, Kentucky. He was married in 1847 to Helen Harpending of Caldwell Co. Next he married Lizzie Moore also of Christian County. His obituary read, "Judge Tyler was a prominent member of the Ninth St. Presbyterian Church and also a Master Mason. He was an honest, Christian man, a devoted husband and parent, a true friend and an upright citizen." He is buried in Hopkinsville's Riverside Cemetery.

In 1895, the decision to finally tear down the old market house on Public Square was announced. Built around 1869, money to construct both the market house and city hall had been raised by Henry Frech, a prominent businessman in town who served as mayor from 1869-1871.

The market house had long fallen into disfavor. The building had been a place to hitch horses or sleep off a night's encounter with spirits of the liquid kind. The market house was described by a local newspaper as "a failure as a market house . . . inadequate as a police headquarters and inhumane to incarcerate offenders in that dirty, cold place called a calaboose." Citizens complained of its bell chiming on the hour every hour, disrupting the sleep of anyone within earshot of the Public Square. Clarksville's most unloved building was garnering criticism as a general nuisance to the public. They pleaded for "a night of unbroken slumber." Even during the Federal occupation of Clarksville, the bell was a vexation when on numerous occasions it was rung out of mischief by "small black children." To read the newspapers of the day, it would seem that citizens were sorry that this unpopular building was not brought down by the great fire of 1878.

Finally, city councilmen Piedmont Gerhart, Gracey Childers and W.S. Payne convinced the powers that be that the building MUST come down! When the market house was finally torn down, a small, central park-like area was added to the square. The newspaper could barely contain its exuberance at the decision. It ran this little farewell salute:

THANKS! THANKS! THANKS! Ha! H!
Goodbye!
The old Market House!
An old eyesore to mar Clarksville's beauty for years will be torn down—
Thanks awfully, gentlemen!

Em Tyler was the hit of the program held October 24, 1895 to benefit the Library Association. In fact, she was called back three times to entertain the audience. She performed comical songs while playing a banjo. She was among many to perform and the evening was pronounced a success in every particular. Her love of music came from both her father and mother's side of her family.

Em Tyler and her banjo. (CV)

The first King's Daughters Circle was organized in Clarksville, who with permission from Judge Tyler, met in the courthouse library. Their purpose was to help physically handicapped persons. Each individual club was called a circle and their benevolent works lasted for decades. Clarksville's oldest circle was the Silver Cross Circle, the first charitable organization in Clarksville outside of churches. The society's roots began in New York.

Joe M. Jarrell, employed by the city as an engineer, mastered a technique that shortened the time needed to ready the horses at the engine house when a fire was reported. Joe installed an electric gong that sounded at precisely the same moment a small crank opened the horse stalls. The horses were trained to quickly position themselves under the suspended harness racks where within minutes; the drivers had them hitched to the firefighting equipment.

Charles' half-nephew, Henry H. Bryan age 50, passed away February 28, 1896. He had been born in Clarksville in 1846 and served in the Confederate Army. Henry received a classical education in Germany, took a tour of Europe and became a lawyer, practicing in Louisiana. He left behind a sister and brother who lived in Galveston, Texas.

In spite of his heavy work load, Tyler always saw to the honoring of Civil War veterans. Meetings were always held in his office and for that year's Memorial Day exercises, Tyler served on several committees: instrumental music, flags and decorations. He also requested for those who lived near him to leave their flowers at his house for the ceremony to be held at both cemeteries.

People wishing that bicycles would somehow disappear had to realize the contraption was here to stay and on June 15, the first bicycle race was held. The race started at Tenth and Madison Streets in front of Robert D. Moseley's home and ran five miles out the Nashville Pike (now U.S. Highway 41-A) and back. It was also reported that the young men of Clarksville were making extensive trips on the "high front with small rear wheel types despite unpaved roads."

On June 30, contractor J.N. Alsop left for St. Louis to finalize the arrangements and purchases for Clarksville's electric railway system. The two engines had already been purchased and were stored at the nearly-completed power house on the corner of Eleventh and Commerce Streets. There were also twelve cars of railroad rails stored on a sidetrack awaiting to be put into use.

A new line was discussed but met resistance from property owners along the newly-proposed Greenwood Avenue route with its terminus at the Greenwood Cemetery. Judge Tyler, in his smooth, authoritative manner did some political maneuvering[136] and made the property owners realize that it was best to just tighten their suspenders and agree to the plan to widen the street.

On July 3, the agreement was reached with the affected property owners. By July 10, the ground was broken to begin the new Greenwood line and by July 14 the line had been constructed to Nannie Johnson's house and by July 25 to George Buck's property. Judge Tyler moved his cast iron fence after his yard was pushed back when the street was widened. On the front gate the iron was forged with his initials "CWT."

Judge Tyler's gate. Photo by author.

In his yard, Judge Tyler battled a particular inhabitant of his garden. For years, he had his yardman chop down what was described as "a

[136] He said he favored incorporating Greenwood and South Clarksville in a new and separate town from Clarksville, in order to raise the money to macadamize Greenwood Avenue.

noxious-looking shrub" which kept sprouting. How could the judge know that by yearly pruning, he was actually helping the plant grow? Finally, a passerby, a young lady visitor from out-of-town, spied the shrub and declared it to be a fig tree. Like a prisoner spared of his sentence at the gallows, the tree grew and flourished and within a year or two the tree showed its appreciation for its commuted sentence and reportedly produced a fine crop of figs.

Judge Tyler had fought long and hard for the bridges over the Cumberland and he was adamant that the public obey his command of no one riding over the new iron bridge faster than a walk. As there was no watchman at this bridge, Tyler issued the instruction on July 14, 1896 that there would be a $5 reward to anyone who reported seeing someone violating his rule.

During the third week in July 1896, the Cumberland Telephone and Telegraph Company had to send a crew out to Greenwood Avenue to replace the short telephone poles with taller ones so as not to interfere with the electric streetway system. The poles were replaced as far down Greenwood to where the turn was made into New Town. Also on July 30, work began to construct the Y's (crossover points where streetcars switched over to another track), to connect the Greenwood line with the Clarksville streetcar line. The route to Greenwood was designated as "route two."

Greenwood summer car, circa 1896. This is the car the Tylers would have used most often. (MB)

Tragedy was to visit the Tylers once more on August 28 with the death of another relative. The young man was Richard Keeling Tyler III, the son of Charles' late cousin, Judge John Duke Tyler and his wife, Helen. This young man had a promising future cut short as he was working with one of the principle ocean steamer houses in New York. The New York newspaper stated his salary as an impressive three thousand dollars a year. His end came while on vacation in the Adirondack Mountains. At age twenty-three, he accidentally drowned while swimming in Lake Placid. He is buried in Riverside Cemetery next to his father. His epithet suggests he died while saving a friend from drowning.

During a meeting on October 1, about the public library that Judge Tyler, "with his characteristic public spirit," offered his office at the courthouse for the use of the library association. The association held a reception on October 20 from 8 until noon to allow citizens to see the progress made with the library and to invite everyone to join in the "good work."

Finally, Judge Tyler ordered that on January 2, 1897 no more tolls would be charged over the lower Red River bridge! Clarksville then had two free bridges. It was said that, "What the city may thus lose in cash revenue will not be a drop in the bucket to what it will gain commercially in being known abroad as a municipality of broad and public-minded citizens."

On February 1, Nannie Tyler Johnson listed her house for rent in the local newspaper. The reason behind her decision was not stated but the house must have been a terribly lonely place with her husband and children gone.

A near fatal streetcar and carriage accident occurred right in front of her house just over two weeks later on February 19. While the streetcar motorman was distracted and not at his post at the front of the car, a couple's horse was startled by the streetcar. It bolted and threw their carriage against the street curb. Mr. and Mrs. William E. Corlew had just entered town around 9:00 a.m. The lady was able to "unbuttoned the curtains and jump without injury," but the gentleman stayed with the carriage and was almost struck by the streetcar when the coupling pole and shafts broke. The motorman was fired and the couple received complete repairs to their carriage, compliments of the streetcar company.

Talk about being on the wrong street at the wrong time. Just three days after the streetcar accident on Greenwood, another incident occurred. It was reported that a "half clad lunatic" was wandering around along Greenwood and "frightening the ladies." His actions were described as strange, as was his appearance. Well, this just would not do to have this person bothering delicate women, including Judge Tyler's two sisters! Constable Clark arrested the poor man and took him before Squire Smith who, on the advice of Judge Tyler, purchased some clothing and dressed him before placing him in jail for his own safety. The man had earlier set fire to a residence where he was employed as a cook.

The duties of police officers in 1897 included: patrolling the train station, the river bridges, the different furnace properties, and walking their beats on the city streets. If necessary, the police were also expected to round up cows that were loose on city streets as well. For this they were paid an average of $78 per month.

Judge Tyler was in charge of collecting Montgomery County's contribution to the upcoming Centennial Exposition to be held in Nashville from May 1-October 31, 1897. The county's exhibit was first opened at the courthouse on April 14 to allow Clarksvillians who may not be able to attend the exposition in the state's capitol city. It ran 4 days before being sent to Nashville.

Judge Tyler put out a public request on April 21, for a man who was an expert in the art of twisting tobacco to meet immediately with him. Tyler offered a few day's work for that person to twist the tobacco in its "natural state"[137] in different shapes to be put on display. Tyler and the volunteer left for Nashville on the *Buttorff* the next evening to take the samples to what is now Centennial Park. The two men returned back to Clarksville the following day.

Thirty-six packages, including casks, barrels, boxes and bags containing Montgomery County Centennial exhibits were shipped to Nashville. Tyler also donated an unusual item: a cross section of a cherry tree trunk and stump; the lower portion of the trunk measured, 5 feet in diameter. The roots, when dug up, reached 33 feet in diameter. It took two yokes of oxen and two mules to haul it from the south side of the river near Lone Oak to Clarksville and then on to Nashville by boat.

The interior of the Agriculture Building where the exhibits from Montgomery County were placed. Annie Keesee, daughter of P.H. Keesee was in charge of the Montgomery County exhibit. Photo by B.F. Langley.

Dr. William M. Goodman professed to be commissioned by God to cure all sicknesses. On June 19, 1897, he was arrested for failure to pay for his license and jailed. He fought against being transferred from the jail to appear before magistrate Squire Sam Caldwell so much so that it took three men to do so. His appearance was said to be "of a man suffering from something out of the ordinary and his condition was more to be pitied than criticized." Goodman was quoted as saying that he will "kill all Masons of the county with the exception of Judge Tyler and if the Judge gets too gay he will cause his head to fall in the basket also." After Caldwell pronounced him insane Goodman was sent back to jail.

This was not the first time Goodman had a run in with the law. Dispensing medicines that were questionable in their ability to cure was the issue. And yet he continued to sell his medicines in Clarksville as late as 1917.

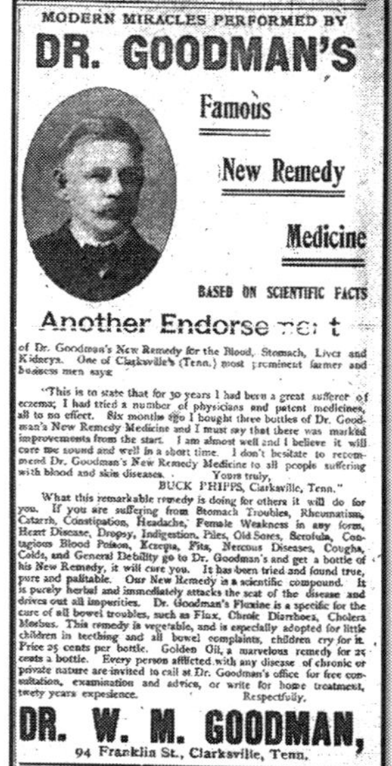

Leaf Chronicle ad in 1905.

Judge Tyler's brother. J.D. was the victim of a near accident. In Hadensville, Kentucky at 4 p.m. on August 22, the attorney drove across a railroad track and either he did not see or hear the train or the engineer failed to blow the whistle as Tyler crossed in front. The train missed Tyler's horse by just feet.

[137] In April, tobacco was just getting planted so the tobacco used here must have been from a previous year's cutting.

An up and coming young black lawyer in town met a terrible death and his murderer was brought before Judge Tyler. General Quarles Boyd was born in Mississippi the year the Civil War ended. He had a reputation as a troublemaker in his teens and early twenties. Years earlier in mid-August of 1885, he and a friend, Tigg Meriwether, had entered Dibble's photography studio on the corner of Franklin and First Streets. Meriwerther had a photo made of himself and after being shown the negative before the print was made, he became angry and combative. His language turned ugly so Dibble ordered both young men out of his business. Boyd, described as a "burly, not passed twenty-two," turned and knocked the "past middle age" and "rather light frame" photographer to the floor.

General Boyd Quarles

Both young men were arrested. Boyd was charged $17.50 and Meriwether, $10.00. Next, a state warrant was sworn out against Boyd who was fined an additional $18.40. He worked off his debt on the county work gang in one day's time.

He worked in the office of William Quarles' law office, attended Wilberforce University, passed the state bar and began his own law office located at 109½ S. First Street. He was a local leader in the Republican party. In the Republican Convention of the Sixth Congressional district of Tennesee held at Clarksville on April 20, 1896, Boyd was nominated for Congress.

A group of 300 black republicans of the Twelveth Civil District led by Nace Dixon met at the courthouse on August 10 and wrote 3 resolutions involving Boyd. They condemned G.Q.Boyd stating that he is, "a dangerous foe to the political and general advancement of intelligent and honorable members of this, the colored race." They openly refused to "support Boyd for Congress or any other position of honor or trust for which he now asks for or is a candidate." Lastly they openly denounced Boyd's verbal attacks towards S.A. Dabney, the black candidate for constable from the same district. Those attacks were said to have been "malicious and without the least cause."

One year later, the 32-year-old Boyd ran into someone who had a grudge against him. On Monday afternoon, August 23, at 2:35, the attorney met his death at the hands of a man related to S.A. Dabney. George Washington "Wash" Dabney fired two shots from his double barrel shotgun at Boyd in the Outlaw and Kates' Tailor Shop that occupied the floor above Shelton and Firse's Barber Shop on Franklin Street.[138] Dabney stated that Boyd had said many slanderous comments about his mother and his sisters. The newspaper described in gruesome detail the shooting that ended the attorney's life. Immediately, Dabney surrendered to police. The tragic affair caused much excitement in town. As for Dabney, he died in 1944 at the home of his daughter on Main Street. It appears that Dabney got off scot-free for the shooting of Boyd.

Boyd had shared his law office with another black attorney, Garland Jones, at 199½ Strawberry Alley. After his death, Judge C.W. Tyler and the Montgomery County Court allowed for Boyd's widow, Susie, to receive the following as her year's support.

One sideboard	**$20.00**	**One wardrobe value**	**$8.00**
One center table	**$8.00**	**Cash**	**$10.00**

For many years, Clarksville needed a building for the sole use of the post office. In 1896 the plans were drawn and approved for a building that was unique from the ground up. This federal building, was constructed diagonally across from the courthouse. It had its groundbreaking ceremony on September 1, 1897. As a customs house, this building served as the location to pay tobacco taxes from the booming tobacco trade in the area. The unique roof displays gabled windows, a spire and Gothic cooper eagles perched at each corner. Built by a young American architect, David A. Murphy, it is one of the most photographed buildings in Clarksville. The building now serves as the Clarksville Customs House Museum.

[138] Later it became the Thomas Rohner Jewelry Store. In recent years, this building was occupied by a lawyer.

The Customs House (MCA).

Tennessee was scheduled to celebrate its Centennial Exposition to be held in Nashville in 1896 but its opening was delayed by one year due to an economic recession affecting the entire nation and "disagreements between the various divisions of the state." Determined individuals labored to see the exposition become a reality. A new group of directors was selected and nearly $1.1 million raised to begin construction. The new director general of the exposition was Maj. Eugene Castner Lewis (1845-1917), the son of George and Margaretta Lewis and the brother of Blanche Lewis who once lived on Madison Street in Clarksville. E.C. Lewis had been one of the exposition's loudest and steadfast proponents, a former Louisville & Nashville Railroad engineer, sales manager and later general manager of the Sycamore Mills of the DuPont Powder Company. Lewis also became the advocate for the construction of Nashville's Union Station, built in 1910. Clarksvillians had to be proud of their former "son."

Eugene Castner Lewis.

When the exposition formally opened, the Nashville newspaper reported, "Montgomery County's exhibit in the Agriculture Building is one of the exhibits in this building that is yet incomplete. The exhibit that has a prominent space being near the center of the building is being put up now." It was understandable that the Montgomery County exhibit did not open until November 10 since dark-fired tobacco was the main focus of the exhibit and the tobacco had to be cut, stripped and cured. Tobacco, corn and other farm products from Montgomery County were also exhibited. Estimates were that 10,000 marched in the parade, 60,000 witnessed the parade and 25,000 people visited the exposition grounds.

A month earlier on October 18, Clarksville lost one of their most noted citizens, Dr. C.W. Bailey who died quietly from stomach issues that had bothered him for years. The former doctor who had lived at Hickory Wild ministering to the boys being schooled there was mourned for his useful life.

Dr. C.W. Bailey. *From Picturesque Clarksville.*

J.D. Tyler was just having a bad streak of luck. He accidentally shot himself in the leg on January 6, 1898 while handling a gun in his office that had been used as evidence during a trial. He was moved from his office in the Bailey block on Strawberry Alley to a nearby apartment to be attended by doctors Johnson, Brandau and Ellis. They removed the 32-caliber bullet from Tyler's leg and dressed the wound. Tyler was then able to be sent home to recover.

In February, Em Tyler gave a Valentine's Day party for her guests at the Tyler home that included a play with 5 acts. Many of the children came in costume. They produced shadow pictures on the wall as part of a guessing game. Em's cousin, Mildred Johnson helped with the party and Mollie was said, "by her dainty refreshments, artistic decorations and easy graciousness (she) proved herself a queen behind the throne."

On August 30, 1898, Grace Stacker displayed the 1st Tennessee's flag draped over the stair rail in the large entrance hall. The occasion was to celebrate the return of the soldiers from the war. It was described as having "floated over its camps at Cavite Bay" in the Philippines. "The folds of the noble insignia were tattered and torn from shot and the strong winds of the bay. Many of the guests and hostesses alike had a loved one who had part in that Philippine campaign and very tender emotions were awakened by the sight of the flag."

The Stacker home. Note the flag. (LC)

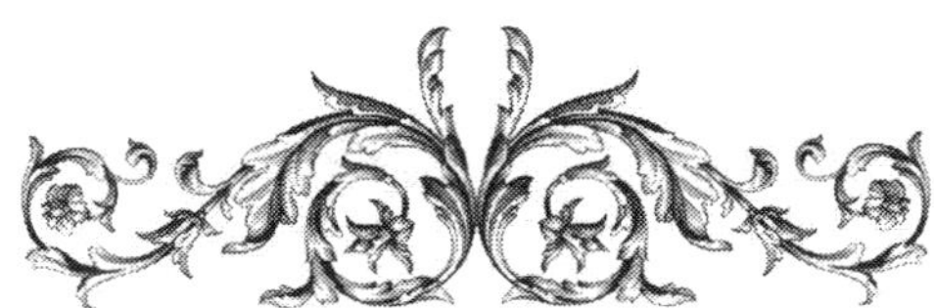

Chapter Eighteen: Another War

For Tyler the news was a jolt. The Tennessee Legislature of January 1898 voted to abolish the Criminal and Chancery Court. The *Jackson Globe* newspaper gloated over the legislative act citing, "Judiciary reform is an accomplished fact and the work of the legislature remains unimpaired. The fight of deposed judges for what they considered right was an able one but they have lost. The sentiment in Tennessee is clearly with the Legislature."

For Tyler it meant he was stripped of the authority given him by legislative acts some years prior. This meant that Tyler retained his office as County Judge but only oversaw probate matters and the administration of insolvent estates and matters of real estate. He could not grant injunctions or try cases of habeas corpus and he no longer had control of the county jail which came under the complete control of the sheriff. An exception was granted if the county needed to use a part of it as a workhouse under the supervision of the workhouse commissioners. The Criminal Court was placed under the jurisdiction of Judge Thomas Munford and the Chancery Court under Judge J.S. Gribble. Judge Munford began trying civil cases beginning the first Monday in May.

Four months later on April 25, the U.S. entered the Spanish-American War. Clarksville men were mustered into service between May 19-26. Forty-seven officers and 975 enlisted men came from Clarksville and the surrounding areas including Springfield, Columbia, Waverly, Big Sandy, Lawrenceburg, McMinnville and Shelbyville. In total, Middle and East Tennessee contributed four regiments—more than 4,000 men.

During July, Tyler's salary was a topic of discussion. As judge he had for years received $2500. Back in 1879, the salary of all inferior judges was reduced to $2000 but the legislature of 1881 re-enacted the law of 1866-67. Attorney Dancey Fort suggested it be increased for the additional services Tyler rendered as judge of the Chancery Court. This was not allowed as Section 7, Article 6 of the State Constitution read,

> **The judges of the Supreme or inferior (lower) courts shall, as stated, receive a compensation for their services to be ascertained by law which shall not be increased or diminished during the time for which they serve.**

Charles' nephew Cave, born on August 11, 1877, entered into service as a private in Company H, 1st Tennessee Regiment and by May was commissioned first lieutenant. Boyd Johnson (son of Hickman Johnson), also enlisted. Cave's early education was under his own half-uncle Professor Quintus Tyler. Next he attended Southwestern Presbyterian College and Kentucky State College in Lexington. Just as he applied to practice law in February 1896, the war with Spain was nearing.

This was a different war from the one Cave's father and uncles had fought in for it was not on American soil. This war introduced American soldier to new diseases.

Col. William Crawford Smith, Lt. Col. Gracey Childers (center row) and soldiers of the 1st Tennessee. (TSLA)

An article in the May 9, 1898 issue of the *New York Times* praised the Tennessee volunteers.

> **Tennessee has maintained the reputation as a volunteer state. The President called for a fraction more than three thousand men to enlist in the war against Spain, for two years, there are now thirty-nine hundred in the camps at Nashville, to be mustered into the**

National service...If the President's call had been for six instead of three regiments, they would have all been in the field now.

The 1st TN would be the only regiment to see action in the Philippines. The regiment's officers were: Colonel William Crawford Smith, Lieutenant Colonel Gracey Childers, Majors Albert B. Bayless, Benjamin Frank Cheatham, John G. McGuire, Major and Surgeon: Richard A. Barr, Captain and Assistant Surgeon R.M. Kirby Smith, Percy Jones, First Lieutenant and Adjutant James K. Polk, First Lieutenant and Quartermaster Andrew J. Duncan, Captain and Chaplain Lewis L. Leland.

While the troops were preparing to enter the war, projects facing Judge Tyler included reviewing requests for such items as an improved concrete fountain (for watering horses), to replace the one already in use at the Public Square. The judge had been aggravated by the newspaper about the trough in three columns. One especially in April 1898 stated

> **Almost every minute of the day it is in use and often the demand upon it is so great that water cannot be supplied fast enough. Almost continually teams and horses are waiting trying to get to the fountain but cannot do so for the number around it. One was formally in operation on Third Street but it was broken down and has never been replaced. The one on the square is insufficient and another should be placed in a more central part of the city.**

He would address this issue later.

Mollie was among several ladies who, on Thursday, May 12, took a round trip to Nashville on the riverboat, *Buttorff.* Rarely did Mollie travel without her husband but this trip was a much needed respite. Mollie was joined by Em, Mildred Johnson, Mrs. Thomas Dade Luckett and her daughter Roberta, Mrs. J.D. Slayden and her daughter Adele, Miss Rosa Whitfield and Misses Lillian and Anna Williams. They returned to Clarksville on Saturday.

In May politics were heating up and accusations arose about Tyler putting men in office that supported him and disallowing the taxpayers' right to choose. With political reform taking hold state-wide, the push by some politicians was to eliminate offices that were considered useless. Leading the opposition was the candidate for the General Assembly, Capt. W.G. Russell. The talk around town was whether or not Judge Tyler's court would be repealed. Heated discussions on both sides took place. The newspaper while, supporting Tyler's past actions as judge encouraged the decision be left up to the taxpayers who "are crying from relief from taxation." Tyler adjourned his court until the first Monday in June and appealed to the Tennessee Supreme Court.

Camp Campbell at the Tennessee-Kentucky border was years away from being created but in August 1898, a possible military camp in Clarksville and the securing of a brigade was being considered by the Secretary of War in Washington. Judge Tyler was sent to the capitol to argue in support of the camp "armed" with resolutions from the city council, the business league, the Tobacco Board of Trade and prominent business people. As history showed, a military camp was constructed many years later in the 1950s with the majority of the camp in Tennessee. But because the post office was located on the Kentucky side, the camp's address was Camp Campbell/later Fort Campbell, Kentucky.

On September 28, Tyler filed a writ of mandamus in Chancery Court in Nashville seeking to recover his salary as he was "still discharging such duties as remain to him since the passage of the act of the last legislature." In 1870 the Criminal Court of Montgomery County was created and the salary of the judge was to be the same as that of the Circuit Judges and Chancellors and to be paid from the Montgomery County treasury. Later this was changed to having their salaries paid through the state treasury.

Tyler's supporters in the matter who were quite vocal became labeled by the press as "Tylercrats." The paper emphasized how any discussion of the matter refers to the court as not the Criminal Court but simply "Tyler's Court" and further that his supporters were crying, "They are fighting Tyler," making it personal. The paper fought against a "Tyler's man representing the county in the legislature" but stated that "if Tyler's court is a useful court, keep it, if Tyler's court is useless, repeal it." The newspaper went further to say, "Our criticism of Judge Tyler is not of Judge Tyler as a judge in the capacity of a judge but it is of him as a man assuming to do things which would be criticized if done by another man and therefore the *Leaf Chronicle* will not hesitate to criticize."

During its time in the war, the 1st TN regiment lost one enlisted man to enemy action. The regiment also lost two offices and twenty-three enlisted men to disease. Two enlisted men were killed in accidents and twenty deserted. The war ended and on December 10. 1898, with the Treaty of Paris signed, the independence of Cuba was guaranteed, Spain was forced to cede Guam and Puerto Rico to the United States.

Judge Tyler got word of a name with which he was all too familiar. On January 16, 1899, in District 9 Deputy Sheriff G.L. "Bose" Welker and Officer Joe Bartee were serving warrants. The first person to be arrested was none other than William Morrow's younger brother Tom, born in 1865. The officers charged Morrow with fraud in regards to some tobacco Morrow had illegally disposed of. The firm of Kendrick and Runyon held a mortgage on the tobacco, and they demanded satisfaction.

The two officers went to Ransom Morrow's house where they made the arrest. While on the Dover Road heading back to town, the officers decided to serve a paper on John Hawkins at his mother-in-law's house. As Welker left Bartee with Morrow, Welker approached her house. He had walked only about eighty yards away from the two when he heard gunshots. Running back to the road, he discovered that Morrow had escaped by sliding off the mule he was riding and scurried off into the night. Bartee was unsure whether any of the shots he had fired found their mark. Since it was 9:30 p.m., they could not follow him to discern whether he was indeed wounded. Guess you could say, "That's another Morrow to the story!"

The new year had begun and in the Philippines, Cave fought in most of the battles around Manila. News of the 1st Tennessee came mostly through personal letters sent home to family. Col. Gracey Childers wrote the following letter to his aunt, Mrs. T.D. Luckett in Clarksville which would be of great interest to everyone who had a loved one in the war.

> **Camp Hughes P.I. (Philippine Islands), January 1, '99.**
>
> **My Dear Aunt Maria,**
>
> **Your much appreciated letter of November 23 received Christmas eve.[139] A number of other letters from home also came in on the ship and made me feel less like you all were so far away.**
>
> **Our camp is located on the bay front with the Paseo de Santa Lucia on the land side. This avenue, as we would call, it is the fashionable drive of the city and between 5 and 10 p.m. is thronged with carriages and people. It is quite warm at mid-day but the mornings, evenings and nights are very pleasant indeed. Our detachment is in tents with bamboo cots for the men to sleep in; many of the other regiments are in barracks, but they were all occupied when we arrived. It is thought our camp is the most healthy as the ground is most hard. It has never been used as a camp or occupied by buildings with fresh breeze and air from the sea while the barracks are mostly old buildings that look as though they were hundreds of years old.**
>
> **Of course the streets are narrow and the ground saturated with the filth of centuries while everything is clean and fresh with us where we are camped. I keep quite well and I think our boys are in better health than when we were in 'Frisco.[140]**

Childers continued his letter mentioning his fellow troops:

> **All our Clarksville boys are with me and are doing finely (sic), in fact, we show up any troops here regulars or volunteers. Boyd Johnson,[141] the Stacker boys, Cave Johnson, (B.N.) Coffman, (Lewis) Drane and all the others are well and our sick report is smaller since we have been in the service.**

The "Stacker boys:" Patrick Lewis Stacker and Clay Stacker, Jr. from GreenwoodFindagrave.

---

[139] This shows that letters between Clarksville and the islands took a month to arrive.

[140] San Francisco was where the troops boarded ships to go to the Philippines.

[141] He and Cave were cousins.

On the same day as this letter was printed in the *Chronicle* another written on December 20 by Lewis Drane, (but received in January), also in Co. H was received by his father, Dr. Henry Tupper Drane. He stated:

It is not nearly so hot here as reported at home and all the tales about smallpox and other diseases are greatly exaggerated. There is no more sickness here than there would be in an army of the same size stationed at any post at home and not nearly so much as there was at 'Frisco when all the troops were there.

Lewis Thomas Drane

However, in a letter written on January 29, 1899 to his mother back in Clarksville, Pat Stacker wrote of Cave. He mentions smallpox breaking out in camp resulting in two deaths. He wrote, "Cave Johnson has been at Corregidor Island where I think the convalescent hospital is. I think it is possible that Cave Johnson will leave on February 10th on the *Arizona* which sails then for Philadelphia via Suez Canal."

There were more than a dozen reports of Cave being in very bad health to the point that it was felt that if he remained in the Philippines, he would die. Cave insisted that he wished to remain with his regiment until all the boys came home. General Elwell S. Otis on January 13, decided to discharge Cave. When Judge Tyler heard of the intention of Otis to discharge Cave on account of ill health, the judge immediately telegraphed Senator Thomas B. Tutley. The senator replied that the war department through Adjutant General Henry Clark Corbin cabled Gen. Otis and ordered him NOT to discharge Cave but instead to issue him a furlough "if the state of his health requires it."

Adj. Gen. H.C. Corbin

The judge simply would have it: he refused to stand aside and allow someone to keep Cave from being honorably discharged to come home to be cared for. It is not known what Judge Tyler said but... Cave was to get his honorable discharge and arrived in Guthrie by train on Sunday, May 7. He was met by his friend Emmett McCulloch. Emmett drove him home arriving at 4 p.m. that afternoon. Clay was described as looking "somewhat pale and thin and troubled to some extent with the asthma which compelled his return."

Cave Johnson and a lady friend he met while in San Francisco attended a large dance held at Idaho Springs on July 11. Cave was able to introduce her to his friends. This appeared to be a serious relationship.

It seemed like old times when on August 25, a streetcar party ran the gambit around town for quite a while until they tired. Cave Johnson, his sister Mildred, cousins Emmie Tyler, Roberta Luckett and Sarah Johnson, Emmett McCulloch, Alice Masten, Polk Smith and Dr. St. George Craig were the merry makers who talked and laughed the evening through.

In September Judge Tyler proposed to replace the little watering fountain near the courthouse. The old fountain was "inadequate to the demands of the place" according to Dr. T.H. Marable who was interviewed by the *Leaf.* He cited that while allowing their horses to drink, wagons tongues kept striking the fountain until it finally fell over, was taken away and stored at the engine house. He complained that Tyler had done nothing about putting up a more suitable one. He also said that a proposal to replace the fountain had been approved by the city board and still Tyler had done nothing about it. Of course Judge Tyler had a response as he always did. He stated

Yes, such action was taken some time ago and I have been waiting for a catalogue which I understand Dr. Marable has in his possession which contains descriptions of various fountains. I will be glad to co-operate in the movement for I believe it is one that will be of real benefit to the people, the country people in particular.

He added,

There is another condition which the city ought to enforce if such a fountain is placed there; that is to prohibit blocking up the street there with carriages or permitting people to stand all along this side of the street where the fountain would be.

Noticing that N.F. Hart, general agent for the Majestic Range Company was in Clarksville and that J.M. Bowling was selling the ranges in his store, Cave Johnson sent in a letter of appreciation to the newspaper. He cited the gift by the company of a large range gifted to Co. H of the 1st Tennessee while the regiment was stationed in San Francisco, California. In the letter printed on October 20, Johnson stated that the range "proved an excellent stove in every way and added much to the comfort of the company."

At the war's end, for weeks, plans had been made, committees formed and delegates selected to travel to San Francisco to welcome the troops on November 7. The Clarksville delegation consisted of: Grace (Mrs. Clay) Stacker, Innes Cheatham, Mrs. C.H. Bailey, Louise Heggie, Kathleen O'Brian, Cave Johnson and Finis Ewing, Jr. Mary Stacker[142] had already arrived in San Francisco. Mary passed away from a stroke on November 14, while staying at the Cliff House in San Francisco. On Monday, November 20, Gen. Brandon and Mrs. John Gracey[143] left San Francisco to accompany the body of Mary home. This lady was greatly mourned because of her life-long charity work. From San Francisco the regiment was moved by rail back to Nashville where a large reception was planned. The official ceremony was held at the Tabernacle (now known as the Grand Old Opry House).

It was just a matter of time before a fatality involving a streetcar occurred, but it also turned out to be the only known streetcar fatality. The accident occurred Friday evening, November 16, when Dr. Byron F. Hadley tried to climb on to a streetcar on the west side of Franklin and First Streets. The thirty-three-year-old physician fell, struck his head and later died. Accidents would occur for years with the streetcars, more often than not, blamed for the injuries that occurred. Demands were made that streetcar drivers sound some type of bell to alert people driving buggies (at each intersection), to warn of the streetcar's presence. Clarksville had to slowly come to grips with the fact that times were changing.

A most happy announcement came on November 17, of Cave Johnson's engagement to the lady he met in San Francisco. Alice Huldine Master was described as being one of the most beautiful and charming ladies in town. This marriage was never to take place.

It was appropriate the addition of a large collection of new books were added to the library in November during the Thanksgiving season. Lena Beach, the librarian submitted a complete list of the books to be printed in the newspaper that included 19 histories of different countries and other non-fiction offerings as well as a variety of fiction books.

Company H of the 1st TN arrived home by train at the L & N Depot the morning of November 30. Brass bands, whistles, bells, yelling and shouting was heard as the men disembarked. The whole day was spent in a parade, speeches on the Public Square, fireworks at 7 p.m. and a banquet and ball at 9 p.m. The men then returned home to their families to fill the rest of the night with stories of their time in the Philippines.

Cave and his sister were present at a bowling party from 7:30-11 p.m. at the Tarlton Alleys on December 1, given by Mr. and Mrs. R.E. Taylor. The private party consisted of over 40 attendees. Refreshments were served and it was said that "its pleasant exercise relieving the stiff conventionality of so many more pretentious social functions."

Christmas 1899 was going to be different at the Tyler house. Em had it all planned: no Christmas tree but in its place, stockings were to be hung in a row, "without regard to age, size, color, or previous condition of servitude." Various articles of stockings were sent in on Christmas eve by those wishing to participate in the festivities the next morning. The little children of the neighborhood joined together to sing a Christmas carol to begin the morning's activities. Next the stockings were all emptied of their precious offerings and a grand time was had by all sans a Christmas tree.

Complaints were heard in the downtown as tramps were milling around for no particular reason. The newspaper compared them to the lilies of the field in that they toil not, neither do they spin! They discouraged the warm-hearted but misguided philanthropists of Clarksville from

---

142 Mary Gracey (Stacker) was born May 3, 1838 in Kentucky to George Gracey and Maria Ann Tilford Gracey. She was the sister of Matthew Gracey (1847-1907).

143 Mary Stacker's sister.

feeding them when "they have no visible means of subsistence and who spurn the offer of work as almost an affront." The paper demanded the law "charge them with vagrancy or build a workhouse; just do something!"

Alex Stafford (seated in front with cap) and the 1899 police department. (MCA)

The beginning of a new year provided a chuckle involving Jo Tyler. After enjoying a meal, Judge W.M. Brandon entered the attorney's office to sit a spell and was invited to take a seat in a revolving chair designed on purpose to spill any occupant out onto the floor. The "weighty judge tilted back, titled back and the chair braced itself and waited. Then he tilted back again and there was a mixture of broken furniture, coat tails, boot heels, dust, sulphur smoke and official dignity and Jo Tyler was assisting the judge to rise." After recovering his breath which took a few minutes, he admonished the attorney, "Jo Tyler, I'll have you indicted by the grand jury, as sure as you tell this to a living soul." The *Leaf Chronicle* reporter, which printed the whole episode then stated," That's why Jo won't talk about it."

The 1899-1900 arrest records for Clarksville were announced: From February 1, 1899-January 31, 1900, the number of arrests were: **February:** 16, **March**: 19, **April**: 36, **May:** 15, **June:** 16, **July:** 31, **August**: 36, **September:** 40, **October**: 19, **November:** 22, **December**: 32, **January:** 6. That year, there were a total of 289 arrests when Clarksville's population was 10,000. The city officials were quite proud of these numbers and used them to assure the public that the police were doing an excellent job of ensuring public safety. Perhaps the increase in fines affected the crime rate. These fines included:

Drunk and fast driving: fine $10.00
Obstructing the street: fine $5.00
Riding a bicycle on sidewalk: fine $2.00
Throwing rocks: fine $2.00
Resisting arrest: fine $50.00
Jumping out of a moving train: fine $4.00
Defacing city property: fine $50.00
Street walking (women) & maintaining himself by undue means (men): arrest
The keeping of a bawdy house: fine $10.00-$50.00
Vagrancy: fine up to $25.00
Keeping a gambling house: arrest
Sweeping the pavement without sprinkling: no fine mentioned. (Dust swept into the air was considered a health hazard and so sprinkling with water was required!)

Road congestion in 1900 Clarksville, Tennessee? Imagine the roads of Clarksville at this time having to be shared between the streetcars, horse and buggies and the more recent bicycle. Citizens were fussing unaware that in just a few years, the roads would have a new competitor, the automobile.

Em Tyler continued as a student at the Clarksville Female Academy on Madison Street. This building, constructed in 1886 replaced the older one that had served as a hospital during the Civil War. Em's report card from the school year 1899-1900, ending May 9 was:

Attendance 60
Deportment 100
Composition 90
Arithmetic 47
German History 58
Music History 80
Spelling 70
Reading 98

Physics 49
American Literature 97
Penmanship 95
Physical Culture 94
Art 80
Piano 98
Scholarship 74
General Average 86

The grading scale:
90-100 Excellent
80-90 Very good
70-80 Good
50-70 Indifferent
0 Failure

Em Tyler (GF)

While at school, she earned the nickname "Tip" while at the academy, participating in the photography and bicycle clubs. It is no surprise that one of her highest grades should be in piano, deportment, American literature and reading. She definitely did not like math or science. If her parents satisfied with these grades, we will never know. What is surprising is the low grade she received for attendance. Since the school was on Madison Street, the judge would pass it every day on his way to and from the courthouse. Was he able to drop Em off in the morning and pick her up in the afternoon?

On March 12, 1900, twenty-two years after its celebratory opening, William Morris, a black porter at the Queen City Warehouse smelled smoke and saw smoke coming out from the southeast courthouse tower just before 8 a.m. Joe Jarrell, foreman, saw sparks and alerted the fire department. The fire began in a flue which served the library room and office of Circuit Court Clerk, C.W. Stanton. By quick action, the court records that had been stored in fireproof safes were saved as were the upper floor Circuit Court records after 1896. The desk and records from Judge Tyler's office were grabbed by concerned citizens. Lost were all the records of the county superintendent of schools and the burial records of Riverview Cemetery. This has been problematic ever since to say the least for families trying to locate graves of loved ones. At 8:25 the clock tower fell. Because of fire-proofing measures initiated after the 1878 fire, only the upper floor and tower were a total loss.

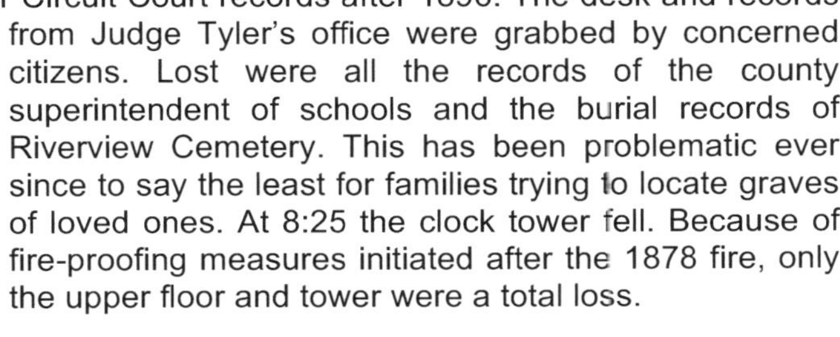

Firefighters fighting to save the courthouse. (LC)

Fortunately, the 200-300 library books were kept in the basement level of the courthouse and just a few of them sustained water damage. The repairs following the fire necessitated the removal of the books to a temporary location.[144]

The heat from the fire caused occupants of the Arlington Hotel to spew out its front doors to seek a cooler location. A fireman, John G. Burchett was injured when struck by a beam while carrying a water hose up some steps. Sparks from the fire spread to the Queen City Warehouse as the wind was blowing from the southeast direction and men stood on the roofs of buildings all the way down Commerce Street and continually fought the sparks that endangered the businesses. Because the lower courthouse floor was constructed with steel girders, beams and cement, it survived the fire.

Judge Tyler was fortunate to be able to move his office temporarily across Second Street to that of his brother's law office in the Glenn building and the mayor and aldermen gave Tyler permission to use the city hall for his court business.

Next came the arguments over whether to tear down or rebuild the courthouse after the fire. The editorial staff of the *Leaf Chronicle* led the outcry to tear the courthouse down citing the building as "a white elephant, a death trap and a fire trap." Judge Tyler showed again his single-mindedness and determination to rebuild it and this he did without increasing taxation. Tyler studied the amount of insurance that had covered the courthouse and found it sufficient to

---

[144] After repeated relocations, during Judge Tyler's lifetime and beyond, the Clarksville-Montgomery County Public Library now is a proud part of the Veterans Plaza off Madison Street.

rebuild. Estimates arrived for insurance compensation included the building itself: $29,981.62 in damages, $4,200 of furniture lost and $500 in books destroyed as a cost separate from the estimate for the building reconstruction. The courthouse rebuilding committee members included Finis Ewing, John A. Rollow, J.H. Achey, Edmund L. Brewer and Judge Tyler who served as the ex-officio chairman.

After the 1900 fire. (LC)

It was during the rebuild that the chimneys were removed as fireplaces were no longer needed with the advent of electricity. Additionally, more changes were made: the former Chancery courtroom was converted into a conference room for the County Judge (Tyler) and his office was moved into the former Clerk and Master's office which adjoined the former Chancery courtroom.

Office space was provided for the director of budgets and accounts and purchasing agent. The walls were given a fresh coat of paint, new drapes were added to the tall windows and new office furniture was purchased.

Repairs being done on a window on March 3, 1900. Courtesy Felix G. Woodward Library.

The courthouse clock was a topic of much discussion. Its importance to the city was expressed in a news article printed on March 14, in the *Leaf Chronicle.*

Remember the Clock

No plan for the restoration of the courthouse of Montgomery County should be considered that fails to include a big clock, with its dials illuminated by electricity, placed even higher than the old one, to be seen for miles around. There is no one feature of the old building so much missed as the clock. Involuntarily the eyes of the people turn yet to the spot it occupied, seeking information as to the flight of time. Rich and poor, young and old, white and black-it was the common friend of all. There is nothing upon which the public money can be expended which will yield richer returns in general service than upon the replacing of the tower clock. The *Leaf Chronicle* has often referred to this matter before, more because so many people have expressed a desire for illuminated dials for the courthouse clock.

It was decided by members of the courthouse committee and announced to the public that the clock tower was to be fully restored. It was indeed to have a glass dial that would be illuminated and the eagle would be replaced at its top.[145]

On April 28, Nannie Johnson escaped serious injury while driving into town from across the Cumberland River. As she was driving her buggy down the bank towards the ferry, a strap broke on the harness causing the buggy to slam into the horse. Nannie showed the cool demeanor often seen in her family and was able to control the animal before all went into the river.

In the second week of June Mollie had what was described as a "severe attack of illness" but was recovering. The vagueness of the diagnosis leaves little information as to what exactly happened.

Judge Tyler wanted a bigger bell, plain and simple: a 4,200-pound bell and an electric fire alarm system for the rebuilt courthouse. The mayor and aldermen approved the requests and the

[145] Uncle Billy Daniel always referred to the previous courthouse eagle as the "old buzzard."

bell was ordered. A contract with Charles A. Moses of Chicago was approved on June 30, 1900 to begin the work needed to restore the courthouse by December 1, 1900. As so often happens, this deadline was not met.

One summer evening in July as a colleague, John B. Allen,[146] was driving Judge Tyler home in his buggy, they met up with one of Clarksville's new streetcars at the corner of Fifth and Madison Streets. As they were pulling out onto Madison, the unexpected appearance of the streetcar frightened the horse. To avoid injury, the always-decisive Judge Tyler, (according to the newspaper), "remembering the days of his youth, executed a flying leap which brought him to safety." The stately judge landed in the First Baptist Church yard. Was this reporter's statement in reference to Tyler's escape from Ft. Donelson? In other words, no one could say that the judge did not recognize when it was time to get out while "the gettin' was good." Horse runaways and carriage accidents occurred often in the city, some resulting in serious injuries and some others proving to be fatal. Judge Tyler had not lived through such an exciting life only to be done in by a frightened horse. Anyone who witnessed this accident must have been amazed at the feat of the stoic, ever-dignified 61-year-old judge, hurling himself off a moving buggy. John Allen did not fare as well with his attempt to escape injury, as he got caught up in the wheels of the buggy. Except for the intervention of a bystander, he could have sustained serious injuries.

Without warning, early Thursday morning August 10, at about 8:00 a.m. Mollie suffered an "apoplectic stroke." Her condition was caused by pressure on the brain, resulting in sudden loss of consciousness and voluntary motion. She passed away at home that night, sometime between 10:00 and 11:00 p.m.

Her funeral was held at 5:00 p.m. the next afternoon at the Trinity Church with services conducted by Rev. William J. Miller. The choir paid tribute to her in song at the church service and then took a special electric car out to the cemetery as a group where they sang once more at the gravesite. The Confederate Veterans of Forbes Bivouac also attended to honor the lady who had shown so much devotion to them. Later, this group issued a proclamation in her honor and entered it into their permanent records:

> **That in the body of Mrs. Tyler, this bivouac and the Confederate soldier body has lost a most devoted and loyal friend; that her voice will be missed from the music that always accompanies the decoration of the graves of our dead; that we extend to our friend and comrade, the bereaved husband, and to their only daughter whose loss cannot be measured, our sincere and earnest sympathy; that a copy of these resolutions be spread upon the minutes, furnished to the bereaved family, and published in our city papers.**

Mollie was buried slightly in front of Nannie in the Tyler family plot in Section 6. The statue of Nannie is seen among the white choir robes. Surrounding her grave is a low fence. Note the openness of the gravesite, nothing like the way it appears today.

Trinity Episcopal Church choir, which sang at the August 10, 1900 funeral for Mollie. Notice the large wreath leaning up against Nannie's gravesite enclosure. Prof. William Emery is seen leading the choir at the grave. Photo courtesy Trinity Church.

Mollie had endured so much sadness during her life but was now reunited with her much-missed daughter Nannie and unnamed baby. On Mollie's impressive seven-foot tombstone carved in the shape of a cross, is the Bible verse, "Blessed are the pure in heart for they shall see God."

The *Leaf Chronicle* August 10 issue ran this article to announce Mollie Tyler's death:

A Noble Woman Has Passed Away

One of the Best Known Women in Clarksville, Her Life Was Devoted to Making the World Better and Happier.

[146] It is possible this was John B. Allen (1842-1910) who served in the Civil War under N.B. Forrest.

This article included a description of her during her years at White Hall as a girl noted for her vivacity and lovable disposition. A special tribute in the same issue, written by a neighbor stated:

> **What more can be said of a woman other than she was the very embodiment of gentleness and refinement, that she had a lovable disposition, and possessed the most splendid character that God ever yet bestowed upon a human being. And still this does not do justice to the beautiful Christian life that has gone out with the breath of Mrs. Mollie Tyler.**

Em at age sixteen was now without a mother. This was where the extended family played its role as Em's aunt, for whom she was named, probably served as her mother from then on. Did the judge ever consider remarrying? We will never know but because of the presence of his sister Emmie in the house and sister Nannie next door, he was not under pressure to do so and it seems he had no interest in it. So began Charles' life without his faithful wife. More than ever, Charles would need to stay busy. That would not be a problem.

Mollie's grand monument at Greenwood. Its design and size denoted the deep love Charles had for Mollie. Photo by author.

The bicycle was increasingly a nuisance and this feeling of resentment was reinforced when on August 26, Rev. Arthur King's horse became frightened as a boy on a passing bicycle rang his bell causing the horse to crash the buggy into a tree with Rev. King in it. The pastor's collarbone was broken and the accident made front-page news. It can be imagined that the bicycle was condemned even more afterwards. To make matters worse, more and more women began riding them. The adopted fashion for female bicyclists was bloomers, which allowed them to straddle the bike in order to pedal, but at the same time revealed the lower legs. Exposing a lady's leg beneath the knees; was it fashion or actually a violation of morals? Judge Tyler probably thought all this amusing compared to the type of problems he saw every day in his courtroom.

Clarksville received the sad news that on September 6, Father Phillip Fitts passed away in his native state of Alabama after a long illness. He lived in Clarksville for eleven years and had taken over the parish at Trinity just after its foundation had been laid.

Ever watchful of the county's finances, Judge Tyler filed a complaint against a five per cent tax addition to the taxpayers of Montgomery County on the basis that it was unfair. Because of his strong objection on this matter, it was announced on September 18, that the added tax was removed. The *Leaf Chronicle* gave Judge Tyler complete credit and further stated that, "When it comes to looking after Montgomery's finances, just let the judge alone."

On October 19, the two 10-foot sheet copper goddesses and an eagle made of the same arrived in Clarksville, sent from the Burlier Cornice and Roofing Company of Louisville. They were carefully stored until their time to be installed.

The county jail took on a new nickname in 1900. Named after the sheriff, Alex C. Stafford, "Hotel De Stafford" was filled with twenty-three prisoners from age ten to almost seventy. They were incarcerated on charges ranging from murder to assault and larceny. The "jailbirds" included two women, a ten-year-old boy and twenty men, including one with only one arm, taking up space in the jail. The little boy was, by that time, a "hardened criminal," according to the newspapers. Incredibly he had already, in his short lifetime, served time on a chain gang but was caught again after stealing a whip.

People were dissatisfied with the quality of the city streets or roads they found leading into Clarksville. The streets in Clarksville were really nothing more than a mixture of gravel, dirt, coal cinders and furnace slag for top dressing. Some of the rocks for the streets were supplied from the Red River Rock Quarry where Judge Tyler sent many an evildoer to break rocks all day. The *Daily Leaf Chronicle* led the outcry for better roads by suggesting that the city start using a new paving material called asphalt, which was more expensive but longer lasting and more durable. They also offered for consideration a new type of gravel, easily quarried in nearby Kentucky. For whatever reason, asphalt was not considered as a viable option and so was not introduced into Clarksville for some years hence. Judge Tyler maintained that gravel was the best option for streets. Large steam-powered rollers would run over the gravel time and again, compacting it down into the ground on public roads and city streets. This process was repeated whenever it was necessary, especially after a wet weather period. The city's large steam roller was given the affectionate name of "willapus-wallipus."

A dozen or so young boys from the Odd Fellows Home (a facility in New Providence that cared for and housed widows and children), would crowd into the cab of the roller to get the thrill of their lives as it steamed over downtown streets. Joe M. Jarrell, the workman in charge of the roller, would even allow some of the boys to steer the huge machine under his guidance. The laughing and "hollering" of the boys could be heard blocks away.

The steam roller in front of the Clay Stacker home on Madison Street near Seventh Street. (MCA)

In November, ten dollars was appropriated by the Board of Mayor and Aldermen for placing stepping stones across Main Street and two hundred dollars to regrade Second Street from Marion to Jefferson Street. The board also directed several property owners on Marion and Franklin Streets to lay brick sidewalks.

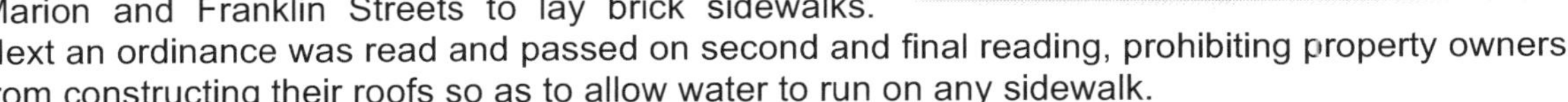

Next an ordinance was read and passed on second and final reading, prohibiting property owners from constructing their roofs so as to allow water to run on any sidewalk.

Whenever a prisoner could not pay his or her fine, Judge Tyler gave him or her the opportunity to work it off at fifty cents per day. The police report of November 2, shows the number of fines "worked out:" Fines paid: $52.00. Fines worked out: $219.56. Fines secured $89.50.

Progress on the courthouse continued and by November 6, the entire weatherproof roof was installed allowing for construction over the winter months on the interior of the building. The new bell for the clock tower was shipped from Shane Bell Foundry in Baltimore arriving in town on November 13. It was inscribed on one side "Court House, Montgomery County, Tenn. A.D. 1900. Weight 4,200 lbs." And on the other side, "McShane Bell Foundry, Baltimore, Md. 1900." The old bell was destroyed in the fire.

Four days later at 2:00 p.m., the bell was raised to hang in the tower. Before lifting it to the tower, Judge Tyler insisted on a moment to inspect the bell and to hear it rung. Raising the bell just a few feet into the air, it was indeed rung rendering a "rich, resonant, mellow sound that was heard all over the city." Judge Tyler turned to the crowd gathered to see the new bell and announced, "There's no crack in that bell, gentlemen."

In 1975, Arthur Travis, courthouse maintenance man, pointing to the manufacturer's inscription on the bell. Photo by Chris Smith of the *Leaf Chronicle*.

An incredible robbery occurred at Judge Tyler's home sometime in early December. The thief was brazen enough to steal an item that had particular meaning to the judge. It was a revolver taken from the Battle of Shiloh when Tyler and a small group of Confederates captured a Union officer with a detachment of men. Tyler took the officer's six-shot Colt revolver, a prize weapon that he carried with him through the reminder of the war, brought it home and placed it safely on the top of his wardrobe. In 1880 Tyler took the gun to Sid Moore who fired the round still in the chamber from the time of the war, cleaned it and reloaded it. Tyler placed it back on top of the wardrobe and again two years later, had Moore repeat the procedure. Tyler had never fired the gun himself but when it came time again to be cleaned, the gun was not to be found. Tyler offered a liberal reward for the gun but never saw it again.

The problem of public roads persisted, so Judge Tyler addressed the issue by employing county prisoners. These chain gangs were noted for doing quality work grading and spreading gravel over the roadways. In fact, during the construction of one road in Oak Plains, the appreciative people living along the road capitulated by sending their own wagons filled with gravel to spread. They further expressed their gratitude to the chain gangs by preparing a barbeque for them before they left to go back to Clarksville. Judge Tyler as well, received public accolades for the superb use of the prisoners.

Four days before Christmas 1900, the two 10-ft. goddesses were placed in position over the east and west door facades. Both statues hold a sword in one hand and the other arm is raised. The copper eagle was waiting its turn to be placed at the apex of the tower.

To reach the bell, clock and roof, one had to ascend through several levels in the tower by wooden ladders. The bell suspended between two heavy beams of wood would be reached first climbing the ladders. The next level housed the clock workings. From that level a ladder ran up to where the eagle sat on the tower.

In 2024, this author was able to climb some of those ladders up into the tower accompanied by a courthouse employee. Much had changed there after the 1999 tornado and all that was visible were the heating and cooling ductworks. Still it was something she always wanted to do.

The courthouse decked out for the celebration of its completion. Pendants hung from the clock tower and the windows displayed draped colors. (MCA)

Several more interior modifications were made: a narrow set of wooden stairs leading to the tower led from the general sessions courtroom instead of the hallway, the tower was rebuilt with heavier timber, an improvement over the previous one, four extra trusses supported the roof, all the brick piers had been reconstructed and the first floor had been repainted. Interior progress continued and by mid-January 1901 the installation of the steel ceilings began at the same time workers were busy painting and doing finishing work on the woodwork. Also, the machinery for the tower clock came to Clarksville awaiting an expert who could be found to set it up and get it running.

The people coming in from the country needed to know the time. While the courthouse clock was absent during the rebuild, Fox & Nichols Grocery on the corner of Third and Commerce Streets placed a large calendar clock for everyone to use especially a "conspicuous time piece especially for the accommodation of people from the country." This was a smart move as shoppers were drawn to his store.

It was requested in 1901, due to increased numbers of people visiting Clarksville, that an additional fountain be purchased for the corner of Madison Street and Greenwood Avenue. Clarksville was indeed growing! By November a contract had been signed for building the new water fountains to William Manning. The new Public Square stock fountain was made of stone and seven feet in diameter. The Third Street fountain was oval and made of concrete. The old stone stock fountain in the Public Square was placed at the corner of Madison and Greenwood.

Chapter Nineteen: Tyler Frees the Ferries

In a total about face on February 5, 1901, the Tennessee Senate approved a bill, Number 186 "to establish a Criminal Court for Montgomery County and to confer criminal jurisdiction on the County Judge (Tyler) of said county." In other words, Judge Tyler had all of his power and jurisdiction reinstated! This had to have been an extraordinary moment for the judge. The bill was to take effect on April 1, 1901.

The rebuilding of the courthouse continued and J.J. Estabrook, secretary of the Standard Electric Time Company of Waterbury, Connecticut came in person to set up the clock and make it operational in late February 1901. The control box of the clock was installed in Judge Tyler's office and the controls not only determined the running of the tower clock but also the seven clocks located inside the courthouse. It was during this time that the tower clock became known as "Judge Tyler's watch." Arriving later were the dials for the clock. By February 22 finishing touches were being completed and the four faces of the clock were in place and the black and white marble tiles[147] on the floors installed.

The first floor with its black and white marble tiles and the staircases to the second floor. (MCA)

The hands of the old clock, being moved by a system of cables often was stopped for a day at a time by winds. The hammer was three times as heavy as the previous, pealing out a sound almost twice as loud. The precision of the clock was explained for example: the striking gear of the tower clock was set in operation two seconds before the actual instant of the hours that being the time required to raise the big hammer and drop it on the bell. Additional rods turned the hands on the clock. The new clock with its updated electrical components was declared as "keeping good time."

Montgomery County lost perhaps the oldest recorded person ever in the county on April 15. "Aunt Rachel" Duke's age was said to be 126 years old[148] as she was reputed to have been born in 1775! She claimed to have "biled (sic) de pot for General Washington and his troops in Virginia." She had been born when her master was age 13 and had acquired the name Duke through a former owner, the family of the second wife of the late W.D. Moss of Clarksville. Her death occurred at her home in the "Old Field" settlement in the eastern suburbs of the city in District Twelve. She had nine children and outlived all but one.

A big change was made in the spring. Owners of the homes along Madison Street were asked on April 15 to permit the city to widen this all important route and to agree to set their fences back in order to accommodate the widening. All 14 homeowners indeed agreed that the fences would be moved no later than May 15. The owners were: B.W. Macrae, Wesley Drane, John Gill Anderson, Wm. M. Daniel, M.H. Clark, Benjamin F. McKeage, C.E. Frey, Ed P. Turnley, James L. Glenn, R.R. Neale, Lewis Rogers Clark, Hugh Matthew Dunlop, E.W. Barker and Joseph Watkins Scales. After its completion, Madison Street was nine feet wider, much to the satisfaction of Clarksville

[147] Two marble floor tiles were purchased by the author at the courthouse auction and donated to the rebuilt courthouse to be displayed with other artifacts in 2024. One tile weighed 12.8 lbs. and another 14.6 lbs. Imagine the tremendous weight of these tiles that made up the entire floor.

[148] How this was possible is a mystery.

citizens. Just three weeks later, all night incandescent streetlights were approved to be installed in various areas of town. Truly Clarksville was making progress towards the future. While some people in Clarksville were forward-minded, others resisted change. This time the subject of interest was changing from oil to electricity to illuminate city streetlights. Those in favor argued it was much cheaper than any other type of light; those opposed complained that you could not look at it because it was so bright. Some smart-witted person then replied that the sun should be abolished for the same reason.

The musical ability of the Tylers was displayed once more when seventeen-year-old Em Tyler, as well as her aunt Emmie was among the Trinity Church choir members who visited the Odd Fellows' Home to perform a special Easter program on April 21. Em must have appeared as the embodiment of her dear mother while singing the well-known spirituals.

Never forgetting the veterans of Forbes Bivouac, Clarksville citizens held a fundraiser for the Confederate Uniform Fund on April 26. Its intention was to raise monies to supply veterans with new uniforms to wear at reunions. Mrs. Henry Lupton coordinated an event at the opera house with performances by the College Mandolin Club, the First TN Quartette and others. Em Tyler performed as well, while sitting upon a pedestal during the playing of "Dixie" while holding "the flag that bore the single star." She later took part in a skit, which was the hit of the evening. The newspaper was quoted as saying that Em Tyler and the other young ladies "electrified the audience with their rollicking song and impersonation." The result of the night's festivities was an impressive amount of $150.00.

One of the honors bestowed upon Judge Tyler included the naming of Company A, Fifth Tennessee Infantry after him. On May 1, the "Tyler Rifles" were named to honor the man they admired for his honorable military service and demeanor as a gentleman. This company had the reputation of being the best within their regiment. Over time the judge was also honored when a fund-raising branch of the public library was named in his honor.

Another reunion for the Confederates was to be held in 1901 in Memphis. In the spring, Judge Tyler received a letter written by his friend, relative and fellow Confederate veteran, Robert T. Mockbee. It read

> **Memphis, Tenn. May 7,**
> **Hon. Chas. W. Tyler, Clarksville Tenn.**
> **Dear friend and comrade-**
> **In anticipation of your attending the reunion on the 27th, 28th, and 29th of the month, I write to you to spend the time as my guest while in the city. Tell all the members of the old Fourteenth[149] Regiment that Gen. William McComb has promised to be here and my house will be his home while here. We live at 1805 Union Avenue. Let me hear from you soon. I am very truly your friend,**
> **R.T. Mockbee**

One of the rare moments of hilarity that occurred inside the Clarksville Montgomery courthouse came on May 9, involving a lawsuit for damages over a dead dog. The case, while beginning in a serious manner went downhill after the lawyer, Dancey Fort, representing Frank Welker, accused George Shearon of killing Welker's hound. To show an increased value for the dog, it was claimed that the dog gave out some of the "sweetest music in the world" while chasing raccoons, squirrels, rabbits and fox. Additionally, the dog had served as an excellent guard dog. H.N. Leech, the attorney for Shearon, replied that Dancey knew absolutely nothing at all about music and that there had never been a case where the music of a dog's voice added value to the animal in a lawsuit. Next Leech was accused of defaming the memory of the dog.

When asked the name of the hound, "Tyler" was put forth. Immediately the accusation was sounded that there had been "an attempt to prejudice the minds of the jury by the statement that this dog was named for Judge Tyler," whereby Leech, tried to show that the dog was named instead for Joe D. Tyler and was of no value and that "fact alone gave the defendant the right to kill the dog." According to newspaper reports, the spectators in the courtroom "got their money's worth of amusement" and that they had been "kept in an uproar of laughter." The result of the suit

---

[149] The battle flag was present at this reunion according to the June 3, 1901 issue of the *Leaf Chronicle*.

was a judgment for the plaintiff in the amount of $25.00 plus costs. Judge Tyler had to have enjoyed every minute of the proceedings.

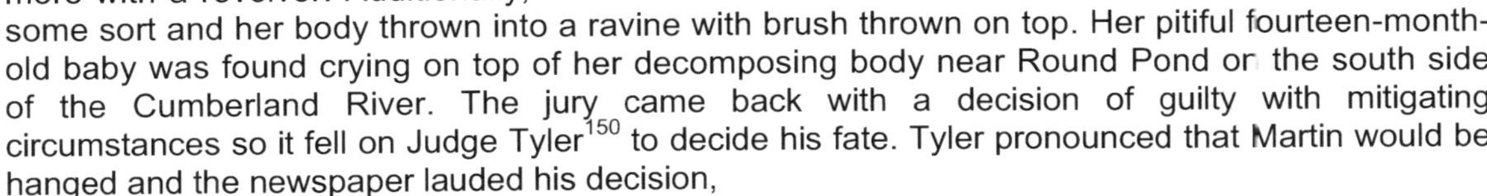

Tyler's friend and supporter, Dancey Fort. (MCA)

On May 27, Judge Tyler appointed his nephew Cave Johnson to the post of Attorney General of Montgomery County. The appointment was a popular one as Johnson was well-respected locally.

At trial on June 28, Doc Martin was charged with the brutal slaying of Lena, his wife of one year. She was shot in the head once with a shotgun and twice more with a revolver. Additionally, her head had been beaten with a club of some sort and her body thrown into a ravine with brush thrown on top. Her pitiful fourteen-month-old baby was found crying on top of her decomposing body near Round Pond on the south side of the Cumberland River. The jury came back with a decision of guilty with mitigating circumstances so it fell on Judge Tyler[150] to decide his fate. Tyler pronounced that Martin would be hanged and the newspaper lauded his decision,

> **For if ever there was a willful, coldblooded and atrocious murder this was one. Judge Tyler is to be commended for promptly assuming the responsibility shifted upon him by the jury. He sentenced Doc Martin to be hanged Friday, August 2nd and we are glad that he religiously sticks to the unwritten law naming Friday for the execution. We have contempt for Judges and Governors whose superstition evades hangman's day- it smacks of Pilate's handwashing.**

Martin appealed his death sentence to the Tennessee State Supreme Court and the argument over the constitutionality of the court, which convicted him, began. The verbal sparring was described as "bitter." Attorney General George Wesley Pickle and Cave Johnson supported the existence of the Montgomery Criminal Court that Judge Charles W. Tyler had been running for twenty-five years and for which Judge John A. Pitts and Martin's defense attorneys fought for its termination. This had no effect on Doc Martin's death sentence.

Sheriff Stafford informed Judge Tyler of a planned trip to Nashville. He left Clarksville on July 17, in order to witness the execution by hanging of three murderers. Stafford felt he needed to "take pointers" in case he had to perform the same duty in the final decision of the Doc Martin case in Clarksville. However, while awaiting his hanging in jail, Martin was found ill with pneumonia on December 26 and died on January 1, 1902 in his jail cell. Thenceforth all other convicted murder felons of Montgomery County were transferred to the state penitentiary to serve their sentence or for execution.

In a shocking incident on July 26, Judge Tyler had his courtroom shot up in a three-way gun battle. Special Chancellor Thomas Frazier Martin was on the bench during the morning to hear a case of a lawsuit from a divorce case of Dill v. Dill that quickly escalated into a scene from the O.K. Corral. The attorneys representing R.T. Dill were William Daniel, Jr. and his father. Felix Grundy Gilbert and George Gilbert represented Mrs. Dora Dill. During the heat of the matter, words were exchanged between F. Grundy Gilbert and Daniel, Jr. Grundy either struck or struck at Daniel, Jr. and in response, Daniel, Jr. pulled out his pistol and shot at Grundy. Grundy reciprocated by pulling out his pistol and firing at William Daniel, Jr. who took cover behind the judge's bench. Daniel, Jr. fired two more shots at Grundy. William Daniel, Sr. was injured in the neck when he grabbed George's gun as he was about to fire and it discharged.

William M. Daniel, Sr. Civil War vet and attorney with a temper. (CV)

When the smoke cleared, William Daniel, Jr, was shot twice. Grundy Gilbert had minor wounds. The Daniels were taken to Tyler's office and seen thereafter by a physician. Grundy and George Gilbert left to go to their law office in the Bailey block where Grundy was treated. The sound of the shooting drew a large crowd to the

150 At this time the option was left to the court to decide to inflict the penalty of life imprisonment or the death sentence.

courthouse. So where was "His Honor" during all of this? Martin stated. "At the first shot I gathered up my papers and retired, standing not upon the order of me going, but going at once as I had pressing business elsewhere." Of the 15 shots fired, 10 holes were located in the walls; one shot went through a chair. One can bet Tyler was furious over this. If Martin had required the men to give up their guns at the door as Judge Tyler always did, the shooting would have not happened at all. The evidence of this episode was still visible in the court room wall until the 1999 tornado.

In the summer of 1901, the members of Forbes Bivouac gathered once more.

Among those pictured are: John William Trotter, William "Billy" Bringhurst, William M. Collier, W.H. Dawson, John Hurst, John Mellon, Dr. John Rogers, J. Hart Balthrop, Hugh Bumpus, J.H. Tabor and of course Judge Tyler (at arrow). (MCA)

Also that summer, at a camp meeting at Hazelwood, near Glenellen, a woman "lunatic" marched straight into the church and commenced swearing at everyone including the minister, as she strolled up and down the aisle. She was brought before Judge Tyler the next morning where the decision was made to send her off to an asylum.

The Tyler house was flooded with guests on the occasion of a gathering by Em Tyler in honor of Nora Monahan of Memphis on the evening of August 12. With an orchestra filling the air with musical delights, Em oversaw the reception described in the press as one in which "Clarksville's society was well-represented and prominent were the pretty and attractive debutantes who are so eagerly awaiting the coming season." This was Em's special night as well for it was her official entrance into society. The who's who among the single female and male attendees were listed by name in the newspaper and since Em had her mother's entertaining skills, it must have been an evening to remember.

At Trinity, change was again necessary as William J. Miller who had served the congregation from 1896 until September 1901 departed for retirement in Colorado. Emmie Tyler, wrote of the church's departed priest,

> **Mr. Miller was particularly devoted the Church and her ways—his sermons, whatever may have been to them, whether the Fatherhood of God or the brotherhood of man, never failed to bring prominently before us the Motherhood of the Church, her gracious teachings, her divinely appointed ordinances. He rendered valuable assistance to the *Diocesan* paper,[151] while here; and his contributions have been sadly missed since he left the diocese.**

The local newspaper once so anxious to see Tyler's authority diminished, was singing his praises in over a resolution put forth by Henry Merritt's committee in an article printed on November 22. Touting the judge's accomplishments, the reporter wrote, "This resolution was a generous and courteous recognition of Judge Tyler, the status which he occupies and the respect due him in the premises." Tyler and the committee were tasked to formulate a practical plan not only for freeing the current pikes and ferries but also to create a system for developing good roads and pikes in every district of the county."

Meanwhile at the "Hotel de Stafford" updates on the "boarders" at the jail were printed in the newspaper on December 10, 1901,

> **There are now twenty boarders at the Hotel de Stafford. The present session of the Criminal Court had reduced the number somewhat, several of them having been given chain gang sentence, which they are working out. They are confined to await trial for various offenses. Three are charged with murder, three with highway robbery, and three carrying pistols and petty larceny.**

[151] A small church newspaper begun by Bishop Thomas Gailor and continued by Miller.

The rising waters of the Red River in late December of 1901, at Port Royal, almost caused the death of a widow and her children as they attempted to cross. Mrs. J.R. Williams had not anticipated the waters rising so much during her two-day visit to Saddlersville, Kentucky. Luckily, bystanders pulled her and her children safely from the river when her horse panicked in midstream and was overcome by the treacherous currents.

Upon hearing of the accident, Judge Tyler once again had the chain gang to retrieve the new ferryboat from the island to which it had floated. The ferry had broken from its moorings on the rainy night of the 13th. Tyler instructed the gang to get the ferry back in "satisfactory working order." It reminded him to commit to re-building a bridge in that spot. Port Royal was so close to where the judge had grown up and he knew many of the families still living in the area.

Port Royal's history is fascinating. It was one of Middle Tennessee's earliest settlement areas as the first permanent settlers arrived in 1784. The first meeting of the Tennessee County Court, North Carolina, was held nearby in 1788, years before the Tylers' arrival. The town itself was organized in 1797, and during the time the Tylers lived nearby, it grew to a population of over twelve hundred.

To help with the Christmas holiday expenses, the decision was made to suspend the toll on the City and Searcy ferries for several weeks until December 29. The city merchants paid the tolls instead for a limited time. The toll on the Russellville Pike was also stopped for a short while. This was greatly appreciated by all those needing to come into town to shop for their families, as was the intention of storeowners. The inference was then made that the ferries next year would be toll free at an even earlier date.

The sleet storm of late January 1902 shrouded Judge Tyler's courthouse in ice. Power lines fell and trees leaned over with the weight of the ice on their limbs. Crews worked quickly to restore telephone lines downed when their poles broke.

After serving in the Spanish-American War, Cave Johnson had become a member of the Clarksville bar and formed a law partnership with Michael Savage in February 1902. The young man had such a promising future...one that would be cut short.

Judge Tyler, as chairman of the Montgomery County Highway Commission, purchased the Edmondson Ferry on March 15, allowing it to remain as a toll ferry, but when the Seven Mile Ferry was also purchased, it operated free to customers as did the City Ferry and Searcy's Ferry. Searcy's Ferry operated under private ownership as usual and the City Ferry converted to gasoline for power. The buoys were removed and the ferry "took on a much-improved appearance." Regardless, the City Ferry for years had been a troublesome item for Judge Tyler as so often it liked to take "little excursions" down river whenever driftwood broke the chains to the buoys.

The City Ferry in 1893. Swift Suiter on the right operated the ferry. He, on several occasions. saved people from injury coming onto the ferry and young boys swimming and boating from drowning. (MCA)

After a long, lingering illness, Judge Tyler's half-nephew, Jesse Averitt Bryan passed away on July 8, in Houston, Texas. It is likely the judge was unable to attend the funeral due to his schedule.

December 15, closed out one of the busiest years since the Criminal Court was re-established in Montgomery County. It was reported that there were: 147 cases, 101 went to trial, which included: 58 convictions, 7 acquittals, 3 mistrials and 21 to be continued into the next year. Nine of the convicted defendants received penitentiary sentences, 23 were given workhouse sentences and the fines against the remaining defendants amounted to $1000 all of which had been paid or secured.

City officials were always able to get crushed stones for use on city streets. The Red River rock quarry was where Judge Tyler sent many an evildoer to break rocks all day. The first week of January, law enforcements promised 2,000 loads of stones to be spread on Clarksville streets.

Trinity was struggling once more as support for the Diocese was intermittent. When the new rector, Gerald R. Messias directed that a parish missionary society be formed. He came to Trinity in 1903 and went so far as to pronounce the society organized and proceeded to appoint its officers. He put the task on the shoulders of the church's Women's Auxiliary. Emmie Tyler described the stunned reaction of the ladies to their newly appointed task, "I shall never forget the blank look of astonishment and meek submission on the face of those present as we filed out of the rectory, feeling the burden laid upon us was greater than we could bear." Messias then left for a six-week vacation on an extended trip. During his absence, there were no church services as he was unable to get someone to cover for him. He was gone from July 20 until September 1.

Emmie and Mrs. Ashabel Patch, committed to the task and attended the convention of Tennessee Churchwomen at Memphis and with renewed energy and hope for expanding the society's membership. But after a visit and sermon by Bishop Gailor to organize "a regular system of meetings with the object of promoting missionary interest in the parish" Emmie realized the support simply was not there.

Judge Tyler took his brother John Duke Tyler along with him on February 12, to inspect the work being done by one of the county's chain gangs and was satisfied by the work the men were doing on the Hopkinsville Turnpike near the state line. In one month's time, the gang had been getting the road in prime condition but it was estimated that to finish the job, two or three more months would be needed. The judge was always able to muster up some deserving bad guys to round out a road crew in stripes.

Once again, inclement winter weather in 1903 directly affected the court's schedule. The regular term of the Criminal Court was adjourned on February 16 because only eight of the thirteen jurymen who had been summoned could report for duty. The high water made it impossible for some to cross the river into town. The court delayed its business one day to start its week-long proceedings.

Rejoicing was in order, when in April 6, 1903, the Edmondson, Seven Mile and City ferries were finally freed. No longer would travelers across the Cumberland have to pay. This issue had been discussed and argued for years.

Under the watchful eye of Judge Tyler as county financial officer who controlled every cent spent by the county, a new covered bridge was constructed in 1903 over the Red River in Port Royal. Other than recording that in 1866 a flood washed the first Port Royal bridge away, nothing else is known. The original stone in the piers came from the Port Royal Mills and dam dating back to about 1800.

Work on the new bridge began in August and then on December 10, 1903, at about 2:30 p.m., as workers removed its false support timbers, 200 feet collapsed, sending three workers and one bystander into the Red River, causing the death of twenty-two-year-old Will Woolridge and injuring Walter J. Jolly and Henry Farmer. Woolridge died two hours after the accident with both legs broken and major internal injuries.

The collapse was so loud and caused the ground to shake that locals believe it was due to an earthquake. This bridge that was 200 feet long and 45 feet high. It cost $5,000 and was almost ready to be opened traffic. Judge Tyler had to be furious after fighting to have the bridge rebuilt. The collapse was found to be due to the breaking of two defective cast-iron plates when they should have been constructed of steel or wrought iron plates. Later it was stated that the collapse occurred because the bridge had no center pier. J.C. McMillian held the contract to build the bridge and since Montgomery County had not accepted the bridge before it fell, McMillan bore the expense of rebuilding it. He promised to add a center pier and rebuild with "more substantial material."

In a regular county court meeting in January of 1904, Squire Johnson moved that Farmer and Jolly should each receive $75 as compensation for their injuries. Jolly who had his leg broken in the collapse and his right foot crushed, fell at home in early March 1904 while walking using crutches and re-broke the same leg. Farmer also had a leg broken in the collapse. A bank in town also collected money to help the men since their families were totally dependent on their income.

Re-opening day. Courtesy Port Royal State Park.

The rebuilt bridge was complete the following year in 1904. On its re-opening day, crowds of people came to inspect the new bridge and to show their appreciation for it being rebuilt. Tyler meant for the bridge to be maintained and last many years and to that end he paid Charlie Norman, a blacksmith, ten dollars to make two signs, each reading, "$10 FINE FOR GOING FASTER THAN A WALK." One of the signs was posted on each end of the bridge. Even thirty-three years after Judge Tyler's death, no one would touch these signs. This bridge existed until 1972 when much of it collapsed once more into the Red River.[152]

Above: Judge Tyler's sign on the bridge. (MCA)

In 1978, state officials built a 75% scale recreation of the 1904 bridge. This bridge was destroyed on June 10, 1998 as heavy rains and tornado-strength winds demolished a large portion of the bridge. Due to funding being unavailable, the bridge, much to the regret of so many, was never rebuilt.

There was an outcry heard around the town over the possible destruction of Spring Street by the laying of the Tennessee Central Railroad tracks. Michael Savage and Cave Johnson filed a petition in the U.S. Circuit Court against the Tennessee Central Railroad to halt the construction of the line along Spring Street on behalf of Mrs. Gamaliel B. Wilson and H.W. Ritter. The suit alleged that

-the construction of the road bed by the TN Central Railroad up Spring Street completely destroyed the usefulness of the street and also cut off egress and ingress to the county jail.

-TN Central Railroad was under a $15,000,000 mortgage and if allowed to progress in the destruction of the street, the county would sustain an irreparable loss and would be without a remedy as the amount of the mortgage was greater than the present value of the road.

-the TN Central Railroad Co. had abandoned its original survey and changed its survey to Spring Street with the hope they might avoid the expense of condemning the property through which it was originally intended that it should run and that it should not be allowed to proceed in the destruction of Spring Street until the same is condemned and the value and damages assessed as required by law.

-the mayor and Board of Aldermen had no power or right to confer this privilege upon this road as granted them in a city ordinance of some time since.

A temporary injunction was filed at the time that allowed more time to decide the suit. Then on Tuesday, April 14, a delegation of lawyers and others connected with the suit met in Lebanon, Tennessee. It would be July before the decision was handed down.

Sad tidings came to the Clarksville Tylers in later April when they received word that the son of Dr. Duke Tyler lost his little son in Hadensville, Kentucky. The boy died after a short bout with tuberculosis. Nannie Tyler Johnson and attorney J.D. Tyler attended the funeral.

The weather did not want to cooperate either for the special Remembrance Day for Civil War veterans at Greenwood Cemetery on May 31. In spite of the rain however, a respectable number

---

[152] Through much public support the bridge was rebuilt using the original stone supports.

turned out for the ceremony to present crosses of honor to the veterans. Rev. W.J. Collier opened the ceremony with a prayer followed by the singing of the hymn, “Onward Christian Soldiers.” Cave Johnson addressed the crowd and read the rules and requirements for the presentation of the crosses of honor. The song, “No, Never Alone” was sung by a quartet composed of Charles Kincannon, Henry Herndon, Campbell Barbee and Robert Daniel. Johnson then conferred the crosses to: Dempsey S. Major, J.L. Owen, Thomas McCabe, Charles Henry Bailey, Alexander W. Manson, John E. Moseley, Drewery F. Marshall, Enoch N. Cooksey, George N. Byers, John Mellon, Mercer W. West, David Halliburton, George W. Buck, T.R. Munford, J.S. Lowe, Gabriel L. Williams, James H. Welles, John F. Woodmore, George W. Warfield, Isaac N. Belote, W.F. Buckner, Charles W. Tyler, John H. Schrodt, Clay Stacker, Sr., Alfonzo “Fonz” Frederick Smith, James L. Lockert, Thomas D. Luckett, Nathaniel O. Lovelace and Thomas D. Johnson. As each name was called, the veteran stepped up to have the medal pinned upon his lapel and receive a buttonhole bouquet. Alfonzo Smith spoke on behalf of the recipients, followed by Dr. John Horace Lacey of the Presbyterian Church addressing the citizens gathered. Members of Forbes Bivouac, the United Daughters of the Confederacy and Sons of Confederate Veterans next decorated the graves of deceased veterans. The ceremony finished with the entire assemblage gathered around the base of the Confederate monument to sing, “Nearer My God to Thee.” The benediction was led by Dr. Lacey.

Emmie’s 54th birthday was celebrated at her home on Greenwood Avenue on June 5. Her actual birthday was the 4th but it was a birthday to remember. A description of the evening made the “Society Notes” of the newspaper.

> **The parlor and hall were decorated gracefully in white bride’s roses and asparagus fern. The dining room was done in scarlet over a hundred scarlet carnations being used. Scarlet was carried out through the entire dinner of seven courses from the red bouillon through the ice course. The place cards were very artistic hearts done in watercolors, a large heart bearing the guests’ names and four small hearts attached by red ribbons bearing the names of the honorees, Miss Bringhurst, Miss Tyler, Mr. Wallis, and Mr. MacComb whose birthday is on the same day as Miss Tyler’s.**
>
> **The occasion was one to be remembered by the guests. Miss Tyler was the recipient of many handsome gifts. After dinner each guest made some happy wish and the ancient ceremony of blowing out a candle apiece was thoroughly enjoyed.**
>
> **The party included Miss Tyler, Mr. MacComb, Miss Anne Belle Bringhurst, Mr. Herbert Morrow, Miss Mary Pickering, Mr. James Kendrick, Mr. and Mrs. H.M. Lupton, Miss Sara Bringhurst, Mr. Deval Wallis, Miss Sarah Kendrick, Mr. Claude Carlisle, Miss Hope Gracey, Mr. Henry Harris.**

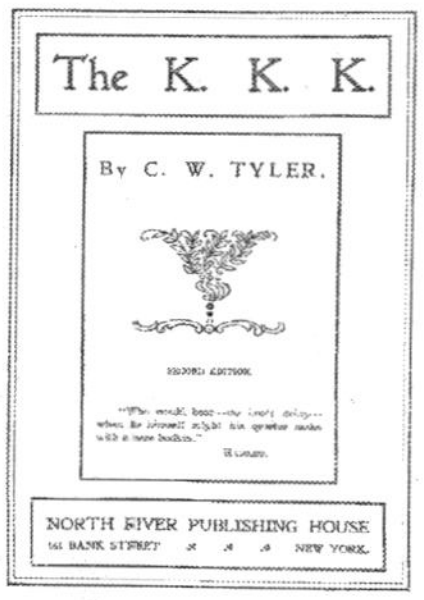

There was no mention of the judge or Em.

Judge Tyler’s first book entitled, *The K.K.K.* was published and released in July of 1903. He candidly wrote about lynchings and self-appointed judges taking the law into their own hands. Tyler condemned mob violence, which he contended, “will never be put down in his section until the criminal statuettes are so amended as to secure the speedy trial of offenders through the medium of the courts.” He carried his case further as he addressed a grand jury after one such lynching in his district when he declared:

> **If masked men at midnight may sit in judgment upon the rights of one citizen, they may do so upon those of another; if the turn of a guilty man comes first, that of an innocent man may next succeed. If earnest and well-disposed citizens presided in the first instance and seal a prisoner’s fate, and there is no appeal from their decision and no subsequent investigation into their acts, men of a very different stamp may handle the next case.**

His description of the jail mentioned in the book matches the city jail in use in 1900. Names such as Kinchen and Gallows Hollow resonate with local attachments. He added:

> **Moreover, when the good people or any community took the law into their own hands they advertised to the world that their laws were inefficient, or that they had no confidence in the officials’ whose duty it was to administer them.**

His book's preface read

Few intelligent persons in this country can have failed to note the rapid growth of mob law among us in the last few years. Formally the punishment of offenders was the business of the courts and illegal executions in the name of justice never resorted to except in rare instances when some deed of peculiar atrocity stirred an entire community to frenzy. Now human beings are frequently sent out of the world by hasty assemblages of excited men, not only in open defiance of the authorities but often where the offense charged would not have been punishable with death under the law. In some instances, to our shame as a people be it said, the irresponsible mob has burned helpless captives at the stake, thus introducing into an enlightened country a practice hitherto unknown except among the cruel savages. Surely the time has come when serious enquiry should be made into the causes back of this rapidly growing evil, with the view of staying its further progress if possible. Having been for a number of years the judge of a court in my State with criminal jurisdiction, I have become convinced that then only reason why good citizens countenance mob violence is that they have lost faith in the ability of the courts to deal effectually with crime. They weary of the delay attending criminal prosecutions and the frequent failure of justice in the end exasperates them. If this be true, then the remedy for mob law is to substitute for it speedy trial and prompt punishment of all offenders through our regularly established courts of justice. In dealing with criminals we had for the present better err on the side of too much dispatch than to pursue further the procrastinating methods that have awakened a protest in the minds of the soberest men in the country and brought some portions of our wide republic to the verge of anarchy.

In framing the present story, it was my purpose to show on the one hand how easily the vengeance of a mob may be misplaced and on the other how provoking to the patience of those interested in the suppression of crime and the preservation of order must be the progress of a modern criminal trial as it drags its slow length along through the courts. Some of the incidents here narrated are real, other fictitious, and I have endeavored to weave them all into a story that while carrying a moral with it would not be without interest to the general reader. The name of the book, I may add, was taken from that of a secret society which soon after the close of the Civil War was organized in my community for the purpose of administering speedy justice to evil-doers at a time when this end could not be attained through the courts. The title, therefore, when chosen was not without significance to me, though doubtless it will be meaningless to most of those who glance over my pages.

I am aware of the fact that this story lacks the polish it would have possessed had it come from polished hands. It was written however for the honest purpose of striking at a grave existing evil and, such as it is, I send it forth without apology, hoping it may find a few friends among the millions of readers in this great country, and be in the end productive of some good.

Finally, on July 28, the Tennessee Central Railroad case was heard in Clarksville by Judge Josiah Wilkins Stout. The TN Central Railroad wished to have the injunction dissolved in order to continue the construction of the new tracks on Spring Street. Finally, the judge rendered his decision that the "injunction be so modified thus to allow the defendants to enter their cross bill to proceed and prosecute their action against complainant for the matters complained of in said bill. In other respects, the motion to dissolve the injunction is disallowed." The newspaper took the side of what they considered to be the majority of citizens in stating their opposition to the plans: unsightly trestles making it impossible to enjoy both sides of the street, private property seriously damaged, warehouses, homes, mills, factories in jeopardy and owners unlikely to get ample compensation.

On the left: the TN Central trestle along Spring Street. On the right: Judge Stout (MCA).

The *Chronicle* which had been favorable for the Tennessee Central to come into town pleaded, "Isn't there some way by which this street can be saved to the public? f there is, let it be done." In the end, the railroad placed the tracks exactly where they wanted them.[153]

Nannie Johnson filed an injunction against the city to prevent them from cutting a limb from a shade tree in her front yard that the city claimed interfered with the street roller. In early December 1903 Judge Stout dissolved the injunction. Needless to say, Nannie Johnson was added to the list of those who did not hold the judge in high regard.

J.B. Killebrew contributed biographies on the prominent men of Montgomery County that was included in The *Nashville Banner* issue of February 13, 1904. He described Tyler, a man he knew personally as

> **A man of nerve, capacity, aggressiveness and high intellectuality. He accomplished results by indefatigable industry. He moves in a quiet, but irrespirable way to secure his ends. Born in Montgomery County, he was mainly educated by his father, Hon. John Duke Tyler and was a good classical scholar at the age of 15.**

In March, Judge Tyler was asked by the chairman of the Tennessee World's Fair Association to prepare a pamphlet to be distributed at the St. Louis World's Fair expounding the advantages of seeking a home in Montgomery County. To that end Judge Tyler publicly advertised through the local newspapers that assistance was needed to gather the appropriate information about the county's resources, business and manufacturing capabilities.

In May, the Daughters of the Confederacy held a fundraiser on the courthouse lawn to help defray the transportation cost for members of the Forbes Bivouac to travel by train to the June Confederate Reunion to be held in Nashville. Tyler must have changed his mind about allowing gatherings on the lawn. The ladies served strawberries and cream to the public from 5:00-10:00 p.m. Judge Tyler, along with John B. Allen, T.W. Walthall, James H. Wells and Squire Major, served on the committee.

It was reported that nearly two hundred participants from Montgomery County attended the reunion, including members and their families of Forbes Bivouac. The long list of Clarksville citizens present was printed on the front page of the newspaper. Listed first was Judge Tyler, accompanied by his sister, Emmie. The railroad honored them by identifying the special cars in which they rode. The event was reported to have been a complete success with the parade five miles long, making the reunion the largest in the history of the association.

During the reunion, the veterans were housed in the luxurious Maxwell House Hotel. Shortly after this reunion, the pastor of Trinity in Clarksville used the event in a sermon to plead for citizens to let their wounds heal and to look to the future in the New South. The war had been over for forty years but emotions still simmered and some found it difficult to reconcile their lives to what had happened by holding onto deep-seated feelings.

Billy Bringhurst, was excited to learn that passengers departing from the Tennessee Central train on Spring Street would no longer have to circumvent the back side of the Public Square in order to reach his hotel. The Tennessee Central Railroad on June 28, announced its plans to construct an overhead foot bridge from the depot to Franklin Street. Stairs were to be built from the street level of the depot up to the bridge.

A Nashville newspaper in November insinuated that Judge Tyler allowed four blacks youths to get off easy after selling their votes to a prominent citizen, working for one of the candidates in an election. When shown the article, Judge Tyler made sure to clarify the action he took in handling the charges. He also insisted that the Clarksville paper publicize the account of his actions. Once Judge Tyler expressed his opinion that such articles do more harm than good. The *Leaf Chronicle* added a final statement in support of Tyler, in that he, "has labored faithfully to suppress election fraud in this county and has never discriminated between black and white."

---

[153] Many citizens alive today remember having to drive under the trestles to get to Riverside Drive.

Forced to act due to economic hardship, tobacco growers in western Kentucky and northern Middle Tennessee formed the Dark Tobacco District Planters' Protective Association of Kentucky and Tennessee (PPA) on September 24, 1904. This group set its own tobacco prices and asked that all farmers support the organization. Those farmers who refused were intimated by a faction of the Association, who became known as the "Night Riders." The self-organized masked vigilantes roamed the countryside terrorizing these farmers. Barns were burned, plant beds destroyed, salted or even littered with dynamite. This bloody period of vandalism, destruction of crops and property, included murder.

Night Riders were required to take an oath, sworn by lantern light on bended knees and with one hand on the Bible,

> **I, _____, in the presence of the Almighty God, and these witnesses, take upon myself these solemn pledges and obligations that I will never reveal any of the secrets, signs or passwords of this order, either by word or writing, to any person or persons who are not entitled to the same, in accordance with the rules and regulations of this order. I furthermore swear and promise that I will never reveal or cause to be revealed, by word or act, to any persons, and of the transactions of this order, in lodge or out of lodge room, etc.**

Nannie T. Johnson who had lost her first son, many years before (born and died August 6, 1878), next lost her son Cave who died at 2:00 a.m. on November 25, at age 27. Although the cause of his death is not listed in the Clarksville obituary, his death described as "slow and painful," was reported in *The Paducah Sun* newspaper as consumption. Either he contracted the disease while serving in the Philippines and it was misdiagnosed as asthma or he had asthma but contracted tuberculosis in Clarksville after his return home. This young man so full of promise and good works was buried in Greenwood in the Johnson family plot with military honors after a service at Trinity. J.B. Killebrew described him in 1904 as

> **having inherited many of the high qualities of his maternal grandfather, the Hon. Cave Johnson for whom he was named. Affable, polite, accommodating with good address and pleasing manners, he enjoys by birth association and a happy temperament, many of the advantages that lead to a triumphant success in the profession of law.**

The inscription on his stone reads: "Here lies interred for a space the earthly temple wherein once dwelt the immortal soul of Cave Johnson who served his country in the war with Spain."

While contending with the Night Rider threat, Judge Tyler's family advocated change in the downtown. The Tyler women signed a petition supporting early closure of town stores.

> **January 21, 1905: A letter: To the Merchants of Clarksville:**
> **Gentleman,**
>
> **We the undersigned ladies of Clarksville, your patrons and friends, do earnestly petition you to close your stores, hereafter at 6:30 p.m. each day except Saturdays and every month except December. We promise to do our shopping before the time designated and also to use our influence to get others to accommodate themselves to the new arrangement.**
>
> **Our grounds of this request are chiefly these: That the married men, employers and employees may spend their evenings with their families to the benefit and happiness of themselves and their wives and children. That young men may have their evenings for self-improvement. That all may be given time for needed rest and recreation Respectfully submitted. Signed by Mrs. Polk Johnson, Mildred Johnson, Miss Tyler (Emmie), Emily Tyler** (and several hundred others.)

Law-breaking in the county continued in its daily rounds. In the report submitted to the mayor in February 1905, the number of arrests made in Montgomery County in 1904 by each police officer were: John Edward Robinson-139, N.H. Dye-128, Dick Perkins-167, John Alsobrooks-127, W.M. Gardner-174, Alex Small-190, Extra officers: 228. The total number of arrests made and tried before the Recorder during the year February 1904-February 1905 were: Number whites: 353, Number colored: 800, Number males: 912, Number females: 241.

This one was a new one for the books: On April 24, a Mississippi sheriff tried to abduct three black prisoners arrested in Cumberland City and jailed in Clarksville. After hearing the details of the arrest, Judge Tyler decided the men were not legally held. The Mississippi sheriff Davis produced three warrants charging the men with embezzlement committed in that state. Tyler refused to hold the prisoners based on the warrants but did agree to keep them in custody until a warrant could be sworn out before a Montgomery County magistrate. This occurred on April 24 before Squire Smith who heard the case and directed the prisoners be held for 10 days to allow Sheriff Davis time to get the appropriate requisition papers. That night, the prisoners were bonded out. When Davis heard this he waited at the jail and re-arrested them. Handcuffed, he took them to the L & N passenger depot to slip them on the train and take them back to Mississippi. Before boarding, one of the prisoners began yelling, "Fire! Murder!" Another yelled, "They are going to kill us!" This drew such a crowd of spectators that the sheriff took off their handcuffs and walked away. This clearly was in contempt of the Montgomery County Court and Judge Tyler issued a bench warrant for the sheriff's arrest.

It was just April and already complaints were flying along with the "clouds of dust" on the Public Square. People were irritated by the lack of sprinkling in the square "where all the dust originates." The argument was that it was totally pointless to waste water sprinkling Franklin Street if the Public Square was not sprinkled as well. At that time the city sprinkler only sprayed water at the head of Franklin Street (at First Street).

On May 29, attorney Michael Savage read to the County Court a petition for the appointment of Nannie T. Johnson as postmaster of Clarksville and asked the magistrates to sign it; each one did so.

Just seven months after his own death, Cave's little sister, Mildred, became ill and passed away at 6:00 a.m. on June 5, 1905. Did she contract the disease from her brother? Nannie withdrew her application for the appointment of postmaster for Clarksville in September due to the death of her two children. Bettie Garland commemorated Mildred's death with a poem she wrote for her friend and relative by marriage:

Yesterday with the morn's waking
Woke she, a pallid smile wreathing!
White lips in languorous waning,
Young lips aweary with breathing.

Where has the sweet spirit wandered,
Whose were the fond arms to bear her,
Seeks she a newly found garden.

There were the lilies grow fairer?

Gateway of high flashing arches
Grander than all we've beholden,
Over the fair rolling pathways
Leading to palaces golden.

Softly she enters there smiling,
Hundreds of white wings surround her,
Voices of welcoming angels,
Chanting melodies around her.

"Little Mildred" Johnson.
Courtesy John Williams.

Mildred was said to have been beloved "for that gentleness and refinement that denotes the highest type of womanhood." Her funeral service was held at Trinity with burial in the Johnson plot at Greenwood. Nannie Tyler Johnson was now alone having lost her entire family.

The Jim Crow Law did not go into effect in Tennessee until July 5, 1905. (House Bill Bo. 87, Chapter 150.) On that morning the Street Railway Company posted signs to show the location of the seats provided for white and colored passengers. White passengers were directed to go to the front of the car and colored to the back. The streetcar driver was given the power to designate seats. It was asked that all passengers, both white and black assist the railway company by carrying out the law and that failure to comply meant the state could fine the company $25 per day.

Chapter Twenty: A Life Out West and Night Riders

On August 16, 1905, at age 21, Em married Harold Gouverneur Mitchell (1884-1930) a wealthy cattleman and mine owner. Their marriage took place in San Francisco. Although Mitchell lived in Montana, his family had their roots in Virginia and Kentucky. Harold's father, Dr. Armistead Hughes Mitchell (1832-1898), and his wife Mary Ellen "Molly" Irvine Mitchell[154] (1851-1927), once lived in Oldham County, Kentucky. Dr. Mitchell was a civic leader in the Deer Lodge community and co-founder of what became the state hospital at nearby Warm Springs. Back in 1895, at the head of First Chance Gulch and the Garnet town site, Dr. Mitchell built a stamp mill to crush ore and a town was born and it first took on Mitchell's name. Two years later, it was changed to Garnet for the brown garnet found along the contact zone of granodiorite and limestone rocks of the area. Mitchell passed away the next year. Inside St. James Episcopal Church at Deer Lodge, is a stain glass window dedicated to Dr. Armistead Mitchell. He is interred in Hillcrest Cemetery in Deer Lodge, Powell County, Montana. Today, Garnet is Montana's best preserved ghost town and the government will pay for people to live there.

CLARKSVILLE BELLE

Weds Wealthy Miner While Touring In Montana.

Clarksvile, Tenn., Aug. 19.—Telegrams received here announce the marriage in San Francisco of Miss Tyler, daughter of Judge C. W. Tyler, to Harold Mitchell, of Butte, Mont. Judge Tyler was with his daughter, but the marriage was a complete surprise to friends here. Mr. Mitchell is interested in the Anaconda copper mines and is reported to be worth $5,000,000. He is a Yale graduate and a man of fine family. Miss Tyler was one of the most popular belles of Clarksville's social history.

The announcement of their wedding in the *Leaf Chronicle*.

Their wedding came as a complete surprise to her friends. Em and her father were on an extended visit out west during which the marriage took place. There is no other information on this whirlwind marriage. With her father being present when she decided to marry Mitchell, did he strongly advise her not to rush into such a serious commitment? Did she ignore his advice and marry Mitchell anyway? These are questions that will probably never be answered now. One can imagine the feelings her father had returning to Clarksville without her, left to answer the many questions her family and friends would confront him with.

The Mitchells began their life together in Deer Lodge, Montana, a town that had prospered after its designation in 1908 as a division point for the Chicago, Milwaukee, St. Paul and Pacific Railroad. Housing, dining and entertainment were then at a premium.

Judge Tyler received word on August 31 that Mollie's aunt, Mrs. Eugene Corbett, living in Nashville fell from the third story window of her home on Vine Street and died instantly. Mrs. Corbett before her marriage was Joella Bayless who once lived at the home of Billy Settle.

Having married someone with "means," Em, Harold and Harold's sister, Mary started for Spain on September 15 with plans to spend the winter abroad. But before leaving the country they toured the west and stopped by Clarksville to visit Judge Tyler. They returned on the *Cedric* on December 1, 1905. The trip which was to last through the winter was cut short due to Em becoming ill while on the trip. However, her condition improved and upon arrival in New York, they decided to spend a few days in Washington, D.C. visiting friends

[154] An interesting fact: Mary's brother, Thomas H. Irvine, was elected sheriff of Custer County, Montana in 1879 and served several terms. He came to Montana in 1864 from St. Joseph, Missouri, settled at Deer Lodge and removed to the Yellowstone River country in the early seventies. He was a scout for Gen. Nelson A. Miles and engaged in many Indian fights, including the Battle of Wounded Knee.

there before coming to Clarksville to visit with her father.

A single alderman on the city council in September 1905 argued that a new market house had been promised to the citizens of Clarksville for six years and he wanted the issue raised again. An estimate of $7,500 was given to build a new market in the exact same location as the last one torn down years before! Opponents reminded the alderman that the last one allowed but a narrow pass on either side of the Public Square and the population of Clarksville was only half of what it was then. It had been an eyesore, a subject of ridicule and nobody patronized it, they said, "The square as it was then, was a good wide open street leading to the Tennessee Central Depot" and that the alderman proposed "building this shed in the middle of the street obstructing the way and the view." Mayor Smith did not support the building project and therefore was able to kill the plans to do so. Since that time until the present Public Square has remained an open space.

Halloween pranks on Judge Tyler's street received public attention. A group of boys hoisted a buggy up a telephone pole about ten feet from the ground and left it hanging there to be discovered in the morning. The buggy was not damaged but the owner could not have been amused by the trickery of the night's festivities. One can bet it was not Judge Tyler's buggy they chose.

A sentence was handed out on December 2 by Tyler on an offense that would seem trivial today. John Hawkins was charged with using profane language in the presence of women while intoxicated. He was disorderly in New Providence, found guilty, sentenced to three months on the chain gang, fined $50 and costs. How many would populate the jail if charged on that offense today?

The chain gang made the news once more in February 1906 as J.D. Tyler accepted a bid offered to rent members of his chain gang out. The bid of Dorrel and Forrest Suitor was filed and stated

> **For all able men we agree to pay the county 31 cents per day per each man, further to board and clothe them. For all boys under fourteen years of age and women we will board and clothe them. We agree to furnish a good place for the gang to live; this is for the gang for the year 1906. We will make responsible bond if required. (signed) Dorrell Suiter and Forest Suiter, L.A. Diffenderfer**

J.D. Tyler's reply was

> **I am willing to take the county convicts on the same terms as last year or upon such conditions as the committee thinks fair and reasonable.**

Simmering all the while was the organizing of the Night Riders and their intended purpose. By the spring 1906 around 2,000 men had taken the Night Rider oath. Dr. David Amoss had clearly stated the Riders' purpose and meant for swift action to be taken:

> **to burn or otherwise destroy the property of growers and to whip them and others who refuse to co-operate with you in winning your fight against the Trust is more than they deserve. There is no reason why a few persons should continue to make the masses suffer when their cooperation would not only be to their benefit, but would increase the earnings and thus improve the conditions of all equally.**

The violence came as close to Clarksville as St. Bethlehem and Fredonia but came no farther because it was said that there was "too much law in Clarksville." Probably the strongest contributing factor was that the tobacco warehouses were located mainly in the downtown area of Clarksville and with the Cumberland River and Red Rivers shaping the town into a peninsula, it might be easy for the riders to enter town but difficult to escape if any destruction was committed.

Things became more personal when Mollie Tyler's brother-in-law Robert B. Rossington who lived in New Providence received a threatening note from a rider.

> **Springfield, Robertson Co.**
> **Mr. Chris Smith**[155]
> **It has been reported to me that you and Mr. Bob Rosington (sic) are the only persons that**

---

[155] This may be Christopher Kimble Smith, a wealthy tobacconist in Clarksville.

you don't belong to the Association. You have some tobacco growing on your farm. You had better get in the Association with your tobacco if you want it to do you any good. Take my advice. Don't want any trouble with you. Show Mr. Rosington this note. Delay is danger.

The threatening letter sent to Robert Rossington.

Plans were formed in May 1906, for a new county jail as Judge Tyler advertised for contractors to bid on the work. The contract awarded to D.A. Dickey of Nashville required that the specifications outlined by the jail committee be met. The new jail was to be built on Commerce Street in front of Ritter's Planing Mill on what was known as the Thomas Herndon lot in "a lovely grove of shade trees." The adjoining street by the jail was Sullivan Street. The estimated cost was $15,790 for a two-story building.

Judge Tyler had to be ecstatic when, on August 15, 1906, he received word that his daughter Em had given birth to a baby son at Deer Lodge, Montana. His father reported that the boy was "well and happy." He was named Armistead in honor of his Mitchell grandfather.

In 1906, the city was proud to finally open its new public high school. Clarksville High School was built diagonally cross the street from Nannie Johnson's home. This school was open until 1969 when a new Clarksville High School was opened on Richview Road. Robert Penn Warren, born and raised in Guthrie, Kentucky just north of Clarksville, attended the school and graduated in 1921, eventually becoming the first Poet Laureate of the United States.[156]

One of the students who attended the new high school was Joseph "Rex" Tyler, (1894-1959), born to Joseph Duke Tyler (1859-1937), and Jessie Settle Tyler (1865-1951). He attended school across the street while living with the judge and his family on Greenwood Avenue.

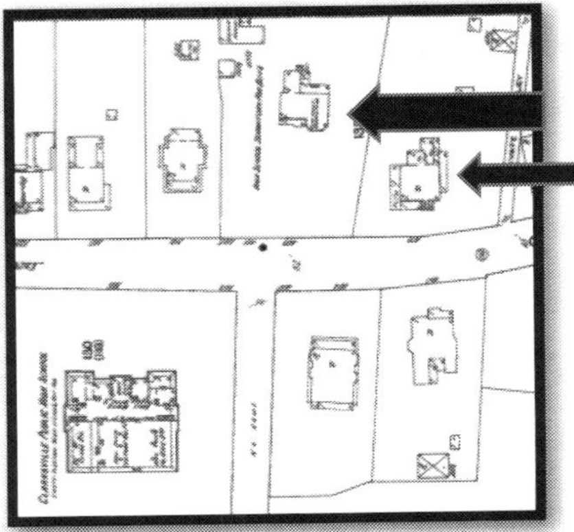

Top arrow: Nannie T. Johnson's house. Bottom arrow: Judge C.W. Tyler's house. The map shows the two houses' proximity to the high school. From Sanborn Fire Maps.

From January through September 1906, records showed that Clarksville was the largest market for Association tobacco at 12,030 hogsheads followed by Springfield with 6,622 hogsheads, Hopkinsville with 5,961 hogsheads and Guthrie, Kentucky with 3,595 hogsheads.

Armistead's father and uncle, William H. Scanland, nearly lost their lives in a car accident in December while in Butte, Montana. While out driving, probably in one of his expensive cars, Mitchell was speeding and failed to take a curve at the intersection of Montana and Copper Streets. He drove through an iron railing and took a flying leap over an embankment missing some trolley wires and went 30 feet through the air. The crash was heard for several blocks. The men were pulled from under the car motor in pools of their own blood and rushed to the hospital. Mitchell was more seriously injured with scalp and facial wounds but no skull fracture. His upper lip was partially torn from his gum and one front tooth knocked out.

[156] The school when vacated and sold, was converted into apartments and now bears the name of the Robert Penn Warren Apartments.

The decade of terror had begun when on November 30-December 1, 1906 nearby Princeton, Kentucky was raided and burned by Night Riders. This raised immediate concerns in Clarksville that it was also to be raided as there were so many large tobacco warehouses in town.

The winter of 1907 was especially difficult on Judge Tyler who was suffering from rheumatism. So much so, that he traveled to the sanitarium at Martinsville, Indiana and spent two weeks trying to regain his health. The spa at 539 E. Washington Street was glowingly advertised:

> **Between 1890 and 1930, Martinsville's economy revolved around mineral water resorts, fed by aquifers of artesian water discovered in 1887. For decades, visitors from near and far traveled to the area to 'take the waters.' The spas offered highly touted treatments – mineral baths, mud wraps, and copious quantities of the water – believed to cure everything from rheumatism to digestive issues.**

The Martinsville Sanitarium, constructed around 1897. Courtesy Indiana Historical Society.

The Martinsville Sanitarium operated as a health resort until about 1957. In ca. 1911 guests paid $18.00 to $35.00 per week for a room and treatments at the sanitarium. Tyler's nephew, J.D., travelled with him to the spa and the pair returned to Clarksville on January 29, 1907 with the judge admitting to improvement in his health.

While Tyler was out-of-town, on January 16, 1907, the county prisoners were removed from the city lockup on the Public Square to the new county jail on Commerce Street, which was nearly finished. The jail was built by the Pauley Jail Company of St. Louis. The jail had a hip roof and the front of the jail had a covered front porch with a pavilion to the right. As before when the jail was on the Public Square, the jailer lived in the building with his family and so this jail had the appearance of being more of a home than what people today would consider a place of incarceration. The jail fronted on Commerce Street and the sheriff was provided with five rooms, bathroom and closets for his family. The jail proper was in the rear, where there were eight cell rooms and ten cages "so arranged that white and black prisoners are kept in separate rooms. There would be special rooms for the youth and also lunatics that might be confined there."

On the left: the new jail. On the right: Hugh Davis standing in front of the jail. His uncle, Robert L. Black, who served as sheriff from 1910-14, hired Hugh to act as a "turnkey" (jailer). (TSLA)

At first, the prisoners were confined in the cell rooms on the first floor, where jail cages were. The second floor of the building was not yet completed. The work was in charge of M.W. Nichols, who bragged that the jail was one of the best of its kind in the state. Judge Tyler was proud that the county could build such a secure jail for prisoners.

On January 30, 1907, the steamer *Buttorff's* captain, James Tyner, received a letter threatening to kill his entire crew and burn the boat if it carried any tobacco raised by non-Association members. The boat had just left Clarksville heavy with Clarksville tobacco on its way to Paducah when the letter was received. Crewmembers were issued 41-caliber Winchester rifles and shown how to use them in case they needed to welcome any of the masked men onboard. No attempt was made to interfere with the shipment and the steamer safely arrived in Paducah.

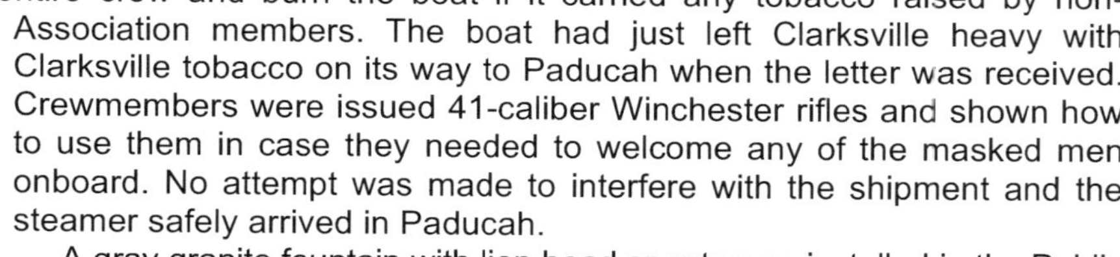

A gray granite fountain with lion head spouts was installed in the Public Square in 1907. Water poured from four spouts into an upper and lower basin. Tobacco farmers would come from miles around and unload their wagons at the loose floor in preparation for the next day's auction.

Afterwards they would lead their tired teams of horses or mules to the fountains for a rewarding drink. The teams were housed in one of the livery stables around Second or Third Streets. Dogs were also allowed to use the fountain since dogs often accompanied their masters to town. This fountain was placed there by the National Alliance, Herman Lee Ensign, Founder.

A fountain exactly like the one in the Clarksville Public Square being used by horses and a dog. How could they know that in just a few years, the automobile would make its appearance in Clarksville and its fountain would eventually lose its purpose.

In late 1947 the fountain was removed to the "old fairgrounds" (what is now the main baseball field at Austin Peay State University.) The newspaper stated,

> **Removal of the obsolete horse watering bowl on the Public Square would afford more room for traffic and at the same time would not injure Clarksville's appearance. The horse trough is a relic of the horse and buggy days and was installed when horse-drawn vehicles were the rule rather than the exception. It belonged to the era when hitching posts and hitch lots were the vogue. The watering trough could be preserved and installed in one of the city's parks if demand warranted but we see no constructive purpose for the trough occupying the space of a parked automobile on a crowded street.**

A new state law on the books that Judge Tyler had to enforce was one that the ladies in town were just absolutely thrilled over: On April 15, Tennessee passed an anti-spitting law. The law was written to "prevent consumption and tuberculosis and the spread thereof and to prescribe the punishment for the violation of this act."

> **Section 1. Be it enacted by the General Assembly of the State of Tennessee that any person or persons who may be the proprietor or proprietors or manager, or managers of a store, factory, shop, office, hotel, theater or any other kind of building wherein business with the public is conducted shall provide cuspidors or spittoons within such place or places of business in sufficient number and shall keep the same disinfected and in a sanitary condition to meet the approval of the local Board of Health either municipal or county as the case may be.**
>
> **Section 2. Be it further enacted that it shall be unlawful for anyone to spit or expectorate upon streetcars, public buildings, or on any floor, wall, or furniture of buildings or any part thereof mentioned in Section 1 of this act and any person who shall willfully or carelessly spit or expectorate upon streetcars, walls or furniture or any part thereof heretofore mentioned shall be guilty of a misdemeanor and fined not less than two dollars ($2.00) nor more than five dollars ($5.00) for each offense.**
>
> **Section 3. Be it further enacted that any person or persons who may be proprietors or managers of any corporation which may be the owner of steam railway passenger coaches operated in this state shall provide cuspidors or spittoons within said coaches in sufficient number and shall keep the same disinfected and in a sanitary condition to meet the approval of the State Board of Health.**
>
> **Section 4. Be it further enacted that it shall be unlawful for anyone to spit or expectorate upon a floor, wall or furniture of any steam railway passenger coach and any person or persons who willfully or carelessly spit or expectorate on said floor, wall or furniture shall be guilty of a misdemeanor and fined not less than two dollars ($2.00) nor more than five dollars ($5.00) for each offense.**
>
> **Section 5. Be it further enacted that said proprietors, managers and owners heretofore mentioned shall keep a copy or copies of the notice prescribed by the local or State Board of Health conspicuously posted in each department of such place of business and on any steam railway passenger coach and on application of the State, municipal and county boards of health (as the case may be), shall furnish such proprietors or managers or owners with a copy or copies of the notice prescribed.**
>
> **Section 6. Be it further enacted that any person or persons or corporations mentioned in this act unless the penalty heretofore in this act is prescribed who shall willfully neglect or refuse to comply with any of the above provisions shall be guilty of a misdemeanor and**

shall be fined not less than ten dollars ($10.00) nor more than one hundred dollars ($100.00) or confined in the county jail for a period of not more than three months one or both in the discretion of the court and upon complaint from any of the said health authorities it shall be the duty of the District Attorney to prosecute the violation of this act.
Section 7. Be it further enacted that every police, health officer, deputy health officer, sheriff and deputy sheriffs shall enforce the provisions of this act as in other cases of misdemeanors.
Section 8. Be it further enacted that this act take effect from and after its passage, the public welfare requiring it.

Passed April 15, 1907
E.G. Tollett, Speaker of the Senate
John T. Cunningham, Jr., Speaker of the House of Representatives
Approved April 15, 1907, Malcolm R. Patterson, Governor[157]

The law went into effect in early May and Judge Tyler was on it! By May 8, Tyler had signs posted throughout the courthouse stating that parties "expectorating" on the floor or wall of the courthouse would be fined $5.00. Businesses placed spittoons inside to accommodate customers who wanted to chew and shop. One business on Franklin Street posted spittoons every couple of feet in front of their display cases. Women had to appreciate the business owner's thoughtfulness.

Clark's Jewelry Store with spittoon on the floor next to Clark. (MCA)

The riders continued to cut telegraph wires, blow up threshing machines and use their bullying tactics. Tobacco farmers carried their shotguns with them to market and stood guard at night over their barns filled with tobacco. Some planters who feared for their personal safety, came to town and stayed at such hotels as the Franklin House. One family moved kit and caboodle into town. James Monroe Rogers, his two sisters and six children first moved to a house on Greenwood Avenue and then next to a 16-room house at 207 Seventh Street that he purchased in 1909 for $2500 from Dr. George Madison Pardue. This house was constructed from log cabins dated to around 1848. In 2024 the house[158] was razed and one of the cabins was able to be salvaged.

May 16, 1907: E.E. Wimpey of Glenellen had his plant beds scraped resulting in a total loss of tobacco plants.
May 18, 1907: Cicero Dowlen of Port Royal had two large plant beds destroyed by someone who poured salt on one bed and pulled all the plants up in the other resulting in the loss of about 25 acres of tobacco. The Dowlen's watch dog had been poisoned the week prior to the raid. Eyewitness reported seeing 12-16 men west of Port Royal riding horses in the direction of Dowlen's farm about 9:00 p.m. One was carrying a sack and another one or two hand guns. Dowlen stated that he had suspicions of who committed the outrage but would not name the persons.
May 20, 1907: Black farmers largely stood with the official PPA and suffered for it as well. (First name not known), Dudley, a black sharecropper who raised his tobacco on Ben Hollins'[159] property near Guthrie[160] was the next victim in Montgomery County. Dudley's wife was kidnapped by 12-15 men and forced to identify his plant beds.

Hollins' house. It has long since been torn down.

[157] Patterson bought the mansion "TipTop" from Hugh and Mattie Dunlop and lived briefly in Clarksville.
[158] The house is remembered as the old Ma Greene boarding house.
[159] B.F. Hollins was born in 1822. He left no family. He was a cousin to Duke Tyler's wife, Helen.
[160] Hollins' house was across the road from the drive leading across a field to Polk Prince's home. Polk Prince was also a member of the Association.

The intersection of Woodson and Trough Springs Roads in 2024 where the shooting occurred. The interstate 24 overpass at mile marker 13 is shown at the top of the photo. This was once known as "the crossroads." Photo by author. Map by Google.

Of course, Earl stated that he, his brother and others were waylaid and fired upon first. Author's note: The riders were actually riding away from town at the time of the shooting.

John Gardner and Walter Hunt fled the county but later returned and turned themselves in. The two were immediately put on trial in the case of Gardner v. State that lasted from September 8 until October 3, 1908 presided over by Judge Tyler. The trial was so emotionally charged that each and every man who entered the courtroom was searched for weapons. To the satisfaction of the Association, both men were convicted of second-degree murder and sentenced to ten years in prison. Meanwhile on September 25th, a vacant tobacco factory owned by Sory was burned in Adams.

The Bennett home on Sango Road stills stands today. Photo courtesy of Robb Hodges and Thomas Murff.

Because of the killings, the Association decided to boycott all Clarksville businesses for a month, causing much distress to business owners not involved in the dispute. A compromise was reached when it was agreed that city officials would keep its guards out of the county unless the sheriff was in charge. The boycott was lifted. The case was appealed to the Supreme Court that reversed the decision of the lower court on December 17 for failing to allow the case to be tried in a different county outside of the Black Patch area. A total of 137 affidavits were filed by the defendants in support of their motions, with no opposing affidavits from the state. The Supreme Court also cited a second ground for reversal which was exclusion of terrorist acts by the Night Rider organization. Three years later on December 5, 1911, in a Nashville court, the judge acquitted the pair. Sory was never convicted.

April 21, 1908: A cropper who lived and worked on the farm of attorney William M. Daniel, Jr. in District Ten was awakened that night by shots being fired into the side of the house. He took it as a warning and moved immediately.

June 6-7, 1908: Rufus Hunter[161] born in 1865, who lived in the Henrietta community on the Oak Plains Road near the Cheatham County line and had been a magistrate and a member of the Montgomery County Court, for six years was killed by the Night Riders. Hunter, a prominent farmer in the community and a member of the Planter's Proactive Association had been threatened twice by the Night Riders for a time before his murder for circulating a petition asking for financial aid for his aunt Mrs. Nichols to rebuild her home after it was destroyed by the riders. Hunter was called out onto his porch after midnight by a group of men standing near the road. He tried to reason with the men, even inviting them in his house to talk since he had been ill with pneumonia. After mortally wounding Hunter, the men sprayed buckshot all over the exterior of the 1½ story house, breaking all the windows. Neither Hunter's wife or six children were harmed as they were in bed upstairs.

Sheriff Stanton rode out to the house and found that Hunter had been hit in the abdomen by only one bullet and that coming from a 32-caliber pistol. Hunter was able to tell the events leading

---

[161] One of the descendants of the Hunter family was named for Felix Ewing, "the Moses of the Association."

up to the attack but could not identify any of the riders. Staton was holding Hunter's hand when he died.

Amid all the upheaval of the Night Riders raids was a wonderfully significant event: Em graduated from the Female Academy on June 11, 1908. The announcement read:

> **The commencement exercises of the Clarksville Female Academy were held and attended by a large audience. The school has closed a successful season and the class of graduates is the largest in the history of the school.[162] Rev. C.D. Graves delivered a short address to the class and presented medals to those who received special marks in their studies. The following were the graduates: Misses Martha Ann Brandau, Natalie Clardy, Mary Irone Davie, Effie Louise Ely, Agnes Gertrude Elliott, Marguerite Hodgson, Karlene Hoy Rudolph, Hettie Smith, Emma Lena Turney, Mildred Emily Tyler, Annie Webb, Elva Nichols and Lizzie Louise Clark.**

Em was 24-years-old, married to Harold Mitchell and living out west. The *Nashville Banner* announced the graduates of the academy naming her as Emily Tyler; Tyler, not Mitchell. How she was able to complete her schooling in Clarksville is a mystery.

This photo was taken of Em when she was chosen to serve as a State Representative for the Richmond Confederate Reunion. She was termed, "Maid of Honor" for the Tennessee Division. (CV)

On Friday, June 13, Hunter's brother Edmund, also a member of the Association, had his barn burned to the ground. Rufus's two brothers William and Edmund, made it publically known they would find who shot their brother and bring them to justice.

This murder was denounced as one of the "most dastardly and unprovoked act that was ever committed in Montgomery County." On June 17, Gov. Patterson offered a $1,000 reward for the arrest and conviction of the person or persons who murdered Hunter. The application for the reward was made by Judge Tyler. The proclamation read:

> **Malcolm Patterson, Governor of the State of Tennessee to all who shall see these presents, Greeting,**
>
> **Whereas, it has been made known to me by Judge C.W. Tyler, Judge of the Criminal Court of Montgomery County and W.M. Brandon, Attorney General that on the night of June 6, 1908 in the 14th Civil District of Montgomery County, one Rufus Hunter was foully assassinated and, as these officials deem it necessary that a reward of $1000 dollars be offered for the arrest and conviction of the unknown parties who committed this deed.**
>
> **Now, therefore I, Malcolm R. Patterson, governor, as aforesaid, by virtue of the authority in me vested, do hereby offer a reward of one thousand ($1,000) dollars payable upon arrest and conviction to any person or persons who may apprehend the said murderers and deliver them to the Sheriff of Montgomery County in order that justice in that behalf may be had and executed.**
>
> **In testimony whereof, I have hereunto set my hand and caused the Great seal of the State to be affixed at Nashville, this 17th day of June 1908.**
> **By the Governor**
> **Malcolm R. Patterson**
> **Jno. W. Morton, Secretary of State**

Malcolm Rice Patterson (1861-1935),[163] was one of Tennessee's most controversial governors. He was given credit for quelling the Night Riders in the Reelfoot Lake uprising in 1908, but was accused of issuing pardons to political allies.

October 4, 1908, a stable on the farm of George Ford was burned along with two mules, a horse, wagon, 27 bushels of wheat, 30 barrels of corn and hay.

---

[162] With the opening of the new Clarksville High School in 1907, the numbers of students at the Female Academy would decrease yearly until its closure.

[163] Gov. Patterson would live for a brief time at Clarksville's Tip Top mansion.

On October 20, 1908, a highly respected lady in the community south of the Cumberland River who had seen her share of upheaval passed away. Mary Baxter Watkins died of a heart attack. This revered lady was remembered for the selfless aid she and her husband rendered to the cause of the Confederacy during the Civil War. Without a doubt, Judge Tyler would have attended the funeral for Mrs. Watkins who hid him from Federal soldiers.

In the Henrietta community the riders visited a sawmill where they cut logs in two, which had been sold to "hillbillies." This was the nickname given to the poorer farmers with small acreage of tobacco who could not afford to join the Association. The activities of this group led local writer Robert Penn Warren to write a fictitious book on the subject entitled, *Night Riders,* published in 1939.

On January 4, 1909, Judge Tyler went on record arguing that every Montgomery County Civil War veteran should receive a pension especially since the county had sent more of its sons to battle than any other in the state. After Tyler's statements, it was found during a census in February 1909, that of the 15 Confederate veterans and 5 widows of veterans in the Corbandale district, only 4 were receiving pensions.

Judge Tyler responded in a long report printed in the January 20, *Leaf* dispelling the article about the state of Montgomery County during the tobacco wars that was printed in the *Uncle Remus Magazine* published at Atlanta, Georgia. Most of which Tyler thought was "reckless" and he really resented the inference that Clarksville was like a military camp. He stated

> **That a sentinel is stationed at night on the court house tower is wholly devoid of truth. So the story that Night Riders have three times formed in the vicinity to attack the town is more fiction. No whipping or bodily injury of any kind has ever been inflicted on any individual in this county by Night Riders or other body of lawless men except by the band of which Vaughn (sic) Bennett was a member when he was killed in March 1908. These youths-for they were such-were out two or three nights in succession. They burned a wheat thresher and whipped two men, not brutally or severely. This was the extent of their depredations. No tobacco warehouse or factory has been burned in this county in the last five years and no barn or other building has been burned where there was reasonable ground for supposing the fire was the work of Night Riders. Some depredations have been committed in the destruction of plant beds and in one instance the pulling up of plants after they had been set out on the field.**

Tyler then explained the events and truth behind each of the recent shootings and whether or not they were related to Night Rider's activities.

On February 9, Judge Tyler went head-to-head with his own lawyer brother John Duke Tyler over an order he issued to the sheriff which stated that no one be allowed to see James Davis or any of the other prisoners confined on a murder charge except on a written order from the court. Duke Tyler and F. Grundy Gilbert were representing Davis. Judge Tyler stated that he had instructed Sheriff Staton not to permit visitors to see the prisoners without a written order from the court. A writ of mandamus was filed against Sheriff Staton for Davis' lawyers to be allowed to see him without permission from Judge Tyler and the Criminal Court. Judge Josiah W. Stout ruled in favor of the attorneys and Judge Tyler appealed the decision.

On February 27, Em Mitchell, who had been visiting her father for several weeks, planned to leave to return home to Butte, Montana but her departure was delayed due to Armistead being ill.

It was reported in the March 8, issue of the *Nashville Banner* that Mrs. Eliza Knott had passed away. Mrs. Knott had taken over as principal at Hickory Wild after her father left that position. Her obituary was quite complimentary of the lady who seemed to have continued the high standards of the academy so instilled by John Duke Tyler.

THE DEATH RECORD.

Mrs. Eliza T. Knott.

Special to the Banner.

Adams, Tenn., March 8.—Mrs. Eliza Tate Knott, one of the most cultured women of Middle Tennessee, died Saturday at the home of her daughter, Mrs. M. B. Webb, of Hampton Station, Montgomery County. Mrs. Knott was born and reared near old Tate's Station, and early in life developed a taste for books. Left a widow in her twenties with two little girls, she turned her attention to teaching, and was for years principal of Hickory Wild Academy, a flourishing school near the Tennessee and Kentucky line, which was liberally patronized by both states.

She was a fluent writer of both prose and poetry, and also wrote several popular plays.

She was 84 years of age and a consistent member of the Christian Church. A daughter and several grand children survive her. The remains were interred in Merrivelle Cemetey.

Also that year, Judge Tyler impressed upon local merchants that failure to comply with the "Cigarette Law" which included selling, offering to sell, keeping in stock or giving away cigarettes or paper to be used to make cigarettes, would result in a fine of $50.

On June 24, 1909, Marcellus Rhinehart,[164] James Davis, Will and Jesse Nicholson went on trial in Tyler's court for Hunter's murder. Labeled as "one of the most important trials in the history of Montgomery County," Judge Tyler issued orders early in the trial to admit no one to the court room except by special permission after all the seats had been filled and he had a guard stationed at the door.

Rhinehart raised crops on the nearby Wall farm. The men with Rhinehart testified they had been forced to ride with him that night after being threatened with death if they refused. Rhinehart, the only one convicted, was sentenced to be to be hanged August 25, 1910 in Nashville. At the reading of his sentence Rhinehart showed, "not the slightest trace of emotion or concern." The other men were acquitted.

RHINEHART FOUND GUILTY

CLARKSVILLE NIGHT RIDER CONVICTED OF MURDER IN THE FIRST DEGREE.

Special to The Herald.

NASHVILLE, Tenn., July 17.—Marcellus Rhinehart was convicted in the criminal court of Montgomery County at Clarksville this morning of murder in the first degree with mitigating circumstances. He was one of the three defendants charged with the murder of Rufe Hunter, killed by night riders some months ago. The other two defendants were Jeff Nicholson and James Davis, who were both acquitted. The trial has lasted 21 days.

From the *Leaf Chronicle.*

One humorous sidelight of this trial that took place during the heat of July: Judge Tyler had an electric fan placed behind two of the defendants, because, as it was reported, "This had materially relieved Lem Davis and James Davis, both of whom are fleshy men and suffered much from the heat before the fan was installed."

[164] In the January 30, 1905 issue of the *Leaf Chronicle*, it was stated that Rhinehart had recanted his break (with the Association) and was restored (under the protection of the Association) at a meeting held that day. The others mentioned included G.N. Gentry (restored) and new member A.G. Warfield. Obviously Rhinehart must have dropped out of the Association at some point. Farmers on either side of the issue switched allegiances during the era of terror.

Chapter Twenty-One: Dealing with Personal Attacks

Judge Tyler spoke in favor of the American Snuff Company locating in Clarksville on July 12, 1909. He, Clarksville mayor M.C. Northington and Chamber of Commerce president M.A. Stratton all voiced their support of the company citing the importance tobacco had on the local economy. The building still exists today on the corner of Tenth and Commerce Streets.

On September 8, J.D. Tyler provided his half-mile mile race track in New Providence for some matinee races. Walter H. Drane's road horse, "Dan," driven by Bud Leigh of New Providence, a noted trainer, was pitted against "Robert, Jr." driven by Leigh F. Sickenberger. Dan won the heat in 1:15 minutes. The pair raced again but in the second heat, Sickenberger's horse was the winner. This racetrack would soon be the center of controversy.

Friday, October 2, saw the death of the Tyler/Johnson families' valued former slave and later servant. Aunt Roxy who was born in 1810 had been a slave of John Duke Tyler's but following emancipation during the war, Aunt Roxy chose to continue to live with Nannie Johnson as her cook after her marriage to Polk Grundy Johnson. She was described as "gentle, loyal and pious, the possessor of unusual intelligence and ability." Roxy was treated with all the consideration accorded a beloved member of the family. Age caused her to retire to St. Bethlehem where she lived her last days with her grandchildren as all of her six children had already passed before her.

J.D. Tyler offered his race track to be used again for races during the week of October 4-11, 1909 as part of the Tennessee Confederate Veterans Reunion to be held in Clarksville. It had been, according to the newspaper, "a number of years" since horse racing had been held in Montgomery County and Tyler's race track was reputed to be one of the best ½ mile tracks in the state." All the activities were sponsored by the Retail Merchants Association and Forbes Bivouac. J.D. would sometimes travel to Nashville to get "blooded" horses for the races.

Forbes Bivouac in front of the Confederate monument in Greenwood Cemetery, just yards away from Nannie's grave. Judge Tyler is seen at arrow. (CMCPL)

The Confederate reunion lasted from October 13-14. Downtown businesses decorated their fronts with bunting and flags. Some even continued the décor inside their stores. One lady from out-of-town sent a generous supply of smoking tobacco and her husband sent buckeyes as good luck favors for the old soldiers. The two gifts were individually wrapped in paper boxes tied with strings that represented the Confederate colors. Judge Tyler issued badges to the veterans from his office to be worn during the two-day reunion. Receptions, business meetings, barbeques and socials highlighted the two-day event aided by the United Daughters of the Confederacy, Forbes Bivouac, the United Confederate Veterans and the Sons of Confederate Veterans. State governor, Patterson attended the event held on Thursday as did state senator James B. Frazier.

From time to time there would appear an article in the newspaper that seemed odd: The Night Rider attacks were *not over* and yet the October 28 issue of the *Leaf Chronicle* wrote that "the phrase 'hard times' is no more heard." Peace and plenty seem to abound and if every man will adopt the Golden Rule, there can be no reason why the city of Clarksville shall not increase its population, business and contentment."

While all the news of the year focused on the Night Riders, there was still plenty of drama going around with Judge Tyler's family. In one instance it centered around Tyler's enforcement of the liquor law. One of the first to step to criticize was Robert B. Rossington, one of Mollie's in-laws. On December 6, 1909, he charged that during the racing event on October 1, 1909 at J.D. Tyler's that liquor was being sold and gambling was being done and that Tyler had ordered the sheriff who was there to basically turn a blind eye if he saw such occurring. Rossington asked under what authority or power the Criminal Court Judge could suspend the laws and tie the hands of the sheriff? He also charged that more than 50 barrels had been shipped to the track by the Gerst Brewing Company from Louisville, stored in J.D. Tyler's old smokehouse and that there was drunken men and boys on the race grounds. He also charged that Judge Tyler knew in advance there would be alcohol delivered there and that was why he issued the order to the sheriff. Tyler did not respond to the charge but M.M. Hussey and W.R. Shelton who were the managers of the Racing Association of the events, did. They stated,

> **We asked Judge Tyler for such an order in our case, and he gave us the order applying alone to games and amusements. He never gave us an order in any way affecting the sale of liquors or drinks of any kind and we never asked for such an order. As for the suppression of liquor selling, drunkenness or disorder of any kind, we would gladly have had the aid of any and all officers in putting it down. We never authorized the sale of beer or another liquor nor was any sold on the grounds with our sanction or knowledge. We make this statement in justice to Judge Tyler and ourselves. We will add that Judge Tyler, as we are informed, was not on the grounds at all during the three races.**

The order actually read: "C.J. Staton: I have appointed M.M. Hussey and W.R. Shelton to look after the games and amusements at the races and you will make no arrests unless authorized by them to do so. (signed) C.W. Tyler.

The disagreement between the judge and Rossington spilled over into the new year. On Wednesday, January 19, 1910, the grand jury was met in session with Tyler presiding. Sworn in on the jury for the term was: T.W. Walthal, foreman, J.G. Rollow, G.A. Crotzer, Horace Ritter, A.S. Hammond, Warner Wesley Riggins,[165] C.S. Daniel, R.W. Holt, T.A. McDaniel, R.H. Edmondson, C.C. Robinson, Bailey Johnson and J.H. Herman. Tyler charged the jurors with their duties in preparation for cases to begin to be heard the following Monday. One name that was specifically mentioned was that of Robert B. Rossington.

> **Gentlemen of the Grand Jury:**
>
> **In the discharge of your duty you will bear in mind the oath you have taken to present no one through malice or ill will, and to leave no one unpresented through fear, favor, or affection. You will bear in mind also that all your proceedings are to be secret. No grand juror is to divulge what takes place in the grand jury room nor is any one to disclose afterward how many members voted on any measure that may come before you.**
>
> **As a general rule you may assume that whatever is a violation of sound morals is also a violation of the criminal law, if done in such a way as to affect the public. A man who is simply guilty of profanity or the use of obscene language is not indictable if his offense be committed in private, but if it be committed in a public place and within the hearing of many others, he is guilty of a misdemeanor for he has committed an offense against the public. So, if one do willful injury to the person or property of another for each citizen is entitled to protection from violence of wrong doing at the hands of another. The general rule is that every man in this country may do as he pleases provided he does not at the same time inflict willful injury upon another.**
>
> **I need not charge you that murder, arson, larceny, offenses against females and many other like crimes are grave felonies and ought to be diligently enquired into wherever committed. But there are other offenses made so by statute which are just as much violations of the law and require as strict investigation at your hands.**
>
> **The practice of going around armed illegally is altogether too common in this community and is not confined by any means to the lower class of people. No one is allowed to carry**

[165] This was Marie Riggins' father.

any pistol, razor or other like weapon concealed about his person but one may carry an army pistol openly in the hand since this is a weapon used in warfare and the right of the citizen to go armed with such weapons cannot be abridged by the legislature.

The sale of intoxicating liquor of any kind is now prohibited by law in this state and it is the duty of the grand juries to see that this law is regularly enforced. The juries should be careful too, in this matter to be no respecter of persons but to enforce the law equally and impartially against high and low, black and white.

Then Tyler got personal...

Not long ago articles were published in this newspaper signed by R.B. Rossington of New Providence in which he charged that the statute against the sale of liquors had been violated upon certain occasions which he named. I instruct you, particularly to summon R.B. Rossington before you and to interrogate him not only as violations of the law in this particular that came under his personal knowledge but also as to what he has heard from other person and when you have thus obtained the names of all of his informants I request you to summon before you these persons also to the end that the charges brought by him may be investigated to the bottom and indictments for wherever the proof in your opinion justifies this course on your part.

I have heretofore instructed grand juries as to what constitutes a sale in this county and there have been several appeals from my ruling in this particular which are now pending in the Supreme Court of the State. In the meantime, I again instruct the jury that whenever one takes orders here for intoxicating liquor and receives pay for same and afterwards delivers the liquor to his customer he is guilty of a misdemeanor for the sale is complete in this county. And if he lends to his customer liquor of his own to be replace when the same amount is brought from another state that is a sale in this county and indictable.

There are many other statutory offenses to which I might call your attention but it does not deem it necessary to do so now. There are several persons in jail, charged with offenses and I ask you to look into their case without delay to the end that they may be either released from prison or tired and punished for their crimes.

You should look into the bonds of all public officers and enquire also into the conditions of the jail and poorhouse and other public buildings. You will be entitled at all times to the advice and assistance of the attorney general and can obtain additional instructions from the court whenever you ask for it. You may now retire in charge of the officer.

Attorney General Charles T. Cates phoned Judge Tyler in April to request that Tyler agree with commuting Rhinehart's death sentence to life in prison as Cates believed, "the ends of justice could be met without the execution of the prisoner." Tyler did so stating that, "the peace and quiet of the entire county could as well or better be served by a life imprisonment than by an execution." An application for communtation was sent to Gov. Patterson. It was granted.

Several important educational strides were made on May 16, when a joint high school board was organized in Judge Tyler's office. Tyler was elected chairman, Charles D. Runyon secretary/treasurer and Prof. Perry Lee Harned, principal of the joint high school. The other members of the board who attended this, the first meeting of the board were: James G. Rollow, county superintendent, Dr. Thomas Hartwell Marable, Mac R. Hanner and Samuel Walker Kelly.

On June 20, Gov. Patterson commuted Rhinehart's sentence to life in prison. He served 15 years and then was released on Christmas eve, 1924 after attorney Austin Peay commuted his sentence to time served on one condition: Rhinehart was ordered to stay out of Tennessee and that, if he violated that provision, the pardon would be revoked.

The Rhineharts seemed to be a bad lot all around. One of Rhinehart's brothers got into a fight a couple of years later and was shot and killed. Another brother was charged with assault with intent to kill in August of 1912 and Tyler put him on the chain gang until he heard from the state.

Ignoring Peay's instruction to stay out of Tennessee, in December 1930, Marcellus Rhinehart was arrested for bootlegging whiskey in Ashland City. Rhinehart of the Henrietta-Fredonia communities was the last of the infamous Night Riders when he died on June 7, 1984, in Marshfield, Missouri. His infamy in Tennessee as a rider was preceded by his time as a teenager in Kentucky when he rode with the silent brigade in several raids. His most daring escapade was the historic raid on Hopkinsville. He helped to commandeer the train that was used in the attack.

The year 1910 was an election year. A young lawyer, J.T. Cunningham, Jr. ran as a candidate for alderman from the First Ward. In 10 years, he would run against Judge Tyler.

Judge Tyler was once more sworn in as County and Criminal Judge of Montgomery County. It had been 37 years since he was appointed to fill out the unexpired term of Judge Thomas King in 1873.

In 1910, the courthouse clock "went on strike" failing to operate correctly causing disgruntled complaints. Immediately someone suggested by way of the newspapers that large sheet metal megaphones be added near the bell on the east and west sides of the tower so that when the clock struck, the bell could be heard all over the county. He stated the megaphones could be made of galvanized sheet iron and would not cost much." The man who signed his name only as "A.O." even gave the names of two men who could make them.[166]

Samuel L. Smith,[167] principal at Clarksville High School needed Judge Tyler's permission to try an experiment, a most unusual one. Smith was anxious to replicate a trial already conducted in Texas, whereby dynamite was used instead of simple plowing to produce higher crop yields. Smith needed some acerage to test the Texas scientist's theory. Having considered the idea, Tyler gave Smith permision to use an old abandoned broomsage field that once served as a baseball lot. On December 12, holes were dug, the sticks of dynamite were inserted in the ground and ignited. The explosion shook the ground, pulveruized the broomsage and blew a tree high up into the air. A corn crop was planted in the spring and in November the results were in: the yield of the planted corn from the dynamited field was four times the average in the county. The experiment was importaant to Smith because he wanted to encourage diversified farming instead of farmers depending on a single crop (tobacco), upon which they risked their whole livliehood. The farmers were not buying the idea as dynamiting fields was a tactic all to familiar with everyone as one used by the Night Riders. It all just left a bad taste in their mouths. It wasn't until banker C.W. "Bill" Bailey came up with the four pillars of income years later that diversification in farming took hold.

Tyler issued an order in the last of January 1911 for the sheriff to arrest persons using the courthouse without permit or authority for dances. The judge also had new locks put on the doors and let it be known that anyone forcing or tampering with the locks would be prosecuted.

Dr. David Amoss was tried in court from March 6-16, in Hopkinsville, Kentucky and acquitted on a technicality. He left the state immediately with his son to New York City. Afterward, the tobacco growers received higher prices for their crops. The U.S. Supreme Court ruled in *United States v. American Tobacco Co.* (1911) that the Duke trust, ATC, was a monopoly and was in violation of the Sherman Anti-Trust Act of 1890. The ATC was ordered to dismantle.

THE PLANTERS' PROTECTIVE ASSOCIATION
OF KENTUCKY AND TENNESSEE

G. B. BINGHAM

Clarksville, Tenn

1911 letterhead for the Association showing D.C. McGregor, treasurer and John Scales, auditor, both of Clarksville as part of the Planters' Protective Association. Courtesy Timothy R. Henson.

On the left: John Scales of Clarksville. He was a long-term member of the Association. Courtesy Timothy R. Henson. On the right: Dr. David Amos, country doctor from Caldwell Co., Kentucky and organizer of the Night Riders; died in 1915.

166 This was Alvie Oscar Harness, a local carpenter.

167 Smith (1875-?) was also the architect involved in school design for Rosenwald Schools.

In 1911, Charles Tyler released his book, *The Scout* and several short stories that were published in the *Southern Magazine*. His book honored the young Tennessee war martyr, Sam Davis. Tyler dedicated the book:

To My Dear Daughter,
Mrs. Harold G. Mitchell of Montana,
This Book is Affectionately Inscribed.
May She Teach Her Little Boy
Ever to Revere the
Memory of the Brave and True Men
Who Fought, and Died for Dixie

In recent years, U.S. Army Ret. Lt. Col. Allen West stated, "History is not there for you to like or dislike; it's there for you to learn from and if it offends you, even better, because then you are less likely to repeat it. It's not yours to erase; it belongs to all of us." Tyler wrote the following in the preface of his book not as a learned college professor who after 150 years passed came up with their own theories on the war or one with a possible political agenda but, as a man who personally witnessed and participated in the events of the war for 4 years, whose family lost everyone they owned.

> **I have often thought if some skillful writer would weave into story, a few of the many stirring incidents of our great Civil War, it would not only prove interesting reading to those of the present day, but would go far forward enlightening them as to the real issue in the contest.**
>
> **Why did the South go to war?**
>
> **Certainly not to preserve the institution of slavery. There was not an intelligent man in the South-certainly not in the border slave states who did not know that slavery was far safer in a union pledged to its protection than it could possibly be in a separate republic, with a hostile Northern government at our doors.**
>
> **Let us glance at the situation as it was then.**
>
> **Mr. Lincoln in his inaugural address had declared that, while he opposed its extension into the territories, he had neither the right nor the desire to interfere with slavery as it existed in the Southern States. The Congress at Washington not long afterward unanimously adopted a resolution to the same effect. This, indeed, was the well-understood attitude of the victorious Republican party on the slavery question. They would not disturb slavery in the states, but they would oppose its extension into the territories.**
>
> **For this reason, and still cherishing sincere attachment for the union, the people of Tennessee, when the question of separation or union was submitted to a popular vote in 1861, by an overwhelming majority determined to remain in the union. Virginia and other important Southern states reached the same conclusion. South Carolina and a few of the cotton states resolved to withdraw and establish an independent government, though in several of these was a strong sentiment that oppose such action.**
>
> **Each of these Southern states, mind you, in gravely weighing and deciding the question, had proceeded upon the idea that every enlightened people on the earth had the right to determine for themselves what form of government they would see fit to live under. Nearly all the influential men and newspapers at the North agreed with them in this opinion and counseled moderation and forbearance. *The New York Herald*, Horace Greeley in the *New York Tribune*, a monster mass meeting about the time of the inauguration of Lincoln, all urged prudence and patience and declared that any attempt at coercion would be madness.**
>
> **It was at the critical juncture that the new government at Washington organized a military and naval expedition with troops and battleships to ordered this to proceed to Charleston harbor for the relief of Ft. Sumter, General Scott, commander-in-chief of the envoy, protested against this and advised the peaceful evacuation of the fort. Stephen A. Douglas in the Unites States Senate joined in the protest and declared, 'This means war, and I am for peace.' Even Major Robert Anderson in command at Ft. Sumter wrote to the Adjutant General of the Unites States, 'I have no heart in this war which now you are about to begin.'**
>
> **For the Confederates in Charleston but one course was left. Before the arrival of the hostile force they threw shells into Ft. Sumter until Major Anderson and his little garrison of seventy men agreed to evacuate. Their surrender was not asked for. With all the honors of war they marched out and Sumter was evacuated as General Scott had advised. Not a man had been hurt on either side. But it was enough. Before Major Anderson had time to report**

at Washington, the President of the United States called for an army of seventy-five thousand men to invade the South and put down the rebellion. The result might have been foreseen and doubtless was foreseen.

Casting every consideration of self-interest to the winds, the people of the entire South—men, women, and children rose indignantly and hurled defiance in the teeth of the government at Washington. For four years the North waged a war of coercion and invasion and the South fought desperately in self-defense. By force of overwhelming numbers, we were conquered in the end; but I stand here today, fifty years after the fall of Sumter and declare it still my deliberate conviction that in the unequal contest the South was right and the North was wrong. No brave people on the earth have ever been submitted tamely to armed invasion of their country or ever will. No government on the earth ever had the right by fire and sword to compel millions of enlightened citizens to yield its allegiance against their will. The South was right and the North was wrong.

A WORD AS TO SLAVERY

Though coming down to us from remote ages and sanctioned at some period of its history by every civilized government on earth, slavery was always wrong. No human being ever did have the right to hold in bondage another human being. The story of the introduction of African slavery into North America is worth reading. On the shores of New York and New England slave ships were openly fitted out. The crews that manned them crossed thousands of miles of water and swooping down like cruel birds of prey upon poor terrified human creatures in far-off lands, bore them home in captivity. These kidnappers went and came from the shores of New York and New England. There was never a Southern ship or Southern man among them. True, when they came to sell their black brethren into slavery they found their best customers in the warmer country below them, but the worst that can be said of the South in this connection is that it was an accessory after the fact. Certainly it was a change for the better with the poor African when he passed from the Yankee pirate to the Southern planter.

For more than a hundred years this inhumane, but gainful traffic was openly carried on, nor did it cease till the African slave trade was abolished by act of Congress in 1808 under the administration of Thomas Jefferson, a Southern president. The conscience of the world was not being awakened against slavery. One by one the European states emancipated the slaves in their colonies. The first to act was Great Britain, which adopted a system of gradual emancipation, paying one hundred million dollars to the slave owners and making liberal provision for the slaves from the national treasury. Other European countries followed the example until all the slaves under their control were peacefully emancipated. The last to act was Holland in 1860.

Next year came the Civil War in America. Everyone realized that the slavery problem was one to be peacefully solved here as elsewhere. Mr. Lincoln, as said, declared he had no desire and no power to disturb it where it already existed. The Congress at Washington the day after the battle of Manassas assured the world the war was not being waged for the abolition of slavery. There was danger of foreign intervention. The world was looking anxiously on. To free millions of slaves as a war measure would be to invite horrors at which civilization might stand aghast. Therefore, the President and Federal Congress gave the world their solemn assurance that this should not be done. Two years rolled by; danger of intervention passed; the battling South held her own. Then the thing the President and Congress had solemnly declared they would not do, they proceeded to do. By proclamation the slaves were freed on all the Southern plantations. At one blow the South was robbed of half her wealth, and the arms of all her soldiers in the field were unnerved by dreadful apprehension for the fate of their loved ones at home.

The flag of the South went down in defeat. Then came the rule of the unspeakable carpetbagger. All the intelligent and respectable citizens at the South were disenfranchised for the grave crime of having defended their own firesides. Millions of ignorant Negroes were left without aid in the midst of the utterly impoverished whites, whom they had been taught to regard as their worst enemies. What followed?

Nearly a half century has passed away. The carpetbagger is dead and rotten, but not forgotten. Together the whites and blacks of the South are working out their own salvation. The latter with few exceptions still dwell in the land into which the cruel new England slave dealers sold them. They till in freedom the soil which their ancestors tilled in bondage, thus bearing mute evidence to the fact that the white people of the South were not hard taskmasters in the days of slavery and have been their best and truest friends since. You

may hear their grateful voices now praising God from hundreds of churches in the Southland. In every locality you will find schoolhouses for the education of their children, maintained by taxes voluntarily levied by Southern people upon themselves. Let any honest man look back across the centuries and say whether the North or the South has been the truest friend to the poor Negro since his forefathers in happy ignorance roamed the wilds of Africa.

Do you say I am an unreconstructed rebel? No, indeed, no indeed. I would have our children and our children's children know that we waged no unworthy combat in the brave days of old. I would have them down to remotest posterity revere the memories of the brave and the true men who fought and died for Dixie, and who sleep now in unmarked graves all over the Southland. This done, I look to the future. The North and South are not as England and Ireland, with independent histories running back into remote ages. Together our ancestors fought the War for Independence. Together they met the problems that confronted them in the after years. We have a common glorious past, and I trust we have a common glorious future. We are living in the greatest and most enlightened country that the ages have seen. Looking forward, I can see no cloud on the horizon that shall arise to darken our future. May our descendants of the North, the South, the East and the West move forward hereafter a common brotherhood—

Till the sun grows old,
And the stars are cold,
And the leaves of the judgment book unfold.

He also wrote in an article for the *Confederate Veteran* entitled, "Patriotism in a Tennessee County,"

A land that could forget its own sons who once took up arms and sacrificed their lives in response to its call is a land whose people must be intrinsically base; and if the cause was lost for which these sons contended, the failure to cherish their memories becomes doubly dishonorable, for then their good name, having no favoring government to uphold it must rest alone in the keeping of the men who shared their convictions and suffered defeat with them. Upon these it devolves as a sacred duty to defend the 'lost cause' against traducers to uphold the motives of their fallen comrades, and to transmit to posterity, as worthy of emulation, the story of their virtue, their courage and their sacrifices.

One must remember that while it is very easy for us to pronounce his statements as too strong, Charles Tyler was an eyewitness to the Civil War and saw the devastation it caused first hand. Tyler saw this when his own father's wealth was lost when his slaves were liberated.

One gets the idea from just reading the preface, that Charles was pouring out feelings on the war, suppressed for years and was using this book as sort of a catharsis. He recalled in June 1861, Montgomery County overwhelmingly voted 2,632 to 32 to join the Confederate States of America; within the city the vote was 561 to 1 to join. According to Tyler, so many men from Montgomery County volunteered to serve that the number, "exceeded the entire white population subject to military duty." Tennessee as a whole was reluctant to remove itself from the Union, as it was the last state to secede in 1861 and the first to rejoin the Union in 1866.

Tyler did not contain his writings to war matters alone but also wrote engaging short stories, which appeared in the *Southern Monthly Magazine*. Certainly these stories were less intense than the previous ones. On writing books, the judge stated, "If the public liked to read as well as I like to write, I would be a successful author." Tyler credited a former student of his father with the first account he found of the actual arrest and hanging of Davis. J.B. Killebrew, previously the Commissioner of Agriculture and Mines for Tennessee, was considered by Tyler to be a "painstaking and accurate writer."

Judge Tyler left on July 24, for a trip to Los Angeles to visit Em. The visit was to last until the latter part of August. Was this a pleasure trip or was there something more significant to him meeting her in Los Angeles instead of her home in Montana? Perhaps trouble was brewing in the Mitchells' marriage as this was the judge's seventh trip he had made out west.

The annual Tristate Fair ran from September 26-30, in Memphis and exhibits were brought in from all over the state. Montgomery County was well represented at the event and its display at the fair garnered first prize for the best arranged and decorated exhibit in the agricultural department and the second place prize for the best tobacco exhibit from a single county. Roy Holman and C.E. Frey were credited with setting up the exhibits.

Montgomery County exhibit from author's collection.

Beulah Rossington, Billy's widowed sister came for a visit in early October. Her husband had passed away earlier in 1908. She stayed with her brother one week and then visited with Charles the next week. Beulah was living in Chattanooga when she passed away on September 10, 1915.

The court docket was full two days before Thanksgiving 1911. Two hundred cases covering all degrees of law violations were presented to Judge Tyler. This included 29 already in jail, 3 murder cases, 2 rapes cases, several for larceny and numerous ones considered to be misdemeanors. The majority of the cases of course, had to be delayed until after the holidays.

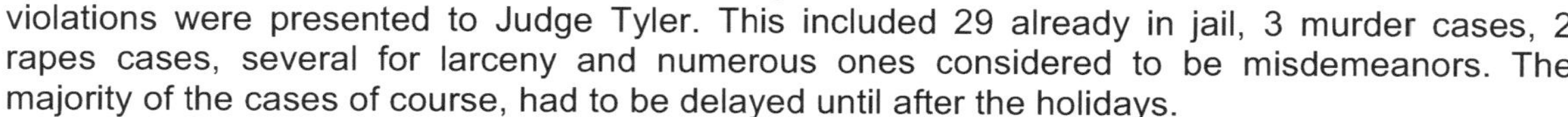

The judge was beside himself with astonishment on December 19. After pronouncing Malcom Mimms guilty of arson and burglary and sentencing him to eleven months and twenty-nine days in the workhouse as prescribed by law, the jury refused to accept the verdict. Judge Tyler sent the jury back to the hotel to reconsider and the next morning their decision had not changed. Tyler gave them a scathing talk stating, "In my experience of nearly 40 years as judge I have never witnessed such action on the part of a jury. I speak without malice when I say I have never had such an indignity heaped upon me before as this jury has done." His talk went on for minutes charging the jury with defiance of the law. The newspaper reported wrote that, "In the delivery of this talk to the jury, Judge Tyler seemed to be very much affected but displayed no anger." Tyler declared a mistrial and on December 6, 1912, Mimms, who had been in jail for 14 months was sentenced to two years at the Boys' Reformatory.

Emmie Tyler moved out of her brother's house sometime in 1912 and temporarily moved in with her sister next door. Something major happened between brother and sister for her to leave the family home she occupied for decades. It seems to have been an argument over money matters and the home and, as seen later, the situation escalated into a lawsuit filed by Emmie. She then took a room at the Farris Apartments on Main Street that faces the rear of Trinity Church on Franklin. For the last twelve years of her life, Emmie lived alone in this apartment, never returning to the home on Greenwood. One can just see her walking out the front door of the apartments headed across the street to her beloved church.

On the left: The Farris Apartments. Below: The Johnson family plot at Greenwood. Photo by author.

On March 24, 1912, Nannie Tyler Johnson passed away and was buried in front of her husband, Polk Grundy and near their three children at Greenwood in Section 5. These, along with Polk's children by his first wife, Emma Robb are all buried in the Johnson family plot that faces the Tyler plot in the cemetery. A cemetery lane separates these two sections. On her gravestone is written, "God shall wipe away the tears from their eyes.[168]

[168] The inscription on Nannie Johnson's tombstone in Greenwood is entirely unreadable due to a large limb damaging it during a severe rainstorm.

Seven year's prior, Nannie Johnson prepared for the inevitable by writing her will dated June 9, 1905:

This is my will written in my own hand. I wish my brother C.W. Tyler to be paid back for all he has expended for me; all else I am possessed of I leave to my sister Emmie Tyler.
June 9, 1905
(Signed) *Nannie T. Johnson*
(Holographic will proven by three witnesses)
Probated and recorded March 28, 1912
C.B. Bailey, Clerk
By S.W. Kelly, Deputy Clerk

As Clarksville grew, so did the need for more police protection. In 1912 the department had seven officers on duty.

The 1912 police department in front of the jail in the Public Square. From left to right: unknown, Alex Small, John H. Allsbrook, Chief J. E. Robinson, Dick Perkins, J. O. Ellarson, J. M. Fowlkes. The building was erected in 1841 as a bank. Dubbed by the newspaper as an old "hoarding place for gold and a bastille for criminals." (MB).

In late March the following report was given by the jail committee: 28 prisoners were in the jail, 23 were on the chain gang currently engaged in quarrying and crushing stone near Ringgold for the Clarksville and Hopkinsville Pike under the supervision of Forest Suitor; the health of the convicts and prisoners were good and the jail was in a sanitary condition.

After unusually heavy rains on April 12, bridges in town gave way as waters tore at their supports. The headline read, "Torrents of Rain Wreck the Bridges and Does Great Damage. Flood Carries Away Structures on West Fork Creek at Peacher Mills and McCauley's Mill, Bridges Across Little West Fork at Ringgold and Gowan's Imperiled." The rain gauge at Southwestern Presbyterian University recorded a fall of 3.06 inches for 24 hours. The Cumberland's waters carried away millions of feet of timber. The City Ferry and Seven Mile Ferry shut down. Judge Tyler sent a crew from town to operate the Edmondson and Seven Mile ferries and Squire Joe Jarrell had the Hickory Point Ferry brought to operate on the Red River to connect New Providence with the city for emergency purposes only. The fast-rising waters took as its victims two men who drowned at the New Providence bridge.

On June 11, Emmie advertised in the newspaper that she was selling household items. The ad read:

FOR SALE

Miss Emmie Tyler has some furniture and other articles which she will dispose of at low rate. She can be seen at the residence of the late Mrs. Nannie T. Johnson from 4 to 6 p.m. every day except Sunday.

On August 19, Judge Tyler convened his Criminal Court addressing two issues that had been reported to him: acts committed violating election and liquor laws. It had been reported that people had been crowding around the ballot boxes and looking over their returns in the last election and that men were openly violating the liquor law in other cities in Tennessee. The judge stated that he would enforce all laws and it mattered not what was done in other places, he would see the law enforced in Clarksville. He reported that in just one day on August 7, 1912, he had issued 21 warrants for the arrest of persons charged with the illegal sale of alcohol. He charged the grand jury to investigate any cases of liquor law violations. "Law is law and whether you like it or not, you know no officer can afford to wink at its violation as it would result in violation of other laws with impunity," he said. "I charge you gentlemen to thoroughly examine the witnesses (to illegal drinking), and make no distinction."

Hickory Wild lost its longest resident on August 20. William Tyler, the grandson of Aunt Roxy, had been born in 1837 and died on the farm, working it for its various owners his entire life. His obituary stated that his grandmother had come from Virginia with Judge Tyler's grandfather in 1912. William's sister had died just a short time previously in Nashville. His death was announced in the newspaper where William was described as "a faithful, upright and honest man, respected by all who knew him." He was lovingly buried at the Hickory Wild cemetery alongside John Duke's family.

The City Council on November 6, passed on first reading an ordinance to purchase the empty lot next to the current police station on the Public Square on which to build the new city hall. F.L. Smith Sons Company won the bid for $11,750 to include the cost of the steel cages to be placed in the basement.

Sports and movie houses were to become part of what historians now call the period of "escapism." Negativism and the harsh realities of life spurred people's desire to forget their troubles, if not for just an afternoon at the ballpark, then a night at the movie theater. Not to be outdone, Clarksville businessmen were jumping on the bandwagon and excitedly investing in these new and popular forms of entertainment. One such example was the Lillian Theater described as "an ornament to Clarksville." Named after the owner, Joe Goldberg's daughter, it was the first theater on the southeast corner of First and Franklin Streets. Remembering the fire of 1878, in 1912, Goldberg had made every attempt to see that this building was as fireproof as possible by designing the main floor to be level with the street, including two large exits in different parts of the building and a lobby he claimed to be sufficient enough to allow a packed auditorium emptied in less than one minute if the need arose. All building materials were fire proof, including brick, asbestos, the concrete foundation, iron columns and glass panels. Clarksville's first "moving picture theater" welcomed its patrons with a great front arch of Italian marble and white tile brick at its entrance.

By 1913, it was said that "formerly kind-hearted people used to establish watering troughs along the country roads but now gasoline stations are needed much more." Yes, the new automobile was taking over the streets and the watering troughs were a thing of the past.

The watering trough near Clarksville High School remained there until the mid-1930s. It must have been a curiosity for people driving down Madison and Greenwood to see the old, obsolete trough still standing there as though any minute an old, tired team of horses might stop to refresh themselves. On one day in September 1935 the officers of the freshmen class were made to "fish" in the horse trough for 30 minutes as part of an initiation to remind freshmen that they were just "frosh." They then were jeered for not "catching anything."

Nannie Johnson's house for a time, served as a dormitory for the boys at Clarksville High School. The city paid $7500 for the house and property in 1913. It was a legal mess as there was an outstanding mortgage on the house and debts associated with the house had not been paid.

After all the fussing and complaining, Clarksville's street sprinkler was finally worth its cost of repairs. On March 17, 1913, the water sprinkler was so impressive that is was said that everyone stopped what they were doing to rush to see it and "almost started a riot."

A typical 1900 street water sprinkler. (Not from Clarksville).

Chapter Twenty-Two: The End of the Night Rider Era

In Montana, Em's husband, Harold was wealthy enough that in 1913, while visiting in Chicago and on their way to New Orleans he purchased two cars: A Pope-Hartford race car and a 1912 touring car. For the remainder of the trip, he drove the racer that could reach speeds up to 100 miles per hour and he let his chauffeur drive the touring car.

In the summer of 1913, Em, Harold and a few of Harold's in-laws travelled to China, Japan and the Philippines. (Em may have wanted to see where her cousin Cave had served during the Spanish-American War). While on the trip, Em and her niece, Mitchell Scanland, saved the life of a drowning man. Mitchell was the daughter of Marie Adele Mitchell Scanland, Em's sister-in-law.

While on board the *S.S. Manchuria* in Shanghai harbor, a bombardment was begun by Chinese government forces at Woosung forts occupied by rebels. The liner steamed out of danger but for some reason an American theatrical manager, Robert McGreer, dove into the sea and was about to drown when both women jumped in the water in and kept him afloat until they were rescued by men in a sampan.[169] His explanation for his distress was that he had "developed a cramp."

S.S. Manchuria

The *Butte Daily Post* ran the headline on September 2, 1913: "Butte Ladies Prove Themselves Heroines in Strange Adventure in Far Japan." The newspaper stated that both women were "accomplished swimmers." Judge Tyler had to be immensely proud of his daughter who, like her aunt Nannie, discounted danger to aid someone in need.

The question of why Judge Tyler was making repeated trips out west to visit his married daughter was finally answered when Em separated from Harold Mitchell stating that by doing so, she was simply seeking "peace." She and Harold had been named constantly in lawsuits over their interests in different mines and properties. At some point a divorce was filed. Em left the West with their son and came home to Clarksville to her father to the house on Greenwood Avenue; to the home where memories of a loving grandmother, mother, aunts and cousins filled the rooms and of an aunt still alive but not present. Em was the first in the line of Tylers to be divorced at a time when divorce was rare. She must have wondered how she would be accepted by the people she knew growing up but it seems that Em was happily incorporated back in the community and social circles of Clarksville.

Always civic-minded, Em picked up with her social functions and involved Armistead in them too. Judge Tyler filled the role of Armistead's father, a male role model every boy needs in his life. Two photos show Judge Tyler and his much-loved grandson, Armistead sitting together in a bright sun-filled room. In one photo Charles is seated in a Queen Anne chair with his right hand resting in an endearing

[169] A small, flat-bottomed boat.

manner on his grandson's back. Em was still married to her first husband when this photo was taken in 1913. Of the picture, Judge Tyler wrote, "I do not consider myself much for looks." But the *Confederate Veteran* replied that "the judge is better looking than the picture of him in the fine group."

On the Lillian Theater's opening day July 28, over 2,000 people attended. It was estimated that an additional 500 were turned away! The Lillian competed with the other theaters in Clarksville at that time which included the Majestic, the Capital, the Lyric[170] and the Elite.

Souvenir from the Lillian's opening day.

On December 12, Emmie released her book, *The Blind Child and the Star,* about "a poor family at Christmas time and the brave efforts of a little boy to keep from his younger sister the secret that Santa Claus is a myth and only comes to the homes of those who are able to buy gifts for their children. It was stated that the book was dedicated to the memory of her cousin Cave Johnson. The 25-cent booklet was described as "neatly bound and tied with a ribbon." Perhaps she was trying to show her brother she was capable of writing a book too or it could be a simple case of sibling competition. A newspaper reporter wrote his critique of the book stating,

> **As a Christmas story, it is far superior to the nonsensical rhymes and tales that are usually gotten out for children. The story is told in a simple and natural way and is well calculated to reach the heart both of grown people and children. The story is well planned and will be interesting reading to all young people and carried with it a beautiful lesson of living for others. The booklet is well printed, beautifully illustrated and neatly bound. It will make a beautiful Christmas present and a souvenir of worth as it comes from the pen and fertile mind of one of our best and most talented women.**

December 15, was the first time in Clarksville's history a movie was made in town. It featured the city's horse-drawn firefighting equipment dashing along Madison Street to the Public Square. In just one year, that fire equipment would be needed to put out another major fire.

The courthouse clock was problematic once again when in January of 1914, it went totally haywire striking unheard hours causing a newspaper reporter to call the clock "dumb." Later that year the hands failed to move and the reporter pronounced the clock "nutty again."

The jewelry store of A.J. Clark on Franklin Street may have seen an increase in sales of their watches to combat the failure of the clock to keep people informed of the correct time. Judge Tyler, in an interview with the newspaper, stated that he had been given the authority to purchase a new clock provided "he saw fit to do so." His response was that at the present time he believed the money could be better spent elsewhere in the county than on the clock.

The situation of the clock was this: because the locations of the mechanical parts of the clock were scattered throughout the courthouse, it was difficult to keep it in good working order. The master clock was located in Tyler's office, the storage batteries were in the basement and the works controlling the striking mechanism and main clock works were in the clock tower. Hurst Lyon, who was an employee of the Gas and Electric Company, said he could keep the clock working correctly if he had access to the courthouse whenever it malfunctioned, usually after closing hours. However, quite often he could not locate the janitor to get the keys to Tyler's office. The newspaper chimed in to state that the master clock needed to be moved out of Tyler's office.

The health report for January was released. Cases of tuberculosis: 4; smallpox: 4, scarlet fever: 4; measles: 1; whooping cough: 1. There were no cases of diphtheria (of special notice of Tyler) and no yellow fever or typhoid.

---

170 The Lyric Theater was across the street where stands the old Elder-Conroy building.

Emmie traveled to Houston, Texas in March 1914 and was the special guest of Mary F. Bryan, her half-aunt. During her stay, she was the recipient of many social invitations and was honored by Mr. and Mrs. J. Stuart Boyles with a motor trip to the San Jacinto Battleground Park.

Judge Tyler was among the participates at the funeral of the Honorable Horace H. Lurton, appointed Associate Justice of the United States Supreme Court in 1910. A respectful crowd lined Clarksville streets in the oppressive heat of July 15, to witness the funeral procession with individual hacks carrying each of the members of the Supreme Court to the Greenwood Cemetery. Tyler opened his home to Chief Justice Edward D. White while he was in town for the funeral. Tyler served as a pall bearer. Lurton was a native son and the brother of Charles' 1872 law partner.

Despite all of Goldberg's efforts to fire-proof his theater, his beautiful theater perished along with the opera house just 4 days after Christmas in 1914 at 6:30 p.m. The cause of the fire was determined to be an overheated furnace in the opera house. The flames crossed the street and ignited the Lillian Theater. Three days previous to the theater's destruction, the movie being shown was, "Playing with Fire," a drama!

On the left: The smoldering ruins of the Lillian. (MCM) On the right: Surveying the ruins of Elder's Opera House. (LC).

People were coming by the hundreds each week starting in July of 1914 to visit wells located on Joe D. Tyler's property for its "curative powers." Tyler refused to charge anyone for the use of the waters and there was talk of a possible health resort being built.

The same month on July 29 via the newspaper, Judge Tyler issued a notice that on August 10 the grand jury was going to meet to investigate all violations of the liquor law before or on the day of the upcoming August 6 election. He stated "I give you fair warning that I shall enforce it to the extent of my ability."

On February 18, 1915, Judge Tyler seated a special grand jury to investigate the recent Night Rider activities around the border of Stewart and Montgomery Counties. Doc Davidson, a suspect in the raids was arrested on the farm of Wyatt Rawlins with a bench warrant issued by Judge Tyler. Davidson and his gang had been threatening blacks and whites for days in Districts 9 and 21. Tyler determined to take on this case "as a warning to those who would disregard the majesty of the law." The following month on March 10, 1915 in Davidson County, the House approved a bill for the creation of a 10 member state rangers militia appointed from "as many sections of the state by the governor" to address "acts of violence that occur in any county of the state wherever the rights of persons are violated or jeopardized by organized forces." This bill reinforced the Night Rider Law. The rangers were appointed to ten-year terms. Judge Tyler suggested they receive $3 per per diem while seeing actual duty since it was quite likely they would have little to do. Alex C. Stafford was appointed as a ranger from Montgomery County.

Former Night Rider Milton Oliver in his tobacco patch guarded by a member of the Kentucky state militia. From the book, *Before Fort Campbell* by M. Jay Stottman, Lorie C. Stahlgren and A. Gwynn Henderson.

It was a benefit to raise money to send Confederate veterans to the much anticipated convention in Richmond, Virginia in June. Yearly these Southern veterans were passing away and each time a convention was held, it was an opportunity to re-connect with old comrades maybe for the last time. In March Judge Tyler appointed Mrs. H. Lupton and Em to prepare the entertainment for the fund-raising event. In mid-June, Stafford and his deputy brought three white men from Stewart County charged with night riding and placed them in the Montgomery County jail for "safe-keeping." This brought the number to six alleged riders in the jail.

The Lillian Theater was rebuilt and reopened in 1915. It was renamed the Roxy Theater in 1941 and four years later, it again burned, was remodeled and enlarged in the art deco style. A sleek exterior, featuring a new lighting called neon, beaconed movie-goers from miles around. Re-opened in 1947, the Roxy entertained Clarksvillians with first-run movies until 1980 Since that time it has been used as a dinner theater and a theater for stage productions.

Celebrations were in order for more good news. The tobacco wars ended when the Association disbanded in 1915. This occurred after tobacco prices rose following the breaking of the trust, earning growers a fair price for their tobacco! What was left behind was more than the charred remains of barns and the loss of tobacco but also resentment, bitterness and a general distrust among neighbors as some of the Night Rider attacks gave the group opportunity to carry out personal vendettas. The conflict became the largest military-style operation in the United States since the outbreak of the terrible Civil War.[171]

Stories of the dreaded Night Riders were told around Clarksville for years. Charles Tyler had seen the workings of the K.K.K. and the Night Riders but his belief in the court system held true. Looking back over this dark period in Clarksville's past, banker C.W. Bailey in his address to the Rotary Club on September 21,1955 said this,

> **Clarksville was under voluntary guard for a number of months. This was effective because there were only four main roads leading into the city and only one of them does not cross a river. No large group could enter undetected. Some damage was done in other tobacco centers which were not so well-protected.**

Judge Tyler was 67-years-old when the Night Rider era began and 78 at its end. He had gotten the county through yet another disturbing and uncertain period and should be remembered for his leadership and decisiveness.

The charges against Tyler of failure to enforce the law ran off and on for years. In 1915, A.R. Gholson charged the same after understanding the judge to say during the mass meeting on June 30, that he disagreed with the State Supreme Court holding that a man could be taxed for selling alcohol *and* also be punished with jail time. Tyler thought this unfair *and* that he stated he would not comply. Gholson stated, "If Judge Tyler could not conscientiously enforce the law as it is now upon the statute books, he ought to have self-respect enough to resign and that he ought not to bring this stain upon his good name near the close of his career after an honorable service of 40 years upon the bench." Was the judge getting soft? Was he thinking he was above the law or was he simply getting too old for the job? These questions may well have had an impact on Clarksville voters in the upcoming election.

Em Mitchell, in early August sold her bungalow on Greenwood to George Fort for $4500. to use as a home. Tyler had transferred the deed of the cottage to her earlier. This was a small house situated to the right of the Tyler's former house and is no longer standing.[172]

Dr. Duke Tyler was inaugurated as mayor of Guthrie, Kentucky on January 3, 1916. This occurred at the meeting of the city board. Just two years' prior, Dr. Tyler had nearly succumbed to a severe case of pneumonia.

Reports of people in mid-January driving above the speed limit set by Judge Tyler as "no faster than a walk" over the Red River Bridge to New Providence spurred the judge to appoint Hershel Walker as a special officer to arrest anyone who violated the order. Additionally, they would be fined by Walker who assured the judge he would enforce the law to the letter.

---

[171] Today, a yearly musical in Adams, Tennessee tells the story of the era of the Night Riders. David Alford, who wrote "Spirit, The Authentic Story of the Bell Witch of Tennessee," He wrote, composed and directed, "Smoke A Ballad of the Night Riders" as well. Performances are held at the Bell School in Adams.

[172] Adolph Hach and his wife would, in the future, use it for a short while as a residence. Phila sold baked goods from this cottage.

Once again the courthouse was utilized as a venue for a major social event. This time on February 26, the famous Smith's Saxophone Trio of Versailles, Kentucky entertained a large crowd who danced the night away on the black and white marble tiles on the main floor of the building.

Tyler's grandson aired his opinions via the local newspaper in a letter to the editor of the *Leaf Chronicle* printed on March 2. The Vitagraph silent film, "My Lady's Slipper" had just shown at the Lillian Theater on February 2. Armistead wrote the following, "Mr. *Leaf Chronicle* I wish you would put this poetry in your paper without charge. It is about Charley Chapman (sic. Charlie Chaplin, the newspaper printed his name incorrectly), and the picture show. This is the poetry:

Good morning Mr. Chapman, you think you are so swell;
You claim to set the fashion, but looks like you're just from___-
There is one thing you are doing that makes the people laugh.
And that is throwing rotten eggs at Wilson and at Taft.
These men are trying to get us in a fight,
And so you give them rotten eggs and Charley you're right.
Armistead H. Mitchell

The editor's reply was "Master Armistead is but nine years old but already seems able to effectively judge political situations. A chip off the old block, he is."

It was unbelievable- on Sunday night, November 19, 1916 the main building of the high school was destroyed at an estimated loss of $40,000. Ironically, the new annex was just completed, doubling the size of the first building due to increased growth. All classes were moved into the new building. To this day, people remark that they were proud to have attended classes in the "old CHS."

Clarksville High School after the fire. The fence is from the Franklin Street courthouse lawn. The trolley tracks are also seen. (MCA)

Another strange weather-related phenomenon was recorded in Clarksville on the night of December 21, when an unusually strong electrical storm occurred at 6 p.m. Citizens were terrified by the tremendous thunderclaps and the startling scenes of ignited gases blowing manhole covers from the streets. Lightning bolts were seen rolling down the streets, striking the post office and several houses. If this was not enough to unsettle nerves, snow, sleet and rain also came down in cascades. Workers at the post office, the former customs house, returned to work and found all the metallic objects in the building were magnetized.

Tyler had a personal interest in the decision of the county to sell his sister's former home, then being used as a boys' dormitory for Clarksville High School. On April 2, 1917 Tyler authorized the sale of the property to Adolph Hach for $10,000.[173] Tyler stated, "It is not the intention of the county to maintain another boys' dormitory. The boys attending the high school can come into town horseback, in buggies, or in other vehicles. Girls cannot therefore a girls' dormitory will continue to be maintained by the county." The money collected from Hach was used exclusively to improve country schools. Other matters before Tyler included:

-increasing the price of coffins for black paupers from $5 to $7.
-raising the cost of board for prisoners in the county jail from 40 to 60 cents per day.
-the rate of taxation was fixed the same as the previous year.
-a request from the United Daughters of the Confederacy was granted for $25 for markers to be placed at the graves of unknown Confederates.
-C.K. Williams was elected a notary republic.
-the new highway committee members were announced: G.A. Crotzer, H.E. Dowlen, John Long and Baxter Watkins.
-a request to have the court decide if the wagon tax should be repealed was thrown out by Tyler.

---

[173] Hach, Jr. served as a pall bearer when Armistead passed away in 1942.

On April 6, the country entered the terrible conflict of World War I. Beginning on June 1, Registration Day, Clarksville boys signed up to fight. On that single day alone, 2,515 registered in Montgomery County. Clarksville's youth were once again going off to war to fight again on foreign soil. There were shortages everywhere and fuel was rationed. Some citizens today still have the rations card books so important during the war years. Victory gardens sprung up all over Clarksville and life revolved around the war effort.

With the war raging in Europe a large crowd gathered in Tyler's courtroom the morning of April 14, to hear the matter of food shortages nationwide and abroad discussed. His courtroom was full with anxious listeners wanting to learn how the county planned to solve the shortage. Merchants and farmers alike were present at the meeting in which Tyler was the first to speak. He admonished everyone: men, women and children to "do his bit" by growing food in gardens and stated he, himself would do the same. It was necessary he said to "not only feed the people at home but to feed the armies fighting in Europe." The matter was settled nationally when a central organization was formed to arrange meetings across the country to encourage the growing of gardens to help in the war effort.

April continued to be filled with business under Tyler's authority. The judge pushed for new roads on the south side of the river citing the terrible conditions of present roads. He stated,

> **The people of the Southside must get to the river the best they can and when they get there they must pay tolls to cross the bridge, and then must pay their taxes just as they do now. How anybody can consider this fair I fail to see. In my opinion they are entitled to first class roads to the Cumberland River and then to free passage across the river, they and their children after them. Our present ferries should be abandoned as soon as possible. In six months Lock C will be completed and we will have deep water the year-round. Then if we wish we can have steam ferries large enough to accommodate the travel and with (river) banks as convenient for us as any pike in the country or any street in Clarksville. I do not say this is the plan we should adopt. I say it is one of the plans we should consider.**

He then asked W.J. Manning to provide an estimate of the cost of such a plan. When given the costs of about $30,000. Tyler suggested caution with the war in Europe continuing that the county should not incur a debt it cannot meet. So the south of the river folks had their hopes put on hold once again.

April also came with some unhappy tidings: Joe Duke Tyler's house in New Providence was totally destroyed in a fire on April 21, 1917 originating from sparks from the chimney igniting the roof. His stable and a neighbor's home caught fire but luckily was extinguished before they were lost. As for the house and its contents; he had partial insurance to cover the cost.

The first meeting to organize a Clarksville and Montgomery County Chapter of the American Red Cross on May 1. Of course the names of Judge Tyler and his daughter Em Tyler Mitchell were offered as members. The following Friday and Saturday a membership campaign was started. Stations to sign up were scattered throughout the city and each person signing up was asked to pay $1 for their membership fee. There were five women's teams and four men's team organized to collect the funds. Em worked May 11-12 at the Mammoth Theater on Franklin Street to signup members and collect dues. Meetings and campaigns to raise money continued until the war's end.

Oh, the poor prisoners on the chain gang. Starting June 1, Judge Tyler ordered their services to pulverize limestone at the Red River Quarry as a source of revenue for the county. He estimated the costs would be much cheaper than as it had been bringing the stones in from Bowling Green. The contract between Tyler and the Red River Iron Works showed that the county agreed to furnish the furnace with from1,000 to 1,500 tons of limestone per month at a rate of about 70 cents per ton. In exchange, the furnace would give the county the use of its rock quarry at Red River and also the use of its big crusher. The crushed limestone was then available to farmers for their use. The stone would also be spread on streets and used in making concrete culverts. It was estimated to save at least $2,000 per year to the county.

The sheriff approved the $3.00 dental bill charged for extracting a prisoner's tooth but a member of the County Court wasn't so satisfied and asked that the bill be reduced to just one dollar. There were other ways to save the city the expense of prisoner tooth extractions that included: hiring a blacksmith to do the job for 50 cents or even better, tie a string to the tooth, tie the other end to the iron cage door and toss the prisoner out the window which would probably cost no more than 15 cents!

An unexpected event happened on July 31, when, during an afternoon electrical storm, a bolt of lightning struck the Confederate monument in Greenwood Cemetery. The strike was so loud that everyone in the area knew something in the cemetery was hit, but was it a tree or something else? Immediately following the storm Herbert Roake, the grounds keeper, walked over to investigate and immediately he discovered the storm's victim. What he found were a series of streaks on each of the four sides of the granite shaft extending from top to bottom. The bottom corner of the bronze figure at the top of the monument had received the hit but surprisingly, the statue itself was not damaged. It was noted however, that some of the lead used in the joints of the monument was melted by the electrical impulse traveling down to the ground. As Greenwood Cemetery did not own the monument, the Daughters of the Confederacy volunteered to take responsibility for the repairs to the monument that meant so much to them. Today no evidence of the lightning strike can be seen on the shaft causing this event to be totally forgotten.

In order to raise money for the Red Cross, a garden party was held on August 3, at Judge Tyler's home. Adults and children alike participated in the event declared a success.

That same year Emmie completed a manuscript, *A History of Trinity Parish*. She wrote about Chaplain Charles Todd Quintard who ministered to the wounded and dying after the Battle of Franklin. Battlefields are non-denominational; they are not selective as to who suffers upon them. This was proven each time Quintard cared for the soldiers in whatever way he could. Emmie wrote the following of Quintard in her booklet, "On week days, he ministered to us physically and on Sundays spiritually. He was one of the purest and best men I ever knew." Her writing is very articulate and shows the education she received as the daughter of the revered schoolmaster, John Duke Tyler of Hickory Wild. In the front she wrote the following dedication:

In Loving Memory of her who first taught me love and reverence for the Church---
My Mother

The church office has two copies of *A History of Trinity Parish* displayed in cases. Included in her book was this endearing story: During a Diocesan convention, two priests each more experienced in oratory skills were overshadowing a young minister. One of the dear ladies of the congregation, fearful that the young minister might feel this situation "a source of mortification to him," decided to pay him the honor of pinning a rose to his coat. As she turned to go find a pin, the young man stopped her and said, "Oh, never mind, Madame, I have one, the ladies are so fond of decorating me that I always go prepared." The lady was Nannie Tyler Johnson.

To raise funds for the church parish house, Emmie donated her late nephew Cave's collection of handsome curios he brought home with him from the Philippines where he served in the military. One item she kept was a trunk made of exotic camphor wood.

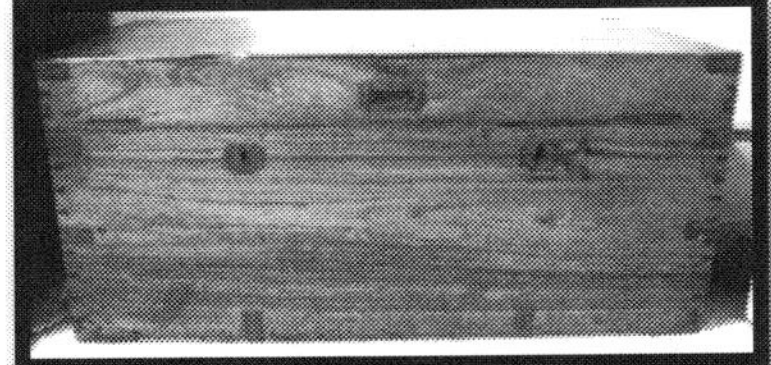

Cave's signature from a book in the author's possession.

In 1917, Em Tyler Mitchell was finally granted a divorce from her husband stating that she and he "were unable to live in peace and quiet." Em had been named with her husband in several lawsuits over the mines. Mitchell's attorney refused to introduce testimony and the decree was granted. In the settlement, Em received from and sold to her ex-husband, rights to some of the mines they owned jointly. Em was given complete custody of their son and through the years, there is no mention of Armistead ever seeing his father again. Harold died in 1930 in San Diego at age 45. He is buried in Hollywood Forever Cemetery.

A "disorderly house" which literally straddled the Tennessee-Kentucky border was the center of a jurisdiction dispute during the summer of 1917. It was well known that liquor was being kept there and sold openly in defiance of the prohibition law. Guthrie wanted something done about it; Clarksville wanted something done about it, but whose jurisdiction was it? Officers on both sides of the state line were not sure about how to handle the matter. Judge Tyler had enough and sent the following order to Deputy Sheriff Oscar Douglas Johnson:

> **I am informed that a man named John Riley is running a saloon near the State line a short distance from Guthrie, Kentucky. I am further informed that his place of business is in Tennessee and that he is selling liquor openly and in defiance of the law. You therefore will proceed at once to the place mentioned and arrest the said John Riley and all persons you may find loafing about his house. You will search the premises and take charge of all intoxicating liquor you may find therein. You will bring this liquor to Clarksville and place it for safekeeping in the County Jail here. You will also bring with you said John Riley and all others arrested on his premises and place them in the County Jail. You will then report your actions immediately to me.**
>
> **C.W. Tyler, Judge**
>
> **This June 24, 1917**

At 10:00 p.m., Johnson and the sheriff of Todd County, Kentucky along with several deputies from each state acted on Judge Tyler's order. When their demand to be admitted inside the house in question was ignored, they broke down the door and arrested John Riley, Lee Wilson and an unnamed black man. They also confiscated the liquor they found on the premises. Indecision over.

The winter of 1917-18 was brutal indeed. The temperatures reached 20 below zero causing the snow to remain from November through March. The weather did not deter the erecting of a memorial boulder on the southwest corner of the courthouse lawn December 8, 1917 to honor Montgomery County pioneer, Valentine Sevier. The stone remained in this spot until the 1999 tornado. During the restoration of the courthouse, it was removed from the lawn and stored until it was placed in its present position near the Customs House Museum parking lot.

Emmie and Em both volunteered to solicit funds for the Red Cross in May 1918. Emmie was able to collect $5 and Em $50. Their team headed by Mrs. Austin Peay, was able to collect a total of $115.50.

By order of the mayor, citizens, businesses and churches were required to oil the street in front of their property. The June 4, 1918 newspaper listed the properties affected. As the judge had 126 feet frontage on Greenwood, he was to pay $17.64 or hire someone to spread the oil for him.

NOTICE TO OIL STREETS

The following property owners are hereby notified to oil the street to the center in front of their property on or before June 8, 1918. The names of the property owners, the frontage to be oiled by each, the estimated cost and the streets to be oiled are given below.

Unless the work is done by the property owners on or before the date named, the City of Clarksville will do the work and charge the cost to the property owners.

E. B. LAURENT, Mayor.

In early June 1918, Dr. Duke Tyler put his 100-acre stock farm on the market. The farm was located 200 yards from the train depot at Hadensville. Age forced him to sell his farm.

Showing respect to his 80-year-old neighbor, Miss Sallie Howard, the beloved school teacher, on June 22, Billy Settle allowed her funeral to be held at his house. Howard had taught three generations of students in her school, her cottage that also served as her home on Commerce Street.

Armistead, in July, performed in a minstrel show that honored the Tylers and Ely families. The purpose of the show was to raise funds in support of the Red Cross as World War I had broken out in Europe. He was continuing his family's legacy of community service as well as displaying musical talent.

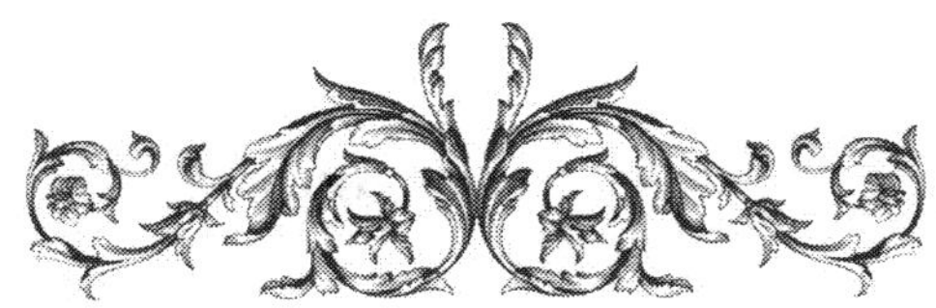

Chapter Twenty-Three: The Final Days

On July 19, 1918 Tyler announced his run for re-election. This election was different and Tyler could sense there was change in the air; change he did not wish to accept. His opponent in the election was a young attorney, John T. Cunningham.

COUNTY AND CRIMINAL JUDGE.
We are authorized to announce
C. W. TYLER
as a candidate for re-election to the office of County and Criminal Judge of Montgomery County.

We are authorized to announce
JOHN T. CUNNINGHAM,
as a candidate for the office of County and Criminal Judge of Montgomery County.

Leaf Chronicle ad July 19, 1918.

Three days later on July 22, Judge Tyler defended himself in the newspaper over charges that, the county's financial records were not properly kept, a charge Tyler called "false and malicious." The judge wrote that

A short time since a well-known citizen saw John T. Cunningham standing in the First National Bank and went in to urge him not to run against me for County Judge. Hearing this conversation, Wesley Drane came from behind the railing and said, 'I intend to see that he runs and I intend to elect him.' He also stated that the people of the Southside were against me due to my stance on the bridge issue[174] and that.... he (Drane) had made arrangements to buy all the purchasable votes of the county so my defeat was assured. Thus I am fighting Wesley Drane and the First National Bank which is the headquarters of the opposition to me in this county. Of the seven county officials who are candidates for re-election, I am the only one who has opposition. They say I am an old man. Chief Justice Wilson of the Tennessee Court of Appeals is an old Confederate soldier of nearly my age and Chief Justice White of the U.S. Supreme Court is also an old Confederate about my age. I hope it is not improper of me to remind the people of the county that I am an old Confederate soldier. I have tried to discharge my duty faithfully in peace and in war. Should the voters of the county see fit to re-elect me for the position I have so long held I would be deeply grateful. Should they fail to do so I will not grumble or think hard of them, but I will be much distressed.
Very truly,
C.W. Tyler

Immediately beneath this article was an affirmation of the truth of Tyler's statement that the books were indeed well kept, signed by Sterling Fort, W.E. Beach and E.L. Brewer of the Revenue Commission, dated July 16, 1918. In the next day's paper was John T. Cunningham's response to Tyler's article that rebuffed the suggestion he was "run by Wesley Drane and the First National Bank. "I wear the collar of no man." This last message before the election is very revealing: first, it shows his mind is as sharp as it had ever been, secondly, his argument takes a personal, almost petty shot at those mentioned and thirdly, the overtone tone of his letter exhibits a true fear that he may not be re-elected. Voters could also sense by his advertisements that Tyler was truly concerned at this point about the upcoming election outcome due to the wording. His past successful elections included:

1878 Tyler v. Col. Thomas Yancey and Gen. Baker D. Johnson
1886 Tyler re-elected with no opposition
1902 Tyler v. W.D. Howser
1910 Tyler v. John T. Cunningham

[174] That Tyler refused to consider funding bridges to the south side of the river during war time.

Tyler's last ad before the election in which he was defeated. July 16, 1918. (LC)

To The People

OF

Montgomery County

Last year I warned you against the Two Bridge proposition. It was defeated by a small vote. Cunningham is running now to carry the same proposition into effect. He says so himself. If he does it will more than double your taxes and your County debt. This is my second warning to you. You can neglect it if you please.

Yours truly,

C. W. TYLER

July 29th, 1918.

His time had finally come. Charles had to accept a final disappointment in life: the end of his political career. This came on August 2, 1918 when he lost re-election. The newspaper headlines announced, "Cunningham Judge by Overwhelming Majority. Unofficial Returns Show That He Carried 15 Out of 22 Districts Giving Him a Lead of 872 Votes. Judge C.W. Tyler, after 45 Years' Continuous Service, Meets Defeat at Hands of Voters."

John T. Cunningham, Tyler's successor.

Tyler was greatly affected by this loss and even though he was seventy-eight years of age, defeat was not a concept he understood. For a man whose entire existence had been so active and totally centered around service to his community, leaving office must have been an extremely difficult pill to swallow. His life as judge defined who he was and it was as if his very identity had been stripped away from him. It seems very likely that Judge Tyler would have preferred to have passed away while in office than to have to pack up his law books and go home to a house full of memories. Fortunately, Judge Tyler was not alone. Em and his grandson, Armistead were there to care for him and give him company. One must remember that Charles Tyler had been raised literally in his father's school house where there could be upwards of thirty to forty people living all at one time. Family members, slaves, boarding and non-boarding students would have made Hickory Wild a core of constant activity. How very different the house on Greenwood must have seemed to the old judge having to step down from the bench! Consequently, he then had time to reflect on his life and inventory the good decisions and the bad. What regrets, if any he had, we will never know. Retrospectively, did he judge himself and pronounce a sentence of well done or not?

So what was Judge Tyler's state of mind in anticipation of long years after the death of his children and wife? This is revealed in one of his books when he wrote of the coming of a new day:

> **In the early morning, yes, in the early morning, my friend, ere yet the weary world is awake. It is then your soul, if you have a soul, thrills with generous emotions and is moved with high resolves to do mighty things during the day...Doubt and despondency are fading with the night, the glad earth wakes again to life and beauty and a voice within us cries, 'rejoice, rejoice.'**

About worry, he wrote:

> **How often it is—I may remark in passing –that divine providence thus steps into our affairs and removes difficulties that have been filling us with unnecessary apprehension.**

About loneliness:

> **The thoughtful man is never lonely. His mind to him a kingdom is, and nature is the great storehouse from which he draws food for reflection.**

About missing a departed loved one:

> **But O for the touch of a vanished hand,**
> **And the sound of a voice that is still.**

And finally about memories:

> **Ah me, what sweet and sorrowful recollections come trooping forth when we touch the secret spring that unlocks the door of memory.**

Still he had to face the fact that his work was over or was it? The *Nashville Banner* was quick to point out that his office was "unique, existing by special statute in Montgomery County, at least the combination of the Criminal Judge with that of County Judge nowhere else exists." They praised him for all his accomplishments through the years and added, "He is a gentleman of culture and most agreeable manners. He was possessed of much vigor and the *Banner*, together with his many friends, hopes that his retirement from the bench does not mean an end of his activities." They needn't worry: Tyler was determined to still have a say in the running of Clarksville.

Then came the highly anticipated news: World War I finally ended on November 11, 1918 and word reached Clarksville by wire. At 6:00 a.m. every whistle and bell in Clarksville was sounded; all over town word spread and by 2:00 p.m. that same day a huge parade was held to celebrate peace.

After the majority of the troops arrived back in Clarksville there was a celebration on May 15, 1919 and its theme was "Blow the Whistles, Ring the Bells, Honk the Horns." There was tremendous flag waving and bands playing. Red, white and blue bunting was displayed from storefronts all over town. Years later the city of Clarksville further honored the men of World War I by changing the name of Strawberry Alley to Legion Street.[175]

Also honored on that same day were the veterans from the Mexican conflict, the Spanish-American War and Civil War. The parade even included two wagons for the aging Confederate veterans. Did Charles Tyler ride with them as a veteran and former member of Forbes Bivouac?

During the year 1919 Tyler, now as a private citizen, addressed several organizations on the question of road building. Clarksville in the early years had numerous toll turnpikes, bridges and roads. After assuming office, Judge Tyler made it a priority to purchase the turnpikes and remove the tolls on roads and bridges that especially benefitted farmers. He was credited with being the great road builder in the state of Tennessee during his tenure in which more than 250 miles of hard surface roads, more than 600 miles of first class dirt roads and a number of well-built bridges were constructed across the numerous streams in the county. Was he contemplating running against Cunningham for the judgeship in two years and so was staying in the public's eye?

Em continued the role of her mother by holding socials at their home. On June 17, 1919, she gave a garden supper party. The newspaper reported that,

> **The stately willow trees and dark green shrubs of the old Tyler garden with long, purple shades of the setting sun formed a never-to-be-forgotten picture. The little winding paths have been left untouched and the borders of rose, hedge and trellis of vines, the blue grass court, a willow tree of nearly a century old, the quaint flowers make up this informal old garden. The buffet supper was served at 7:30 from two beautifully appointed tables. Crystal bowls of sweet peas were effectively used as center pieces.**

Charles's brother-in-law, Billy Settle died suddenly at home of a heart attack on October 26, 1919. He was a lifelong member of Trinity and sang in the choir. He was survived by a daughter, Maggie Settle McKeage and a son, Matthew Gracey Settle (? -1937) who was married to Susan Daniel.

In probably the last photo taken of Judge Charles Tyler, he still exuded a dignified bearing yet was very frail and thin from a life spent in an aggregate of personal accomplishments, tempered with loss.

Charles Tyler was not ready to give up law and so joined with his nephew Joe D. Tyler to form the law firm of Tyler & Tyler in May of 1920. Their office had been previously occupied by Dr. T.D. Johnson on Strawberry Alley. Even so, during the last two years of his life, Charles was not seen out in public as much; his friends noted his inactivity and were concerned about his failing health. It was during the last months of his life that Charles began writing another book on the Civil War, a book he was to never finish.

175 And yet years later a portion of the street had its name returned as Strawberry Alley.

If Tyler was thinking of challenging Cunningham for the judgeship in the next election, we will never know for on Thursday, May 27, 1920, at 5:30 in the afternoon, Tyler passed away at the age of eighty-one.[176] A lifetime spent in an aggregate of personal accomplishments, tempered with loss, stress, political fights and rheumatism all culminated in robbing strength from the man who served Montgomery County with his whole being. Right or wrong in his decisions, liked or disliked personally, he never lost the respect he earned from his labors. If his little daughter Nannie had survived to adulthood, she would have been 39 years old at the time of her father's death.

The parish records listed the cause of death as "old age." Although he had been ill for several months, in truth, he never recovered physically from his defeat in the 1918 election. Charles had been born poor and died poor monetarily, but he recognized and understood that true riches come from giving back to the community he so loved.

As with his father's death, upon the announcement of his death, the courts adjourned for the day and businesses closed out of respect for his passing. His funeral was held at his house, Saturday morning at 10:00 a.m. with the Rev. Warner L. Forsyth conducting the service. The final rites included a solo by Charles Stratton and a hymn by the church choir. Members of the bar and Forbes Bivouac, along with county officials and friends of all backgrounds, attended the service. The list of pallbearers included Dr. Frank J. Runyon, Laurin B. Askew, W.J. Manning, Sterling Fort, Dancey Fort, E.R. Tandy and Boyd Johnson. Finally, the aged judge was interred alongside the graves of his mother, half-brother, wife, grandson and, of course, Nannie. In stark contrast to the much larger, more elaborate tombstones of his family, Judge Tyler's plain tombstone only gives his name and dates. He had erected large, expensive monuments for his mother, wife and daughter Nannie. He had also paid for Quintus's burial expenses. Not being wealthy, these were paid for entirely out of love. The death notice printed in the May 28 issue of the *Leaf Chronicle* stated:

> **Ending of Life of This Splendid Citizen Marks Distinct Period in History of Montgomery County-His Public Record One of Untiring Service**
>
> **He was never of robust constitution; he lived notwithstanding a vigorous, strenuous life. The ending of his life marked a distinct period in the history of Montgomery County. The histories of communities and states are written in the lives of their dominant or central characters—the men who do things, the men who lead. There are but few leaders among men; they are like the peaks of a mountain chain—here and there a peak—here and there a leader. Charles W. Tyler was a leader and lived in a period that required leadership. He lived a poor man and died a poor man. While he handled millions of dollars during the forty-seven years as Financial Agent for Montgomery County, not one dollar, except his salary, ever stuck to his hands. Judge Tyler was a kind-hearted man. He loved to see men succeed; he was especially considerate of young men and aided many of them. It was hard for him to resist appeals to the heart. He gave men the benefit of the doubt and never was heard.... to say an unkind, ungenerous word about any man.**

The obituary in the next day's paper read:

> **And thus ended the earthly career of a man who has long been a conspicuous figure in a community for which he had so much unselfishly wrought for almost half a century. Peace to his memory.**

The Clarksville Bar issued a long tribute to the judge and concluded with this:

> **As members of the Clarksville bar we write his record thus that the world may know that his brother lawyers, those who were most closely associated with him, those who strove both with him and against him, those who at times turned the fierce light of criticism on his acts and deeds, all without exception, appreciate and attest his long life of useful and able service to this county and revere his memory.**
>
> **William M. Daniel** **Austin Peay**
> **Q.C. Atkinson** **Matt G. Lyle**
> **Michael Savage** **Dancey Fort**

---

[176] The *Nashville Banner* reported Tyler died at the Clarksville hospital.

There was a generation of Americans who could remember FDR as the only U.S. President they had known for as long as they had lived. Others today in 2025 remember Queen Elizabeth II of Great Britain as being the only British monarch during their entire life. Such was it for many Clarksvillians when Charles Tyler served as judge and county financial officer. For forty-seven years, Tyler guided Clarksville through post-Civil War reconstruction, the great fire of 1878, the tobacco wars and racial strife. He lived to see the streets filled with horses, mules and carriages, then streetcars and finally automobiles. For years, people remarked of how things had been "when Charles W. Tyler was judge." What a life!

In his will probated on June 14, 1920, Judge Tyler left the house and lot on Greenwood "where we now reside" to his daughter Em. Charles further directed that his debts first be paid from his insurance money and then the rest should be equally divided between Em and his sister Emmie. He concluded by writing, "All else I may own I give to my dear daughter Mrs. Em Tyler Mitchell, and with it, her father's blessing." Em stated, "My precious father once said to me, 'I am not leaving you rich in this world's goods, my dear, but I have given you a good mind and taught you to use it.'" He would touch the pages of an open book and say, "Remember, these are the minds of men. Ready to talk to you at any time." She praised her father when she stated, "No parent could leave a more enriched heritage nor a greater insight for searching the past to realize the potential of the future." She related that her father would never reveal his age; only that he was born in 1839. Proudly, she said that her father was a walking encyclopedia of information who could speak both Greek and Latin fluently.

Because Em had inherited the house, the judge's sister Emmie filed a suit against her niece for its possession. This brings up the story that all family members knew the contents of Mildred's will and therefore this was the reason why the will was never probated. Family dynamics are strange beasts. Emotions suppressed for years sometimes pour forth after a death. It seemed unimaginable that a niece was being sued by an aunt for whom she was named. As it was a suit, its contents were recorded and on the books and the private affairs of the family were then made public. Why Emmie filed the suit at all was a mystery and even back to the reason she moved from the house in the first place. She had lived there free of charge and Charles saw that she had everything she needed. Now at her late age and with no descendants, who would benefit from the suit? Why did she choose to sue? Sadly, suits such as these ruined family relationships often beyond repair. Perhaps since it was in Charles personality to always be in control, Emmie just sought to have some control herself.

Also named in the suit was Charles' administrator H.M. Perry. Under the will of their mother Mildred Tyler, Emmie believed she should receive a share of her estate and that of her late sister Nannie T. Johnson. The three cases were grouped into one suit. In the first, it was charged in the bill that Mrs. Mildred S. Tyler willed her home place on Greenwood Avenue to both Charles and Emmie Tyler. The bill conveyed her interest in the property to Charles for $2,500, the deed reciting that the consideration had been paid in cash. Another paper executed by Judge Tyler on the same day the deed was made, recited however, that the $2500 had not been paid and it constituted a lien on the property and if the indebtedness was not paid at his death, the complainant would have the right to sell the property to collect. In this case, Chancellor Josiah W. Stout held that recovery was barred by the statute of limitations and did not apply because the collection was not enforced until after Judge Tyler's death. The court disagreed since the note involved in the transaction was made to mature one day after death.

In the second bill, Emmie was given a judgment for about $4500 over the ownership and sale of Nannie Johnson's home on Greenwood then owned by Adolph Hach. Nannie Johnson, having no living heirs, it was contended, left all her property to her sister with the exception of certain expenses Judge Tyler had borne for Emmie.

Judge Tyler had sold the property for about $10,000. These expenses, the chancellor stated were estimated to be about $5,500 and so Emmie was to receive the remainder of the sale price. Even though $4500 does not seem to be a large amount, in today's money it would be $109,552.12. An appeal was then filed on both sides to the State Supreme Court. Emmie was represented by Dancey Fort and Em by Matthew G. Lyle. The suit would take years to settle.

If Judge Tyler had lived just two more months he would have witnessed a most historic event. On

August 18, 1920, Tennessee became the last state needed to ratify the 19th Amendment giving women the right to vote. Clarksville women celebrated this advancement, which gave them a voice in government in the new century. One has to wonder what his reaction would have been? If his daughter Nannie had lived, and if she had been taught to be an independent thinker like her grandfather and father before her, would she have been among the Clarksville women suffragettes?

Within a short period of time, Judge Tyler's successor, John T. Cunningham, had the library books removed from Tyler's old office in the courthouse and placed in the Women's Club Building after its purchase by a federation of some thirty-five individual women's clubs. This federation was chartered in 1918 with the purpose of securing a building for a public library. Forty-six years later in 1964, the library was moved to the corner of Main and Fourth Streets and later to its present location off Madison Street in the Veterans Plaza Center.

After Judge Tyler's death, a club named in his honor, the Tyler Club, was organized to benefit the Public Library and honor its founder. As of 2025, the library's collection includes 88,972 books for adults, 81,887 children's items, 12,500 young adult materials, 3,272 CDs, 13,399 VHS tapes/DVDs and 4,351 CDs audio for adults.

Having been divorced from her first husband for years, Em Tyler Mitchell married Lt. Col. Robert Albert Bailey, Jr. (1882-1964), of Franklin, Tennessee on August 23, 1920 in Chattanooga. He was the son of Robert Albert Bailey, Sr. (1849-1916), and Leonora Mayberry Bailey (1851-1934). Robert, Sr., served in Co. G, 4th TN Cavalry during the Civil War.

Where Em met her husband is not known. Robert was also a military man, having served in the 114th Field Artillery during World War I. Some members of this unit came close to capturing the Kaiser himself! Robert was discharged from the army in 1919 with the rank of major. The couple honeymooned for several weeks in Glacier National Park, Lake Louise and Banff in the Canadian Rockies. Upon their return they lived in Birmingham, Alabama.

Robert A. Bailey, Jr. and Em Tyler Bailey.

Em sold her father's house on December 10, 1924. The Baileys lived in several locations. In the 1930 Census, she and Robert were living in Los Angeles at 520 South Hobart Street at the Greystone Apartments, a very prestigious address and just a block over from Hollywood Blvd. Their final move was to Franklin, Tennessee where, in the 1940 Federal Census, they were living on Bridge Street but by 1950 their home was on Third Avenue North. Robert was shown as being a business manager in the State Adjutant General's office.

Greystone Apartments.

Em worshipped at St. Paul's Episcopal Church near Five Points in Franklin. It stands as the oldest Episcopal Church in Tennessee and the oldest Episcopal Church building in continual use west of the Appalachian Mountains. The church was not far from the brick apartment house in which Em and Robert lived. That apartment house, at the corner of 5th Avenue and Bridge Street no longer stands.

In late November 1922, Emmie in Clarksville gathered up a bundle of doll clothes and took them to the church's parish house to sell. The sale lasted from December 3 until Christmas. Will Allen Dromgoole, a female writer from Clarksville, ran a column in the *Nashville Banner* entitled "Song and Story." In it she praised the sewing ability of Em Tyler in making doll clothes. She wrote,

> **Dolls have furnished food for thought, for laughter for tears even; but it isn't every day that they furnish real food to eat as they do for Miss Tyler. That is when this gentle folk too busy to do their doll sewing remember the gentle lady and transmit their orders to her. You might ask her about it; there's a big, brave heart beat in the story.**

On December 9, 1922, Emmie had an insolvency notice placed in the newspaper attached to her brother's estate.

The last photo of Emmie Tyler. (GF)

Emmie gave a party on Tuesday, February 15, 1923, presumably at her Farris apartment that included a 5-act play. Emmie and Lucy Gracey wrote the play but no mention of how many or who attended the party was mentioned in the local newspaper.

In preparation for the inevitable, Emmie wrote out her will on March 8, 1929:

Miss Emmie Tyler
Will
This is my will written in my own hand.
I appoint Mr. Alf Killebrew[177] executor of my estate and request that he will see that my wishes concerning my funeral and burial are carried out. I wish above everything else that my body shall be embalmed. <u>I urge that this shall be done.</u>
I wish a simple funeral in Trinity Church and to be buried by my mother in Greenwood Cemetery. After all of my debts and expenses have been settled I wish a simple marker to be placed at my grave like at the graves of my brothers and sister Mrs. Nannie T. Johnson. I give $500.00 (five hundred dollars) to Nannie Tyler- daughter of Dr. Duke Tyler of Guthrie, Ky. The rest of my money I leave (which is in land bonds) I give to Trinity Church, Clarksville, Tenn. I give to Mildred Tyler Gill my pin with the word 'Mother' set in small pearls, my bracelet set with small diamonds and a small silver ladle to Nannie Tyler, daughter of Dr. Tyler and the rest of my jewelry and silver to Dr. Tyler's three daughters Donie, Mary, and Helen. The rest of my effects, furniture, clothing, pictures (I would like what few books I have to be given to the Old Woman's Home in Nashville) are to be given to the families of Joe and Duke Tyler.
March 8, 1929
(signed) Emmie Tyler
Witness: (signed) Mary Dishman
C.W. Brooks
If any of Joe or Duke Tyler's families should care for the books, I wish them to have them.

March 9, 1929
Have my <u>body embalmed, please do this</u>.[178] Have a simple funeral in Trinity Church and bury me by my mother in Greenwood Cemetery. I want you and Mr. Alf Killebrew to attend to everything necessary to be done. I have bonds and money in the First Trust and Savings Bank. Mr. Killebrew will know about it. May God bless you always my dear friend for your sympathy and kindness to me.
(signed) Emmie Tyler

June 30, 1930
My will
Mr. Kimbrough in the First Trust and Savings Bank has. I wish my small mahogany table which was my mother's, given to Mildred Tyler Gill who has my mother's name. If there should be anything among the clothes I leave that Jessie- Joe Tyler's wife or Mildred or Duke Tyler's daughters should want, let them divide them accordingly and if not, let them be given to someone in need. Lucy Duffy if she should care for them.
(signed) Emmie Tyler
Also give my camphor wood chest, brought from the Philippines by Cave Johnson to Mildred Gill. Probated August 26, 1932.

Judge Cunningham inherited a chronic headache known as the courthouse clock. In 1930, W.R. Gaisser got the clock operational again after weeks of not working…for a while. It continued

---

177 The son of long-time friend, J.B. Killebrew.

178 What caused her to be so insistent about being embalmed? One can guess it had to do something she saw with Nannie's death.

to cause trouble for decades such as when it was nonoperational 1933 until 1940.

On April 1, 1932 an unusual ad was seen the *Leaf Chronicle*:

> **WOMAN TO TAKE CHARGE**
> **of Montgomery County, one with theses qualifications: capable, pleasing personality and educated. Write F.B.P. Montgomery Hotel, Clarksville, Tenn.**
> **Miss Emmie Tyler, ticket.**

Finally, years after the suit was filed, the court decided the case of Emmie Tyler v. Mrs. Em Tyler Mitchell. Chief Justice McKinney of the Supreme Court in Nashville on April 7, 1932 ruled that Emmie was not entitled to recover on a note for $2500. Due to the sensitive nature of the suit, the Clarksville newspaper was silent on the outcome however, the *Nashville Banner* printed the decision on page 5 of the issue in small print with typos as "Miss Emmy Tyler vs. Mrs. M. Tyler Mitchell." It was meant to read "Em" Tyler Mitchell of course. It was over.

With the suit now settled, Em sought to take care of other pressing matters and so wrote to Greenwood Cemetery to make her wishes known. By the letter it is seen that Em originally planned to be buried next to her father. The letter dated June 4, 1932 read:

> **I had intended to come in about this while at home but I ran into the 'flu' and it was a 'better man then I was, Gunga Din.'**
>
> **While I was there I went over my cemetery lot carefully as I had forgotten exactly how it lay. . . These are my wishes in regard to future burials there. I will draw it out below so there can be no confusion. As the original stock was my father's and John Daniel paid me it a few years ago, I presume that there can be no question as to my ownership of the lot. Aunt Emmie Tyler and I are the only immediate members of the family left. The lot runs into a V-shape. In this V-shape is the grave of my grandmother Tyler. There is ample room beside her for Aunt Emmie and it is there that I wish her placed at the time of her death. The upper tier consisting now of first- little Nan, my mother then my father- I wish preserved in its entirety for myself. I wish to be buried next to my father. Then Armistead, my son, next to me if such be his desire in the future years. I am naturally supposing that Mr. Bailey will wish to lie with his own people but there is ample room for him if he so desires. I suggest you file this letter for future authority.**
> **Emily Tyler Bailey**

On a visit to Clarksville, Em Bailey was riding in a car with Louise Perry[179] and Mrs. Scott Winn[180] and her two daughters with whom Em was related, late Friday afternoon on May 6, 1932 when they had a serious accident on Franklin Street near Eighth Street. A motorcycle ridden by two men ran into the back of Perry's car. The men received compound fractures of their right legs. The ladies in Perry's car were uninjured.

At age 82, Emmie died August 22, 1932 at 3:20 p.m. after her last months were spent in failing health. She continued to take part in affairs of the church. How much the stress of the lawsuit contributed to her passing will never be known.

According to her specific instructions, her 3 o'clock funeral service was preached at Trinity the next day by the Rev. Charles B. Romaine of Franklin, TN. Her pall bearers were: Edward Aylett Cooke, Charles E. Cooke, Dr. Roland Bain Macon, Charles Haddox Drane, Alf Killebrew, Lawrence Newton Byers, Thomas Bledsoe Foust, Weaver David Posey. Honorary pallbearers were; Isaac Piedmont Gerhart, Charles Curtis Gerhart, John Owen McKeage, Clive Wilcox, John B. Baker, Alfred Clebsch, Horace T. Mallon, Fred Seip, Dr. Maurice Langdon Hughes, Martin Lee Cross, Adolph Hach and Claybourne Walton Brooks. This lady whose life was dedicated to God and her church was buried in the Tyler family plot at Greenwood with a large crowd in attendance. Emmie outlived her brother Charles by 12 years.

The Baileys remained living in Franklin and Em was active as her mother had been in her church and social circles. Em spent her days visiting friends, reading, playing bridge and enjoying

---

[179] Louise Perry Dickson was the daughter of McClain and Hope Gracey Perry, the niece of Donald Gracey and the widow of James M. Dickson. Em knew her from church. Louise passed away in 1970.

[180] This was Louise Gracey Winn (1885-1962) and her daughters Hope Gracey Winn (1918-1928) and Emily Tyler Winn (1920-1992).

the company of her husband. Her niece, Louise Nunnelly Green of Franklin described the couple as very attractive. Em, according to Mrs. Green, was an extremely interesting person, one, in fact, who was psychic. She related that there were two houses in Franklin that Em refused to enter because of "bad spirits there." She also believed strongly in reincarnation, thinking herself to have previously been a Roman soldier. She recalled how Em was interested in everything and that her favorite book was *Atlantis: The Antediluvian World* by Ignatius Donnelly, published in 1882. An immediate success at its release, the book became an instant classic as it explored the possible existence of the lost continent. It is fascinating to think of this woman so ahead of her time, of course, encouraged to be such by her devoted father. It was also natural for Em to be interested in Greek history since she was the granddaughter of John Duke.

Due to failing health, Em move to the Lofton Nursing Home on Columbia Avenue. Em's estate was sold at auction before she moved there. Em's upright piano is now in the possession of Mrs. Green's family.

On Sunday, October 9, 1932, Trinity Parish celebrated its 100th anniversary. During the 11 o'clock service, Rev. Arthur E. Whittle read a portion of the church's history prepared in print by Emmie.

Many years later, Robert Bailey died on January 19, 1964 in Franklin. Em buried him at the Mount Hope Cemetery there. It speaks volumes that one of his pall bearers was Brig. Gen. Rufus Ramey, a highly decorated officer that served in both World Wars. She remained busy with social functions, church-related work and trips and hosting special parties

Having been widowed for eight months, Em wrote her will on August 12, 1964, one she typed herself on her own typewriter. It read, with misspellings/typos unchanged:

Will

Emily Tyler Bailey

This is my last will and testament nullifying any will made by me before this date. To Betty Anne Mitchell and Robert Charles Mitchell- I leave my entire block of <u>Mitchell Huesighbrod minning Carrnberry</u> shares (sic). Numbers -13-14-15-16-38 total 51,563 shares. Also whatever remaining interest I hold in the Mitchell estate. This and nothing more as they have already received more than their share of my personal property.

To Louise Perry Dickson- the sum of $500 from my personal savings account at the Williamson County Bank.

To Capt. Tom Henderson from the same account $300 for friendship rendered.

To John Will Gosey- for faithful service.

To Aaron Douglas $50.

I have given the <u>Britanican</u> (sic) and the big dictionary & (stand this and silver to Irene Gracey, the big clock and the painting of Armistead and his dog to Irene Gracey Stapp). in parenthesis: these words are stricken out.

To Grady (sic) Stapp the one <u>Revolutionary</u> toddy spoons-silver

I have given to Emily Tyler Winn my diamond ring and the gold card case, the pearl crescent.

To H. Scott Winn and Emily Tyler Winn all the rest of my personal possessions. (including the Meissen figurine and the cloisonné vase, the ivory elephant from chia, 3 oriental rugs, the contents of my room not otherwise disposed of). These words are stricken out as well.

To <u>Sophraino</u> Mayberry Eggleston the enamel dog collar, the old Johnson silver spoon. Whatever money is left in the Williamson County Bank after the conditions of this will are carried out to be added to my account at the Harpeth Bank. From this account my funeral expenses are to be paid. Any residue of what I die possessed of to be evenly divided between Louise Perry Dickson, Irene Gracey Stapp, H. Scott Winn and Emily Tyler Winn. I appoint Henry Mayberry as executor to carry out the terms of this will.

Signed

August 12, 1964 /s/ Emily Tyler Bailey

<u>The inventory of her estate:</u>

Entire block of Mitchell-Mussigbrod Mining Company shares:	**worthless**
Balance in Harpeth National Bank 11-16-68	**$508.04**
Remaining interest held in Mitchell estate	**none**
Britannica, big dictionary and stand	
Blue and silver vase	

Painting of Armistead and his dog
Gold card case and pearl crescent $50
Meissen figurine
Cloisonné vase
Two pairs cuff links
One typewriter
Two pearl scarf pins
One medal, one dog tag and gold watch and chain.
Record of watch (slip of paper)
One dresser
One T.V. set
Ivory elephant from China
Box with seven stick pins
One platform rocker

There are questions: In the divorce settlement, did her husband leave her stocks he knew were worthless and because she never touched them, she never found out? Why would she leave them to her children if she thought they had no value? The money she left to friends simply was not there. Em must not have realized what a perilous financial state she was in at her death. If she had lived much longer, she would have not been able to pay for her expenses at the home. How sad that Judge Tyler's daughter should end her life in such a sad situation.

Em died at age 84 on November 18, 1968 at the nursing home and was buried the next day, not at Greenwood next to her father but instead near the center of the Mount Hope Cemetery, beside her husband, who preceded her in death by four years. Why she changed her mind over this matter is unknown. Unlike Greenwood Cemetery, whose grand trees provide shade for its inhabitants and their visitors, Mount Hope Cemetery is nearly devoid of trees save for one large one, near Em's grave in the Bailey family plot. Her obituary in the *Tennessean* described her as an artist and musician.

Entrance to the Mount Hope Cemetery in Franklin, Tennessee. Photo by author.

When asked if Em ever talked about her sister Nannie, Louise Green replied in the negative. Mrs. Green never met Em's son Armistead, but recalled from a family portrait that he had a huge German shepherd as a pet. Armistead as an adult, was described as being 5'7", 140 lbs. with a light complexion, light brown hair and blue eyes.

In 1929, Armistead married Annette "Ann" Klemt (1907-1971) Their daughter Betty Anne (1930-2004), was born the same year as Armistead's father's death in San Diego. Their son Robert Charles (1936-1988), was born in Nashville. The couple moved to West Palm Beach, Florida where in 1940 Armistead was working at Monmouth Plumbing Co. and living in a lovely, small, white stucco house just two blocks from the beach. Armistead passed away at age 36 on September 18, 1942 after becoming ill months previously in April. His body was brought back to Clarksville, accompanied by his wife[181] and her sister, Mrs. John Strickland. His daughter Betty Ann was age 12 at the time of his death and his son Robert Charles, age 6. Armistead was laid to rest next to his grandfather, Judge Tyler. This spoke of how close the two must have been while the judge was still living. Services were conducted by the Rev. Earl Gilbreath of the Episcopal Church.

[181] Armistead and his wife were planning to divorce; it is unclear whether they did or not.

Chapter Twenty-Four: The Statue and the Tylers' Legacy

Although it was later determined to have been stolen as early as May 19, Nannie's statue was reported missing, on June 1, 1996. Immediately the Clarksville police were called in to investigate the crime, with Detective Charles Abernathy leading the investigation.

Eleanor and Stephen Score stand beside Paul Schaaf after the statue was placed back upon its pedestal. Photo by author.

The theft was announced in the *Clarksville Leaf Chronicle* on June 5. The headline read, "Neighbors Feel Sense of Loss After Theft." An article in the next day's issue of the paper read "Search Intensifies for Statue Missing from Cemetery." The citizens of Clarksville were outraged at how someone could disturb the resting place of this dear little girl. It became the topic of conversation throughout Clarksville as people expressed their contempt for the abhorrent act.

On June 19, the police department was contacted by Stephen Score, an antiques dealer in Boston, who reported that the statue of Nannie Tyler was safe. Stephen and his wife Eleanor Score reported that they had purchased the statue believing that it came from an estate garden. Later they found that the statue was the one stolen from a cemetery in Clarksville, Tennessee. This was enough for Mr. Score to call authorities. Clarksvillians were overjoyed to hear the Scores intended to return the statue back to Clarksville.

Stephen Score, inc. 6/20/96

Mr. Paul Schaaf
Heritage Bank

Dear Mr. Schaaf:
Enclosed is a photo of the marble statue. Please do let me hear from you as soon as you are able. The height is approx. 35 inches.
Yours truly,
Stephen Score

73 Chestnut Street, Boston, MA 02108 (617) 227-9192

The letter from Score to Paul Schaaf held in Greenwood Cemetery office files.

The statue's journey proved to be an extensive one. From Clarksville, it was transported to St. Charles, Missouri, Richmond, Virginia, Indiana and then to Boston, Massachusetts. This is what is now known: A person possessing the statue entered an antique store owned by dealer Bo Wiechens in St. Charles. The person offered to sell the statue for $1700 cash, stating that the statue had come from the Bommarito estate in St. Louis, which was liquidated in 1995. From all appearances, the statue showed no indication that it came from a cemetery and so the deal was made. The next day, Ms. Weichens packed the statue into her van and headed for The Heartland Antique Show in Richmond, Virginia. Unfortunately, while loading the statue, she broke the right arm. Upon arriving at the show, she set a dealer's price of $2800 for the statue. On June 1, Mr. Score purchased the statue for $2250. He immediately had the arm professionally reattached and advertised the statue in the Wilton (Connecticut) Antiques

Marketplace Show supplement in the June 21 *Antiques and The Arts Weekly*.

Nannie's pedestal missing the statue. Photo by author.

For the repaired statue, Score asked $6000. It was on Wednesday, June 19 that a New York state dealer called Score to inform him that the statue resembled one reported in *Antiques Week* as missing from a cemetery in Clarksville, Tennessee.

On July 1, 1996, at 11:30 a.m., over fifty people watched with anticipation as a white station wagon pulled slowly into Greenwood Cemetery. Stephen and Eleanor Score had driven 23 hours in their un-air-conditioned car to Clarksville with the statue lying in the back. After speeches and presentations from city and county dignitaries, the trustees of the Greenwood Cemetery respectfully raised the statue of Nannie Tyler back to its rightful position on its pedestal, as singing of the Doxology broke out in the crowd. "Praise God from whom all blessings come…" Arrangements of flowers decorated her grave that day. The note, which had set upon the pedestal that read, "Little Nannie has been found. Thank you God for helping us," was removed before the statue was reset.

Grateful citizens desiring to thank the Scores for the return of the statue were on hand with camcorders and cameras taking it all in. Mr. Score stated as he addressed the crowd,

> **Initially I was shocked and deeply anguished at having bought a desecrated piece. I felt wretched. However, when I contacted Clarksville civic leaders to return the statue, suddenly I realized their relief and jubilation with its recovery. Now I feel it's been a positive experience. If I hadn't advertised the piece, it might not have gone back during this generation.**

Visitors to Nannie's statue cover it with gifts because of the story that Nannie's toys once placed on her grave in a glass case had been stolen years ago

The statue being returned to its base. Stephen Score stands next to Nannie's statue. Photos by author.

Also present at the ceremony was Charles Haddox Gill, his wife, Sue and their son, Tyler Gill, a Kentucky judge. The Gills who were married December 11, 1920, brought with them a family photo album, which held the very photo of Nannie, sent by Judge Tyler to be used to sculpt the statue. After the ceremony, the civic leaders and the Gills attended a luncheon in the Scores' honor and then stopped by the former home of Judge Tyler on Greenwood Avenue.

How sad for this thievery to have occurred at all, when in 1887, W.P. Titus wrote that:

> **Benjamin Grove, esq., of Louisville, an engineer of much reputation for skill in artistic landscaping and ornamenting grounds was employed to lay out this most beautiful city in home for the dead, where the dust of loved ones may ever rest under the green sod, free from the despoiler's hands and protected against all intrusions.**

This beautiful place of repose was laid out into sections, complete with crushed gravel avenues and filled with flowerbeds, shrubbery, exotic trees and evergreens. White border stones were placed at the corner of each section. A superintendent's house was built to the left of the entrance of the cemetery with its own garden planted in back.

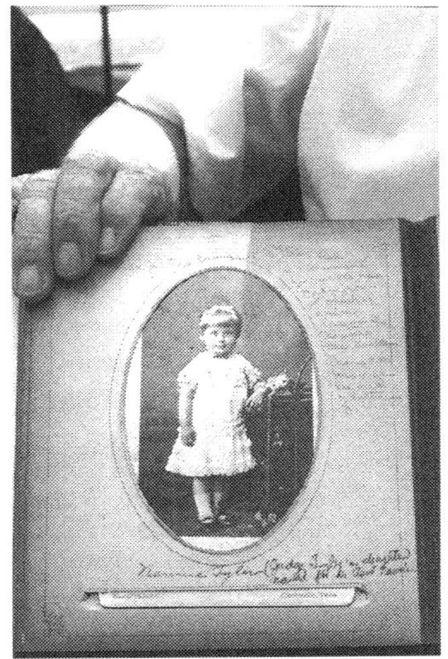

Charles Haddox Gill, Jr., a Tyler family descendant, holds a family photo album with a picture of Nannie. Written on the page is the following: "This picture was sent to **Italy**[182] and a monument in marble was made from it which is now in Greenwood Cemetery, Clarksville. Nannie was four when she died of diphtheria. Nannie Tyler, Judge Tyler's daughter, named for her Aunt Nannie." This aunt was Nannie W. Tyler, the daughter of John D. Tyler and Mildred Tyler. Photo by author.

The question is asked, "Why this child's statue? There are many others in Greenwood. The reason was that the statue did not belie that it came from a cemetery and so it was easily sold as simply as statue of some unknown little girl.

But, of course, this was not just a statue of any little girl; it was the exact size and likeness of one particular little girl. Certainly nearly every Clarksville family suffered the loss of one or more children in the 1800s. If one examines the records, an overwhelming number of children died not just from disease but what could be termed "freak accidents" almost to the extent that if a child lived to adulthood, it was more of a surprise than if they did not. Whenever a family experiences the death of a loved one, the wound is deep but deeper still if it is a child.

One common method to get through the grieving process is to find a way to memorialize the lost one. Human hearts cry out, "Do not forget our loved one! Please remember how great our love was for our child! Remember her, remember her, REMEMBER OUR LITTLE DARLING!" Judge and Mrs. Tyler must have felt this when they had the statue carved. So again, what made Nannie so well known among the other children who died at that time? It was her parents' simple refusal to let their daughter be forgotten, and the statue would serve that purpose.

Today Greenwood is still the most admired cemetery for miles around and is made even lovelier by the presence of this sweet child's spirit. The people of Clarksville have never forgotten Nannie. Marie Riggins, who, on the day the statue was returned to Greenwood was nearing 95 years of age, said, that for as long as she could remember flowers were placed in the statue's hand. She believed them to have been placed there by generations of cemetery workers. Now because of her damaged hand, flowers are left at its base or wired to the remnant of her hand.

At the time, Stephen and Eleanor Score, along with their seventeen-year-old son Avery, lived in the Beacon Hills district of Boston, their antique shop beneath their apartment. Stephen specialized in buying and selling antiques such as hooked rugs, painted furniture, artwork, especially Americana and Continental pieces and had been in the business for over thirty-five years. He was able to deal on the highest level in the purchase of antiques as seen in 2006 when he paid $1,080,000 at a Christie's Antiques Auction for a rare Philadelphia-made weather vane.

The Score's antique store in Boston.

This author spoke with the Scores in July of 2009 while in Massachusetts. Stephen again stated how upsetting it had been to discover that the statue of Nannie was a stolen one, and not from an estate as he was informed. He said, "I was so disturbed to discover that I was involved in something so

[182] The descendants, mistakenly believed the statue was carved in Italy as it was carved out of Carrara marble that is quarried there.

tawdry." He went on to say how pleasant his visit to Clarksville had been and how graciously everyone had treated them both.

If anyone has ever wondered what happened to the Scores who generously returned Nannie's statue to Clarksville, the story is startling. Once again, the Scores went out of their way to help turn a bad situation into a positive but this time, on the night of March 19, 2003, the end result could have been disastrous.

A few years after returning Nannie's statue back to Clarksville, their kindness on this occasion nearly cost them their lives. The Scores hired a man in need to paint their shop, took him in for meals on several occasions, carried him to the hospital once, and even paid for his medicine. One night, the Score family was awakened by loud banging at the front door. The door was in the process of being kicked in by an intruder who turned out to be the man the Scores had helped. For one hour, the mentally unstable man terrorized the Scores until police finally took him away.

Stephen himself had to be taken to the hospital; so distraught was he from the incident. Eleanor stated that she could not ever again think about trying to help someone. "If he had had a gun, we would have been dead."

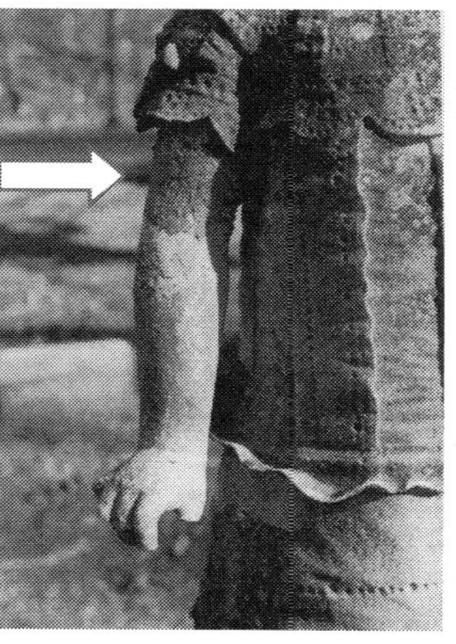

Score passed away from cancer on September 9, 2023. It was 139 years to the day that Nannie died. He was described in the *Boston Globe* newspaper as, "a husband, a father, a mensch and an icon in the art and antiques world."

The statue today is one of the most visited sights in Clarksville. As is now known, marble does not stand the test of time well. One hundred and thirty-nine years of weather and pollution have done their work upon the stone.

On the left: The right hand once held a rose but over time, the piece has been broken off. Photo by Chris Crow. On the right: Repairs done to the statue's right arm. Below right: Vandals in 1999 damaged the edge of the dress. Photos by author.

As one drives along Greenwood Avenue to enter the cemetery, seven stately ginkgo trees are seen standing between the blacktop of the street and the low wall in the front of the cemetery. Although it seems peculiar that they were planted outside the wall, one must remember that the trees were there well before cars existed and even the street when it was nothing more than a well-traveled dirt road, would not have needed to be very wide. What sorrowful events those towering trees have witnessed over the years as family after family passed by them to lay their loved one into eternal slumber. Nannie's grave is near the front center of the cemetery in one of the oldest sections. As one stands there by Nannie's statue, it is easily imagined that when the judge visited Greenwood Cemetery nearly every Sunday for almost thirty-five years, he placed his hand ever so lovingly on the head of his daughter's statue and perhaps even spoke to it. Then, turning he conversed with Molly who also left him too soon.

The inscription on Nannie's pedestal. Photo by author.

Crossing the lane over to the Johnson family plot, he may have paid his respects to the sister who risked her life, he always proudly recalled, to get past the Yankee lines to smuggle clothes and supplies to him after the fall of Ft. Donelson.

Even today, people feel compelled to touch the statue as though desiring to comfort the child, but certainly to let her know she has not been forgotten. People feel something when they see the statue, for Nannie represents that one person we all have lost who was dearest to us.

For many years, hanging on a wall inside in the stately antebellum home of Sue Gill was a large portrait of Nannie. This portrait was executed using the MacCormac photo of Nannie. The only difference is the addition of color. The ribbon, which held back her hair from her face, is blue and her dress white. Her perfectly formed, delicate face shows a quiet gentleness and sweetness that only a child could radiate. To look at that face is to realize the tremendous feeling of loss endured by her parents after her death.

In November 2015, after her mother's death, Dr. Charlotte Gill, donated the portrait to the Customs House Museum in Clarksville. It was put on display during the exhibit "A Time of Mourning," in April 2016. This was the first time the portrait had ever been on exhibit. The museum also received a portrait of Judge Tyler, donated by Charlotte's brother, Tyler Gill.

One wonders what kind of individual Nannie would have been. Would she have become a teacher like her grandfather teaching classes across the street at the new high school? Or would she have contented herself to be involved in social events and fund-raising for needed causes?

Nannie's home on Greenwood Avenue has been greatly modified over the years. Originally, the two-story house had a full-length covered front porch. Evidence of that still remains on the exterior brick on the front of the house. Entering the vestibule and then through the original front door, there is a double parlor with the upstairs staircase on the right. The hard wood floors are unique in that the wood is laid at a diagonal.

Em sold the house on December 10, 1924 to Capt. Benjamin H. Hiett, a lawyer, civil engineer and distinguished Army officer who purchased the property as an investment and at the time had not decided what to do with the property. Adolph Hach, Sr. purchased the house from Hiett later that year paying $5,000.

The design of the house has been greatly altered over the years. It was Hiett who renovated the house in such a way as to make two separate apartments. The staircase was blocked off on the lower floor and a front first floor window opened into a doorway using the stairs as the means to reach the second floor apartment. J.H. Ellarson & Son Architects were contracted to do the work estimating its completion in the middle of November. Each apartment was constructed to have five rooms, a bath and its own separate entrance. Ellarson had begun the work about mid-October. Hach also had exterior repairs done, although what those were, is unknown as well as when the house's exterior brick was painted white. It is likely that Hach paid to have it done. Also, when the paint was sand-blasted off is not known, but today the residence is its natural brick color.

Judge Tyler Home Being Remodeled

The old Judge C. W. Tyler homestead on Greenwood Avenue, purchased some time ago by Adolf Hach, is being remodeled into a modern double apartment house, the owner revealed today.

Work started about a week ago and includes a complete renovation of the interior and outside repairs. The two apartments will each have five rooms and a bath with two separate front entrances.

J. H. Ellarson & Son are doing the work under contract and plan to finish the job about the middle of November.

Mr. Hach plans to rent the apartments.

Adolph and Phila Hach with guests Betty White and Minne Pearl.

On April 29, 1939, Hach advertised that the Tyler home "had two good apartments. Near new school. A bargain. Jim Northington, agent." The house remained in this arrangement during the ownership of the house later to Sarah Beth Haynes who passed away in 2015. The house in 2024 is currently being renovated after Kitty Harvill and her husband Christoph Hrdina purchased it in 2021. They remodeled the kitchen, opened the stairwell, totally restructured the screened-in side porch, re-plastered the walls, brought the electricity up to code, added a large closet to the main floor bedroom as well as other improvements. The staircase that was once enclosed has been reopened and one can imagine the judge's two little girls giggling as they descended the steps to play outside. Kitty and Christoph have committed their time, energy and talent to the house, understanding and appreciating not only its architectural but historical value. The house seems to have come alive once more and with each room's restoration, it is assured that Judge and Mollie Tyler would have thoroughly approved of their efforts. Christoph has named the house, "the Pearl' since promising

Kitty he would have it looking like a pearl in two years. The stairwell has since been opened up as it existed when the Tylers lived here.

On the left: The parlor before renovation by Kitty Harvill and Christoph Hrdina. On the right: The entrance hall looking toward the front door of the house with the vestibule beyond. Also shown is the enclosed stairwell on the left with a built-in bookcase below. Photos by author.

The parlor after its renovation by Kitty and Christoph.

The two-story vestibule was added by the Hachs and not present at the time of the Tylers. It provided a space for a small kitchenette on the second floor for use by the apartment renters. Adolph Hach closed off the parlor stairway to make the upstairs separate from the rest of the house for apartments. The only way then to get to the second floor then was to go outside and enter the window transformed into a door. Judge Tyler's two daughters' bedrooms were in the back of the upstairs. Another bedroom was in the front along with a sitting room. Probably, this bedroom was the one used by Emmie. The presence of the austere judge can still be felt in the house.

The hardware is original to the house. Sarah Elizabeth Haynes, a previous owner of the house, recalled that a man offered her to buy the door handles inside the house, "just name the price and I will buy them," he said. Fortunately, Miss Haynes decided against the sale. And a workman once told her that if ever the roof collapsed, she would most certainly be crushed by the weight of the huge wooden beams from the attic. The exterior bricks of the house, once painted white, have been sandblasted. Miss Haynes bought the Tyler home in 1992.

The Tyler house when painted white. (MCA)

As for the Polk and Nannie Johnson's home, it remains a private residence today after an extensive renovation by its former owners, Marlin and Lisa Huddleston, who spared no expense in preserving the house. He filled it with grand antiques, proudly showing his efforts on the show, "History and Heritage" hosted by Rosalind Kurita. After living in the house for a few years, Huddleston sold the house and its contents at auction.

When the Hach family lived here, Adolph installed a large swimming pool, Clarksville's first, in the back yard. Tennis courts were added in the far back corner of the yard. There were also stables, a log cabin and extensive gardens behind the house, the space now occupied by apartments. If people remember one thing about the Hachs, they without fail recall that Adolph and Erna had a large St. Bernard named Bruno who carried a monkey called Chico around on his back all over town. This former home of the Johnsons and Hachs has a story to tell with a hidden room behind a bookcase and bars on the basement windows. The secret room hidden behind a bookcase in one of the rooms has doors, which were meant to be latched from the inside. To get into the room, which can hold about eight people, one has to step on a stool. Its intended purpose is unknown, but one theory that has been circulated is that during World War II, Clarksville citizens of German descent were feared to be Nazi sympathizers. Did the government consider the Hachs, with Camp Campbell so close, as possible sympathizers? One source says Erna Hach was placed under house arrest. So was the room built there to hide her friends also suspected of being in league with the Germans?

Another possibility is that Polk Grundy Johnson had the room built in case the Civil War re-ignited and the family could hide their valuables there. Regardless, there is no mention of this room on the application for the house to be listed on the National Register or on other documents.

One other interesting note about the house: Lisa Huddleston told how the workers on the house have told her of seeing the face of a black lady looking in the window and handprints of a child. Could Roxy still be overlooking the care of the house?

As for Judge Tyler's crowning achievement: the courthouse, a complete remodel of the courthouse began in 1963 with the county clerk's office. The following year, the register's office, trustee's office and County Judge's office were remodeled and changes made.

The trustee's office ca. 1937. Shown are Lauren Martin, deputy and Paul Thompson, trustee.

Two years later, under the guidance of Chloe Cunningham Northington, head of the Montgomery County Beautification Committee, old stumps from the lawn were removed, trees were shaped and grass sown. Shrubs, shade and ornamental trees were added next to the basement entrances. Boxwoods, azaleas, dogwood trees, linden trees, Austrian pines, cotoneaster, Burford holly and convex leaf hollies were purchased and planted from Frank Murphy's nursery on a bid basis. Parking was no longer allowed on the north side of the courthouse. Large-scale lighting and landscaping were completed by April of 1966. The exterior brick walls were sandblasted, tuck-pointed and "pigeon proofed." The bell and tower clock were repaired, the brick walkways, basement entrance canopies, stone benches, ornamental railings and aluminum doors were all in place by May 15, 1966 and a dedication ceremony was held to herald the completion of the renovation. The total cost for the project was $30,000 and by anyone's standards, it was a welcome improvement to the crown jewel of the city.

Next in 1977, came a three phase renovation undertaken by Rufus Johnson and Associates. The courthouse basement was redesigned to add an elevator and heating and cooling for the whole building was upgraded. The second phase focused on restoring the main floor's heavy walnut molding and twin oak staircases. Out-of-date fluorescent light fixtures were taken out and care was taken to install chandeliers similar to the courthouse's original lights and the basement and main floor received a new telephone system. The second phase was almost completed by July of 1979 and monies were soon available for the third and final phase to begin in January of 1980. This final part required the temporary removal of some offices and courtrooms from the second floor to the Public Library basement costing $28,000. The renovations were complete at the end of 1981 and the courtrooms and offices returned to the second floor ready for business. The total cost of this massive renovation was $750,000.

Through the years it was necessary to sand-blast the exterior, tuck-point the brick and pigeon-proof the roof. The Chancery courtroom was relocated upstairs next to the circuit courtroom and the former Chancery courtroom was converted into a conference room to be utilized by the County Judge. It also allowed space for the office of budgets and accounts and the purchasing agent. Judge Tyler's old office was moved into the former Clerk and Master's office adjacent to the former Chancery courtroom. Interior improvements included paint, drapes and new furniture for some of the offices.

The Archie Wood-Frank Adkins Post of the American Legion donated a flagpole that was installed on the south side of the lawn. Terrazzo tiles on the porches were laid in the entrances and extended to the interior main floor inside. The basement restrooms were remodeled and a sprinkler system installed. At one time, the eagle had to be reset on top of its perch and this was accomplished by a 60-year-old worker.

The eagle titled on its perch. Photo by George Ene.

The indirect lighting was improved and repairs were done on both the clock and bell in the tower. The four entrance stairs were re-concreted and new ornamental railings added. At the remodel's conclusion, the following was written in the newspaper,

No longer regarded as a just an ancient landmark, the courthouse proudly stands amid trees, flowers and shrubbery-credit to Montgomery County. Her clock now chimes the hours as time passes by. Barring fires and tornado she should for decades continue as our temple of Justice-blind but not deaf, stern but not heartless and rugged but beautiful.

On the left: The courthouse steps, before and after repairs. Photo by L.J. Dancey. On the right: In 1938, Robert Lawrence Pyland, a firefighter and part-time painter was hired to paint aspects of the clock tower and the eagle perched on top of the steeple. (LC)

The courthouse lost its long-term custodian when Alex McKinnon passed away on January 9, 1933 after suffering from paralysis. He died at his son's home on Main Street. County officials sent a large floral arrangement to honor the man who kept the courthouse in top condition for 30 years prior to 1914. Following his retirement, his son, Hurley took over his job. McKinnon was born into slavery in Wayne Co., Tennessee and was around ninety-years-old according to Hurley. Burial was in Golden Hill Cemetery.

Sittin' and spittin' was the problem on the wall that surrounded the courthouse in the 1960s. Farmers that came in with their families on Saturday would often congregate together and sit in the shade passing the time chewing their tobacco, whittling, and spitting. It became such a

problem that to remedy the situation the county put up strips of spikes on the walls. Park benches were installed and it seemed to make everyone happy so the spikes were eventually removed. They had better be glad Judge Tyler was not alive to see the spitting on his courthouse sidewalks or someone would have to go get Uncle Billy.

David Clinard, long-time firefighter remembered when, in the mid-1980s, lightning struck the clock tower. The firemen had to break through the heavy glass doors of the courthouse main floor and race up inside the tower to determine how best to fight the fire. He recalled climbing a rickety old 80-year-old spiral, wooden staircase twice hoping and praying they would not collapse beneath him and impede their ability to stop the fire from spreading. This they accomplished with mere hand-held fire extinguishers.

An F-3 tornado was the cause of the courthouse's destruction in 1999. The tornado tore through Clarksville during the early morning of January 22 at 4:12 a.m. Crossing the Cumberland River the tornado totally leveled the Petri Cigar Factory on Crossland Avenue and laid waste to Valleybrook Park, whose trees fell like matchsticks in its path. Next the tornado with 200 miles per hour winds plowed through the historic Dog Hill district and continued its destruction downtown until 4:27 a.m. The tornado hit numerous downtown buildings including the courthouse, Trinity Episcopal Church, Madison Street Methodist Church and the Madison Street Church of Christ. It wreaked havoc on the campus of Austin Peay State University before tearing through the Red River housing district. The width of this tornado was estimated to be 880-feet as it passed through Clarksville. For 4.3 miles the tornado left its mark on the landscape. Fortunately, because the tornado struck at such an early hour in the morning, no one was killed or severely injured. Among the rubble of the courthouse's bricks were the pieces of slate roofing (one of the fire proofing materials after the 1878 fire) and the bell that fell through to the basement.

One of the two new statues of justice sans blindfold. Note the lightning rod attached to the back.

The eagle, so much a topic of debate when the courthouse was built in 1900, was nowhere to be found. In fact, to this day, neither hide nor feather has been seen of it since. Guesses are that it landed somewhere in Kentucky with all of the other debris dropped onto the fields and pastures. Whoever found it has not come forward and its location is still unknown today.

Other courthouse casualties of the tornado included the original gears, brass workings, chains and drives of the previous clock, left in in an unused room nearby and the original clapper for the bell that was lost in the 1900 fire.

The courthouse immediately after the tornado. The building is gutted in preparation for its rebuilding.

History repeated itself as the decision had to be made to either tear the building down or rebuild. At one of many public meetings to debate the issue, Miss Marie Riggins, voiced her strong feelings in front of the county commissioners and County Executive Doug Weiland, about the matter by declaring, "This was Judge Tyler's courthouse and he would want it to be rebuilt!"

Salvaged items from the courthouse after the 1999 tornado. On the left: Brass window hardware. Courtesy Thomas Murff. On the right: A beautifully detailed door hinge. In author's collection.

The courthouse was indeed rebuilt after many months of emotionally charged meetings. The firm of Lyle, Cook and Martin were selected to rebuild the courthouse but with major interior changes. One of the tasks in rebuilding the courthouse was to fill in the old openings for the numerous fireplaces that were present in the exterior walls. The exterior was rebuilt to look like the original but the interior was totally modified to meet current needs. The county mayor's office is located on the second floor and a single courtroom on the same floor displays the photos of the county judges that have sat on the bench throughout the county's history, Judge Tyler's among them. In addition to restoring the courthouse's ornate exterior and redesigning its interior, a new courts center was built next door as well. Lane Lyle stated that he would receive numerous phone calls from Miss Riggins who was making sure he was doing the job correctly.

Amazingly, the 4200-pound bell was not destroyed when, during the 1999 tornado, it came crashing through the roof dropping three stories to the ground level of the courthouse. It is a distinct credit to the foundry that forged the bell that it was discovered to be intact. After the courthouse was rebuilt, the decision was made to simply display the bell in the courthouse yard on the southeast corner of Commerce and Third Streets where it remains today.

The photo on the right shows the broken beam upon which the bell was once suspended. Photos by author.

As before following the fire of 1878, the local newspaper, the *Leaf Chronicle* showed incredible spirit by printing its editions in spite of this horrendous event. A statue, entitled "The Day After," to commemorate the newspaper's tenacity and dedication is seen as a seated figure (Joe Public) reading the January 23, 1999 edition of the newspaper on a city bench across from the *Chronicle's* office on Commerce Street. This statue was created by the local firefighter and sculptor, Scott Wise, who is also responsible for the John Montgomery statue on the Public Square.

On the extremely cold day of the official dedication ceremony, January 22, 2003, a time capsule was placed in the corner of the new courts center building. Several of the invited dignitaries curtailed their speeches because of the cold conditions, which was much appreciated by the large crowd assembled.

The old time capsule had been opened during the demolition work on the old courthouse after the tornado. Sadly, after 120 years, the tin box placed there by Judge Tyler had simply corroded. The few salvageable contents, are now displayed in the atrium on the main floor of the restored courthouse. Not all of the listed contents were found with no explanation as to why they were not. A complete list of the contents was listed in the *Clarksville Semi-Weekly Tobacco Leaf* May 16 edition of the 1879 paper. The list below reflects the efforts of Christine Young, noted paper conservator who restored the contents of the salvageable items of the time capsule.

Expected Contents of the Cornerstone Box:

1. A written history of Montgomery County from April 12, 1780 to 1879; a list of the white and black portions of the population according to each of the census taken for each decade along with all the names of the magistrates who had served during the time, by Judge C.W. Tyler. *Fragments found but unsalvageable.* 2. The contract entered into between the contractors, (MacCormac & Sweeney) and the county commissioners for building the new courthouse, cost $55,000. Contract dated October 23, 1878. *Found and encapsulated.*
2. A copy of the *Clarksville Chronicle* dated May 10, 1879. Actually it was a copy of the *Clarksville Weekly Chronicle*. *Found and encapsulated.*
3. A copy of the *Clarksville Tobacco Leaf* with the account of the 1878 fire. April 13 & 14th, 1878. Actual name of the newspaper was the *Clarksville Semi-Weekly Tobacco Leaf* dated Friday, April 18, 1878. *Fragments found but unsalvageable.*
4. A copy of the *Clarksville Tobacco Leaf* date of laying cornerstone, May 13, 1879. *Fragments found but unsalvageable.*
5. Constitution and by-laws of The Clarksville Tobacco Board of Trade. *Found. Cover encapsulated; contents unsalvageable.*
6. Charter, constitution and by-laws, Citizens' Building and Loan Association. Found and encapsulated.
7. List of names of all officers of Montgomery County. *Not found.*
8. List of contractors and employees of the building. *Not found.*
9. A copy of the *Cincinnati Enquirer*, with the inscription "G.W. Bunting, architect, MacCormac & Sweeney, Columbus, Indiana, contractors C.G. Rosenplaenter, superintendent." May 12, 1879. *Found and encapsulated.*
10. A calling card of Mrs. Ida Redmond, wife of one of the contractors. *Found and encapsulated.*
11. A copy of the *Louisville Evening Post and News* furnished by Mr. H.C. Batts of that newspaper, *Fragments found, but unsalvageable.*
12. A copy of the "Cornerstone," a paper by the *Tobacco Leaf Press* in procession. *Not found.*
13. A copy of the *Louisville Age* (dated May 10, 1879) *Fragments found and encapsulated.*
14. A list of the city officers at the time of the incorporation of Clarksville (1819) and the present board of officers (1879). *Found and encapsulated.*
15. Date of charter, 1865, of First National Bank of Clarksville, list of the officers now and then (1879) *Found and encapsulated.*
17. A foreign coin, by Mr. Samuel Ramey valued at $1.50. Not found.
17. Several bills of U.S. currency; bank notes in denominations of $5, $10, $20 and $50. *Only one found and encapsulated: U.S. one-dollar bill, 1875, serial number N598873E.*
18. An old British coin: British half-penny copper, 1862. *Found.*
19. Confederate money. *Fragments of paper money found but unsalvageable.*
20. Various little articles and coins.

Found but not on the list:

21. Catalogue and announcement of the Clarksville Female Academy, 1878. *Encapsulated.*
22. Newspaper *Clarksville Weekly chronicle*, May 3, 1879. *Encapsulated.*
23. Charter and by-laws of the Tobacco Board of Trade ,1878-79. *Encapsulated.*
24. Proceedings of the Clarksville Tobacco Board of Trade, October 14, 1875. *Encapsulated.*
25. Two trade cards from M.H. Clark & Brother, *Leaf Tobacco* Brokers, Clarksville, Tenn., Hopkinsville, KY and Paducah, KY. *Encapsulated.*
26. Coins found: 1867 nickel, 1876 dime, 1877 quarter. Also found, a brass uniform button from the University of the South (Sewanee).

***An auction was held to sell off remnants of the staircase, light fixtures, doors and floor tiles.

This author was honored to be a member of the choir for the courthouse dedication ceremony on the fourth anniversary of the disaster. Among the crowds of people gathered to celebrate the salvation of the historic building was Marie Riggins. The pride in the restored courthouse was evident that day on the faces of Clarksvillians and in the speeches of the dignitaries.

In 2005 the crumbling courthouse exterior steps were repaired, a project left over from the rebuilding of the courthouse that concluded in 2003. Control joints were installed on the three entrance steps to control cracking. The 4th (north) entrance is completely modified for the disabled and no longer has steps and inside there is an elevator to make all floors of the courthouse handicapped accessible.

Today there is a neighborhood within 1-2 miles of Hickory Wild, named after John Duke Tyler's former school. The names of the streets bear the names of Tyler family members. The entry into the neighborhood is John Duke Tyler Boulevard and there is also Judge Tyler Drive, J.A. Tate Drive, Old Duke Drive, Tate Lane, Black Gum Lane, Teacher Drive and Judge Circle.

A celebration to commemorate the anniversary of the creation of the public library by Judge Tyler was held at the current library in 2019. The special guest was Judge Tyler Gill[183] descendant of the Tyler family.

Clarksville Mayor Joe Pitts, Tyler Gill, Gerald Beavers, library board member and library director Martha Hendricks cutting the ribbon. Photo by author.

In 2024, the Customs House Museum, courthouse, F & M Bank Arena and L & N railroad bridge added an exciting feature to the nighttime sky: they are lit up with appropriate synchronized colors for special holidays and recognized causes. This new addition to the downtown is happily appreciated by all who visit the historic downtown. Also the same year, ground was broken in March for the construction of a new library that will serve the north side of the county.

From 1820 until 1920 the Tyler family had exerted their influence on the history of Montgomery County. Like the Biblical verse which says, "For what is your life? It is even a vapor that appears for a little while and vanishes away," so was it was this family. Sadly, few if any descendants of John Duke Tyler are left in Montgomery County.

The tremendous contributions of Charles Waller Tyler to Montgomery County are like the threads loomed permanently into the tapestry of its history. This remarkable person will, as all others who pass away, simply evaporate from our memories, unless we make an effort to record their existence. He was a multifaceted man, one who was required by circumstances to view situations in black or white, never grey.

Under Judge Tyler, the county debt was paid off, a public library became a reality, improvements were made in the county jail system, the ferries were made free to the public which laid the path for the construction of new bridges, the roads were improved and many more built to accommodate the county's growth.

His magnificent courthouse still stands in 2025 as the gem of the downtown that has suffered several fires and a tornado. Although many disagreed with his methods and use of his authority, no one can say that everything he did was not in the best interest of the county. Judge Tyler never wavered in his belief in the law and administered his rulings accordingly. Montgomery County's first historian, Ursula Smith Beach felt that Tyler affected Montgomery County the most. She said of Tyler in 1976, "He was a gentleman. A fair judge and he was concerned with Sevier Station (its preservation), as I have been for ten years."

Here was a man who had tremendous power and influence and knew how to use it. No one can now argue that he used that power for personal gain and not for the greater good of Clarksville. Tyler was never a rich man and never sought to benefit monetarily from his office.

---

[183] Judge Tyler Gill carries on the Tyler family love of music. In 2024 he participated in the choral production, Handel's Messiah at the Madison Street Methodist Church, enjoyed so much by the author and the entire audience.

After Judge Tyler left office in 1918, a complete audit was ordered by his successor. What Judge Cunningham found in the monetary records was a complete and total accounting of every cent that passed through the hands of Judge Charles Tyler in his forty-seven-year career!

Four years after the death of Tyler, Sterling Fort, in a speech, told of how the judge had dreamed of having a proper high school built to educate the youth of Clarksville. Fort stated because of Judge Tyler, "that dream became a reality and changed a gully-marked field into a splendid high school."

Concurrently while serving as judge, Charles exhibited his capability as the County Financial Agent by taking the county from considerable debt and reducing it by half. When he came to the office the county's finances were in a detestable state. The county owed a bonded debt of $357,423 as well as $8,443 in "floating debts." It took years but he was able to erase all of these debts. The courthouse clock, known as "Judge Tyler's watch" still illuminates the time of day that can be seen for miles. Yet remarkably, even so now 105 years after his death, he may be best remembered for being the father of little Nannie.

From *Picturesque Clarksville*

Photo of Judge Tyler in the Montgomery County Library

Nannie Tyler's statue with the Confederate monument in the background. Photo by author.

Hickory Wild in 2025

Present day aerial photo of the old Hickory Wild property at 3245 Kirkwood Road. Arrow #1 may show the location of the destroyed Tyler family cemetery and arrow #2 shows the house built on the original foundation of the school/home. Photo by Google Maps 2025.

Afterword

"Someone really needs to write a book about this," was a comment I heard while standing that day in the cemetery when Nannie's statue came home. Ten years later I decided to undertake writing a manuscript that I prayed would dignify the story surrounding the statue and the death of the little girl it symbolized, for this is a story that deserves to be told. This was my first manuscript.

It seems that little Nannie Tyler was denied so much by her terrible passing and unfortunately over a century after her death, persons exhibiting the worst side of human nature disturbed her rest. It is the intent of this writer to make her sweet story known and maybe in some way give something back to her.

Whenever possible, dates and details were checked and double-checked but as anyone can tell you who has preceded this "author" in such efforts, historical research is problematic because of inaccurate spellings of names and incorrect dates. So much has been written and taken for fact that even the smallest item needs to be verified. Marie Riggins warned me "there are a lot of fairy tales out there." In this re-write, I found a few!

I sincerely hope I have compiled a manuscript of which she would approve. It is also my intent here to encourage anyone who knows their family history, or has a story to share, to write it down and make it available for others. So much of history is lost to time, the elements, or to natural disasters that it becomes incumbent upon each of us to stay the evaporation of our past. As is well known, Clarksville lost a great deal of its records on that terrible day in January 1999 when the tornado struck.

One can never predict what will be found during genealogical research but it turned into one of those strange coincidences that, while researching the story of Nannie's life that this writer should come upon an obituary of a great uncle that died within the same year and month. His name was Clifton Farrar, son of Pridgen and Mary Farrar, this writer's great grandparents. Clinton was just three years old when he too died of diphtheria. He had an older sister whose name was Genie Farrar. Montgomery County's first female Clerk and Master. This sister was to serve as Judge Tyler's successor, Judge John T. Cunningham's secretary for many years. She would have been among those checking the accounting of the county treasury after Tyler's exit from office. She was to find that every single penny was accounted for during Tyler's stay in office.

That was 2006….it is now 2025: nineteen years ago and ten books later. Somehow this author miraculously put forth books that many people have enjoyed. However, sometimes a book needs to be revisited: additional information is discovered, surprise facts uncovered and corrections needed. This accounted for the pressure to write a second edition Nannie's story. In this I believe I have succeeded in many ways though realizing that the true history of a family can only be known to its members, no matter how much it is researched.

There, of course is much more information on the Tyler family here than that of little Nannie for she lived such a short life. But, understanding her family and ancestors may lead us to understand what type of individual she may have become. Hopefully I have captured their story and done it justice. With each visit to Nannie's grave, I feel satisfied knowing she and her family are all together where only peace may touch them.

Carolyn Stier Ferrell
2025

Appendix A

The Tyler Family Plot at Greenwood Cemetery

Emmie Tyler
Charles' younger sister
October 11, 1849
August 22, 1932

Anna Waller Pettus Dingee
Mildred's relative
April 13, 1861
January 18, 1912

Quintus Marcellus Tyler
Charles' half-brother
August 6, 1816
May 15, 1888

Mildred S. Tyler
Charles' mother
November 23, 1809
January 25, 1884

Nannie Tyler
Charles' daughter
March 16, 1881
September 9, 1885

Tyler Baby
Charles' son
December 7, 1886
December 7, 1886

Armistead Hughes Mitchell IV
Charles' grandson
August 15, 1906
September 18, 1942

Charles Waller Tyler
July 11, 1839
May 27, 1920

Mollie Settle Tyler
Charles' wife
April 21, 1849
August 9, 1900

Note: Mollie (Settle) Tyler's family members are also buried at Greenwood Cemetery in Sections 7, 9, 11 and 23.

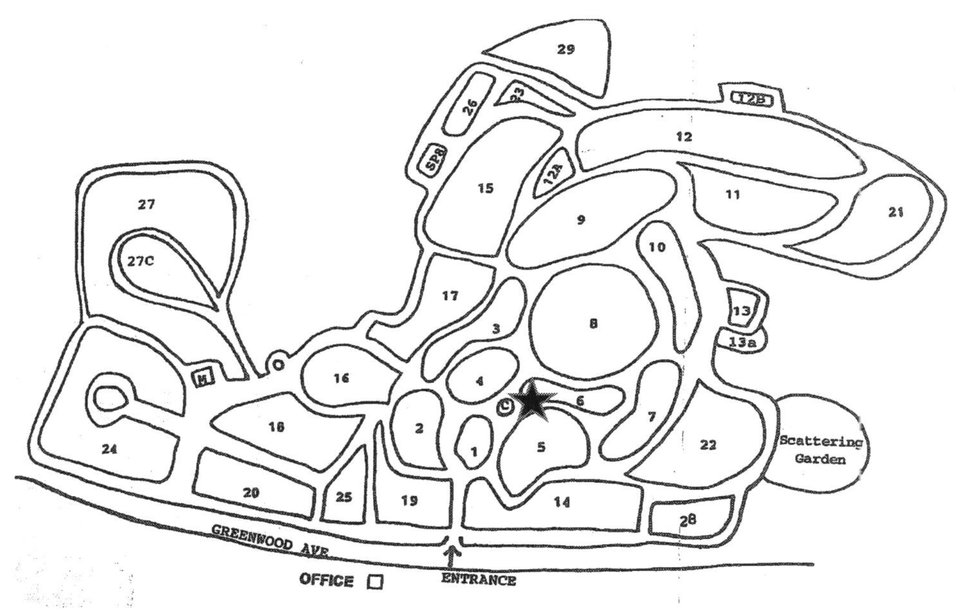

Map courtesy Greenwood Cemetery

Appendix B

Tyler's Law Service Record:

1872: Tyler earned his license to practice law from Cumberland College's School of Law.
1873: Tyler partnered with Edmund B. Lurton in law office.
1873: Tyler appointed by Gov. John C. Brown to fill vacancy in office of County and Criminal Judge of Montgomery County by the death of Judge King.
1874: Tyler elected to fill unexpired term of Judge King. Ran against Henry C. Merritt.
1878: Tyler defeated Col. Thomas L. Yancey and Baker D. Johnson.
1886: Tyler re-elected without opposition.
1894: Tyler re-elected without opposition.
In 1899 the legislature took from Tyler the criminal jurisdiction and gave it to Judge Munford who held it until 1901. It was then restored to Tyler who still acted as County Judge during those two years.
1902: Tyler defeated W.D. Howser.
1910: Tyler defeated John T. Cunningham by a small majority.
1918: Cunningham defeated Tyler by a large majority.

Civil Rights Acts During Tyler's Terms:

The Civil Rights Act of 1866: On April 9, 1866, Congress passed the Civil Rights Act declaring that all persons born in the United States were citizens with full rights under the Constitution.

The Civil Rights Act of 1871 made it a crime to deny any citizen equal protection under the law by means of "force, intimidation or threat."

The Civil Rights Act of 1875: An Act to protect all citizens in their civil and legal rights, declared that all persons were entitled to use public accommodations, and that all persons were allowed to serve on juries. It gave citizens of every race and color equal rights to make contracts, testify in court, purchase, hold and dispose of property, and enjoy full and equal benefit of all laws. It provided punishment for anyone denying this right to any citizen. But on the basis of Dred Scott, the Supreme Court found that the Civil Rights Act of 1875 was unconstitutional, and that under the Constitution, Blacks were not people as "people" is used in the Constitution. Overturned on October 15, 1883.

The Civil Rights Act of 1883: This may have referred to a series of cases that were heard by the Supreme Court on October 15, 1883.

Appendix C

The Criminal Court During Charles W. Tyler's Terms

In some counties of Tennessee, a separate court has been established which has the Criminal law jurisdiction of the Circuit Courts. The Criminal Court has appellate jurisdiction over Criminal law matters decided in the General Sessions Courts.

The Criminal Court of Montgomery County, by general law found in 16-2-506 of Tennessee Code Annotated, is part of the 19th judicial district.

For the general law pertaining to Criminal Courts, see title 16, Chapter 10 of Tennessee Code Annotated. For the general law pertaining to Criminal Court Clerks, see title 18, Chapter 4 of Tennessee Code Annotated.

The following acts once pertained to the Montgomery County Criminal Court, but are no longer current law. Also referenced below are acts which repeal prior law without providing new substantive provisions.

1. Acts of 1841-42, Chapter 27, set the second Monday in January as the day the criminal cases would be heard in Circuit Court in Montgomery County. All civil cases then pending in Circuit Court would be adjourned over until the first Monday in March, the date for beginning the first of three regular terms of Court.
2. Acts of 1847-48, Chapter 171, created a Criminal Court for Montgomery, Rutherford, and Wilson Counties, to be held at Nashville, Clarksville, Murfreesboro and Lebanon, which would be presided over by the Criminal Court Judge of Davidson County. Each Court would be held three times a year. The Circuit Courts in the three affected counties would retain criminal jurisdiction so far as to empanel a grand jury at the regular terms of Court for the finding of bills of indictment and presentments.
3. Acts of 1853-54, Chapter 55, provided that after the next term of the Criminal Court in Montgomery County, the Court would be held on the first Monday of January, May and September.
4. Acts of 1855-56, Chapter 158, provided that the Circuit Court for Sumner County would be transferred to and held by the Judge of the Criminal Court of Rutherford, Davidson and Montgomery Counties.
5. Public Acts of 1857-58, Chapter 98, provided that the Criminal Districts of Davidson, Rutherford and Montgomery would hold three terms of Court in each year at Nashville, Clarksville and Murfreesboro.
6. Public Acts of 1869-70 (2nd Sess.), Chapter 115, established a Criminal Court for Montgomery County to be held in Clarksville. The Court was vested with the same jurisdiction then held by the Circuit Courts of the State for the trial and presentment of crimes and offenses against the State occurring within Montgomery County, and to the exclusion of the Circuit Court. The Circuit Court Clerk would be the clerk for the new Court and the sheriff would perform all 79 duties then required relating to criminal cases in the Circuit Court. Terms of Court would begin on the first Wednesday of each month. The Judge of the County Court would be the Criminal Court Judge and the act conferred upon the judge all the powers and jurisdiction of a Circuit Judge and the Judge would receive the same compensation as did Circuit Judges, payable from the County Treasury.
7. Public Acts of 1870-71, Chapter 63, amended Public Acts of 1869-70 (2nd Sess.), Chapter 115, above, the act creating the Criminal Court for Montgomery County, by providing for four terms of Court beginning on the fourth Monday in January and the Fourth Monday in April, the second Monday in August and the second Monday in November, and authorized special terms of Court within the discretion of the Judge of the Criminal Court.
8. Public Acts of 1873, Chapter 53, fixed the salary of the Judge of the Criminal Court for Montgomery County at $1,800 per year, payable from the State Treasury.

9. Acts of 1885 (Ex. Sess.), Chapter 20, amended Public Acts of 1873, Chapter 53, to set the salary of the Criminal Court Judge at $1250 annually.
10. Public Acts of 1895, Chapter 13, provided that the Judge of the County and Criminal Court would also hold the Chancery Court for Montgomery County which was detached from the Eighth Chancery District.
11. Public Acts of 1899, Chapter 302, repealed Public Acts of 1869-70 (2nd Sess.), Chapter 115, and Public Acts of 1895, Chapter 13.
12. Public Acts of 1899, Chapter 409, directed that the criminal jurisdiction of Montgomery County be conferred upon the Circuit Court to be exercised by the judge of that court at the times then specified by law.
13. Acts of 1901, Chapter 396, established a Criminal Court for Montgomery County to be held at Clarksville and to have all the jurisdiction then conferred upon the Circuit Court in the presentment and trial of offenses against the State, to the exclusion of the Circuit Court. The Clerk of the Circuit Court was designated to act also as the Clerk of the Criminal Court. The Judge of the County Court was to be the Judge of the Criminal Court and the terms of the new Court would be held on the first Monday in February, June and November, and the third Monday in August. The County Judge's salary was fixed at $2,500 and he would receive no further compensation for holding Criminal Court.
14. Acts of 1909, Chapter 579, amended Private Acts of 1901, Chapter 396, by providing that the Criminal Court Judge would be paid a salary equal to that of Circuit Judges and Chancellors in the State, to be paid one-half from Montgomery County funds and one-half from State funds.

Jails and Prisoners

The following acts once affected jails and prisoners in Montgomery County, but are no longer operative.

1 Acts of 1806 (Ex. Sess.), Chapter 43, appointed as commissioners, James Elder, Hugh Bell, John Shelby, Henry Small, and Charles Stewart and authorized them to fix a site in Clarksville and erect a courthouse and a prison for the District of Robertson. Montgomery County would levy a tax for the year 1807 and for two years thereafter to pay for the construction. Robertson, Dickson, and Stewart Counties would also levy a tax to defray a portion of the expenses of building the prison.
2 Acts of 1809, Chapter 50, amended Acts of 1806 (Ex. Sess.), Chapter 43, by appointing Joseph Woolfolk to replace Hugh Bell as Commissioner for the courthouse and prison and providing that if additional vacancies were to occur, they were to be filled by the remaining commissioners.
3 Acts of 1809, (Sept. Sess.), Chapter 66, amended Acts of 1806 (Ex. Sess.), Chapter 43, above, by authorizing Montgomery County to levy additional taxes to pay for the courthouse and prison and directing the Counties of Robertson, Dickson, Hickman, Stewart and Humphreys to levy additional taxes to pay their proportional share of the expenses for the prison.
4 Private Acts of 1826, Chapter 82, allowed the County Court of Montgomery County to levy a tax for the purpose of repairing the county jail or building a new one.
5 Public Acts of 1867-68, Chapter 77, provided that the Jailer of Montgomery County would be elected by the qualified voters for two-year terms.
6 Public Acts of 1883, Chapter 111, directed the County Court of Montgomery County to elect three persons to be Commissioners of the county jail along with the County Judge. The commissioners would have complete jurisdiction and control of the jail and workhouse. They would employ a physician to attend the inmates, examine and approve all accounts for clothing and supplies, work prisoners on the roads with the approval of the District Road Commissioners, or place them at other employment not dangerous or injurious to their health. They were to appoint a superintendent to supervise the jail. The act was declared invalid by the Court because of its defective title in an unreported case styled Staton v. Montgomery County which is cited in Collier v. Montgomery County, 103 Tenn. 705, 54 S.W. 989, 991 (1900).

7 Public Acts of 1889, Chapter 155, provided for the control and management of the jail and workhouse, and the prisoners therein. The act contained most of the provisions of the 1883 Act, above, and also authorized the County Court to appoint a superintendent of the jail and workhouse who would be the Sheriff of the County, if the Sheriff properly notified the County Judge of his intention to fill the office. This Act was the basis of litigation in the case of Collier v. Montgomery County, 103 Tenn. 705, 54 S.W. 989 (1900). It was held invalid on the grounds that it unconstitutionally deprived the sheriff of custody of prisoners not convicted and sentenced to the workhouse.

Sheriff

The following acts have no current effect but are included here for reference purposes since they once applied to the Montgomery County Sheriff's Office.

1. Acts of 1903, Chapter 69, declared that the Montgomery County Sheriff would not be required to give an additional bond on account of his duties regarding the newly created Criminal Court.
2. Private Acts of 1931 (2nd Ex. Sess.), Chapter 17, authorized the Sheriff to appoint one First or Chief Deputy, at a salary of $150 monthly.
3. Private Acts of 1933, Chapter 600, fixed the salary of the Montgomery County Sheriff at $3,600 annually. In the event the fees and commissions collected by the office equaled or exceeded that amount, the excess would be turned over to the Public Treasury, but if such fees and commissions amounted to less than $3,600 then the Sheriff's salary would be the lesser amount.
4. Private Acts of 1935, Chapter 812, provided a scheduled of salaries for several officials of Montgomery County, the Sheriff's being fixed at $3,600 per year.
5. Private Acts of 1941, Chapter 427, authorized the Sheriff to appoint two Deputies of his own choice who would receive, in addition to the fees allowed by law, a salary of $80 monthly paid out of County funds on warrant from the County Judge. The Sheriff was not precluded from hiring other Deputies but they would be paid only the legal fees for work actually done. The Deputies would be required to submit a detailed report showing that they had met all the conditions of the act and had devoted their full time to the duties of office.
6. Private Acts of 1949, Chapter 115, amended Private Acts of 1941, Chapter 427, by increasing the salary of the two Deputies from $80 monthly to $125 monthly.
7. Private Acts of 1951, Chapter 135, authorized the Sheriff of Montgomery County to appoint four Deputies of his own choice, one of whom would be assigned to duty in the District Attorney's office. Each Deputy was to be paid $150 a month over and above the fees then allowed by law.
8. Private Acts of 1953, Chapter 249, authorized the Sheriff to appoint seven Deputies of his own choice, one of whom would be Chief Deputy. A salary of $175 per month would be paid the Deputies.
9. Private Acts of 1957, Chapter 154, amended Private Acts of 1953, Chapter 249, allowing the Sheriff to appoint eight Deputies of his own choice, each to receive a salary of $200 a month in addition to their ordinary fees.
10. Private Acts of 1976, Chapter 262, made it unlawful in Montgomery County for any person except a law enforcement officer duly authorized to make arrests and holding a first, second, or third class radio operator's license, or a member of the Sheriff's Department, or a member of a police force to have in his or her possession or to have installed in a motor vehicle any mobile radio or any other apparatus capable of receiving or transmitting messages or signals on the same wave length or frequency as that assigned to police radios. The act was not approved by local authorities and did not become effective.

Criminal Court

The following acts once pertained to the Montgomery County Criminal Court, but are no longer current law. Also referenced below are acts which repeal prior law without providing new substantive provisions.

1. Acts of 1841-42, Chapter 27, set the second Monday in January as the day the criminal cases would be heard in Circuit Court in Montgomery County. All civil cases then pending in Circuit Court would be adjourned over until the first Monday in March, the date for beginning the first of three regular terms of Court.
2. Acts of 1847-48, Chapter 171, created a Criminal Court for Montgomery, Rutherford, and Wilson Counties, to be held at Nashville, Clarksville, Murfreesboro, and Lebanon, which would be presided over by the Criminal Court Judge of Davidson County. Each court would be held three times a year. The Circuit Courts in the three affected counties would retain criminal jurisdiction so far as to empanel a grand jury at the regular terms of Court for the finding of bills of indictment and presentments.
3. Acts of 1853-54, Chapter 55, provided that after the next term of the Criminal Court in Montgomery County, the Court would be held on the first Monday of January, May and September.
4. Acts of 1855-56, Chapter 158, provided that the Circuit Court for Sumner County would be transferred to and held by the Judge of the Criminal Court of Rutherford, Davidson, and Montgomery Counties.
5. Public Acts of 1857-58, Chapter 98, provided that the Criminal Districts of Davidson, Rutherford, and Montgomery would hold three terms of court in each year at Nashville, Clarksville, and Murfreesboro.
6. Public Acts of 1869-70 (2nd Sess.), Chapter 115, established a Criminal Court for Montgomery County to be held in Clarksville. The Court was vested with the same jurisdiction then held by the Circuit Courts of the State for the trial and presentment of crimes and offenses against the State occurring within Montgomery County, and to the exclusion of the Circuit Court. The Circuit Court Clerk would be the Clerk for the new Court and the Sheriff would perform all duties then required relating to criminal cases in the Circuit Court. Terms of Court would begin on the first Wednesday of each month. The Judge of the County Court would be the Criminal Court Judge and the act conferred upon the Judge all the powers and jurisdiction of a Circuit Judge and the Judge would receive the same compensation as did Circuit Judges, payable from the County Treasury.
7. Public Acts of 1870-71, Chapter 63, amended Public Acts of 1869-70 (2nd Sess.), Chapter 115, above, the act creating the Criminal Court for Montgomery County, by providing for four terms of Court beginning on the fourth Monday in January and the Fourth Monday in April, the second Monday in August and the second Monday in November, and authorized special terms of Court within the discretion of the Judge of the Criminal Court.
8. Public Acts of 1873, Chapter 53, fixed the salary of the Judge of the Criminal Court for Montgomery County at $1,800 per year, payable from the State Treasury.
9. Acts of 1885 (Ex. Sess.), Chapter 20, amended Public Acts of 1873, Chapter 53, to set the salary of the Criminal Court Judge at $1250 annually.
10. Public Acts of 1895, Chapter 13, provided that the Judge of the County and Criminal Court would also hold the Chancery Court for Montgomery County which was detached from the Eighth Chancery District.
11. Public Acts of 1899, Chapter 302, repealed Public Acts of 1869-70 (2nd Sess.), Chapter 115, and Public Acts of 1895, Chapter 13.
12. Public Acts of 1899, Chapter 409, directed that the Criminal jurisdiction of Montgomery County be conferred upon the Circuit Court to be exercised by the Judge of that Court at the times then specified by law.

13. Acts of 1901, Chapter 396, established a Criminal Court for Montgomery County to be held at Clarksville and to have all the jurisdiction then conferred upon the Circuit Court in the presentment and trial of offenses against the State, to the exclusion of the Circuit Court. The Clerk of the Circuit Court was designated to act also as the Clerk of the Criminal Court. The Judge of the County Court was to be the Judge of the Criminal Court and the terms of the new Court would be held on the first Monday in February, June and November, and the third Monday in August. The County Judge's salary was fixed at $2,500 and he would receive no further compensation for holding Criminal Court.
14. Acts of 1909, Chapter 579, amended Private Acts of 1901, Chapter 396, by providing that the Criminal Court Judge would be paid a salary equal to that of Circuit Judges and Chancellors in the State, to be paid one-half from Montgomery County funds and one-half from State funds.

Sheriffs during Tyler's terms:

1872-1874: Irwin Beaumont
1874-1876: James H. Achey
1876-1882: James E. Mosley
1882-1886: James M. Collier
1886-1888: George R. Harris
1888-1892: C.W. Staton
1892-1898: James M. Collier
1898-1904: A.C. Stafford
1904-1910: Charles W. Staton
1910-1914: Robert L. Black
1914-1920: G.L. "Bose" Welker

Mayors during Tyler's terms:

1872-1873: George Harris
1874: George Ligon
1875-1877: Mike Sullivan
1878-1879: George Ligon
1880-1881: J.J. Crusman
1882-1885: Arch Howell
1886-1889: James N. Smith
1890-1891: G. Ligon/T.H. Smith
1892-1897: Dr. N.L. Carney
1898-1899: James H. Smith
1900-1901: W.B. Young
1902-1903: Dr. T.H. Marable
1904-1905: James H. Smith
1906-1910: M.C. Northington
1911-1912: M.R. Hanner
1913-1914: D.B. Wood
1915-1917: Dr. T.H. Marable
1917-1918: E.E. Laurant

Bibliography

"A Bad Bridge," *Clarksville Tobacco Leaf,* April 24, 1886.
"A Ballad of the Night Riders," www.smokenightriders.com, Tennessee Arts Commission.
Abernathy, Charles. Personal interview, January 8, 2006.
"A Bigger Bell, *Leaf Chronicle*, September 29, 1900.
"About Insurance," *Leaf Chronicle*, January 29, 1892.
"About the 19th Century Decades," http://kclibrary.nhmccd.edu/19thcentury1880.htm, April 19, 2006.
"Accident Averted," *Daily Leaf Chronicle,* February 20, 1897.
"Accidents and Incidents," *Clarksville Tobacco Leaf,* April 18, 1878.
"Adee Hickman Murdered Near the Electric Light Station," *Weekly Leaf Chronicle*, March 15, 1892.
"Adolph Hach Buys Tyler Home from Hiett," *Leaf Chronicle*, May 23, 1939.
"A History of Masonry," *Semi-Weekly Tobacco* Leaf, November 2, 1900.
"A Homecoming," *Leaf Chronicle*, June 25, 1996.
"A Just Sentence," *Leaf Chronicle*, July 3, 1901.
"The Alarming Floods," *Clarksville Weekly Chronicle*, January 22, 1882.
"A Lawless Case," *Clarksville Leaf Chronicle,* April 23, 1892.
"Alex M'Kinnon Buried Monday," *Leaf Chronicle*, January 10, 1933.
"Almost a Serious Fire," *Leaf Chronicle*, September 4, 1896.
"An Accomplished Fact," *Leaf Chronicle*, November 22, 1901.
"A Matter of Interest To Public," *Leaf Chronicle*, January 30, 1914.
"An Alleged Night Rider," *Leaf Chronicle*, February 17, 1915.
"A Narrow Escape," *Leaf Chronicle*, April 28, 1900.
"And Great Was the Fall," *Clarksville Weekly Chronicle*, October 12, 1878.
"Angered by Yankees," Special Bicentennial Edition, *Clarksville Leaf Chronicle*, June 3, 1984.
"An Indignation," *Leaf Chronicle*, August 11, 1896.
"Anniversary of High School Fire," *Leaf Chronicle*, November 20, 1917.
"A Noble Woman Has Passed Away," *Clarksville Daily Leaf Chronicle*, August 10, 1900.
"Another Fallen Hero," *Clarksville Tobacco Leaf,* October 24, 1878.
"Another Letter from Manila," *Semi-Weekly Leaf Chronicle*, February 10, 1899.
"Another Little Waif," *Clarksville Leaf Chronicle*, March 12, 1892.
"Another Nightmare," *Weekly Leaf Chronicle*, July 24, 1896.
"Another Plant Bed Destroyed," *Clarksville Leaf Chronicle*, May 23, 1906.
"Annual Reports of the City Officials," *Clarksville Leaf Chronicle*, February 6, 1905.
"An Unique Occasion," *Leaf Chronicle*, December 26, 1899.
"Appertaining to the Old Confederate Reunion," *Leaf Chronicle*, October 12, 1909.
"A Public Benefit," *Leaf Chronicle*, October 19, 1896.
"Area History During the War Between the States," http://oldspencermill,com/page4.html, December 3, 2006.
"A Spook in District No. 9," *Clarksville Leaf Chronicle*, April 19, 1892.
"As to Underpinning," *Clarksville Semi-Weekly Tobacco Leaf*, July 9, 1895.
"Attention Ladies and Gentleman," *Leaf Chronicle*, July 3, 1903.
"Attention Merchants," *Daily Tobacco Leaf Chronicle*, November 4, 1892.
"Attorneys Want to See Prisoners," *Leaf Chronicle*, February 6, 1909.
"Auto Leaps Thirty Feet," *Powell County Call*, December 1, 1906.
"A Water Fountain," *Leaf Chronicle*, April 8, 1898.
Baggett, Lonnie. Personal interview March 6, 2006.
Barker, John Nick, unpublished diaries (1843-1868), Microfilm, Genealogy Room, Clarksville-Montgomery County Public Library.
"Baseball," *Clarksville Weekly Chronicle*, July 6, 1886.
"Baseless, Absolutely No Foundation for the Insinuation in an Article," *Clarksville Leaf Chronicle*, November 19, 1904.
Beach, Ursula Smith. *Along the Warioto*: *A History of Montgomery County, Tennessee.* (Nashville, TN: McQuiddy Press, 1977) p. 108, 251.
Beach, Ursula. "History of Law Enforcement," Printed copy, March 13, 1974.
Beach, Ursula S. and Eleanor Williams. *Nineteenth Century Heritage, Clarksville, Tennessee* (Oxford, MS: The Guild Bindery Press, 1989) p. 8, 12-13, 42-43, 74, 90-94, 110-113, 153, 161,185, 187-88, 193-194, 200-205, 213, 215-216, 220, 223, 231-233, 251, 257-260, 262, 264, 269, 275, 283, 284-286, 289, 303-305, 362-365.
"Beautiful Lillian Theater Will Be Opened Monday," *Leaf Chronicle*, July 26, 1913.
"Beautiful Tribute," *Clarksville Daily Leaf Chronicle*, September 29, 1900.
"Beecher on Gallows Gush," *Clarksville Semi-Weekly Tobacco Leaf,* March 29, 1881.
"Bell Was Raised Today," *Daily Leaf Chronicle*, November 14, 1900.
Ben M., Eva P., Kristen S., and Marcus S. "Clothing of the 1880s," http://www.pkwy.k12.mo.us/northeast/tapp/clothingofthe19th.html, April 19, 2006.
Bentley, Rick. *Bicentennial Focus, 1776-1976, Clarksville/Montgomery County,* (Clarksville, TN, 1976) p. 6-7, 38, 56-57, 62.
"Big Bell," *Daily Leaf Chronicle*, November 14, 1900.

"Big Dance," *Leaf Chronicle*, February 7, 1916.
"Black Dress Goods," Advertisement, *Clarksville Weekly Chronicle*, November 27, 1880.
"Blacksmithing," Advertisement, *Clarksville Jeffersonian*, January 8, 1850.
"Blade and Bullet," *Clarksville Weekly Chronicle*, October 15, 1887.
"The Blind Child and the Star," *Leaf Chronicle*, December 12, 1913.
Blissland Parish Vestry Book at the Episcopal Theological Seminary, near Alexandria, Virginia, p. 21.
"Bloodiest Fight of Modern History," *Daily Leaf Chronicle*, April 11, 1901.
"Boat Trip," *Leaf Chronicle*, May 12, 1898.
"Bold, Bad Burglars," *Leaf Chronicle*, October 15, 1881.
Browning, Elizabeth Barrett. "Grief", http://quotations.about.com/cs/poemlyrics/a/Grief.htm, July 29, 2006.
"Building Lots," Advertisement, *Clarksville Tobacco Leaf*, May 2, 1878.
"Bustle Era Hair Styles, Natural Form Period 1877-1882," http://demode.tweedlebop.com/vic_hair.html, April 19, 2006.
"Called Meeting of the County Court," *Clarksville Tobacco Leaf*, April 18, 1878.
"Campaign for Red Cross Work," *Leaf Chronicle*, May 4, 1917.
Campbell, T.E. "Colonial Caroline*: A History of Caroline County, Virginia*," (Richmond, VA: The Dietz Press, Inc., 1954) p. 160, 347, 357, 370, 431, 432.
i.b.i.d. "Map of Parishes," p. 430.
"Can't Afford a Bond Issue," *Leaf Chronicle*, April 25, 1917.
"Capable Judges Have Guided the Fiscal Affairs of this County," *Leaf Chronicle*, August 31, 1933.
"Captured," *83rd Illinoisan*, March 17, 1865.
"Card from R.B. Rossington," *Leaf Chronicle,* December 6, 1909.
"Caroline County, Virginia," http://www.rootsweb.com/vacaroli/caroline.html, January 18, 2006.
Caroline and Spotsylvania County Records, Letters and Times of the Tylers, Vol. III.
Caroline County, Virginia Court Records. Will Book 1793-1897, Will and Plat Book 1742-1840, Will Book 19, 1814-1818. Abstract by Kimberly Curtis Campbell, (Athens, GA: Iberian Publishing Co., 1998) p. 14-15, 32, 35, 65, 92.
Carpenter, David. Superintendent of Riverview Cemetery, Personal interview, December 27, 2006.
"Caused Big Excitement Up Town," *Leaf Chronicle*, March 17, 1913.
Cecil, Jill Noelle. "Nannie Statue May Return Next Week," *Leaf Chronicle*, June 27, 1996.
i.b.i.d. "Nannie Statue Coming Home Monday," *Leaf Chronicle*, June 29, 1996.
i.b.i.d. "Statue Turns Up in Boston Shop," *Leaf Chronicle*, June 22, 1996.
i.b.i.d. "Neighbors Feel Sense of Loss After Theft," *Leaf Chronicle*, June 5, 1996.
i.b.i.d. "Search Intensifies for Statue Missing from Cemetery," *Leaf Chronicle*, June 6, 1996.
Cemeteries of Caroline County, Virginia. Vol. 1, Compiled by Herbert Ridgeway Collins, (Westminster, MD: Family Line Publications, 1994) p. 136.
"Charles W. Tyler," *Confederate Veteran Magazine*, Vol. 21, No. 7, January 1913, p. 600.
"Charles W. Tyler," Printed copy, Vertical files, Genealogy Room, Clarksville-Montgomery County Public Library.
City Directory of Clarksville, Tennessee 1911-1912, Complied by Ernest Miller, (Ashville, NC: Piedmont Directory Co., 1912) p. 200.
City Directory of Clarksville, Tennessee 1917, (Quincy, IL: Hoffman Directories, 1917) p. 10, 452.
Claggett, David McKee. Personal Diary, October 1, 1862 to January 2, 1865, Genealogy Room, Clarksville-Montgomery County Public Library, p. 24, 27.
Clarke, Lucy Bailey, "The History of Howell School," Printed Copy, Vertical files, Genealogy Room, Clarksville-Montgomery County Public Library.
"Clarksville, A Comprehensive View of Montgomery County's Capital City," *The Daily American*, May 2, 1886.
"Clarksville Bar Takes Action," *Leaf Chronicle*, June 4, 1920.
"Clarksville Does Honor to the Memory of Micajah Clark," *Clarksville Leaf Chronicle,* February 10, 1912.
"Clarksville High School," Advertisement, *Clarksville Tobacco Leaf*, August 13, 1880.
"Clarksville Hit by Tornado," *Clarksville Semi-Weekly Tobacco Leaf*, February 22, 1884.
"Clarksville Local Market," *Clarksville Semi-Weekly Tobacco Leaf*, March 8, 1881.
"Clarksville Marble Works," Advertisement*, Clarksville Semi-Weekly Tobacco Leaf,* August 18, 1880.
"Clarksville Marble Works," Advertisement, *Leaf Chronicle*, August 20, 1880.
"Clarksville Reading Club," *Clarksville Tobacco Leaf*, June 29, 1880.
"Clarksville's Great Calamity," *Clarksville Tobacco Leaf*, April 18, 1878.
Clarksville Sesqui-Centennial 1783-1934, Printed copy, in possession of author, p. 13, 27.
"Clarksville: The Gem of the Cumberland," Unpublished manuscript, Genealogy Room, Clarksville-Montgomery County Public Library.
Clarksville, Tennessee City Directory 1885-1886, Adam Woodbridge, proprietor, (Chattanooga, TN: C.W. Norwood and Company, 1886) p. 10-11, 67, 71.
Clarksville, Tennessee City Directory, 1895-96, (Paducah, KY: Zorn Printing Co., 1895) p. 116.
Clarksville and Montgomery County in Tennessee, Chamber of Commerce of Clarksville and Montgomery County, (Cleveland, OH: Bryan Printing Co.) no publication date given.
Clinard, David. Personal interview, October 27, 2024.
"Committee Decides on County Jail," *Leaf Chronicle,* May 22, 1906.
"Committee's Action on County Convict Matter," *Leaf Chronicle*, February 17, 1906.
"Complete Plans for Red Cross," *Leaf Chronicle*, May 10, 1917.
"Complimentary," *Clarksville Weekly Chronicle*, February 28, 1874.
"Compliments to a Rising Young Man," *Daily Leaf Chronicle*, May 27, 1901.
"Conestoga," http://www.en.wikipedia.org/wiki/Conestoga_(ship), November 29, 2006.

Confederate Rolls, Microfilm, Tennessee State Library and Archives, Nashville, TN.
"The Confederate Soldier," http://www.nps.gov/archive/gett/gettkidz/reb.html, December 22, 2006.
"Constitution and By-Laws," *Daily Tobacco Leaf*, October 4, 1894.
"Contract," *Leaf Chronicle,* November 22, 1901.
"Contract for the New City Hall Let," *Leaf Chronicle*, November 7, 1913.
"Cooke Sells Out Jewelry Store," *Leaf Chronicle*, April 26, 1922.
The Corn Sheller, March 1979, Vol. II. #3.
"Corner Stone Laying," *Clarksville Semi-Weekly Tobacco Leaf,* May 6, 1879.
Correspondence Relating to the War with Spain Including the Insurrection in the Philippine Islands and the China Relief Expedition April 15, 1898 to July 30, 1902, Vol. 1, Center of Military History United States Army, Washington, D.C., 1993, Library of Congress, U.S. Government Printing Office.
"Council in Session," *Leaf Chronicle*, June 11, 1895.
"County Court-April Term," *Leaf Chronicle*, April 12, 1873.
"County Court Meets in Called Session," *Daily Leaf Chronicle*, May 29, 1905.
"The County Court Met in Quarterly Session," *Leaf Chronicle*, April 6, 1903.
"County Judge, The Tyler Family," *Cumberland Lore, Leaf Chronicle*, April 30, 2002.
"County Sells Boys' Dormitory," *Leaf Chronicle*, April 2, 1917.
"Courted Death; Met It Calmly," *Clarksville Daily Leaf Chronicle,* July 19, 1902.
"The Court House Bell," *Clarksville Weekly Chronicle*, August 14, 1880.cunningh
"Court House Clock Bell's Inscription Found in Records," *Leaf Chronicle*, March 9, 1940.
"Court House Clock Goes Wrong Again, *Leaf Chronicle*, January 16, 1914.
"The Court House Clock Nutty Again," *Leaf Chronicle*, June 29, 1914.
"The Court House Clock," *Leaf Chronicle*, October 26, 1910.
"Court House Getting Along Nicely," *Daily Leaf Chronicle*, December 21, 1900.
"The Court House Wrecked by Fire," *Semi-Weekly Leaf Chronicle*, March 13, 1900.
"Court House Lawn," *Leaf Chronicle*, May 8, 1894.
"Courtroom Crowded to Hear Argument in Hunter Murder Trial," *Leaf Chronicle*, July 14, 1909.
"Crazy Woman Breaks Up Camp Meeting," *Daily Leaf Chronicle*, July 25, 1901.
"The Criminal Court and County Judgeship," *Leaf Chronicle*, March 18, 1881.
"Criminal Court," *Clarksville Weekly Chronicle*, June 14, 1875.
"Criminal Court," *Clarksville Semi-Weekly Tobacco Leaf*, November 11, 1887.
"Criminal Court," *Leaf Chronicle*, May 25, 1899.
"Criminal Court," *Clarksville Chronicle,* February 6, 1875.
"Criminal Court," *Leaf Chronicle*, February 3, 1875.
"Criminal Court," *Clarksville Tobacco Leaf*, March 6, 1880.
"Criminal Court to Convene," *Leaf Chronicle*, November 11, 1911.
"Criminal Court Still Grinding," *Leaf Chronicle*, December 6, 1912
Cunningham, Bill. *On Bended Knees*, McClanahan Publishing House, Nashville, TN, 1983, p. 134,139, 188-189.
"Cunningham Judge by Overwhelming Majority," *Clarksville Leaf Chronicle*, August 2, 1918.
"Dance at Idaho Springs," *Leaf Chronicle*, July 12, 1899.
Darnell, Jones, Alley and Hogan. *Cemetery Records of Montgomery County, Tennessee,* Vol. I, 1968, Vol. II, (Clarksville, TN: Ideal Printing Co.)
Davis, Marna Jean. *Children's Clothing from the Victorian Era,* http://www.shootingstarhistory.com/children.html, April 19, 2006.
"Death and Funeral of Henry H. Bryan, Esq.," *Clarksville Chronicle*, December 21, 1878.
"Death Comes to Cave Johnson," *Clarksville Leaf Chronicle,* November 25, 1904.
"Death of Captain John D. Tyler," *Clarksville Weekly Chronicle,* May 25, 1860.
"Death of Miss Mildred Johnson," *Clarksville Leaf Chronicle*, June 5, 1905.
"Death of Mr. J. Tyler Bryan," *Clarksville Semi-Weekly Tobacco Leaf*, November 9, 1880.
"Death of Mrs. Mary F. Bryan," *Clarksville Leaf Chronicle*, March 11, 1892.
"Death of Quint. M. Tyler," *Clarksville Semi-Weekly Tobacco Leaf*, June 12, 1888.
"Death of Respected Colored Man," *Daily Leaf Chronicle*, August 21, 1912.
"Death Summons Miss Em Tyler," *Clarksville Leaf Chronicle,* August 22, 1932.
"Death of Tyler Bryan," *Clarksville Weekly Chronicle*, November 13, 1880.
"Declined to Deliver Ben Rhinehart," *Leaf Chronicle*, August 21, 1912.
"Decoration Day," *Clarksville Tobacco Leaf Chronicle*, May 18, 1892.
"Delightful Reception," *Clarksville Daily Tobacco Leaf,* December 13, 1894.
Detroit Toy Store 1870, http://www.detroithistorical.org/exhibits/streetsoflldetroit/toy.asp, April 19, 2006.
Dickinson, Emily. "Vanished," *Collected Poems of Emily Dickinson*, (New York: Crown Publishers, Inc., 1982) p. 202.
i.b.i.d. "A Book," *Collected Poems of Emily Dickinson*, (New York: Avenel Books, 1982) p. 34.
i.b.i.d. "I Went to Thank Her," *Collected Verses of Emily Dickinson,* (New York: Crown Publishers, Inc., 1982) p. 244.
Dicken, Emma. *Terrell Genealogy*, (San Antonio, TX: The Naylor Company) no date given.
"Dick Tyler," *Hopkinsville Kentuckian*, August 31, 1904.
"The Difference was Dynamite," *Leaf Chronicle*, July 30, 1996.
"Diphtheria," Directors of Health Promotion and Education, http://www.astdhpphe.org/infect/dip.html, December 26, 2005.
"Divorce Actions," *The Palm Beach Post*, March 29, 1940.
"Doc Martin Sentenced to be Hanged August 2," *Leaf Chronicle,* July 3, 1901.
"Dr. Goodman Is Insane," *Leaf Chronicle,* June 21, 1897.

Dolan, Maryanne. *Vintage Clothing, 1880-1960, Identification and Value Guide*, (Florence, AL: Books Americana, Inc., 1987) p. 1-4, 10, 18.
"Doomed Man. Wm. Morrow Awaiting His Execution This Afternoon," *Clarksville Semi-Weekly Tobacco Leaf,* June 19, 1885.
Doran, Michael F. *Atlas of County Boundary Changes in Virginia 1634-1895*, (Athens, GA: Iberian Publishing Co., 1987) p. 41.
Dorris, William Pvt., 83rd Illinois Infantry. Letter to his wife from Ft. Donelson, April 21,1863, *Cumberland Lore, Leaf Chronicle,* March 18, 1985.
"Dreams and Premonitions," *Leaf Chronicle*, October 5, 1906.
"Dr. Cunningham Passes Away," *Leaf Chronicle*, November 22, 1910.
Dunn, Brian. "Nannie in Protective Custody," *Leaf Chronicle*, October 26, 1999.
i.b.i.d. "Tears Flow for Nannie," *Leaf Chronicle*, October 25, 1999.
Durrett, Nancy Dozier. Personal interview, January 27, 2007.
"Dwelling House Fired into," *Clarksville Leaf Chronicle,* April 23, 1908.
"Edmund Hunter Loses Barn and its Contents," *Leaf Chronicle*, June 12, 1908.
"Education," Advertisement, *Clarksville Gazette*, December 12, 1819.
Ellerton, John Lodge. "Now That the Laborer's Task Is O'er," *The Best Loved Poems of the American People*, (New York: Doubleday, 1936) p. 348.
Elson, Henry W. *The Civil War Through the Camera*, (New York: McKinlay, Stone & MacKenzie, 1912).
Encyclopedia of Virginia Biography, Vol. 1. Lyon Gardiner Tyler LL.D. ed., (Baltimore, MD: Genealogical Publishing Co., 1998) p. 284-285, 346-347.
"The End of a Famous Case in Montgomery County," *Leaf Chronicle*, December 6, 1907.
"Entertainment at Hickory Wild Academy," *Clarksville Tobacco Leaf*, February 25, 1874.
"Epitaphs," *Courier-Journal*, August 3, 1889.
"Erin Enterprise," *Clarksville Democrat,* March 24, 1883.
Evans, Ronn, *Memorabilia of Clarksville and Montgomery County*, unpublished manuscript, Genealogy Room, Clarksville-Montgomery County Public Library, p. 3-9, 14-18, 22-23, 25, 35.
"Evening of Encores," *Leaf Chronicle*, October 25, 1895.
"Every Man to the Front," *Clarksville Tobacco Leaf*, April 18, 1878.
"Execution," *The Watchman*, June 15, 1821.
"The Execution of Ben Harbert," *Clarksville Jeffersonian*, March 12, 1856.
"The Execution of Elias," *Clarksville Jeffersonian*, April 11, 1855.
"Executive Committee Adopts a Program," *Leaf Chronicle*, October 18, 1899.
"Ex-Night Rider Now Bootlegger," *Leaf Chronicle*, December 24, 1930.
"Expert Tobacco Twister," *Daily Tobacco Leaf*, April 21, 1897.
"Eye Sore Comes Down," *Semi-Weekly Tobacco Leaf-Chronicle*, July 5, 1895.
"Fall Millinery," Advertisement, *Clarksville Weekly Chronicle*, December 11, 1880.
"Fall of Clarksville 1862," *Cumberland Lore, Leaf Chronicle*, Howard Winn, ed. June 16, 1986.
"Fall of Fort Donelson," *Tennessee Historical Quarterly*, William T. Alderson, ed. Vol. 21, (Nashville, TN: Tennessee Historical Society, 1962) p. 71, 83.
"Farm for Sale," *Clarksville Chronicle*, December 7, 1866.
"Farmers' Meeting Today," *Leaf Chronicle*, January 30, 1905.
"Fashionable Furniture," Advertisement, *Clarksville Chronicle*, June 25, 1858.
"Fast Driving Through Bridge," *Leaf Chronicle*, January 15, 1916.
"Fatal Shooting Affair at Clarksville," *The Tennessean*, November 7, 1880.
"Female School at White Hall," Advertisement, *Clarksville Jeffersonian*, August 30, 1851.
*50th Tennessee Infantry Regiment", Tennesseans in the Civil War. A Military History of Confederate and Union Units, Part 1, (*Nashville, TN: Civil War Centennial Commission, 1964) p. 285-288.
"First Brick," *Clarksville Weekly Chronicle,* April 27, 1878.
"First Meeting of the Joint High School Board," *Leaf Chronicle*, May 17, 1910.
Fleet, Beverley. *Virginia Colonial Abstracts*, Vo. II, (Baltimore, MD: Genealogical Publishing Co., Inc., 1968) p. 116.
"For Atlanta," *Leaf Chronicle Weekly*, September 27, 1881.
"For Liberty," *Weekly Leaf Chronicle*, December 20, 1889.
"For Sale," Advertisement, *Clarksville Jeffersonian*, March 15, 1851.
"For Sale," Advertisement, *Tennessee Watchman*, January 20, 1821.
"For Sale," Advertisement, *Leaf Chronicle*, June 11, 1912.
Forbes Bivouac Attendance Roll, unpublished copy, Genealogy Room, Clarksville-Montgomery County Public Library.
"Forbes Bivouac Makes Preparation for Decoration Day," *Clarksville Leaf Chronicle*, May 11,1892.
"Former Judge Charles W. Tyler Passes to His Eternal Reward," *Clarksville Leaf Chronicle*, May 28, 1920.
"Fort Donelson National Battlefield," http://www.nps.gov/fodo/, December 4, 2006.
"Founders of Trinity Parish Honored in Memorial Service," *Leaf Chronicle*, October 10, 1932.
"Free Bridges," *Leaf Chronicle*, January 5, 1897.
"Free Vaccinations," *Clarksville Tobacco Leaf*, February 10, 1882.
"Frey and Holman Get Premiums," *Leaf Chronicle* September 30, 1911.
"Fully Exonerated," *Clarksville Daily Tobacco Leaf Chronicle,* May 29, 1894.
"Funeral of Cave Johnson," *Clarksville Leaf Chronicle*, November 26, 1904.
Funk, William H., "Brutal Saviors of the Black Patch," https://www.historytoday.com/miscellanies/brutal-saviours-black-patch.

Gannaway, Richard and Bristol. *Obituaries Complied from Clarksville Newspapers, Montgomery County, Tennessee*, Vol. 1, 1869-1910, published 1991.
i.b.i.d. 1883-1870, Vol. 2. i.b.i.d. 1893-1884, Vol. 3.
i.b.i.d. 1903-1894, Vol. 4.
i.b.i.d. 1913-1904, Vol. 5.
i.b.i.d. 1914-1921, Vol. 6.
i.b.i.d. 1922-1926, Vol. 7.
i.b.i.d. 1927-1930, Vol. 8.
i.b.i.d. 1931-1934, Vol. 9.
Genealogies of Virginia Families, Vol. III, (Baltimore, MD: Genealogy Publishing Co, Inc., 1981) p. 793.
i.b.i.d. Vol. V, (Baltimore, MD: Genealogy Publishing Co., Inc., 1982) p. 235-242.
"Gets a Furlough, *Weekly Leaf Chronicle*, February 28, 1899.
Gildrie, Richard. "Bill Morrow Expiates His Crime Upon the Gallows," *Cumberland Lore, Leaf Chronicle*, March 18, 1985.
i.b.i.d. *Heirs Through Hope, A History of Trinity Episcopal Church,* Trinity Episcopal Church: 1983, p. 74, 79, 82, 88-89.
i.b.i.d. and Kemmerly, Phillip and Thomas H. Winn. *Clarksville, Tennessee in The Civil War: A Chronology*, September 1984, p. 5-6, 18, 42.
i.b.i.d. "Lynch Law and the Great Clarksville Fire of 1878: Social Order in a New South Town," *Tennessee Historical Quarterly,* Vol. 42, (Nashville: Tennessee Historical Society: Robert B. Jones, ed., Spring, 1983) p. 58-77.
Gill, Sue. Personal interview, January 14, 2006.
Gill, Tyler. Phone interview, January 8, 2024.
"Going after Drink Dealers," *Nashville Banner*, August 19, 1912.
"Good Races and Sport," *Leaf Chronicle*, September 9, 1909.
Goodspeed History of Tennessee, Illustrated, Montgomery, Robertson, Humphreys, Stewart, Dickson, Cheatham and Houston Counties, (Nashville, TN: Woodward and Stinson Publishers, 1886) p. 773, 791-799, 1110-11.
Goodspeed Tennessee History and Biographies, Montgomery County, (Signal Mountain, TN: Mountain Press, 2002) p. 31-32.
"Goosetree on Trial," *Clarksville Weekly Chronicle*, March 25, 1892.
"Governor Offers $1000 Reward," *Leaf Chronicle*, June 18, 1908.
Gower, Stanley, "Beautified Courthouse is Credit to County," *Leaf Chronicle*, May 15, 1966.
"Grand Jury in Session," *Leaf Chronicle,* January 19, 1910.
"Grand Jury in Session," *Leaf Chronicle*, February 19, 1915.
Grant, Ulysses S. *Personal Memoirs, 1885-1886*, http://classicbook.info/books/personal- memoirs-of-u-s-grant-complete-/chapter-27-page-1, December 5, 2006.
"Grant's Visit," Charles Waters, ed., *Cumberland Lore*, *Leaf Chronicle*, May 1, 1994.
Gray, Mary Winters. "Greenwood Summers Evoke Memories," *Cumberland Lore, Leaf Chronicle*, September 1990.
"Great Crowd Flocks to Criminal Courtroom," *Leaf Chronicle*, November 29, 1907.
"Greenwood Cemetery," Pamphlet, Greenwood, Inc. 2006.
Greenwood Cemetery Records, November 1884-May 1926, Greenwood Cemetery Office.
Griffey, Irene M. "The Old Indian," *Cumberland Lore*, *Leaf Chronicle*, April 29, 2003.
Guest, Edgar A. "As We Prayed," *Collected Verse of Edgar A. Guest*, (Chicago, IL: The Reilly & Lee Co., 1934) p. 588.
Gowan, Hugh and Judy. *Blue and Grey Cookery Authentic Recipes from The Civil War Years*, (Altoona, PA: Daisy Publications, 1983) p. 13.
i.b.i.d. *Stories, Anecdotes and Humor from the Civil War*, (Altoona, PA: Daisy Publications, 1983) p. 2.
"Grandson of Late Judge Tyler Dies," *Clarksville Leaf Chronicle*, September 19, 1942.
Green, Louise. Personal interview. June 21, 2006.
Griffey, Irene M., *Montgomery County Courthouses, 2003*, p. 3-16, 26.
i.b.i.d. "Courthouse Ceiling Collapses," *Cumberland Lore*, *Leaf Chronicle*, January 21, 2003.
Griffey, Irene M. and Rubye Patch. "Clarksville Historic Cemetery Trails, Riverview Cemetery," *Cumberland Lore*, *Leaf Chronicle,* November 1, 1999.
"Guerilla Chase," *83rd Illinoisan*, April 7, 1865.
"Had A Narrow Escape," *Clarksville Leaf Chronicle*, July 24, 1900.
"Half Clad Lunatic," *Daily Leaf Chronicle,* February 19, 1897.
Halliburton, John H. *Clarksville Architecture*, (Nashville, TN: Parthenon Press, 1977) p. 1-9, 31-34, 63, 67.
"Halloween Pranks," *Clarksville Leaf Chronicle*, November 1, 1905.
"Harold Mitchell Buys Two New Automobiles," *The Anaconda Standard,* January 29, 1913.
Harris, Steven B. "Death by Hanging," http://yarchive.net/med/hanging.html, May 4, 2006.
"Hatton Fund Association," *Clarksville Chronicle*, April 27, 1866.
Hays, Ruth. Handwritten manuscript on Hickory Wild: no date given.
"Head Brace for Wet Plate and Daguerreotype," http://thephotopalace.blogspot.com.
"Health Seekers Coming This way," *Leaf Chronicle*, July 11, 1914.
"He Has Returned," *Leaf Chronicle*, March 2, 1899.
"Henry H. Bryan," *Clarksville Semi-Weekly Leaf Chronicle*, February 28, 1896.
Henson, Timothy R. *Armed and Dangerous, Civil War in the Tobacco Patch*, printed copy 2005, p. 8-9.
"Hickory Wild Academy," *Clarksville Weekly Chronicle*, July 25, 1873.
"Hickory Wild Academy," *Leaf Chronicle*, July 30, 1873.
"Hickory Wild Academy," *Leaf Chronicle*, June 28, 1877.
"Hickory Wild," *Clarksville Semi-Weekly Tobacco Leaf,* June 10, 1879.
"Hickory Wild Academy," Advertisement, *Clarksville Semi-Weekly Tobacco Leaf,* September 5, 1879.

Hicks, Mrs. Ellis. Personal Interview, December 16, 2006.
Hiden, M.W. "The Late Governor J. Hoge Tyler's Family of Essex and Caroline Counties," *William and Mary Quarterly,* Vol. III, (Baltimore, MD: Genealogy Publishing Co., 1981*)* p. 780-796.
"Historical Emporium," https://www.historicalemporium.com/mens-late-victorian-clothing.php#styleguide, July 21, 2024.
"Historical Marker Honors Dr. Burt," Charles Waters, ed., *Cumberland Lore*, *Leaf Chronicle*, July 1,1993.
"Historic Court House," *Leaf Chronicle*, March 12, 1975.
"Historic Old Colt's Revolver," *Leaf Chronicle*, December 14, 1900.
History of Tennessee, Illustrated. Montgomery, Robertson, Humphreys, Stewart, Dickson, Cheatham and Houston Counties, (Nashville, TN: The Goodspeed Publishing Co., 1886) p. 784, 791-793, 803, 813.
"Home of J.D. Tyler Wrecked by Fire," *Leaf Chronicle*, April 23, 1917.
Hooper, J.J. "Hills and Hollows," *Nashville Banner*, May 26, 1852.
Hopkins, William Lindsay. *Caroline County, Virginia Court Records and Marriages, 1787-1810,* (Athens, GA: Iberian Publishing Co.,1995) p. 44-45, 78, 92-93, 118.
"Horse and Buggy Days," *Leaf Chronicle*, October 23, 1947.
"Horse Ran Away but Kept Stopping," *Daily Leaf Chronicle*, October 10, 1900.
"Hotel De Stafford is Very Populous," *Daily Leaf Chronicle*, November 21, 1900.
Hunt, Arthur, Jr. *Time Was 1922-1946*, Printed 2006.
"Hurricane Springs," Advertisement, *Clarksville Semi-Weekly Tobacco Leaf*, June 17, 1879.
"Impeachment Trial," *Clarksville Semi-Weekly Tobacco Leaf*, March 25, 1881.
"Important Bill is Now Pending," *Leaf Chronicle*, March 10, 1915.
"Improved Highways," *Leaf Chronicle*, January 11, 1895.
"Infant Dead," *Leaf Chronicle*, May 1, 1903.
"The Injunction," *Leaf Chronicle*, August 15, 1903.
"Injunction Sustained," *Leaf Chronicle*, August 19, 1903.
"Injunction Dissolved," *Leaf Chronicle*, December 4, 1903.
"In Memoriam, Tyler Bryan," *Clarksville Weekly Chronicle,* November 13, 1880.
"Inside Facts," *Leaf Chronicle,* November 12, 1887.
"In Society," *Daily Leaf Chronicle*, February 15, 1898.
"In Society, A Bowling Party," *Leaf Chronicle*, December 2, 1899.
"It is a Five Dollar Reward," *Daily Leaf Chronicle*, July 14, 1896.
Jackman, Bob. "Widely Loved Statue Returned," *Maine Antique Digest,* http://www.maineantiquedigest.com/articles/nann0896.htm, 1996.
"Jail Committee Holds Meeting," *Leaf Chronicle*, April1, 1912.
"J.D. Taylor Lost Plant Beds," *Leaf Chronicle,* May 21, 1907.
"J.D. Tyler Accidentally Shoots Himself in Leg," *Leaf Chronicle*, January 6, 1898.
"Jeff Davis Church," *Clarksville Tobacco Leaf*, November 5, 1886.
"Joe D. Tyler is Buried Sunday," *Clarksville Leaf Chronicle*, March 1, 1937.
John Calvin Jordan, Personal Letter, 49th Tennessee Infantry, June 10, 1863. http://members.aol.com/jweaver303/tn/49tnltr.htm, December 3, 2006.
"John Duke Tyler," *Republican Banner*, March 3, 1853.
Jones, Dianne A. VAGenWeb Hanover County, "Virginia Map, Genealogy Project," http://www.rootsweb.com/~vahanove, January 18, 2006.
Jordan, Thomas and J.P. Pryor, *The Campaigns of Lieutenant-General N.B. Forrest and of Forrest's Cavalry,* (Dayton, OH: Morningside Bookshop, 1973) p. 88-93.
"Joseph D. Tyler," *The Tennessean*, February 28, 1937.
"Joseph D. Tyler Kicked by Horse," *Leaf Chronicle*, July 11, 1907.
"Jubilee at Hamptons," *Leaf Chronicle*, October 26, 1876.
"Judge Brandon's Experience," *Leaf Chronicle*, January 23, 1900.
"Judge C.W. Tyler," *Nashville Banner*, August 23, 1918.
"Judge C.W. Tyler," *Leaf Chronicle*, March 3, 1894.
"Judge Stout Renders Opinion," *Leaf Chronicle*, February 9, 1909.
"Judge Thomas W. King," *Leaf Chronicle,* July 30, 1873.
"Judge Tyler," *Clarksville Daily Tobacco Leaf Chronicle*, April 6, 1893.
"Judge Tyler," *Clarksville Weekly Chronicle*, February 6, 1875.
"Judge Tyler and County "Politics," *Leaf Chronicle*, May 23, 1898.
"Judge Tyler and Sheriff Staton at Loggerheads," *Clarksville Semi-Weekly Tobacco Leaf*, May 21, 1889.
"Judge Tyler Back from Biloxi," *Clarksville Leaf Chronicle*, April 29, 1904.
"Judge Tyler Caned," *Clarksville Daily Tobacco Leaf Chronicle,* July 20, 1894.
"Judge Tyler Home Being Remodeled," *Leaf Chronicle*, October 25, 1939.
"Judge Tyler Issues Warning," *Leaf Chronicle*, July 29, 1914.
"Judge Tyler Mentioned Among 'Writers of Today,'" *Daily Leaf Chronicle*, December 17, 1901.
"Judge Tyler Much Better," *Leaf Chronicle*, January 29, 1907.
"Judge Tyler Sets Aside the Verdict in the Malcolm Mimms Case," *Leaf Chronicle,* December 19, 1911.
"Judge Tyler's Case," *Clarksville Tobacco Leaf*, March 22, 1881.
"Judge Tyler's Friends Coming to the Rescue," *Nashville Banner,* March 18, 1881.
"Judge Tyler's Report," *Clarksville Tobacco Leaf,* January 9, 1880.
"Judge Tyler Succeeds in Getting the Five Percent Addition to Our Taxes Removed," *Clarksville Leaf Chronicle*, September 18, 1900.

"Judge Tyler to Prepare an Important Statement of the County's Resources," *Clarksville Leaf Chronicle*, February 25, 1904.
"Judge Tyler Writing Up the County's Resources," *Clarksville Leaf Chronicle*, March 3, 1904.
"Judge Tyler's System of Road Building," *Daily Leaf Chronicle*, September 25, 1901.
Kalman, Bobbie. *Early Settler Children*, (New York: Crabtree Publishing Co., 1991) p. 6, 42, 46, 49, 56, 58, 60-61.
"The Kindergarten," *Clarksville Semi-Weekly Tobacco Leaf*, February 26, 1895.
Kentucky, U.S., County Marriage Records, 1783-1965.
Killebrew, Joseph B. *Recollections of My Life,* Printed, Vol. I, Genealogy Room, Clarksville-Montgomery County Public Library, 1896.
i.b.i.d. "Middle Tennessee, Montgomery County," *Nashville Banner*, January 30, 1904.
i.b.i.d. "Middle Tennessee, Montgomery County" *Nashville Banner*, February 13, 1904.
Kimbrough, Ben. Personal Interview, January 15, 2007.
Kirchberger, Joe H. *The Civil War and Reconstruction, An Eyewitness History*, (New York: Facts on File, Inc., 1991) p. 115, 117, 175.
"Ladies Hair Dressing and Manufacturing," Advertisement, *Clarksville Tobacco Leaf,* May 30, 1878.
"Large Audience Saw Patience Last Night," *Daily Leaf Chronicle*, April 26, 1901.
"Last Rites for Judge Tyler," *Clarksville Leaf Chronicle*, May 29, 1920.
"Leaflets," *Clarksville Tobacco Leaf*, November 7, 1878.
"Leaflets," *Clarksville Tobacco Leaf*, November 14, 1878.
"Leaflets," *Leaf Chronicle*, April 7, 1885.
Ledbetter, Bill. "Musings of a Former Paper Boy," *Cumberland Lore, Leaf Chronicle*, May 1993.
"Leg Broken," *Leaf Chronicle,* March 11, 1904.
Letters and Times of the Tylers, Vol III., p. 226.
"Let the Public Square Be Sprinkled," *Leaf Chronicle*, April 10, 190∞.
"Lime," Advertisement, *Clarksville Weekly Chronicle*, May 11, 1878.
"Limestone for Iron Furnace," *Leaf Chronicle*, May 11, 1917.
Lindsley, John L. "Fiftieth Tennessee Infantry," *The Military Annals of Tennessee, Confederate,* (Spartansburg, SC: The Reprint Company, 1974) p. 558-566.
Littlefield, Holly. *Children of the Trail West*, (Minneapolis, MN: Carolrhoda Books, Inc., 1999) p. 13, 18-19, 20-21.
Lockert, Robert. "The Gray Bat's Survival," http://www.batcon.org/batsmag/v20n2-02.html, November 19, 2006.
Logsdon, David R. *Eyewitnesses at the Battle of Fort Donelson,* (Nashville: Kettle Mills Press, 1998) p. 71, 83.
"Lynching," *Clarksville Semi-Weekly Tobacco Leaf*, March 7, 1878.
"MacCormac's Art Gallery," *Clarksville Tobacco Leaf,* October 31, 1878.
"Madison Extension to be Widened," *Daily Leaf Chronicle*, April 16, 1901.
"The Majestic Range Co.," *Leaf Chronicle*, October 20, 1899.
"Many Plant Beds Burned," *Clarksville Leaf Chronicle*, February 15, 1915.
"Many Visitors Go to The Nashville Reunion," *Clarksville Leaf Chronicle*, June 14, 1904.
"Marble Hall," *Clarksville Semi-Weekly Tobacco Leaf*, July 28, 1882.
"Market House," *Clarksville Semi-Weekly Leaf-Chronicle*, July 9, 1895.
"Market House Bell," *Clarksville Weekly Chronicle*, May 18, 1878.
Marshall, Charlotte O. "Parlor Tricks," *Cumberland Lore, Leaf Chronicle*, April 30, 2002.
i.b.i.d. "Back Page: Lore and Legends," *Cumberland Lore, Leaf Chronicle*, October 7, 2008.
Marshall, Pattie. "White Chapel School," *Clarksville-Montgomery County Schools, Pictorial and Historical Collection,* Vol. 1, (Clarksville, TN, 1999) p. 48.
"Martha Washington Tea," *Leaf Chronicle*, February 22, 1908.
"Matrimonial," *Clarksville Leaf Chronicle*, October 26, 1878.
"Mayor of Guthrie," *Nashville Banner*, January 5, 1916.
McBride, Robert M. and Sam Robison. *Biographical Directory of the Tennessee General Assembly 1796-1861*, Vol. I, (Nashville, TN: Tennessee State Library, Archives and The Tennessee Historical Commission, 1975) p. 746.
"McMillan," *Leaf Chronicle,* December 19, 1903.
McSherry, Patrick, "A Brief History of the 1st Tennessee Volunteer Infantry," https://www.spanamwar.com/1sttennessee.html, June 24, 2024.
"Meeting of the Clarksville Bar," *Clarksville Leaf Chronicle*, May 29, 1920.
"Memorial Day," *Leaf Chronicle*, May 19, 1896.
"Mildred Waller Johnson," *Leaf Chronicle*, June 6, 1905.
"Military!" *The 83rd Illinoisan*, March 17, 1865.
Minniehan, Edna. Personal interview, November 18, 2006.
"Miss Emmie Tyler, Doll Dress Maker," *Leaf Chronicle*, November 28, 1922.
"Mississippi Officer Tries to Kidnap Three Negroes," *Leaf Chronicle*, April 25, 1905.
"Miss Scanland and Mrs. Mitchell are Heroines," *The Anaconda Standard*, September 3, 1913.
"Miss Tyler of Clarksville the Guest of Mrs. M.E. Bryan Houston, Texas," *Leaf Chronicle*, March 28, 1914.
"Miss Tyler's Reception," *Leaf Chronicle*, August 13, 1901.
"Mitchell-Tyler," *Leaf Chronicle*, August 17, 1905.
Montgomery County Will Books, Microfilm, Vol. T-U, Reel # 99A, p. 6, 87, 353-354.
"Montgomery County Court Meets in Quarterly Session," *Leaf Chronicle,* January 4, 1904.
Montgomery County Courts in Session Official Dedication, January 22, 2003, (Clarksville, TN: Sites Etc. Advertising and Jostens Printing Co., 2003) p. 9-11, 20, 95, 102.

"The Montgomery County Exhibit," *The Tennessean*, April 21, 1897.
"Montgomery County Exhibit," *Nashville Banner,* May 3, 1897.
"Montgomery's Exhibit," *Nashville Banner*, April 14, 1897.
"More Alleged Night Riders," *Leaf Chronicle*, June 14, 1915.
Morris, Andrew J. "Dating Portraits-Clothing Styles, 2003," http://www.ajmorris.com/roots/photo/datep18.htmClarksville, March 19, 2006.
Morrow, Gene Juneau. *Historical Notes of Clarksville, Tennessee, 1784-1865, (*Clarksville, TN: Clarksville Sesqui-Centennial, 1934) p. 6-7, Article 10-11, 17.
"The Morrows," *Clarksville Weekly Chronicle*, January 3, 1885.
"The Morrows," *Semi-Weekly Tobacco Leaf,* June 6, 1884.
"Mr. Ben Hollins Loses Plant Bed," *Daily Leaf Chronicle*, May 29, 1907.
"Mr. Fort Buys Beautiful Home," *Leaf Chroni*cle, August 16, 1915.
"Mrs. Em Tyler Mitchell and Mr. Bailey of Alabama," *Nashville Banner*, August 23, 1920.
"Mrs. Johnson Withdraws Her Application," *Leaf Chronicle*, September 12, 1905.
"Mrs. Mary G. Stacker," *Leaf Chronicle*; November 17, 1899.
"Murder on Public Square," *Clarksville Semi-Weekly Tobacco Lea*f, January 8, 1858.
Murff, Thomas, "Vigilantes in Sango," *Sango Community News*, September, 2013, p. 18-19.
"The Music of John Philip Sousa," http://www.worldmilitarybands.com/sousamus.htm, March 26, 2005.
"Must Stop Using Court House," *Leaf Chronicle*, January 30, 1911.
"The Name and Family of Redd," compiled by The Media Research Bureau, Washington, D.C., http://reddhistory.weebly.com/uploads/5/9/2/0/5920265/the_redd_family_name.pdf, June 22, 2024.
"Nathan Bedford Forrest, a North Georgia Notable," http://ngeorgia.com/people/forrest.html, February 10, 2006.
"The Nature Conservatory Purchases Bellamy Cave," http://www.nature.org/wherewework/northamerica/states/tennessee/press/press2, November 21, 2006.
"Negro Woman Confesses to Writing Anonymous Letter," *Leaf Chronicle*, February 5, 1908.
"New City Hall Better looking," *Leaf Chronicle,* June 15, 1914.
"New City Hall Model in All Arrangements," *Clarksville Leaf Chronicle*, February 7, 1914.
"The New Clock Keeps Perfect Time," *Leaf Chronicle*, February 13, 1901.
"New County Jail," *Leaf Chronicle*, January 17, 1907.
"New Court House," *Clarksville Semi-Weekly Tobacco Leaf*, July 29, 1881.
"New Court House," *Clarksville Tobacco Leaf*, April 23, 1878.
"New Jail," *Clarksville Weekly Chronicle*, February 5, 1881.
"New Law Firm is Launched," *Leaf Chronicle*, May 27, 1920.
"New Port Royal Bridge Collapses with a Fearful Crash of Timbers," *Leaf Chronicle Weekly,* December 11, 1904.
"Night Riders After Hervey Collier," *Clarksville Leaf Chronicle*, July 1, 1907.
"Night Riders at Work," *Daily Leaf Chronicle*, May 17, 1907.
"Night Riders Destroy Beds," *Daily Leaf Chronicle*, May 18, 1907.
"Night Riders Give a Warning," *Clarksville Leaf Chronicle*, May 29, 1907.
Olson, Sigurd F. "Pine Knots," http://www.uwm.edu/Dept/JMC/Olson?articles/columns/pine_knotsoct01.htm, November 2, 1954.
"Open Forum," *Daily Leaf Chronicle*, July 23, 1918.
"Open Forum," *Leaf Chronicle*, July 7, 1913.
"Open Forum," *Leaf Chronicle*, March 2, 1916.
"Opening of Idaho Springs," *Clarksville Semi-Weekly Tobacco Leaf,* June 10, 1879.
"The Opera House," *Clarksville Weekly Chronicle*, July 16, 1887.
"Organize for Raising Food," *Clarksville Leaf Chronicle*, April 14, 1917.
"Our Boys at San Francisco," *Leaf Chronicle,* November 17, 1899.
"Our Criminal Court," *Clarksville Weekly Chronicle*, March 12, 1881.
"Overcome by Heat," *Nashville Banner*, September 16, 1897.
Page, Sue Baggett. Phone interview, January 7, 2024.
Paine, Donald F. "The Black Patch Tobacco War Trials," *Tennessee Bar Journal*, September 2006.
"Passing of a Faithful Old Servant," *Leaf Chronicle*, October 11, 1909.
Patch, Rubye. "All About Henry's Emerald Hill," *Cumberland Lore*, *Leaf Chronicle*, April 1, 2000.
i.b.i.d. "Clarksville's Historic Trails, The Military," *Cumberland Lore, Leaf Chronic*le, July 1, 1999.
"Personal,*" Leaf Chronicle*, October 5, 1911.
"Personal," *Leaf Chronicle*, November 3, 1883.
"Petition for Cummutation," *Leaf Chronicle*, April 5, 1910.
"Petition for Writ of Mandamus," *Semi-Weekly Tobacco Leaf*, September 29, 1899
"Plant Beds Were Scraped," *Daily Leaf Chronicle*, May 16, 1907.
Podell, Louise. Personal interview, November 15, 2008.
"Private Acts Compilation," UT Press, Knoxville, TN, https://www.ctas.tennessee.edu/private-acts/law-enforcement-historical-notes-57, accessed August 30, 2024.
"Private acts of Montgomery County, Tennessee," Revised edition, county technical assistance service the University of Tennessee Institute for Public Service, Nashville, TN, original compilation by William C. McIntyre, legal specialist revised and edited by Gary S. McKee, legal specialist 1988 updated by Stephen Austin, legal consultant 2013.
"Proceedings of the City Council," *Clarksville Semi-Weekly Tobacco Leaf*, June 6, 1879.
"The Program of Exercises," *Leaf Chronicle*, November 30, 1899.
"Progress Marled by Courthouse Changes," *Leaf Chronicle*, May 15, 1966.

"Questions Presented to the Supreme Court at Jackson Settled," *Clarksville Semi-Weekly Tobacco Leaf,* June 11, 1889.
"Quiet Meeting of the City Board," *Leaf Chronicle*, November 2, 1900.
"Quintus Tyler," *1860 United States Federal Census*, http://www.AncestryLibrary.com, June 12, 2006.
"Races, Carnival and Confederate Veterans," *Leaf Chronicle*, September 6, 1909.
"Rare Fun in a Court Room Occasioned by Dog Lawsuit," *Daily Leaf Chronicle*, May 9, 1901.
"Reader Recalls Old Thrill Here," *Leaf Chronicle*, June 27, 1927.
"Realty Transfers," *Leaf Chronicle*, May 27, 1939.
"Reception of Ex-President Jefferson Davis," *Clarksville Tobacco Leaf,* October 13, 1875.
"Red Cross Note," *Leaf Chronicle*, July 26, 1918
"Remember the Clock," *Leaf Chronicle*, March 13, 1900.
"Resolutions Presented to American Snuff Company," *Leaf Chronicle*, July 12, 1906.
"Rhinehart Unconcerned," *Leaf Chronicle*, April 4, 1910.
"Richard Keeling Tyler," *Clarksville Daily Leaf Chronicle*, September 1, 1900.
Riggins, Marie. Personal interview. January 8, 2006.
"Riley Darnell's Croppers Have Beds Destroyed," *Daily Leaf Chronicle*, May 30, 1907.
"Rites Held for Beloved Woman," *Clarksville Leaf Chronicle*, August 23, 1932.
"River Items," *Leaf Chronicle*, April 21, 1883.
Roberts, Mardee. "Little Nannie Statue Will Grace Cemetery Again," *Leaf Chronicle,* March 25, 2001.
Robinette, Jesse. "Fidelity Was First with Rogers family," *Cumberland Lore, Leaf Chronicle*, October 1999.
i.b.i.d. "County Law Enforcement from 1796," *Cumberland Lore, Leaf Chronicle,* March 2000.
i.b.i.d. "Three of Veterans Pictured Came Home to Clarksville," *Cumberland Lore*, *Leaf Chronicle*, May 1989.
Robinson, Renee. "Clarksville Reunited with 'Little Darling'," *The Tennessean*, July 2, 1996.
Ross, Dan. "A Town of Seven Ponds," *Cumberland Lore*, *Leaf Chronicle*, May 18, 1987.
i.b.i.d. "A Sense of Place," *Leaf Chronicle*, June 20, 1989.
i.b.i.d. "The Town Is Built on Seven Hills," *Cumberland Lore, Leaf Chronicle*, November 1, 2001.
Ross Family Journal 1851-1871, Microfilm, Genealogy Room, Clarksville-Montgomery County Public Library.
Ross, James. *Life and Times of Elder Reuben Ross*, (Philadelphia, PA: Grant, Faires and Rodgers, 1977) p. 90-92, 96-97,107, 355-357.
"Rotary Told of History of City and County," *Clarksville Leaf Chronicle,* September 23, 1955.
"Rufus Hunter Killed in Cold Blood by Midnight Assassins," *Leaf Chronicle*, June 8, 1908.
Russell, Hansi Orgain, Personal Interview, January 15-16, 2007.
Schimpky, Bobbie and Bobbie Kalman. *Children's Clothing of the 1800s.* (NY: Crabtree Publishing Co. 1995) p. 11-13.
Schladweiler, Jon. Historian of the Arizona Water Pollution Control Federation, http://wwww.sewerhistory.or/misc/rosie.htm, February 19, 2002.
"Scorching Reply to Judge Tyler," *The Tennessean*, January 31, 1909.
Score, Stephen and Eleanor. Personal interview, July 2, 2009.
"Scraping of the Wimpey Plant Beds," *Daily Leaf Chronicle,* May 17, 1907.
"Senate Bill No. 186," *Daily Leaf Chronicle*, February 8, 1901.
"Seniors Remind Freshmen that They Are Just Frosh," *Leaf Chronicle*, September 25, 1935.
"Sentenced to be Hung," *Clarksville Jeffersonian*, June 4, 1851.
"Serious Accident to Rev. Arthur King," *Daily Leaf Chronicle*, August 27, 1900.
Severa, Joan. *Dressed for The Photographer, Ordinary Americans & Fashion, 1840-1900*, (Kent, OH: Kent State University Press, 1995) p. 387-389, 393-397, 401.
"Sermon by Dr. Ringgold at Trinity Church, Sept. 15th," *Clarksville Chronicle*, October 5, 1872.
"Severe Storm at Hadensville," *Leaf Chronicle*, August 23, 1897.
"Sheriff's Sale," Advertisement, *Clarksville Gazette*, November 1, 1820.
Shull, Thelma. *Children's Toys of Victorian Days.* http://www.mechanicalbanks.org/scrapbook/1940s/pages/1943_hobbies.htm, March 19, 2006.
Sichel, Marion. *History of Children's Costume*, (New York: Chelsea House Publishers, 1983) p. 40, 44.
i.b.i.d. *History of Women's Costume*, (New York: Chelsea House Publishers, 1984) p. 44, 55-57.
"Smallpox," *Clarksville Weekly Chronicle,* January 5, 1884.
Smith, Wiley, "Open Forum," *Leaf-Chronicle*, February 26, 1913.
"Society Events," *Leaf Chronicle*, July 31, 1912.
"Society," *Leaf Chronicle*, August 17, 1914.
"Society," *Leaf Chronicle*, December 12, 1912.
"Society," *Leaf Chronicle*, January 6, 1914.
"Society," *Leaf Chronicle*, June 18, 1919.
"Some Extracts from a Letter," *Leaf Chronicle*, March 14, 1899.
Soodalter, Ron. "Terror in the Night," *Kentucky Monthly*, September 23, 2014.
Spaulding, Lily May and John, ed. *Civil War Recipes, Recipes from the Pages of Godsey's Lady's Book*, (Lexington, KY: The University Press of Kentucky, 1999) p. 15-16.
"Special Grand Jury to Convene," *Clarksville Leaf Chronicle,* February 18, 1915.
"Special Music to be Rendered," *Daily Leaf Chronicle*, April 18, 1901.
Speer, William S. "Hon. Joseph Buckner Killebrew, A.M. Ph.D.," *Sketches of Prominent Tennesseans*, (Nashville, TN: South Historical Press, 1978) p. 82-83.
Speth, Alma. Personal interview. December 2, 2005.
"Spirit of Mud Alley," *Clarksville Tobacco Leaf*, September 30, 1874.
"Spirit of Mud Alley," *Cumberland Lore*, *Leaf Chronicle*, Louis Tatum, ed., March 1, 1985.

"Spring Street Should Not Be Destroyed," *Leaf Chronicle*, August 29, 1903.
"Squabble Settled," *Leaf Chronicle*, April 11, 1980.
"State and County Boards of Health," *Leaf Chronicle*, April 17, 1886.
Steele, Valerie. *The Corset, A Cultural History*, (New Haven, CT: Yale University Press, 2001) p. 67, 69, 72, 76-77.
Storring, Rod. *A Doctor's Life: A Visual History of Doctors and Nurses Through the Ages*, (New York: Dutton Children's Books, 1998) p. 26-27.
"Streetcar Party," *Semi-Weekly Chronicle*, August 29, 1899.
"Suicide," *Clarksville Jeffersonian*, July 16, 1861.
"Supreme Court to Hear Local Lawsuits Feb. 7," *Leaf Chronicle*, January 31, 1923.
"Supreme Court Opinions," *Nashville Banner*, April 7, 1932.
Sutton, Bettye; Goodwin, Sue; Bradley, Becky; Welling, Sheilda; Whitley, Peggy. *American Cultural History 19th Century 1880-1889*, Kingwood College Library, http://kclibrary.nhmccd.edu/19thcentury1880.htm, April 19, 2006.
Tackett, Doug. Personal interview. "Montgomery County Sheriff's Office," May 10, 2006.
"Tchaikovsky in the 1880s'," http://www.animactionsunlimited.com/Tchaikovsky.the%201880's.htm, April 19, 2006.
"Teethina," Advertisement, *Clarksville Semi-Weekly Tobacco Leaf*, September 21, 1880.
"Telephone Changes," *Leaf Chronicle*, July 25, 1896.
"Tell Me About the Mattaponi River," http://www.itsyourenvironment.net/alliance/matriver1.html, March 4, 2006.
"Ten Mile Road Race," *Leaf Chronicle* June 22, 1896
"Tennessee Inventor Makes Connection," *Nashville Banner*, November 15, 1923.
"Tennessee Legislature," *Clarksville Weekly Chronicle*, April 2, 1881.
"Tennessee Now Has an Anti-Spitting Law," *Leaf Chronicle*, May 3, 1907.
Tennessee, U.S. Marriage Records, 1780-2002.
Tennessee, U.S. Wills and Probate Records, 1779-2008.
"That Baby," *Clarksville Leaf Chronicle*, March 16, 1892.
"That Pond Again," *Clarksville Weekly Chronicle*, May 4, 1878.
"These New Books," *Weekly Chronicle*, November 24, 1899.
"Thinks Mind Was Unbalanced," *Clarksville Daily Leaf Chronicle*, July 21, 1902.
"This Clock," *Leaf Chronicle,* May 8, 1900.
Thomas, Irene Farrar. Typed manuscript on Current House/Burt Infirmary, In possession of author, January 26, 1976.
"Those Monuments," *Clarksville Leaf Chronicle,* April 13, 1892.
"Three Cornered Pistol Duel at Close Range," *Leaf Chronicle*, July 26, 1901.
"Thursday Night's Fire Alarm," *Clarksville Weekly Chronicle*, December 10, 1881.
Titus, W.P. *Picturesque Clarksville, Past and Present,* (Clarksville: Wm. P. Titus Publishers, 1887. Reprint: Ann E. Alley and Ursula S. Beach, 1976) p. 47, 68, 81, 88, 90, 93, 107, 128-29, 171, 208-216, 268, 285-87, 308-10, 319, 364-365.368, 380, 390, 400.
"Today's Mass Meeting in the Interest of Law Enforcement," *Leaf Chronicle*, June 30, 1913.
"To Offer Reward for Night Riders," *Daily Leaf Chronicle,* May 23, 1907.
"To the People of Montgomery County," *Leaf Chronicle*, July 22, 1918.
"Torrents of Rain Wreck the Bridges and Does Great Damage," *Leaf Chronicle*, April 12, 1912.
"Touching Tribute," *Daily Leaf Chronicle*, October 2, 1900.
"To Witness the Triple Execution," *Daily Leaf Chronicle*, July 18, 1901.
"Town Ordinance, Extract from the Minutes of the Corporation," *Clarksville Gazette*, May 13, 1820.
"The Tragic Fate of Mrs. Eugene Corbett," *Leaf Chronicle*, August 31, 1905.
Travers, Bridget & Freiman and Fran Locher, ed. *Medical Discoveries: MedicalBreakthroughs & The People Who Developed Them.* Vol. 3 (U-X-L, Detroit, MI: 1991) p. 361-362.
i.b.i.d. Vol. 2, p. 175.
Travis, Jeannie. "Southern Family Man," *Cumberland Lore, Leaf Chronicle*, February 7, 2006.
"Treatment for Diphtheria," *Clarksville Weekly Chronicle*, November 6, 1880.
"Tribute of Respect," *Clarksville Jeffersonian*, May 23, 1860.
Trinity Episcopal Church Parish Records, Vol. I, 1875-1896, Vol. II 1897-1965.
"Trinity History Briefly Related," *Leaf Chronicle*, October 10, 1932.
"The Truth About Woolly Bears," http://www.alamnac.com/preview2000/woollybears.html, November 16, 2006.
"They Have Gone," *Leaf Chronicle*, November 3, 1899.
"To the Workhouse," *Leaf Chronicle*, February 25, 1898.
"Twenty-one Years a Judge," *Leaf Chronicle*, July 11, 1894.
"Two Serious Hurt in Crash," *Leaf Chronicle*, May 7, 1932.
"Two Tornadoes," *Clarksville Weekly Chronicle*, February 28, 1884
Tyler, Charles. Letter to Editor. *Clarksville Weekly Chronicle*, November 13, 1880.
Tyler, Charles W. *The K.K.K.,* (Nashville, TN: Publishing House M.E. South, 1903) Preface, p. 5-6 21, 23, 52, 55, 59,139, 294.
i.b.i.d *The Scout. A Tale of the Civil War,* (Nashville, TN: The Cumberland Press, 1911) Preface, p. 17, 37, 39, 40, 108, 180, 191, 230, 242, 248, 296, 331.
i.b.i.d. "Patriotism in a Tennessee County," *Confederate Veteran*, Vol. VI, p. 125.
i.b.i.d "Sealed Proposals," *Clarksville Tobacco Leaf*, May 2, 1878.
Tyler, Emmie. *History of Trinity Church*, unpublished manuscript, Trinity Church Archives, 1917.
"Tyler Family of Essex, Spotsylvania and Caroline Counties," *William and Mary Quarterly*, Vol. I, (Baltimore, MD: Genealogy Publishing Co., 1982) p. 279-286.

"Tyler Inquiry," *Clarksville Weekly Tobacco Leaf*, March 29, 1881.
"Tyler Inquiry," *Clarksville Weekly Tobacco Leaf,* April 5, 1881.
Tyler, Lyon Gardiner. *Encyclopedia of Virginia Biographies*, Vol. I, (New York: Lewis Historical Publishing Co., 1915) p. 346-347.
i.b.i.d. *The Letters and Times of the Tylers,* Vol. 3, (Williamsburg, VA: Higginson Book Co., 1896) p. 221-226.
Tyler, Quintus. Unpublished manuscript on Tyler Family, typed by Em Tyler Bailey, undated.
"Tyler Rifles," *Daily Leaf Chronicle*, May 1, 1901.
"Tyler's Court," *Leaf Chronicle*, August 23, 1898.
"Tyler's Court," *Weekly Leaf Chronicle*, August 30, 1898.
"The Union's First Great Victories," http://www.military.com/forums/0,15240,80756,00.html, November 27, 2006.
"Until the 2d Monday in May Next," *Clarksville Weekly Chronicle*, April 27, 1878.
Untitled Article of Scalded Child at Greenwood Cemetery, *Clarksville Democrat*, June 3, 1887.
Untitled Article on Black Baptisms, *Clarksville Weekly Chronicle,* May 21, 1887.
Untitled Article on Boys Arrested at Greenwood Cemetery, *Clarksville Semi-Weekly Tobacco Leaf,* August 1, 1884.
Untitled Article on Captain Phillips and the Tramps, *Clarksville Weekly Chronicle,* November 23, 1878.
Untitled Article on Captured Rebel Letters, *83rd Illinoisan*, November 20, 1864.
Untitled Article on the Circuit Court, *Clarksville Tobacco Leaf*, January 28, 1874.
Untitled Article on City Fights, *Clarksville Weekly Chronicle*, August 24, 1878.
Untitled Article on Death of Four Children from Diphtheria, *Clarksville Weekly Chronicle*, September 14, 1878.
Untitled Article on Death of Scott Child, *Clarksville Semi-Weekly Tobacco Leaf,* March 28, 1879.
Untitled Article on Diphtheria, *Clarksville Leaf Chronicle,* September 19, 1885.
Untitled Article on Eclipse Stables, *Clarksville Semi-Weekly Tobacco Leaf*, April 16, 1880.
Untitled Article on Emma Tyler, *Clarksville Semi-Weekly Tobacco Leaf*, March 3, 1882.
Untitled Article on Exoneration of Frank Phillips, *Clarksville Semi-Weekly Tobacco Leaf,* May 2, 1878.
Untitled Article on False Fire Alarm at College, *Clarksville Semi-Weekly Tobacco Leaf,* May 2, 1878.
Untitled Article on Fire Engine, *Clarksville Tobacco Leaf*, May 2, 1878.
Untitled Article on Greenwood Streetcar, *The Democrat*, July 17, 1890.
Untitled Article on Henry Whitlow, *Daily Leaf Chronicle*, November 9, 1918.
Untitled Article on Hickory Wild Academy, *Clarksville Semi-Weekly Tobacco Leaf*, August 29, 1882.
Untitled Article on Idaho Springs and J. A. Tate, *Clarksville Semi-Weekly Tobacco Leaf,* March 28, 1879.
Untitled Article on Judge Tyler and Coleman Burr, *Clarksville Tobacco Leaf,* August 1, 1878.
Untitled Article on Judge Tyler Inquiry, *Clarksville Weekly Chronicle*, March 19, 1881.
Untitled Article on Judge Tyler Speaking at Vernon Furnace, *Clarksville Semi-Weekly Tobacco Leaf*, October 12, 1880.
Untitled Article on Judge Tyler, *Clarksville Semi-Weekly Tobacco Leaf*, January 7, 1890.
Untitled Article on Large Crowd Witnessing Baptisms, *Leaf Chronicle*, December 18, 1886.
Untitled Article on Madison Street Bridge, *Clarksville Semi-Weekly Tobacco Leaf,* September 30, 1879.
Untitled Article on Marcellus C. Rhinehart, *The River Counties*, 1984.
Untitled Article on Mildred Settle, *Clarksville Weekly Chronicle,* April 16, 1887.
Untitled Article on Miss M---t R---g, *83rd Illinoisan*, March 7, 1865.
Untitled Article on Mrs. Rosenfield, *Clarksville Semi-Weekly Tobacco Leaf*, April 25, 1878.
Untitled Article on Night Riders, *Clarksville Leaf Chronicle*, January 30, 1907.
Untitled Article on Quintus Tyler, *Clarksville Semi-Weekly Tobacco Leaf*, October 6, 1882.
Untitled Article on Replacement of Downtown Sidewalks, *Clarksville Tobacco Leaf,* September 5, 1878.
Untitled Article on Scalded Child at Greenwood Cemetery, *Clarksville Democrat*, June 3, 1887.
Untitled Article on Shooting of Tyler Bryan, *Clarksville Semi-Weekly Tobacco Leaf,* November 5, 1880.
Untitled Article on Shooting of Tyler Bryan, *Clarksville Weekly Chronicle*, November 6, 1880.
Untitled Article on the Old Plank Walk at Passenger Depot, *Clarksville Weekly Chronicle*, November 18, 1876.
Untitled Article on Theft at Sam Lung's, *Clarksville Weekly Chronicle*, January 30, 1886.
Untitled Article on Threatening Letter, *Clarksville Leaf Chronicle*, January 30, 1907.
Untitled Article on Water Pipes Bursting in City Jail, *Clarksville Semi-Weekly Tobacco Leaf*, October 6, 1882.
Untitled Poem about Covered Bridges, http://www.philsbridges.com/questions.php, March 11, 2009.
"Valuable Land for Sale," Advertisement, *Clarksville Gazette*, October 14, 1820.
Van Steenwyk, Elizabeth. *Frontier Fever*, (New York: Walker Publishing Company, Inc. 1995) p. 114, 118-119.
"Very Serious Accident," *Leaf Chronicle*, January 6, 1898.
Victorian Fashions and Costumes from Harper's Bazaar: 1867-1898. Edited by Stella Blum, (New York: Dover Publications, Inc., 1974) p. 114-187.
"Victim of Consumption," *The Paducah Sun*, November 26, 1904.
"The Views of a Citizen on County Government, *Clarksville Semi-Weekly Tobacco Leaf*, May 28, 1889.
"Vigorous Defense of Clarksville and People," *Leaf Chronicle,* January 20, 1909.
"Violations of the Election and Prohibition Laws," *The Tennessean*, August 20, 1912.
Virginia Military Record, (Baltimore, MD: Genealogy Publishing Co., Inc., 1983) p. 110, 643-644, 704.
Virginia Will Records, (Baltimore MD: Genealogy Publishing Co., Inc., 1982) p. 76.
Waldrep, Christopher. *Night Riders: Defending Community in the Black Patch, 1890-1915.*
Wallace, Betty Joe. "A Woman's Life in the 1800s," *Cumberland Lore, Leaf Chronicle*, November 1, 1992.
Walston, Larry L., e-mail to author, March 20, 2008.
"The Water Fountains," *Leaf Chronicle*, December 3, 1901.
Waters, Charles M. "Appearance' Was a Key Word in Lives of Our Proper Victorian Ancestors," *Cumberland Lore*, *Leaf Chronicle, May* 2, 1991.

i.b.i.d. *Historic Clarksville. The Bicentennial Story 1784-1984,* (Clarksville, TN: Historic Clarksville Publishing Co., 1983) p. 16-17, 42, 75, 77, 80-82, 89-90, 93, 95, 99, 102, 104-106, 112, 119, 122, 132, 147, 155.
Waters, Dorothy Faxon. *A Line of the Faxon Family from Thomas Faxon 1601 to William Elliott Faxon 1982*, (Tallahassee, FL: Rose Printing Company, 1982) p. 13-15.
"What It Means," *Weekly Leaf Chronicle,* August 11, 1899.
"What They Think About the Matter," *Leaf Chronicle*, September 8, 1899.
"Which Is Paid Here to the Memory of a Noble Woman," Records from Meeting, Forbes Bivouac, 1890, Genealogy Room, Clarksville-Montgomery County Public Library.
Whitman, Walt, "Pioneers! O Pioneers!" *Complete Poetry and Collected Prose*, (New York: Viking Press, 1982) p. 371.
"Who Wants a Pretty Girl Baby?" *Daily Tobacco Leaf Chronicle*, January 28, 1892.
Wilbur, C. Keith, M.D. *Civil War Medicine, 1861-1865*, (Old Saybrook, CT: The Globe Pequot Press, 1998) p. 105.
"Wildlife Nature's Weatherman," http://www.youngbucksoutdoors.com/wildlife/031113YBNature.html, November 16, 2006.
"William and Mary Quarterly," Vol. 19, No. 4 (Apr., 1911) p. 282.
"William Buck's Fashionable Barber Shop," Advertisement, *Clarksville Semi-Weekly Tobacco Leaf,* August 1,1882.
Williams, Eleanor. "Renovations Ease Courthouse into 20th Century," *Leaf Chronicle*, July 2, 1988.
Williams, Eleanor. *Cabins to Castles,* (Jackson, TN: The Guild Bindery Press, 1992) p. 202.
Wingfield, Marshall. *A History of Caroline County, Virginia from its Formation in 1727 to 1924. Compiled from Original Records and Authoritative Sources and Profusely Illustrated,* (Press of Trevvet Christian & Co., Richmond, VA, 1924) p. 212-213.
i.b.i.d. "Tyler Club Named for Controversial Judge," *Cumberland Lore, Leaf Chronicle*, December 1990.
i.b.i.d. *Worship Along the Warioto*, (Self-printed, 1995), p. 338-340.
Williams' Clarksville Directory City Guide 1859-60, (Clarksville, TN: C.O. Faxon, Publishers, 1859. Reprint: Ursula Smith Beach, 1976) p. 10-11, 40, 73, 79.
Williams, Eleanor and Beach, Ursula. *Homes and Happenings*, (Oxford, MS: Guild Bindery Press, 1990) p. 21-23, 27-28, 33-35, 42, 51-53, 84, 93, 99-105, 107, 115 -117.
Williams, Nannie Haskins. Unpublished Diary, Genealogy Room, Clarksville-Montgomery County Public Library, 1869-1890.
"William Woolridge Succumbs to Injuries Sustained in Bridge Collapse," *Leaf Chronicle,* December 11, 1903
"Will Serve the Sentence," *Leaf Chronicle*, May 25, 1893.
Wingfield, Marshall. "Caroline County, Virginia," http://www.rootsweb.com/~vacaroli/caroline.htm, January 18, 2006.
Winn, T. Howard. Personal interview. June 11, 2006.
Woog, Adam. *A Cultural History of the United States, The 1900s,* (San Diego, CA: Lucent Books, Inc.,1999) p. 40.
"Work on Certain Street Improvements to Begin at Once," *Leaf Chronicle*, June 29, 1904.
1730-1735 Essex County, Virginia Will Book 5, Antient Press, p. 264-266, 282-284.
"Workmen Razing Historic Building," *Leaf Chronicle*, April 8, 1914.

Made in the USA
Columbia, SC
07 May 2025

57630768R00167